US Trotskyism 1928–1965
Part III: Resurgence

Historical Materialism Book Series

The Historical Materialism Book Series is a major publishing initiative of the radical left. The capitalist crisis of the twenty-first century has been met by a resurgence of interest in critical Marxist theory. At the same time, the publishing institutions committed to Marxism have contracted markedly since the high point of the 1970s. The Historical Materialism Book Series is dedicated to addressing this situation by making available important works of Marxist theory. The aim of the series is to publish important theoretical contributions as the basis for vigorous intellectual debate and exchange on the left.

The peer-reviewed series publishes original monographs, translated texts, and reprints of classics across the bounds of academic disciplinary agendas and across the divisions of the left. The series is particularly concerned to encourage the internationalization of Marxist debate and aims to translate significant studies from beyond the English-speaking world.

For a full list of titles in the Historical Materialism Book Series available in paperback from Haymarket Books, visit:
https://www.haymarketbooks.org/series_collections/1-historical-materialism

US Trotskyism 1928–1965
Part III: Resurgence

Uneven and Combined Development

Dissident Marxism in the United States, Volume 4

Edited by
Paul Le Blanc
Bryan Palmer

Haymarket Books
Chicago, IL

First published in 2018 by Brill Academic Publishers, The Netherlands
© 2018 Koninklijke Brill NV, Leiden, The Netherlands

Published in paperback in 2019 by
Haymarket Books
P.O. Box 180165
Chicago, IL 60618
773-583-7884
www.haymarketbooks.org

ISBN: 978-1-64259-058-6

Distributed to the trade in the US through Consortium Book Sales and Distribution (www.cbsd.com) and internationally through Ingram Publisher Services International (www.ingramcontent.com).

This book was published with the generous support of Lannan Foundation and Wallace Action Fund.

Special discounts are available for bulk purchases by organizations and institutions. Please call 773-583-7884 or email info@haymarketbooks.org for more information.

Cover design by Jamie Kerry and Ragina Johnson.

Printed in the United States.

10 9 8 7 6 5 4 3 2 1

Library of Congress Cataloging-in-Publication data is available.

Contents

1 Introduction: a Party of Uneven and Combined Development   1
   Paul Le Blanc

2 New Stirrings   21
   Paul Le Blanc
   1 Jean Blake, 'The Continuing Struggle for Negro Equality'   25
   2 Murry Weiss, 'McCarthyism: Key Issue in the 1954 Elections'   33
   3 Evelyn Reed, 'The Myth of Women's Inferiority'   43
   4 Marjorie McGowan, Jeanne Morgan, Jack Bustelo (Joseph Hansen), 'Debate on Cosmetics'   65
   5 Harold Robins, 'Automation – Menace or Promise?'   89
   6 Murry Weiss, 'The Vindication of Trotskyism: Khrushchev's Report on Stalin's Crimes'   100
   7 James Robertson, 'New Stage for the Youth'   112
   8 Evelyn Sell, 'Really Beat?'   119
   9 James P. Cannon, 'United Socialist Political Action in 1958'   130

3 New Pathways   139
   Paul Le Blanc
   1 Tim Wohlforth, 'Youth Report to the Eighteenth National Convention'   149
   2 Frances James, 'Africa's Bid for Freedom'   153
   3 Joseph Hansen, 'Theory of the Cuban Revolution'   161
   4 Hedda Grant (Hedda Garza), 'Still a Man's World'   180
   5 Melba Baker (Melba Windoffer), 'Women Who Work'   183
   6 Myra Tanner Weiss, 'Kennedy: The Candidate and the President'   193
   7 Political Committee, Socialist Workers Party, 'Preparing for the Next Wave of Radicalism in the United States'   204
   8 Theodore Edwards (Edmund Kovacs), 'Kennedy's War in Vietnam'   220
   9 Farrell Dobbs and Joseph Hansen, 'Reunification of the Fourth International'   229
   10 Evelyn Reed, 'A Study of the Feminine Mystique'   244
   11 James P. Cannon, 'The Triple Revolution: Political Implications and Program for Action'   255

4 Challenges of Black Liberation 272
    Paul Le Blanc
    1 Lois Saunders, 'The South's Dilemma' 275
    2 Fred Halstead, 'The Jackson Freedom Ride' 287
    3 George Breitman, 'How a Minority Can Change Society' 298
    4 Robert Vernon (Robert Des Verney), 'Why White Radicals Are Incapable of Understanding Black Nationalism' 316
    5 Socialist Workers Party, 'Freedom Now: The New Stage in the Struggle for Negro Emancipation and the Tasks of the SWP' 347
    6 Richard Kirk (Richard S. Fraser), 'Revolutionary Integrationism' 373
    7 George Breitman, 'Malcolm X: The Man and His Ideas' 390

5 Divergences and Consolidations 403
    Paul Le Blanc
    1 Sam Marcy (Sam Ballan), 'The Global Class War and Destiny of American Labor' 406
    2 V. Grey (Vincent Copeland), 'China, Hungary, and the Marxist Method' 413
    3 Tim Wohlforth, 'Summary for Minority on World Movement' 415
    4 James Robertson, 'The Centrism of the SWP' 420
    5 Tim Wohlforth et al., 'Call for the Reorganization of the Minority Tendency' 426
    6 Richard Kirk and Clara Kaye (Richard Fraser and Clara Fraser), 'Radical Laborism Versus Bolshevik Leadership' 428
    7 Farrell Dobbs and George Novack, 'The Organizational Character of the Socialist Workers Party' 436

6 Debates and Interventions 460
    Paul Le Blanc
    1 Joseph Hansen, 'Deutscher on Trotsky' 466
    2 George Breitman and Joseph Hansen, 'Exchange of Views on Deutscher Biography' 483
    3 Arne Swabeck and John Liang (Frank Glass), 'The Chinese Revolution – Its Character and Development' 489
    4 Tom Kerry, 'Maoism and the Neo-Stalin Cult' 502
    5 James P. Cannon, 'Don't Strangle the Party' 517

CONTENTS

7 **History and Theory** 533
   Bryan Palmer and Paul Le Blanc
   1   Grace Carlson, 'The Myth of Racial Superiority'   539
   2   Joseph Hansen, 'Hayek Pleads for Capitalism'   550
   3   Harry Frankel (Harry Braverman), 'Three Conceptions of Jacksonianism'   566
   4   William F. Warde (George Novack), 'A Suppressed Chapter in the History of American Capitalism: The Destruction of Indian Communal Democracy'   576
   5   William Gorman, 'W.E.B. Du Bois and His Work'   594
   6   Jean Simon (Jean Tussey), 'Tom Paine – Revolutionist'   608
   7   George Breitman, 'How Stalinism Will Be Ended'   620
   8   Myra Tanner (Myra Tanner Weiss), 'Sternberg vs. Karl Marx'   625
   9   Joyce Cowley, 'Women Who Won the Right to Vote'   639
   10 John G. Wright (Joseph Vanzler), 'Feuerbach – Philosopher of Materialism'   658
   11 James P. Cannon, 'Intellectuals and Revolution: The Case of C. Wright Mills (Letter to George Novack)'   666
   12 William F. Warde (George Novack), 'C. Wright Mills' *The Marxists*'   669

Bibliography   689
Index   700
Dissident Marxism in the United States   720

CHAPTER 1

Introduction: a Party of Uneven and Combined Development

Paul Le Blanc

This is the concluding volume in a trilogy of documentary materials covering the history of Trotskyism in the United State from 1929 to 1965. It is part of a broader multi-volume project on 'Dissident Marxism in the United States', involving the development of US Marxism outside of the Communist and Socialist parties in the period from the late 1920s to the early 1960s. This includes an already published volume on the Communist Party Opposition headed by Jay Lovestone, and forthcoming volumes on 'independent Marxism' unaffiliated with the specific groups mentioned here.

The people who were drawn to the Trotskyist banner sought to forge a genuinely revolutionary pathway from the violence and oppression of capitalism to a better future of socialist democracy, the control of the world's economic resources by laboring majorities for the good of humanity – a cause which they believed had been betrayed by the bureaucratic leaderships and badly compromised programs of the mass reformist-Socialist parties and by the global Communist movement led by Joseph Stalin. The overall history of US Trotskyism is covered in a number of other works and cannot be rehearsed in this introduction (though the introductions of all three volumes provide some of the essentials). The most ambitious effort to date in mapping a general history is Robert J. Alexander's *International Trotskyism*, but also useful and serviceable is the recently republished *Trotskyism in the United States: Historical Essays and Reconsiderations* containing contributions by George Breitman, Paul Le Blanc, and Alan Wald.[1]

A limitation of the three large volumes presented here is that they do not cover the subsequent history of those groupings which broke from the Trotskyist mainstream – such as those associated with Hugo Oehler, Max Shachtman, C.L.R. James and Raya Dunayevskaya, Bert Cochran, Sam Marcy, Clara Fraser and Richard Fraser, Tim Wohlforth, James Robertson, and others. The disputes which resulted in those splits are recorded here, and work by others

---

1   See Alexander 1991 and Breitman, Le Blanc and Wald 2016.

provides much useful material on what happened next, but obviously there is room for more work on such matters.

It is hoped that these three volumes – and the entire set of 'Dissident Marxism in the United States' – will stand as a useful resource for scholars and activists. What is offered in the rest of this introduction attempts to provide ideas and information that may be helpful in making sense of the mass of documentary material that follows.

Using a Theoretical Construct

Leon Trotsky's 'law of uneven and combined development' (decisive in the development of his distinctive *theory of permanent revolution*) can be generalized to help elucidate many complex phenomena, including what happened to the Trotskyist movement as it made its way from the mid-1950s to the mid-1960s.

Trotsky described uneven development as characterizing different areas and different countries which are just that – different. These different regions have had their own particular characteristics, and for various reasons, technological and cultural and ideological innovations arose first in one area and then had an impact on other areas at different times – leading to uneven development in the history of the world as a whole. This leads to another historical law expressed by Trotsky in this way:

> Unevenness, the most general law of the historic process, reveals itself most sharply and complexly in the destiny of backward countries. Under the whip of external necessity their backward culture is compelled to make leaps. From the universal law of unevenness thus derives another law which, for the lack of a better name, we may call the law of combined development – by which we mean a drawing together of the different stages of the journey, a combining of separate steps, an amalgam of archaic with more contemporary forms.[2]

Similar dynamics can be found in a left-wing organization, particularly one spread over different geographic areas, with a diverse social composition, embracing different generations, and interacting with co-thinkers in various

---

2 This draws from a brief biography of Leon Trotsky and discussion of his ideas: Le Blanc 2015, pp. 78–9.

INTRODUCTION: A PARTY OF UNEVEN AND COMBINED DEVELOPMENT   3

other countries as well as with the complex and evolving society within which it is embedded. The dialectical contradictions of such 'uneven and combined development' can sometimes be found not simply within a revolutionary organization, but even within an individual who is a leading member of such an organization.

Before exploring this further, however, it is worth considering the applicability of an additional conceptualization.

A Sect and Not a Sect

In the view of many, the Socialist Workers Party in the 1950s fits the classic definition of a sect. In a polemical analysis of 1954 – aimed precisely at the SWP – sociologist Lewis Coser wrote: 'A sect ... consists of men [now we would say 'people'] who have cut themselves off from the main body of society. They have formed a restricted and closed group which rejects the norms of the inclusive society and proclaims its adherence to a special set of rules of conduct'. Acknowledging 'fundamental differences between a [religious] fundamentalist sect and the political sects of the modern socialist movement', Coser explains:

> The original radical impulse of the sectarian was likely to be born out of a revolt against the injustice, the cruelty, the insensitivity of American capitalist society; it was nourished by moral indignation and Utopian idealism. The political sectarian, as distinct from the religious sectarian, didn't want to save his own soul; he wanted, out of the generous impulse of his conviction, to change the human condition of his fellowmen.

The problem, Coser notes, is that 'the twists of history in nineteenth and twentieth century America' resulted in the failure and isolation of the would-be social revolutionaries. 'The socialist movement either adapted itself to prevailing strands of opinion, thus losing much of its radical inflection, or was thrown into isolation and in a reflex of defensiveness accentuated its sectarian characteristics'.[3]

At this point, patterns similar to what can be found in religious sects kick in. 'The sect, by its exclusive structure, creates a morality opposed to that of the rest of society', Coser explains. 'Since it regards the outsider as not parti-

---

3   Coser 1954, pp. 360, 368.

cipating in grace, as not belonging to the select, as not having the fortitude or capacity to adhere to revolutionary principles, it sees him as an exponent of a lower morality'. He adds: 'The sect does not strive for large membership. On the contrary it may even find it advantageous to suffer a loss of membership if this involves the elimination of men inclined toward compromise and mediation'.[4] Hence the prevalence of factional fights, expulsions, and organizational splits among organizations aspiring to be revolutionary. Apparently, all such groups must be seen as sects.

This suggests a highly problematical aspect of Coser's analysis. If one is opposed to racism, gender and sexual oppression, war, and class exploitation and seeks to build a movement and struggles against such things – thereby 'creating a morality opposed to that of the rest of society' – then one is by definition a sectarian. This is the case, presumably, even if one's movement wins majority support and culminates in a successful revolution – since Coser quotes Lenin's writings as presenting classic sectarian perspectives.

In fact, Coser's sweeping generalities are challenged by Lenin's more precise discussion of sectarianism in *Left-Wing Communism, An Infantile Disorder*. Here Lenin identifies three key elements that are essential for what he considers to be a genuinely revolutionary party (in contrast to an ultra-left sect): 'First, by the class-consciousness of the proletarian vanguard and by its devotion to the revolution, by its tenacity, self-sacrifice and heroism'. By 'proletarian vanguard' he is not referring to a small self-proclaimed elite, but a minority layer of the working-class that is drawn to the party. 'Second, by its ability to link up, maintain the closest contact, and – if you wish – merge, in certain measure, with the broadest masses of the working people – primarily with the proletariat, *but also with the non-proletarian* masses of working people'. Only then is it possible to refer to the final necessary element: 'Third, by the correctness of the political leadership exercised by this vanguard, by the correctness of its political strategy and tactics, provided the broad masses have seen, *from their own experience*, that they are correct'.

Lenin adds, significantly: 'Without these conditions, discipline in a revolutionary party really capable of being the party of the advanced class, whose mission it is to overthrow the bourgeoisie and transform the whole of society, cannot be achieved. Without these conditions, all attempts to establish discipline inevitably fall flat and end up in phrasemongering and clowning'. He concludes that 'these conditions cannot emerge at once. They are created only by prolonged effort and hard-won experience. Their creation is facilitated by a cor-

---

4 Coser 1954, pp. 361, 362.

rect revolutionary theory, which, in its turn, is not a dogma, but assumes final shape only in close connection with the practical activity of a truly mass and truly revolutionary movement'. What is particularly important is this outward-looking engagement with experience, which for the Russians from 1903 to 1918 was in fact a

> wealth of experience. During those fifteen years, no other country knew anything even approximating to that revolutionary experience, that rapid and varied succession of different forms of the movement – legal and illegal, peaceful and stormy, underground and open, local circles and mass movements, and parliamentary and terrorist forms. In no other country has there been concentrated, in so brief a period, such a wealth of forms, shades, and methods of struggle of *all* classes of modern society, a struggle which, owing to the backwardness of the country and the severity of the tsarist yoke, matured with exceptional rapidity, and assimilated most eagerly and successfully the appropriate 'last word' of American and European political experience.[5]

What is projected here – reflecting the actual, historical experience of Bolshevism – is something that in no way conforms to the kind of sect that Coser discusses. It is in large measure because of his own engagement with and assimilation of this historical experience that James Cannon, writing to his friend V.R. Dunne in 1955, after reading correspondence of Engels regarding would-be Marxists in the United States, commented: 'I am on the warpath against any sign or symptom of sectarianism myself. I intend to write about it too, in a "preventative" way, and to appeal to Engels for help'. Keenly aware of the larger social circumstances alluded to by Coser, Cannon asserted: 'I know that sectarianism – in one form or another – is an ever-present danger to any small organization of revolutionists condemned to isolation by circumstances beyond their control, regardless of their original wishes and intentions'. Like Lenin, however, he reaches for a greater precision than Coser's formulation will allow: 'The moment such an organization ceases to think of itself as a part of the working class, which can realize its aims only with and through the working class, and to conduct itself accordingly, it is done for'. He elaborates:

> The key to Engels's thought is his striking expression that the conscious socialists should act as a 'leaven' in the instinctive and spontaneous move-

---

5 Lenin 2008, pp. 305–7.

ment of the working class. Those are winged words that every party member should memorize. The leaven can help the dough to rise and eventually become a loaf of bread, but can never be a loaf of bread itself.

Every tendency, direct or indirect, of a small revolutionary party to construct a world of its own, outside and apart from the real movement of the workers in the class struggle, is sectarian. Such tendencies can take many forms, and we should not delude ourselves that the well known illustrations exhaust the possibilities.[6]

And yet this by no means exhausts the question of SWP sectarianism. While Cannon and his comrades may have assimilated the powerfully anti-sectarian tendencies associated with Russian Bolshevism, they were also immersed in the kinds of difficult US realities that both Cannon and Coser allude to, generating sectarian impulses which Cannon explicitly tagged as 'ever-present'. Careful observation reveals combined elements – non-sectarian and sectarian – blended within the reality of the SWP of the late 1950s and early 1960s.

Case Study: George Breitman and the Detroit SWP

To get an adequate sense of this, it may be helpful to give some attention to the Detroit branch of the SWP in the period of 1954 to 1967.[7] George and Dorothea Breitman moved to Detroit in the wake of the dispute and split with the Cochran faction, joining Frank and Sarah Lovell, who had transferred in during the last stages of the fight. Their collective political understanding and experience were certainly challenged by the situation in which they found themselves. Detroit had been a stronghold of the Cochranites, and young activist Evelyn Sell later recalled that the split 'left us with only eight members, no headquarters, [and] no mailing list or mimeograph machine or basic resources'. All of them had to get jobs to support themselves, but for Breitman his 'real' job was to function as an effective organizer of the Detroit SWP branch. In a 1958 letter to a comrade, he described his view of this work:

> Those who sent me to Detroit didn't intend that I should stay there; they thought in terms of a year or two, an improvement in the internal situation, etc. I told them I was going for good. ... I had my heart set on ... helping younger comrades, so far as I could, to develop all their powers,

---

6 Cannon 1955.
7 This draws from Le Blanc 2005, pp. 372–7.

to realize their potential. I think I make a beginning at it. I know some a little, some substantially, some not at all. I know that I helped to create a healthier climate in the branch, in which development could be encouraged in the right direction.[8]

Over the next dozen years, the Detroit branch of the SWP attracted a growing number of people, especially with the youth radicalization of the 1960s. According to one observer, Breitman was 'adored by the younger party members'. Melissa Singler was a teenage activist involved in the 1960 picketing of Woolworths during the early days of the civil rights movement, and the first socialist class series she attended was taught by Breitman. 'I was terribly excited by the classes', she remembers. 'George was able to take a roomful of young people, most of whom had gone from six to sixteen in the silent 1950s, and have us hanging on his words'. Impressed by 'his straightforwardness and his creativity', Singler notes that 'there was tremendous admiration on the part of those teenagers for this man who could so easily and humorously tell us about a history we had not been told about before'.[9]

Evelyn Sell recalled, 'he devoted special time, energy, and thought to helping younger comrades realize their potential', and he 'paid extra-special attention to the development of women comrades'. Breitman's commitment comes through in his discussion of Simone de Beauvoir (the existentialist he 'admired the most'):

> In all of her novels there is much that is good, and some that's very good. ... But her best book, and I think the best of that school is her [pioneering feminist] study, *The Second Sex*. ... [I]ts dissociation from Marxism is feeble and quibbling, I think. The spirit and tone of the whole work is Marxist to me. It is the work of a truly talented and cultured writer. (Maybe I felt a special impact; it had long been one of my conceits that I understood the woman question better than anyone else, including most women; and I was shaken up to find that after all I didn't know much about how hard it is to be a woman).[10]

Breitman's comprehension of working-class realities necessarily intersected not only with those of gender but also with those of race. As Michael Smith

---

8   Allen and Lovell 1987, p. 22.
9   Wohlforth 1994, p. 271; Allen and Lovell 1987, p. 137.
10 Allen and Lovell 1987, pp. 22–3.

puts it, 'He learned about black nationalism in Detroit. It was all-pervasive in that extremely nationalist and political city, and he was thus able to educate others, many others, about black nationalism and about its shining prince and chief spokesman, Malcolm X'.[11] Evelyn Sell captures an essential aspect of Breitman's achievement:

> His empathy enabled him to have unique insights into the feelings and aspirations of blacks – and this gave the Detroit branch a special advantage in responding to the exciting developments in the black community: the emergence of a generation of black youths seeking militant and revolutionary solutions to racism; the outpouring of almost the entire black population for the 1963 civil rights march through downtown Detroit; the nationalist character of the Michigan Freedom Now Party. George's ability to be in tune with these developments didn't come solely from his brain but from the very core of his being.[12]

'I thought he was black like me', commented one reader of Breitman's works who was surprised, upon meeting him, to find that he was white. 'I felt as if he was in my skin'. Another young black student commented that initially 'I looked upon the world struggle and the world situation as that of black vs. white – as oppressive whites who were responsible for oppressing nonwhites'. Contact with Breitman contributed to a shift in perspective: 'The struggle is really against avaricious capitalists who use racism and sexism as weapons in order for them to continue their exploitation and oppression of the working class of the world'.

Paul Lee, in a perceptive discussion of Breitman's writings on Malcolm X, has added another important point:

> It has been rare in my experience to meet white people who define themselves as *people* before they define themselves as *white*. That is, most whites that I've known see themselves and their culture as the norm, which implicitly or explicitly expresses itself in an attitude of superiority.
>
> In George's case, I'm not sure if he had *any* attachment to his so-called whiteness or to his ethnicity. I am sure that I never felt judged or 'different' in his regard because of my so-called blackness. I've been told the

---

11   Allen and Lovell 1987, p. 139.
12   Allen and Lovell 1987, p. 23.

same thing by other African Americans who knew him, including the late Wilfred Shabazz [brother of Malcolm X], who was an exceptionally perceptive person.

I can't account for *why* this was so, but I do know that it gave him an advantage in dealing with people defined as black, who, after all, just wanted to be treated as people. He related to black people with an ease and unselfconsciousness that won him their respect and trust. Another revolutionary who happened to be white, John Brown, is said to have had a similar relationship with black people.[13]

With his path-breaking work on Malcolm X, it became possible for Breitman to break out of two ghettoes. One ghetto was the rarefied circle of allegedly 'sectarian' politics to which small left-wing groups (especially Trotskyists) were often restricted, certainly in the conservative political and cultural atmosphere predominant in the United States during the 1950s and early 1960s. The other ghetto was much larger – that of so-called white America, which was traditionally sealed off from people of color in general and especially from African Americans. But this was consistent with Breitman's distinctive qualities over a number of years, which involved the persistent integration of his creativity with a deep and ongoing commitment to consistent revolutionary organizational work, which meant an engagement with more and more people across the boundaries of age, gender, and race. From semi-retirement in the mid-1950s, James P. Cannon went out of his way to hail the Detroit branch for its 'combination of all-sided activity' (which, according to Frank Lovell, was actually 'a tribute to George Breitman').[14]

The Friday Night Socialist Forum was one key element in bringing everything together. 'Working closely with his wife Dorothea, along with Frank and Sarah Lovell and Evelyn Sell, Breitman converted the group's Friday Night Socialist Forum into a tool for discussion and recruitment, and he continued to oversee the forum from 1954 until he left Detroit in 1967', writes historian Angela Dillard. 'Although African Americans did not join the SWP in large numbers … the forum and the *Militant* deeply influenced a number of young activists', Dillard emphasizes, commenting that the forum 'attracted dozens of young radicals, many of whom would go on to work with [the prominent black activist who led the Freedom Now Party] Reverend [Albert] Cleage and found some of the most important organizations of the late 1960s, including the League of

---

13 Lee 2002.
14 Allen and Lovell 1987, p. 50.

Black Revolutionary Workers and the Revolutionary Union Movement (RUM), the West Central Organization (WCO), and the Black Economic Development Conference'.[15]

Evelyn Sell described the Friday Night Socialist Forum as 'a primary means of party-building, of educating members and nonmembers, of developing young comrades as speakers, and of creating a center for political and radical activities in the Detroit area', elaborating:

> From its inception, the Friday Night Socialist Forum invited speakers from a range of organizations. Although most of the topics were political, there were many dealing with art, music, and literature. A humanities professor from Wayne State University not only gave talks about music but brought his portable keyboard and played excerpts to illustrate his points. A comrade who was a relatively well-known sculptor gave a series of talks on art, including taking the whole forum audience to the Detroit Art Institute for a guided lecture tour. The forum devoted a weekend to an exhibit of Daumier prints along with showing a film on the revolutions of 1848. The Friday Night Socialist Forum had theater nights when we presented portions of the writings and plays of Bertolt Brecht. As George wrote in a letter to me, Brecht was 'the creative writer with whom I identify the most closely'. He made Brecht fans out of many of us, and this was reflected in the Friday Night Socialist Forum.[16]

The forums would be held at the SWP headquarters that Breitman and his comrades established, which combined offices and a modest bookstore with a large meeting room and was dubbed Debs Hall to honor the great socialist leader Eugene V. Debs. Independent radical Dan Georgakas, coauthor of *Detroit: I Do Mind Dying*, frequently attended the Friday Night Socialist Forum, 'the only regularly scheduled Left event in the city at that time'. The initial presentations 'were always followed by often spirited question/answer/statements/debate periods', an intellectually stimulating format that added to its appeal. 'Looking over the list of those who attended the various forums, one will find a virtual who's who of the Detroit Left in the period which immediately followed [from the late 1960s through the 1970s]', as well as 'individuals who became part of the liberal establishment: at least one congressman and several judges, college administrators, union leaders, and city officials'. Once the weekly forums

---

15 Dillard 2010, pp. 23, 231.
16 Allen and Lovell 1987, p. 21.

became an SWP institution through the country, Georgakas notes, 'over a period of time, in any given location, hundreds of people might attend one or more such forums', and although most of those attending never joined the Socialist Workers Party, 'the cumulative impact of such forums was considerable'.[17]

During this period of 1954–67, it should be noted, Breitman played several important roles. According to Ernest Mandel (well-known Belgian Marxist theorist and a central leader of the Fourth International), Breitman was 'one of the few in our movement who have made a genuine contribution to the development of theory, in his case in the field of black nationalism, and more generally the nationalism of the downtrodden and the oppressed everywhere in the world'. Beginning in 1956, Breitman also played a key role in pushing forward the discussion that brought about a reconciliation among many Fourth Internationalists, culminating in formal reunification in 1963. Breitman's role in this, recalled Frank Lovell, was 'little known to most members of his branch in Detroit at that time'.[18]

To most members of the Detroit branch of the SWP, however, Breitman did provide a model of what Sell called 'a well-rounded, professional revolutionary', who 'set an example simply by the way he did things' – specifically, as someone who was prepared to assume responsibility in all phases of political life in the branch, including the most 'mundane'. Sell emphasizes: 'He took a serious attitude toward every task and assignment, whether it was functioning as a branch organizer, or bringing a wealth of ideas to executive committee meetings, or mopping the hall floors as a member of the headquarters committee'.[19]

Life and Leadership in the SWP

Tim Wohlforth had been a prominent activist in the Young Socialist League, youth group of the organization led by Max Shachtman – Independent Socialist League (formerly the Workers Party) – that was evolving from Trotskyism to social democracy and preparing to merge into the Socialist Party of America. Disagreeing with this perspective, Wohlforth and others broke away in 1957 in order to join the Socialist Workers Party and then to help create an SWP youth group, the Young Socialist Alliance (YSA), which came into being in 1960. Serving on the SWP's central leadership body, the Political Committee (PC), for several years, Wohlforth offers an interesting perspective. 'The main problem

---

17   Georgakas 1992, pp. xv–xvi.
18   Allen and Lovell 1987, pp. 49, 71.
19   Allen and Lovell 1987, 20.

with the Political Committee was that it was not very political', he complains. 'Unlike the YSA, the Socialist Workers Party in general in the late 1950s was a dull place, and Dobbs's PC was no different. A typical PC meeting was a two-hour battle to keep awake'. (He also describes the SWP's weekly newspaper, the *Militant*, of this period as 'exceedingly dull'). Going on to describe political differences and factional tensions which he discovered in his new organization (some of which are indicated in the documents gathered here), he added:

> I do not want to suggest that the SWP in this period was some kind of factional jungle. Actually life in the party was peaceful to the point of boredom. Most factionalism was of an underground character, conducted by individuals who claimed to have no political differences with the leadership. Dues were paid and the *Militant* was always sold. The party was run in a modest, but smooth and professional manner. The problem was that the party comprised a generation of workers and intellectuals – those recruited in the 1930s and during World War II – that was getting old and tired. Cannon did a better job than Shachtman in holding on to his aging cadres, and on the whole, he and his followers kept the revolutionary faith. But because will and energy had departed, faith was about all they had left. Cannon could not defy the general trends affecting the working class in the 1950s.[20]

Yet there were rank-and-file members who would not have accepted Wohlforth's characterizations. 'The Party has many needs. There is a constant and continuous whirl of activity', commented Ben Stone, an active member from 1945 to 1966. 'These activities include attending branch meetings at least once a week, attending special meetings – committee meetings, forums, classes'. He adds: 'Then there are the subscription campaigns (selling subs to the Party newspaper, the *Militant*, and other periodicals)'. Describing the *Militant* as 'the agitator for the Party and its best recruiting tool', he noted that it was 'sold at public places, rallies, demonstrations, meetings, factory gates, and on the streets'. More than this, 'the Party believes in proclaiming its ideas openly before the widest audience and election campaigns provide one of the best forums for dissemination of its views'. All in all, for an activist like Stone, 'life in

---

20 Wohlforth 1994, pp. 77, 82, 91. 'I tried to be interested in the *Militant*', confesses Leslie Evans, 'but the paper had about it a certain flatness, a humorless and artless nagging, endlessly recycling clichés' (Evans 2009, pp. 174–5) – in contrast to the more lively and penetrating weekly news magazine *World Outlook* (later renamed *Intercontinental Press*), which Joseph Hansen edited for the Fourth International.

the revolutionary Marxist party is one of total commitment', since 'the cause of socialism takes precedence over everything else'.[21]

The fact remained that the first decade of Stone's membership was one of dramatic erosion and decline. Coming into the SWP and YSA in the late 1950s were Barry Sheppard and Peter Camejo. With fewer than 600 members (the largest concentrations in New York and Los Angeles), 'the party nationally was composed largely of blue-collar workers, along with some outstanding university-educated intellectuals, such as George Novack, and young people whom we were beginning to recruit from the college campuses', according to Sheppard. 'While the membership was small, it consisted of very dedicated people ("cadres" was the term we used) who gave a great deal of their time and money to the party'.[22] Camejo described the Trotskyist leadership this way:

> The central core of the older party leadership had consisted mainly of several men who had all been involved since the early 1930s. In addition to Farrell Dobbs, who [as part of a team headed by V.R. Dunne] had led the Minneapolis Teamster strikes of the mid-thirties, and Tom Kerry from the seamen's unions on the West Coast, these leaders included Joseph Hansen, who had been Trotsky's secretary and was the SWP's main writer on international politics; George Breitman from Detroit, who undertook the publication of Trotsky's collected writings as well as the speeches of Malcolm X; and the party's principal intellectual, George Novack. A slightly younger second tier included Fred Halstead, Nat Weinstein, Harry Ring, and Ed Shaw. All these men remained active in the SWP after the transition to the younger team. The SWP's founder, James P. Cannon, had retired to Los Angeles in 1952 but occasionally sent his comments to the New York leadership until his death in 1974.[23]

Another young recruit, Leslie Evans, has indicated the way some members sized up the national party leadership: 'Hansen and George Breitman were theoreticians, the highest superlative, while Tom Kerry and Farrell Dobbs were at best politicians, able to carry out policy but not to formulate it. George Novack ranked lower still, an educator'.[24] In SWP branches throughout the country were worker-intellectuals (such as Larry Trainor in Boston) who played the essential role described by Barry Sheppard:

---

21 Stone 1978, pp. 68–9.
22 Sheppard 2005, p. 29.
23 Camejo 2010, p. 114.
24 Evans 2009, p. 158.

Larry imbued us with three aspects of the SWP tradition, above all. First was fierce loyalty to the working class and confidence in its power. Second was recognition of the great importance that the Russian revolution of 1917 held for the future socialist revolution and support for the Leninist ideas that led to the victory of that revolution. Third was support for the ideas of Leon Trotsky and the Trotskyist viewpoint as an alternative to the perversions of socialism that had been brought about during the Stalin era and after. The SWP that we had joined embodied all three aspects of that tradition both in its ideas and in its members, even though we were a small group and we lived at a time during which the working class and the popularity of socialist ideas had suffered great blows as a result of the Cold War witch-hunt period.[25]

The expectation of such stalwarts as Trainor, Stone, and others was that sustaining such steady outreach and radical educational efforts would attract precisely such younger activists as Wohlforth, Camejo, Sheppard, and Evans, as the natural functioning of capitalism (as it periodically seemed to) would yet again impact on new and youthful layers of the population and send them looking for precisely the sort of revolutionary organization that the SWP aspired to be.

Program, Method, Theorization, Reality

Camejo recalls: 'At one point SWP national secretary Farrell Dobbs told me: "The program has been developed. Our job is to implement it". In one form or another I heard this idea repeated by many SWPers, old and new'. Related to this is the way Cannon had begun a 1956 talk, 'Trotsky on America', with the comment: 'Original thinkers are as rare in the social sciences as in every other. In the hundred years of the modern movement of workers' emancipation we know only four genuinely creative minds. These are the masters of scientific socialism, Marx and Engels, and their great disciples, Lenin and Trotsky'.[26]

---

25 Sheppard 2005, p. 29.
26 Camejo 2010, p. 115; Cannon 1960, p. 99. Related to this is Irving Howe's recollection of one of the dynamics in the 1939–40 SWP majority's fight against the Shachtman-Burnham faction: 'When the American Trotskyist movement was torn by a debate in 1939 over the nature of Stalinism (a matter of great importance), there soon began to hover over us the delusionary specter of dialectics, as a result of a strange complicity between Trotsky and his factional antagonist, James Burnham. Few of the intellectuals close to the Trotskyist group cared about dialectics, indeed, they smiled tolerantly at the scholasticism of it all. But a good many of the proletarian leaders and members, those who had laboriously

What might be termed the non-creative approach – perhaps related to the dullness of which Wohlforth complained – was seen by Camejo as connected to a 'concept of the "program" [which] was a defining aspect of Trotskyism'. He explained:

> The early Trotskyists ... saw their primary role as trying to win people over from the mass Communist parties in order to fight for a return to the values of the socialist movement prior to its Stalinist degeneration. Gradually this fight led to a solidifying of the idea that the Trotskyists were the defenders of the true 'program'. This idea of the defense of the program became detached from the real, material development in the mass movement. Among Trotskyists the idea of the true 'program' gradually became its own icon to be defended.[27]

Yet within SWP ranks – including in its leading circles – there was also a much greater intellectual alertness, political engagement, and theoretical creativity than this. Much of this finds reflection in materials gathered in this volume. In large measure it flows from a methodology described by George Breitman in 1964. Breitman insisted on the recognition of what he saw as one of the most important features of Marxism: 'its richness, its variety, its ability to cope with changing situations, its unfinishedness. Marxism is not only what Marx worked out a century ago, nor only what Lenin and Trotsky added when they applied Marx's method to the conditions of their time, but also what subsequent Marxists did, do and will do as they apply this theory to other situations, including some that do not even exist yet'. His elaboration pushes dramatically against the static approach to 'program' of which Camejo complained:

> *Marxism is a theory in process of development*, which grows in power and scope as it is applied to specific situations and to new conditions. It developed when Lenin and Trotsky applied it to the specific conditions of Russia in the epoch of imperialism ('Russianized' it). It developed further when the Socialist Workers Party applied it to the specific conditions of America ('Americanized' it). And it continues to develop as the SWP applies it to the specific conditions of the Negro community in the

---

struggled to master the mystery of how "quantity turns into quality", were upset. By no means were they prepared to give up their belief in the universal applicability of the dialectic just because it was being mocked by a snobbish professor from NYU – and by the way, he really was snobbish'. Howe 1981, pp. 10–12.

27   Camejo 2010, p. 115.

United States ('Afro-Americanizes' it, as the SWP put in the 1963 convention resolution, *Freedom Now: The New Stage in the Struggle for Negro Emancipation* ...).[28]

The methodology personified in Breitman pushes uncompromisingly against the insular and 'purist' dogmatism to which Lewis Coser and others refer:

> Theory is derived from reality; the more closely a theory corresponds to reality, the better a theory it is. Marx studied the conditions and struggles of the west European workers, learned from them, and incorporated those lessons in his theory. Lenin and Trotsky did the same with the Russian workers and peasants. And from its inception the Socialist Workers Party has been doing this with the conditions and struggles of the American Negro people, which have always been unique in many respects. Embodied in its theory and program are many lessons learned from the Negro struggle, and from the ideas, feelings and outlook of the masses in the black ghetto.
>
> The SWP has been studying these changes, trying to understand their causes, find out their direction and fit their revolutionary aspects into a theory and program of action capable of replacing capitalism with socialism. It has been listening to and learning from non-Marxist figures – such as Malcolm X, Rev. Cleage, William Worthy, Jesse Gray, Daniel Watts, James Baldwin, the exiled Robert F. Williams and Julian Mayfield, even Harold Cruse sometimes – who to one degree or another express the thinking, feeling and aspirations of the black ghetto which, as Robert Vernon recently pointed out, is 'more solidly working class and revolutionary in outlook than the trade unions, or anything else in America today'.[29]

The late 1950s and early 1960s saw an anti-racist upsurge spearheaded by the civil rights movement, anti-colonial revolutions and the triumph in Cuba of the radical insurgency of Fidel Castro and Che Guevara, protests against nuclear weapons, a radicalization among college-age youth, the beginnings of protests against the Vietnam war, and more. This dramatically changing context brought an influx of radicalized youth into the SWP and YSA, which doubled and tripled the size of the US Trotskyist movement. By 1960, when he

---

28   Breitman 1965b, p. 20. For an elaboration on the approach to program, theory and method indicated here, see Le Blanc 2016.
29   Breitman 1965b, pp. 20–1. The comment 'even Harold Cruse sometimes' refers to the black nationalist whose sharp criticism of the SWP Breitman's essay is responding to.

was 48 years old, Ben Stone felt the political ground slipping from under his feet. 'Now the rank and file member was much younger, a generation removed, most of whom I hardly knew', he recalled. 'For the first time I began to feel like an old man in the Party, almost a stranger in my own house'. As the 1960s proceeded, 'the Party attracted even younger members, kids in their teens and early twenties. ... The 60s was a time of radical ferment on the college campuses and the Party attracted some of these youth, certainly in greater numbers than ever before'.[30]

The result was both revitalization and crisis. 'The older, primarily worker-based segment of the party had grown concerned that the SWP would be changed by its newer members, mostly middle-class youth', according to Camejo. 'Many of the older members opposed our support for what they saw as contemporary issues, such as gay liberation, and in general were nervous that the SWP might abandon its roots in Trotskyism and begin to alter its "program"'.[31]

George Breitman emphasized a point missed by many at the time – that a significant working-class component was integral to the mass protest movements opposing racism, the Vietnam war, etc. 'It is idiotic and insulting to think that the worker responds only to economic issues', Breitman stressed. 'He can be radicalized in various ways, over various issues, and he is'. Breitman developed this point at length:

> The radicalization of the worker can begin off the job as well as on. It can begin from the fact that the worker is a woman as well as a man; that the worker is Black or Chicano or a member of some other oppressed minority as well as white; that the worker is a father or mother whose son can be drafted; that the worker is young as well as middle-aged or about to retire. If we grasp the fact that the working class is stratified and divided in many ways – the capitalists prefer it that way – then we will be better able to understand how the radicalization will develop among workers and how to intervene more effectively. Those who haven't already learned important lessons from the radicalization of oppressed minorities, youth and women had better hurry up and learn them, because most of the people involved in these radicalizations are workers or come from working-class families.[32]

---

30 Stone 1978, p. 86. For an outstanding source on the broad, diverse and multifaceted radicalization, see Gosse 2005.
31 Camejo 2010, p. 114.
32 Breitman 1971, p. 25.

Factional Crises, Future Triumph, Eventual Collapse

The combination of uneven qualities explored here generated tensions and factional conflicts within the SWP, as comrades reached for the most effective and appropriate balance of political principle and political relevance, and as they struggled to understand the complex and changing world around them.

There proved to be sufficient strengths in the underlying political program and theoretical perspectives to enable the SWP to grow dramatically in the 1960s, to provide influential and often creative analyses of emerging realities, and sometimes to play a serious role in the social struggles of the time.

To many who were paying attention, the SWP of the late 1960s and 1970s seemed an incredibly vibrant organization: between 1,000 and 2,000 activists animated by high ideals and dynamic Marxism, with a conception of socialism both democratic and revolutionary, and a proven capacity to organize – in impressive united front efforts – effective social movements and struggles capable of bringing about positive change.

Among the new recruits were important clusters of African-American and Latino activists, and also a significant percentage of women, some of whom assumed a significant leadership role in the efforts of the SWP and YSA. The party's earlier work on issues of race and nationalism, and its serious-minded engagement with Malcolm X, contributed to the ability of some comrades to play a role not only in African-American but also in Chicano and Puerto Rican struggles.

The fact that in the 1950s and early '60s the SWP had seriously engaged with not only such works as Friedrich Engels's *Origin of the Family, Private Property, and the State*, but also Simone de Beauvoir's *The Second Sex* and Betty Friedan's *The Feminine Mystique*, made it more sensitive and responsive to early feminist stirrings coming out of the new radicalization and enabled it to connect very positively to the rising women's liberation movement. In addition, the recruitment of a growing number of gay and lesbian comrades – combined with influences and insights that were part of the new radicalization – enabled the SWP finally to scrap a narrow and destructive policy that had banned homosexuals from membership.

Perhaps the SWP's most profound accomplishment involved its central role in the creation of the massive and powerful anti-war movement, through persistent united front efforts, that proved capable of helping to end the US war in Vietnam. The details of that story were told in Fred Halstead's classic *Out Now! A Participant's Account of the Movement Against the Vietnam War*.[33]

---

33 Halstead 1978.

From 1965 to 1980 the SWP seemed in the process of becoming a hegemonic force on the US Left and within a variety of social movements. Along the pathway to this seemingly promising outcome, however, there was a glossed-over failure to fully resolve (or adequately combine) the uneven and contradictory elements that had been part of the party's experience in the 1950s and 1960s. Related to this, there was also a cropping up of organizational measures and norms that (in the words of James P. Cannon) had the potential to 'strangle the Party'.

After a new leadership drawn from the 1960s radicalization took control within the SWP, an extremely complex and difficult situation developed in the world and the country – as the 1970s gave way to the 1980s and 1990s. There are multiple sources and analyses of what happened next, as the SWP imploded.[34] Amid growing political uncertainty combined with accumulating mistakes and disappointments, the new leadership became increasingly authoritarian in the name of 'Leninism', abandoning the historic program of Trotskyism in order to embrace a utopian understanding of Castroism, and initiated incredibly damaging waves of expulsions. What remained of the once-promising organization shriveled into what in the opinion of many on the Left, including a substantial number of once-dedicated members, proved to be a politically irrelevant sect.

Future Resources

The very nature of the capitalist economic system – whose incredible, undeniable global dynamism has the result, over and over again, that 'all that is solid melts into air', and that 'all that is holy is profaned' – blends equally dizzying creativity and destructiveness as one decade gives way to another. Multiple variations of corruption, pollution, tyranny, and violence seem to proliferate with the passage of time.

If it is the case, as some have argued, that this is necessarily and inevitably so, then there will continue to be waves of rebellion and resistance, organized by hopeful heroines and heroes seeking to create the possibility of another, better world. Even those who have no such hopes may find it enlightening to consider the perceptions, insights, and efforts of earlier generations of rebels to be found in these volumes. In many cases these can shed light on what happened

---

34 See, for example, Alexander 1991, pp. 880–98; Sheppard 2012, pp. 278–320; Evans 2009, pp. 292–309; and extensive materials in the sets of documents edited by Lovell 1992 and Le Blanc 1992.

in a past that has shaped our present. And those who struggle for a more hopeful future may also have something to learn from those who sought to pass on resources to such people as themselves.

CHAPTER 2

New Stirrings

Paul Le Blanc

The second half of the 1950s saw – both despite and because of the heady combination of Cold War repression and fear of nuclear war, relative prosperity mixed with rampant commercialism and consumerism, and what many found to be a stultifying cultural conformism – the initial stirrings of a new wave of radicalization that would, within a decade, sweep through the United States. All of this was taking place within a global context of Stalinism's crisis and collapse, and the seemingly inexorable rise of anti-colonial revolutions throughout Asia and Africa.[1]

One of the decisive developments of this period was the rise of the civil rights movement, sparked by the 1954 Supreme Court decision finding racial segregation in public schools to be a violation of the 14th amendment of the US Constitution – a development reflected in the thoughtful analysis of Jean Blake, 'The Continuing Struggle for Negro Equality'.[2] While this development and the SWP's evolving engagement with it are reflected in this and the next chapter, we have – as with the previous volumes in this documentary trilogy – gathered most of the materials dealing with these defining realities into a unified section, such as the third chapter of the present volume, in order to highlight various dimensions of racism and the anti-racist struggle.

Also of profound importance was a development related to the extreme repressiveness of Cold War anti-Communism that had reached a reaction-

---

1 Parallel postwar developments of prosperity in the advanced capitalist countries, anti-colonial struggles, and anti-Stalinist ferment are succinctly laid out in Heller 2006, pp. 75–136. Among the books providing cultural and intellectual background are Pells 1985; Jezer 1982; Lipsitz 1990; Stone 1969. A fine survey of the US Left largely shaped in this period can be found in Brick and Phelps 2015.
2 Outlines of the early civil rights struggle are detailed in Branch 1988, with focused attention on the Northern urban areas within which the SWP was concentrated in Sugrue 2008. Analytical framework is provided by Allen 1990 and Marable 2007 – corresponding in significant ways with perceptions advanced by libertarian-socialist Guerin 1956, seeing racism in the US as flowing from capitalist and imperialist economic dynamics, comparing it with the racism related to the colonialism of his native France. This work was translated into English by one US Trotskyist, Duncan Ferguson, and formally distributed in the United States by another, George L. Weissman.

ary crescendo through the efforts of right-wing Republican Senator Joseph McCarthy. When McCarthy's smear tactics, designed to advance his own political influence and career, were unleashed on fellow Republicans, the Eisenhower administration, and the Department of Defense, he was discredited and marginalized by the powers-that-be. The beginnings of this process are analyzed in Murry Weiss, 'McCarthyism: Key Issue in the 1954 Elections'. Worthy of note was the tendency of the SWP to join in the estimate of others in this period to characterize McCarthyism as 'incipient fascism'. The SWP had played a significant role in challenging the anti-Communist red scare and McCarthyism through a persistent and ultimately effective defense around James Kutcher. A veteran of the Second World War, Kutcher lost both of his legs in combat, but later was able to secure a clerical job with the Veterans' Administration. When he lost this job, because of his membership in the officially 'subversive' SWP, a broad array of liberals, radicals, labor activists, and others rallied to what was dubbed 'the case of the legless veteran' – which lasted from 1948 until the Veterans' Administration was finally forced to rehire him in 1956.[3]

Among the early stirrings would be those culminating in the rise of a new wave of feminism. There had long been an interplay between socialism and feminism in the United States, and within and around the US Communist movement there were particularly important developments in the 1940s and 1950s – with the controversial efforts of Mary Inman to develop a Marxist theory of women's liberation with *In Defense of Woman* (for which she was eventually challenged and expelled by party leaders), the pioneering research efforts of Eleanor Flexner culminating in the 1959 classic *Century of Struggle: The Women's Rights Movement in the United States*, and the writings of left-wing fashion designer Elizabeth Hawes with such books as *Fashion is Spinach* (1938), *Why Women Cry, or Wenches with Wrenches* (1943), and *It's Still Spinach* (1954).[4]

Within the SWP, as well, there were a number of strong women. In his reminiscences of the 1950s, Tim Wohlforth recalls Sylvia Bleeker (whose roots had been in the Russian revolutionary movement before she immigrated to the United States, where she became a Communist and then a Trotskyist) – 'Sylvia

---

3   General accounts of the phenomenon of 'McCarthyism' are presented in many studies, including: Schrecker 1998; Fried 1996; Morgan 2004. Goldstein 2001 places this in historical context. The Kutcher case is the focal-point of Kutcher 1973, Goldstein 2016, and also a documentary film by Howard Petrick, 'The Case of the Legless Veteran', available at: https://www.youtube.com/watch?v=9sbdlIdt9HY.

4   For a documentary overview, see Schneir 1972 and Schneir 1994. Important works are Inman 1941 and Flexner 1968, both discussed in Weigand 2001. Such feminist writings as Hawes 1938, Hawes 1943, and Hawes 1954 receive insightful attention in Berch 1988.

had a disdain for routinism and bureaucratic procedure and was the bane of local organizers', and similar qualities could be found particularly in the younger and vibrant Myra Tanner Weiss, the only woman on the SWP's governing Political Committee – opinionated, articulate, who 'did not approach other party leaders with undue reverence'. Wohlforth added: 'There was a layer of women in the party who, like Myra, were politically strong and refused to accept a secondary role because they were women. These party feminists included Evelyn Reed, George Novack's wife, who made a special study of anthropology, Frances James …, and Clara Fraser (Kaye), a leader of the Seattle branch'.[5] Such sensibilities are manifest in the anthropological-sociological exploration by Evelyn Reed on the alleged inferiority of women, and on both sides of a debate that unexpectedly flared up within Trotskyist ranks about the issue of cosmetics, involving Marjorie McGowan, Jeanne Morgan, and Joseph Hansen.

As with race and gender, we can see significant attention being given to issues of culture and radical stirrings among youth – highlighted by James Robertson's exploration of what would turn out to be the early seedlings of the 1960s youth radicalization, and by Evelyn Sell's discussion of the so-called 'beat generation'. Although the 1950s have been seen as, in many ways, a time of both cultural and political conservatism and conformism, alert minds among the US Trotskyists were picking up on countervailing tendencies in the very same period.[6]

Some analysts have suggested that this growing attention to what would later be termed 'identities', instead of the traditional Marxist focus on *class*, reflected the deeper trends identified by the 1955 article by Harold Robins on automation. Potentially far-reaching technological changes in the economy certainly had important implications for capitalism, the working class, and the class struggle. The themes explored by Robins have remained a focal-point decades after,[7] and – as with other issues touched on in this chapter – we will see a revisiting of these questions in the next chapter. That the time was fast-approaching to say 'farewell to the working class',[8] however, was not a notion that US Trotskyists were inclined to embrace – although a growing number of left-wing commentators (C. Wright Mills, Herbert Marcuse, James Boggs, Paul Sweezy,

---

5 Wohlforth, pp. 82–3.
6 Relevant to this are Charters 1992, Farrell 1997, Duberman 2011, pp. 7–78, Jamison and Eyerman 1995, and Goodman 1964.
7 Scholarship generated on this issue in later decades includes: Gordon, Edwards and Reich 1982; Shaikin 1985; Noble 1986; Wilson 1997.
8 The phrase comes from Gorz 1982.

André Gorz, Ernesto Laclau, Chantal Mouffe) would, at various moments and with varying levels of consistency, be saying such things out loud in coming decades.

In fact, the mood among Trotskyists as the 1950s flowed into the 1960s was that History was going their way. This was especially the case in regard to one of the most profound changes of the time – a deepening crisis within the world Stalinist movement. This comes through clearly in the public forum presentation by Murry Weiss, which described in detail the revelation by Nikita Khrushchev of Stalin's crimes as 'the vindication of Trotskyism', and it certainly ruptured what had been a hegemonic position within the Stalinized Communist movement in the Left.[9]

As a self-critical mood, a rethinking of basic perspectives, was spreading within what remained of the Left, and with the proliferation and growth of insurgent moods and social struggles, it seemed to many, including within Trotskyist ranks, that a reshuffling and regroupment of left-wing forces might be possible, with beneficial results. Efforts to make this so, and the thinking behind such efforts, are indicated in the remarks made by James P. Cannon at a regroupment gathering in 1958.

---

9 See Starobin 1972 and Isserman 1987. Murry Weiss, along with his companion Myra Tanner Weiss, played a particularly important role in the SWP from the early 1950s to the 1960s. Information on Weiss can be gleaned from: *New York Times* 1981; Kovacs 2000, made available through a site operated by Louis Proyect: http://lists.csbs.utah.edu/pipermail/marxism/2000 -October/043492.html (accessed 22 June 2016); Evans 2009, pp. 141, 146–7, 179–80; Sheppard 2004, pp. 58–61; Stone 1978, pp. 75–6; Alexander 1991, pp. 936–8.

1 The Continuing Struggle for Negro Equality[10]
(*1954*)

Jean Blake

Developments since the May 17 US Supreme Court ruling that segregated public schools are unconstitutional have made clear that whatever decrees are issued by the Court to implement the decision following the submission of additional briefs in October, school segregation will not be abolished in fact in the United States until all forms of racial discrimination are ended.

From an historical perspective, the Court's action was simply the latest in a series of shifts in policy on official discrimination, resulting from the particular political needs of the capitalist class.

A brief summary of these shifts demonstrates the contradictory interpretations of the Constitution possible under democratic capitalism. The only underlying principle involved is the maintenance of the capitalist system. Consequently no court decision on segregation is irrevocable or irreversible.

- March 4, 1789, the Constitution went into effect, specifically recognizing slavery and discrimination.
- Dec. 15, 1791, the Bill of Rights went into effect, including the Fifth Amendment, with the clause 'No person shall be … deprived of life, liberty, or property, without due process of law …'. But this guarantee did not apply to Negroes' rights, since Negroes were considered property, not persons.
- March 6, 1857, in the Dred Scott decision, the Court held that a Negro who had been a slave could not become a citizen by residing in an area where slavery was banned.
- Dec. 18, 1865, the Thirteenth Amendment, abolishing slavery, was declared ratified. But it was still necessary to pass the Fourteenth (July 28, 1868), and Fifteenth (March 30, 1870) Amendments, specifically granting the 'equal protection of the laws' and the right to vote.
- 1873–1879, in the first cases interpreting the Fourteenth Amendment after its adoption, the Court held that the amendment banned all state-imposed discrimination against Negroes.

---

10   Blake 1954.

- 1896, in the notorious Plessy v. Ferguson case, the Supreme Court ruled that segregation was not unconstitutional so long as the separate facilities provided were equal.
- 1954, in cases from Kansas, South Carolina, Virginia, Delaware and the District of Columbia, the Court holds that 'separate educational facilities are inherently unequal' and therefore violate the Fourteenth Amendment and the Fifth Amendment.

What is the reason for the Court's reversal of its previous interpretation, in the Plessy case, that segregation is not unconstitutional? Chief Justice Warren, in delivering the Court's opinion, specifically cited only one new factor in the situation, 'the extent of psychological knowledge'. Modern psychology, he said in effect, reveals that separation of Negro children from white in public schools has a detrimental effect upon the colored children even though the material facilities provided are equal. 'Any language in Plessy v. Ferguson contrary to this finding is rejected'.

Psychology was a major element in the new interpretation – that is true.

But it was not the psychology of the effect of segregation on colored children. It was the psychological effect of US Jim Crow on the colored colonial peoples, and the political needs of American capitalism's propaganda campaign for domination of the world, that were decisive in reversing the Court's previous position.

While not a word of this appears in the decision, it was clearly the policy of the administration in Washington to secure an interpretation aimed at convincing the opponents of American capitalism abroad that the 'imperfections' in US democracy are being corrected internally. That was why the Justice Department filed a brief as friend of the court specifically requesting a re-examination of the 'separate but equal' doctrine. That was why Vice President Nixon, on his return from a 'good-will' trip abroad, publicly reported that the practice of discrimination in this country is harmful to US foreign policy.

And that was also why the *Voice of America* began broadcasting the news of the decision within two hours after it was rendered, so that the peoples in Asia and Africa and Europe heard it before many Americans.

Reactions to Ruling

In the weeks following the ruling, reactions at home varied. The National Association for the Advancement of Colored People, which led the fight against segregation, and supporters of the struggle for Negro equality, saw the ruling as an important legal victory. On the whole, they recognized that it would be necessary to follow up this moral victory with additional court actions as well as organizational and other measures, in order to implement the decision and to combat attempts at delay, evasion and circumvention.

Southern extremists varied in their comments. Governor Talmadge of Georgia, who had repeatedly declared 'there never will be mixed schools in Georgia while I am governor', expressed his intention to defy the court ruling. He challenged the authority of the Court and threatened to abolish the public school system rather than end segregation. On an NBC-TV *Meet the Press* program, he said his state would not 'secede from the union', but he indicated that troops would be used to uphold the state laws.

Senator James O. Eastland of Mississippi declared: 'The South will not abide by or obey this legislative decision by a political court. Integrated schools are not desired by either race in the south. An attempt to integrate our schools would cause great strife and turmoil'. Senator Harry F. Byrd of Virginia said that the decision 'will bring implications and dangers of the greatest consequence'.

Senator Eastland and his fellow Mississippian in the House, Congressman John Bell Williams, have introduced resolutions asking Congress to approve a constitutional amendment which would destroy the Court's jurisdiction in matters of racial segregation.

But the dominant opinion of the Southern ruling class was better expressed by Governor James F. Byrnes of South Carolina, who said he was 'shocked', but proceeded to note that the Court did not order an immediate end to separate schools. He went on to advise South Carolinians to 'exercise restraint and preserve order' while he – the 'benevolent Bourbon', as one Negro writer characterizes him – studies the decision and decides on recommendations to the Legislature.

The Bigots Mobilize

That, on the whole, is shaping up as official policy in the South: continue segregation, since there is no order in the Court decision banning it; and devise ways and means to continue segregation by legal and extra-legal trickery, whatever the Court may rule.

Unofficially, other methods are being prepared to maintain segregation. These methods range from social, economic and political pressure and intimidation of Negroes, to outright force and violence.

On June 10, for example, a group of former Ku Klux Klansmen announced that they have reorganized under the name of the 'White Brotherhood', pledged to preserve segregation by legal means and to '*try* to avoid killing and violence'. (My emphasis – *J.B.*). Bill Hendrix of Tallahassee, Fla., former KKK Grand Dragon, is spokesman for the group.

At the same time, as though to emphasize the fact that the old forms of intimidation in the South have not been entirely abandoned, a *Pittsburgh Courier* headline on June 5 reported: *Lynching in Alabama!* The victim, unnamed when the paper went to press, was found hanged in a wooded section near a Negro church outside of Vredenburgh.

Earlier, on May 26, the new home of a Negro dentist in Birmingham, Ala., was damaged by arson. The following weekend the pattern of segregation by intimidation was repeated in the northern city of Cleveland, Ohio ('best location in the nation'), with three new cases of attacks on homes by paint-smearing, rock-hurling bigots, and a similar incident in nearby Lakewood.

Law Needs Teeth

The long history of incidents such as these and similar attacks in Chicago and elsewhere apparently have influenced the thinking of Southern white supremacists. They are beginning to hold meetings of governors and other law enforcement officers to consider how to segregate Negroes, as the North has done, without legal sanction.

Negro leaders, too, recognize that the Supreme Court decision and further decrees can remain a dead letter from the outset unless the action of the Negro people and their allies puts teeth into the law.

In an *Atlanta Declaration* adopted by a southern conference of the organization, the NAACP announced a campaign by branches in all areas affected by the Court decision to petition local school boards for immediate ending of racial segregation in schools and to offer assistance in working out problems.

The next day the Supreme Court acted on six more cases involving segregation. In three cases the Court denied hearings, thereby letting stand lower court decisions
1. banning segregation in low-rent housing projects in San Francisco;
2. banning segregation on the old 'separate but equal' doctrine at Hardin Junior College of Wichita Falls, Texas; and
3. ordering the city of Houston, Texas, to permit Negroes to use municipal golf courses on a segregated basis.

Only the first case involved a principled opposition to segregation.

In the three other cases, involving admission of Negroes to the University of Florida and Louisiana State University, and to a city-owned Louisville, Ky., amphitheater, the Supreme Court merely ordered the lower courts to reconsider their decisions 'in the light of' the May 17 ruling and 'conditions that now prevail'.

These actions should make it clear that the Court does not intend to take a clear-cut, principled stand extending its ruling against segregation in the schools to segregation in all other fields, as some had hoped. If they intended to do so, they could have commented on the cases they refused to hear, or they could have heard them and ruled to uphold the decision of the lower courts while clarifying the basis for the decision as the unconstitutionality of segregation.

In the three cases that were referred back to the lower courts for re-examination, the Court could have been less ambiguous if it had wished to outlaw segregation.

But the Court did none of these things, because the main task had already been concluded May 17 with the ruling on school segregation: the Voice of America had its story.

There will be other by-products of the Supreme Court decision. Machine politicians already are attempting to credit or blame the Democrats or the Republicans, or one candidate or another in primary elections, for the decision against school segregation, in order to win votes in the November elections.

McCarthyite Smears

McCarthy-type smears will be dragged in to discredit opponents of segregation. Senator Eastland started this process on May 27 when he asserted that the 'court has been indoctrinated and brainwashed by left-wing pressure groups'. His proofs: Justice Black received an award April 14, 1945, from: the Southern Conference for Human Welfare, which Eastland called a notorious 'Communist-front' organization; Justice Minton, who was then on the US Circuit Court of Appeals, made a speech at the same affair; Justice Douglas accepted a $1,000 Sidney Hillman award from the CIO in December, 1952; Justices Reed and Frankfurter gave character-witness testimony in behalf of Alger Hiss, former State Department official convicted of perjury in 1950.

But such developments are secondary to the main line of policy on segregation. There is no basic disagreement between the Democratic and Republican parties on this question. The history of the past half century and more demonstrates that the ruling class, through both capitalist parties, has no intention of ending discrimination against Negroes. At present, in the attempt to make Washington's foreign policy less objectionable to the world's colored millions,

Wall Street is willing to grant a concession: a statement that public school segregation is unconstitutional.

At the same time, a small legal victory might strengthen the arguments of those Negro leaders who preach support of capitalism as the system under which equality will eventually be achieved.

But will the Supreme Court ruling achieve either of its real aims – winning the confidence and support of the colonial peoples, and of the American Negroes, for capitalism?

In the first place, it won't win the support of the Chinese, Koreans, Indo-Chinese or any other colonial peoples fighting for freedom from imperialist domination. Their distrust of the United States is based on more than the obvious hypocrisy of the US claim to leadership of the 'free world' while practicing discrimination at home.

The basic antagonism is between people who have been super-exploited for generations by foreign imperialism, and the capitalist rulers of the US who must find new fields of exploitation in order to maintain the profit system. This antagonism would exist even if there were no problem of Jim Crow in America. The US government knows this, too, and is not halting A-bomb and H-bomb production in favor of Supreme Court rulings as a means of winning world domination.

Similarly at home, a few colored politicians, or others with a vested interest in a segregated community, may be satisfied with democratic platitudes and abstractions; but the mass of Negro workers want integrated schools so that their children – not some great-great-grandchildren of the future – can have the same education and the same opportunities for jobs as other children. They want equal job opportunities and equal pay right now, so that they can provide decent homes for their families and get out of the demoralizing slums. They want their right to live wherever they wish, under civilized conditions, without danger of threats and violence.

They also want, like other working men and women, freedom from the fear of war and of unemployment, and all the traditional freedoms they have been taught are theirs – the right to think, speak, write, meet, vote.

But the Supreme Court ruling will not even result in the one limited objective of integrated schools. The majority of the states now requiring or permitting segregation will, it is true, get in line with the Court ruling by revising their laws and ordinances requiring separate schools – though whether they effect these legal reforms sooner or later or not at all depends on how principled, militant and uncompromising a struggle the NAACP and the Negro people and their allies conduct.

New Forms of Segregation

But the outlines of the new forms of segregation in the US, even though state laws requiring separation of colored and white children in schools may be wiped off the books completely, are already clear. Numerous Northern newspapers and magazines have pointed out that in most cases colored children will 'naturally' continue to go to the same schools they went to previously, since they live in segregated ghettoes and could logically be expected to attend schools in their own neighborhoods.

For the majority of Negro children, the Supreme Court decision will mean no change at all. Only those living on the borders of the 'community within a community' will be faced with the problem, of enforcing their right to attend mixed schools.

The NAACP recognizes this and has announced it will now broaden its campaign to combat segregated housing and discrimination in employment, while at the same time it seeks implementation of the ruling against school segregation. Employment of Negroes in the least skilled jobs in heavy industry or the dirtiest, most difficult and lowest paid jobs in consumer goods industries, tends to make it difficult or impossible for them to move out of the ghettoes because of the higher cost of transportation and of buying or renting newer homes.

Finally, those few who are able to overcome the legal and economic barriers find that the white supremacists do not hesitate, as a last recourse, to use naked force. Bombings, arson, destruction of property, beatings and even murder are the means. Very seldom do the law enforcement authorities take action against their silent partners who carry out the dirty work. Local police subversive squads can track down every detail in the history of a socialist, a militant unionist, or a persistent fighter for equal rights; but they plead helplessness in discovering who bombed the home of a new Negro resident in a 'white' neighborhood.

The struggle for equal rights, like the struggle of the unions, is essentially a defensive struggle. In both, the problem is to hold on to gains already made, and to fight for their extension in order to counteract the efforts of the ruling class to restrict all progress that threatens its power and privileges. As long as these struggles are conducted within the limited perspective of isolated reforms – a legal decision here, a temporary wage increase there – the gains are superficial and transitory.

To repeat an old but time-tested analogy: some of the most painful or ugly symptoms of a disease may be temporarily soothed by surface medication, drugs or minor operations; but until the basic cause of the illness is found and cured, the infection will recur or break out in other forms.

That is why labor's gains in wages and working conditions will not secure the workers' standard of living until the whole wage system, and the organization of production for profit on which it is based, is attacked fundamentally and replaced with a rational socialist system of production in keeping with mankind's present stage of material and technical progress.

And that is why racial segregation will be eliminated, not by court decisions, but only when its role in relation to our American capitalist system of production and all the institutions developed to maintain and support it is recognized and similarly attacked fundamentally.

The Supreme Court ruling on school segregation can have historic significance if it is utilized by the united working people as a wedge in the revolutionary struggle to demolish the old superstructure of capitalism and build a new society for mankind on modern foundations.

2 McCarthyism: Key Issue in the 1954 Elections[11]
(1954)

Murry Weiss

Senator McCarthy took the 36 days of the Army-McCarthy TV hearings as a priceless opportunity to shape a political image before millions of viewers – the image of himself as savior of America. He played up to the mass audience, pandering to their prejudices, shocking, arousing, repelling them – and at the same time fascinating them with his brazenness, his arrogant assurance, his utter contempt for his opponents. Above all, he pounded tirelessly on his fascist charge of '20' and '21 years of treason'.

The hearings over, the Wisconsin fascist leader retired to a secret hide-out to recuperate and plot his next move. The sudden relief the liberals felt from the daily fascist rasp on their nerves induced reckless speculation: they told each other that McCarthy was finished, and they held funeral services for him in their newspaper columns. He had turned out to be his own worst enemy, the liberals assured themselves. The American people, they declared, had got a good look at McCarthy and his methods and had decided they didn't want any part of either.

But life is unkind to illusions. McCarthy returned, and it became clear that the fascist beast was still alive and kicking, and that the nightmare wasn't over by any means.

The next act of this political drama is now to be played against the backdrop of the 1954 elections. What will McCarthy's role be? Will he split from the Republican party after the primaries and form a separate fascist party? Or will a new *modus vivendi*, based on common determination to win a witch-hunting victory over the Democrats, be established between McCarthy and the other Republicans?

To assess the role of McCarthyism in the coming elections, it is first necessary to make a realistic estimate of the results of the Army-McCarthy hearings.

---

11   Weiss 1954.

It is possible to draw a pleasing sketch of McCarthyism in decline since the beginning of the year. A superficial comparison of McCarthy's power before and after the hearings has led commentators to the hasty conclusion that McCarthyism is routed. Not only the highly impressionable liberal columnists but some of the more sober observers, including those in the official trade union camp, have drawn this conclusion. *Labor's Daily*, July 13, announces in a headline, 'Joe's Strength Ebbing Fast', and opens its story: 'Sen. Joseph R. McCarthy was under attack from all sides today and it appeared his strength was ebbing even in his home state'.

There is some truth to the contention that McCarthy has suffered a setback. But only a grain of truth. And this grain cannot be properly understood unless it is put in context. For while suffering blows and tactical setbacks, McCarthyism has in the same period made important advances in its basic development as a fascist movement.

The year 1954 opened auspiciously for McCarthy. Early in February, he went on national tour under the official sponsorship of the Republican National Committee, and proceeded to denounce the Democrats for their '20 years of treason'.

Within the Senate, McCarthy seemed unassailable. On Feb. 2 the Democrats and Republicans collapsed and voted 85 to 1 for the appropriations he demanded for his committee. McCarthy's Senate power was further strengthened by his appointment to the all-important Rules Committee.

McCarthy's prowess as a witch hunter was at a high point. In his first public skirmish with the Army, over the Peress and General Zwicker affair, McCarthy scored a hands-down victory, the Army beating a fumbling and apologetic retreat before him. The extent of his power in relation to the Army Department was revealed in the fantastic picture that came out later, in the Army-McCarthy hearings, of Army Secretary Robert T. Stevens chasing up and down the country trying to curry favor with Pvt. G. David Schine, a McCarthy protégé.

And McCarthy's success in building a spy network in government agencies was evidenced in the appointment of his personal henchman, Robert E. Lee, to the Federal Communications Commission, and the placing of his lieutenant, Scott McLeod, in charge of State Department security.

A Pleasing Score Card

If we now list the tactical blows and reverses McCarthy has suffered during the last few months, without examining the situation further, it is quite possible to draw the altogether erroneous conclusion that McCarthy's power is being smashed.

Since the hearings, McCarthy's faction has been on the defensive. A majority bloc of the three Democrats on McCarthy's committee, plus Republican Sen. Potter, has forced McCarthy to accept the resignation of his personal favorite, Roy M. Cohn, chief counsel of the committee. Sen. Flanders' resolution to remove McCarthy from his committee chairmanships is still pending. McCarthy's attempt to investigate the Central Intelligence Agency has been temporarily blocked. And President Eisenhower himself has finally spoken out against McCarthy, censuring him for his 'reprehensible' methods.

Even the press seems to have swung against McCarthy. The mass-circulation pro-McCarthy press has adopted a more cautious attitude, and the mildly critical tone of such papers as the *New York Times* and *Herald Tribune* has given way to a crusading anti-McCarthy editorial policy.

In the electoral field there are indications of a shift against McCarthy. The outspoken anti-Semite and McCarthyite, Jack Tenney, was badly defeated for State Senator in the California primaries. And in the Maine primaries, Robert L. Jones, McCarthyite opponent of incumbent Sen. Margaret Chase Smith, was swamped by a 5 to 1 margin.

Finally, it can be said that McCarthy's prestige as a witch hunter has suffered. The fact that he was forced to defend himself at the hearings, and to demand rights he never gave others, damaged his awesome appearance as the grand inquisitor who stood above all questioning.

And yet, despite this superficially comforting picture of McCarthy's fortunes in decline, it would be disastrous to fail to see that actually American fascism experienced a profound development precisely during the last months.

Deepening of the Process

The point we must grasp is that while the incipient fascist movement has experienced tactical setbacks, these setbacks are related to the deepening of the process of formation of a distinct fascist faction in the administration and in the Republican Party. They are also related to the mobilization of a fascist mass following. Without such blows a fascist movement does not develop. The blows from the old-line capitalist political machines represent their resistance to the emergence of a powerful fascist threat to their own form of capitalist rule. Historically, the fascist movement has always used such attacks to enhance its appearance as the party of the 'underdog', the 'little people' who hate the powers that be.

If we listen to pollsters who have sampled public opinion since the hearings and who prove that McCarthy has no more than 25 or 30% of the populace in his camp, we might conclude that McCarthyism is no longer a threat. But the conclusion is false – for the simple reason that fascism is not running for election in America. Is it necessary to recall that the Nazis suffered a serious election defeat immediately before Hitler took power?

When we look: at McCarthyism as a fascist movement in the process of formation, the figure of 'only' 25 percent looms as the most ominous political fact of 1954.

If we regard the events of the first six months of 1954 as a test of whether McCarthyism was just another strain of the reactionary breed of capitalist politics, or something qualitatively different, then the fact that the McCarthy faction has withstood all attempts to integrate it into the Republican machine is a strong indication that McCarthyism is no ordinary current. The growing differentiation of a fascist faction within the capitalist parties is a sign of the maturity of the threat to the working class.

One of the gravest signs of the extent of the fascist danger is the hardening of the core of McCarthy's following through the 'ordeal' of the hearings. The fascist movement is crystallizing, not only among government functionaries and national politicians, but at the grass roots. The selection of a fascist cadre with a broad following is taking place: The process is by no means complete, and before it is complete the working class will have its opportunity to reverse it; but it is already developing in outline form. We leave it to people who believe in miracles and the Democratic party to ignore such a phenomenon.

We must look at the social base of McCarthy's mass support. Who are the hard-core McCarthy supporters that make up 25 percent of the population? Unfortunately the pollsters do not take their point of departure from the reciprocal relations between the three social classes in American society – capitalist, middle class and working class. Nevertheless, they do indicate in their findings that the main support for McCarthy comes from sections of the lower middle class and among unorganized workers. Insofar as social composition is treated in the polls, there is a high percentage of the uneducated, the small farmers, small businessmen and declassed elements in the pro-McCarthy columns.

Will this mass following go all the way with the fascist movement? That depends. It depends above all on what the workers' organizations do. During the hearings the labor officials stood aside and watched the Democrats carry the ball. All they did was to cheer a little from the sidelines. As a result McCarthy gained where it hurt labor most – in the consolidation of a mass following. History will not permit many blunders like this without visiting severe punishment on the working class.

A New Test

The army-McCarthy hearings, which disclosed the whole anatomy of a conspiracy to shackle the United States with a fascist dictatorship, should have been the signal for a mighty offensive of the labor movement against this ominous threat. The moment was missed. And now a new test is before us – the 1954 elections.

The elections will not pass without McCarthy utilizing them in the same way he utilized the hearings – to build a mass following, to cultivate the legend of invincibility, and to grab every bit of radio and TV time possible for his fascist propaganda. He is planning to open his first big skirmish with the labor movement precisely during the election campaigns. What else does his plan to investigate 'subversion' in defense plants signify?

But the labor bureaucracy persists in its strategy of leaving the defeat of McCarthy to the Democratic party. They preach that with the election of a Democratic majority in Congress in 1954, and a Democratic president and administration in 1956, all the basic problems of the working class, including the problem of McCarthyism, will be solved.

The Democratic strategists, in their turn, also promise that McCarthy will be taken care of if a Democratic majority is elected to the Senate. They argue that if they are the majority McCarthy would be removed as chairman of the Permanent Investigations Subcommittee without even a struggle – since under the ordinary rules of Senate procedure McCarthy would then be replaced by the senior Democrat on the committee.

Can anything more asinine be imagined? The whole problem of defeating American fascism is reduced to the electing of Democrats instead of Republicans – to a maneuver in Congress – to a re-shuffling of posts! And all this, after the experiences of Italy and Germany and Spain!

Perhaps salvation lies not with the Democrats but with the Eisenhower Republicans? After all, they have been doing the main fighting, even though they are somewhat inept and at times downright idiotic.

The extent to which the Eisenhower Republicans can be depended on to handle McCarthy can be measured by the fact that McCarthy has no reason to split from the Republican party at this time. McCarthy aims at 1956 and the presidency. The organization of a separate fascist party can wait until the experiment of capturing the Republican party has played itself out. In the meantime, the GOP is a perfect arena for McCarthy at this stage of development of his fascist movement.

The fact that McCarthy doesn't have the support at this time of the main sections of the Big Business rulers of the Republican party is not decisive in his calculations. His is a long-term perspective. The crisis of world capitalism is having an explosive effect on the stability and inner equilibrium of the American capitalist political structure. McCarthy obviously senses this. He is ready for sharp turns, sudden upsets, and for any number of cleavages and weaknesses to develop in the most solid and conservative section of the bourgeoisie.

Those who think that the biggest and most powerful sections of American finance capital will never throw in their lot with McCarthy do not know these capitalists, their moods or their problems. It is not only the new and fabulously rich oil tycoons who are fascist-minded. The key sectors of America's rulers would turn to fascism in a moment if they thought that it could solve their problems. That's what McCarthy must prove to them, and that's all he must prove.

Aim to Win the Elections

The Republican aim is to win the elections. That's the Democratic aim also. This is not meant to be facetious. American capitalist politics is unprincipled to the core, dominated as it is by an overriding concern for the enormous advantage that control of the administration gives to the capitalist group in power. In order to win, each side will resort to any lie, trick or device that can bring victory.

Last November Brownell showed how the Republican strategists operate. He accused Truman of harboring and promoting a Russian agent. The whole charge was calculated to swing the tide against the Democrats in the California Congressional race then pending. The string of Democratic victories in the nationwide off-year elections had unnerved the Republican high command, and they resorted to this smear to discredit the Democratic party and stop the Democratic election trend.

What was the result? In answering Brownell, Truman characterized Brownell's method as 'McCarthyism'. Whereupon McCarthy demanded and got equal time with Truman to answer him. Having seized the initiative, McCarthy took over the debate and beat the Republican party and even Eisenhower himself over the head with the same club he used on Truman. From then on it was McCarthy's show.

But this experience didn't inhibit the Republican high command from playing ball with McCarthy. They sent him out as their chief spokesman in opening the 1954 election campaign.

Feeds on Witch Hunt

McCarthy took advantage of this opening so aggressively and skillfully that the Republican administration had to make a stand against him. The line between the permissible and the impermissible had to be drawn – and the administration made its stand through the Army-McCarthy hearings. But it is precisely these hearings which revealed that their strategy is not to destroy McCarthy but merely to establish a *modus vivendi* in which the fascist demagogue would voluntarily restrict himself within certain limits. These limits are exactly what McCarthy *must* overstep in order to build his fascist movement. He overstepped them before, in taking advantage of the openings his Democratic and Republican opponents gave him. Such openings arise from, the official witch hunt and its inevitable consequence – inter-party and inner-party witch hunting. Is there any reason to believe that McCarthy's opponents will now at long last refrain from creating new openings for him? It can be confidently predicted that the temptation to witch hunt opposing candidates in the prevailing fetid atmosphere will not be heroically resisted by the power-hungry contenders.

While McCarthy makes the 'treason' charge the kernel of his fascist program to 'save America' and to establish his own dictatorship, the old-line machine men of the Republican party can see a lot of merit in that charge as a formula for winning elections – if the necessary hysteria can be worked up to swing it into high gear. And isn't the Republican administration, with Eisenhower and Brownell in the lead, working day and night to build the hysteria and create precisely such a national lynch atmosphere?

The moment another episode like Brownell's smear of Truman last November takes place, McCarthy will at one stroke wipe out any tactical losses he suffered in his fight with the Army and the administration. He will be completely vindicated. All grounds for anti-McCarthy maneuvers within the party and administration will be removed. McCarthy will then be able to make a new and powerful push in building his fascist network in all government and military agencies, as well as in mobilizing a mass following.

The present relationship of forces between Democrats and Republicans in Congress is very close in both the Senate and the House. The Democrats are obviously depending on the usual mid-term swing against the 'ins' during periods of economic decline. The Republicans also are worried that the recession – which looks very much like a depression to the workers – will provoke a swing to the Democratic party in 1954 that could roll on to 1956. At the same time, the farm vote hangs in the balance, and there is already evidence that a section of Eisenhower farm support has turned against him. Under all these circumstances, with the fate of their whole administration at stake, it can hardly be expected that the Republicans will not use the witch hunt technique.

There is no getting away from it. The witch hunt has a logic of its own, independent of the intentions of its authors and users. It was inevitable that the witch hunt, started by the Democrats under Truman, would develop until the capitalist politicians began to devour one another. And in this process, a fascist movement can maneuver with ease, gaining the initiative at every critical turn.

A New Force in Politics

This election year of 1954 is not merely another year in the see-saw between the two capitalist parties. Something new has been added. For the first time in American history a powerful fascist movement is on the political scene. And the defeat of this fascist movement is now the main order of business before the working class of this country.

When the Socialist Workers Party says that the drive of a fascist movement toward power must be met by a counter-drive of the workers toward power, the labor officials and liberals smile indulgently and return to the 'practical' questions of the day. But there were a lot smarter labor officials and liberals in Italy, Germany and Spain, who rejected the reality of the struggle with fascism – and woke up in concentration camps or in exile.

Other elements in and around the ideological fringe of the labor bureaucracy talk airily about 'fighting fascism', but are too sophisticated and too lacking in revolutionary faith in the capacity of the American proletariat, to talk of such 'clichés' as a 'struggle for workers' power'.

The worst of these elements within the labor bureaucracy (or trying to crash the bureaucracy) is the Stalinists. The Stalinists not only refuse to talk of an orientation toward workers' power; it is their prime objective to prove that they have nothing to do with such 'irresponsible' perspectives. For them, all strategy in fighting McCarthyism is reduced to the slogan: Get into the Democratic party.

And yet any sober reflection on the real situation in the United States and the experience of Europe shows that we face precisely that alternative: workers' power or fascist power.

It may be objected: Are you serious? To whom are you addressing this program of struggle for workers' power as the only means to smash the fascist menace? To the American labor movement, with its corrupt, capitalist-minded labor bureaucracy? Isn't this somewhat ludicrous?

The need for a revolutionary socialist strategy to successfully fight McCarthyism is not a laughing matter. What is ludicrous is not the distance between our socialist program and the program of the labor bureaucracy, but rather the disproportion between the program of the labor bureaucracy and the objective reality. That is both ludicrous and tragic.

The Reality in America

Our program conforms to reality. It is based on both theoretical analysis and historical experience. But the program of the American labor bureaucracy is based on memories of the past, on a relation of class forces that is about to be blown up by the deepening of the world capitalist crisis within the American sector. That's why it is a worthless program.

The reformist program of the bureaucracy and the Stalinists had some semblance of 'realism' in the epoch of the rise of capitalism, or in countries like the US where the crisis of capitalism was delayed by way of imperialist expansion – that is, by way of thrusting the rest of the capitalist world into a deeper crisis.

As long as capitalism operates more or less efficiently, the relations between the three classes, capitalist, middle class and working class, are maintained with a degree of equilibrium. The middle class follows the capitalist class, and even drags the workers along with them through the labor bureaucracy. The class struggle, while constantly upsetting this equilibrium, doesn't fundamentally destroy it.

But as soon as capitalism enters its decline, this relationship of class forces is sharply altered and the brittle political superstructure resting on the previously stable class relationships begins to crack up.

The crisis of capitalism brings ruin and despair to the middle class and the working class. The alternating currents of boom and bust resolve into the alternatives of catastrophic war or catastrophic depression. This whole process creates an unbearable social tension, and a collective conviction arises that a change must absolutely be made.

In such times the working class is presented with the opportunity to take the helm and steer society out of the capitalist morass. The middle class, suffering acutely from the effects of the capitalist crisis, is at that point the natural ally of the working class and would readily follow its lead toward a fundamental change in the social system.

But should the working class falter, should it prove unable to rise to the tasks imposed by revolutionary times, then the whole situation deteriorates. All the worst features of the middle class – its prejudices, its inability to act as a cohesive class pursuing its own interests, its collective hysteria in times of crisis – become favorable factors for the rise of a fascist movement.

The fascists then issue a counterfeit of the revolutionary program that the workers' organizations failed to present. They turn the program into its opposite. While appealing to the mass feeling that some change is absolutely essential, the change which they offer is a counter-revolutionary fascist change. All this is dressed up with whatever unrestrained demagogy the moment requires.

At the same time the capitalists, who have lost the ability to rule through middle-class liberal politicians and the labor bureaucracy, become receptive to the idea of using the fascist movement to establish their unquestioned rule by means of a blood-nurse of the working class and the establishment of the iron-heel dictatorship of Big Business.

This, in broad outline, is the perspective that confronts this country. There is no use looking the other way, or bemoaning our fate. There is no use complaining that the alternatives of fascism or socialism confront us too soon – that we need more time.

The alternatives are here, now. The fascist movement is not waiting. The workers cannot and dare not wait.

Thus the problem of problems now before us is to hasten the awakening of consciousness in the working class to the fact that the next few years will decide who will rule in the United States. A showdown crisis is before us. Either the capitalists will rule through a fascist dictatorship, or the workers will rule through a Workers and Farmers Government.

Those who think that all is lost and that fascism must succeed are the worst traitors and liars. The American workers have a tremendous capacity to rise to historic needs. The workers have learned a great deal since they first organized and beat the corporations, in the Thirties. Everything intelligent, everything heroic, everything that made the American workers the most productive and most militant working class in the world will become aroused and active in the mortal struggle with fascism.

For our part, we proceed with the utmost confidence. The present labor leadership will be shoved aside. Its pro-capitalist political program will be rejected by the new, young, militant layers of leader-fighters which are today taking shape even during the darkest moments of reaction. And the program and leadership of the revolutionary socialists will be embraced by these millions of proletarian fighters who will smash and scatter the fascist movement.

July 10, 1954

3 The Myth of Women's Inferiority[12]
(1954)

Evelyn Reed

One of the conspicuous features of capitalism, and of class society in general, is the inequality of the sexes. Men are the masters in economic, cultural, political and intellectual life, while women play a subordinate and even submissive role. Only in recent years have women come out of the kitchens and nurseries to challenge men's monopoly. But the essential inequality still remains.

This inequality of the sexes has marked class society from its very inception several thousand years ago, and has persisted throughout its three main stages: chattel slavery, feudalism and capitalism. For this reason class society is aptly characterized as male-dominated. This domination has been upheld and perpetuated by the system of private property, the state, the church and the form of family that served men's interests.

On the basis of this historical situation, certain false claims regarding the social superiority of the male sex have been propagated. It is often set forth as an immutable axiom that men are *socially* superior because they are *naturally* superior. Male supremacy, according to this myth, is not a social phenomenon at a particular stage of history, but a natural law. Men, it is claimed, are endowed by nature with superior physical and mental attributes.

An equivalent myth about women has been propagated to support this claim. It is set forth as an equally immutable axiom that women are *socially* inferior because they are *naturally* inferior to men. And what is the proof? They are the mothers! Nature, it is claimed, has condemned the female sex to an inferior status.

This is a falsification of natural and social history. It is not nature, but class society, which lowered women and elevated men. Men won their social supremacy in struggle against and conquest over the women. But this sexual struggle was part and parcel of a great social struggle – the overturn of primitive society and the institution of class society. Women's inferiority is the product of

---

12   Reed 1954.

a social system which has produced and fostered innumerable other inequalities, inferiorities, discriminations and degradations. But this social history has been concealed behind the myth that women are naturally inferior to man.

It is not nature, but class society, which robbed women of their right to participate in the higher functions of society and placed the primary emphasis upon their animal functions of maternity. And this robbery was perpetrated through a two-fold myth. On the one side, motherhood is represented as a biological affliction arising out of the maternal organs of women. Alongside this vulgar materialism, motherhood is represented as being something almost mystical. To console women for their status as second-class citizens, mothers are sanctified, endowed with halos and blessed with special 'instincts', feelings and knowledge forever beyond the comprehension of men. Sanctity and degradation are simply two sides of the same coin of the social robbery of women under class society.

But class society did not always exist; it is only a few thousand years old. Men were not always the superior sex, for they were not always the industrial, intellectual and cultural leaders. Quite the contrary. In primitive society, where women were neither sanctified nor degraded, it was the women who were the social and cultural leaders.

Primitive society was organized as a matriarchy which, as indicated by its very name, was a system where women, not men, were the leaders and organizers. But the distinction between the two social systems goes beyond this reversal of the leadership role of the two sexes. The leadership of women in primitive society was not founded upon the dispossession of the men. On the contrary, primitive society knew no social inequalities, inferiorities or discriminations of any kind. Primitive society was completely equalitarian. In fact, it was through the leadership of the women that the men were brought forward out of a more backward condition into a higher social and cultural role.

In this early society maternity, far from being an affliction or a badge of inferiority, was regarded as a great natural endowment. Motherhood invested women with power and prestige – and there were very good reasons for this.

Humanity arose out of the animal kingdom. Nature had endowed only one of the sexes – the female sex – with the organs and functions of maternity. This biological endowment provided the natural bridge to humanity, as Robert Briffault has amply demonstrated in his work *The Mothers*.[13] It was the female of the species who had the care and responsibility of feeding, tending and protecting the young.

---

13   Briffault 1927.

However, as Marx and Engels have demonstrated, all societies both past and present are founded upon labor. Thus, it was not simply the capacity of women to give birth that played the decisive role, for all female animals also give birth. What was decisive for the human species was the fact that maternity led to labor – and it was in the fusion of maternity and labor that the first human social system was founded.

It was the mothers who first took the road of labor, and by the same token blazed the trail toward humanity. It was the mothers who became the chief producers; the workers and farmers: the leaders in scientific, intellectual and cultural life. And they became all this precisely because they were the mothers, and in the beginning maternity was fused with labor. This fusion still remains in the languages of primitive peoples, where the term for 'mother' is identical with 'producer-procreatrix'.

We do not draw the conclusion from this that women are thereby naturally the superior sex. Each sex arose out of natural evolution, and each played its specific and indispensable role. However, if we use the same yardstick for women of the past as is used for men today – social leadership – then we must say that women were the leaders in society long before men, and for a far longer stretch of time.

Our aim in this presentation is to destroy once and for all the myth perpetuated by class society that women are naturally or innately inferior. The most effective way to demonstrate this is to first of all set down in detail the labor record of primitive women.

Control of the Food Supply

The quest for food is the most compelling concern of any society, for no higher forms of labor are possible unless and until people are fed. Whereas animals live on a day-to-day basis of food-hunting, humanity had to win some measure of control over its food supply if it was to move forward and develop. Control means not only sufficient food for today but a surplus for tomorrow, and the ability to preserve stocks for future use.

From this standpoint, human history can be divided into two main epochs: the food-gathering epoch, which extended over hundreds of thousands of years; and the food-producing epoch, which began with the invention of agriculture and stockbreeding, not much more than 8,000–10,000 years ago.

In the food-gathering epoch the first division of labor was very simple. It is generally described as a sexual division, or division of labor between the female and male sexes. (Children contributed their share as soon as they were old enough, the girls being trained in female occupations and the boys in male occupations). The nature of this division of labor was a differentiation between the sexes in the methods and kinds of food-gathering. Men were the hunters of big game – a full-time occupation which took them away from home or camp for longer or shorter periods of time. Women were the collectors of vegetable products around the camp or dwelling places.

Now it must be understood that, with the exception of a few specialized areas in the world at certain historical stages, the most reliable sources for food supplies were not animal (supplied by the man) but vegetable (supplied by the women). As Otis Tufton Mason writes:

> Wherever tribes of mankind have gone, women have found out that great staple productions were to be their chief reliance. In Polynesia it is tare, or breadfruit. In Africa it is the palm and tapioca, millet or yams. In Asia it is rice. In Europe cereals. In America corn and potatoes or acorns and pinions in some places.
>
> *Woman's Share in Primitive Culture*

Alexander Goldenweiser makes the same point:

> Everywhere the sustenance of this part of the household is more regularly and reliably provided by the efforts of the home-bound woman than by those of her roving hunter husband or son. It is, in fact, a familiar spectacle among all primitive peoples that the man, returning home from a more or less arduous chase, may yet reach home empty-handed and himself longing for food. Under such conditions, the vegetable supply of the family has to serve his needs as well as those of the rest of the household.
>
> *Anthropology*

Thus the most reliable supplies of food were provided by the women collectors, not the men hunters.

But women were also hunters – hunters of what is known as slow game and small game. In addition to digging up roots, tubers, plants, etc., they collected grubs, bugs, lizards, mollusks and small animals such as hares, marsupials, etc. This activity of the women was of decisive importance. For much of this small game was brought back to the camp alive, and these animals provided the basis for the first experience and experiments in animal taming and domestication.

Thus it was in the hands of women that the all-important techniques of animal domestication began, which were ultimately climaxed in stockbreeding. And this domestication has its roots in maternity. On this score, Mason writes:

> Now the first domestication is simply the adoption of helpless infancy. The young kid or lamb or calf is brought to the home of the hunter. It is fed and caressed by the mother and her children, and even nourished at her breast. Innumerable references might be given to her caging and taming of wild creatures ... Women were always associated especially with the milk and fleece-giving species of domestic animals.
> Ibid.

While one aspect of women's food gathering activity was thus leading to the discovery of animal domestication, another aspect was leading to the discovery of agriculture. This was women's labor in plying their digging-sticks – one of the earliest tools of humanity – to procure food from the ground. To this day, in some backward areas of the world, the digging-stick remains as inseparable a part of the woman as her baby. When the Shoshone Indians of Nevada and Wyoming, for example, were discovered, they were called 'The Diggers' by the white men, because they still employed this technique in securing food supplies.

And it was through this digging-stick activity that women ultimately discovered agriculture. Sir James Frazer gives a good description of this process in its earliest stages. Using the natives of Central Victoria, Australia, as an example, he writes:

> The implement which they used to dig roots with was a pole seven or eight feet long, hardened in the fire and pointed at the end, which also served them as a weapon of offense and defense. Here we may detect some of the steps by which they advanced from digging to systematic cultivation of the soil.
>
> The long stick is driven firmly into the ground, where it is shaken so as to loosen the earth, which is scooped up and thrown out with the fingers of the left hand and in this manner they dig with great rapidity. But the labor in proportion to the amount gained, is great. To get a yam about half an inch in circumference, they have to dig a hole about a foot square, and two feet in depth. A considerable portion of the time of the women and children is therefore passed in this employment.
>
> In fertile districts, where the yams grow abundantly, the ground may be riddled with holes; literally perforated with them. The effect of digging

up the earth in the search for roots and yams has been to enrich and fertilize the soil, and so to increase the crop of roots and herbs. Winnowing of the seeds on the ground which has thus been turned up with the digging sticks would naturally contribute to the same result. It is certain that winnowing seeds, where the wind carried some of the seeds away, bore fruit.
The Golden Bough

In the course of time, the women learned how to aid nature by weeding out the garden patches and protecting the growing plants. And finally, they learned how to plant seeds and wait for them to grow. On this, A.S. Diamond writes:

Some of the food-gatherers discovered, for example, that the crowns of yams, after removal of the tubers for eating, would grow again when put back into the earth. Once the technique was learned for one plant or root or grain, it could be extended to others. In the process of cultivation, not only was quantity assured, but the quality began to improve.
The Evolution of Law and Order

Not only were quantity and quality improved, but a whole series of new species of plants and vegetables were brought into existence. According to Chapple & Coon:

Through cultivation, the selective process had produced many new species or profoundly altered the character of the old. In Melanesia people grow yams six feet long and a foot or more thick. The miserable roots which the Australian digs wild from the ground is no more voluminous than a cigar.
Principles of Anthropology

Mason sums up the steps taken in agriculture as follows: 'The evolution of primitive agriculture was first through seeking after vegetables, to moving near them, weeding them out, sowing the seed, cultivating them by hand, and finally the use of farm animals'. (Op. cit.).

According to Gordon Childe, every single food plant of any importance, as well as other plants such as flax and cotton, was discovered by the women in the pre-civilized epoch. (*What Happened in History*).

The discovery of agriculture and the domestication of animals made it possible for mankind to pass beyond the food-gathering epoch into the food-producing epoch, and this combination represented humanity's first conquest over its food supplies. This conquest was achieved by the women. The great Agricultural Revolution, which provided the food for beast as well as man, was the crowning achievement of women's labor in plying their digging-sticks.

To gain control of the food supply, however, meant more than simply relying upon nature and its fertility. It required, above all, woman's reliance upon her own labor, her own learning and her own capacities for innovation and invention. Women had to find out all the particular methods of cultivation appropriate to each species of plant or grain. They had to acquire the techniques of threshing, winnowing, grinding, etc., and invent all the special tools and implements necessary for tilling the soil, reaping and storing tie crop, and then converting it into food.

In other words, the struggle to win control over the food supply not only resulted in a development of agriculture, but also led to working out the first essentials in manufacturing and science. As Mason writes: 'The whole industrial life of woman was built up around the food supplies. From the first journey on foot to procure the raw materials until the food is served and eaten, there is a line of trades that are continuous and born of the environment'. (Op. cit.).

Women in Industry, Science and Medicine

The first division of labor between the sexes is often described in a simplified and misleading formula. The men, it is said, were the hunters and warriors; while the women stayed in the camp or dwelling house, raised the children, cooked and did everything else. This description has given rise to the notion that the primitive household was simply a more primitive counterpart of the modern home. While the men were providing all the necessities of society, the women were merely puttering around in the kitchens and nurseries. Such a concept is a gross distortion of the facts.

Aside from the differentiation in food-getting, there was virtually no division of labor between the sexes in all the higher forms of production for the simple reason that the whole industrial life of primitive society was lodged in the hands of the women. Cooking, for example, was not cooking as we know it in the modern individual home. Cooking was only one technique which women acquired as the result of the discovery and control of fire and their mastery of directed heat.

Uses of Fire

All animals in nature fear fire and flee from it. Yet the discovery of fire dates back at least half a million years ago, before humanity became fully human. Regarding this major conquest, Gordon Childe writes:

> In mastery of fire man was controlling a mighty physical force and a conspicuous chemical change. For the first time in history, a creature of Nature was directing one of the great forces of Nature. And the exercise of power must react upon the controller ... In feeding and damping down the fire, in transporting and using it, man made a revolutionary departure from the behavior of other animals. He was asserting his humanity and making himself.
> *Man Makes Himself*

All the basic cooking techniques which followed upon the discovery of fire – broiling, boiling, roasting, baking, steaming, etc. – were developed by the women. These techniques involved a continuous experimentation with the properties of fire and directed heat. It was in this experimentation that women developed the techniques of preserving and conserving food for future use. Through the application of fire and heat, women dried and preserved both animal and vegetable food for future needs.

But fire represented much more than this: Fire was the tool of tools in primitive society; it can be equated to the control and use of electricity or even atomic energy in modern society. And it was the women, who developed all the early industries, who likewise uncovered the uses of fire as a tool in their industries.

The first industrial life of women centered around the food supply. Preparing, conserving and preserving food required the invention of all the necessary collateral equipment: containers, utensils, ovens, storage houses, etc. The women were the builders of the first caches, granaries and storehouses for the provisions. Some of these granaries they dug in the ground and lined with straw. On wet, marshy ground they constructed storehouses on poles above the ground. The need to protect the food in granaries from vermin resulted in the domestication of another animal – the cat. Mason writes: 'In this role of inventing the granary and protecting food from vermin, the world has to thank women for the domestication of the cat ... Women tamed the wild cat for the protection of the granaries'. (Op. cit.).

It was the women, too, who separated out poisonous and injurious substances in foods. In the process, they often used directed heat to turn what was inedible in the natural state into a new food supply. To quote Mason again:

'There are in many lands plants which in the natural state are poisonous or extremely acrid or pungent. The women of these lands have all discovered independently that boiling or heating drives off the poisonous or disagreeable element'. (Ibid.)

Manioc, for example, is poisonous in its natural state. But the women converted this plant into a staple food supply through a complicated process of squeezing out its poisonous properties in a basketry press and driving out its residue by heating.

Many inedible plants and substances were put to use by the women in their industrial processes, or converted into medicines. Dr. Dan McKenzie lists hundreds of homeopathic remedies discovered by primitive women through their intimate knowledge of plant life. Some of these are still in use without alteration; others have been only slightly improved upon. Among these are important substances used for their narcotic properties. (*The Infancy of Medicine*).

Women discovered, for example, the properties of pine tar and turpentine; and of chaulmoogra oil, which today is a remedy for leprosy. They invented homeopathic remedies from acacia, alcohol, almond, asafoetida, balsam, betel, caffeine, camphor, caraway, digitalis, gum, barley water, lavender, linseed, parsley, peppers, pomegranate, poppy, rhubarb, senega, sugar, wormwood, and hundreds more. Depending upon where the natural substances were found, these inventions come from South America, Africa, North America, China, Europe, Egypt, etc.

The women converted animal substances as well as vegetable substances into remedies. For example, they converted snake venom into a serum to be used against snake bites (an equivalent preparation made today from snake venom is known as 'antivene').

In the industries connected with the food supply, vessels and containers of all types were required for holding, carrying, cooking and storing food, as well as for serving food and drink. Depending upon the natural environment, these vessels were made of wood, bark, skin, pleated fibers, leather, etc. Ultimately women discovered the technique of making pots out of clay.

Fire was used as a tool in the making of wooden vessels. Mason gives a description of this technique; and it can be easily understood how the same technique was extended to the manufacture of the first canoes and other sailing craft:

> They burned out the hollow part, keeping the fire carefully checked and controlled. Then these marvelous Jacks-all-trades removed the fire and brushed out the debris with improvised brooms of grass. By means of a scraper of flint which she had made, she dug away the charcoal until

> she had exposed a clean surface of wood. The firing and scraping were repeated until the dugout assumed the required form. The trough completed, it was ready to do the boiling for the family as soon as the meat could be prepared and the stones heated.
>
> Op. cit.

In this remarkable conversion, a substance, wood, which is ordinarily consumed by fire, was fashioned into a vessel for cooking food over fire.

The industries of women, which arose out of the struggle to control the food supply, soon passed beyond this limited range. As one need was satisfied, new needs arose, and these in turn were satisfied in a rising spiral of new needs and new products. And it was in this production of new needs as well as new products that women laid down the foundation for the highest culture to come.

Science arose side by side with the industry of women. Gordon Childe points out that to convert flour into bread requires a whole series of collateral inventions, and also knowledge of bio-chemistry and the use of the micro-organism, yeast. The same knowledge of bio-chemistry which produced bread likewise produced the first fermented liquors. Women, Childe states, must also be credited with the chemistry of pot-making; the physics of spinning, the mechanics of the loom and the botany of flax and cotton.

From Cordage to Textiles

Cordage may appear to be a very humble trade, but cordage weaving was simply the beginning of a whole chain of industries which culminated in a great textile industry. Even the making of cordage requires not only manual skill, but the knowledge of selecting, treating and manipulating the materials used. Chapple & Coon write:

> All known peoples make some use of cordage, whether it is for binding haftings on implements, making rabbit nets and string bags, or tying ornaments around their necks. Where skins are used most, as among the Eskimo, this cordage may consist mostly of thongs cut from hides and animals sinews; people who use few skins and live in forests, use vegetable fibers, such as rattan, hibiscus, fiber and spruce roots, where no secondary treatment is necessary to make them serviceable. Other fibers are short, and must be twisted together into a continuous cord or thread.
>
> Op. cit.

Out of the technique of weaving, there arose the basket industry. Depending upon the locality, these baskets were made of bark, grass, bast, skins, roots. Some were woven, other types were sewed. The variety of baskets and other woven articles is enormous. Robert H. Lowie lists some of these as follows: burden baskets, water bottles, shallow bowls, parching trays, shields (in the Congo), caps and cradles (in California), fans, knapsacks, mats, satchels, boxes, fish-creels, etc. Some of the baskets are so tightly woven that they are waterproof and used for cooking and storage. (*An Introduction to Social Anthropology*).

Some, writes Briffault, are so fine that they cannot be duplicated by modern machinery:

> The weaving of bark and grass fibers by primitive woman is often so marvelous that it could not be imitated by man at the present day, even with the resources of machinery. The so-called Panama hats, the best of which can be crushed and passed through a finger ring, are a familiar example.
>
> *The Mothers*

In this industry, women utilized whatever resources nature placed at their disposal. In areas where the coconut is found, a superior cordage is made from the fibers of the husk. In the Philippines, an inedible species of banana furnished the famous Manila hemp for cordage and weaving. In Polynesia, the paper mulberry tree was cultivated for its bark; after the bark was beaten out by the women, it was made into cloth, and from this cloth they made shirts for men and women, bags, straps, etc.

The textile industry emerged with the great Agricultural Revolution. In this complex industry there is a fusion of the techniques learned by the women in both agriculture and industry. As Gordon Childe writes: 'A textile industry not only requires the knowledge of special substances like flax, cotton and wool, but also the breeding of special animals and the cultivation of particular plants'. (*Man Makes Himself*).

A textile industry, moreover, requires a high degree of mechanical and technical skill, and a whole series of collateral inventions. For such an industry to develop, Childe continues,

> ... another complex of discoveries and inventions is requisite, a further body of scientific knowledge must be practically applied ... Among the prerequisite inventions, a device for spinning is important ... most essential is a loom.

> Now a loom is quite an elaborate piece of machinery – much too complicated to be described here. Its use is no less complicated. The invention of the loom was one of the great triumphs of human ingenuity. Its inventors are nameless, but they made an essential contribution to the capital stock of human knowledge.
>
>   Ibid.

Hunting, apart from its value in augmenting the food supply, was an extremely important factor in human development. In the organized hunt, men had to collaborate with other men, a feature unknown in the animal world where competitive struggle is the rule. On this point, Chapple & Coon state: 'Hunting is fine exercise for body and brain. It stimulates and may have 'selected for' the qualities of self-control, cooperation, tempered aggressiveness, ingenuity and inventiveness, and a high degree of manual dexterity. Mankind could have gone through no better school in its formative period'. (Op. cit.).

Leather Makers

However, because hunting was man's work, historians are prone to glorify it beyond its specific limits. While the men, to be sure, contributed to the food supply by their hunting, it was women's hands that prepared and conserved the food, and utilized the by-products of the animals in their industries. It was the women who developed the techniques of tanning and preserving skins, and who founded the great leather-making industries.

Leather-making is a long, difficult and complicated process. Lowie describes the earliest form of this type of labor as it is still practiced by the Ona women of Tierra del Fuego. When the hunters have brought back a guanaco hide, the woman, he tells us,

> ... kneels on the stiff rawhide and laboriously scrapes off the fatty tissue and the transparent layer below it with her quartz blade. After a while she kneads the skin piecemeal with her fists, going over the whole surface repeatedly and often bringing her teeth into play until it is softened. If the hair is to be taken off, that is done with the same scraper.
>
>   Op. cit.

The scraper that Lowie speaks about is, along with the digging-stick, one of the two most ancient tools of humanity. Side by side with the wooden digging-stick that was used in vegetable collecting, and later in agriculture, there evolved the chipped stone, scraper, or 'fist-axe' used in manufacturing. On this subject Briffault writes:

> The 'scrapers' which form so large a proportion of prehistoric tools were used and made by women ... Much controversy took place as to the possible use of these scrapers. The fact that went farthest toward silencing skepticism was that the Eskimo women at the present day use instruments identical with those their European sisters left in such abundance in the drift gravels of the Ice Age.
>
> The scrapers and knives of the Eskimo women are often elaborately and even artistically mounted on handles of bone. In South Africa the country is strewn with scrapers identical with those of Paleolithic Europe ... From the testimony of persons intimately acquainted with the Bushmen, these implements were manufactured by the women.
> Op. cit.

Mason corroborates this: 'Scrapers are the oldest implements of any craft in the world. The Indian women of Montana still receive their trade from their mothers, and they in turn were taught by theirs – an unbroken succession since the birth of the human species'. (Op. cit.).

Tanning

But leather-making, like most other trades, required more than manual labor. Women had to learn the secrets of chemistry in this trade too, and in the process of their labor they learned how to use one substance to effect a transformation in another substance.

Tanning is essentially a chemical alteration in the raw hide. Among the Eskimos, writes Lowie, this chemical change is achieved by steeping the skins in a basin of urine. In North America, the Indian women used the brains of animals in a special preparation, in which the skin was soaked and the chemical alteration thus achieved. True tanning, however, requires the use of oak-bark or some other vegetable substance containing tannic acid. As part of the process of leather-making, the women smoked the leather over a shouldering fire. The shields of the North American Indians were so tough that they were not only arrow-proof, but sometimes even bullet-proof.

Leather products cover as vast as basketry. Lowie lists some of the uses of leather: Asiatic nomads used it for bottles; East Africans for shields and clothing; among the North American Indians, it was used for robes, shirts, dresses, leggings, moccasins. The latter also used leather for their tents, cradles and shields. They stored smoking outfits and sundries in buckskin pouches, and preserved meat in rawhide cases. The elaborate assortment of leather products made by the North American Indian women never ceased to excite the admiration of visitors to the museums in which they are collected.

Briffault points out that women had to know in advance the nature of the particular hide they were preparing, and to decide in advance the type of product for which it was best suited:

> It varies infinitely according to the use for which the leather is intended; pliable skins smoothed out to a uniform thickness and retaining the layer to which the hair is attached; hard hides for tents, shields, canoes, boots; thin, soft washable leather for clothing. All these require special technical processes which primitive woman has elaborated.
> Op. cit.

Mason writes:

> On the American continent alone, women skin dressers knew how to cure and manufacture hides of cats, wolves, foxes, all the numerous skunk family, bears, coons, seals, walrus, buffalo, musk ox, goats, sheep, antelopes, moose, deer, elk, beaver, hares, opossum, muskrat, crocodile, tortoise, birds, and innumerable fishes and reptiles.
>
> If aught in the heavens above, or on earth beneath, or in the waters wore a skin, savage women were found on examination, to have a name for it and to have succeeded in turning it into its primitive use for human clothing, and to have invented new uses for it undreamed of by its original owner.
> Op. cit.

Pot-Makers and Artists

Pot-making, unlike many of the other industries of women, entailed the creation of entirely new substances which do not exist readymade in nature. On this point Gordon Childe writes:

> Pot-making is perhaps the earliest conscious utilization by man of a chemical change ... The essence is that she can mold a piece of clay into

any shape she desires and then give that shape permanence by 'firing' (i.e., heating to over 600 degrees C). To early man this change in the quality of the material must have seemed a sort of magic transubstantiation – the conversion of mud or dust into stone ...

The discovery of pottery consisted essentially in finding out how to control and utilize the chemical change just mentioned. But, like all other discoveries, its practical application involves others. To be able to mold your clay you must wet it; but if you put your damp plastic pot straight into the fire, it will crack. The water, added to the clay to make it plastic, must be dried out gently in the sun or near the fire, before the vessel can be baked. Again, the clay has to be selected and prepared ... some process of washing must be devised to eliminate coarse material ...

In the process of firing the clay changes not only its physical consistency, but also its color. Man had to learn to control such changes as these, and to utilize them to enhance the beauty of the vessel ...

Thus the potter's craft, even in its crudest and most generalized form, was already complex. It involved an appreciation of a number of distinct processes, the application of a whole constellation of discoveries ... Building up a pot was a supreme instance of creation by man.

Man Makes Himself

Indeed, primitive woman, as the first potter, took the dust of the earth and fashioned a new world of industrial products out of clay.

Decorative art developed side by side with all of these industries in the hands of the women. Art grew out of labor. As Lowie writes:

A basket-maker unintentionally becomes a decorator, but as soon as the patterns strike the eye, they may be sought deliberately. The coiling of a basket may suggest a spiral, twining the guilloche, etc. What is more, when these geometrical figures have once been grasped as decorative, they need not remain riveted to the craft in which they arose. A potter may paint a twilled design on his vase, a carver may imitate it on his wooden goblet.

Op. cit.

The leather products of women are remarkable not only for their efficiency but also for the beauty of their decorations. And when women reached the stage of cloth-making, they wove fine designs into the cloth, and invented dyes and the techniques of dyeing.

Architect and Engineer

Perhaps the least known activity of primitive women is their work in construction, architecture and engineering. Briffault writes:

> We are no more accustomed to think of the building art and of architecture than of boot-making or the manufacture of earthenware as feminine occupations. Yet the huts of the Australian, of the Andaman Islanders, of the Patagonians, of the Botocudos; the rough shelters of the Seri, the skin lodges and wigwams of the American Indian, the black camel-hair tent of the Bedouin, the 'yurta' of the nomads of Central Asia all are the exclusive work and special care of the women.
>
> Sometimes these more or less movable dwellings are extremely elaborate. The 'yurta' for example is sometimes a capacious house, built on a framework of poles, pitched in a circle and strengthened by a trellis-work of wooden patterns, the whole being covered with a thick felt, forming a dome-like structure. The interior is divided into several compartments. With the exception of the wood, all its component parts are the product of the Turkoman woman, who busies herself with the construction and the putting together of the various parts.
>
> The 'pueblos' of New Mexico and Arizona recall the picturesque skyline of an oriental town; clusters of many storied houses rise in terraced tiers, the flat roof of one serving as a terrace for that above. The upper stories are reached by ladders or by outside stairs, and the walls are ornamental crenellated battlements ... courtyards and piazzas, streets, and curious public buildings that serve as clubs and temples ... as their innumerable ruins testify.
>
> Op. cit.

The Spanish priests who settled among the Pueblo Indians were astonished at the beauty of the churches and convents that these women built for them. They wrote back to their European countrymen: 'No man has ever set his hand to the erection of a house ... These buildings have been erected solely by the women, the girls, and the young men of the mission; for among these people it is the custom that the women build the houses'. (Quoted by Briffault, op. cit.).

Under the influence of the missionaries, men began to share in this labor, but their first efforts were greeted with hilarity by their own people. As one Spanish priest wrote: 'The poor embarrassed wretch was surrounded by a jeering crowd of women and children, who mocked and laughed, and thought it the most ludicrous thing they had seen – that a man should be engaged in building a house!' (Ibid.)

Today, just the opposite is laughed at – that women should engage in the building and engineering trades!

On Women's Backs

Women were not only the skilled workers of primitive society. They were also the haulers and drayers of goods and equipment. Before domesticated animals released women from part of their loads, it was on their backs that primitive transportation was effected. They conveyed not only the raw materials used in their industries, but entire households of goods being moved from one place to another.

On every migration – and these were frequent before settled village life developed – it was the women who took down the tents, wigwams or huts, and put them up again. It was the women who transported the loads, along with their babies, from one settlement or camp to another. And in everyday life, it was the women who carried the heavy loads of firewood, water, food and other necessities.

Even today, the women among the Ona tribes of Tierra del Fuego, as Chapple & Coon point out, carry loads of well over 100 pounds when they change camp sites. Of the Akikuyus of East Africa, the Routledges write that men were unable to lift loads of more than 40 to 60 pounds, while the women carried 100 pounds or more: 'When a man states: 'This is a very heavy load, it is fit to be carried by a woman, not a man', he is only stating a fact'. (W. Scoresby and Katherine Routledge, *With a Prehistoric People*).

Regarding this aspect of women's work, Mason writes:

> From woman's back to the car and stately ship is the history of that greatest of all arts which first sent our race exploring and processing the whole earth ... I do not wonder that the ship-carpenter carves the head of a woman on the prow of his vessel, nor that locomotives should be addressed as she.
> Op. cit.

Does all this extensive labor activity mean that women were oppressed, exploited and ground down, according to our modern notions? Not at all. Quite the reverse was true. On this score, Briffault writes:

> The fanciful opinion that women are oppressed in savage societies was partly due to the complacency of civilized man, and partly to the fact that the women are seen to work hard. Wherever women were seen engaged in laborious toil, their status was judged to be one of slavery and oppression. No misunderstanding could be more profound ...
>
> The primitive woman is independent because, not in spite of her labor. Generally speaking, it is in those societies where women toil most that their status is most independent and their influence greatest; where they are idle, and the work is done by slaves, the women are, as a rule, little more than sexual slaves ...
>
> No labor of any kind is, in primitive society, other than voluntary, and no toil is ever undertaken by the women in obedience to an arbitrary order ...
>
> Referring to the Zulu women, a missionary writes: 'Whoever has observed the happy appearance of the women at their work and toil, their gaiety and chatter, their laughter and song ... let him compare with them the bearing of our own working women'.
>
> Op. cit.

It is not labor, but exploited and forced labor, that is galling to the human being.

When women began their labor, they had no one to teach them. They had to learn everything the hard way through their own courage and persistent efforts. Some of the first hints they probably took from nature itself. Mason writes:

> Women were instructed by the spiders, the nest-builders, the storers of food and the workers in clay like the mud-wasps and termites. It is not meant that these creatures set up schools to teach dull women how to work; but that their quick minds were on the alert for hints coming from these sources ... It is in the apotheosis of industrialism that woman has borne her part so persistently and well. At the very beginning of human time she laid down the lines of her duties, and she has kept to them unremittingly.
>
> Op. cit.

The First Collective

But because women began their labor in so humble a fashion, many historians have presented women's industries as merely 'household crafts' or 'handicrafts'. The fact is that before machines were developed there was no other kind of craft than hand craft. Before specialized factories were developed in the towns and cities, there was no other factory but the 'household'. Without these households and their handicrafts, the great guilds of the Middle Ages could not have come into existence. Nor, indeed, could the whole modern world of mechanized farms and streamlined industries have come into existence.

When women began their labor they pulled mankind out of the animal kingdom. They were the initiators of labor and the originators of industry – the prime mover that lifted humanity out of the ape-like state. And side by side with their labor there arose speech. As Engels points out:

> The development of labor necessarily helped to bring the members of society closer together by multiplying cases of mutual support and joint activity ... the origin of language from and in the process of labor in the only correct one ... First comes labor, after it and then side by side with it, articulate speech.
> *The Part Played by Labor in the Transition from Ape to Man*

While men undoubtedly developed some speech in connection with the organized hunt, the decisive development of language arose out of the labor activity of the women. As Mason writes:

> Woman, having the whole round of industrial arts on their minds all day and every day, must be held to have invented and fixed the language of the same. Dr. Brinton, in a private letter, says that in most early languages not only is there a series of expressions belonging to the women, but in various places we find a language belonging to the women quite apart from that of the men.
>
> Savage men in hunting and fishing are kept alone, and have to be quiet, hence their taciturnity. But women ate together and chatter all day long. Apart from the centers of culture, women are still the best dictionaries, talkers and letter writers.
> Op. cit.

What labor and speech represented, first of all and above everything else, was the birth of the human collective. Animals are obliged, by nature's laws, to remain in individualistic competition with one another. But the women, through labor, displaced nature's relationships and instituted the new, human relationships of the labor collective.

'Household' the Community

The primitive 'household' was the whole community. In place of individualism, social collectivity was the mode of existence. In this respect, Gordon Childe writes:

> The neolithic crafts have been presented as household industries. Yet the craft traditions are not individual, but collective traditions. The experience and wisdom of all the community's members are constantly being pooled … It is handed on from parent to child by example and precept. The daughter helps her mother at making pots, watches her closely, imitates her, and receives from her lips oral directions, warnings and advice. The applied sciences of Neolithic times were handed on by what today we should call a system of apprenticeship …
>
> In a modern African village, the housewife does not retire into seclusion in order to build up and fire her pots. All the women of the village work together, chatting and comparing notes; they even help one another. The occupation is public, its rules are the result of communal experience … And the neolithic economy as a whole cannot exist without cooperative effort.
>
> *Man Makes Himself*

Thus the crowning achievement of women's labor was the building and consolidation of the first great human collective. In displacing animal individualism with collective life and labor, they placed an unbridgeable gulf between human society and the animal kingdom. They won the first great conquest of mankind – the humanizing and socializing of the animal.

It was in and through this great work that women became the first workers and farmers; the first scientists, doctors, architects, engineers; the first teachers and educators, nurses, artists, historians and transmitters of social and cultural heritage. The households they managed were not simply the collective kitchens and sewing rooms; they were also the first factories, scientific laboratories, medical centers, schools and social centers. The power and prestige of women, which arose out of their maternal functions, were climaxed in the glorious record of their socially useful labor activity.

Emancipation of the Men

So long as hunting was an indispensable full-time occupation, it relegated men to a backward existence. Hunting trips removed men for extended periods of time from the community centers and from participation in the higher forms of labor.

The discovery of agriculture by the women, and their domestication of cattle and other large animals, brought about the emancipation of the men from their hunting life. Hunting was then reduced to a sport, and men were freed for education and training in the industrial and cultural life of the communities. Through the increase in food supplies, populations grew. Nomadic camp sites were transformed into settled village centers, later evolving into towns and cities.

In the first period of their emancipation, the work of the men, compared with that of the women, was, quite naturally, unskilled labor. They cleared away the brush and prepared the ground for cultivation by the women. They felled trees, and furnished the timber for construction work. Only later did they begin to take over the work of construction – just as they also took over the care and breeding of livestock.

But, unlike the women, the men did not have to start from first beginnings. In a short time, they began not only to learn all the skilled crafts of the women but to make vast improvements in tools, equipment and technology. They initiated a whole series of new inventions and innovations. Agriculture took a great step forward with the invention of the plough and the use of domesticated animals.

For a fragment of time, historically speaking, and flowing out of the emancipation of the men from hunting, the division of labor between the sexes became a reality. Together, men and women furthered the abundance of food and products, and consolidated the first settled villages.

But the Agricultural Revolution, brought about by the women marks the dividing line between the food gathering and food producing epochs. By the same token, it marks the dividing line between Savagery and Civilization. Still further, it marks the emergence of a new social system and a reversal in the economic and social leadership role of the sexes.

The new conditions, which began with food abundance for mounting populations, released a new productive force, and with it, new productive relations. The old division of labor between the sexes was displaced by a new series of social divisions of labor. Agricultural labor became separated from urban industrial labor; skilled labor from unskilled. And women labor was gradually taken over by the men.

With the potter's wheel, for example, men specialists took over pot-making from the women. As Childe writes: 'Ethnography shows that potters who use the wheel are normally male specialists, no longer women, for whom potting is just a household task like cooking and spinning'. (*What Happened in History*).

Men took over the ovens and kilns that had been invented by the women – and developed them into smithies and forges, where they converted the earth's metals: copper, gold and iron. The Metal Age was the dawn of Man's Epoch. And the most common name today, 'Mr. Smith', has its origin in that dawn.

The very conditions that brought about the emancipation of the men brought about the overthrow of the matriarchy and the enslavement of the women. As social production came into the hands of the men, women were dispossessed from productive life and driven back to their biological function of maternity. Men took over the reins of society and founded a new social system which served their needs. Upon the ruins of the matriarchy, class society was born.

From this labor record of the women in the earlier social system, it can be seen that both sexes have played their parts in building society and advancing humanity to its present point. But they did not play them simultaneously or uniformly. There has actually been an uneven development of the sexes. This, in turn, is only an expression of the uneven development of society as a whole.

During the first great Epoch of social development, it was the women who pulled humanity forward and out of the animal kingdom. Since the first steps are hardest to take, we can only regard the labor and social contribution of the women as decisive. It was their achievements in the fields of production, cultural and intellectual life which made civilization possible. Although it required hundreds of thousands of years for the women to lay down these social foundations, it is precisely because they laid them down so firmly and so well that it has taken less than 4,000 years to bring civilization to its present estate.

It is therefore unscientific to discuss the superiority of men or women outside the framework of the actual processes of history. In the course of history, a great reversal took place in the social superiority of the sexes. First came the women, biologically endowed by nature. Then came the men, socially endowed by the women. To understand these historical facts is to avoid the pitfalls of arbitrary judgment made through emotion or prejudice. And to understand these facts is to explode the myth that women are naturally inferior to men.

4 Debate on Cosmetics[14]
(*1954*)

Marjorie McGowan, Jeanne Morgan, Jack Bustelo (*Joseph Hansen*)

[This debate was generated by a column in the *Militant* regarding the question of cosmetics, written by Joseph Hansen, under the pen-name of Jack Bustelo. The debate found its way into a special internal bulletin, to which Evelyn Reed also contributed, in defense of the Bustelo column.]

On Cosmetics
Marjorie McGowan

I wish to enter the discussion in the paper on the subject of cosmetics with the blunt statement that I found Jack Bustelo's article 'Sagging Cosmetic Lines Try a Face Lift' both offensive and presumptuous in tone, and false in content and implications. I believe that the editors should exercise more discrimination in the publication of articles concerning which there may be controversy – or quite possibly what is indicated is a controversy which will clear up for the editors in what way they should be discriminating. At any rate, it seemed clear to this reader that the Bustelo article was sharply out of place in the paper with its high standard of revolutionary journalism. Bustelo's subsequent letter of August 16, a fabric of half-truths laid out in a pattern of fancy but meaningless prose, only carried to its logical conclusion the implications and undertones of the first article, and for this reason, I wish to deal with the letter rather than the offending article.

His entire August 16th letter is rooted in an erroneous assumption; that the revolution will create, out of the whole cloth, entire new standards of morality and beauty, and that 'not much in the lumberroom of bourgeois morals and beauty will prove very useful'. I believe this to be both false and unscientific.

---

14 McGowan, Morgan and Hansen 1954.

The revolution in technology and science which reached its highest development under capitalism in the last 40 years or so, has wrought a partial revolution in all phases of life – in the relation between the sexes, in sexual morality, in medicine, in nutrition and health, in architecture, in art, in beauty, in hobbies for leisure, in city-planning, in child-rearing, in methods of education, in psychology – a revolution in life and in living which cannot be completed and consummated until released from the restrictions and bonds imposed by the private ownership in the means of production. These new, progressive and highly creative developments in all phases of life stand in sharp opposition to and are caught up in dynamic contradiction with the antiquated economic system of capitalism. They cannot be deepened and extended throughout the entire social body and find their expression as the new and modern way of life until freed by the world-wide socialist revolution. Only then can the new and revolutionary developments expand unhindered throughout the world.

It is unscientific to conceive, as does Bustelo, that socialism will throw out everything which it inherits from capitalism and create everything new starting from the beginning. Rather, socialism will keep all that is revolutionary and progressive and all that men and women by their demands and desires wish to keep as good and worthy of further development. In my opinion, there will be a vast indebtedness which the socialist world will, in hindsight, accredit to capitalism, including much of its 'lumberroom of morals and beauty'.

Socialism, for instance, will not throw out the morality of bourgeois society in toto and create a new one out of the whole cloth. Morality has been in the process of evolution during all of the centuries of mankind and the socialist society is not going to write off a part of the historical heritage of the human race as being totally useless. Rather, socialism will extract the hypocrisy and the mysticism out of bourgeois morality and leave the universal ideals of human brotherhood and make a reality of the Golden Rule.

Nor will socialism throw out the revolution which is taking place in modern architecture, with its unity of the natural and the man-made; nor the trend toward the decentralization and planning of cities going on before our eyes in the creation of tracts with their schools, stores and social services – anarchistic, to be sure, at the hands of the builders and realtors. Rather, socialism will free this revolution from the bonds of the profit system, and cities will be planned for the use, convenience and beauty of living, rather than for the profit of the realtors, investors, speculators and contractors.

Nor can we conceive of socialism rejecting the revolution which is taking place in art. Art has pervaded all phases of life. Pots, pans, fabrics, furniture, lamps, stoves, landscaping, architecture – *all* objects in the environment have become mediums for the creative expression of the artist and the designer.

Art is no longer restricted to formalistic classifications, as sculpture or pictures hung on the walls of the wealthy or in museums, but is diffused and coordinated in the beauty and the unity of *all* objects in the environment of the wealthy, the upper middle class, and even in the homes of some of the more privileged workers. Socialist man is not going to dismiss these manifestations of new and vitally progressive art forms, starting all over with something new and different and inconceivable to our minds because unknown and unrelated to its past development. Rather, the revolution in art forms will no longer be just for those who can afford them, or be shackled with mortgages and time-payments, but will be the rightful heritage of every citizen in the communal world. Communist man will make an art of his way of life, surrounding himself with the creative outpourings of his inherent talent.

Nor will the socialist world create entire new forms of occupation for leisure hours out of the whole cloth. As an example, Comrade Cannon's theory of the resurgence of handicrafts is taking place on all social levels in the tremendous boom in the do-it-yourself crafts. The revolution will complete and free this trend which clearly expresses and fulfills a driving need in man, and will make it economically possible to have both the leisure and the material means to engage in craft activities.

These are only a few examples of what is meant by the revolution in living. We could go on with further illustrations, but suffice it to say that socialism will not create entire new standards in medicine, health, nutrition, child-rearing, psychology, methods of teaching, etc., unrelated from their historic past and their present development. Instead, it will extend and continue the revolution which capitalist technology has already commenced, but freed from the contradictions and restrictions imposed by a decadent, reactionary political-economic system.

What holds true for the rest of life also relates to beauty in the female form around which the discussion on cosmetics revolves. The development of the future must be sought out in the seeds of the present. The beauty of tomorrow will not be created out of nothing, but out of the living forces and tendencies of today. This is the only scientific way to proceed in any question; we do not engage in a star-gazing or crystal-ball divining. Jack Bustelo, however, didn't look at what 40 or 50 million women want today as a basis for deciding what they might want in the future. Rather, in pompous disregard for the aspirations of modern women, he rejects these aspirations as false and depicts the women as mere ignorant dupes of the capitalist hucksters.

I personally find it inexcusable that column space should be given to a self-appointed judge of what constitutes feminine strivings and what constitutes a social norm of female beauty all under the pretext of a survey of one phase of the American economy. I wholeheartedly endorse the right of self-determination in the very personal matter of what strikes the individual as beautiful, but *social* norms of beauty are determined *socially*, not by the dictates of some individual or other. Bustelo has a right to his own opinion of what he considers beautiful. However, involved here is not his opinion, per se, but the fact that he has set up his opinion against the strivings of millions of women in capitalist society and said, in effect: 'The well-scrubbed look shall be the standard of tomorrow and should be the standard of today. Let us not gild the lily. I see all this in my crystal ball'.

Not only does he show a remarkable ignorance of female psychology, but as remarkable an ignorance of the history and meaning of cosmetics. As he points out with considerable flourish, the mores in beauty change, evolve and grow along with developing civilization. However, all of this change and the course of its development cannot be reduced to one source as he attempts to do – to the dictates of a ruling class in a class society. However the mores might change, the strivings for beauty are the product of profoundly powerful forces implicit in the human personality and in the relation between the sexes, and have a more direct relation to the forces of reproduction than to those of production. The use of cosmetics and other means of bodily decoration are older than written history and women were gilding the lily long before the class struggle came into existence, and from all the signposts of today, they shall continue to do so long after the class struggle has passed out of existence. As such, this is a question which both transcends the confines of the class relationships, and, at the same time, is contained and determined by it.

The fact is, as in all other phases of life in capitalist America, a revolution has been going on in standards of beauty side by side with and flowing out of the revolution in technology. This revolution is more than cosmetic-deep. It involves the glow of physical health and good nutrition which stands in direct relation to the higher standards of living of the American economy. It also involves the freer and more informal mode of attire, the more natural gestures and grace of movement, which flow out of and parallel the concurrent revolution in sexual morality of the last 35 years or so. The long-stemmed American beauty, full of natural vitality and physical grace, with shining hair, clear eyes, smooth skin and natural cosmetics with a trace of accent here and there, is no fiction but an American commonplace. This type of beauty is the American social standard, whatever Bustelo might think of it, but by and large it is the exclusive property of first of all youth, and secondly of wealth. If this American beauty is also neurosis-ridden, as our observant Bustelo comments upon, this only demonstrates that things are considerably more complicated than they seem. But why throw out the baby with the bath?

The cosmetic industry and their hucksters do not thrive on the natural beauty which is the birthright of youth of whatever class. It thrives on the lilies who have begun to fade, a phenomenon of nature which strikes every woman in her thirties. And in days of yesteryear, a woman was rated old by the time she reached her forties. It is an inherent part of every normal female ego to strive toward the preservation of youthful beauty, and this is a proper female goal worthy of the considered attention of a revolutionist. The goal of preserving youth as long as reasonably possible has always occupied the attention of the human race, but for the woman of the working class to achieve this goal, considerable effort and expense is entailed. Once the fresh bloom of youth is gone, the working-class woman has neither the means to patronize the beauty shops nor the energy after wrestling with pots, pans and children to devote to the preservation of personal beauty, and soon she has joined the ranks of the drab millions, cheated of a good part of life's thrill. But one look at the radiance of movie stars in their middle forties, achieved solely through a higher standard of living and the alchemy of the modern beauty temples, is enough to convince millions of women that this is something they want too. Who, we may ask, is Jack Bustelo to leave us with the implication that this is something ridiculous? And who is he to set himself up as a self-styled authority on the merits of soap and water (not to speak of rice-powder!) as opposed to all the women who find that creams and lotions do a better job? And who is he to say that the quest for personal beauty is not a legitimate goal of all women; that character is more the ticket?

This finding of beauty in the spirit and character of the working class woman is legitimate for a revolutionist. But let us not confuse means and ends. There is nothing beautiful in the dishpan hands, the premature wrinkles, the scraggly hair, the dumpy figures in dumpy housedresses, the ugly furniture and the hodge-podge accessories of the working-class woman and her home. To find beauty there is nothing other than the ultra-leftism of the radical snob – an affectation – belonging to the days when long hair and dirty ears were the hallmark of the real honest-to-goodness radical. If the hungry spirit of the working-class woman did not yearn for the beautiful surroundings which are the exclusive property of the leisure and upper middle class; if the women did not hunger for personal beauty in their bodies; in their clothes, in their environment, there wouldn't be any struggle, nor any revolution, nor any socialism. The spirit is, indeed, a beautiful thing because it is alive, vital and progressive. But the spirit moves out and away from the dirt, squalor and the grind of today toward the beauty of the free world of tomorrow. He who finds magnificence in squalor, or even satisfaction in it, will never rise above it. But he or she whom the spirit moves shall find at the end of the struggle the true goals of the human race.

More on Cosmetics
Jeanne Morgan

Jack Bustelo's article on cosmetics and his letter entitled 'Is Beauty Deeper Than Cosmetics?' makes the point that the beauty of working class women, like the beauty of the pioneer women 'lies in their character and it is manifest not in the cosmetics they indulge in but the deeds they perform'.

Let me say, first of all, that working class women do not 'indulge in' cosmetics. Our use of cosmetics is far from an indulgence – it is basically an economic necessity and from this has become an esthetic necessity.

If a woman applying for office work, a waitress job or domestic work forgets about her personal appearance and ignores it, she will surely be the last to be hired, unless she has some really exceptional skill or background.

In unskilled factory work the appearance of physical strength and stamina counts the most. But even in this case, the appearance of stamina, youth and vigor is augmented by cosmetics. You can't go out hunting even a factory job, looking as tired as you might feel – cosmetics brighten up a weary face and give the illusion of the necessary vigor and youth.

Do you know, Mr. Bustelo, that a young woman who has only minor office skills, is already a glut on the labor market at the age of 25? Employers advertising for office help will very often indicate that 'under 25' is all they are considering. Youthfulness is admired by the employer not for esthetic reasons at all, as one might imagine, but merely because it indicates a greater capacity for energetic work. Do you disapprove if women 'indulge in cosmetics' to acquire the bright-eyed, youthful, healthy and vigorous look needed to get such jobs?

But all women cannot work and support themselves. Jobs are not as plentiful for women as for men. Those jobs which are open to women pay a great deal less. And this simple economic fact creates the great competitive enterprise known as 'getting and keeping a husband'. (One would think that men would recognize this and fight for equal job rights for women, if only to free themselves of the compulsive element in marriage).

This grandiose competition, which has countless forms, both open and subtle, consumes a great part of women's time and thought. And one of the major tools of this competition is sexual accentuation through the use of cosmetics.

Although this is often viewed as more of 'women's trickery' it is not something to be laid at their doorstep. At bottom it is an economic problem. Capitalism cannot provide jobs for all the members of the working class – male and female. The male half of the population is expected to support the female half – marriage is the medium for this – and the most complex, fantastic and subtle attitudes of morality and esthetics are developed to help bring this male-female relationship into operation. (And by the way, this relationship which was once taken for granted, breaks down in the decline of capitalism and forces many married women to take on the double burden of domestic service in her home and wage-work in the outside world).

Accentuation of sexuality through cosmetics is necessary in the competition for a husband and economic security. This may be unfortunate, or ridiculous, or degrading, but it is also a bare fact of contemporary existence, stripped of all its romantic trimmings.

Mr. Bustelo may laugh at cosmetic 'improvement' and sexual accentuation and ridicule the women victims who concentrate on this to the detriment of the rest of their personalities, but the capitalist system has conditioned him, and men in general, to respond to this kind of sexuality – often without even knowing what he is responding to.

However, it is true that if all the 'ordinary women' had good health, a buoyant, optimistic attitude, well-made clothing, it would go a long way toward the destruction of the cosmetic industry. Good health, a good figure, a clear skin, sparkling eyes, lustrous hair – all these things come first of all from a good diet – not a starch-filled diet of too much bread and potatoes but a diet that includes plenty of eggs and steak and fresh vegetables. And a buoyant, optimistic attitude is the product of a happy life with perspectives for the future. Can capitalism give these things to all women?

Bustelo may be able to retain a warmth and affection toward the working class woman who has had too little rest and too much anxiety and worry – he may admire her 'moral beauty' but she herself and her husband and her friends will not find this consideration too useful. Very few people today can go along with Bustelo's attitude that 'ordinary' women 'are beautiful no matter how toil-worn' – especially very few men. This moral beauty which is treasured by those who are more conscious than the average is not much use to the 'ordinary' husband and wife whose esthetic and sexual ideals are built on the 'ordinary' standards.

Why shouldn't a woman paint her face, dye her hair, use perfume and whatever else is necessary to help fulfill the esthetic and sexual desires of both herself and her husband? Between Mr. Jack Bustelo and the world at large, she is damned if she does and damned if she doesn't.

It is quite true that the great use of cosmetics today is 'one of the signs of the barbarism of the times', but not as Bustelo understands it. (Cosmetics are ancient, and have been used for many reasons, good and bad. They will probably be used even under socialism, by both men and women, for the pleasure of personal adornment). The great use of cosmetics today is 'a sign of barbarism' because it is *obligatory* and necessary. Because we do not always use cosmetics simply because we choose to do so. This is the barbarism, not the thing in itself. And it is a sign of barbarism because it exposes the fact that the physical appearance of women is made to assume such a great and decisive importance in this society, and the other aspects of her personality are subordinated almost to the point of extinction. But I for one, want to have my cake and eat it too. I wish to improve and enjoy my physical appearance and at the same time improve and develop all the other sides of my personality. And I think all women have a right to both these things.

Why doesn't Mr. Bustelo advocate good wages, plenty of money to *meet the necessity* of cosmetics – or a good diet and high standard of living to *lessen the need* for cosmetics?

Don't offer us 'moral beauty' or a new esthetic standard as a solution for today's 'ordinary woman' in today's every-day world. Let's look forward to socialism for that, when everyone can develop new cultural and esthetic ideals.

The point is this, Mr. Bustelo: AS LONG AS THE WORLD DEMANDS COSMETIC IMPROVEMENT, either for economic or esthetic reasons, WOMEN HAVE EVERY RIGHT TO WHATEVER MEANS ARE NECESSARY TO MEET THAT DEMAND. And to ridicule us for bowing to that demand is rather poor taste, and an example of that cheap humor which makes a butt out of an easy victim. This alone is unworthy of the pages of the paper.

However, in addition, your point of view contains a political error. We are not going to change the world by revolting against such a side-line issue as this – and that seems to be what your article would have us do. If working class women boycotted all cosmetics I doubt very much if it would help build a Labor Party or lessen Jim Crow or halt the war drive.

∴

The Fetish of Cosmetics
Jack Bustelo

Is the use of cosmetics worth the attention of a Marxist? At first sight, it might seem we should say no. What difference does a question, seemingly so remote from the class struggle, really make? After all, the great problems of unemployment, fascism, war, and the struggle for power reduce everything else to subordinate importance. And surely, in the list of subordinate questions that Marxists do feel constrained to consider, cosmetics comes at least close to the bottom. Yet among readers of the *Militant* recently, a minor article, aimed at no more than showing how the 'recession' had affected the cosmetics business and what the hucksters intended to do about it, evoked the kind of response that only an important issue deserves. How are we to explain this?

A possible answer is that I displayed prejudice against women in writing about the cosmetics purveyors and their 'public relations' department and that this display of prejudice in the *Militant* naturally aroused indignation. (An example: 'Maybe you, Jack, want to laugh and ridicule my using popular cosmetics to overcome some of these difficulties of working for a living. Laugh if you want ...' – F.J. in the *Militant*). I must admit that the accusation is not easy for me to answer. First, the evidence that I was guilty of prejudice is not submitted. How then can I decide rationally who is at fault, myself or the critics, or whether an element of misunderstanding is involved? Moreover, in the absence of explanation as to what my prejudice consisted of, I am given no opportunity for self-correction.

The absence of a specific indication as to the prejudice leads me to suspect that only feeling is involved on the side of my critics, a feeling that perhaps does not correspond with the real facts. In this predicament I may be excused perhaps for referring to what Hegel had to say about judgments that are not made explicit:

> Since the man of common sense appeals to his feeling, to an oracle within his breast, he is done with any one who does not agree. He has just to explain that he has no more to say to any one who does not find and feel the same as himself. In other words, he tramples the roots of humanity underfoot. For the nature of humanity is to impel men to agree with one another, and its very existence lies simply in the explicit realization of a community of conscious life. What is anti-human, the condition of mere animals, consists in keeping within the sphere of feeling pure and simple, and in being able to communicate only by way of feeling-states.

Whether we agree or disagree that I am consciously or unconsciously prejudiced for or against women, the key issues of the dispute over cosmetics still remain and have to be considered on their own merits. A discussion of these issues I think will prove fruitful no matter what nuances of differences over them we may finally end up with.

'Cosmetics are a Grim Necessity'

In her letter to the *Militant*, Helen Baker of Seattle says: 'Far from being a luxury (and they are taxed as such), cosmetics are a grim necessity for the older or not physically blessed woman worker'. Leaving aside the relation between cosmetics and the older or not physically blessed woman worker, which I will consider later, I agree completely with Comrade Baker's conclusion that 'cosmetics are a grim necessity'. They are a grim necessity in the current decades of capitalism, particularly in the United States. Just how grim it is we will see presently, but let us start with the necessity.

This was well expressed by Antoinette Konikow, one of the pioneer American Trotskyists, in a letter in the June 9, 1945, *Militant* called to my attention by Gustie Dante of Boston. The letter, which seems aimed at partially correcting an article by Grace Carlson in the April 21, 1945, *Militant* is worth quoting in full:

> Your article on 'The Right to Be Beautiful', in which you discuss the use of cosmetics and beauty aids, awoke a few thoughts that I should like to share with your readers. I have lived for almost three-quarters of a century and in my youth we never used cosmetics. In fact, the use of them was considered indecent. And still we had beauty and romance. How do you explain the present situation? It seems to be that woman's entry into industry has a great deal to do with it.
>
> While rich ladies use cosmetics to cover up their pale faces acquired during Society's winter whirl of endless nights of drinking and dancing, women who work in factories and shops have pale and tired faces because of physical exhaustion due to overwork, bad air, hurried lunches and their whole life of rush and worry.
>
> The working woman uses cosmetics, not only for her own satisfaction – to have a nice appearance or to attract possible romance – but she has to look well and attractive to keep her job. I think that if women would lead a healthy and normal life, their faces would look different. They would acquire the rosy cheeks that we had in our youth and the bright eyes and the red lips.
>
> To me cosmetics are an expression of our unhealthy life under capitalism. It is not an important issue but it is just as well to understand that changes in women's work affect even the most minute forms of their life. This doesn't mean that I condemn cosmetics. I think that we shall have to use them for quite a while yet!

Despite its shortness, this letter says a great deal. Note especially the last paragraph: 'To me cosmetics are an expression of our unhealthy life under capitalism'. It is quite clear that just as Antoinette could recall that in her youth beauty existed without cosmetics so she could visualize a time in the future when beauty would again exist without cosmetics. Her attitude was revolutionary. At the same time, so far as a woman has to use cosmetics 'to keep her job' or for 'her own satisfaction', Antoinette didn't condemn cosmetics. This necessity, she recognized, is forced on us by the times and we have to bow to it 'for quite a while yet'.

But Do Cosmetics Bestow Beauty?

The necessity of using cosmetics will be granted, I think, by almost everyone. We also have to use money. But then a most important question arises. Do our norms of beauty include either money or cosmetics?

Comrade Jeanne Morgan of Los Angeles starts I think from the same grounds as I do when she says, 'Our use of cosmetics is far from an indulgence – it is basically an economic necessity ...'. However, she then draws the following conclusion: '... and from this has become an esthetic necessity'.

All right, but an esthetic necessity to what class in what kind of society? If we were to continue the train of thought indicated by Antoinette Konikow we would have to say that it is an esthetic necessity in capitalist society, one that is *imposed* on us insofar as we can't escape that society. Knowing this, however, we no longer consider it beautiful. We have a different norm as class-conscious workers just as our norm of morality is different from that of the capitalists.

But Comrade Morgan puts cosmetics in a supra-historical category: 'Cosmetics are ancient, and have been used for many reasons, good and bad. They will probably be used even under socialism, by both men and women, for the pleasure of personal adornment'.

Let's put it in a somewhat different way: It's human nature to use cosmetics for the pleasure of adornment. People have always wanted this pleasure and always will. You can't change human nature.

If we were to agree to this, what happens to the grounds we started out with in common, that our 'use of cosmetics is far from an indulgence – it is basically an economic necessity ...'? Isn't it obvious that to take the view that cosmetics bestow beauty is to make a concession to bourgeois ideology?

The Language of Cosmetics

Up to now we have talked *about* cosmetics without permitting them to speak for themselves; yet there are few sectors of the commodity world gifted with more eloquent tongues. Let us pause in our discussion long enough to hear a word from them; and taking a hint from Comrade Morgan let us turn the floor over to a cosmetic used – not by the socialist man of the future – but by the capitalist and proletarian men of the present.

When my electric razor breaks down, I go back to the old safety razor. Afterward I splash on a cosmetic that stings at first but seems to help take away the raw feeling you get from scraping a razor across your hide. I bought it because it says '50% alcohol' on the label and legend has it that alcohol reduced the chances of infection from using a razor. On the back of the label is a short message in which Mennen Skin Bracer tells about itself. It is demagogically silent about the risk and annoyance of shaving. It doesn't say a single word about the *economic necessity* that compels me to go through the daily ritual in order to keep a job. Instead, it proclaims: 'A delightful after-shave lotion. Cooling, refreshing, mildly astringent. A pleasant easy-to-use deodorant. Use Skin Bracer any time day or night – it peps you up. And the intriguing aroma wows the ladies!'

That last sentence is intriguing isn't it? If it were really true, think how simplified some of life's problems could become for our hard-working proletarian. When he comes home unstrung from the terrific pace of eight hours on the belt line and goes to the bathroom to pep himself up with Mennen Skin Bracer, he suddenly sees the way out. No more drab, endless perspective of a lifetime of poverty and toil. He shaves with a new sparkle in his eyes, puts on the intriguing aroma, goes to the right part of town, astutely sidles around an heiress until he gets her down wind, 'wows' her and from then on lives the life of Riley. Why even Bustelo might use a dash of the intriguing stuff and wow the women who think he is prejudiced against their sex. Isn't it sheer sorcery what magic has been captured and sealed in a bottle of Mennen Skin Bracer?

Now surely the public relations department of the Mennen Company wouldn't put something on millions of bottles that no man would possibly believe. But what is it that the men users of the cosmetic are induced to believe? Obviously that there is a *thing* that can help smooth out their relations with women. And that means, doesn't it, that there is something basically wrong on a wide scale in the *relations* between men and women? What is it? And what is its cause?

Lest we jump to a too hasty generalization from insufficient cases, let's try another cosmetic. In September, Max Factor ran an advertisement in the newspapers for a 'color-fast' lipstick 'to make men go mad over you ...' says the ad, 'wear "SEE RED". This lipstick is a rich, true shade ... a hot tempered red that can make *you* maddeningly pretty. Looks fiery-bright for hours and hours, too – amazing "stay-on lustre" won't fade or blot away. Come in for "See Red" today. But careful ... don't start anything you can't finish!' The accompanying illustration shows two men forehead to forehead, pushing their noses against each other like two starts seeing red at the Marigold wrestling matches and a girl, her lips highly colored, looking sidelong at them with a kind of pyromaniac pleasure.

Again we note the demagogic silence about the economic necessity of wearing lipstick. Nothing is even said about the lipstick making you look young. The emphasis is not at all on how lipstick helps you get and hold a job. The emphasis is on how 'to make men go mad over you ...'.

Again we ask what sorcery it is that has captured and sealed this magic power in a few inches of colored grease. And we have to say that the sorcery is in the fact that a *thing* can be endowed with the capacity to smooth out women's relations with men. We are forced to add to our conclusions that from the side of women something must be basically wrong on a wide scale with their *relations* with the opposite sex.

Let us try one more, a recent half-page ad. Two drawings: A reclining nude woman discreetly seen from the rear – a bottle of perfume called 'ishah'. Sandwiched above and below these eye-pullers are the following sensational words: 'THE VERY ESSENCE OF WOMAN ... HER BEAUTY ... HER ALLURE ... ishah ... discovered by Charles of the Ritz. Bottle, packaged, sealed in France ... $10 to $2.50 (plus tax)'.

This is not a new scientific discovery enabling a lonely man to buy the very essence of woman, her beauty, her allure, all bottled, packaged and sealed in France. It is aimed at women. Are you a woman who is not a woman? Has no beauty? No allure? Take heart. All this has been fixed up now. The very essence of woman, her beauty, her allure has now been discovered, captured and sealed in a bottle. Everything that all the different kinds of cosmetics and beauty-aid gadgets offer is now available in a single bottle from $10 to $2.50 (plus tax). And it's all marvelously easy, no inconvenience, no plastic surgery, no torture. Just touch a drop or two of the essence behind your ears and wow!

Long ago in analyzing the strange powers of money, Marx called attention to this projection by which human beings see their relations not as relations but as *things* which they endow with remarkable powers. Indicating the parallel to certain magic objects in primitive beliefs and religions he called it fetishism. What we have in cosmetics is a fetish, a particular fetish in the general fetishism that exists in the world of commodities. The special power that cosmetics have derives from the fact that in addition to economic relations, sexual relations attach to them. That is the real source of the 'beauty' both men and women see in cosmetics.

The Duality of Cosmetics

As we can see by now, the use of cosmetics, although it need not be placed among the unsmiling questions, has a most serious side from the viewpoint of Marxist philosophy. Every student of *Capital* who has really pondered over 'The Fetishism of Commodities and the Secret Thereof' will know what I mean. But even without going into it that deeply I think it is possible to grasp the essence of the matter through a special case with which most people are familiar.

At a certain age, girls – sometimes very young ones – begin trying out lipstick, powder and rouge. In almost every case, this either causes or is associated with a sharpening of relations with their parents. At the same time they often seem to leap ahead of their age group so far as their former boy associates are concerned. If they can get away with it, they go out with youths considerably older than they are. The reason such girls use cosmetics is to facilitate this *by appearing older than they are*.

What they seek to say is quite obvious. Through the magic of cosmetics they express their wish to cut short their childhood and youth and achieve the most desirable thing in the world – adulthood. Why they want to be adults can be surmised in the light of how capitalist society treats its youth. Precisely at the age when the sexual drives begin to appear and an intense need is felt for both knowledge and experience, capitalist society denies both to them. Just when the developing human being must set out to establish normal relations with the opposite sex, capitalist society through the family intervenes and attempts to suppress the urge.

The relation with the other sex thus tends to become distorted and the interest that belongs to the relation shifts to a considerable degree to a symbol. The powers and allure of the relation – some at least – are likewise transferred to the symbol. Lipstick, for instance, comes to signify adulthood; that is, the adult capacity and freedom to engage in activities forbidden to children. By smearing her lips the child says, this gives me the power to do what I want. Naturally it's only a wish and an imaginary satisfaction – or at least that's what most parents imagine it to be or wish to rate it as, and the real power of the drive toward relations with the opposite sex, disguised by the fetish, is not always recognized. The symbol becomes beautiful or ugly, beneficent or malignant. In Antoinette Konikow's youth, for instance, lipstick was 'indecent'. Today it is a 'must'.

This interesting alternation in time of the esthetics of cosmetics is accompanied by an even more striking duality in its powers. To a child, as we have noted, cosmetics are a means of hiding and disguising youth, a means of appearing to be at the age when it is socially acceptable to gratify the urge for knowledge and especially experience in sexual relations. Thus the same fetish displays opposite powers at one and the same time – the power to make old women young and young women old. Mother uses cosmetics to hide her age and bring out her youth by covering up the dark circles under her eyes. Daughter uses them to hide her youth and even touches up her eyes with blue shading to bring out her adult beauty.

Now what shall we say of children who use cosmetics because of the social necessity to look old? Shall they be denied that right? My inclination would be to tell them to go ahead and use cosmetics if they feel like it. At the same time I would be strongly tempted to explain what a fetish is, how it comes to be constructed, what is really behind it and how this particular society we live in denies youth the most elementary right of all – the right to grow naturally into a normal sexual relationship – and gives them instead the fetish of cosmetics as an appropriate companion to the fetish of money.

The application of Marxist method has thus forced cosmetics to yield two important results. We find ourselves touching two problems of utmost moment in capitalist society – the inter-relation of men and women and the inter-relation of youth and adults; that is, the whole problem of the family. In addition, we have discovered that these inter-relations as shaped by capitalist society are bad, for it is from the lack of harmony and freedom in them that the fetish of cosmetics arises. Existence of the fetish, in turn, helps maintain the current form of inter-relations by creating a diversionary channel and an illusory palliative. Thus we have uncovered a vicious cycle. Bad inter-relations feeds the fetish of cosmetics; the fetish of cosmetics feeds bad inter-relations.

Our application of Marxist method has given us even more. If we deny that beauty is inherent in a *thing*, then it must be found in a human relation; or at least its source must be found in such a relation. Doesn't that mean that the beauty associated with sex is at bottom the beauty not of a thing but of a relation? If we want to understand that beauty we must seek it first in the truth of the relation; that is, through science. Is it really so difficult to see that in the society of the future, the society of socialism where all fetishes are correctly viewed as barbaric, that beauty will be sought in human relationships and that after science has turned its light into the depths that seem so dark to us – the depths of the mind – the great new arts will be developed in those virgin fields?

Intimations of it in the class society that is our heritage may be seen, I believe, in such relationships as Marx and Engels achieved. Whether they were fully aware of it we do not know. But we ourselves touch such forms of beauty, I think, in a one-sided way in the admiration and love we feel for our comrades in the socialist struggle. It is their *character* that attracts us, not the smoothness of their complexion, the regularity of their features, their age, or the color of their skin. And character, as we all know, is determined in action, that is by the deeds we perform. That is where a revolutionary socialist looks for beauty in people.

'The Corporate Taste'

Antoinette Konikow, let us recall, noted that in her youth girls never used cosmetics. 'And still we had beauty and romance'. This may sound strange to us of this day and age, particularly if we have come to regard cosmetics as a sign of beauty and romance. What has caused us to adopt this attitude?

We might find hints as to the reason from the theoretical point of view if we carefully searched the Marxist classics. George Plekhanov, in his *Fundamental Problems of Marxism*, for instance, notes the following about a previous period:

> In Chesneau's work, *Les chefs d'école*, Paris, 1883, pp. 378–379, we find an extremely acute observation concerning the psychology of the romanticists. The author points out that romanticism made its appearance soon after the days of the revolution and the empire. 'In literature and art there was a crisis similar to that which occurred in morals after the Reign of Terror – a veritable crisis of the senses. People had been living in a condition of perpetual fear. When their fear was over, they abandoned themselves to the pleasures of life. Their attention was entirely engrossed in external appearances, in outward forms. The blue heaven, the splendor of sunlight, the beauty of women, sumptuous velvets, iridescent silks, the sheen of gold, the sparkle of diamonds – these were the things that filled them with delight. People lived only with the eyes and had given up thinking'. In many respects this resembles the psychology of the period which we are now (the years immediately after 1905) passing in Russia.
>
> pp. 74–75

The period Plekhanov refers to was a period of reaction such as we are living in, the difference being that the reaction we are suffering from is incomparably deeper than the one that afflicted the Russian socialists. Plekhanov's hint might well direct a study on this question, particularly on how the weight of the reaction affects the revolutionary vanguard through such indirect avenues as capitalist norms of beauty. In place of sumptuous velvets, iridescent silks, the sheen of gold, the sparkle of diamonds we could readily substitute sumptuous ranch houses, iridescent TV screens, the sheen of a new automobile and the sparkle of tile in a modern kitchen. There would be no lack of material!

We would even enjoy a considerable advantage over Chesneau and Plekhanov, for the influence of capitalist norms appears to be far more direct in America than it was in either Russia or France.

For example, take the following ad from the latest issue of *Charm* magazine (Oct. 1954): A glamorized photograph of a conventional female beauty on a date to see 'The Pajama Game' with a conventional male beauty. (Both of them are the long-stemmed Aryan type). And here is the message: 'alive after five ... thanks to her Remington Electric typewriter. And no wonder – *electricity does the work* – helps today's smart women of letters turn out such truly beautiful work in *so little time*, with *so little effort* and so pleasing to the boss'. This is accompanied by a picture of the fetish itself – a brand new electric Remington typewriter, artfully streamlined to make it wind resistant.

The reference to the relationship behind the fetish ('The Pajama Game') is not what makes this a remarkable ad. It is the inference that a typist, stenographer or secretary can leave the office more dead than alive. This and the open admission that the really interested party is the boss. A fetish that permits a speed-up ('so little time') is ballyhooed almost like an after-shave lotion. Compare the 'it peps you up' of Mennen Skin Bracer with the 'alive after five' of a Remington Rand typewriter. What sorcery there is in the typewriter of a huckster!

Lest anyone still doubt how directly the American capitalist class is involved in this question of beauty, let me quote the following words from a recently published book, *The Tastemakers*, written by one of them, Russell Lynes, Managing Editor of *Harper's Magazine*:

> There are pressures on our tastes from all sides, pressures that even the most reluctant among us can scarcely ignore. The making of taste in America is, in fact, a major industry. Is there any other place that you can think of where there are so many professionals telling so many nonprofessionals what their taste should be? Is there any country which has as many magazines as we have devoted to telling people how they should

decorate their homes, clothe their bodies, and deport themselves in company? And so many newspaper columns full of hints about what is good taste and what is bad taste? In the last century and a quarter the purveying of taste in America has become big business, employing hundreds of thousands of people in editorial and advertising offices, in printing plants, in galleries and museums, in shops and consultants' offices. If the taste industry were to go out of business we would have a major depression, and there would be breadlines of tastemakers as far as the eye could see.

That strikes me as pretty plain speaking about the source of one of the pressures bearing down on us. However, Lynes puts it still more baldly in the very next paragraph:

This is not, however, a catastrophe we are likely to encounter, because the taste industry has gradually become essential to the operation of our American brand of capitalism. It is in the nature of our economic system not merely to meet demand but to create it. One of the ways that demand is created is by changing people's tastes, or at least inviting them to change, and by making the pressures to give up what seemed good yesterday for what should seem inviting today so strong that they are almost impossible to resist.

How difficult the pressures are to resist we may judge from cases of good revolutionists who succumbed to the prosperity that has endured since the outbreak of World War II. Some of them did it silently, without seeking to find a political difference as excuse or rationalization. The lure of a ranch house in the suburbs with a picture window as laid out in the lush colors of *Better Homes and Gardens* proved impossible to resist. The overwhelming pressure has a name; it is 'bourgeois'. The proletarian became 'bourgeoisified'. In other words, he gave up thinking and became an addict of the opium of commodity fetishism.

Lynes describes the days we live in as the days of 'The Corporate Taste'. 'The corporation has, in fact', he says, 'become one of the most powerful and conscientious (does he mean "conscious"?) art patrons of our day, and has established itself not only as a purveyor of tasteful objects but as an arbiter of taste as well'. He even dates the beginning of 'The Corporate Taste': 'It was inevitable that sooner or later business, in its efforts to reestablish itself in the confidence of the public, would embrace culture. And this it began to do in earnest in the early 1940's while the war was on'.

The imperialist war thus had its reflection in the development of an imperialist taste in culture in America.

'If we are to understand this influence of the corporation on the taste of our time, there are three ways in which the corporation must be looked at – as a consumer of the arts, in its role as patron; as a purveyor of the arts, in its role as the manufacturer or dispenser of the objects with which we surround ourselves; and finally as a new kind of society in which taste has a new kind of significance'. This Managing Editor of an influential bourgeois magazine obviously knows what it is all about. He even admits that the motive of the corporations in the field of culture 'no matter how indirectly expressed, has been profit'.

He cites examples of forays in this field by such corporations as Dole Pineapple, Capehart Phonograph-Radio, the Container Corporation of America, Standard Oil of New Jersey, the Pepsi-Cola Company and Corning Glass. And he explains in some detail what the calculations of these patrons of the beautiful are:

> To a great many manufacturers the problem is not how to improve taste but how to keep it fluid so that what looked new and attractive last year will seem old-fashioned this year and downright archaic ten years from now.
>
> Just as the public relations counselor is concerned with the corporation's psychological warfare, the industrial designer is concerned with the logistics of taste. His function in other words is to fight the corporation's battles on the taste front.

It is a temptation to continue citing Lynes to show how consciously American Big Business goes about fixing and unfixing our ideas of beauty, but one more paragraph will have to suffice:

> It is the men who make and sell refrigerators and rugs, automobiles and baby carriages, furniture and dresses whose sales charts would have a dismal downward inclination to the right unless they managed to redesign their wares in ways that make last year's 'latest word' seem today's drab cliché. An 'old-fashioned' stove with its oven at a reasonable eye level may be more efficient than a brand-new one that forces the housewife to bend double to see the roast, but the manufacturer will do his best to make her long for a new model because it is more 'up to date' and, euphemistically, 'better designed'. The same is, of course, true of automobiles – even more true. Ever since 1905 the automobile industry has been second only to the women's fashion industry in its insistence on the glamour of 'this year's model' compared with 'last year's model'. In fact,

a man clothes himself in his car in much the same spirit that a woman dresses herself in her clothes, and he is subject to the calculated whims of Detroit just as his wife is subject to the equally calculated whims of Paris.

In the whole history of capitalism, has the bourgeoisie ever gone about cultivating the fetish of commodities more cold-bloodedly than American Big Business?

'Art has pervaded all phases of life', Marjorie McGowan declares, criticizing my exposure of the cosmetics peddlers. 'Pots, pans, fabrics, furniture, lamps, stoves, landscaping, architecture – *all* objects in the environment have become mediums for the creative expression of the artist and the designer'. I must admit that there is a grain of truth in what she says. It is 'Corporate Art' – perhaps best exemplified in the singing commercial – that has pervaded all phases of life in America today.

Should We Accept Battle on This Front?

Marjorie McGowan accepts the 'logistics' of the corporation battle on the tastefront as a 'revolution in living'. I appreciate her frankness and think she does the party a service by stating precisely what her views are on this question, for it is bound to help all of us in clarifying our attitude in this difficult field. But I must add that critical as she is of my exposure of the cosmetic hucksters and profiteers and my subsequent letter in the *Militant*, she is uncritical in a more important direction. 'Socialism, for instance', she says, 'will not throw out the morality of bourgeois society in toto and create a new one out of the whole cloth … Rather, socialism will extract the hypocrisy and the mysticism out of bourgeois morality and leave the universal ideals of human brotherhood and make a reality of the Golden Rule'.

I will not belabor the point of how far this departs from the view of the authors of the *Communist Manifesto* who held that the socialist revolution 'involves the most radical rupture with traditional ideas'. I am sure that on thinking it over, Comrade McGowan will agree that she has conceded to bourgeois morality more than is its due. The ideals of human brotherhood are the very antithesis of bourgeois morality – not the morality they preach on Sunday, naturally, but the morality they practice 365 days of the year – which puts naked self-interest above all other considerations as we have seen even in the case of cosmetics. The ideals of human brotherhood are incompatible with the norms of any class society.

Marxists have been critical of bourgeois standards or morals and beauty from the beginning. Today in America where the most powerful capitalist class of all time has decided quite consciously to pay some attention to esthetics it is not simply a theoretical duty to meet them on this field; it is a burning practical necessity. It is part and parcel of the whole ideological offensive we must conduct to maintain our Marxist heritage and build a combat party. We cannot leave this field to the bourgeoisie!

However, it might be objected that this is a hopeless struggle. 'We are not going to change the world by revolting against such a side-line issue as this – and that seems to be what your article would have us do', declares Jeanne Morgan. 'If working class women boycotted all cosmetics I doubt very much if it would help build a Labor Party or lessen Jim Crow or halt the war drive'. (By this time, I hope, it is unnecessary to explain that I don't advocate 'boycotting' cosmetics any more than I advocate boycotting money).

F.J. likewise is not interested in revolt on this issue: 'But for me, I live in the world as it is today, with its standards of beauty and *its* social customs'.

Marjorie McGowan makes the task seem insuperable and even quixotic: 'But one look at the radiance of movie stars in their middle forties, achieved solely through a higher standard of living and the alchemy of the modern beauty temples, is enough to convince millions of women that this is something they want too. Who, we may ask, is Jack Bustelo to leave us with the implication that this is something ridiculous?'

(But doesn't the struggle against Jim Crow involve breaking down the Nazi-like racial standard of beauty in Hollywood? Is that ridiculous?)

On this question I think E. Patrick of Los Angeles was dead right when she pointed in the *Militant* to the working-class women for leadership in this battle as well as on other fronts of the struggle for socialism. Referring to women's 'present adherence to bourgeois society' as indicated 'by their devotion to the standards of beauty of the ruling class', she is of the opinion that 'working class women, like the working class generally, are abandoning these bourgeois standards'. This may be stated too strongly but it is certainly correct insofar as the whole direction of development tends in that direction. We can confidently expect women of the revolutionary socialist movement to transcend bourgeois standards and give leadership as Marxists on this important ideological front.

And we may be sure that they will find allies among the petty-bourgeois women – yes, even among the movie stars made radiant by the alchemy of Hollywood. Does that sound far-fetched? Let us listen to an expert on the question, Gloria Swanson, who, born March 27, 1899, still looks radiant at the age of 55.

Her testimony at the same time offers us an opportunity to check some of our conclusions about cosmetics with the virtual rigor of a laboratory control, since she isn't even faintly aware of our discussion; and, in addition, approaches the whole question not from the basis of beauty but of morality.

The Necessity to Lie

In an article in the Sept. 26 issue of *This Week*, she discusses the question, 'Should a Woman Lie About Her Age?'

'I can work up a full head of steam about the entire subject, which I feel is a tip-off on a sad state of affairs existing these days', the noted actress says. 'I mean simply this: Nearly every woman in America develops a strong consciousness of age when the 30th milestone looms on the horizon'. From then on nearly every woman begins to lie about her age.

Gloria Swanson very correctly expresses her indignation at those men who 'stand snickering on the sidelines'. But lying about her age is not the fault of the women. 'A woman, you see, would never stoop to lying about her age if the men of America didn't put such a premium on youth. We are without doubt the most age-conscious country in the world and the male has set the pace. *The masculine point of view makes a woman feel that age is some sort of contagious disease or a dirty word*'. (Miss Swanson's emphasis).

Then she strikes hard: 'Our shallow men go gaga about screen stars who only yesterday – in some cases quite literally – played hopscotch on the corner after school. They crane their necks to ogle the Bikini-clad saplings on the beaches and dig each other in the ribs as they nod in the direction of the new office girl, over-dressed, overbearing and under 20'.

And so the older women try to keep up by snipping off the years. Is this moral? Here Gloria Swanson adopts a viewpoint that a Marxist must agree corresponds with proletarian morality: 'I am convinced that a woman is justified in fibbing if her livelihood and happiness, as well as those of her family, are at stake. But only then'.

Where a competent woman might be denied a job because of her age, this defender of women's rights does 'not hesitate one moment' to advise: 'Give the prospective employer any age you can reasonably get away with. If he's so foolish as to set an arbitrary limit, ignoring experience and proved ability, he deserves to be lied to. Besides, you must look out for yourself and your family'.

It is perfectly evident that Gloria Swanson's approach on this point parallels that of a Marxist – if economic necessity compels you to lie about your age of course you lie. (The form of the lie, whether a phony employment record or use of cosmetics is not important here).

But does this economic necessity hold as an absolute? Shall we convert it into an esthetic necessity? No, says Gloria Swanson. 'This reasoning, I believe, is perfectly sound when self-protection is genuinely and seriously involved. But in all other circumstances, I can see no real point in camouflage'.

Her grounds for this reasoning, deserve the attention of all of us: 'First, because deception about age only serves to abet this silly glorification of youth. And second, whom are you kidding, anyway?'

That in my book rates as a principled stand on this question, showing that to some degree at least, Gloria Swanson has seen through some powerful fetishes.

Then she indicates that not all men fall in the category of 'shallow'. '... sociological studies have shown that there's a high degree of marital happiness when men (the more intelligent ones!) consider other qualities more important than age and marry women older than themselves'. We would say this was an indication not so much of intelligence as of freedom from certain fetishes cultivated today under capitalism. This freedom from fetishism is sometimes accidental and in any case not in one-to-one ratio to intelligence.

To illustrate her point, Gloria Swanson tells about a girl who lied about her age and married a man who thought she was much younger. When he found out, he was hurt and angry. 'Not because she was older than he thought (he, too, had some brains) but because she had lied to him. And if she held the truth lightly in one case, he thought, what was her character like in others'.

This man, who sought character in his mate, was however intelligent enough to understand why she had lied and he had sufficient character himself 'to forgive her'.

In Gloria Swanson's opinion any man to whom a few years makes any difference 'isn't worth marrying in the first place'. She advises an older woman considering marriage with a younger man to tell him her age. 'Let him know the facts. If it bothers him, let him go his merry way, chasing the young, clinging things who don't have the fascination of an older woman'.

Finally, Gloria Swanson indicates what her norm is.

> The Europeans have the right idea about these things. Over there, a woman isn't really interesting to a man until she is in her 40's. The European male seeks more than a youthful figure and candy-box face. He wants some imagination, some sense, some of the essential fineness of mind and spirit that maturity brings to a woman.
> But over here it's different and it bothers the girls no end.

Thus from this former Hollywood star we learn that if economic necessity demands it, of course we lie about such things as our age and looks. But from any other viewpoint the camouflage is pointless and even vicious. After all, what really counts is character. Since the current American standard is seriously wrong, we must seek a better one. Gloria Swanson finds it in Europe, whereas a Marxist looks to the working class, but both can agree that there are many women today and at least some men who have reached the conclusion that things are not right.

Well, Gloria Swanson's article could stand some sharpening and modification from a Marxist point of view – she leaves out, for instance, the class struggle and its influence, and she under-rates the maturity of some youth, overlooks their need for camouflage, and misses the special problems they face – but her article indicates that she for one thinks something might be done about the false standards 'over here'.

Is it really so daring to venture the opinion that there are other American women, especially in the working class, who will agree with her on that and begin doing something about breaking down the capitalist standards of beauty? Why shouldn't the Marxists stand in the forefront of such a development, offering it leadership and theoretical clarification, especially on the secret of the fetish of cosmetics that deludes both men and women?

5 Automation – Menace or Promise?[15]

(*1955*)

Harold Robins

A revolution in the method of production is taking place in American industry through introduction of *automation*. The tendency itself is not new. Karl Marx was familiar with it, calling the factory 'in its most perfect form' the 'automatic factory'.[16] What is new is the extent to which automatic systems have been introduced on production lines, especially in the United States since the end of World War II.

In the production of atomic materials it is generally known that the lines are completely automated. No human being can handle radioactive products in any quantity or even come near them without fatal injury. This industry, consequently, began in 1942 on the basis of automation. The atomic industry, however, only holds the mirror of the future to other industries. A survey of some of the principal ones will show how about 13,000,000 workers are already being more and more directly affected by the deep inroads automation has made.

Auto

A report of the United Automobile Workers, CIO,[17] has the following to say:

> Although the Ford Motor Co. has received a good deal of publicity about its automated plants, it is not alone in its modernizing efforts. GM, Chrysler, and the independent producers are installing similar machinery

---

15 Robins 1955.
16 **Footnote by Robins:** See his illuminating analysis of the evolution of automatic machinery and factory and its effect on the working class in 'Machinery and Modern Industry', *Capital*, pp. 405–556. Kerr edition.
17 **Footnote by Robins:** *Report on Automation*, delivered at the Economic and Collective Bargaining Conference, Nov. 12–14, 1954.

> ... it is clear that industry has embarked on a full scale program of automation. Each company is contesting with the next to see how fast it can automate its plant and thereby reduce its unit labor costs. The changes in effect, and those yet to come, require that the union give careful attention to manpower displacement problems.

The UAW's conclusion is generally correct. The key is in the following statement: '... one man will do at least the work now done by five men'. This may sound like the panicky statement of an alarmist. If anything, however, it is a conservative estimate. It was supported by such illustrations as an automatic machining unit at Nash Motors that reduced man hours by 80% and by the statement of a Ford spokesman that direct labor has been reduced by 25–30%.

Actually in given units, the change – a change pointing to the future for the whole industry – is much greater. *Mill and Factory* for December 1953 reported that Buick had introduced two automatic engine-head production lines and two engine cylinder-block lines on which every bit of machining was completely automatic, *eliminating every single production worker*.

A Ford spokesman, commenting on the installations at Cleveland and River Rouge, said that the entire cost of the Cleveland modernization would be returned in the first year in labor 'savings'.

A Buick representative boasted that one machine costing about $350,000 had replaced 17 machines on the production line. The labor 'savings' from the production workers displaced along with the 17 machines would no doubt easily repay the cost of the new equipment within a year.

Iron Age reported August 12, 1954, that Buick had a fully automated *foundry* for producing cylinder blocks, cylinder heads, valve guides, etc. The November 1, 1954, *Automotive Industry* described Packard's new engine plant at Utica, Mich., as having fully automatic engine-head and engine-block lines. A single operator is required at the control panel. *No production workers are needed at all*. The installation is said to have cost more than $20,000,000. Its capacity is rated at 50 engine heads and blocks an hour.

De Soto, Pontiac and other companies have installed similar production lines. In making Chevrolet V-8 engines, one worker stands by each of some 18 machines for tool changes. Other machining operations too, from GM roller-bearing production to radiator caps and bumpers, have completely eliminated production workers.

General Motors reports that it spent $750,000,000 for modernization last year and plans to spend at least another $500,000,000 in its US plants this year. In Britain GM plans to spend $100,000,000 in the next five years for automation. In Germany GM has already spent $100,000,000 and is slated to spend another $71,000,000 for modernization. Realization of GM's plans will make possible a 15% increase in overall production *within a year and a half* (spring of 1954 to fall of 1955). Figures on how many workers will be displaced at the same time are not given.

Chrysler borrowed $250,000,000 from Prudential Life Insurance Co. to finance a change-over. Ford is reported to have spent $600,000,000 for its huge re-equipment costs. And in England Ford has a five-year plan calling for the expenditure of $181,000,000.

The same logic that operated in Marx's time indicates that the competition in production line changes in auto must spread to other branches of industry, must challenge every large producer to do likewise or die.

Will the auto workers perhaps find jobs through the expansion of total production, or in maintenance of equipment, as the new technology spreads throughout the industry? It is true that some of the companies are calling up displaced workers for other, non-automated jobs. Yet at the same time they are crowding a year's production into roughly half a year. That fact alone spells out how permanent the new jobs will be.

As for the creation of new jobs, the new machinery generally requires less servicing than older equipment. But we need not depend on impressions as to how many workers can find such jobs. A typical plant will show what is involved. Ford's Cleveland plant has a 'guestimated' capacity of half a million engines a year. According to *Mill and Factory* (October 1953) a labor force of 500 men is required. About 100 of them are cleaners and sweepers. About 50 are carpenters and millwrights. The balance is made up of lubrication and hydraulic specialists, machinists and toolmakers, pipefitters, electricians and electronic technicians. The only labor shortage Ford ran into was electronic technicians. Ford hired electricians and schooled and trained them on the job and after work.

Iron and Steel

The continuous rolling mill has been an automated set-up for more than 20 years. That process shapes cast ingots into rolled sheets, strips and bars. Despite this highly developed technique, the industry employed almost 800,000 production workers in blast furnaces, steel works, iron and Steel foundries as well as rolling mills.

Iron Age, in its March 4, 1953, issue tells about a new mill built by the Great Lakes Steel Corp. near Detroit. An automatic process was introduced in the slabbing mill, scarfing unit and soaking pit. All production workers were replaced by automatic mechanisms. A chief operator and assistant sit in an air-conditioned pulpit controlling the entire works.

In 1954 US Steel opened a new mill at Morristown, Pa., reportedly the most modern in the industry. As yet no details have appeared as to its production methods or the number of workers that will be displaced in other, less modern mills. The previous example, however, gives us an indication of the enormous productivity of a handful of workers using automated equipment.

The September 24, 1953, *Iron Age* informs us that Atlas Steel of Canada opened a new continuous casting mill that '... threatens change in steel-making methods ... eliminates the need for all ingot casting and stripping equipment except the ladle crane ... Conventional steelmaking generates about 25–30% scrap'. The new mill reduced scrap to 3–10%, according to the same source November 4, 1954.

'Overall cash savings ... are figured at 3 cents per pound for stainless, 8 cents per pound for valve steel, 20 cents per pound for high speed steel'. 'There is less equipment to maintain ...'.

> The report indicates that continuous casting eliminated the 'need for all ingot casting and stripping equipment, soaking pits and blooming mills which are the largest and most expensive units in conventional steel mills'.

A new automated molding plant is reported in operation at Cleveland. Owned by the Eberhardt Mfg. Co., the new unit is said to take only one-fourth the floor space required by other processes for the same production. According to the November 4, 1954, *Iron Age*, it performs 12 operations, among them, molding, closing, clamping, cooling, stripping and shake-out. It is a package unit laid out in multiples of flask length. Controls are electrical and pneumatic and operate in conjunction with cycle time. The number of production workers eliminated by any of these changes is not given.

The manufacture of steel pipe and tubing has become automatic. *Iron Age*, July 16, 1953, reports that Pittsburgh Steel opened a new plant to make casings for oil pipe lines automatically. This put the company in position to compete with Colorado Fuel and Iron, Republic Steel and the Lone Star Steel Co.

In this way the steel industry is attempting to better its position in the world steel market. They are well aware that in the fight for a narrowing market whoever doesn't automate will be automated out of business.

Machine Tools

On January 3 of this year, the *New York Herald Tribune* reported that the machine tool industry faces the pleasant prospect of big sales because 'New machine tools offer greater opportunities than ever for speedier production and more fully automatic operations'.

Iron Age, however, reported in November of last year that at the Leipzig Fair in East Germany the machine tool industry there made significant dents in the markets of 'Central American countries, the Near East, Indonesia, and Japan'. The East German factories, it seems, buy the latest automatic machines from Western Europe. With these set up on automated lines they manufacture 'old look' (about 1948 model) lathes and other machine tools of fine construction, low price and easy credit terms that cannot be matched anywhere. (The same report states that the balance of trade between East Germany and West Germany has now been brought into balance – by the export from East Germany of cheap hardware – probably produced on automatic production lines).

Tremendous orders were placed with the US machine tool industry in 1953–54 ($1,100,000,000 in 1953 and $900,000,000 in 1954), but the end of 1954 saw a slackening off. However, an upswing now seems to have occurred in the section turning out automatic machinery, which is good news for them but bad news for those turning out standard equipment. They must now compete with a flood of second-hand equipment displaced by automated set-ups.

Oil and Pipelines

The UAW-CIO *Report on Automation* states that in the petroleum industry, according to an unnamed spokesman of the industry, 'The average refinery which would employ 800 people without instrumentation would employ 12 people were instrumentation utilized to the fullest extent possible'.

R.T. Neuschel, writing in the January 1953 *Mill and Factory*, says:

> More and more industries are becoming increasingly mechanized. Process industries (chemicals and oils) were among the first to show this trend. As an example today, almost half the employees in some petroleum refineries are engaged in keeping the vast network of mechanical equipment in good working order.

Neuschel says tersely of the scope of automatic machine processes in other fields:

Fabricating industries are following the same trend. Mechanization of manufacturing processes is on the upswing in metals, plastic moulding, textiles, to name a few. Even in the distribution field there is a growing trend toward mechanization.

According to *Instruments and Automation*, 'Pipeline instrumentation is expanding – including automatic pumping stations operated by microwave and telephone line telemetering. Radioactive isotopes are being used for locating batches in stream ...'.

The relatively new pipeline industry is rated as sixth largest in terms of capital investment. It maintains 167 storage fields (generally exhausted petroleum fields) for storage of natural gas. At distribution points workers control the flow of products to trucks, railroad cars and tanks by push-button methods. Fleets of light airplanes inspect the vast lines that reach every section of the country except the Columbia River Valley. (Gas is due there next year from Canada and the San Juan Basin in Arizona).

In the closely related petrochemical industry, 80% of which is located in the South, the investment per worker now runs from $20,000 to $30,000 according to the Southern Association of Science and Industry. Most of the big oil companies have entered into competition with independent chemical plants. The large rubber, steel, paper and other corporations are also in the field. Petrochemicals make up about 25% of the chemical industries' $20,000,000,000 in sales.

The January 3 *New York Times* reported that the average investment per worker in the chemical industry 'now exceeds $25,000 and may run four times that much in certain new, highly mechanized plants'. How high productivity is in the chemical industry can be gauged from the fact that behind the $20,000,000,000 in products stands only 527,000 production workers, according to the **Times**. ('The industry provides direct employment to about 780,000 persons', says the same source).

Electronics

The effect of automation in the electronics industry is particularly dramatic since up until very recently manufacturing was done by hand methods of assembly construction. Expansion under such relatively primitive methods could occur only by employing more workers and using more space.

The federal government financed the research that finally made possible electronic-stage manufacture where the product is assembled like a Tinkertoy set, the kind used by youngsters to build derricks, bridges, houses, etc. After three years of research, *Mill and Factory* reports, November 1953, that a process of printing electronic circuits on a ceramic wafer was developed. Other components, too, are printed and automatically assembled by machine soldering instead of the older hand methods. Resistors, capacitors and coils are printed by the new process. Inspection of every circuit is automatic. The result is better units that stand more strain and cost considerably less. The press turns out about 2,800 wafers an hour. (It too is automatic of course). With this new process, 'circuits may be developed to amplify signals, generate and shape wave forms, scale count, and perform customary electronic functions'.

The UAW *Report on Automation* states that '... a radio assembly line geared to produce 1,000 radios a day requires only two workers. Hand assembly lines it replaced required 200 workers'.

At the CIO Convention last December Reuther mentioned a machine that turns out 90,000 electric light bulbs a day.

T.J. Watson, Jr., president of International Business Machines Corp., was quoted by the *New York Herald Tribune*, January 16, as declaring: 'Machines are being made that have thousands of times the speed of machines only ten years ago, and there appears to be almost no limit to the possibilities of electronics as applied to the American business office'.

Coal

A brief review of changes in the coal industry, printed in *Reader's Digest* last December, indicates that the coal miners of the 1950s, displaced by mechanization like those of the 1920s, will continue to migrate in search of jobs. But unlike the 300,000 miners of the previous generation, the present generation will not find many jobs. Today all the basic mass production industries, as well as agriculture, are increasing productivity and at the same time cutting the size of the labor force.

To strip the ground away from coal seams in Pennsylvania, the Hanna Coal Co. has built a 1,700 ton derrick and ordered another one of 2,800 tons. This machine will have a capacity bite of some 10 tons.

Remote-control mining equipment in West Virginia produces six times the national average production per man. (This average includes high-production strip mines). The result is coal delivered at $5 a ton in Charleston, W.Va.

A coal pipeline is under construction from western Pennsylvania to Cleveland. It will deliver coal at a cost saving of $1.25 a ton. *Iron Age* (April 29, 1954) reports other lines are now being planned.

Railroads

The January 3 *New York Herald Tribune* reports that 'push-button freight yards, centralized traffic control, and even electronic brains in the accounting office' are new features being introduced in the railroad industry. Electronic 'brains' rent for $13,000 to $40,000 a month (IBM rates) and are tremendous payroll savers. As a matter of fact, these more than human 'intelligence' machines are operated by ordinary humans who, it seems, unlike the machines, expect wages.

This sampling of various industries should be sufficient to indicate the impact of automation. The use of automatic machinery may not be as all-inclusive in many industries as in atomic production but it is affecting virtually all to one degree or another and the logic of its development is clear enough. A few additional facts will indicate how widespread it is becoming:

Western Union has introduced a nationwide automatic switching system. Saw mills and paper mills are going in for automation. Bottles coming from automatic bottling machines are automatically placed in cartons. The Roman Cleanser Co. formerly employed nine men to stack filled cartons coming off a conveyor line. This is now done by a machine – and with less breakage.

The painter in factories is being replaced by machines. Studebaker reports introduction of automatic spraying of the prime coat. This eliminates all sprayers and water sanders who formerly rubbed down the prime coat. According to the January 15 *Automotive Industries*, all painting on new Chryslers is completely automatic.

Ward's Automotive Report, cited by the UAW-CIO *Report on Automation*, reveals that a 'passenger car plant which formerly employed 36 men to feed fenders into a conveyor for spray painting, now has modernized equipment which automatically feeds six sets of fenders to a fast merry-go-round where various colored finishes are applied simultaneously'.

Richer Living?

Capitalist propagandists hail the promise of automation but give little consideration to the tragic consequences for working people thrown out of jobs. An example is the article by Wm. F. Freeman in the January 3 *New York Times*. The headline declares, 'Automation Aims at New Freedom' and the subhead adds, 'Devices that Run Factories Promise to Release Men for Richer Living'.

That would be good news if it were true. However, although the *Times* boasts that it gives 'All the News That's Fit to Print', it did not see fit to print any proof of this optimistic forecast for automation. It did not even admit that it is the drive for profits that impels the use of more and more automatic machinery. Instead it is introduced 'to the end of freeing workers from drudgery, monotony and fatigue of repetitive work, of reducing worker hazards, of opening the avenue to more important and better paying jobs and of improving the quality and uniformity of product'.

An industry spokesman quoted by *Fortune* magazine (cited in the UAW-CIO *Report on Automation*) was more honest when he confessed: 'I don't think we are consciously trying to ease the burden of our workers, nor consciously trying to improve their standard of living. These changes take care of themselves'.

A Union Problem

The union bureaucracy has shown some signs of alarm at the development of automation. The UAW-CIO *Report on Automation*, with its displacement figure of four out of five workers is a case in point. But the program proposed up to now to meet the problems arising from the revolution in technique now sweeping industry at truly American speed leaves much to be desired.

The report speaks of re-training displaced men at company expense for other jobs in auto. The re-training proposal is excellent – if it is actually fought for; but just what 'other' jobs will be available remains a mystery. They could be created by establishing a much shorter work week and thus spreading the available employment. But that is not Reuther's program.[18]

The report also demands that the government help re-train the displaced men for other jobs. Another excellent proposal – if fought for. How much of a fight is required can be gathered from the fact that the government is unwilling to provide adequate schooling even for children. According to the National Citizens Commission for Public Schools, America is falling behind its growing population by some 67,000 classrooms a year. (*New York Herald Tribune*, December 27, 1954).

The *Report on Automation* takes as its major demand the so-called 'Guaranteed Annual Wage'. If the full demand were won, and if it were applied retroactively so as to cover displaced workers, it would provide the cushion of one year's

---

18 Footnote by Robins: The attitude of the auto barons on this question may shed some light on Reuther's position. For instance, Harlow H. Curtice, President of General Motors, 'explained that he is a definite opponent of the 35-hour week'. (See *In Europe, too, He Found the Future BRIGHT*. Issued by General Motors Department of Public Relations).

severance pay. Reuther's record, however, leads one to doubt that any promise of militant struggle under his guidance is worth a great deal.

A test of his willingness and capacity to fight is provided by the threat automation presents to the entire bracket of older workers with high seniority who are approaching the retirement age of sixty-five when company-financed pensions will be due. If these workers can be dumped before then by introducing automatic processes, the companies stand to make a sizable saving, a consideration of which they are quite conscious. The *Report on Automation* admits that in the new automated plants preference in hiring is given to younger workers. The youth, too, must have jobs; but if Reuther were seriously concerned about placing the older workers shouldn't he be concerned about their senior right to work where automation is going into effect today?

Another point in Reuther's 'solution' is the 'Annual Improvement Factor'. 'The immense productivity gains of automation should be assessed and then shared equally by all workers in coming negotiations', says the *Report on Automation*.

Good. The workers should share in the benefits of automation. But two considerations are sufficient to judge the worth of Reuther's 'solution'.

1. The strength of a union is based on the members it has in the plants. This is steadily being cut down by automation.
2. Under the Reuther program, the four out of five displaced from their jobs have a dim chance to share 'equally' in anything but a search for jobs.

To these displaced workers Reuther really has nothing to offer, unless an invitation to support the Democratic Party can be considered an 'offer'. And what does the Democratic Party promise beyond meager unemployment insurance and relief handouts? What happens to the standard of living of the displaced workers as automation cuts deeper and deeper? And with the fierce competition for jobs sure to follow, even those on the automatic production lines will find their standard of living dangerously threatened.

It should be evident that the problem of automation, as it affects the working class, demands a far-reaching solution, one that can be carried out in the final analysis only on the political level, for it involves much more than the worker-capitalist relation in this or that corporation or even industry. It concerns the working class as a whole in its relation to the entire productive system and the capitalist class in America. To effectively struggle for their interests on such a scale, the workers must turn to independent political action. That means formation of a fighting Labor Party, one of whose first tasks must be to draw up a program that approaches automation as a national problem requiring the whole power of government to be brought to bear in protecting the worker as he becomes displaced by the machine he created.

Beyond that, of course, looms the still bigger problem – how to convert automation into a positive benefit for the working class so that the leisure and freedom from drudgery it promises is converted into a reality and not allowed to fade like a mirage. That can be accomplished only under socialism, under a scientifically planned economy. Automation gives fresh urgency to consideration of the socialist solution in America.

6 The Vindication of Trotskyism: Khrushchev's Report on Stalin's Crimes[19]
(1956)

Murry Weiss

The Soviet Union is today in a stronger position in relation to the capitalist world than at any point since the revolution of October 1917. It is sufficient to mention that 600 million people of China after expelling the imperialists and overthrowing the capitalist regime of Chiang Kai-shek, are now allied to the Soviet Union.

Economically, the USSR has attained with unprecedented speed the status of the second industrial power in the world.

The authority and prestige of the Soviet Union is at an all-time high among the colonial and semi-colonial peoples who are fighting for their independence.

It would seem that the regime in power in the USSR should be enjoying its greatest stability and popularity. And yet, there is unmistakable evidence that the very progress the Soviet Union has made, the improvement of its position in relation to world capitalism, and the enlargement of its orbit of influence, has brought about the eruption of the deepest contradictions in Soviet society.

What are these contradictions? How will they be resolved? What place does the present turmoil in the Soviet Union and Eastern Europe have in the struggle for world socialism? These are the questions before us.

The most recent clue to the nature of the crisis unfolding in the land of the October Revolution is the revelations issuing from the Twentieth Congress of the Communist Party of the Soviet Union last February and in particular the report on Stalin made by Khrushchev to the closed session of the Congress.

Let us therefore consider the most important revelations contained in Khrushchev's speech:

In the first group are those pertaining to Stalin's regime of mass murder and terror. On this point Khrushchev admitted:

---

19   Weiss 1956.

- The Moscow Trials of the thirties were frame-ups.
- The charge that the Trotskyists were spies, wreckers and terrorists was fabricated.
- The confessions that formed the basis of the Moscow Trials were obtained by means of psychological and physical torture summed up by Stalin in the formula: 'Beat, beat, and again beat!'
- The assassination of Kirov, which was the starting point of the Moscow Trials, appears to have been carried out by Stalin's secret police.
- The whole generation of Bolsheviks associated with Lenin in the leadership of the Russian Revolution of October 1917 was murdered, many of them after being tortured into confessing falsely that they were spies and terrorists.
- Frame-ups, false confessions and mass murder were practiced on tens of thousands of members of the Communist Party and hundreds of thousands of workers and peasants.
- Revolutionary legality and workers' democracy were destroyed and replaced by police rule under the direct supervision of Stalin.

The second group of Khrushchev's admissions relate to the question of nationalities. As you know, the Soviet Union is a federation of numerous Republics. The October 1917 revolution gave freedom and autonomy to the national minorities, who had lived under the oppression of Great Russian chauvinism in what was called 'the Czarist prison of the peoples'.

Under the Stalin regime, Khrushchev revealed a number of small nations were subjected to mass deportations to faraway places in the course of which millions perished.

The third set of revelations deals with Stalin's crimes and blunders as a war leader: Here Khrushchev recounts how Stalin ignored all evidence of political reality and refused to believe Hitler would attack the Soviet Union.

Thus, Khrushchev points out, the Soviet Union was unprepared economically and militarily for the fascist onslaught in 1941.

Moreover, thousands of the best officers of the Red Army, from the company level up to the general staff had been liquidated in the purges and this badly disorganized the army.

Stalin, according to Khrushchev, was demoralized and helpless in the first stage of the war. Later he exerted his authority to commit military blunders that in one instance alone cited by Khrushchev cost the lives of hundreds of thousands of soldiers.

In short, Khrushchev shows that contrary to his own words at the Nineteenth Congress, in which he assigns the credit for the victory of Russia in the war to 'Stalin's genius', the truth was that Stalin's regime brought the USSR to the edge of disaster during the war and cost the lives of millions of soldiers and civilians.

The fourth group of Khrushchev's counts denouncing Stalin pertain to the 'cult of the individual'.

Khrushchev goes into considerable detail on this point. He describes how Stalin replaced the government, the party, the Central Committee and the courts and established a one-man system of rule. He describes how Stalin demanded of one and all, not merely obedience to his command, but the utmost servility. Those who failed to shower Stalin with declarations of unbounded praise for his Godlike genius were immediately suspect and subsequently fell under Stalin's terror.

In connection with the cult of the individual Khrushchev relates how Stalin personally edited histories and biographies to falsely depict his role as the all-wise, infallible, genius-leader.

The fifth group of revelations concern the relations of the Stalin regime to other workers' states, notably Yugoslavia. It is likely that a fuller text of the speech will reveal a lot more regarding China. But the evidence contained in Khrushchev's speech, plus what is already well known, establishes fully that Stalin adopted the same attitude toward the new workers' states outside the Soviet Union as he did toward the national minorities within the USSR.

The sixth and final point of Khrushchev's indictment of Stalin deals with Soviet agriculture. Khrushchev shows that contrary to the myth that Stalin was a deep student of the agrarian question and the leader of the great social transformations in Russian agriculture since the revolution, he was in reality abysmally ignorant of the problem. According to Khrushchev, Stalin's only contributions to the solution of agrarian problems consisted of sabotaging all serious efforts to alleviate severe crises and proposing fantastically unreasonable taxation. (At one point Stalin proposed to tax the peasants an amount greater than their total income for the given period).

Unrevealed Atrocities

There are many things that Khrushchev did not reveal in his report. The atrocities against the leaders of Jewish culture were not mentioned. Neither was Stalin's international murder-machine. Nor was anything said on how this machine was used in Spain, how it was used to liquidate Trotsky's secretaries, and how it was used to assassinate Leon Trotsky himself. We can expect that more revelations will come and more details will be given on what was already admitted.

The truth, as is well known, makes its way slowly, for long periods of time – but once it gains momentum it moves with great speed.

Now it is irrefutably established that the Trotskyist movement told the world working class the truth about the crimes of Stalinism. Each and every crime revealed by Khrushchev was exposed by the Trotskyists many years ago. Any fair-minded person can verify this by consulting the record of our movement – merely by looking through the files of *The Militant* since 1928.

∴

The Twentieth Congress disclosed one gigantic fact: The Russian workers are beginning the historic work of overthrowing the bureaucratic caste and restoring the democratic foundations of the revolution. This is the basis for a Marxist understanding of the feverish movement on the surface and at the summits of Soviet society.

The US State Department propagandists are attempting to depict the Khrushchev revelations as a proof of the 'inherent evil of communism'.

∴

In the first place this pitiful effort rests on accepting the Stalinist falsehood that socialism has been victoriously achieved in one country – the Soviet Union. On that premise, it is, of course, not difficult to prove that socialism is not what the founders of the socialist movement said it would be.

However, Marx, Engels, Lenin and Trotsky and the whole Bolshevik party, including Stalin up to 1924, never dreamed of a reactionary utopian concept like achieving socialism within the boundaries of one country. The Russian Revolution established a society transitional to socialism. Socialism itself will be achieved only on the premise of the victorious revolution over capitalism in its main centers. The socialist society will be founded on the highest technological achievements of capitalism, as a world-wide productive system liberated from the fetters of national boundaries and capitalist private property.

State Department Propaganda

But let's take the State Department propagandists on their own premise for a moment. If the crimes of the Stalin cult are the expression of the 'evils of communism', what is the exposure of these crimes? Why are these crimes being repudiated?

The New York Times, US News and World Report, and other authoritative spokesmen for Big Business, agree that the only plausible explanation for the repudiation of the Stalin cult – the only factor that can explain why the present rulers would take the grave risk of destroying the very keystone of the whole Stalinist structure, is the movement of the Soviet people from below. But they don't dare say that this movement is pro-capitalist in its thought or direction!

Any hopes they had, that an uprising against Stalinism in Eastern Europe or the Soviet Union would favor the return of capitalism were smashed by the June 17, 1953 insurrection of the East German working class. This working-class insurrection, highly organized and magnificently disciplined, and embracing the entire East German industrial working class was anti-capitalist and socialist through and through.

As a matter of fact, only the Stalinist bureaucrats, tried to pin the label of a pro-West, imperialist-inspired movement on this revolutionary uprising. The capitalists knew better, as all the evidence shows. They were therefore unable to intervene.

Evidently, therefore, the so-called 'evils of Communism' are being countered by an insurgent movement of the working people who have no thought of returning to capitalism but are bent on removing the barriers in the path to the free society of world socialism.

And then, if the bureaucratic degenerations that gripped the first workers state in history are to be depicted as the 'evils of communism' what term will the State Department propaganda flunkeys use to describe the two world wars, the world depression, the ten-year hell of Hitlerism, the 20-year rule of Mussolini and the dictatorship of the fascist butcher Franco? Are these not the expression of the 'inherent evils of capitalism'?

Correctly understood, Stalinism itself is an expression of the evils of capitalism besetting an isolated workers' state. While the October Revolution established the foundations of a new social order, the weight of the Czarist past and the pressure of capitalist encirclement of a backward country imposed a cruel burden of bureaucratic parasitism and terror on the Russian people.

∵

Khrushchev opened his speech with a dissertation on the views of Marx, Engels and Lenin on the 'cult of the individual'. But although he uses the term 'Marxist-Leninist' in practically every other paragraph of his speech, Khrushchev's method has nothing in common with Marxist thought on this question.

He reduces the question to one of modesty versus vanity. Marx was modest, he tells the audience. So was Engels; Lenin was *very* modest. But not Stalin. Stalin ceased to be modest and raised himself above the party and what is worse the Central Committee. Then he began to murder people who disagreed with him, and then still others for no reason at all. He began to commit all kinds of hideous crimes – all because he forgot that a Marxist-Leninist is modest.

Empty Explanations

Khrushchev says: 'It is clear that in the situation of Socialist victory there was no basis for mass terror in the country'. Then why the mass terror?

Khrushchev answers the question of 'Why the Stalin cult?' with an empty tautology. The Stalin cult arose because Stalin raised himself above the Party and the Central Committee. It's the same as explaining the crimes of Stalin by his criminal conduct.

If a socialist society has been established, this signifies that mankind has raised its productive powers to the point where the class division of society has been eliminated. The elimination of the class struggle eliminates the need of a state with its special body of armed men to impose by force the rule of the dominant class.

If the Soviet Union has indeed entered the domain of socialism, then, how explain the fact that instead of witnessing the withering away of the functions of the state, it experienced, during the last three decades, the enormous growth of an oppressive state apparatus that maintained its rule by perpetrating the most heinous crimes against those subjected to its rule.

Surely, a Marxist-Leninist must see in such phenomena the expression of extremely acute, social contradictions. But, no, Khrushchev views the phenomenon of the growth of a repressive state which practiced mass murder for 22 years according to his reckoning, as a result of an erroneous theory, that somehow got into Stalin's head, namely, the theory that precisely with the advent of socialism class strife sharpens.

How did this theory get into Stalin's head despite the achievement of a socialist society? Apparently it is associated with Stalin's tendency to lack modesty and to raise himself above the Central Committee. Purely arbitrary and half-baked idealist constructions! In Khrushchev's explanations there is not a trace of the Marxist method of materialist dialectic in which the role of the individual in history is regarded as a function of the struggle of classes and social strata within classes.

Trotsky's Method

The method of the cult of the individual is not abandoned in this type of explanation – it is only turned inside out. Instead of a god – we are presented with a devil. Contrast to this method the method of Trotsky, who 20 years ago, in his basic work *The Revolution Betrayed*, explained the Stalin cult as follows:

> The increasingly insistent deification of Stalin is, with all its elements of caricature, a necessary element of the regime. The bureaucracy has need of an inviolable super-arbiter, a first consul if not an emperor, and it raises upon its shoulders him who best responds to its claim for lordship. That 'strength of character' of the leader which so enraptures the literary dilettantes of the West, is in reality the sum total of the collective pressure of a caste which will stop at nothing in defense of its position. Each one of them at his post is thinking: *L'état – c'est moi*. [I am the State.] In Stalin each one easily finds himself. But Stalin also finds in each one a small part of his own spirit. Stalin is the personification of the bureaucracy. That is the substance of his political personality.

The 'personification of the bureaucracy' – that is the clue to understanding the role of Stalin. The bureaucracy that rose to power after the Russian Revolution is an historically illicit force. It came to power on the wave of reaction – in a country exhausted by years of imperialist war, revolution and civil war.

The vanguard of the proletariat was bled white. The great ocean of petty peasant enterprise predominated over industry. The initial defeats of the European revolution further sapped the strength and revolutionary vitality of the Russian workers. With every defeat of a workers revolution abroad the bureaucratic tendencies in the Soviet Union were strengthened and with the strengthening of the bureaucratic caste in the Soviet Union it was able to crush the revolutionary wing of the party of Lenin. And then utterly crush the party itself.

Bureaucratic Usurpation

The bureaucracy expressed its hunger for privilege amidst universal poverty in its adherence to Stalin. Stalin had the best qualifications for the job. His record as an old Bolshevik provided the necessary disguise for the process of bureaucratic usurpation.

That's why Khrushchev must say over and over again in his speech that Stalin was politically right as against Trotskyism. He means by that to justify the triumph of the bureaucratic caste over the Bolshevik party of Lenin and Trotsky.

Fundamentally that is what the great struggle was about. It was a struggle between a bureaucratic reaction which lifted the Stalinist oligarchy to power and the proletarian Left Opposition led by Trotsky that fought to defend the Bolshevik party, the Soviets and the trade unions from strangulation by the bureaucracy. It was the re-enactment on a vast historical scale, of the same kind of struggle that has taken place in many unions, which started under fighting leadership, practiced wide internal democracy, conducted a policy of militant class struggle, reached out the hand of solidarity to workers in every industry – but subsequently, under different social conditions, with the receding of the class struggle, became bureaucratized and headed by what Daniel DeLeon described as the 'labor lieutenants of capitalism in the ranks of the working class'.

Khrushchev Refuted

Khrushchev says:

> We must affirm that the party fought a serious fight against the Trotskyists, rightists and bourgeois nationalists and that it disarmed ideologically all the enemies of Leninism. The ideological fight was carried on successfully ... Here Stalin played a positive role.

The facts refute Khrushchev as completely on this question as on the later frame-ups in the Moscow Trials.

1. Trotskyism was not defeated by ideological means. The record shows that bureaucratic usurpers, utilizing the pressure of a deep social reaction to the revolution, silenced their opponents from the beginning by methods of frame-ups and terror. If Stalin defeated Trotsky's Bolshevik opposition by 'ideological means' what were thousands of Trotskyists doing in jail from 1927 on?
2. The Stalinist faction did not fight for Leninism. On the contrary, as documentary evidence shows, Lenin opened a fight in the last years of his life against the Stalinist faction as the expression of the ominous bureaucratic tendency. Lenin fought the rise of Stalin and Stalinism from his deathbed and Trotsky continued the fight after Lenin's death.

Khrushchev says that Stalin was right in the fight against Trotskyism because without that fight Russia would have failed to industrialize or collectivize agriculture. One is almost compelled to stand in awe before the sweep and audacity of this lie.

Actually, it was the Trotskyist opposition that as early as 1923 proposed that the Soviet Union embark on a central industrial plan and that a struggle be opened to collectivize agriculture as a weapon against the growing kulak (capitalist) element in the countryside. This proposal was hooted down derisively by the Stalinist faction. Trotsky was called a fantastic super-industrialist, a dreamer and a charlatan. Stalin, the great expert on agriculture, said what the Russian peasant needed was not a plan but a good rain.

For his proposal to fight the growing power of the rich peasant kulak, Trotsky was accused of 'underestimation of the peasantry'. In a bloc with the right wing of the party, led by Bukharin, the Stalin faction conducted reactionary propaganda among the kulak elements to incite them against Trotskyism. They didn't even refrain from using anti-Semitism in this campaign.

Thus, while leaning on the social pressure of the capitalist elements, the bureaucracy throttled the opposition and expelled it from the party, drove the workers who supported the Left Opposition out of the factories and opened a reign of terror.

Left Opposition Confirmed

Within months after the expulsion of Trotsky, the position of the Left Opposition was confirmed to the hilt. The kulak threat, which the Stalinists claimed did not even exist threatened to engulf the Soviet regime. The Stalinist faction then made a 180-degree turn. They took over Trotsky's program, and applied it. Industrialization? The first five-year plan was launched and it quickly confirmed the Left Opposition's estimates of the possibilities of planned economy. However, the bureaucracy gave its own distorted version to these measures – relying not on the creative power of the masses but on bureaucratic decree.

These historical questions are of urgent importance to the revolutionary movement. Not a single question confronting the radical workers today can be understood without tracing the struggle waged by Trotskyism from 1923 down to the present day. And the struggle of Trotskyism was only a continuation of the line of struggle of Marx, Engels and Lenin as it was tested and enriched by the October revolution.

Take the question of peaceful coexistence and the peaceful road to socialism – these so-called new theories of the Twentieth Congress, revising Lenin's conception of our epoch as 'the epoch of imperialist war, proletarian revolution and colonial uprisings'. Khrushchev and Company have not announced new theories, as the Stalinist leader in the US, Eugene Dennis, would have us believe. Peaceful coexistence between capitalism and socialism is the basic theory of Stalinism. That question was fought out in the great dispute over the theory of 'socialism in one country' versus the Leninist-Trotskyist conception of permanent revolution.

The peaceful road to socialism? A bloc with the liberal capitalist? A multi-class coalition government? That was the program of the reformist right wing of the Second International which was vigorously opposed by Lenin, Trotsky, Luxemburg and Liebknecht.

In the Russian workers' movement these were the questions that demarcated Bolshevism and Menshevism since 1903.

Bolshevism and Menshevism

It was the essence of Menshevism to seek to ally the working class with the liberal bourgeoisie. Such an alliance results in the defeat of the proletariat, with the liberals turning up in the camp of reaction.

The essence of Bolshevism, defended by Lenin and Trotsky from 1905 through 1917 and to the end of their lives, was to organize the working class independently, against the parties of capitalism.

The arguments of the CP leaders about why we must work in the Democratic party are the very arguments, the sophistries of the lesser evil, that Lenin waged a life-long struggle against. It is all the more important to go back to the basic teachings of Lenin on these principled questions because his name and authority are invoked by the Stalinist falsifiers – to support the very theories and arguments Lenin demolished.

The Basic Question

The question of class collaboration versus class struggle – this is at bottom the question dividing Stalinism and Trotskyism in the United States, in the Soviet Union and throughout the world.

The Daily Worker editors berate themselves for having blindly and subserviently parroted all the lies of Stalin. Why don't they ask themselves: How did it happen that a revolutionary party, which by its very nature must be headed by critical-minded independent leaders, tested in the class struggle, became headed by spineless bureaucrats who defended every crime, no matter how monstrous, that issued from the Kremlin?

The answer isn't hard to find. The CP in the US, like all Communist Parties, was destroyed as an independent revolutionary party, following the expulsion of the Trotskyists in 1928. The Stalinist bureaucracy used its power and prestige to pervert the Comintern into its factional instrument. All communist leaders who opposed this were bureaucratically driven out of their respective parties. Those who were willing to become the creatures of the Stalinist bureaucracy in the USSR lost their capacity to be revolutionists at home. They lost their class bearings. They became capable, as a matter of course, of any deed of treachery.

The position of the Soviet Union in relation to the capitalist world has, as we stated in the beginning, become considerably stronger since World War II. At the same time the power of the Stalinist regime has been undermined. For those who identified the destiny of the Soviet Union with Stalinism, this comes as a completely unexpected and bewildering phenomenon.

The Trotskyists, however, foresaw and were completely prepared for this development. They alone analyzed the basic contradiction in Soviet society as the contradiction between the new property forms of nationalized and planned economy established as a result of the October revolution and the domination of the workers' state by a bureaucratic oligarchy.

This contradiction, Trotskyism taught, manifested itself in the struggle between the Soviet working class and the dictatorship of the bureaucratic caste. The fate of the struggle between the workers and the bureaucracy was tied to the fate of the world-wide struggle of classes. Stalinism, the politics of the bureaucracy, was born and prospered in an epoch of defeats of proletarian revolution – it was the refraction of capitalist pressure and reaction within the Soviet Union and the world workers' movement. A major factor in promoting defeats, Stalinism became strengthened by them.

The Thunder of Revolution

But despite the obstacle of Stalinism the anti-capitalist forces in the world and the Soviet Union have become enormously strengthened. The Soviet working class, now 50-million strong and augmented by the industrial working class of Eastern Europe, expresses this profound shift in the world relationship of forces by a revolutionary resurgence. The Twentieth Congress heard the echo of this revolutionary thunder in the halls of the bureaucracy. Everything they did there and everything they have done since is in the nature of panicky preparations for the onrushing revolutionary storm.

The world revolution and the world working class movement have entered a new stage marked by the appearance of the Soviet masses in the political arena. This stage can only culminate in the downfall of the Soviet bureaucratic caste, the victory of Russian bolshevism and the triumph of the world socialist revolution.

7 New Stage for the Youth[20]
(1957)

James Robertson

Since its inception as an organized force, the radical youth movement in the United States has gone through two major stages of development. First came the wrenching away of the socialist youth from the old Socialist party under the impact of the World War I, the Russian Revolution and the formation of the Communist International. These constituted the basis of the Communist party youth movement in the twenties. Second came a turning away from the Comintern as Stalinism moved to the fore. The Spartacus Youth League, founded by the American followers of Leon Trotsky, was a point of attraction, while larger numbers of youthful militants went to the revivified Young People's Socialist League. The most active elements in these two organizations merged and affiliated to the Socialist Workers party. But this promising development gave way under the impact of World War II and the factional struggle that broke out in the SWP over the question of defense of the Soviet Union.

The postwar period up to the death of Stalin, the Khrushchev revelations and the East European revolts and uprisings saw little socialist activity and organization among the youth. The socialist youth groups were small and largely ineffectual; Communist party work in the youth field in terms of education and activity was a kind of middle-class liberalism compounded by subservience to the dictates and interests of the Russian Stalinist state machine.

Today the radical youth movement stands at the threshold of a new stage of development, one of great importance and opportunity for the revolutionary socialist movement. It is now possible to create a new pool of potential Marxist leadership among the American youth. What we do in the immediate future can set the tone and pattern for a whole period.

Conditions are favorable for a renascence of a propagandists radical youth movement. The witch-hunt has receded, murmurings are apparent in the economy, developing antagonisms are visible between the rank and file and the

---

20   Robertson 1957.

hidebound trade-union bureaucracy, the East European class struggles have had an impact as has the latest round in the colonial struggle against imperialism.

Against this background the principal fact is the dissolution of the (Stalinist) Labor Youth League. Only a few years ago this organization still had as many as 5,000 members. Now it has fallen to pieces – a direct consequence not of domestic events but of Khrushchev's revelations and the massive struggles in the Soviet bloc which showed the workers of East Germany, Poland and Hungary pitted against the Stalinist regimes. Having no independent roots in the American class struggle, the Labor Youth League existed by ideas alone, with a certain amount of bureaucratic glue to hold them together. The enormous discrepancy between the avowed aims of the Labor Youth League and the practice of its principal heroes, such as Stalin, was too great a contradiction to be bridged.

The formation disintegrated and ordered its own dissolution.

This was accompanied by a breakdown of the long-existing hostility of former LYL members toward other radical youth organizations. Among these in turn, as among the organizations of older people, it became generally recognized that a regroupment of forces was in order and that this could be reached only through friendly discussion over programmatic questions, no matter how sharp the differences over particular proposed answers to the common problems faced by the working people. The forum movement started up around the country and various broad and loose clubs appeared, providing a platform for speakers representing various tendencies. The interest in this development has been particularly high among the radical-minded youth.

Within the general flux, of course, some of the older people have refused to recognize that they were faced with new tasks and new opportunities. Among the more notable of these is the Socialist Labor party, an encrusted organization that remains decades behind the times.

Because the turn was not due to a rising class struggle in this country that might have brought tens of thousands of new people into action in a massive way, the issues have primarily revolved around an ideological assessment affecting a relatively thin stream of younger people. Among these, however, the ferment has been profound.

A great shattering of illusions about Stalinism has occurred. In contrast to those in the Communist party and its periphery, who were led to believe that today's leadership of the Soviet Union represents the socialist ideal, are those who felt they had to reject everything associated with the Soviet Union, even socialism itself. Seeing Russia as a horrible, totalitarian monstrosity, where the workers are turned into dehumanized slaves and brutes and all class-consciousness is eradicated, they felt it better to stick with John Foster Dulles. The feeling is well expressed in George Orwell's novel *1984* – the hopelessness of everything in face of such phenomena as Stalinism. For many youths in the Social Democratic and liberal movements, this illusion, too, has been shattered. The actions of the workers in East Europe have demonstrated that the working class can move and exert its pressure despite Stalinism. The dual shake-up in thinking has shown that the old order is dead – a new movement is required in the youth field.

The actual process of regroupment, naturally, has not been straightforward. A number of alternatives have been advanced on what to do.

The simplest is 'stand-patism'. The hope is to ride out the storm. The attempt to wish away the present is characteristic of those who really have nothing to offer. The Socialist party, for example, having finally achieved re-unification with the Social Democratic Federation, responded to the regroupment process by urging everybody to join them. This is nice of them, but not well calculated to meet the challenge of the big change that has occurred. The SP-SDF leaders recognize that something peculiar called the forum movement has developed, but they are so far removed from reality that they actually believe Khrushchev's revelations were part of a plot aimed at sucking in the Socialist party.

Those who are under the illusion that the Socialist party represents a hope for the future should make it a practice to read the *Socialist Call* more attentively, for it reveals what a thoroughly hidebound, ossified and miserable grouping this really is.

The Communist party likewise takes a 'stand-pat' position. Of course they are progressively losing their following of youth, but they still hope to ride things out. If they no longer label opposing tendencies as 'fascist agents', they nevertheless regard them as irrelevant. As in the case of the Socialist party, this represents a complete loss of touch with reality. At one time the CP was a formidable barrier to the socialist movement. But that's not true any longer. The former strength of the Communist party remains today only as an illusion among some of its followers, who begin to sit in little rooms, isolated from the social process.

Another tendency, the one grouped around the *Monthly Review*, while not numerically significant perhaps, carries considerable ideological weight, especially among those who have retreated from the Communist party zone. This tendency, too, has clearly indicated its lack of interest in community relations or discussion with other tendencies. In reply to an invitation to participate in the forum initiated by A.J. Muste, Paul M. Sweezy, one of the editors of the *Monthly Review*, declined, suggesting that others should follow his course of abstention.

Such rigidity, having much in common with the sectarian ossification of thought most clearly represented by the Socialist Labor party, was, of course, to be expected among some of the radical currents in abrupt turns of this kind. In other groups underlying instabilities rose to the surface. This was especially true of the one nationally established youth organization outside of the Labor Youth League; that is, the Young Socialist League, which is more or less affiliated to the Independent Socialist League.

The Young Socialist League had the possibility, perhaps, of becoming the nucleus for a new independent youth movement. But it has undergone an internal crisis. The right wing, tailing after the Shachtmanite leadership of the Independent Socialist League, which proposes to become part of the Socialist party, is preparing to enter the Young People's Socialist League on any terms whatever; and the left wing, resisting this course, has its attention centered on the problem of bringing together the elements really capable of building a new youth movement.

The possibility of achieving a regroupment around a broad common denominator of militant socialist activities is very attractive to segments in the youth field of the most diverse political background. For example, in the Bay Area, with which I am most familiar, we in the left wing of the Young Socialist League have met with a most friendly response from many young people who generally regard the *National Guardian* as their paper. On a nation-wide scale, the forum movement has given impetus to these get-together tendencies. At the present stage, exploratory discussions are going on about political minimums and organizational forms. These are occurring among the left wing of the Young Socialist League, young people in and around the Socialist Workers party, some of the youth supporters of *The American Socialist*, sympathizers of the *National Guardian*, former members of the defunct Labor Youth League, and just plain independents and youth first, coming to radical politics.

This is quite a list. If anyone had suggested two years ago that there was a possibility of a united youth organization with such components, it would have been taken as prima facie evidence for certifiable insanity. This in itself shows what an enormous wrenching we've gone through in the youth field in this country.

All these young people taken together are an impressive force – at least potentially. The various tendencies are not negotiating as crystallized national formations. They are found in varying proportions in a whole series of clubs and local groups in youth forums and the like across the country. In New York, for instance, the Young Socialist Forum has a good-sized contingent sympathetic to the views of the Socialist Workers party as well as left-wing members of the Young Socialist League. In Philadelphia the proportion of former members of the Labor Youth League is larger. In Chicago the tendencies are spread more evenly. The Minneapolis club has mainly an *American Socialist* complexion. In Detroit it is Socialist Workers. In the Bay Area several groupings have appeared besides the left-wing caucus of the Young Socialist League, among them the Mark Twain Club which came out of the Labor Youth League. In Los Angeles, Socialist Workers partisans have done much toward getting a united group independent of all parties. These main areas indicate what is happening nationally.

It is important to understand that the desire for unity, the desire to reverse the fragmentation of the radical movement, is not sufficient in and of itself to bring about a healthy unification. The basis for unity requires the fullest and most careful consideration. Here, by way of preliminary, it might be well to indicate a difference in attitude that is important for those coming from the Labor Youth League and those from a background such as the Young Socialist League.

Former LYL members, used to an organization numbering in the thousands that suddenly went to smash, feel that a terrible vacuum has been created in the socialist youth field. Large numbers quit completely after the Khrushchev revelations. Others who did not renounce their socialist views feel dispirited and demoralized. We of the YSL on the contrary saw the self-demolition of the LYL as a progressive development, since it removed a big barrier. True, it involved the loss of a good number of young people from the radical movement; but it opened the possibility of a new beginning since it broke the monopoly of a false program and a false control in the American youth field.

The question of program once again asserted its predominance over mere numbers. After all, of what use is an organization, no matter how large, if its purposes run counter to the interests of socialism? The end of the Stalin cult and the confirmation of the crimes and betrayals charged against Stalin's rule was a most healthy development. Now we are able to discuss in an atmosphere free of the vilification with which the Labor Youth League customarily responded to issues raised by its opponents.

The elements of a new youth movement that must be considered in their interrelationship are, first, its independence, secondly, its broadness; thirdly, its militancy. These must be combined in such a way as to lead to an effective and democratic movement of young socialists, and at such a tempo as to maximize the opportunities at hand.

To avoid leaving these as just words, it is necessary to specify our meanings. By independence I mean free from the organizational control of specific parties, that is, groupings adhering to fully formulated political programs. It is true that there is a long-term instability in 'independence' of the youth, since people grow up, and in growing up they settle on a political program. After debate, experience and participation in political activities, the most independent youth movement will eventually reach an outlook more or less parallel to one or another of the various parties.

Right now, however, a little bit of youth 'vanguardism' in political matters is a desirable thing. Because of the more rapid break down of old organizational ties in the youth field – a kind of running ahead of the general socialist field – any seeking after adult link-ups would have to be with groups as they were rather than as they will be. The regroupment process is reaching maturity more rapidly among the youth than among the adults. Thus there exists a considerable discrepancy in developments in the two areas. Gradually the adult level will pull parallel and that may raise problems, but that is for the future.

Another important consideration in favor of independence is that one of the legacies of Stalinism is an exceptionally suspicious attitude among young people who have been in politics. A great many – and by no means the least worthy – former members of the Labor Youth League want no part whatsoever of subordinating themselves to adult groups. This antagonism toward the older generation in general is a result of the specific experiences of these youth with Stalinist practices.

In addition to this a good many young people who want to participate in a new youth movement look toward definite adult organizations or periodicals. Any enclosing and narrowing down of the youth movement would simply chop them off.

From the considerations regarding independence, I think it follows directly that the new youth movement must seek an extremely broad scope. Maximum diversity within a basic common denominator is, moreover, a really precious asset, in my opinion, because it brings into play a great deal of experience, bodies of knowledge and insight from different tendencies. Speaking from personal experience, the Bay Area YSL has been labeled as a bunch of 'hard-boiled Bolsheviks' and also as an 'all-inclusive political zoo'. We drew no line against anarchists, social democrats, sectarians, or those with illusions about the Soviet Union, yet we engaged in a good deal of militant action. The lesson we drew from it is the need not merely for tolerance but for genuine interest in the ideas of others, their contributions, and mutual exploration of views, while at the same time placing a lot of emphasis on militant activity without, however, using a disciplinary whip in any fashion or making any kind of attempt at compulsion.

It so happens that about ninety-eight percent of the activity that a youth organization might undertake is in any case of the type an extremely broad range of tendencies can subscribe to. Differences that could appear through participation in working-class struggles are not very great at present.

However, there are certain limitations to broadness. The main one, I think, is the political hostility of groups that are opposed to an independent youth organization. Among these are the Socialist Party – Social Democratic Federation, the Socialist Labor party, the Shachtmanite ISL and so on. Yet even here there will be individual members who might like to participate. Even a member of the Young Democrats might like to see for himself what an organization with socialist aims offers. You don't treat such seventeen-year-olds, who want to argue for Stevenson, like aged betrayers of the working class. The opportunity should be open for them to develop into Marxists. On the other hand there are groups in this country who proclaim their Marxism to be second to none yet who would refuse to touch an independent socialist youth organization with a ten-foot pole. In practice the question of just how broad 'broad' is will be determined by the attitudes of those who wish or don't wish to participate.

As for militancy, this can be a cloudy word. It should be sufficient, it seems to me, to classify an organization as militant if it seeks to take a genuinely socialist position on issues as they arise, to decide on practical steps and to discuss in comradely fashion the various theoretical ramifications. Aside from what it means in programmatic implications, militancy involves a conscious attempt to break with the study-group habits of withdrawn young people and to undertake actions energetically, with a great deal of commitment.

In conclusion I would like to stress the urgency of youth regroupment. The breaking of the Stalinist grip in the American youth field has opened opportunities not seen for decades. But these opportunities will not remain indefinitely. They can be dissipated, leaving the arena free for backward or even reactionary tendencies. On the other hand, resolute action can signify the early appearance of a new socialist youth movement in America with a great future before it in the coming period of working-class radicalization.

8 Really Beat?[21]
(1958)

Evelyn Sell

There seems to be an unwritten law in America that every generation must be labeled. The 'Lost Generation' of World War I was followed by the 'Socially Conscious Generation' of the thirties. Various tags have been placed on the present generation – those who grew up during World War II, fought in the war that wasn't a war at all but a 'police action', and are now on the roller-coaster ride of an up-and-down American economy. This has been called the Brain-Washed ... the Waiting ... the Go ... the Silent ... and, finally, the 'Beat Generation'.

Bewailing the apathy of today's youth, *Time* and *Life* called them the 'Silent Generation' because the young people in America seemed completely content to let the world go by while they sought regimented living in a ranch house with a swimming pool. In a symposium of college professors in the *Nation* last year, the same criticism was voiced. College students were characterized as 'earnest but dull ... the mass of college students lead lives of quiet enervation ... many undergraduates acknowledge no heroes, profess only lukewarm admirations, shun causes, are suspicious of joinings and flinch from commitments'. The professors (and *Time* and *Life* before them) were appalled at the 'indifference to either politics or reform or rebellion ...', which they noted in 'our intellectual elite. In twenty years they will run the most powerful nation on earth'.

The spokesmen of the present group who 'run the most powerful nation on earth' are worried not about the next set of rulers so much as the next set of 'ruled'. Science fiction writers enjoy describing mythical lands where the masses are drugged into political apathy, where the dictators mold the thoughts and actions of their workers through TV. We do not live in such a push-button world as yet. We live in a world where wars – even atomic wars – must be fought by people who believe in what they are fighting for. Those who 'run the most powerful nation on earth' need a generation of Americans who acknowledge

---

21   Sell 1958.

heroes like McCarthy, admire brink-of-war diplomacy, believe in capitalism, like nothing better than to fight in another and another and another 'police action'.

That is where the apathy hurts – young people shun, to a great extent, commitments to socialist actions but they also shun committing themselves to new Koreas, to economic insecurity, to witch-hunts. Most young people play it cool – to both sides. They are nursing their passion, waiting (in the unemployment lines), watching (uprisings throughout the world), listening (to reports of the poisoning of our atmosphere by nuclear tests).

But there are other young people who do not withhold their passion, who live fast and furiously, at fever pitch. They commit themselves totally – some to motorcycles and endless races down the roads of America, some to drugs and the sensations of 'flipping', some to the exotic intellectuality of Eastern philosophies, or to defiant homosexuality, or promiscuous heterosexuality. They are the loud-mouths of the generation. They attract the spotlight. Books are written about them. Magazines photograph and describe them. Movies are made about them. But at bottom they are not so different from their more silent brothers and sisters. They share a deep-going rejection of the values of our society and a fervent stressing of the value and importance of the human being as a person.

The label 'Silent Generation' failed to win popular acceptance. Now, however, writers claiming to speak for their kind have adopted a name for themselves that seems to be catching on. In 1952, the same year that *Time* and *Life* wrote of 'The Silent Generation', John Clellon Holmes published an article in the *New York Times* entitled *This Is the Beat Generation*. Since then the phrase has gained popularity and notoriety through the literary successes of writers such as Jack Kerouac and Allen Ginsberg. Kerouac has not only hit the best-seller lists with his *On the Road*, he has become touted as the spokesman of the people of whom he writes: people who live on the bum; who restlessly seek their 'kicks' in modern jazz, marijuana, fast cars and faster motorcycles, crime, defiant sexual amorality, Zen Buddhism; who have as their heroes James Dean, Dylan Thomas, Charlie Parker; who say to each other, 'We gotta go and never stop going till we get there'. 'Where we going, man?' 'I don't know, but we gotta go'.

These are the 'hipsters', the Beat Generation. Kerouac calls them 'seekers'. What are they seeking? 'God', answers Kerouac; 'I want God to show me His face'. Kerouac defines Beat: 'Beat means beatitude, not beat up'. The hipster is one who is on the beat, in tune with things, in the know, a cool cat who takes drugs and then says, 'But, man, last night I got so high I knew *everything*. I mean I knew *why*'. In his second published novel *The Subterraneans*, Kerouac writes that they are 'hip without being slick, they are intelligent without being corny, they are intellectual as hell and know all about Pound without being pretentious or talking too much about it, they are very quiet, they are very Christlike'.

The real hipsters, the actual 'pros' of the Beat Generation, are numerically very small. The select group is swelled, however, by the curious and the bored and the sometimes rebellious who like to season their suburban solid-citizen safe lives with a dash of bitter-sweet Bohemianism.

The rest of the world lives in Squaresville. The squares don't dig anything. They wear Brooks Park suits, drive MGs, hunger after the dollar and are

> burned alive in their innocent flannel suits on Madison Avenue amid the blasts of leaden verse & the tanked up clatter of the iron regiments of fashion & the nitroglycerine shrieks of the fairies of advertising & the mustard gas of sinister intelligent editors, or ... run down by the drunken taxicabs of Absolute Reality ...

This last is from Allen Ginsberg's *Howl*. In this poem he mourns not only the wasted lives of the squares but also that of the hipsters 'who drove cross-country seventy-two hours to find out if I had a vision or you had a vision or he had a vision to find out Eternity ...'.

John Clellon Holmes, in an *Esquire* article, defines 'beat' in this way:

> Everyone who has lived through a war, any sort of war, knows that beat means, not so much weariness, as rawness of the nerves; not so much being 'filled up to *here*', as being emptied out. It describes a state of mind from which all unessentials have been stripped, leaving it receptive to everything around it, but impatient with trivial obstructions. To be beat is to be at the bottom of your personality, looking up ... [The] conviction of the creative power of the unfettered individual soul stands behind everything in which the members of this generation interest themselves ... a generation groping toward faith out of an intellectual despair and moral chaos in which they refuse to lose themselves.

The letters *Esquire* printed in response to Holmes' article speak for themselves:
- From Connecticut: 'This is the Beat Generation, all right. Dead-beat!'
- From Pennsylvania: 'I know I am speaking for a lot of young men who just want to be left alone and not continuously bugged by people who don't take time to know us ... I, too, am searching for something, I don't know what, but it's there inside of me'.

- From Maryland: 'I'm tired of hearing us called freaks, renegades, and generally inferior human beings ... The Beat Generation you refer to is made up of a minority of people who have used the times as an excuse for their shortcomings'.
- From New York: 'We live in a terrible world. We do not know when the big blast will go off and boom, we will be no more. So we must live for today, for tomorrow may never come. That is why we must live fast. We have simply got to get all our living in while we can. In other days, people could plan their lives ... Today, however, while we must keep part of ourselves aware of the future and must plan for it, the rest of us, unfortunately, have to be aware that there may be no future and we had better live now and not then. This is a terribly morbid philosophy, but perhaps the only one that keeps us from degenerating altogether'.
- From Nebraska: 'How can you have the gas to lump all the teenagers into one glob? Generations as a group do not exist. They are a myth perpetrated by know-it-alls with the magic key to our mysterious youth's minds ... so they believe'.
- From New York: 'Now to separate the different phases of our so-called Beat Generation: There are Rock and Roll teen-agers, and the mentally hip, us. The R&Rs like wild parties, fast cars, crime, violence, fighting, drugs, sex and death, if you like. They are uncluttered and primitive. Our group – the cool – we have a goal. We are striving to find beauty in a world that shuns it.

    'Our feelings are not gutty; they are cool. We do not depend on the bizarre, and crimes without object are not ours. We consider physical violence and argument very square. We enjoy continental coffee shops and the like ... Our feelings can well be described in one word, indifferent, indifferent to the world of squares which surrounds us ... The statement "They refuse to lose themselves", is the most profound part of your article.'

Who Belongs

In this letter the writer touches the problem of definition. Who belongs to the Beat Generation? Is the hipster clothed in the motorcyclist's black leather jacket, or does he wear the gray flannel of disillusioned Madison Avenue sophisticates, or does he slouch in a San Francisco bar in nondescript working clothes? Although the bickering is considerable over what is a 'real' hipster, these three groups are usually included in discussions of the Beat Generation: the gangs (leather-belted, sideburned, jeaned and garrison belted), the Bohemians (replete with drugs, sex, jazz, poetry and knapsack), and the sorrowfully sedate suburbanites who wander down among the dregs of society for relief from the routines of ordinary middle-class life.

The latter group can be considered more as 'fellow travelers' than the hard core of hipsterism. An article in the *Reporter* calls them 'people who are merely curious, who want to see the vision but not be in it, who have a contempt for Squaresville but live there, who dig jazz but don't live it'.

The Bohemians and the juvenile gangs 'live it'. There is no well-paid job or middle-class security for them to run back to when the last musician has played the last note or the last rock is thrown by the last standee of a rumble. They are in deadly earnest about 'being with it'. In writing about the juvenile gangs, John Clellon Holmes shocked many when he said,

> Even the crudest and most nihilistic member of the Beat Generation, the young slum hoodlum, is almost exclusively concerned with the problem of belief, albeit unconsciously. It seems incredible that no one has realized that the only way to make the shocking juvenile murders coherent at all is to understand that they are specifically moral crimes ... Such crimes, which are no longer rarities and which are all committed by people under twenty-five, cannot be understood if we go on mouthing the same old panaceas about broken homes and slum environments and bad company, for they are spiritual crimes, crimes against the identity of another human being, crimes which reveal with stark and terrifying clarity the lengths to which a desperate need for values can drive the young. For in actuality it is the *longing* for values which is expressed in such a crime, and not the hatred of them. It is the longing to do or feel something meaningful, and it provides a sobering glimpse of how completely the cataclysms of this century have obliterated the rational, humanistic view of Man on which modern society has been erected.

Holmes points out that what the juvenile gangs are turning to, in their search for a code of ethics, is one of the oldest types of human organization, the tribe. The inviolability of comradeship, the high regard for personal courage, the oath to present a united, fighting front to the rest of the world, the concept that you and your brother belong and the others are all enemies to be destroyed or circumvented – these are the mores of the primitive tribe. What Holmes does not point out is that these are also the ethics of the capitalist society we live in drawn out to their most crude and saddening extremes. In trying to find his way in this world he never made, the juvenile gang member responds to the society that condemns him, 'OK, you made the rules. I'll go you one better'. In a class society, where one group is constantly engaged in struggle against another, the juvenile gangs plot rumbles, one gang against another. In a society that fosters prejudice, the juvenile gangs make raids on the 'sheenies', or the 'niggers', or the 'wops', or the 'japs'. In a society of permanent war, the gang member has his own versions of flame throwers, bazookas, bombs and grenades.

The third group included in the Beat Generation is the Bohemians. In *The Social History of Art*, Hauser writes of the difference between the Bohemians of the romantic and naturalistic periods. What he says of the latter could be published about the hipster today in *Playboy* or the *Nation*:

> The *bohème* was originally no more than a demonstration against the bourgeois way of life. It consisted of young artists and students, who were mostly the sons of well-to-do people, and in whom the opposition to the prevailing society was usually a product of mere youthful exuberance and contrariness ... [they] parted from bourgeois society, not because they were forced, but because they wanted to live differently from their bourgeois fathers. They were genuine romantics, who wanted to be original and extravagant. They undertook their excursion into the world of the outlaws and the outcasts, just as one undertakes a journey into an exotic land; they knew nothing of the misery of the later *bohème*, and they were free to return to bourgeois society at any time. The *bohème* of the following generation, that of the militant naturalism with its headquarters in the beer cellars ... was ... a real *bohème*, that is, an artistic proletariat, made up of people whose existence was absolutely insecure, people who stood outside the frontiers of bourgeois society, and whose struggle against the bourgeoisie was no high-spirited game but a bitter necessity. Their unbourgeois way of life was the form which best suited the questionable existence that they led and was in no sense any longer a mere masquerade.

It is the Bohemian artist of the Beat Generation who has established his headquarters in San Francisco. That city is being hailed by some as the Paris of this generation; and the 'San Francisco School' of art is lauded as the fountainhead of a renaissance in American art today. Those associated with this school include Kerouac, Ginsberg, Rexroth, Ferlinghetti.

Most San Francisco poets and writers are in the ranks of the longshoremen, migratory agricultural workers, seamen, and others whose work keeps them on the move. Allen Ginsberg, for example, makes a trip to the Arctic and then has enough money to go to Mexico and Europe for a while. Jack Kerouac, after achieving a minor success with a novel years ago, became disgusted with the

New York literary life and said, 'I have to make my choice between all this and the rattling trucks on the American road. And I think I'll choose the rattling trucks ...'. He chose the trucks and the odd-job life of the lumpen-proletariat. Young writers of the San Francisco school don't debate the theoretical questions of the class struggle in Bohemian coffee shops – they engage in that struggle on the picket line. They don't join the picket line to soak up atmosphere – they work at the place being struck.

The ranks of this artistic proletariat have been swelled by the conscientious objectors who were quartered nearby during the war. The anarcho-syndicalist traditions of the once powerfully influential IWW have reasserted themselves somewhat as the disillusionment with Stalinism has grown. Add to this a strong anti-war movement and you have the political temper of the San Francisco Bohemian climate. The school has been aptly termed 'the new anarchist Bohemianism'.

All the publicity about the school has resulted in a tourist invasion into the Bohemian life of the city. In a 'fanzine', RUR, put out by David Rike of Berkeley, California, it is explained that the Beat types

> aren't pleased about all the publicity since that means commercialization, the turning of North Beach into a tourist hang-out, higher rents, and the coming in of all sorts of squares, and week-end Bohemians and out-right gawkers. With commercialization, their bars are no longer places where you know you can meet all of your friends at since they are now squeezed out by the tourists who simply have to dig these cuh-razy people they read about in *Life*, *Playboy* and *Esquire*. The rents have gotten so high that even Lawrence Ferlinghetti has moved out of the Beach and down to the Potrero Hill district, besides numerous other persons. And the squares; you know the type, they have a nice Respectable job, white-collaring it somewhere, during the day, but wow, man, they gotta be with the Crowd and be Hip and, like that, so they don their turtle neck sweater, sandals, and frisco jeans and drive out to the Beach in their MGs (discreetly parking them in some dark alley, of course). But that's the way things go here in America.

As Hauser pointed out, the *bohème* consists of both artists and students. Student beats usually refuse to admit any ties to either the slum hood or the arty hipster. During a discussion held by the Young Socialist Club in Detroit, the question was asked by one of these Beat-type students, 'Is this movement progressive or reactionary?' The consensus among those present was that the movement is progressive in that it questions and rejects the capitalist philosophy of life. Its reactionary features consist in the inability to do more than reject, in the lack of understanding of the social forces spawning the movement.

The observation was made during this discussion that young people generally are beginning to seriously question the *status quo*, that they are restlessly turning this way and that in search of a guide to life in keeping with the ideals of democracy. The youth of the thirties went through the same process of questioning and seeking. The answers came then in the shape of the powerful upsurge of industrial unionism, which rallied to its struggle the youth, the intellectuals, artists and middle class of that day. The present generation seeks but has not yet found such an answer.

A word much in popularity among students today is 'humanism'. Over and over they insist on their belief in humanist principles. One of them said to me, referring to a mutual friend,

> He is what I call a *real* socialist. He really believes in helping people. When he talks about sharing the wealth he really means it. I don't know if you're a real socialist. You call yourself that but I don't know how you really feel about other people.

David Rike made the following observations about the Beat types:

> … they want a Change; they want to be able to Dig-the-Scene as human beings, before there isn't any Scene to dig at all. If it was October, 1956 and we were in Hungary, they'd be behind the barricades with the Freedom Fighters and participating in the Workers' Councils that sprang up. Some of them would very much like to be down in Cuba, with Castro. And, on Easter Sunday of this year, a lot of them were marching in the pouring rain in front of the AEC offices in Oakland, protesting nuclear tests.
>
> H-Bomb protests and maybe they'll, in the future, come out and give support to strikes and labor struggles, especially when there might be students scabbing … Deep Down, they're Waiting. Waiting for something like Spain, 1936; or Berlin, 1953; Budapest, 1956; or maybe even San Francisco, 1934 or Oakland, 1946 …
>
> When I first dug the Beach and the Beat-types more than a year ago, I noted that they appeared to be no more than Pachucos who read books, had social consciousness, and didn't resort to violence so readily. This isn't coincidental, because as intellectuals, they play a vanguard role in Awareness. In Hungary, 1956, things got started by mass action on the part of the students, but when the chips were really down and the Russians moved

into Budapest, it was the young workers from the factories who were manning the barricades, chucking molotov cocktails at tanks, and directing actions in the Workers' Councils. And the Beat-types have the potential for doing the same thing in this country.

The middle-class 'fellow traveler', the juvenile hood, the Bohemian – this is the Beat Generation. And yet there is one other member of this group that is included as a kind of minister without portfolio, the Negro. Norman Mailer and Herbert Gold in magazine articles have stressed the relationship between the Negro and his struggle in society and the hipsters. In fact, the argument is that to be a hipster is to be a white Negro. Mailer has written that when the Bohemian and the juvenile delinquent came face to face with the Negro the 'hipster was a fact in American life'.

This kinship with the Negro is often expressed. Kerouac writes,

> At lilac evening I walked with every muscle aching among the lights of 27th and Welton in the Denver colored section, wishing I were a Negro, feeling that the best the white world had offered was not enough ecstasy for me, not enough life, joy, kicks, darkness, music ...

Highly romanticized, yes, but indicative of the bond between the Beat Generation and the Negro – two groups who are forced to live on the edges of society. The most obvious bond between them is their common language and their common responsiveness to jazz. Hip, cool, man, beat, to be with it – these terms originated among and through those who created and those who dig jazz.

The members of the Beat Generation are spread across America (and, if the reports are accurate, it seems they may even exist in England's Teddy Boys, Japan's Sun Tribers, and in Russia). The dominant characteristics of the group have emerged and crystallized since the end of World War II. The exact number is difficult to determine although Norman Mailer has estimated that 100,000 Americans are conscious hipsters and millions more are Beat and don't know it, or refuse to admit it. Holmes' *Go* was published in 1952 but it wasn't until several years later that books such as his became popular, touted and commented upon in large-scale fashion. By the time *On the Road* was presented to the public, growing numbers responded to sentiments expressed in these works with, 'Yeah, man, that's the way it is. You're hip, you're hip'.

What we see today is not a qualitative change in the phenomena of the Beat Generation but a growing recruitment to its ranks. Young artists and students turn to a Beat way of life as an expression of their revulsion against capitalist society and their indetermination about what to do about it. They are caught in the vacuum caused by the relative apathy of the working class and its failure as yet to take the road to independent political action.

And their literary spokesmen say,

> Man, don't bug me about dope. What hallucinations could I have that could compare with the reality of atomic bombs on Hiroshima and Nagasaki? Don't get horrified at my little crimes – stealing cars to play chicken, cutting up a few people here and there. What could I do that could compare with World Wars and the theft of security and shelter and sustenance from millions? Don't tell me I live a crazy life, man. What's more insane than sealing up food in caves or dumping it in the ocean when millions are starving? What's crazier than laying off tens of thousands of workers when they want to and could be producing cars and refrigerators and clothes and homes?
>
> Don't stop me from living it up. I'm me, you're you. You get your kicks your way; I'll get mine my way. So don't push me into the organization, man. I'm not one of the bunch. Each one of us is something beautiful and wonderful. Cherish each little spark, let each blaze up in his own way. Don't smother anyone under the ashes of conformity.
>
> Don't tell me to live in Squaresville – the squares themselves know that underneath the slick suburban surface there's a sickness that can't be cured and every sweet dream of love and tenderness is long gone. Don't give me the-little-wife-and-sweet-kiddies-around-the-fireplace bit. Man, like that went the way of dodo-bird things like free enterprise, the horse and buggy and the worship of tree spirits. We're living in the now – and the now is changing so fast we have to run faster and faster just to stay in one spot!
>
> So, don't hold me back. I gotta go and keep going till I get there; where? I gotta find out where – and I can't find out if I can't go, go, go, if I'm caught like those 'who chained themselves to subways for the endless ride from Battery to holy Bronx on benzedrine until the noise of wheels and children brought them shuddering mouth-wracked and battered bleak of brain all drained of brilliance in the drear light ...'.

Those who gasp and raise their eyebrows over the antics of the hipsters see only the negative, run-away-from-it-all, self-destructive aspects of this group. 'Why don't they live *normally*?' the raised eyebrows ask.

Wouldn't it be the negation of all personal worth, wouldn't it be really self-destructive, really horrifying if they did live by the rules of a society where war, depression and the suppression of the individual have become normal? If they didn't thumb their noses at a moral code that no longer satisfies the needs of our changed human relations?

The Beat Generation does more than reject a world they never made and don't want. They are seeking for a world worth living in. Their search has led them into blind alleys so far, it is true, but over and over again, they affirm, 'There must be an answer to the whys and wherefores of life. Maybe the next kick I go in for will reveal the truth behind it all. The answer is somewhere. I'll find it ... in my own way ... in my own time'.

9 United Socialist Political Action in 1958[22]
(*1958*)

James P. Cannon

The subject assigned to us tonight, as it appears in the advertisements, reads: 'United Socialist Political Action in 1958 – and the prospects for American socialists'. This two-sided subject proposes action today and suggests, at the same time, that we look ahead and try to see where we are going.

In my opinion, the two sides of the subject are equally important, and they are properly joined together. Unless we consider our outlook it's not easy to take any kind of meaningful action. On the other hand, if we content ourselves with looking at the future as we would like to see it, and do nothing about it today, take no action in the direction of our goal, we debase our vision into a daydream of mopers and idlers.

Direction without motion is just about as useless as motion without direction. If we want to do anything meaningful and purposeful in the present day, we have to look ahead and see the general direction of our goal. And if we want to reach the desired goal without too much delay we have to get started. We have to get going. That, I think, is the double meaning of the subject assigned to us for our discussion tonight.

Our vision and our goal, to which our lives are committed and which make our lives worthwhile, is the socialist society of the free and equal. And as a next practical, experimental step on the road to that glorious objective, we ought to take a census of the socialist population of this country. We should try to find out how many people will make out their ballots for socialism if the issue is presented to them squarely. To that end we are proposing an electoral coalition of socialist forces for united socialist political action in 1958.

I believe that a survey of the present situation in the American socialist movement will show the feasibility and the timeliness of this proposed next step. There are important historical precedents for this procedure as I will relate a little later on.

---

22   Cannon 1958.

We have to start from where we are. In the discussion and exchange of views that have been taking place, particularly in the past two years, many writers in different publications have turned their attention to this question of just where we stand right now. The trend of opinion seems to range from sober to gloomy.

Some say we're 'at rock bottom'. Others say 'we have no place to go but up'. And then some real calamity howlers have expressed the opinion that we can't even go up or down or sideways; that all we can do is just sit there and 'think', and twiddle our thumbs, and perhaps wait for a new Moses to be discovered in the bullrushes who will lead us out of this capitalistic Egypt.

Well, I don't believe in unfounded optimism at all, but, as I see it, the reality is a little better than some socialists picture it. There is no doubt, no doubt whatever, that the present position of American socialism is far from good, and far from strong. That's obvious. But what about the other side of the present reality – what about the position of American capitalism? Well she ain't what she used to be, that's for sure.

This small capitalist segment of the world that aspired only yesterday to rule the whole world, has fallen on evil days and everybody knows it. Even the professional boasters are singing the blues. As I read the comments, ranging all the way from the colonial world to the very centers of American power in these days, the general opinion of American capitalism is that it's in a hell of a fix. I am only telling you what I read, but I must admit that I think so too. Nobody has any confidence except Eisenhower. And he's out on the golf course and doesn't know what's going on. They say he doesn't even read the newspapers.

Now, we socialists don't need to conceal our own troubles – we have plenty of them. We who have survived the storms of these last terrible years know very well that we have been hurt. The socialist movement in the United States has suffered heavy blows, one on top of another, for at least 17 consecutive years.

First, there were the terrible reactionary effects on the labor movement, and on all American radicalism and even liberal thought, of the Second World War. And the cold war that followed it. And the Korean war. The effects were reactionary in all directions.

A Turn of the Tide

Then we had to contend with the conservatizing influence of the long, artificially propped-up prosperity, which sapped the strength of American radicalism in all its departments.

And then we had to put up with the devastation and terror of the long witch-hunt, which decimated the ranks of American radicalism and liberalism and all sections of the socialist movement.

And then, last, but not least, the socialist movement has been sapped by a moral sickness – the calculated lies and slanders, the suppression of free and independent thought, the violations of class solidarity, the disruption of fraternal relations and free discussion among socialists of different tendencies. All this dirty business has worked to demoralize the movement and to discredit the name of socialism.

We have been hit hard from all sides. But in spite of that – and this is our great capital for the future – a considerable nucleus of undaunted and incorruptible socialists have survived all this adversity. More than that, the adverse factors have been changing in recent times. For several years now, if we have looked closely enough, we have seen a turn of the tide.

Anti-war sentiment is stronger in this country today than it has been at anytime in the last quarter of a century. The most striking proof of that is the fact that, for the first time since the early thirties, Hollywood dares to make anti-war movies again. And they are turning out to be the most popular movies on the screen today. There is a world of significance in this simple fact which the movie manufacturers never dreamed of when they were making something to sell.

Not only is the anti-war sentiment strong and growing, but economic troubles are beginning to engender a new radicalism. The unprecedented boom, propped up by military spending, was dragged out so long that many people began to think that capitalism finally had found a way to escape from its own laws. This artificial boom, according to what I read in the most conservative financial journals of the country, has entered into a decline. They call it a 'recession', but they admit there are five million unemployed in this country; and that means that there are probably six to seven million actually unemployed.

And nowhere have I been able to read in the financial and economic columns of the various journals – nowhere except in Eisenhower's speeches – any promise that it will get better 'next month'. Or, more correctly, this month – this is the first of March already, and Eisenhower is already one day down on his fatuous prophecy

Anti-war sentiment is growing, the capitalist economy is in decline and with it the conservatizing influence of prosperity is spending its force. And also in recent years we've seen the witch-hunt slow down. It isn't stopped, by any means, but the witch-hunt terror that all sections of American radicalism had to contend with in the past ten years, has been decidedly moderated. People are raising their courage again in wider and wider numbers. All that is in our favor.

A New Atmosphere

And no less important than these favorable turns in the situation, is a new atmosphere in the circles of American radicalism – in all circles. Socialists of different tendencies have begun to think of each other as comrades. Free discussion and fraternization, and sentiment for united action and regroupment of all the scattered forces are the order of the day now everywhere. I say that's a good day for us and for our cause – the cause of American socialism.

It doesn't bother me at all that, in a meeting such as ours, we have some criticism of each other; and some things are said by one speaker that another can't fully endorse – that's not the significant thing about this great meeting tonight. The significant thing is that socialists of different tendencies stand together here on the same platform and urge united action against the capitalist class.

All these changes I have mentioned are in our favor, and we should take advantage of them. We should see in them the opportunity for American socialism to enter a new stage of revival which will carry it to new heights on the road to victory over American capitalism.

In spite of all that has happened to discourage, to terrorize, to weaken and demoralize the movement there are still a lot of socialists in this country. The sentiment for socialism in the United States, even today after all that has happened, is much bigger than any of the organized parties and groups; bigger than all of them put together. And the potential sentiment for socialism, which the bankruptcy of American capitalism will generate in the next period, is a hundred or a thousand times greater than the conscious socialist sentiment at this present moment. That's the real situation as I see it, and the real prospect before us. We ought to take it as the starting point in a new struggle to put socialism on the map and wipe capitalism off the map.

The Starting Point

The basic aim in rebuilding for the future, as I think all present will agree – the basic aim to which we are all striving – is to regroup the scattered socialist forces, and eventually to get all honest socialists together in one common party organization. But that can't be done in a day. The experience, of the last two years shows that it will take time. We'll have to take the process of collaboration and unification in stages, one step at a time.

The starting point of the process is for all genuine socialists of all tendencies, whether presently affiliated to one organization or another, or independent at present, to recognize that we are all part of one movement, and that we ought to work together fraternally in one field of action after another. Work together against the injustices and oppressions of capitalism. That sounds almost like a revolutionary assertion after the terrible experience of the disruption of solidarity. But it used to be the unvarying practice and tradition of the old socialist and radical movement in America.

In the time of Debs and ['Big Bill'] Haywood and Vincent St. John, there were many differences of opinion and different organizations, and many quarrels and squabbles and debates. But it was taken for granted, as a matter of course, that when there was an issue of common interest against the class enemy – whether it was a strike, or a labor leader arrested, or some act of injustice committed against any section of the movement – that all should work together in solidarity against the injustice.

On this point I am a reactionary – I want to turn the clock back to the good old days of solidarity and cooperation in practical action against the common enemy. Fraternal cooperation and solidarity in practical action does not exclude differences of opinion, does not exclude discussion and debate as we go along. There is no socialist life without free discussion of differences. But while we discuss our differences, we should also remember what we have in common as socialists and act together in support of it.

Many different opinions are being expressed in the course of debate on the American road to socialism. I think all suggestions and ideas should get an attentive hearing. But however one may think socialism is going to come to the United States, one thing is sure – it's not going to be smuggled in. It's a shame to have to say that, isn't it?

The cause of socialism can be advanced only by counterposing it to capitalism – simply, honestly, openly and directly. Clever tricks designed to fool people into socialism are self-defeating as well as dishonest and contemptible. I think we have had more than enough of that indecent horseplay already. The revival of the American socialist movement will really begin to get under way when we get back to fundamentals and come out in the open as socialists every day in the week and twice on Sunday.

When we say that socialists should find a way to work together, especially in electoral campaigns, we mean of course real socialists, socialists who, to use the words of the *Communist Manifesto*, 'disdain to conceal their aims'. Socialists without false faces.

What is a socialist? Well, I can tell you very quickly what he is not. He is not a Republican. And he is not a Demo-Dixiecrat. And he is certainly not a shame-faced supporter of the war program of the US State Department. He is not a member of or supporter of any capitalist party whatever. I'm not submitting this as an argument. I'm stating this as the summary conclusion from established facts.

Marx, Engels and Debs

Capitalism rules and exploits the working people through its control of the government. That's fact number one. And capitalism controls the government through the medium of its class political parties. That's fact number two. The unconditional break away from capitalist politics and capitalist parties is the first act of socialist consciousness, and the first test of socialist seriousness and sincerity. That's fact number three.

Where did I learn that? Marx and Engels explained it over a hundred years ago, so it's not hot off the wire. I personally heard Debs explain it fifty years ago. That's what they said – Marx and Engels and Debs.

They were very simple fellows who couldn't understand that the way to get what you want is to vote for what you don't want. They couldn't understand that the really slick and clever way to get socialism is to vote for capitalism. And to tell you the truth, we don't understand it either. And we don't intend to play that game.

About 20 years or so ago there was an aviator who flew out of the New York airport on a trip to Los Angeles and landed in Ireland. They called him 'Wrong Way' Corrigan, and he became a popular symbol of the man who doesn't know where he's going. That's the trouble with the Wrong Way Corrigans of politics – they don't seem to know where they're going, and it would be imprudent to follow them.

This is not a general public meeting, but a sort of invitational meeting of socialists of different tendencies. All of us present here, I take it, are socialists of one tendency or another. Now let us ask ourselves, honestly and directly: How did we become socialists? How did we acquire our certain confidence in the bright socialist future of humanity – the great vision which has transformed and inspired our lives and sustained us through the darkest days of struggle against this insane social system? Did we acquire our socialist consciousness because of our superior wisdom? I don't think so. We became socialists, each and everyone of us, in the same way – because others who went before us explained it to us in earlier years. They wrote pamphlets and books, and distributed journals, and made speeches, and explained things – and from them we learned.

And the fact that we had to learn from others – does not that suggest the idea that others may learn from us? Does not that impose upon us the obligation to explain socialism to others yet to come? And if we socialists don't speak up for socialism, who will? Who will spread the inspiring word of a socialist outcome of this mad world of capitalism if we don't? And if we have to do it, when do we begin? I believe the sooner the better.

And here comes the importance of the subject we have under discussion tonight. The best time of all – the most fruitful time to explain socialism – is during election campaigns, when public interest is highest, and we stand the best chance to get a hearing. The capitalist class rules this country in a complicated way, through the machinery of bourgeois democracy. They can't shut off all avenues of public communication, even to minority parties – although they try their best.

Socialist Propaganda

The Socialist Workers Party, even with its limited forces, has demonstrated in these recent years, how we can get through cracks in the wall and compel them to give us access to TV and radio audiences and to carry notices in the newspapers. We get a greater hearing for the ideas of socialism in the few months of the election campaign than in all the rest of the time put together. That makes every election campaign a socialist success.

The main purpose of participating in elections, as a socialist organization or as a coalition of socialist organizations, is to take full advantage of the expanded opportunity to make socialist propaganda. And in the economic and social storm that is now beginning to blow up in this country, with fear and insecurity about war, and making a living, or even existing on this planet – there will be more interest in social and political questions, and more people will be listening than at any time in recent decades.

What can we do to make the most of this exceedingly favorable opportunity to advance our cause? The National Committee of the Socialist Workers Party has expressed the opinion and made the proposal in an announcement in the *National Guardian* and in the *Militant* – the proposal that all socialists get together for united political action – for socialism and against capitalism – in the state and congressional elections of 1958. And that this action in 1958 be regarded as the springboard for a united Presidential campaign in 1960.

That's an outlook worth looking at, isn't it? It opens up the prospect, if accepted by other groups and tendencies, of pushing the whole socialist movement a bit forward. It is really a first-class idea, but there is nothing new or original about it. We learned that, where we learned so many things, by looking at the books and studying the history of what others have done before us. Electoral coalitions were a common practice of socialists of different tendencies in the past.

A Historical Precedent

In the year 1900, Debs was a candidate for President, not of a single party, but of a coalition – exactly what we are proposing today. A split-off section of the Socialist Labor Party, headed by Hillquit and Harriman, and the Social Democratic Party of Debs and Berger agreed upon a common election slate with Debs for President, from the Social Democratic Party, and Harriman for Vice-President, from the split-off Socialist Labor Party. The coalition ticket was supported by the *Appeal to Reason* and other independent socialist papers. The united presidential campaign in 1900 aroused so much enthusiasm and so much sentiment for unity, that nine months later they were able to bring the forces together in a new party. That's the way the Socialist Party of America was founded in August 1901.

There are other examples. In Russia the Bolsheviks and the Mensheviks were split and at loggerheads over many issues. But when it came to the elections to the Duma they conducted a poll among themselves to determine the proportion of candidates for each side, and ran a joint electoral slate in the general election. At the outbreak of the First World War, there were Bolshevik and Menshevik deputies in the Duma, the Russian parliament, all elected on a joint slate.

Besides the historical examples, some actions taken by individuals and by groups in recent times have led up to our proposal and made it realistic and timely. You recall that in 1956, the SWP, at the cost of tremendous effort and sacrifice, and the immeasurable labor of comrades bucking the reactionary election laws to get on the ballot, ran a Presidential slate of Dobbs and Weiss. In that election campaign a new note of socialist solidarity was sounded. Whereas for many years in the recent past no socialist or radical party ever cooperated with or supported or helped another party, in that election campaign in 1956, Vincent Hallinan in San Francisco and Clifford McAvoy in New York came out in support of the SWP candidates.

That was the first break in the log jam. Then again last year, in the municipal elections in San Francisco, where Frank Barbaria and Joan Jordan, ran as candidates of the SWP, Hallinan and Billings and Hitchcock and Olshausen and others, all not members of the SWP, differing with us on many points, nevertheless recognized the importance of a socialist vote and endorsed our candidates and helped the campaign. The *National Guardian* supported the SWP candidate in Detroit, New York and San Francisco on the same grounds. The *National Guardian* played a role in this progressive development similar to that of the independent *Appeal to Reason* in the early days.

It seems to us that these new developments, taken all together, have set the stage for another step forward. The SWP National Committee has taken the initiative and made the proposal for a more formal electoral coalition after full deliberation. We mean every word we say, and we are ready to go through with it. The matter is now under discussion throughout all sections of the movement, and we hope for a favorable outcome.

The American socialist movement has been badly battered in the storms of recent years. But the new events, which I have briefly summarized, show that the movement is still alive and kicking and is even looking up a bit. The prospects are brighter than they have been for a long time. We should take heart and hope, as Debs used to say, and work diligently in the coming days to turn the bright prospects into new achievements and new advances.

The forces for an imposing demonstration of socialist sentiment in the 1958 elections are already present. They are waiting for the go-ahead signal. They need only to be aroused and encouraged and organized. And for this, as is almost always the case, there is no eloquence equal to the eloquence of action. United socialist political action in the 1958 elections will be the right action at the right time.

CHAPTER 3

New Pathways

Paul Le Blanc

As the 1950s gave way to the 1960s, the early stages of the youth radicalization were in full swing – widespread involvement in civil rights struggles, defense and active use of civil liberties, opposition to nuclear weapons and the threat of nuclear war, challenging 'the American Century' thrust of US foreign policy, support for 'third world' liberation struggles, cultural rebellion (including, for some, participation in a rich folk music trend), growing struggles for educational and campus reform, and college and university students, etc.[1]

Within this context, the significantly expanding number of young Trotskyists were active in all of these activities and working to help build a young socialist movement – culminating in a Young Socialist Alliance (YSA). First experimenting with a regroupment ethos that would reflect a broad range of perspectives, the group quickly reoriented to become openly and explicitly aligned with the Socialist Workers Party – as discussed in the report by leading participant Tim Wohlforth presented here.[2]

Engagement with the civil rights and black liberation struggles in the United States shaped much of the evolving 'new left' that was growing powerfully in the United States, and this was also central to the new growth in US Trotskyism. As previously noted, an entire chapter of the present volume focuses on these 'Challenges of Black Liberation', although references to such realities necessarily pepper items in the present chapter too.

As indicated in the 1960 essay by Frances James, 'Africa's Bid for Freedom', US Trotskyists were among those who perceived the ferment and insurgency among African-Americans as dovetailing with similar ferment and insurgency sweeping through the colonial and former colonial regions of Asia, Africa, and Latin America.[3]

---

1 On the history of the radicalization of this period, see: Gosse 2005; Bloom and Breines 2003; Sale 1973; and Cantwell 1996.
2 Information on the formation and early period of the Young Socialist Alliance can be found in: Wohlforth 1994, pp. 51–122; Camejo 2010, pp. 23–36; Sheppard 2005, pp. 11–97; Williams 1973.
3 African-American author Richard Wright wrote three books in this period relevant to this theme: *Black Power* (1954); *The Color Curtain* (1956); and *White Man, Listen!* (1957). They are collected in Wright 2008. W.E.B. Du Bois and Frantz Fanon were also in the vanguard on

The Cuban Revolution was a defining feature of this period, and a majority within the SWP came to identify with it deeply and powerfully, although not uncritically. This comes through in Joseph Hansen's review of two early books on the revolution, C. Wright Mills's *Listen Yankee*, and *Cuba: Anatomy of a Revolution* by *Monthly Review* editors Leo Huberman and Paul Sweezy. Hansen's own evolving and influential analysis, gathered in the 1978 collection *Dynamics of the Cuban Revolution* (published the same year as his death), manifesting an extremely positive understanding of strengths in the revolution and in the revolutionaries (Marxist-influenced, but not Stalinist) who made it, is at the same time tempered with an underlying critical edge informed by the analytical approach absorbed from Trotsky. His comrade George Weissman, under the name George Lavan, would soon edit the bestselling collection *Che Guevara Speaks* (a sort of companion piece with his friend George Breitman's *Malcolm X Speaks*, indicating SWPers' successful outreach and influence in this period).[4]

In this same period, Hansen began elaborating a new conceptualization of 'the workers and farmers government', a term which had its roots in the early Communist International, but which he sought to creatively develop in order to account for unexpected postwar realities. Marx, Engels, Lenin, Trotsky and others had originally utilized a number of terms as synonyms: workers' state, dictatorship of the proletariat, workers' rule, workers' democracy. Later, in the 1939–40 debates, Trotsky argued that even though a bureaucratic dictatorship had politically disenfranchised the working class in the USSR, the country was a bureaucratically degenerated *workers' state*, because the social-economic conquests of the 1917 revolution (particularly a nationalized and planned economy, combined with a variety of social gains) remained intact. He argued that this workers' state should be defended (1) in any conflict with capitalist-imperialist powers, and (2) by carrying out a political revolution to overthrow the bureaucratic dictatorship and replace it with genuine, democratic workers' rule. Hansen utilized this to argue that a *workers' state* involves two components: (a) workers' rule replacing capitalist rule politically; and (b) the transition from a privately-owned market economy to a nationalized, planned economy. He went on to utilize the term 'workers and farmers government' to describe a

---

such matters, as brilliantly demonstrated in Hudis 2015 and Mullen 2016. On African liberation struggles of this period, see Davidson 1978. An informative and influential work on Latin America, also from this period, is Gerassi 1963.

4   Hansen 1979 and Lavan 1968. For biographies of Hansen and Weissman, see Lubitz 2004, and Editors of the *Bulletin in Defense of Marxism* 1985. For additional material on the Cuban Revolution itself, and post-revolution developments, see: Huberman and Sweezy 1969; Karol 1970; Habel 1991; Fitzgerald 1994; Farber 2006; and Le Blanc 2007.

genuinely revolutionary movement (such as that led by Castro in Cuba) that smashed the capitalist state and established some form of 'popular power' supported by the workers and peasants, but which had not (or not yet) moved forward to replace capitalism with a nationalized, planned economy. When the Castro regime did that, it became a workers' state – although in some cases (for example, in Algeria in the 1960s, and other former colonial countries) this forward movement was not realized, and the 'workers and farmers government' eventually devolved into a variant of 'bourgeois state'. This conceptualization would become central to SWP perspectives in the 1970s and, with new twists, in the 1980s and beyond.[5]

We have noted that Myra Tanner Weiss was seen as one of the strongest 'party feminists' in this period, and she was a leading spokesperson for the SWP as its Vice Presidential candidate in 1952, 1956, and 1960 (along with Presidential candidate Farrell Dobbs). Rather than focusing on 'the Woman Question', however, she generally chose a broader canvas – such as the analysis here of John F. Kennedy as the Democratic Presidential candidate of 1960 and the ruling President afterward. Not only were the points she made typical of SWP perspectives, but they also found some corroboration afterwards regarding Kennedy and the political process in general.[6] Along lines similar to Weiss's 1962 analysis is the 1963 perspectives document developed by the SWP leadership

The 'Woman Question' was, in this period, evident in the very early beginnings of what was later tagged the Third Wave of Feminism (the first emerged from the 1848 Seneca Falls conference, the second was associated with the struggle for women's suffrage in the late nineteenth and early twentieth centuries, and the third blossomed in the late 1960s and1970s). Reproduced here are responses from Hedda Garza and Evelyn Reed to the publication of new feminist classics – Simone de Beauvoir's *The Second Sex*, and Betty Friedan's *The Feminine Mystique*. Under the surface of both works are, in complex ways, strong Marxist influences – and both reviews, in fully embracing the books, don't hesitate to make explicitly Marxist points in favor of women's liberation.

---

5   Hansen 1974; Barnes 1999; Barnes 2002. In the process of leading what would become an open break from Trotskyist perspectives, in the late 1970s and early 1980s, new SWP leader Jack Barnes made use of Hansen's conception – although it is reported by those who knew both that 'Joe didn't agree with Jack on anything by the time he died [in 1978]'. See Evans 2009, p. 257, and Sheppard 2012, pp. 278–9, 286–7.
6   Much information on Myra Tanner Weiss can be gleaned from the following diverse sources: Thomas 1997; Edwards 1997; International Bolshevik Tendency 1997. Also relevant is Kovacs 2000.

Also distinctive is the substantial 1962 analysis of women workers, a cutting-edge work, by Melba Windoffer.[7]

The radicalization traced in this and the previous chapter was not simply taking place on the American scene – it was a global phenomenon, impacting on both of the major wings of the Fourth International that had ruptured in 1953. Given the fact that the SWP was reacting with some similarity to world events as the majority of the opposing faction of the Fourth International (whose leading personality at this point was Ernest Mandel), a process of rapprochement culminated in a 1963 reunification, described in the major article presented here by Farrell Dobbs and Joseph Hansen.[8]

Another international development – related to Myra Tanner Weiss's discussion of the Kennedy Presidency – is the 1963 reportage and analysis by Theodore Edwards, 'Kennedy's War in Vietnam'. This growing US involvement would dramatically escalate two years later, leading to the SWP playing a central role in building an incredibly effective anti-war movement. This was made possible by the hard, sustained, creative efforts of those who had remained in the SWP and helped build it up, recruiting a new layer of young members out of the 1960s radicalization, and helping to transform many of them into activists cadres with significant insights and skills.[9]

On the other hand, the new forces flowing into the party were quite different from the class-conscious industrial proletarians that had been seen as the ideal recruits of a bygone era. As the 1950s flowed into the 1960s, and as that decade continued to unfold, it became clear to many in the Trotskyist movement that the realities in which their lives were being lived were incredibly dynamic and ever-changing, even if certain underlying patterns and elements identified by Marx remained constant. Cannon had pointed to this in 1952:

> We have eleven years of unchanged prosperity. For us that is an episode, comrades. Why do we say it is an episode? Because we took the advice of Comrade [Murry] Weiss, and we studied Comrade Marx, and we think

---

7 Valuable information on Simone de Beauvoir and Betty Friedan can be found in Bair 1990 and Horowitz 1998. Substantial information on Evelyn Reed can be found in Lubitz 2004b. Melba Windoffer left the SWP in 1966, joining with Clara Fraser, Richard Fraser and others to form the Freedom Socialist Party; biographical information can be found in Durham and Windoffer 1978 and Freedom Socialist 1993. Biographical information on Hedda Garza can be found in Quinn 1995.
8 On the reunification, see: Frank 1979, pp. 91–122; Stutje 2009, pp. 119–23; Alexander 1991, pp. 321–850.
9 On the war itself, see Karnow 1997. The anti-war movement and the central SWP role in building it is presented in Halstead 1978.

> in historic terms and we know it is only an episode but that it is going to change and it must change as a result of the contradictions of the capitalist system itself. But how does it impress the ordinary worker? All he knows is that for eleven years he has been working more or less steadily and enjoying better wages and living conditions than he knew before. Do you mean to say that has not had a conservatizing effect on his psychology? I don't think you read it correctly if you say it hasn't.[10]

As the 1950s became the 1960s, the general reality described by Cannon had extended for an additional decade and more, but new developments had also come into play and were increasingly impacting on social reality and consciousness. There was a global human rights movement – related to the massive anti-colonial and national liberation upsurges, in some ways to the crisis of Stalinism, and very definitely to the anti-racist struggle in the United States. There was the development of automation (some used the term cybernation to emphasize the importance of computers in this development), which seemed destined to disrupt traditional employment patterns even as it seemed to ensure dramatic increases in productivity and wealth. And there was the ominous development and proliferation of nuclear weapons, which linked with the Cold War power struggle in ways that threatened the continued existence of humanity.

These developments were seen by some analysts of the time as constituting an interactive Triple Revolution – a notion that was explored by a fairly broad sampling of liberal and radical intellectuals, some prominently involved in the study of social and physical sciences, others involved in political an social activism, under the auspices of the Center for the Study of Democratic Institutions, a component of the prestigious Fund for the Republic. A statement was issued entitled 'The Triple Revolution', opening with the following assertion:

> This statement is written in the recognition that mankind is at a historic conjuncture which demands a fundamental reexamination of existing values and institutions. At this time three separate and mutually reinforcing revolutions are taking place:
> *The Cybernation Revolution*: A new era of production has begun. Its principles of organization are as different from those of the industrial era as those of the industrial era were different from the agricultural. The cybernation revolution has been brought about by the combination of the

---

10   Cannon 1973b, p. 47.

computer and the automated self-regulating machine. This results in a system of almost unlimited productive capacity which requires progressively less human labor. Cybernation is already reorganizing the economic and social system to meet its own needs.

The Weaponry Revolution: New forms of weaponry have been developed which cannot win wars but which can obliterate civilization. We are recognizing only now that the great weapons have eliminated war as a method for resolving international conflicts. The ever-present threat of total destruction is tempered by the knowledge of the final futility of war. The need of a 'warless world' is generally recognized, though achieving it will be a long and frustrating process.

The Human Rights Revolution: A universal demand for full human rights is now clearly evident. It continues to be demonstrated in the civil rights movement within the United States. But this is only the local manifestation of a worldwide movement toward the establishment of social and political regimes in which every individual will feel valued and none will feel rejected on account of his race.

... We affirm that it is the simultaneous occurrence and interaction of all three developments which make evident the necessity for radical alterations in attitude and policy. The adoption of just policies for coping with cybernation and for extending rights to all Americans is indispensable to the creation of an atmosphere in the US in which the supreme issue, peace, can be reasonably debated and resolved.[11]

The Triple Revolution analysis captured the imagination of a significant number of people on the Left in 1964 and 1965, including James P. Cannon, whose 'take' on it all is presented here.

And yet there were certainly questions at the time about the Triple Revolution analysis, both from the left and the right. A dismissive view – unfortunately distorting the content of the analysis – has been expressed by James Robertson (at the time a leading oppositionist in the SWP, on the verge of launching the Spartacist League), commenting ten years after the fact:

---

11   'The Triple Revolution' can be found in full in Goodman 1964, pp. 396–413. The statement was signed by the following: Donald G. Agger, Dr. Donald B. Armstrong, James Boggs, Lois Fein, W.H. Ferry, Maxwell Geismar, Todd Gitlin, Philip Green, Roger Hagan, Michael Harrington, Tom Hayden, Robert L. Heilbroner, Ralph L. Helstein, Frances W. Herring, Hugh B. Hester, Alice Mary Hilton, Irving Howe, Everett C. Hughes, H. Stuart Hughes, Gerald W. Johnson, Irving F. Laucks, Stewart Meacham, A.J. Muste, Gunnar Myrdal (with reservations), Linus Pauling, Gerard Piel, Michael D. Reagan, Bayard Rustin, Ben B. Seligman, Robert Theobald, John William Ward, William Worthy.

At that point some members of the SWP were playing with – it sounds so funny – today something called the 'Triple Revolution': poverty's been abolished, war's been abolished, racism's been abolished by new technology. Now there's been this triple revolution, what are we going to do next? Doesn't that sound absurd today? But it's a fancy idea and Cannon was kind of drawn into it.[12]

More carefully, and with no reference to Cannon, the prominent semi-socialist, semi-conservative sociologist Daniel Bell devoted critical pages to it in his *The Coming of Post-Industrial Society* – dismissing it as simply a social-science fiction of the early 1960s, because 'the cybernetic revolution quickly proved to be illusory', since 'for the last two decades [i.e. from 1953 to 1973] there had been no sharp changes in productivity'. He concluded: 'Cybernation had proved to be one more instance of the penchant for overdramatizing a momentary innovation and blowing it up far out of proportion to its actuality'.[13] At the same time as Bell's critique, even one of the signers, moderate socialist Michael Harrington, confessed that 'the Triple Revolution analysis was wrong' – although his reasoning was different from Bell's:

> We had accurately identified a tendency of the economy to produce more and more goods with fewer workers because of accelerating technological innovation since World War II. We had rightly rejected the complacent Keynesian faith that some judicious fiscal planning would allow the nation to cope with all of the resulting problems. But we had wrongly and mechanistically assumed that the trend would express itself only through mass unemployment. ... But in the sixties some job seekers were absorbed into the army and war production for Vietnam, and still others were sent to college.[14]

Within the SWP itself, central leaders – already less than happy with the presumptions of the opinionated retiree – were suspicious and critical of Cannon's inclinations toward innovative theorization. Leslie Evans reports that, in fact, Cannon had hoped to use the Triple Revolution analysis to shake the party out of what he perceived as a potentially fatal routinist lethargy. 'The party is too

---

12   Robertson 1986. Despite limitations in Robertson's reminiscences, his relatively respectful (even affectionate), impressionistic comments on the occasion of Cannon's death (1974) contain much interest.
13   Bell 1976, pp. 461–3.
14   Harrington 1973, p. 156.

ingrown', Cannon complained. 'It doesn't work with real people in the world'. He added: 'All of its activity is self-generated – *Militant* sales drives, election campaigns for our own candidates, forums in our own hall of ourselves talking to ourselves. This isn't a way to build a live organization'. After Evans agreed to research the issue, however, one young honcho from the Political Committee, associated with a rising star in the swp firmament, warned him: 'The Political Committee has had a meeting about that and has ruled that it is prohibited to discuss it. Cannon is completely out of line to try to raise it and if he pursues it any further he will be expelled. You had better shut up about it'. As it turned out, this threat may have reflected the mindset of a particular clique within the swp Political Committee, but was a grotesque exaggeration. Nonetheless, Evans did end up dropping it after concluding that 'robotics were not nearly developed enough to produce significant changes in the unemployment rate in the next few years'.[15]

Over fifty years later, however, it can be argued that while the impact of the so-called 'cybernation revolution' was perceived too simply by the authors of *The Triple Revolution*, it identified trends destined to have a powerful impact, intertwining with other trends later tagged as *globalization*. 'Dizzying technical change in the late twentieth century strengthened supporters of global economic integration', according to economic historian Jeffry Frieden. 'Innovations in transportation and telecommunications shrank the costs of international exchange'. Sociologist Patricia Cayo Sexton emphasizes a class-struggle aspect to this. 'Technological change is hardly unique to the United States', she commented in 1991, 'but the speed and extent of it are unusual, as is the strong preference for investing in machines rather than workers'. She added: 'It is generally agreed by analysts that much of the huge investment in new machinery is intended no only to improve operating efficiency, but also to control the work force, limit its powers, deskill it, and create a managerial monopoly of skills and knowledge'.[16] Labour analyst Kim Moody, 15 years later, summarized what had happened in this way:

> In the thirty years from the mid-1970s to the mid-2000s, the world of the worker in the United States was turned upside down. The industrial centerpieces of the us economy shrank or reorganized and the cities, towns, and unions based on them went into decline and/or dramatic changes in make-up. The industrial 'heartland' became a rust belt. The

15 Evans 2009, pp. 155, 157, 158.
16 Frieden 2006, pp. 394–5; Sexton 1991, pp. 216, 217.

'industries' that appeared to replace them were low-wage and mostly non-union. Technology 'employed with ferocity' in a more competitive world, as one economist put it, eliminated some jobs and intensified others. ... In the 1970s, thirty years of economic gains for working-class people stopped and began to go in reverse.[17]

This obviously poses the question as to whether aspects of the Triple Revolution analysis, and of Cannon's 'take' on it, have greater relevance than seemed to be the case to many in the late 1960s or early 1970s.

This is further suggested by a new uptick in twenty-first-century analyses suggesting, as Paul Mason has argued – in terms consistent with the Triple Revolution analysis Cannon was advancing – that 'capitalism cannot sustain the scale of automation that is possible, and the destruction of jobs implied by the new technologies'.[18] It is interesting to see left-wing analysts Nick Srnicek and Alex Williams making points in 2015 that were anticipated in 1964, while taking the analysis even further, based on the continuation of the technological revolution that imaginative radicals were contemplating half a century earlier:

> Through popular political control of new technologies, we would collectively transform our world for the better. Today, on one level, these dreams appear closer than ever. The technological infrastructure of the twenty-first century is producing the resources by which a very different political and economic system could be achieved. Machines are accomplishing tasks that were unimaginable a decade ago. The internet and social media are giving a voice to billions who previously went unheard, bringing global participative democracy closer than ever to existence. Open-source designs, copyleft creativity, and 3D printing all portend a world where the scarcity of many products might be overcome. New forms of computer simulation could rejuvenate economic planning and give us the ability to direct economies rationally in unprecedented ways. The newest wave of automation is creating the possibility for huge swathes of boring and demeaning work to be permanently eliminated. Clean energy technologies make possible virtually limitless and environmentally sustainable forms of power production. And new medical technologies not only enable a longer, healthier life, but also make possible new experiments with gender and sexual identity. Many of the classic demands of

---

17   Moody 2007, pp. 11, 79.
18   Mason 2016, p. 215.

the left – for less work, for an end to scarcity, for economic democracy, for the production of socially useful goods, and for the liberation of humanity – are materially more achievable than at any other point in history.[19]

Simply because a similar argument is being articulated today, of course, does not necessarily mean that the previous analysis (or the analysis as such) is correct. But the innovative and creative approach of many US Trotskyists of the twentieth century is certainly indicated by the fact that pathways they envisioned would continue to have resonance half a century later.

---

19   Srnicek and Williams 2015, pp. 1–2.

1 Youth Report to Eighteenth National Convention[20]
(*1959*)

Tim Wohlforth

The placing of this point on the agenda of the convention signifies that the party recognizes the importance of the creation of a revolutionary youth movement to our work today.

In assisting the establishment of a youth movement the party is basing itself on the experience of the Marxist youth movement from the time of Karl Liebknecht on. It was the early socialist youth movement which carried on the struggle in the pre-World War I period against militarism and the preparations for war. In so doing the youth came into direct conflict with the general reformist drift of the social democratic parties which culminated in the betrayal of the anti-war struggle in 1914.

Virtually the whole socialist youth movement went over to the new Communist International in 1918 and helped not only to create the Young Communist International but also participated in the building of the Communist parties in their respective countries. The formation of the Fourth International again attracted youth and young people, again raised the banner of Liebknecht. Our youth today are the legitimate inheritors of this tradition.

The present forces which make up the *Young Socialist* movement grew out of independent movements within the radical youth forces in this country which the party responded to and helped along. First came the struggle within the Young Socialist League. The conception of an independent revolutionary youth movement was worked out by the YSL Left Wing as an alternative to the Right Wing's capitulation to the social democracy engineered by Shachtman. On the basis of agreement on this conception the Left Wing began collaboration with the SWP which led to the fusion of the Left Wing with the SWP youth.

The fusion with the Left Wing was crucial to the development of a revolutionary youth movement not so much because of the numbers (which were

---

20 Wohlforth 1959.

small) this added to the revolutionary youth cadre but because the fusion gave the youth formation a broader independent stamp and thus made it a pole of attraction to other youth. The Left Wing fight also gave the youth a political tradition – a political past. The documents written in the YSL struggle form the 'In Defense of Marxism' of the youth movement.

These fused forces then turned their attention to the turmoil existing among the Stalinist youth, turmoil created by the Khrushchev revelations and the Polish and Hungarian events. By energetically pursuing a regroupment line towards these elements we were able to further the crisis and thus postpone the consolidation of the Stalinist youth. To this day the crisis continues and the possibility of the Stalinists to launch a national youth formation is put off for some time to come. We recruited some of the best people in this milieu to our youth movement and to the party. Finally, we created a milieu within which our youth forces could work – people for us to talk to and to explain our ideas to.

The ability to develop a revolutionary youth cadre through fusion with the YSL Left Wing and then recruitment from the Stalinist milieu was made possible because of the energetic policy of the party. Without the SWP forces this youth movement could not have been created. The *political* line of the party also was attractive to young people looking for a road out of their crisis. Finally, the *organizational* approach of the party was crucial. The party based its policy on a recognition of the organizational independence of the youth. It did not attempt to dictate to the youth. Without such a flexible policy we would not have been able to fuse with the Left Wing or reach out to the young people formerly around the Stalinists.

As a result of its support to the youth movement the party has benefited. At our Detroit Conference of the YS supporters the majority present were either non-party members or party members (and this was the largest figure) who had joined the party since the beginning of youth work.

Even more important the youth experience has developed young party and non-party members so that we now have a functioning organization with its own press, its own internal life and its own skilled youth cadres which acts as a companion movement to the party reaching out to young people and winning them over to revolutionary socialism.

The key to the progress we have made in the youth field has been our conception of the relation between the youth movement and the party. Basically we can put it as follows: *The content of party-youth relations in any period is political solidarity between the youth and the party but organizational independence for the youth.* The form this relationship takes varies from period to period. It may be expressed in open affiliation between party and youth, or in fraternal relations or, as is presently the case, in informal cooperation.

The youth movement is neither an opponent organization within which the party members operate as a fraction nor a simple appendage of the party. The youth should rather be looked upon as a section of the revolutionary movement united with the party by bonds of political solidarity. However, the youth movement must have its own organizational life with its own leadership, internal discussions, etc. Its program must be worked out jointly by party and non-party members of the youth organization. No young person in his right mind (and these are the only young people we want) would join a youth group if its policies were determined by a caucus of that group composed of members of an adult party. The quickest way to kill the youth movement is to impose that type of discipline within it.

It is precisely because of the independent nature of the youth movement that I am not presenting to this body a full report on the many tactical problems facing the YS that the YS National Plenum will be shortly discussing. I am emphasizing here those questions which relate to party-youth relations and party policy towards the youth.

Our experience of the last two years has shown that wherever there is smooth working relations between the party and the youth, locally and nationally, both organizations benefit and grow.

As a result of our aggressive participation in the regroupment process and our correct understanding of party-youth relations we have been able to assist in the development of a functioning national youth movement. The youth now have a basic political and organizational cohesiveness worked out at our Detroit Conference. We have functioning groups in nine local areas with influence in an additional eleven areas. Our publication, the *Young Socialist* has the largest circulation among young people of any radical publication in the US. We all feel we have a period of modest but highly important growth ahead of us. Many of our worst difficulties are now in the past and we are all united in our desire to start really building a fighting youth organization in this country.

In order to ensure this development we are proposing that the party continue its policy of:

1. Favoring the development of an independent revolutionary socialist youth movement in this country.
2. Encouraging its growth with the forces – personnel, financial and otherwise – available to it.
3. On the basis of the political solidarity between the YS movement and the party recognizing the necessity of organizational independence of the youth.

In return we can assure you that the youth will provide a constant flow of new forces into the party. It will act as a training ground for young party members and thus raise the quality as well as the quantity of new members. The youth will carry on a political campaign in opposition to bourgeois influences among youth whether in direct form or indirectly through the social democrats (who are strong among youth) or the Stalinists. Finally we will build a youth cadre that will be capable of building a mass revolutionary socialist youth movement under favorable objective circumstances and thus ensuring the young working class forces necessary to build a party capable of bringing socialism in the US.

2 Africa's Bid for Freedom[21]
(1960)

Frances James

The 'revolution of rising expectations' in sub-Sahara Africa has startled the world with its speed and scope. Within the last four years seven African countries have acquired formal independence status. The enormous energy released by Negro Africa's fight for independence has rocketed the 'dark continent' into the brilliant orbit of the mid-twentieth century's anti-imperialist movement.

Arab North Africa has long been seething with wars for national independence; the Middle East is a whirlpool of anti-colonialist revolution; all of Asia, and indeed the entire world, has been struck with admiration and awe by the giant socialist revolution of 600 million people in New China; now Cuba has taken the road of revolution against the US capitalist colossus and kindled new hope and self-confidence among the oppressed colonial people throughout Latin America.

No wonder gloom and foreboding characterize the mood of Western capitalist, spokesmen as they observe the turbulent African scene. 'Can it be that Africa is going the way of China?' they ask. The question is highly pertinent.

What has brought about this change in sub-Sahara Africa? And what chance do the African people have to realize their hopes and expectations?

The political awakening of Negro Africa, first of all, is conditioned by the economic boom of the last two decades. This boom has transformed the economic and social structure of a large part of the continent at an almost unbelievable rate. The extent of the change is indicated by the fact that in the post-World War II years exports from these countries have increased on the average of four to five times their pre-war level. The investment of foreign capital in the last ten-year period reached almost six billion dollars. This is approximately equivalent to the total foreign capital investment in sub-Sahara Africa in a period of seventy years – from the discovery of the Kimberly diamond mine in 1871 up to the second world war. (*London Economist*, Dec. 13, 1958).

---

21   James 1960.

Economic expansion in the Union of South Africa set the impressive record of nearly tripling its industrial production and more than doubling total national output of goods and services in the first post-war decade. In the Belgian Congo there were only 4,200 industrial enterprises in 1947. Ten years later there were 21,000. Kenya petroleum consumption between 1950 and 1957 rose by 500 per cent and consumption of electric power rose by 1,600 per cent. Hydroelectrical projects of enormous capacity are planned or are already under construction in almost every part of the continent.

The construction of dams, of course, is designed primarily to increase production of raw materials for export: rubber, cocoa, cotton, peanuts, etc. But it also affects subsistence farming on lands 'reserved' for the African peoples. *Africa Digest* (London) reports that in Kenya (where production of cash crops on 'reserved' lands was prohibited until only recently) 'there has been something like an agrarian revolution'. In one province scattered holdings have been consolidated 'as a model for others ...'.

Modernization of agricultural methods in Southern Rhodesia's African farms has resulted in production of eight to fifteen bags of grain per acre where previously only two to three were produced. The production per acre on the European farms averages only four to six bags.

Modernization filters down into the most remote villages. Progressive chiefs begin to seek ways and means of putting running water and electric lights in village housing units. The economic boom brings with it the African's desire and his constantly more forceful demand for a greater share in the continent's wealth.

By far the most important product of Africa's boom, however, is the growth of the working class – a social force that could unite the people and resolutely lead the revolution to its logical goal – the establishment of a Pan-African Socialist United States.

The demand for labor in the cities combined with the expectation, especially among the younger generation, of educational and cultural advancement, has resulted in an enormous population shift. The size of the major towns in Northern Rhodesia, for example, was doubled from 1948 to 1950. John Gunther in 1957 estimated that forty million rural inhabitants were moving away from 'tribalism' toward urbanization.

This growing proletarian force, living in terrible poverty, suffering discrimination and filled with hatred for the white-supremacist rulers, possesses some unique qualities. Foremost among these is its migratory character.

Migrant labor is established by forcing the African into 'native reserves', then demanding he carry a pass in order to leave the reserve, work in mines, on white settlers' farms or in industrial centers. This is true even of the largest urban centers and in the technically more advanced areas in Kenya, the Union of South Africa, the mining areas of the Central African Federation and the Belgian Congo.

In Leopoldville only about twenty-one per cent of the working population has broken with rural and tribal ties and is considered permanently city dwelling. In the copper belt of Northern Rhodesia only sixty-five per cent of the workers have their families living with them.

This semi-slave status of the African worker was designed to prevent organized resistance to the intense exploitation practiced by the white rulers. And for a time it had its effect. But today the situation is altering. Workers with experience in union and political struggles periodically return to their villages bringing with them the new ideas of militant freedom struggle.

Despite the difficulty of organizing migrant labor and despite the added difficulty of a segregationist policy of the official union movement, African unions have grown to an estimated one-half million members.

Moreover, the very nature of the workers' problems – government-enforced color bars, legal limitations on job upgrading, etc. – have compelled the unions to face political questions from the outset. This is why leaders of the trade unions, like Tom Mboya, head of the Kenya Trade Union Federation, become leaders of the Pan-African independence movement.

Africa's industrial development was accelerated enormously by the war economy of the West. The economic and social impact of this process, combined with the influence of the colonial revolution at large, aroused hope and expectation among Africans that they too could build a new life and reap some of the benefits of industrialization. These hopes, however, cannot be realized without uprooting the whole system of colonialism and returning Africa to the Africans. Thus the fight for genuine independence. Thus the revolution of rising expectations. And thus Western capital has acted as the unwitting agent of its own downfall in Africa.

The British, in their east and west African colonies, have long followed a policy of concessions to the rising independence movement to which the name has been attached: 'Gradual Self Rule'. This policy permits, when the demand is strong enough, formal independence without loss of capital to British interests. British diplomats have explained that the secret of success of this policy is to 'give before the giving is demanded'. Today, there is not a single British colony that is not already 'demanding'.

The French held to the 'French Union' policy with all power concentrated in the Paris government. Last year the pressure of the colonial revolution forced a change in policy to the concept of autonomous republics within a 'French Community'. Threat of withdrawal of all economic aid, arms, police protection, technicians, etc., if a country voted '*non*' to remaining within the Community kept all territories except Guinea within French control. Already, less than a year later, in the French colony of Dahomey, African political leader M. Apithy's party passed a motion demanding independence in 1960 and urging a referendum to consult the electorate, and the Mali Government has made an official demand for independence as soon as possible.

In the Belgian Congo the political movement of the Africans in Leopoldville last January forced an end to the old policy of Belgian 'paternalism' and moves toward future self-rule were conceded. So-called 'riots' and increased political debate, organization and conflict throughout the Belgian Congo have now won a promise of independence and immediate self-rule.

Imperialist attempts to control Africa through concessions runs immediately counter to the wishes of the white settlers (*colons*) and mining interests. They, being a small minority holding political power over Africa's millions, know full well that concessions often sow the seeds of bolder demands. Even the most elementary bourgeois democratic rights would mean the complete isolation and ultimate ruin of the colons. They fear the mass of the African people and can conceive of protecting their privileges only through terror. The political and military strength of the colons in sub-Sahara Africa lies in the Union of South Africa where 'apartheid' (complete segregation) policy is projected as the white man's answer to African expectations.

Increased *colon* power as an answer to the Freedom movement is pushing upward from the Union of South Africa through East Africa and the Central Federation of the Rhodesias and Nyasaland. The *colon* power is attempting to destroy the African movement of Nyasaland through arrest of its leaders (Dr. Banda and 500 others are now in prison). Britain sent troops to back up the colons in the 'emergency' of last year.

The United States, with its 'dollar diplomacy', i.e., economic control combined with the granting of formal political independence, presents itself more than any other single or combined power, as the 'new' liberal imperialism. Last year a special sub-division of the US State Department was set up to handle African Affairs with Assistant Secretary of State Joseph C. Satterthwaite in charge. Official policy toward the Independence movement was stated by him as follows: 'Insofar as these objectives are progressive, just, and constructive, insofar as the methods employed to achieve the objectives are nonviolent and equitable, our attitude – in accordance with our national history, character, tradition – should obviously be one of sympathy and support'. (State Department press release, Oct. 8, 1958).

Even such guarded words as these have brought a protest from European powers and accusations that the US is encouraging the nationalist movement.

Underlying the 'free world' problems of political control lie the economic difficulties of the boom-recession cycle of capitalism. The 'slump' of 1957 resulted in a ten per cent average drop in raw material prices on the world market. The loss to Africa due to the drop is estimated to exceed the total of US and USSR aid to Africa for the last five years. Copper production in the Belgian Congo fell by fifty per cent, resulting in mass unemployment in Leopoldville.

The consequence of periodic recessions is by no means the sole economic problem facing capitalism in its drive to 'contain' the African revolution. Capital, in the form of government loans and private investment for industrial and development projects is seen by the 'free world' colonial 'experts' as the only hope of maintaining political control. Yet in areas where the revolution rises to the heat of open conflict, capital tends to move out. This happened in the Central African Federation when the 'emergency' was declared and in the Belgian Congo concurrent with the strike wave and 'riots' of January 1958.

Still another problem for imperialism is the growing influence of the Soviet Union and China in Africa. The politically conscious forces in the independence movement are wary of the Kremlin and this is not due entirely to their pro-American illusions. Many of them recall with bitterness the exhortations of Moscow to support the imperialist democracies in World War II. They are still waiting for a little of this democracy for Africa.

What the African leaders see immediately, however, is the contrast between the role of the USSR in supporting UN recommendations on the racial situation in South Africa and West Africa and the US abstaining from voting until recently. Moreover, the Soviet Union has loaned money to the independent African states totaling approximately the same as the US loans at about half the interest rate.

The unfavorable situation confronting the US-dominated cold-war bloc has compelled it to 'moderate' its tactics. Premature attempts at solving problems by purely military means and naked terror have been curbed. This tactical shift is of course closely linked to the objective of gaining a new foothold for imperialism by the use of two familiar devices:

a. Split and atomize the movement and paralyze its capacity to act against the common foe.
b. Gain control over sections of the leadership by means of economic pressure, bribery, threats, concessions, blackmail and playing off one segment against another.

These imperialist calculations have the following basis in reality: The African people are divided and fragmented along religious, tribal, cultural and linguistic lines. Over 700 languages exist on the continent. Divide and rule has been the age-old policy of the colonial powers. They have allotted powers in the 'reserves' or labor contracts in the ports and mines to hand-picked tribal leaders or chiefs. They fostered tribal loyalties and made these loyalties economically significant. Behind 'tribal' riots reported in the news lie many jurisdictional disputes over work opportunities, land tenure and other economic issues. All these conflicts are continuously sharpened and encouraged by the white rulers.

Another factor that favors the success of the 'new' imperialist policy is the limited bourgeois and reformist program and outlook of the present leadership of the independence movement. This weakness is strikingly expressed in the illusion that a formally 'neutral' but in reality pro-American orientation in the cold war can serve the cause of the African freedom movement. Understandably, the African leaders want the aid of Western capital to help in the industrialization and modernization projects. The idea, however, that such capital can be secured by commitments to line up with the cold-war bloc is, of course, a deadly trap which the capitalist West has adroitly sprung on many occasions.

While these factors are not to be underestimated and constitute a grave danger to the success of the struggle, there are important reasons why the independence movement resists atomization and will not easily lend itself to piecemeal destruction. There are also reasons why the movement is forced by the logic of its development to overcome the limitations imposed by its bourgeois reformist program and leadership.

As we pointed out, the economic exploitation of Africa by Western capital has had consequences far beyond what the capitalist intended. The growth of industry, the proletarianization and urbanization of large sections of the population have served to enhance the interdependence of all areas of the continent. Thus the independence movement tends from its earliest manifestations to acquire a continent-wide scope and perspective.

Here we witness not a mere historical repetition of the old 'nationalism' that shaped the modern countries of Europe in the course of their bourgeois revolutions. In the concrete circumstances of the combined historical development of Africa, the tasks of the bourgeois revolutions of the eighteenth and nineteenth centuries must be solved in the middle of the twentieth century. In the light of the world pressures imposed on Africa, as well as the peculiarities of the African national problem itself, the solution of these tasks requires an all-continental scope.

The economic and technological problems the newly formed independent African states must face, illustrate this conclusion. Take the hydroelectric plant projected for the Volta River in Ghana. It would supply power to Ghana, Togoland, Nigeria and the French community countries of Dahomey and the Voltaic Republic. The plant on the Congo river will supply parts of the Belgian Congo,

Angola and the French equatorial countries. The problems of one-crop economies – coffee in Kenya, cotton in Uganda, cocoa in Ghana – cannot be solved by diversifying crops and developing internal markets within the narrow limits of each separate country. Economic cooperation in broad areas is a technological necessity. Already technical assistance programs exist in several areas. Ghana-Guinea being a significant case among the newly independent states.

In the eighteen-seventies when the European powers staked out their colonial domains in Africa, no concern was given to the social and political problems of the African people. Land tenure, language, tribal structure, religious groups, etc., were all ignored by the European land grabbers and are still ignored by them when labor needs have to be met in mines and on plantations. For example, the Bakango people at the mouth of the Congo River were arbitrarily divided into territories controlled by French, German, Belgian and British powers. Thus a narrow, 'nationalist' struggle, such as the struggles that established the present national boundaries in Western Europe, is not at all congruent with the freedom and independence aspirations of the Bakango people who live in five separate countries.

The growth of a pan-African concept is reinforced by the fact that European capital dominates the entire area. The African miner sees little difference between Belgian capital in the Congo or British capital in the Rhodesias and the African peasant gets the same vile treatment from European farmers whether on British cotton plantations in Uganda or on Portuguese peanut farms in Mozambique. They all represent European exploitation of African natural resources and labor power for the benefit of foreign capitalists.

As modernization and urbanization preceded the African National Congress movement sprang up around issues of education, work passes and voting rights. The leadership of these Congress organizations, in their early stages, came primarily from the tribal elders, chiefs, the educated elite and others who served the interests of colonial powers as a rule.

Today, when independence has become the dominant and immediate issue, it is the leaders with a pan-African outlook that are winning quite rapidly a dominant position in the Congress movement, the trade unions and in all African political organizations. The Accra Conference of 1958 and the permanent organization of the All African People's Conference demonstrated that the initiative and the leadership in the immediate future lie in the hands of pan-African leaders such as Dr. K. Nkrumah of Ghana, Tom Mboya of Kenya, Touré of Guinea, Dr. Banda of Nyasaland, etc.

What is most important, however, is not the momentary composition of the leadership but the debates over program that are seething in the whole politically active mass of the population.

Last year the African Congress movement in Northern Rhodesia split over the question of militant mass action *versus* the passive-resistance methods of the old National Congress. Those supporting the use of violence when necessary in the struggle for freedom formed the Zambesa National Congress which was almost immediately suppressed only to reappear as the United Independence party. This party has just fused with a new split-off from the old Congress movement to form the United People's party which demands 'secession of Northern Rhodesia from the Federation and self-government for Northern Rhodesia now by Africans'.

The issue of international trade-union affiliation (International Confederation of Free Trade Unions, dominated by the cold-war bloc, *versus* World Federation of Trade Unions, supported by the Soviet bloc, or 'neutrality') broke into open conflict last May when Mboya called a conference in Lagos, Nigeria, to form the first All-Africa ICFTU organization. It was attended by union leaders from twenty-one countries. K. Nkrumah who supported trade-union neutralism, countered with the calling of a trade-union conference in Ghana at the same time. This conference had delegates only from Guinea, Morocco and the United Arab Republic.

These programmatic and organizational clashes reflect the strivings of the African independence movement to achieve clarity in its concept of where the struggle is going and how it is going to get there. The concept of pan-Africanism, so overwhelmingly dictated by the course of Africa's historical development, still leaves open the questions: What class in African society can realize a continent-wide organization of the economic struggle to industrialize and modernize? Can such a struggle be led to victory by any group that isn't ready to break with the capitalist exploiters internationally and take the road of building a planned socialist economy in Africa?

Those who would reject the socialist road for Africa on the grounds that Western capital is required to make progress, fail to take some weighty facts into account. Western capital cannot be obtained by political subservience to Western capitalism without accepting exploitation.

On the other hand, if through the promising development of the African working class, a Marxist program and leadership can be forged that will take the road of socialist revolution – that would indeed contribute immensely to solving the problem of Western aid. The African revolution, taking the Chinese path of expelling imperialism and overthrowing the exploiters, would strike a mighty blow at world capitalism. It would speed the day when the British, French, Belgian and American workers would establish their own power and thereby form an economic and political alliance with Africa and with all the oppressed to build a world socialist society.

3 Theory of the Cuban Revolution[22]
(*1961*)

Joseph Hansen

> *No revolution has ever anywhere wholly coincided with the conceptions of it formed by its participants, nor could it do so.*
> — LEON TROTSKY

∴

LISTEN, YANKEE – *The Revolution in Cuba* by C. Wright Mills. Ballantine Books, New York. 1960. 192pp. 50 cents.

CUBA – *Anatomy of a Revolution* by Leo Huberman and Paul M. Sweezy. Monthly Review Press, New York. 1960. 176pp. $3.50.

In the first stages of the Cuban Revolution, not much appeared about it in the way of searching analysis. Publicity was largely agitational, whether for or against. Consequently the worth of most early writings hinges largely on the accuracy of the reporting and the extent to which documentary material is included. This is especially true of some items, highly laudatory of the Revolution and its leaders, by authors who have since gone over to the counter-revolution.

The situation today is quite different. The character and meaning of the Cuban Revolution, of the government that displaced the Batista dictatorship and of the state now in power are under intense discussion throughout the radical movement on an international scale. The theoretical questions have come to the fore.

This reflects the course of the Revolution itself. It began as an ill-reported and ill-understood revolutionary democratic movement in a small island ruled

---

22   Hansen 1961.

by one of a dozen strong men in Wall Street's empire. Today it stands as a colossal fact in world politics – the opening stage of the socialist revolution in Latin America, the beginning of the end of American capitalist rule in the Western Hemisphere.

The two books under review are among the best in a new literature appearing about the Cuban Revolution, a literature written by serious thinkers accustomed to probing for the deep-lying forces and trends in modern society. These thinkers are fascinated by what this Revolution has revealed, for they feel that perhaps here may be found clues to titanic revolutionary events now drawing near. As Huberman and Sweezy express it: *'In Cuba they are actually doing what young people all over the world are dreaming about and would like to do'*. (Emphasis in original).

Let's begin with *Listen, Yankee*. In writing this book C. Wright Mills displayed considerable courage. The author of *The Power Elite* and *White Collar*, to mention his best known books, staked a big reputation and high standing in academic circles when he decided to support the Cuban Revolution with such forthrightness. That he weighed the issues is evident from the following statement:

> Like most Cubans, I too believe that this revolution is a moment of truth, and like some Cuban revolutionaries, I too believe that such truth, like all revolutionary truth, is perilous.
>
> Any moment of such military and economic truth *might* become an epoch of political and cultural lies. It *might* harden into any one of several kinds of dictatorial tyranny. But I do not believe that this is at all inevitable in Cuba. And I do believe that should it happen it would be due, in very large part, to the role the Government of the United States has been and is continuing to play in Cuban affairs …
>
> The policies the United States has pursued and is pursuing against Cuba are based upon a profound ignorance, and are shot through with hysteria. I believe that if they are continued they will result in more disgrace and more disaster for the image of my country before Cuba, before Latin America, and before the world. (Emphasis in original).

To help enlighten his fellow Americans and as a service in countering the hysteria, Mills presents the Cuban revolutionary case. As a succinct presentation of the main facts that led to the revolutionary explosion, of the achievements since then, and of the aims, attitude and outlook of the main rebel forces, the book is a remarkable accomplishment. I cannot recommend it too highly to anyone seeking a quick briefing, particularly as a knowledgeable Cuban revolutionist, leaving aside diplomatic considerations, might give it to you on a visit to the island.

It's Not Stalinist

The salient feature of *Listen, Yankee* is the clarity with which it presents the anti-Stalinist aspect of the Cuban Revolution. Most readers of the *International Socialist Review* will understand at once, I am sure, that this has nothing to do with the anti-Communism of the House Un-American Activities Committee or similar bodies of witch-hunters and counter-revolutionaries. Even in most Communist parties where the cult of the late dictator was once the first commandment, it is generally accepted today – since Khrushchev's Twentieth Congress revelations about Stalin's crimes and paranoia – that to be anti-Stalinist does not automatically put you in Hitler's camp.

An understanding of the attitude of the Cuban revolutionists toward Stalinism is particularly important. The Cuban Communist party supports the revolution. The government, in turn, has respected its democratic rights, as it has the democratic rights of other radical groupings. It has refused to engage in any witch-hunting and has denounced anti-Communism as a divisive weapon of the counter-revolution. This, plus the aid solicited from the Soviet bloc countries (which undoubtedly saved the Cuban Revolution from going down), has been utilized to falsely picture the Cuban government as having succumbed to Stalinism.

The issue happens to be crucial in the United States for winning support for the Cuban Revolution in sectors of the trade-union movement, among intellectuals and on the campus. It is not just a matter of attempting to overcome hysterical Stalinophobia. In these circles the truth is widely known about Stalin's suppression of proletarian democracy, his frame-ups of working-class political opponents, mass deportations and assassination of socialist leaders. Many rebel-minded people in the United States, who offered their support to the Soviet Union, felt betrayed on learning the facts about Stalinism. Consequently, out of fear of being burned again, they are cautious. On the other hand, the appearance of a genuinely democratic socialist revolution could reanimate them. Besides constituting the only sectors of the population ready at present to give a fair hearing to the Cubans, they are an essential link in rebuilding a mass socialist movement in America.

Mills gives the question the importance it warrants, citing many facts to indicate the profoundly anti-Stalinist nature of the revolution. Among these he notes the stress placed on immediate benefits for the people, the readiness to listen and learn in all fields, the freedom that makes Cuba so exhilarating to radicals, above all those on vacation from the stifling atmosphere of McCarthyland.

On the decisive political fact of leadership, Mills has his Cuban protagonist write an entire letter (No. 5), explaining why the Communist party is not in power in Cuba and why it is highly unlikely even to seek power.

> The plain fact is, our revolution has outdone the Communists on every score. From the beginning up till today, always at every turn of event and policy, the revolution is always faster than the Cuban Communist Party, or individual Communists. In all objective facts, then, we are much more radical, much more revolutionary than they. And that is why we *are* using them, rather than the reverse; they are not using us. In fact they are being very grateful to us for letting them in on the work of the revolution.
>
> In fact, this is the case generally with local Communist parties in Latin America. In a real revolution today, in Latin America at least, the local Communists are to the right of the revolution. Here in Cuba, certainly the revolution has outpaced them and does on every front. They always arrive too late and with too little. This has been the case in Cuba and it still is the case: They lag behind our revolution. (Emphasis in original).

The truth is that Stalinism proved to be an insuperable handicap for the Communist party of Cuba, no matter how revolutionary-minded its ranks were; and it was by-passed by Castro's July 26 Movement.

Capitalist Base Destroyed

On the theoretical assessment of the Cuban revolution as it stands today, Mills offers some interesting opinions. 'The Cuban revolution', he observes, 'has swiftly destroyed the economic basis of capitalism – both foreign and Cuban. Most of this power was foreign – in fact, North American. It has now been destroyed with a thoroughness unique in Latin-American history'.

In his sociological estimate, Mills says, 'The Cuban revolutionary is a new and distinct type of left-wing thinker and actor. He is neither capitalist nor Communist. He is socialist in a manner, I believe, both practical and humane. And if Cuba is let alone, I believe that Cubans have a good chance to keep the socialist society they are building practical and humane. If Cubans are properly helped – economically, technically and culturally – I believe they would have a *very* good chance'. (Emphasis in original).

As to political power, in Mills' opinion, 'The Government of Cuba is a revolutionary dictatorship of the peasants and workers of Cuba. It is legally arbitrary. It is legitimized by the enthusiastic support of an overwhelming majority of the people of Cuba'. In letter No. 6, the Cuban spokesman specifies that it is not a Stalinist-type dictatorship:

> In the most literal sense imaginable, Cuba is a dictatorship of, by, and for the peasants and the workers of Cuba. That phrase, 'dictatorship of workers and peasants', was turned into a lie by Stalin and under Stalinism. Some of us know that. But none of us is going about our revolution in that way. So, to understand us, you must try to disabuse yourself of certain images and ideas of 'dictatorship'. It is the pre-Stalin meaning of the phrase that is accurate for Cuba.

It is in the political area that Mills expresses the greatest worry for Cuba. 'I do not like such dependence upon one man as exists in Cuba today, nor the virtually absolute power that this one man possesses'.

However, Mills believes that '... it is not enough either to approve or to disapprove this fact about Cuba. That is much too easy; it is also politically fruitless. One must understand the conditions that have made it so, and that are continuing to make it so; for only then can one consider the prospects of its development'.

The conditions include the form of struggle needed to overthrow Batista, the enormous counter-revolutionary pressure of the United States, and the fluidity of the present situation in which democratic forms have not yet been worked out in the living experience of the revolution.

Castro's leadership in the difficult revolutionary struggle brought him this exceptional personal power, but it is Mills' conviction that Castro is opposed to any leadership cult, is aware of the danger and will help the revolution to pass through it.

'In my judgment', says Mills, 'one must take seriously this man's own attempts to shift roles, even in the middle of his necessary action, and his own astute awareness of the need to develop a more systematic relation between a government of law and the people of Cuba'.

'Anatomy of a Revolution'

Let us turn now to the book by Leo Huberman and Paul M. Sweezy, the editors of the *Monthly Review*. They wrote this after a three-week visit to Cuba in

March 1960 publishing it as a special edition of their magazine. Events soon dated parts of it. The authors took another trip to Cuba and have now published a supplement, *Cuba Revisited* (December 1960 issue of the *Monthly Review*), which, I understand, is to be included in a new edition of the book.

The strong side of *Cuba – Anatomy of a Revolution* is its emphasis on economics. The authors do a good job of summarizing the main facts about Cuba under Batista, available in such books as Lowry Nelson's *Rural Cuba*, then turn to current problems where they offer the results of their own investigations on the scene. The facts they have assembled are encouraging indeed. Instead of collapsing, as the capitalist press has been predicting, the Cuban economy has grown stronger. Consider, for instance, the main crops, which have been the center of a planned expansion drive:

> Their total volume increased by almost one third in the first year of the Revolution, and there is no doubt that a comparable rate of expansion is being maintained this year. China, it seems, is not the only country capable of 'big leaps forward'! But what other country has ever staged such a leap forward in the very first year of a Revolution and in the midst of a far-reaching agrarian reform? It can be said without exaggeration: in the Cuban Revolution the world is witnessing a process of socio-economic transformation and vitalization that is in many important respects without any precedent. Let the world look hard and draw the appropriate conclusions! (Emphasis in original).

When the agrarian reform was put through, predictions were freely made in the big press that the Cubans with their 'lack of know-how' would speedily bring the cattle industry to ruin by slaughtering the breeding stock, some of it of top quality. The spiteful forecasts of the dispossessed cattle barons were not borne out. Huberman and Sweezy cite a representative of the United Nations Food and Agriculture Organization who said that while no figures were available for the island as a whole, Havana was eating 60 to 70 per cent more beef in March, 1960, than the previous year while the supply of beef cattle had also been sharply stepped up 'chiefly owing to better feeding methods'. The authors conclude: 'There could be no better evidence than this that (1) the Revolution has already transformed the standard of living of the Cuban masses, and (2) this new and higher standard of living has come to stay'.

Some Flaws

In political matters, Huberman and Sweezy in general leave much to be desired, in my opinion. A few indications:

They manage to 'credit' the 'administration of Franklin D. Roosevelt' with having 'abrogated' the Platt Amendment. They also criticize the same administration for withholding recognition of the Grau government and granting it to Batista; but the political necessity of tipping their hats to the FDR myth blocks them from seeing Roosevelt's role in establishing the foul Cuban dictator and maintaining his brutal rule.

In lauding the readiness of the Cuban peasantry to go directly to agricultural cooperatives, Huberman and Sweezy refer to the views of bourgeois land reformers who have aimed at breaking up large landed estates into small peasant holdings.

'More radical thought, at least from the time of Marx', they say, 'has generally rejected this aim on the dual ground that small-scale peasant cultivation of the soil is hopelessly inefficient and that a small peasantry is inevitably a reactionary, counter-revolutionary force. However, the Russian Revolution showed the difficulties which confronted any attempt to go directly from a system of *latifundia* to some form of collective agriculture. In spite of themselves, the Russian Bolsheviks were forced to distribute the land to millions of small peasants, and it was only much later after fierce and bloody social struggles and frightful agricultural losses that they succeeded in establishing the system of collective and state farms'.

Thus they amalgamate Lenin's adherence to the political position of Engels with its direct opposite, that of Stalin. Engels held that collectivization in agriculture, despite its obvious economic advantages, could proceed only in accordance with the will of the peasants themselves. A revolutionary government could seek to convince them by argument and examples but in no case force them. That was how Lenin proceeded. Stalin, after first pandering to the rich peasants, collectivized Soviet agriculture by force. The catastrophic consequences still plague the Soviet Union. If a real lesson is to be drawn from the Cuban experience, it is the advantages to be gained by following the method worked out in theory by Engels and put into practice by Lenin in contrast to the brutal method used by Stalin. Huberman and Sweezy credit Cuba's success to Castro's knowledge of the peasantry and sensitivity to their deepest wishes. If Castro is not aware of the theoretical and historical background, the confirmation of the Marxist view is all the more notable.

A serious political error which Huberman and Sweezy themselves admit in their postscript to the book was the estimate that Washington would not slash the Cuban sugar quota. We remain uncertain as to why they made the error. Did they calculate that it was not in the best interests of capitalism to do this and that the powers that be would recognize this? Or did they underestimate the deeply reactionary character of both the Democratic and Republican machines? Fortunately, the politically astute Cuban leaders were not caught by surprise. As Castro indicated in his speech at the United Nations, they are well aware of the true relationship between 'the shark and the sardine'.

I mention these items with no thought of disqualifying *Cuba – Anatomy of a Revolution*. They are minor, if annoying, flaws in an excellent report and strong defense of the Cuban Revolution. My intent is to suggest that if the authors have any predilection it is in the direction of the Communist party. This gives certain of the things they say about Cuban politics much greater weight than they would otherwise have; for, representing a break with their predilection, these views were undoubtedly pondered many times over before being expressed.

Made by Non-communists

From the origin of the July 26 Movement in 1953 until the rebel army was well on the way to victory, Huberman and Sweezy declare, 'the Cuban CP was cool to and sometimes critical' of Castro's organization. The leadership of the revolution 'owed absolutely nothing to the Communists …'. Only Castro, if he should join the Communist party, could persuade any of the others to follow him. 'Since no responsible observer, to the best of our knowledge, has ever suggested that Fidel has done any such thing, we conclude that the hypothesis of Communist infiltration of the leadership is a pure figment of the anti-Communist imagination'.

Can the Communists get into position to 'wrest leadership of the masses, of the revolutionary movement itself, out of the hands of Fidel and his colleagues in the army and government?' Huberman and Sweezy ridicule the possibility, pointing to the smallness of the Communist party and its lack of standing as against the size of Castro's following and their revolutionary record.

The authors go even further:

> In our judgment, for what it is worth, the Communists could make no bigger mistake, now or in the foreseeable future, than to challenge Fidel and his close associates for the leadership of the Revolution. They would lose, and in losing they might easily do irreparable damage to the cause of the Revolution, which of course is also their cause. On the other hand, if they continue to pursue their present course, they may play an important, and

in some respects perhaps an indispensable, even if subordinate, role in the building of socialism in Cuba.

To make their meaning still clearer, they compare the Cuban Communists with the American Communists in the New Deal period.

> They worked hard and often effectively, trying of course always to push matters somewhat further to the Left than they would otherwise tend to go. While they won control in some unions, they were never in a position to make a bid for political leadership in the country and never caused any serious problems except in the minds of the right-wing lunatic fringe.

In short, although the authors do not say it, since the thirties neither the Cuban nor the American Communists have played the role of *revolutionists*.

> All the charges and accusations concerning the alleged Communist character of the Cuban government and/or Revolution tend to hide what may turn out to be historically one of the most important facts about the Cuban Revolution: this is the first time – ever, anywhere – that a genuine socialist revolution has been made by *non-Communists!* (Emphasis in original).

Castro and the rebel army, 'calling themselves neither socialists nor Communists, in fact without any clearly formulated ideology, seized power in Cuba after two years of bloody civil war and proceeded with élan and dispatch' to do what needed to be done. 'No one can now foretell the full implications of this startling fact', Huberman and Sweezy believe, 'but no one need doubt that it will open up new vistas not only in the realm of social thought but also in the realm of revolutionary action'.

Although there is considerable difference in the angle of view, in emphasis, in political inclination, and in the way they express what they observed, it is clear that the impressions which the Revolution made on C. Wright Mills on the one hand and Huberman-Sweezy on the other were not greatly different. The similarity extends to other fields.

What kind of social order does Cuba have? 'For our part', declare Huberman-Sweezy, 'we have no hesitation in *answering: the new Cuba is a socialist Cuba*'. (Emphasis in original).

How did it get that way? After the seizure of power, 'the aspect which the Cuban Revolution first presented to the world was that of a quite respectable middle-class regime'. This gave rise to many misunderstandings. However, the real power remained in the hands of Castro. 'A sort of dual system of government began to emerge, with Fidel on one side and Urrutia and the cabinet on the other'. The 'paradox between the essentially revolutionary character of the regime and the predominantly liberal-to-conservative personnel which represented it before the world' was resolved by March 1960. Two of the landmarks were Castro's resignation in July 1959 to force the resignation of Urrutia and Che Guevara's assumption of the presidency of the National Bank in November in place of Felipe Pazos. The Castro regime carried the revolution through to the establishment of a planned economy.

Communist Party Viewpoint

Cuba – Anatomy of a Revolution was saluted with vexed criticism from spokesmen of both the Cuban and American Communist parties. (At this writing they have not yet got around to reviewing Mills' book). The CP finds it obnoxious to think that the label 'socialist' should be applied to Cuba. It's a national democratic revolution, you see, in which the national bourgeoisie still plays an important role and in which the need for 'unity' is foremost. In addition, Huberman-Sweezy slight the role of the Communist party in the Revolution and the increasingly important role it will play after the proletarian stage opens.

The two derelict authors answer the criticism somewhat disrespectfully with a footnote in their postscript:

> Now that the big majority of the means of production are in public ownership, and the regime is rapidly developing a consciously socialist ideology, the Communist argument against classifying Cuba as socialist appears more and more clearly as mere verbal gymnastics. The reason for the Communists' adopting this position, however, is straightforward enough: they don't want to admit that it is possible for socialism to be built under non-Communist leadership.

One wishes that Huberman and Sweezy would venture to analyze this reluctance of the Communists. The question would seem not unimportant and very definitely related to their own belief that the Cuban Revolution has opened up 'new vistas not only in the realm of social thought but also in the realm of revolutionary action'. Isn't the failure of the Cuban Communist party central to this far-reaching conclusion? Wouldn't a knowledge of the reasons for the failure be of considerable value to other Communist parties – to the revolutionary-minded rank and file if not to leaders who never cause 'any serious problems'?

In the dispute between the Communists and the editors of the *Monthly Review*, it appears to me that Huberman and Sweezy have the stronger case. In fact they hanged the Communist party theoreticians with their own terminology. If each of the countries in the Soviet bloc, including Albania, is 'socialist', then why should this term be denied Cuba, which now has a planned economy – and far greater freedom than any of them?

The fact is that 'socialist' was used by Stalin in the years of his psychosis as a mislabel for Soviet society. It was a way of proving that you can build 'socialism in one country'. This played into the hands of the worst enemies of the Soviet Union, for they never tired of agreeing and even emphasizing that socialism was what the Soviet Union had all right and therefore Stalinism and socialism were one and the same thing and if America went socialist you'd lose democracy and get frame-up trials and concentration camps here, too. To confer the badge 'socialist' on Cuba may thus – unfortunately – be taken as a somewhat dubious honor. The repugnance the Cubans feel for much that goes by the name of 'theory' is not without good political justification.

In the early days the Soviet Union was called a workers' state; 'with bureaucratic deformations', Lenin added. It was socialist in *tendency*; that is, it was a transitional formation on the road to socialism but not there by a long shot. Nor could it reach socialism on its own resources – such a concept, had anyone suggested it in Lenin's time, would have been dismissed as self-contradictory. The Soviet power was a working-class conquest in the international struggle for a world-wide, scientifically planned society built on the foundation of capitalism as a whole, or at least on the combined resources of several industrially advanced countries.

The concern the Bolsheviks felt for terminology was not due to an aesthetic pleasure in splitting hairs. Precision in applying labels reflected their concern over knowing exactly where they stood in relation to the goal still to be achieved. It was a good tradition, well worth emulating, like much else in Leninism.

What Is It?

If Cuba is not 'socialist' and is highly unlikely to achieve socialism by itself on one small island, what is it?

The Cubans themselves have been reluctant to say. Professing some disinterest in abstruse questions of theory, they have politely invited those of their supporters and well-wishers who are better informed in such matters to have at it. Meanwhile they propose to move ahead, with or without labels, to work out problems that permit no delay and that have kept their limited personnel going twenty-four hours a day. As their own guide, they find it sufficient to follow the broad generalizations of a humanism concerned with the fate of the humble. If you can tell a *guajiro* from an imperialist and hold government power, it seems to work out all right.

This pragmatic approach has added to the theoretical puzzle. If the Cubans don't know whether Cuba is socialist or not, how is anyone else to know? Jean Paul Sartre, on visiting Cuba, came away with the conviction that the world was witnessing something completely novel – a revolution impelled by blows from an imperialist power to respond with counterblows, each more radical than the previous. Would a revolution driven forward by such a process create its own ideology? That remains to be seen. In any case, Sartre found it a refreshing contrast to what he considers the sectarian approach – applying a preconceived ideology to a revolution.

Others, stimulated like Sartre by the Cuban Revolution, have decided that even Marxist theory breaks down before such phenomena. What provisions are there in Marxism for a revolution, obviously socialist in tendency but powered by the peasantry and led by revolutionists who have never professed socialist aims; indeed, seem to have been limited to the bourgeois democratic horizon? It's not in the books!

If Marxism has no provisions for such phenomena, perhaps it is time provisions were made. It would seem a fair enough exchange for a revolution as good as this one. On the other hand, what books do you read?

Paradox of Russia

The Cuban Revolution is not the first to have given the theoreticians something fresh to consider. The Russian Revolution exceeded it in that respect. In 1917 the entire world socialist movement was caught by surprise, including the Bolshevik party – not excepting even Lenin. Socialists wielding power at the head of the workers and peasants in a backward country like Russia! It wasn't in the book. Well ... most of the books.

The Russian Revolution was fortunate in having a leadership as great in theory as in action. Four decades ago it was common knowledge in the socialist movement that one at least of the Russian leaders had accounted in theory for the peculiarities of the Russian Revolution in all its main lines – *some twelve years before it happened*. His name was Leon Trotsky.

Trotsky's theory of the Permanent Revolution greatly facilitated the Bolshevik victory by giving the revolutionary cadre the clearest possible conception of the import of their action. But if Trotsky had not been there, had not made his great theoretical contribution, we may be sure that Lenin, consummate socialist politician and man of action that he was, would have led the Bolsheviks to power just the same and an accurate reflection in theory of the Revolution would have come later.

I mention this not only to defend the right of the Cuban Revolution to have its own peculiarities but to draw from Bolshevik theory to attempt to explain certain of these peculiarities.

The main power in the Cuban Revolution was the peasantry (as in Russia). But this peasantry shaded into the powerful mass of agricultural workers, which, because of the role of the sugar industry, constituted the most dynamic section of the Cuban proletariat. The agricultural workers solidly backed the Revolution. The city workers favored the Revolution but were not in position to head it (unlike Russia) for two reasons. (1) The unions were strapped in the strait jacket of 'mujalismo'; that is, a bureaucracy tied directly to the Batista dictatorship. (2) The political leadership was held by the Communist Party, an organization devoted to 'peaceful coexistence', 'people's frontism', and the cult of Stalin, an organization which, as Huberman and Sweezy put it diplomatically, 'never caused any serious problems'. (The CP leaders actually went so far in avoiding causing any serious problems for Batista that they pictured him as a man of the people and took posts in his government).

The main demands of the peasantry were an end to hunger, an end to Batista's savage killings, and agrarian reform. (In Russia: Bread! Peace! Land!) These demands became the slogans of the July 26 Movement. By all the criteria of origin, aims and social following the July 26 Movement was a petty-bourgeois formation, but an extremely radical one. It had one plank in its program which separated it from all similar groupings and which was to prove decisive. It made a principle of armed struggle without compromise against the Batista dictatorship. To carry out this aim, it organized a peasant guerrilla movement that has been compared to Tito's and Mao's. Parallels can also be found, however, in the rich revolutionary experience of Latin America, including Cuba itself. Its formation was not as novel as its success.

Character of Government

On coming to power, the July 26 Movement set up a coalition government that included well-known bourgeois-democratic figures – and not in secondary posts. In retrospect these may have seemed middle-class decorations or mere camouflage hiding the real nature of the government. It is more accurate, I think, to view this government as corresponding to the political aims of the revolution as they were conceived at the time by its leaders.

But such a government stood in contradiction to the demands of the insurgent masses and to the commitment of the July 26 Movement to satisfy these demands. The Revolution urgently required far-reaching inroads on private property, including imperialist holdings. As Castro and his collaborators moved toward fulfillment of the agrarian reform they met with resistance from their partners in the coalition, a resistance that was considerably stiffened by support from Wall Street, which viewed them as the 'reasonable' elements in a regime packed with bearded 'wild men'.

As Huberman and Sweezy correctly observe, 'a sort of dual system government began to emerge'. The displacement of Felipe Pazos by Che Guevara in November 1959 marked a decisive shift and the resolution of the governmental crisis, whatever hang-overs from the coalition still remained. The government that now existed was qualitatively different from the coalition regime.

Its chief characteristics were a genuine interest in the welfare of the bottom strata of the population, readiness to entrust the defense of the Revolution to them by giving them arms, clear recognition of the identity of the main enemies of the Revolution and resoluteness in disarming and combating them. It was even free from fetishism of private property. Yet it did not think of itself as socialist. It did not proclaim socialist aims. What should we call such a strange government?

Among the great discussions organized by the Bolsheviks in the first four congresses of the Communist International was one precisely on this question. Deeply buried under landslides of Stalinist propaganda, the minutes and resolutions of that discussion are not readily available. When you unearth them, your feeling is one of shock at their timeliness. Did the Bolsheviks really discuss such a question four years before Castro was born!

The Bolsheviks analyzed several varieties of 'workers and peasants government'; that is, radical petty-bourgeois governments, indicating differences that would cause a revolutionary-socialist party to offer support or to refuse support. They also left open the possibility in theory of variants they could not readily foresee at the time. The general label they used for such regimes was 'Workers and Farmers Government'. Here we must expostulate a bit with the Bolsheviks; they also called the dictatorship of the proletariat a 'Workers and Farmers Government'. A representative from theoretically backward America might have asked for distinctive labels so he could more easily tell them apart. But the Bolsheviks discussed this point, too, and felt that it would not be confusing so long as everyone was clear on the difference in content, since the first kind of government would likely prove to be only a transient form preliminary to the latter type.

Of course, the Communist delegates in 1922 could not visualize such a change without the helpful presence of a genuine revolutionary-socialist party such as the Russian workers had in the Bolsheviks. A key question requiring our attention, therefore, is the absence of this factor in Cuba. To find the answer we must turn to the world situation in which Cuba is locked.

Death Agony of Capitalism

The most prominent conditioning force in international politics today is the deep decay of the capitalist system. Leaving aside the effect of such general threats as another major depression or atomic annihilation in a third world war, Cuba has experienced the decay of capitalism in two specific ways: (1) the deformation of national life through imperialist domination – monoculture, super profits, hunger, disease, ignorance, dictatorial rule, etc. (2) the economic and diplomatic strangulation a power like the US applies to a colonial nation seeking independence. The moves emanating from Wall Street and the State Department, as many observers have noted, powerfully accelerated, if they did not make inevitable, the radicalization of the Cuban Revolution. Eisenhower 'lost' Cuba much the way Truman 'lost' China.

Next in importance to the death agony of capitalism is the existence and the growing power of the orbit where capitalist property relations have been transcended and planned economies constructed. Showing what can be achieved in economic, scientific and cultural progress, not to mention sovereign standing, these countries serve as practical object lessons. Their tendency to magnetize attention, especially in the underdeveloped areas, has become an active political factor that is now powerfully strengthened by the possibility of securing material aid from this source. The Soviet Union, by its mere existence, has always been – even in the terrible years under Stalin – a radicalizing force among oppressed peoples. The attraction was enormously increased by the Chinese Revolution and the fresh example which China has provided of how to break out of age-old stagnation and imperialist oppression. Cuba has been affected by all this in the most vivid and concrete way.

The third feature of world politics is the long default of the Communist parties in providing revolutionary-socialist leadership to the working class. For decades this signified betrayal and defeat in the most promising of revolutionary situations. Today it has finally begun to signify the emergence of alternative leaderships – the masses in the underdeveloped areas, having lost fatalistic acceptance of hunger, misery, ignorance and ruthless exploitation, have become impatient and are pushing forward whatever leaderships are at hand. Nationalists have filled the vacuum at least temporarily in many areas, but the tendency is toward much more radical currents. Nowhere is this to be seen with greater clarity than in Cuba.

Finally, there is a tendency among the nationalist movements and newly emerging countries in the Far East, the Middle East, Africa and Latin America to seek mutual encouragement and support. The Cuban revolutionists for example, are in close touch with the Algerian freedom fighters. They have diplomatic relations with Yugoslavia, India, Ghana, etc. Sekou Touré and Soekarno have been honored guests in Havana. Lumumba is a hero in Cuba. A radical move taken by any of them that proves successful has big impact on all the others. For instance, Nasser's seizure of the Suez Canal when Egypt suffered the combined attack of Britain, France and Israel made a lasting impression.

In the light of this international background, the series of countermeasures taken by the Cuban government under pressure from the State Department are seen to have an ideological origin that does no violence to Marxist theory; in fact these countermeasures are explainable only by a theory grounded in the international class struggle.

Character of the State

Whatever the consciousness of the Cuban revolutionists may have been, not a single major measure undertaken by them was unique. 'Intervention' of the *latifundia* and domestic and foreign capitalist holdings was undoubtedly as Cuban as the royal palms, but it finds a precedent in the 'control' exercised over private enterprises under the Bolsheviks prior to the establishment of workers management of industry. A similar stage appeared in the Chinese Revolution. The expropriations and nationalizations are likewise far from novel. A government monopoly of foreign trade is in the Russian tradition; and the planned economy which Cuba has now begun is, of course, recognized by everyone as in the pattern initiated by the Russian workers and peasants.

In the October, 1960, issue of *Political Affairs*, James S. Allen, a spokesman of the Communist Party, labels these as 'measures of a state-capitalist type'. This effort to avoid the label 'socialist', as advanced by Huberman and Sweezy, is not very satisfactory. Are the measures of similar kind in the Soviet Union, Eastern Europe, Yugoslavia, Albania and China also to be labeled as 'of a state-capitalist type'? Evidently not.

Aside from this, Allen's position has another flaw. What about the state? Is it capitalist? Can a capitalist state carry out such measures and still remain capitalist? Judging from the shrieks of the counter-revolutionaries and the froth on Wall Street's mouth, it is not possible.

The fact is that the state structure began to undergo alteration upon Castro's coming to power January 1, 1959. For good and valid political reasons, Castro insisted on smashing both the old army and the old police force. The lesson of Guatemala had been well absorbed by the July 26 Movement. A new army and a new police, based on the rebel forces, replaced the old. A nationwide militia was organized.

One could have decided that this was enough to require us at the time to call Cuba a workers state. But the premise for such a conclusion is that the conscious aims of the leadership are revolutionary-socialist, openly proclaimed, so that it remains only a question of time until the entire state structure is altered to conform to the needs of a planned economy. This political premise, of course, did not exist. It remained to be seen what course the pragmatic leadership would take and whether their proclaimed political aims would become altered as they sought to put into effect the reforms they advocated; or whether in sticking to their political positions they modified or gave up their social and economic aims. The outcome could only be determined by the struggle itself.

The results are now in. In the two years since the victory, the holdovers from the old state have been sloughed off in the key positions although they may still hold authority in some sectors. With the completion between August–October, 1960, of the nationalizations in the major areas of Cuban industry, a new state had come into being so deeply committed to a planned economy that Cuba's course in this direction cannot now be changed save by an imperialist invasion and a bloody civil war.

Since the transcending of capitalist property relations and the construction of a planned economy correspond with the economic interests of the working class and are objectively socialist in tendency, we must, if we are interested in exact terminology, call this a 'workers state', signifying that it is a state committed to the task of carrying Cuban economy and society forward through the transition from capitalism to socialism.

Proletarian Democracy

It is true that this workers state lacks, as yet, the forms of proletarian democracy. This does not mean that democracy is lacking in Cuba. Far more democracy exists today in Cuba than ever existed under any previous regime. It does mean that a government based on workers, peasants and soldiers councils, or some form of councils in democratic control of the government, has not yet been worked out. Mills' observations about the concentration of power in one person are accurate.

Marxist theory admits the possibility of situations in which no alternative exists save such concentration of power. However, it regards this as exceptional and dangerous to the revolutionary interests of the workers and peasants. It is a sign of weakness in the organization of the struggle. The norm is the extension of democracy into all phases of the nation's life. It is not just a question of democratic rights but of organizing the most powerful defense and bringing the maximum power to bear in carrying out the structural changes and constructing the planned economy. Consequently, while defending the present Cuban government from attack from all quarters, Marxists advocate the earliest possible development of proletarian forms of democracy in Cuba. It would seem self-evident that this would add greatly to the political defense of the Revolution, above all as an example to be emulated in other countries.

This is the tendency in Cuba, as Mills notes, and one must join him in ardently hoping that the ferocious pressure from American imperialism will not lead to retrogression.

What Next?

A new stage in the Cuban Revolution is now opening up of the greatest interest and importance. The leaders have convincingly demonstrated that they really meant it when they said they were prepared to carry the Revolution through to its necessary conclusion no matter where it took them. What have been the consequences in their thinking?

Looking back, they must note with some astonishment, I imagine, that it proved impossible to carry through simple humanistic aims, all of them long proclaimed by the bourgeois society that toppled feudalism, without taking measures that transcended capitalist property relations. Capitalism doesn't work for the poor. To fulfill their desire to turn the promise of a better life for the humble into reality, these men of powerful will found they had to put Cuba on the road to socialism. They discovered this through practical experience and not through preconceived notions. It is almost like a laboratory test. What theories did it confirm or disprove, or must we wipe the slate of theory clean and start fresh?

Is this experience not worth evaluation? Wouldn't the way be smoothed for revolutionists in other Latin-American countries, for example, if they knew the reasons for the course that had to be taken in Cuba? Surely the experience will be similar elsewhere in Latin America and other continents as revolutionists follow the example of the Cuban vanguard and bring their peoples into the mainstream of history.

Up to now the Cuban leaders have appeared as great revolutionists of action. Perhaps some of them may now venture into the field of theory with commensurate contributions. It is time, we think, to attempt to bring the theory of the Cuban Revolution up to the level of its practice. From such a development all the friends and supporters of the Cuban Revolution stand to gain – not least of all in the United States where the success of the July 26 Movement has brought new hope and inspiration to the radical movement.

4 Still a Man's World[23]
(1962)

Hedda Grant (Hedda Garza)

The Second Sex by Simone de Beauvoir. Translated from the French and edited by H.M. Parshley, 705pp. New York: Bantam Books, 1961. $ 0.95

Although there are no segregationist laws in the State of New York, few people would deny that the Negro is subjected to unequal treatment; and that out of those inequalities in education, employment, housing, social status, etc., the Negro emerges less educated, in menial jobs and with less social status.

Though much subtler and ambivalent too, woman's struggle does take similar lines to the Negro struggle, except that women have not organized. They have identified instead with the various struggles of 'their men'. Thus the Negro woman must first battle white men and white women to attain her racial equality, before she can join with her white sisters to battle for her sex equality. Yet Simone de Beauvoir says, '… there are deep similarities between the situation of woman and that of the Negro. Both are being emancipated from a like paternalism and the former master class wishes to "keep them in their place" …'.

There are many people who would deny that in 1962, women are still the second sex. It is easy for Americans to see the crushing antifeminist laws and traditions of 'backward countries' but in countries where women have the vote and the automobile, it is harder to see the subtle indignities that corrode and change even the basic character of women.

This is a task that Simone de Beauvoir pursues with great intensity in *The Second Sex*. It stands out as a brilliant pioneering effort among books written on the subject of women. There are available many earnest and scholarly works in specialized fields, i.e., women in history; biology of women; anthropology; feminist struggles, etc. There are also many books which attempt to mutilate any feeble effort on the part of women to become 'at par' with the first sex. Usu-

---

23   Grant 1962.

ally written by men, often with the assistance of women (there are Uncle Toms in the second sex too), they urge the undefeated woman back to her kitchen, implore her to once again 'be womanly' (like telling a Negro to keep his place and be a 'good darky'). Even the author of *America's Sixty Families*, Ferdinand Lundberg, wrote one of the most vicious pieces on the subject of women, *Modern Woman, the Lost Sex*, in which he proposes laws prohibiting single women from working, thus forcing them into marriage!

The works of feminists are sincere, but often limited by a misunderstanding of the causes or nature of the dilemma. They often waste their energies insisting that women have been, and always were equal to men and trying vainly to document their claim. It is true that Bebel wrote a stirring protest against the treatment of women; Virginia Woolf also penned a moving plea to women writers to leave their parlors and write in broader arenas. But neither she nor he could tell them how they got into the parlor in the first place or how to get out of there.

But Simone de Beauvoir examines the problem from every conceivable aspect. The reader emerges with a knowledge of the nature of the problem, in a position to understand even the most despicable and backward aspects of womanhood. Mme. de Beauvoir does not either apologize for or champion women, but describes them as they are and reveals the historic origins of their predicament. Her basic viewpoint is that women, in all societies, and continuing into the present, have been the 'other' rather than 'another'. Even when women have had prestige, it has often been in the negative sense, as symbols, as idols, as heroic mothers. The devastating effect this has had on women still has not caused them to consistently and concretely struggle against their invisible bondage.

Not content merely to do a complete study of the subject, this brilliant author attempts to analyze and criticize almost every major theory pertaining to women; Freud and his theories of women's basic longing to be men are refuted; Engels' theory of the matriarchy is partially disputed. Her challenge is not made in terms of ridiculing or total rejection, but rather from the point of view of a rigorous critique of these thinkers.

A careful study of the laws, myths, literature and economic reasons relating to woman's lot is presented in the first volume. The second volume covers women today; both serving to back up the author's portrayal of that subtle form of discrimination that creates a creature without projects of her own; a creature that has been and still largely is the mirror of men and the mirror of their ideas. A man's fondest projects are but a woman's hobbies; love and marriage and children become her projects, supported by the myths of maternal instinct and womanly role.

The independent woman, who instinctively or consciously shuns this role of 'other' faces a terrible struggle. Often she turns to lesbianism, or woman-of-the-worldism, both negative approaches that defeat her entirely. Mme. de Beauvoir demonstrates this in careful chapters devoted to women in marriage, in love, in childhood, i.e., in her many relationships; coming up with a total portrait that is hard to dispute.

It is true that the basic philosophy and much of the language of the book is existential. But existentialism is in flux; the terminology, easily translatable into ordinary words, seems uncontradictory to Marxist thinking; her concept of the 'existent' easily translated to the concept of the total person who can only develop to full potential under democratic socialism. One may dispute Simone de Beauvoir's analysis of the original causes of woman's situation, but her description of the dilemma and her solution seem beyond genuine argumentation.

The author's perspective for the future, her assurances to the male world that real women with their own projects will make better friends, better lovers; her declaration of the need for an end to capitalism as the only permanent solution to the problem, and yet her insistence that the struggle must start now – all are in tune with revolutionary socialist thinking. But it is in the factual and careful presentation of many things that have been unclear to both men and women, that *The Second Sex* can be called a significant contribution that belongs in the realm of 'must' knowledge of every serious thinker.

5 Women Who Work[24]
(1962)

Melba Baker (Melba Windoffer)

The material conditions for the complete emancipation of woman have long existed. But it has been only in the last few decades that woman's strategic position, her assimilation in industry, has so altered as to make that emancipation an urgent necessity.

For many centuries, the separate, private labor of the woman was essential to the well-being of the family unit. She rendered fat, dipped candles, made the soap, prepared the food, wove cloth and made clothing. Her labor was socially necessary. But her productive activity was largely restricted to the household and was remunerated only through her husband's pay. Man's labor developed in the broader arena of society. He bargained for his pay. His economic and political dominance was fixed by law.

Modern industry, however, made much of woman's labor not only unnecessary but uneconomical as well. A wire brings in the light. A simple touch of the switch turns it off or on. Bread is baked in great continuous-mix factories. The arduous and most unpleasant part of food preparation is performed by truck gardeners and food processing plants. It is pre-measured and pre-cooked. Giant machines, operated by relatively few men and women, can make, launder, clean, press and mend the clothes of hundreds of families.

This simplification of the labor of the household, its potential elimination, has destroyed the challenge and creativity it once offered. It has left housework empty, dull and monotonous, almost an insult to the intelligence and ingenuity of the modern woman.

Child care is a challenge to an individual who has specialized in the well-being and development of children. But it is not that to the vast majority. For most mothers, trapped alone in the house all day with small children, child care is a prison sentence in which association is restricted to her social and intellectual inferiors, the children, relieved only by the more sensible collective education of the child in the public school.

---

24   Baker 1962.

Ashley Montagu, in the book *The Natural Superiority of Women*, expresses the view that 'the mother alone with kids all day becomes a non-social, often anti-social being, and therefore, a bad parent. Housework claims her time, more than the child's needs. And the latter in today's complex world demands extensive professional training to understand'.

It is the quality of mothering that counts and not the quantity. If a mother looks forward to going to work and to coming home to her children, she will be a happier person and contribute more to the happiness of her family – so said Dr. Edith S. Taylor, psychiatric director of the Jewish Social Agency's non-sectarian Child Guidance Clinic, in a recent interview.

Motherhood is not the glorious end-all for a woman. It is one aspect of her life, just as fatherhood is for the man and the kind of mother she is depends upon the kind of person she is. It happens to demand more biologically from the woman than from the man, but the pleasures and the problems of each new generation are the responsibility of both sexes.

The growth of capitalism, the development of industry, has reduced the necessity for woman's labor in the home. And the decline of capitalism, World War II and the continuous war economy since, has forced open the door to the social employment of women on a mass scale. Women have replied to the old reactionary formula that 'a woman's place is in the home', by walking through that door to escape the household tedium and win at least a measure of economic independence and freedom. The US Department of Labor survey in 1960 found that one out of every three workers in the United States was a woman.

Under capitalism, however, social progress is not rational, the result of a plan. Profit is the motor force. Progress is only a by-product, appearing, when it does, in uneven stages, often raising new problems and imposing new burdens before the old ones are eliminated. Women are still under pressure to maintain the primary responsibility of the household and at the same time, their labor is demanded in industry. Her burden therefore is increased.

Frederick Engels wrote in the *Origin of the Family, Private Property and the State*, 'The emancipation of women will only be possible when woman can take part in production on a large scale and domestic work no longer claims anything but an insignificant amount of her time. And not only has that become possible through modern large scale industry which does not merely permit the employment of female labor over a wide range, but positively demands it, while it also tends toward ending private domestic labor by changing it more and more into a public industry'.

Although modern industry has made possible the complete abolition of the duties of the housewife, as we now know them, the majority of women still perform many traditional tasks and maintain their traditional role. They have not yet realized the benefits of modern industry.

Women find themselves in a dual position. With one foot they are stepping into the future while the other foot is trapped in the past. For most women, ours is a period of transition, filled with doubts and misgivings. Is she an unnatural mother? Is she failing in her duty as a housekeeper and wife? She feels damned if she does and is damned if she doesn't.

This partial freeing of women from domestic labor has brought a large section of them into the working class and in addition has freed another large section to participate in politics and community projects of one kind or another. The very participation of women in many of these areas is a recent historical development. Women who work may also participate in a number of community organizations of one kind or another as well as in politics and to a more limited extent in labor organizations. Their political activity is generally limited to the lower echelons, as is their participation in fund raising, community efforts, church activities, etc. The bulk of the 'Jimmy Higgins' work is done by women.

Many of these activities were denied to the great majority of women not so very long ago. Today virtually every woman is in some activity that takes her out of the home for varying periods of time. The woman going to work and going into public life has found a new self. She is becoming a new personality. She is becoming a socially conscious individual, more aware of the economic and cultural realities of life and developing a new interest and new confidence in herself.

Twenty-three million women are today at work in the United States on a full-time basis. Another six million work part-time, making for a total work force of twenty-nine million women. One-half of these working women are married. Of the single women in the United States, from 20–64 years of age, about 75 per cent are working. The work pattern of the single working woman is generally the same as the working man's. The married woman may lose time for child birth and the care of small children.

These women are involved, to a greater or lesser extent, in the class struggle which goes on all the time in one form or another. During the last 20 years, when the class struggle has been relatively muted, the only section of workers who built a new union were the telephone workers. They built their union from a company union. In the best traditions of union militants, they withstood attacks by firemen with high pressure hoses, police clubs, company intimidation and trips to the local jails. In the process they developed new methods of fighting, peculiar to their industry.

This union was brought into existence by that section of society that has always been considered impossible to organize. These workers were primarily young women who, it was said, were only interested in 'getting married and settling down with some man to support them'. Many of these young women still lived at home and were not under compulsion to provide themselves with the necessities of life. In fact they were supposed to have it pretty good. But they just didn't like 'Ma Bell' and her low wages.

Women constitute about one quarter of all manufacturing employees. This number includes the women working in the factory offices as well as the production workers. In the lighter manufacturing industries, such as textiles and apparel, more than nine-tenths of the workers are women. The largest employment of women in the durable goods industries is in the electrical machinery industries.

Two-thirds of the women who work are engaged in the distribution of goods and services, with the greatest concentration of women in business services. Ninety-four per cent of all stenographers, typists and secretaries are women. The next largest section of women workers are bookkeepers and telephone operators. About half of the women workers are concentrated in twenty-eight occupational groups. In twelve occupations, women supply nine-tenths of the labor power.

The women who go to work are reaching out toward the future. They find an identity with their fellow workers along class lines. Having gone to work, the problems of women are recognized as basically social problems. This makes it easier to seek a means to solve them in common.

Of course, the woman who goes to work is not on easy street. In fact, she takes on a new load that is, for the most part, added to her old burden of kitchen and cradle. Some in despair turn back to the protection and shelter of four walls and a husband. To them, the struggle for emancipation is too difficult; they will settle for the status quo. Others lack the physical energy necessary or the emotional stability to form consistent work habits or the ability to work in an organized unit with other people. Some, of course, play the same part as the 'Uncle Tom's' play in the movement of the Negro people. Some are so demoralized as to be content with social parasitism. And others are pushed out of a labor force that is put to use only when profits are high.

The first thing a woman discovers when she enters the market place with her labor power, is its value. Even though she comes with a skill, such as typing or bookkeeping, her labor power is valued lower than that of a male worker, and many times this is in relation to a male worker without a skill.

In general, labor unions have concentrated on organizing men, and usually the more skilled men. This concentration resulted in a higher general wage scale for men as against women.

With the large influx of women into industry in the last two decades, the unions have defaulted in relation to women. Although one-third of the present labor force is composed of women, only 15 per cent of them are organized into unions. A good number of unions make little or no attempt to organize the white collar workers, who are predominantly women.

This callous disregard of the needs of the women workers is a direct concession to management by the union bureaucrats. They go one step further and add insult to injury by using the bosses' age-old argument that women are only working for 'pin money'. This was the fiction invented to excuse the low wages paid to women and children by factory owners at the dawn of the manufacturing period. It still is a good excuse for employers eager to make more profit, but a very bad reason to be accepted by a union.

In a number of industries that are primarily composed of women workers there is often a union settlement of the contract on the basis of outright sex discrimination. The practice of settling for ten cents an hour more for men and three cents an hour more for women is very common. The result is that over the years the spread becomes greater and greater. Needless to say, the employer with 100 women and ten men in his work force is very glad to make a deal of this nature – after a little shadow boxing of course.

There is a very accurate measure of the value of discrimination and prejudice to the employer that is apparent at a glance in the wage scale of different sections of the population.

Wage and salary income of white and nonwhite men and women for the year 1958

	All workers	
Group	**Women**	**Men**
White	$2,364.00	$4,569.00
Nonwhite	$1,055.00	$2,652.00

These figures from the US Department of Commerce give the dollar value of discrimination and prejudice. The nonwhite male is somewhat better off than the white female, but the nonwhite female worker pays the highest price for her color and sex. Her yearly income is at the bare point of existence.

In relation to family 'head' (it is automatically assumed, of course, in our equalitarian paradise, that it is the man) the figures are equally unpleasant.

Families with males at the head received a median yearly income in 1958 of $5,292.00. One-tenth of the families in the United States have females at the head and they had a median yearly income in 1958 of $2,741.00. Thus the family headed by a woman has just half as much food, clothing, shelter, recreation, health benefits, etc., as the one headed by a man.

When the union officials speak of vast sums of money to organize the unorganized they rarely mention the women workers. It is almost as if this group of workers did not exist.

And their silence is not difficult to understand. To organize women workers would present the union officials with a problem they do not want. It would upset the status quo to bring this great section of exploited workers into the general stream of organized labor. To equalize the wage scale would require battles of major proportions. In addition the unions would find themselves grappling with much broader problems than just economic ones. There would of necessity arise renewed and greater pressure from the ranks for independent political action to meet the general social problems of child care, peace, slums, etc.

The low pay of women is linked with the low pay of national and racial minorities. Certain classifications of work are commonly done by women or by men and women of these minorities.

Discrimination is rampant in job classification as well as in rates of pay. Of the twenty-eight occupation groups for women in the United States, a good number are virtually closed to women of the minorities who find their job openings primarily in the lowest-paid categories.

Forty-five per cent of the nonwhite women work outside the home and constitute one out of every eight women working. They work generally in three fields: private household workers, other service workers and operatives in factories, laundries and other work places. Economic necessity is greater in this group and undoubtedly accounts for 45 per cent of the nonwhite women working as against 35 per cent of the white women.

In twenty states there are laws demanding equal pay for equal work, but most of these states insert two exceptions: for domestic labor and for agricultural labor. These are areas where the greatest exploitation and also the most miserable working conditions exist.

Twenty-three states and Puerto Rico have minimum wage laws. Here again, exceptions are made with regard to agricultural labor and domestic labor.

Forty states have laws that regulate hours of employment and days of rest, meals, rest periods, night work, etc. Twenty states have a maximum of a six-day working week to protect the health of women workers. However, these laws all are strangely blind to the plight of agricultural workers.

While many of these laws look good on paper, they have no real significance unless there is a union organization to enforce them. If each woman, as an individual, is compelled to demand the enforcement of the legal provisions that are supposed to protect her, they will not and cannot be enforced. In most cases, the woman does not even know about protective laws. The bosses have legal staffs to advise them. Small businessmen generally belong to trade associations that provide legal service or information. But what working class family has access to this general information outside of the trade union movement?

One of the largest unions of women workers in this country is the International Ladies Garment Workers Union. This bureaucratically run union still allows the piece work system. Each woman is forced to work to the limit of her strength for the bare necessities. Many of the food processing unions allow the operation of the same principle, or permit a quota system that introduces speed-up. The unions generally have permitted speed of the belt system in mass production to be determined by the boss. (In the 1930s the workers fought to have their say in the tempo of their labor).

Women are also blocked in their hope of advancement to higher pay categories of labor. This problem is another reason the male-dominated unions are reluctant to organize women. They would also have to make at least a token effort to fight for their advancement. This would mean many women would reach higher-level job categories than men and those men who are reluctant to give up their illusion of superiority would resent this. A male 'B' mechanic in a crew under a female 'A' mechanic would find his ego a bit bruised. Union officials are undoubtedly uncomfortable in the presence of skilled women workers who won't be treated with the old arrogant and condescending paternalism.

Nation's Business for September, 1961, gives some interesting figures on women's place in the business world. In 1940 four per cent of the executives in the United States were women. In 1950 this figure rose to five per cent. It was still at this level when the 1960 census was taken and is believed to be only slightly higher at the present time. This must be compared to a 1960 work force of 23.5 million women – estimated as close to 25 million in 1961.

Nation's Business goes on to say,

> Most firms feel women are too much of a risk to put into administrative jobs. Many companies shy away from giving women top jobs because they fear the effect this will have on other employees – particularly men. Of the nation's approximately seven million managers, officials and proprietors only 1.1 million are women and about half that number are self employed.

This means that about half of the 1.1 million women executives are owners of beauty shops, restaurants, child care centers, boarding houses, nursing homes, etc.

Women are also excluded from top posts in fields of work that are traditionally theirs. For example, in the library field women fill a very large proportion of the staff positions but a very small proportion of the administrative positions.

Likewise, in the field of education, there are relatively few women in the administrative staffs of the schools. In elementary schools nine-tenths of the teachers and half the principals are women. In secondary schools where women fill about half the teaching posts, they represent about nine per cent of the principals. Women constitute over one-quarter of the administrative staffs in colleges and universities, but they are concentrated in women's colleges. Less than one-tenth of all college board members in coeducational colleges are women.

The 20,000 women teachers in colleges and universities comprised about one-fifth of the college faculty in 1959–60. Of the college instructors, about one-third were women, and of full professors, about one-tenth were women.

The discrepancy between men and women in administrative bodies of unions appears to be even greater than in the business or professional world. Material available in the Seattle Public Library failed to reveal *any* woman in *any* policy making body of *any* union.

The universal discrimination against women tends to unite them in the struggle for equality. But even more of a unifying factor is the problem of child care which all women share, actually or potentially. The extent of the problem in its actuality can be seen in the fact that one out of every seven mothers in this country is in the labor force. One out of every two mothers in the labor force has a child or children under 12 years of age.

Apart from the public school, there is no general provision for the care of children of working mothers. The public school is the only area in which society intervenes in any organized fashion in the welfare and development of the child. Today, seven million women are attempting to solve the same problem of child care, each in her own individual way. Needless to say, this is not the best way for the emotional and physical development of the child or for the peace of mind of the mother.

The task of finding a baby sitter is an arduous one, not to speak of the expense. An individual mother must read newspaper ads, solicit friends, relatives, neighbors and fellow workers.

In general the women who are available for baby sitting and housework are those who for one reason or another are excluded from industrial work. Most often this is due to discrimination in relation to age, health, color or nationality. These women are forced into this occupation. It is not a vocation which they freely selected and for which they have been specially trained.

But all too often, the baby sitter is an emotionally unstable woman. A scandalously high percentage of damage is done to children by emotionally sick individuals. Only a most fortunate few working mothers can afford the luxury of trained baby sitters and housekeepers to relieve them of these tasks and worries.

The United States Children's Bureau regards the most fortunate child of all is the child of the working mother who has the good fortune to attend a good group child care center. But this is the privilege of only one out of every four children of working mothers. The majority of children are cared for by neighbors, relatives and friends. About one child in every thirteen is expected to look out for himself.

This problem, again, is the most severe at the lower income level of working women. This is the bracket of nonwhite working mothers. When we add job discrimination to their extremely low wage scale, and the fact that she may also head a family, the magnitude of the problems she faces in this society is one of truly staggering proportions.

Technically all of these problems can be solved. Social labor is productive enough to be able to provide child care centers staffed by full-time professionals. And there is no reason why the housework that remains to be done, cannot be done by a section of the working class sufficiently equipped and trained to do it in the most economical time – as office buildings are now scrubbed, dusted and put in order for the next day's work.

Ashley Montagu proposes the four-hour working day for those who are married – so that both parents can be equally parents and wage earners to the advantage of all. He goes on to say,

> Women's going to work has forced the father back into the family, and this is good, for his 'responsibility' to his children is no less great than his wife's. When men abandon the upbringing of their children to their wives, a loss is suffered by everyone.

In whatever specific way women will solve their problems, the first essential, if one is not naive, is to win a society that poses all questions for rational solution. That means, above all, the elimination of capitalism where profit alone is the determinant – even when it means the waste of human labor power of millions of human beings and billions of working hours.

Women can, and will, play a key role in this general historical task. They cannot expect to solve their problems without a struggle. Freedom will not be given them as a gift. It must be fought for and won as a human right.

The super exploitation of the women workers adds fuel to the fires of revolutionary struggles everywhere. These women, new to the direct clash of social forces, will supply militants and leaders to the working class in its struggle for freedom. They will give impetus to independent political action. The labor movement will find itself greatly reinforced, not only with the working women but with other sections of the female population who will be in sympathy or will feel the need for the demands of the women workers.

Men and women who have already begun to learn to work together, will also learn how to fight together for the complete emancipation of all. This is the inevitable historical trend. And in the struggle itself the confusion, the doubts that plague women in this transition period will dissolve in the new-found hope for the future.

6 Kennedy: The Candidate and the President[25]
(1962)

Myra Tanner Weiss

At the close of the 1960 election campaign, a small item appeared on the front page of the *New York Times*. An 'authoritative source' announced,

> The Pentagon is expanding its plans to develop bacteriological and chemical weapons for use in limited war situations.
>
> According to an authoritative source, plans call for the use of the weapons in 'brushfire' hostilities, short of all-out nuclear warfare, in an effort to achieve conquest without destruction of life and property …
>
> The Air Force budget for the fiscal year beginning next July 1, now being prepared, will call for the first time for equipping airplanes with nozzles and sprays to deliver 'nonlethal' blows against military installations and population centers, the source said.
>
> Nov. 2, 1960

At the time this item appeared a battle was raging in the United Nations over Cuban charges that the United States was preparing an invasion of its tiny island neighbor. James J. Wadsworth, representing the US, denounced these charges as 'monstrous distortions and downright falsehood'. (*NY Times*, Nov. 2, 1960).

Subsequent events, of course, demonstrated conclusively that Foreign Minister Roa of Cuba spoke the truth and that Wadsworth was either not informed enough to answer the charges or he was lying.

There is probably no way for the average American to know if the Air Force actually equipped its planes with nozzles for use of chemical and bacteriological weapons or if the release in the *NY Times* was just designed to frighten Cubans, and any other people interested, with the thought that they could be beaten simply by being put into a mass state of vomiting or sleep.

---

25   Weiss 1962.

The idea seems to come straight out of science fiction where some occupants of another planet with a superior technology take over the earth by slipping into the human unconscious mind. But if our real world is taking on the character of science fiction, perhaps we can use our imaginations to see a little more of the reality of American politics.

Let's imagine that Cuba had an air-force equipped with nozzles and chemical weapons. Let's imagine that the weapon selected for its big neighbor on the continent was a truth gas that compelled all candidates in election campaigns to tell the whole truth – and furthermore, that this wonderful gas gave its inhaler the knowledge of what he would do when elected to office. About a year has gone by since Kennedy was elected, so it will be easy now to imagine what his campaign speeches would have been like if such a 'truth' gas had hit his nostrils.

Election Year Begins

'In the beginning is the word', quoted Mr. Kennedy, Jan. 1, 1960, in the opening statement of his book, *The Strategy of Peace*. And he continued, 'Surely, then, the first duty of an officer in a democratic government is to uphold the integrity of words used in public debate; and to do this by himself using them in ways where they will stand as one with the things they are meant to represent'.

From the Bible to the American political scene. That's a pretty good start. But if Kennedy had been hit with our imaginary 'truth' gas, he would have added:

> When I am President of the United States, Mr. Roa will again charge us with preparing an invasion of his country. I shall denounce this as a lie. My appointee in the United Nations, Adlai Stevenson, will also denounce this charge as a lie and he will back his stand by quoting me as saying, 'I wish to make it clear also that we would be opposed to the use of our territory for mounting an offensive against any foreign government'.
>
> BUT in a matter of days the world will know that I and the CIA, using Cuban exiles, equipped, trained and financed by the United States organized the invasion. In doing this, I will of course violate my country's pledge to respect and defend the 'right of self-determination of nations' and I shall violate the laws of my country (my brother, Bobby, will then be the Attorney General, and he will list these violations). Cuban sands will soak up human blood and Castro will shame my country before the world by exposing our role in discussions with captured invaders on national tele-

vision broadcasts. All this is what I mean when I promise to 'uphold the integrity of words used in public debate'.

The Promise of Peace

The dominant theme of Kennedy's election campaign, however, was not integrity, but peace. He undoubtedly won the support of the largest of the minority groups of American voters by virtue of his speeches on the need for peace. One of his major campaign weapons was his book, *The Strategy of Peace*. On this issue he voiced some of the yearnings of the American people for an end to the incessant threat of war.

The *New York Times*, Sept. 15, 1960, reported on Kennedy's visit to New York City: 'Hitting hard at every stop, the Democratic Presidential nominee called for a "march toward peace to replace the drift toward war".' On the same day the *NY Times* reported that Kennedy told 2,500, mostly women, that 'his program would take the United States far on the pathway to peace'.

On Sept. 7, 1960, in Portland, Oregon, Kennedy assailed Eisenhower's foreign policy. Many peoples, Kennedy said, sincerely wonder

> how strongly America desires peace ... They are afraid of diplomatic policies that teeter on the brink of war. They are dismayed that our negotiators have no solid plans for disarmament. And they are discouraged by a philosophy that puts its faith in swapping threats with the Russians. For they know it can lead in only one direction – to mankind's final war.

Kennedy likened the Administration's 'massive retaliation' defense system to 'a fire department that can put out a fire only by blowing up houses'.

Kennedy, the candidate, was astutely aware of the growing concern, in this country as well as elsewhere, for the radioactive contamination that increases with the nuclear weapons race. (At that time there was a '*de facto*' ban on nuclear tests due to Russia's unilateral ban on tests – violated only by France). Kennedy promised his audiences that he would provide the leadership that would end the menace of radioactive fallout.

At UCLA, Nov. 2, 1959, he said,

> ... no problem in a world full of problems calls for greater leadership and vision – than the control of nuclear weapons, the utter destruction which would result from their use in war, and the radioactive pollution of our atmosphere by their continued testing in peacetime.

In Portland, Oregon, Aug. 1, 1959, he said,

> There is no serious scientific barrier to international agreement – despite increasing difficulties in problems of inspection and implementation. The only difficult barriers now are political and diplomatic. If we could mobilize the same talents and energy and resources to meet this challenge that we did to split the atom in the first place, then we should be able to persuade friend and foe alike that continued neglect of this problem will make the world a loser ...

It is safe to presume that a few at least in his audience, worried about the Strontium 90 accumulating in their bones, vowed to pull the cord in secret polling places and vote for the 'political and diplomatic' leadership that would mobilize the needed 'talents and energy and resources' to end radioactive fallout.

But if our imaginary truth gas had hit the candidate, this is what his listeners might have heard:

> Within a year, my 'new frontier' will begin to take shape. For most of you this will mean, not progress west, nor east, nor up into space where a Russian will be first to travel. Our frontier will be down – under the ground. The big question Americans will discuss will be how deep to dig, what to store, and if Christian morals permit shooting a neighbor or his children if they should come to you for shelter.

Welfare Promises

As a candidate Kennedy created the image of a man who was deeply sensitive to the sufferings of Americans less fortunate than himself. He promised aid to the aged, who could be utterly ruined by the soaring costs of doctors, medicines and hospitals; to the unemployed, condemned to idleness and poverty in this richest of all lands; to those Americans who, because of race or religion or national origins, were daily robbed of their dignity as human beings, discriminated against, segregated and even submitted to terror in this land of 'free' men and women.

To an estimated audience of 4,000 older citizens who had gathered hopefully in New York City, Kennedy appeared and promised (*NY Times*, Sept. 15, 1960) 'that if elected he and a Democratic Congress would put through a medical care program that would be part of the Social Security system'.

In Detroit, on Sept. 5, 1960, Kennedy eloquently ridiculed the Republican slogan, 'You never had it so good'. He replied with a show of feeling,

> But let them tell that to the four million people who are out of work, to the three million Americans who must work part time. Let them tell that to those who farm our farms in our depressed areas, in our deserted textile and coal towns.
>
> Let them try to tell it to the five million men and women in the richest country on earth who live on a surplus food diet of $20 a month ...

In a television broadcast in Texas on Sept. 12, 1960, Kennedy included in his list of important issues,

> ... the hungry children I saw in West Virginia, the old people who cannot pay their doctors' bills, the families forced to give up their farms ... These are the real issues which should decide this campaign.

And on Sept. 2, 1960, the *NY Times* reported,

> Mr. Kennedy centered his news conference on the civil rights issue and a promise to put the power of the White House, if he is elected, behind a fight to get the broadly liberal Democratic plank passed early in the next Congress ...

Kennedy was no novice as a capitalist politician. He was aware that many voters have become cynical about campaign promises over the years. So part of Kennedy's campaign strategy was to put before the voters the image of a man who not only made promises, but one who had the energy, the youth and the determination to keep his promises.

The *NY Times*, Sept. 10, 1960, reported Kennedy's promise in Los Angeles that

> he would not content himself with drafting programs and transmitting them to Congress ... but would actively fight for their enactment, taking his case to the people if Congress was slow in acting.

He spoke of the crucial period in a new administration – its first 90 days. In this context, on domestic issues, he told an audience in Washington,

> ... the next President of the United States must be prepared in the first three months of his office to send to the Congress messages that will deal

with wiping out poverty here in the United States, which will deal with the problem of full employment ...

Kennedy, the candidate, appeared to meet all needs. He was sensitive; he cared about the welfare of the American people; he thought something should be done about it; and he was ready to go to extreme measures to see that something was done about it. But if Kennedy had taken a whiff of our imaginary truth gas, this is what he would have told his attentive and hopeful audiences:

To the aged and ill:

> Many of you may survive my first year in office as President. But you will not get any help from my administration for your monstrous medical bills. What savings you may have toward a pleasant and secure retirement will continue to disappear if you get ill. But do not give up. After my first year in office has passed, I shall solemnly extend my promise to my second year in office. For some of you, this help, if it comes, will come too late. This is most regrettable. But there are more important things for the President to do.

To the unemployed, Kennedy would sniff our truth gas and say,

> After my first year in office, most of you will still be without jobs. Unemployment will decrease less than 1% of the civilian labor force. And this despite a successful effort to get the biggest military budget passed in peacetime history. And despite the fact that I shall take off their jobs over 100,000 reservists and put them back in the army to show the Russians that we mean business in the Berlin crisis. I shall attend the AFL-CIO Convention in December of 1961 and express my continued concern. But my Administration will pit its full strength against any attempt to find jobs for the unemployed by introducing a shorter work week or a shorter working day without a cut in pay. That might spread the jobs that still exist, but it would cut into profits. We who get profits wouldn't like that.
>
> I shall especially express concern for the one million or more youths who can't find jobs. American youth is in a bad way. And they are the ones who must do the fighting in the wars we are preparing. In December of 1961 I shall urge the youth to become 'fit'. I shall point out that 'To get two soldiers, the United States Army must call up seven men. Of the five rejected, three are turned down for physical reasons and two for mental disability ... and the rejection rate is increasing each year'. But I won't

give them a chance to work. Nor will I subsidize athletic activities – that would be socialistic. But I will continue to pass out surplus government food – it's too expensive to store, anyway – and I shall extend unemployment compensation payments, which may not save a worker's house, or the fund for the kids' education, but will keep him off the dole. And I shall pass legislation to make loans available for the development of industry in depressed areas. That's the free enterprise way.

To those who are fighting for freedom in America, Kennedy would sniff the truth gas and say,

Although 'freedom' is a word I use almost every time I open my mouth, when I am President of this country, the filibuster in Congress will continue to tie my hands. That will prevent me from delivering my promises on civil rights, as it prevented those who went before me. Brave youth will continue to risk their lives for freedom in the South. They will continue to be beaten bloody and put in jail. Their fight will continue to make gains, but I will be too busy with important affairs of state to join them in their struggle, or take their case 'to the American people'.

As for those civil liberties that constitute the basis of the freedom that's always on my lips – the right to form political parties and run candidates freely for public office – these liberties will be seriously impaired in the first year of my Administration. It will be my job to enforce laws passed previously to outlaw the Communist Party. If we succeed – and we shall try – it will be the first time any political party has been legislated out of existence. That will be quite a 'first' for any administration.

As far as the law is concerned, all a political party in power will have to do is to claim that a rival party is controlled by a foreign government. Even if this is denied – even if it can't be proved – that party can be forced to register its members as agents of a foreign government or go to jail. It's not enough that the capitalists own all the means of communication – daily papers, television, radio – it's not enough that we can afford to spend hundreds of millions of dollars in one election campaign to get our candidates elected – we also must persecute one of the small working class parties in opposition.

Russia may be emptying its prisons of political prisoners, but US prisons will continue to fill up with those who are jailed for opinions, for opposition to those in power. This may be confusing to some when we talk about risking human existence for freedom. But then, that's because they really don't understand what kind of freedom I, and millionaires like me, are talking about – the freedom to invest our capital and take our profits anywhere in the world.

Kennedy – the President

But no truth gas existed in the 1960 election campaign. Kennedy successfully created the image of a man of peace, concerned primarily with human welfare. And he became the President of the United States.

Does this mean that Kennedy was just a cheap liar – deceiving the electorate with the usual empty campaign promises in order to fulfill a personal ambition?

The matter is not that simple. To understand Kennedy both as a candidate and as President, it is necessary to begin with the self-evident fact that he is a capitalist politician. He probably believes that peace, full-employment and broad economic progress can be realized under capitalism. The deception of the voters was also a self-deception.

Kennedy, like most historically conscious proponents of capitalism, sees an ideal economic system – one that has overcome its recurrent and incessant crises through wise government guidance, thus permitting continuous enrichment of the deserving few without the impoverishment of the majority. In this thinking there are big blind spots born of self-interest.

It is clear that since the great depression, the government has succeeded in maintaining a relatively steady rate of economic growth. To the liberal capitalist the cyclical problems of capitalism have been solved. But there is the equally obvious fact that it took World War II and a continuous war economy ever since to maintain that growth. The capitalist crisis merely changed its form. From a permanent depression America moved to a permanent war economy from which there is no escape except back to the permanent depression.

However, the subsidization of capitalist economy through militarism is not a *solution*. It requires that the capitalist state borrow on the future labor of society for its holding operation today – at a continuously increasing rate. And even so, the crisis asserts itself through inflation which has quantitative limits beyond which monetary and class stability are both impossible.

The realities of the capitalist crisis are confronted by Kennedy as President. Peace, full-employment and other desirable objectives have to be pursued, not directly but through the assuring of markets and profits to the capitalists, leaving human welfare to appear, if it will, as a by-product.

Basically a capitalist politician, Kennedy also is the son of a millionaire. The profit system has been very good to him. He never knew the poverty, hunger and insecurity that most of the human race knows or has known at some time.

He is confident to the point of arrogance. He is rash. He is anxious for quick victories, impatient and accustomed to getting what he wants. He is petulant when frustrated. And as President, he is dangerous for he is fighting for a cause that can't be won.

The real Kennedy pierced through the 'image' in the first crisis of his Administration. After his criminal and stupid attempt to carry out the plans for an invasion of Cuba, he spoke to American editors gathered in Washington. He spoke quite frankly of the 'sobering' lessons of the Cuban fiasco. His final words, spoken with evident emotion, were, 'Let me then make clear as the President of the United States that I am determined upon our system's survival and success, regardless of the cost and regardless of the peril'.

In this peroration, he dropped his usual use of the diplomatic, euphemistic term 'freedom', and made his meaning amply clear with the brass-knuckle term 'system', i.e., capitalism.

Kennedy's Leadership

Kennedy's real occupation in the White House was revealed in his speech to the National Association of Manufacturers on Dec. 6, 1961. Here the President and the millionaire were merged into one. He was at ease. He spoke well, permitting himself impromptu departures from a prepared text. And he was far more frank than older, more experienced men like Franklin D. Roosevelt would ever have permitted themselves to be.

The burden of this speech dealt with the immediate critical problems of capitalist economy. Kennedy talked about the 'payments balance' between the US and the rest of the world, especially Europe. He pointed out that US businessmen now own about $45 billion in capital invested abroad. In 1960 the 'long-term outward flow of capital funds was $1,700 million. The return was $2,300 million'. So far so good – for US Big Business.

But the American people, with their tax money, spend annually about $3 billion abroad for military bases designed to protect this capital and keep the profits rolling into the pockets of the American rich. As a result of this and other factors, the US has suffered a payments deficit of nearly $4 billion a year, with a net loss in US gold reserves of $5 billion over a 4-year period. (Let no one propose to look for a solution of the US 'payments problem' to the underdeveloped sector of world economy. The 'take' from there of $1,300 million for an investment of $200 million is already so 'balanced' to the US benefit that revolution is now the problem. It is better to deal with a potential than an actual revolution).

Kennedy proposes to change tax and trade policies in order to stop, or slow the flow of capital to Europe. And he proposes to soften the blow that will be dealt European economy by having the US workers and small businessmen (those who lacked enough capital to get on the European gravy train) share the blow by submitting to direct competition with lower European costs of production.

It also 'happens' that Kennedy's proposals answer the immediate problems of US capital in Europe. US industrialists moved into Europe after World War II on an unprecedented scale, and asserted their domination by unifying Europe into the European Economic Community. But this expansion and growth within Europe is reaching its apex. There is no longer room for all 'to make an honest buck'. Competition is growing acute and Europe, under US domination, must once again expand outward. Where? Kennedy's answer: to the United States.

Cars produced in Europe by General Motors, for example, will then compete with cars produced in the US by General Motors. General Motors is the winner, no matter what the outcome. The ultimate effect of this competition will be to lower the wage differential between the two continents.

Having conquered Europe economically, US industrialists hope to conquer the US, using its lower labor costs in Europe as the battering ram.

Certainly Kennedy's program contains 'risks', 'sacrifices' and requires 'courage'. If he succeeds in stopping or even slowing the flow of capital to Europe, the stabilization of capitalism in Europe will be disrupted. And there the working class is powerfully organized as an independent political force. At the same time, class relations in the US will be disrupted.

The immediate peril that Kennedy confronts therefore, is that the axis of the world revolution will shift back from the undeveloped areas of the world to the industrial heart of world capitalism, the US and Europe. He hopes that class-collaborationist control of both labor movements can be maintained. But in any event, the gamble must be made.

Kennedy will have some more 'sobering' experiences in the period ahead. He will learn that the American working class will not take kindly to a lowering of its living standards. He will be reminded that the American workers have never been defeated in struggle. He will discover that American labor is not dead – it has been only sleeping. Kennedy will need much more than a monolithic and servile press. He will need more than admonitions 'to be calm'. And his pleas for sacrifice will not be welcomed by those who lack Kennedy's stake in the system.

Not the 'Communists' but the capitalist crisis itself is preparing to draw onto the world scene the powerful revolutionary forces of Europe and the United

States. The embattled poor in the rest of the world will soon find an ally worthy of their own heroism. Their victory, and all humanity's, will thus be assured.

7 Preparing for the Next Wave of Radicalism in the United States[26]
(1963)

Political Committee, Socialist Workers Party

1. Today the Socialist Workers Party is in a situation where its prolonged isolation is drawing to a close but is not yet over and where any breakthrough into the mass movement has barely begun. This stage of transition presents difficult problems of adjustment and activity to our cadres. It demands a clear understanding of the course and aims of our movement from its origins and a firm grasp of its irreplaceable role in reenergizing, educating and leading the vanguard forces of socialism in the United States.

2. From its inception in the Left Opposition of the Twenties that rebelled against Stalinization of the Communist Party, the SWP has worked to build a revolutionary working class party in this country. We seek to break through all forms of class collaboration and lead the workers in struggle against capitalist rule, with the aim of taking power under the democratic rule of the workers themselves. In domestic policy we advocate nationalization of the means of production under workers control, as the fundamental starting point from which to assure economic prosperity, social betterment and equal rights for all. We call for an end to the capitalist war policy intended to perpetuate imperialist exploitation of peoples in other lands. Our country's full power must be mobilized in support of the quickening advance toward an international system of planned economy as the basis for a world socialist society of peace prosperity, freedom and equality. We hold that war dangers, economic insecurity restrictions of democracy, and racial discrimination will continue until the workers of the United States take the socialist road.

3. Throughout our 35-year history adverse objective conditions have kept us in a minority position within American radicalism. Only today does the situation show promise of a change for the better. Until recent times both the Stalinist and social democratic tendencies considerably outweighed us in the mass

---

26   Socialist Workers Party Political Committee 1963.

movement. Although politically motivated by subordination to wholly different power centers in Moscow and Washington, both of these tendencies follow reformist policies. The cost to mankind has been great. The resurgent labor movement of the Thirties was prevented from passing beyond simple unionism to the formation of an independent working class party. A class collaborationist bureaucracy was able to impose its dictatorial rule over the unions. The workers were kept tied to support of capitalist foreign poiicy at increasing expense to their own class interests.

4. These reformist policies could predominate for so long because of a combination of objective factors. New Deal concessions served to stem the rise of anti-capitalist sentiment among the masses in the Thirties. The stage was thus set to halt labor s upsurge at the union level and keep the workers under capitalist domination through the labor-Democratic coalition. Only a class struggle policy could have saved the workers from this political trap, but the reformist line of the Stalinists and social democrats tipped the scales toward labor subservience to the Democratic Party. These political ties have since been maintained under conditions of relative economic stability thanks to limited capitalist concessions that have given labor the illusion it can prosper under the present social order. To help maintain acceptance of the status quo in the face of deteriorating social conditions, the capitalist rulers resort to witch hunt measures ranging from vicious attacks on opponents of their regime to continuous encroachment on the democratic rights of labor as a whole. Under these conditions all radical tendencies became seriously isolated from the mass movement and had to fight for their very survival.

5. The prolonged ebb in the class struggle since 1947, combined with the witch hunt, served to whittle down the forces and resources of the SWP. Some individual members dropped out from plain discouragement. Others broke away in groups, seeking a quick and easy way to get around the adverse objective conditions, only to abandon all the sooner their previous principles and any identification with serious revolutionary politics. Tendencies arose to make programmatic compromises in an attempt to reach broader forces. Ideas were cooked up to launch valiant actions by a handful as a substitute for mass struggle. On the opposite side the SWP had to consciously counteract the danger of adjustment to a sectarian vegetation apart from the real working class movement. Time kept taking its toll on our human material, while few young people were finding their way into our ranks. The party was put to severe trials of its capacity to retain theoretical clarity, programmatic firmness, and realism in action. Our ability to do what was necessary and possible without trying to race ahead of actual political developments was tested along with our capacity to keep abreast of whatever opportunities opened up in the class struggle.

6. Years before the worst of our isolation set in, a new revolutionary ascent had begun elsewhere in the world. This period started during World War II with the advent of social revolution in Yugoslavia. Then came extension of the Soviet bloc into Eastern Europe and emergence of the Soviet Union itself as the second-greatest world power. The victorious revolution in China was the first of the colonial uprisings to eject and push back the imperialists, and even to checkmate their intervention in the Korean War. One result of these developments was the emergence within the Soviet bloc of a rise in mass opposition to bureaucratic dictatorship and special privilege. The 1953 workers uprising in East Germany, Khrushchev's attack on Stalin at the Twentieth Congress of the Soviet Communist Party and the 1956 struggles for workers control in Poland and Hungary marked the beginning of a crisis of Stalinism. The repercussions of this crisis inside the US Communist Party gave rise to a general shakeup in the radical movement. Sincere revolutionaries who had long trusted the Kremlin bureaucrats learned they had been betrayed. Some who were already worn thin simply quit radical politics. Others solved their personal crisis by moving toward political adaptation to imperialism. Those who had become case-hardened stuck with the CP. But the sturdiest fighters in the CP ranks began to search for a new revolutionary course.

7. In an energetic search for new allies and recruits the SWP intervened in the radical shakeup with a regroupment policy. Leaving open the question of organizational forms if a substantial regroupment should become possible, we put our stress on revolutionary principles and genuine democratic-centralism in the construction and operation of the revolutionary party. Although some new forces were won over to our revolutionary-socialist concepts, in the end we had to draw a largely negative balance sheet concerning the potential for allies or adherents within opponent radical tendencies. Experience revealed that significant reinforcements to our ranks can now come only from the mass movement, primarily from the worker, student and minority youth. It also became clear that a new relationship of forces is developing within the radical movement, giving new advantages to our revolutionary-socialist tendency as against the Stalinists and social democrats.

8. Generally speaking, the crisis of world Communism has acted as a depressant upon many one-time revolutionists. Already wearied and disillusioned, they have reacted by retreat and withdrawal from political life, reducing the effective forces of the radical movement as a whole. The main offset to that trend has come from the impact of the Cuban revolution within the United States. The Cuban developments have served as an energizing factor, attracting young reinforcements to radical politics. Cuba lays bare the class truth about imperialism. It puts all radical tendencies to the test of revolutionary principles,

exposing the social democrats as political hacks for the State Department and the Stalinists as servile agents of the Kremlin bureaucracy. The outbreak of the Moscow-Peking dispute over policy in the struggle against imperialism has still further divided and demoralized the CP circles. With firm adherence to revolutionary principles and the necessary tactical flexibility, the SWP can intervene in these favorable developments to increase its specific weight and attractive power within the radical movement. We can expect our prospects of expansion to be improved still further by the sharpening of social contradictions within this country.

9. The impact of the ascending world revolution of our time steadily worsens the situation of capitalism and sends shock waves into the imperialist strongholds. The overturn of capitalist property relations in the expanding bloc of workers states has produced a corresponding shrinkage in the number of countries remaining open to imperialist exploitation. Intensification of independence struggles within the exploited countries leads toward curtailment of imperialist profits and nationalization of capitalist holdings. This drives the imperialist powers to stiffen their competition on a contracting world market and look for ways to edge into one another's internal markets. These general trends combine to intensify class contradictions within the imperialist countries and undermine the social equilibrium needed to safeguard capitalist rule.

10. Pushed back toward their own borders by the advanced of revolutionary forces abroad and threatened by social unrest internally, the imperialists prepare and keep in reserve the ultimate and catastrophic solution of all-out war. Their immediate aim is to stem the revolutionary tide in the hope of rolling it back and extending capitalist exploitation once again throughout the world. But their strategic aims are blocked by powerful forces. Since the Soviet Union possesses a nuclear arsenal no less deadly than that of the United States, global war would mean the virtual extermination of humanity. Mass consciousness of this grim prospect tends to restrain the imperialists from shaping a direct course toward general war as the central feature of their foreign policy. Instead they proceed from the initial premise of 'limited' non-nuclear wars, using the pretext of a 'deterrent' against general war as the excuse for continuing to stockpile nuclear weapons. Military interventions occur repeatedly and on an ascending scale in an effort to snuff out anti-capitalist revolts (South Vietnam). These imperialist interventions often run up against one or another form of counteraction by the Soviet bloc. When that happens the imperialists do not shrink from going right to the brink of nuclear war in the showdown, as did Kennedy, most recently and most recklessly, in the Cuban crisis.

11. The basic alternative is clearly posed: either the workers revolution in the industrially-advanced countries will disarm capitalism, or the world will

continue to risk nuclear destruction. Above all American imperialism must be disarmed by the people of the United States. That iron fact must be central to the consciousness of revolutionists in this country. In fighting to replace capitalist rule, the Marxists must proceed from a realistic appraisal of developing class struggle trends in this country. American imperialism has passed the apex of its world power and today stands subject to a process of decline. Compelled to sustain crippled allies in the fight against ever-stronger revolutionary forces abroad, its foundations become undermined by all the weaknesses of world capitalism. Its worsening world position tends to become converted into a domestic crisis, which in its further unfolding can arouse the greatest power of all within the United States, the working class. The capitalist rulers confront the following contradiction: They need relative class peace at home in order to carry out their foreign policy. Yet their increasingly severe problems abroad impel them toward austerity measures at home. They must stiffen their resistance to mass demands for social and economic concessions and move toward stronger repressive measures to curb mass opposition to their policies. As a consequence the equilibrium of class forces is becoming undermined.

12. American imperialism as passed the apex if its world power and today stands subject to a process of decline. Compelled to sustain crippled allies in the fight against ever-stronger revolutionary forces abroad, its foundations become undermined by all the weaknesses if world capitalism. Its worsening world position tends to become converted into a domestic crisis, which in its further unfolding can arouse the greatest power of all within the United States, the working class. The capitalist rulers confront the following contradiction: They need relative class peace at home in order to carry out their foreign policy. Yet their increasingly severe problems abroad impel them toward austerity measures at home. They must stiffen their resistance to mass demands for social and economic concessions and move toward stronger repressive measures to curb mass opposition to their policies. As a consequence the equilibrium of class forces is becoming undermined.

13. During the Cuban crisis the people of the United States were put through the wringer as never before. Nuclear death seemed imminent unless one man, the same Kennedy who had precipitated the danger, backed off from playing chicken with hydrogen bombs. Most poignant was the plight of the young. Children in grade school asked one another, 'What are you going to be *if* you grow up?' People are told to have faith in a government repeatedly caught lying; a government that cynically asserts it will continue to withhold vital facts; a government that takes witch hunt reprisals against those who openly disagree with its foreign policy.

14. Worsening social conditions blights the lives of millions. Children in the city slums have no place to play, and except for brutal police control they get little attention from the government. The nation's school system has become a disgrace. Decent housing at relatively low rentals is in short supply. Old-age pensions fall short of minimum needs; many retired citizens get no pension at all. Millions hunger while the government stockpiles surplus food. Even among those able to eat and live reasonably well there is a growing sense of economic insecurity.

15. A capitalist crisis of overproduction has gradually been developing. At present there is a gap of $50 billion between consumer demand and productive capacity, according to government estimates. There is a serious lag in capital investment for plant and equipment, as indicated by the sluggish annual rate of industrial growth. Loss of boom incentive from this key source portends a new recession. To make matters worse, the United States faces stiffer international competition on a contracting world market. These difficulties, together with related factors, are preparing a critical economic situation.

16. Thus far government intervention has delayed and modified the economic troubles inherent in the capitalist cycle. Massive expenditures for war, hiked to unprecedented billions by Kennedy, have been pumped into the economy with some stimulating effect. Capitalists have received lucrative war orders at a handsome profit, along with subsidies and tax write-offs. The economy has paid a price for this shoring up of the profit system. The national debt has soared, weakening the dollar. Inflation has been further accelerated by the unfavorable balance in international payments and the consequent gold drain. For the people generally government economic policy has meant stiff taxes and rising prices. Waning consumer purchasing power has been sustained because they have turned to heavier installment buying, mortgaging tomorrow's income in order to acquire comforts today.

17. Government pump-priming has not brought uninterrupted prosperity. It has achieved relative economic stability within the framework of a series of boom-recession fluctuations. Now several factors indicate a downturn within the cyclical pattern. Each boom becomes more sluggish, more short lived. The time gap between recessions narrows. Every oscillation leaves in its wake a larger residue of chronic unemployment. Meanwhile under-employment and inadequate purchasing power intensifies the search for jobs, giving rise to the national pastime known as moonlighting. Stated generally the economic trend is one of a turn from relative prosperity, through a process of developing stagnation, to a pattern of more precipitous decline.

18. Concerned about the dangers to capitalist stability and earnings, the Kennedy administration has advanced a program of corporate tax cuts, inten-

ded to stimulate capital investment. The masses are promised a slight drop in individual income taxes, but for them the main result will be newly-inflated prices caused by further government borrowing. Kennedy's basic aim is to counteract the declining rate of profit by inducing capital investment for automation, general technological change and overall cuts in production costs. That means intensified exploitation of labor with the prospect of even fewer jobs at a time when prosperity is already by-passing millions.

19. Nothing more graphically expresses the bankruptcy of our economic system than the rise in chronic unemployment. According to Department of Labor figures, which notoriously understate reality, the average rate of unemployment for 1962 stood at 5.6 percent. For unskilled and older workers, youth, Negroes and other minorities the rate was at least double this national average. Government figures show that creation of new jobs through general economic growth has slowed down to about one-half million a year. On the other hand at least a million workers are displaced annually through technological change, while another million young people are entering the labor market. The result is a built-in yearly rise of around one and one-half million in chronic unemployment apart from the victims of slumps in production. These cold statistics spell economic catastrophe for the millions of people affected, doubly so when half of them are denied jobless benefits.

20. Hardest hit are the minority peoples who suffer discrimination not only in employment but also in housing, education, medical care, social welfare and all other spheres of ordinary life. They have no stake in the foreign policy of a government that offers them little more than empty promises and the discipline of a cop's club. Nor do they have any reason to subordinate the struggle for their democratic rights to the capitalist-defined 'national interest'. Drawing that conclusion for themselves, the Negro people stand in the vanguard of the battle to win equal rights for all minority peoples. With increasing militancy and on an ever-broader scale, they are rejecting policies of gradual reform and fighting for freedom now, not at some vague future time. They are breaking the old patterns of white domination over their movement and asserting their right to have decisive leadership in their struggle for emancipation.

21. This radicalization of the Negro people constitutes the most important single political development within the country. It can be expected to have more profound repercussions throughout the population, generating new militancy among all whose basic interests are violated under capitalist rule. First to be aroused are the youth. The vanguard role of Negro students in the civil rights struggle is paralleled to a certain extent by the increased participation of students in the fight against the war danger. Still to be heard from are the young

workers, although their worsening situation goads them toward action against the bosses and the capitalist government.

22. Growing campus support to Negro freedom fighters gives evidence of revulsion against the status quo. Student unrest is building around the war issue. Many listen with an open mind to socialist views in the struggle for peace. Currents of sympathy with the Cuban revolution flow through the schools. Some students are coming to identify themselves with the aims of the socialist movement. Although the bulk of the student body has yet to become politically active, those who are turning rebel show youth's normal impulse to want to do something about a situation they consider intolerable.

23. Student rebels and aroused women who mean business in the fight against war have been entering the peace movement in substantial numbers. They come as critical-minded people looking for a way to achieve their aims. Many are uncommitted to any program or affiliation. Their entry is changing the general features of the peace movement. Not having a class struggle orientation, their outlook has overtones of pacifism and reformism. But they are neither professional pacifists nor typical reformists. Even less are they conscious radicals, though they keep pushing beyond the bounds set by pacifist and reformist leaders. What they want is an effective program of action and the strongest possible force from which nobody who fights against war should be excluded. They don't trust the foreign policy of the capitalist government and they want to do something about it. Seeing no other place to turn many put their hopes in the United Nations. Young people do not look instinctively to the labor movement for help, because all their lives the trade unions have appeared conservative and ineffective where major social issues are involved.

24. The capitalist-minded bureaucrats who dominate the unions give unqualified support to the imperialist foreign policy. In return they hope to secure voluntary economic and social concessions from the bosses, or at least from the government. Within industry they side with the bosses against union militants. Through support to the Democratic Party, they keep the workers captive to capitalist political rule. Under this bureaucratic control labor has lost virtually all its capacity to influence national policy, job conditions have steadily worsened, union growth has failed utterly to keep pace with the expanding labor force. In short, trade unionism has fallen into stagnation through adaptation to the capitalist status quo.

25. Saddled with a conservative union bureaucracy, the workers now face a capitalist drive to solve the economic difficulties at labor's expense. The bosses have launched a three-pronged offensive: on the job, in contact negotiations and through the government. Through technological change and intensified speedup they are whittling down available jobs. They oppose union demands

for reduced hours with no cut in pay. They are determined to hold the line on wages and demand wage cuts if they think there is any chance of getting away with these. To cripple union resistance capitalist politicians call for stiffer anti-labor laws, including a ban on industry-wide bargaining, further curbs on the right to strike and use of anti-trust laws against the unions. Kennedy openly wields his presidential authority on the side of the bosses. The mounting attacks on the unions are revealing to an increased extent the basic conflict of interests between labor and capital.

26. Unemployment has become the major problem confronting labor. As concern for their job security becomes aggravated by boss provocations, more and more workers grow angry and militant. Skilled workers, not being exempt from job attrition and boss attacks, share this changing class mood. Conditions become increasingly favorable for a fighting leadership to forge a high degree of class solidarity, reducing the danger of the bosses using one or another strata of the workers to split their ranks as a class. So strong are the pressures that the bureaucrats find themselves forced to do something. At the lower levels of the bureaucracy, among those closest to the ranks, some capacity is shown to give the bosses a fight. At the summit Meany, Reuther and Co. have asked the government to legislate a shorter work week, and after Kennedy had vetoed the idea even repeated politely that it still ought to be done. The union ranks are not so timid. In several places they have struck for a shorter work week and in resistance to the boss attacks on their conditions. Wage demands have usually represented an attempt to offset rising prices rather than an effort to raise living standards. When a strike achieves even a very modest victory on the work-week issue, other workers take new courage to do battle in their industry. This trend can rise sharply with contract negotiations coming up this year in several basic industries.

27. Every partial union action poses larger issues confronting the workers. The need for a change in leadership grows more acute. Splits in the bureaucracy, such as occurred when the AFL-CIO threw the Teamsters Union to the Kennedy wolves, weaken its monolithic control. Teamster officials, fighting for their union lives, have gone so far as to propose a labor march on Washington to protest the union-busting drive, an action unthinkable to Meany, Reuther and Co. Rifts in bureaucratic solidarity can help open the way for the ranks to assert their views on policy issues and fight for more democratic control over union affairs. These changing trends open new possibilities to promote consciousness of the need for a left wing founded on a class struggle program.

28. Labor on corporation farms has little or no union protection. Worst off are the migratory workers, composed mainly of sharecroppers and small farmers uprooted by growth of monopoly on the land, or Latin Americans brought

in temporarily at times of peak employment. Whole families live as nomads, seeking work by moving from region to region according to seasonal variations in agriculture. Parents and children toil in the fields at starvation wages, living from hand to mouth even when there is work. During slack periods they get no jobless pay nor do they receive other social security benefits. For them daily life is grinding poverty, the future under capitalism a bleak one. Theirs is a burning need to have a labor government.

29. Working farmers are being hard hit by the chronic crisis of overproduction in agriculture. Operating small units and having little investment capital, they are unable to compete successfully with the big corporation farms. Caught between rising production costs and falling prices on farm produce, they are driven toward bankruptcy. Those who go under have little choice but to seek work as agricultural laborers or enter the rat race for jobs in the cities. Excluded by corporate interests from any control over old-line farm organizations, the working farmers are getting together on their own. An outstanding example is the National Farmers Organization founded in 1955. At the outset the NFO tried to compete with the corporations in exerting political pressure on the capitalist government. Failing to get anywhere with that policy, it turned to withholding produce from the market in a demand for better prices. In conducting these strikes the NFO has tended to study union methods of struggle and welcome fraternal relations with the labor movement. Today many working farmers, disenchanted with Big Business policies, would be ready for an anti-capitalist political alliance with the trade unions.

30. At present only the Negro struggle shows a consistent rise in militancy. Upsurges among other sections of the masses remain much more limited in scope and are usually followed by ebbs of some duration. Union struggles run up against government interference on behalf of the bosses. Attempts to influence foreign policy through protest actions, as in the recent Cuban crisis, fail to get any response from the government. A sense of frustration develops, bringing a temporary decline in militancy. But the worsening situation compels a return to action and deepens the search for more effective means of struggle. Each clash with the capitalist class brings into sharper focus the need for a basic change in the power structure and generates new motion toward a break with capitalist politics.

31. Pronounced shifts in political outlook are developing within the Negro movement. Significant forces nationally are beginning to call for independent Negro candidacies in opposition to both the Democrats and Republicans. The stiffening battle for Negro voting rights in the South infers motion in the same direction, even though Southern Negroes can also be expected to intervene as a voting bloc within the two-party system. As the trend toward independent

Negro political action gains momentum it will cut across the labor-Democratic coalition and stimulate labor party sentiment in the unions.

32. A potential for anti-capitalist political action is building up within the peace movement. Militants want to run people for office who will really fight for peace, even though their limited grasp of the class issues involved leaves them subject to political deception. They tend to ask only for a bare assertion of peace aims and take at face value the pretensions of middle class intellectuals who offer themselves as candidates. These liberal practitioners of reformism and pacifism then present the peace issue as though it were an abstract question, divorced from and standing above the class struggle for power in decision-making. As a result the peace fighters are held back from a break with capitalist politics. Parallel misleadership in the unions helps to disorient them so that labor loses the support of potential political allies within the peace movement.

33. Basic weaknesses plaguing the unions stem primarily from the labor-Democratic coalition. Subordination to capitalist political rule undermines labor's ability to influence national policy and correspondingly strengthens anti-labor tendencies. Eisenhower's election in 1952 marked a definitive end to any significant expression of working class interests through factional intervention in capitalist politics. Kennedy's later defeat of Nixon raised false hopes of a return to the New Deal, but meaningful concessions to the unions are no longer in the cards. The relative economic stability on which the labor-Democratic coalition has rested has begun to disintegrate. To ease its own difficulties the capitalist class is moving to intensify its exploitation of labor; the Democratic administration dutifully obeys its master's command. The inevitable result of such a trend will be clashes between capital and labor, occurring in new political forms and reaching new degrees of intensity.

34. As the struggle sharpens, class collaborationist policies become less and less tenable. Relations between the unions and the government grow strained. Breaks in the customary patterns of the workers' lives produce changes in their political thought. They will begin to reappraise the whole question of support to the Democrats. Limitations in union power, manifested at the industrial level under conditions of economic decline, will tend to steer the energies of frustrated workers onto the political arena in new and higher forms. Class battles that start in traditional union fashion will lead in the direction of open clashes with the government. Conditions will ripen for a leap from simple unionism to formation of an independent labor party. Once in being, a labor party would experience rapid growth, drawing to its support unorganized, retired and unemployed workers, minority peoples, students, peace fighters, farmers and sections of the urban middle class. Although a labor party can be expected to start with a reformist leadership and outlook, its radicalization would be

speeded up by reactionary counter-attacks from the capitalist class. The repercussions would tend to pose point blank the need for labor to take complete power and proceed to a basic reorganization of society.

35. Capitalist reaction to a potential labor radicalization is previewed by existing trends on the right. Since the McCarthy period incipient fascist cadres have been crystallizing as a reflex to the deepening capitalist crisis. The latest manifestation of this process is the rise of the Birchites. Rightist groups are beginning to enter candidates in primary elections and put up their own tickets in general elections, seeking to build conservative blocs within the two-party system. Labor's political default helps them gain unwarranted support among potential allies of the working class. However, the ultra-right remains a minority force which receives only limited capitalist support. With labor tied to their political setup, most capitalists favor continuance of the political status quo which enables them to rule over the country and implement an aggressive foreign policy to promote their own interests.

36. Thanks to the misleaders of labor, liberalism still serves as a bellwether to lead the masses into the capitalist political fold. The workers are told that, if only they will help to elect more liberal Democrats, their interests can be protected through reforms under capitalism. But official liberalism headed by the Kennedy administration is moving steadily to the right, shaving down its promises of reform and exposing its political impotence. Instead of reacting sympathetically to union struggles in defense of the workers interests, liberals deplore 'immoderate' demands and 'stubborn' strikes as they help prepare the way for new anti-labor laws.

37. Despite these cold political facts, the union bureaucrats cling harder than ever to the liberals as they try to maintain the outlived labor-Democratic coalition. Communist Party leaders urge the masses to unite with the liberals against an alleged rival power center outside the White House, which means in effect to support the Kennedy Democrats. The Norman Thomas socialists call for a realignment within the two-party system in order to concentrate the liberals with labor under the Democratic Party banner. In the name of defending liberalism against reaction, Negroes are tied to a Jim Crow party, peace fighters to a war party and labor to a capitalist party.

38. The common line advanced by all these misleaders of labor is twice-dangerous because of the devious arguments they present. They succeed in tricking people who want a political change but don't know how to achieve it, putting them at the mercy of the same old policies dressed up in new words. These deceived rebels can develop into conscious political opponents of capitalism with the necessary help. Their problem is to understand that the social difficulties plaguing them, no matter what precise forms they may take, all

stem from one fundamental cause, the bankruptcy of the capitalist society in which we live. They need political analysis, education and leadership capable of mobilizing the full power of the working class and its allies in all-out struggle against capitalist rule. As the first step in that direction they need help to make a clean break with capitalist politics and form an independent labor party.

39. Fulfillment of the political needs of such newly radicalized people becomes central to our activity as a revolutionary vanguard party. Our main task is to develop a propaganda offensive around the key issues of the day, with all party activities related directly to the general campaign perspectives. This means application of the appropriate slogans and demands from our transition program (sliding scale of wages and hours, labor party, etc.) which are becoming more pertinent every day. Our political analysis and proposals for action should be focused on the fight for peace, civil rights, economic security, social welfare and civil liberties. New militancy developing around these issues will in turn help to promote class struggle policies in the mass movement and demonstrate the need for an independent labor party. Our polemics against reformist ideas should be addressed primarily to politically inexperienced people who are interested in explanations rather: than denunciations. Our press should serve as the spearhead and main organizer of the propaganda offensive, with its key functions reinforced through circulation of our general literature. Propagation of our views should be intensified through forums, public debates and other available means.

40. At the present stage, our work on the electoral arena remains concentrated primarily on running party candidates where possible for public office. While continuing our present efforts to enter party candidates in local elections wherever practical, we must also prepare to run our own presidential ticket in the 1964 elections, viewing the presidential campaign as our foremost propaganda action.

41. Our mass work must be linked with the general propaganda offensive. So far as we have party militants functioning in mass organizations they will find new opportunities to participate in spontaneous actions and to advance our class struggle policies. But whether or not we have anyone in a given situation, the party's general propaganda efforts will gradually extend our influence among the masses. Where comrades are engaged in mass work the broad ideological offensive will be vital to their functions, since their own activity remains essentially propagandistic. Looked at in larger terms, the overall party campaign serves to generalize, coordinate and impart a central focus to the various forms of work in mass organizations. It also enables us to step up recruitment, which helps to reinforce party cadres where they now function in the mass movement and to develop fresh nuclei elsewhere through new people won over

to our program. These primary considerations must be kept in mind in deciding the division of labor between mass work and general party activity.

42. Party growth may be accomplished in two ways. One is patient, persistent recruitment of individuals. Though this process is never out of season, it should not blind us to any realistic opportunities through the second form of growth. We must remain alert for signs of any trend toward our programmatic positions that might develop among other radical groups or within larger formations. Should such a trend arise, we would reach out toward those coming our way, seeking to win them over completely to our program. But we do not water down our program and adapt ourselves to the political views of others in eagerness to gain numerical strength. Such a course would only disorient our cadres and compromise the party. We proceed always on the premise that only the program can create the party. To act on any other basis would lead to political ruin.

43. There are small groups now functioning on their own after having broken away from Communist Party control but none of them measure up to our programmatic criteria for a radical regroupment. They tend either to cling to Democratic Party politics or to give little more than lip service to independent socialist and labor political action. They show pronounced tendencies to substitute a small band of radicals for the necessary mass force in impatient efforts to speed up the class conflict. They also incline to resort to factional exploitation of actual mass struggles where they are able to intervene, doing injury to the struggle itself and thereby compromising the whole radical movement. We must frankly express our criticisms of these false policies and explain our counter-views. Political firmness toward these opponent tendencies does not prevent us from maintaining fraternal relations with them or with dissidents in the SP. We are ready to cooperate with all other radicals in opposition to the witch hunt, in counter-rallies against the ultra right, in peace demonstrations, in defense of the Cuban revolution, in support to civil rights and trade union struggles. But in no case will we go along with reckless attempts to substitute a radical vanguard for the masses.

44. Our paramount task is to reach out for people now becoming radicalized. Major attention must be given to work in support of Negroes and other minority peoples fighting for their civil rights. In addition to doing all we can to support the general battle for full equality, we have a special role to play. If the Negro minority is to achieve its objectives, it must split the white majority and win one section over to its side. Such a division among the whites can develop only along class lines. Our special task is to help win white workers over to active support of the Negro freedom fighters and in the process promote an anti-capitalist alliance of the labor and Negro movements. We begin

this attempt by pressing for union support of the civil rights struggle and by backing demands of Negro workers for democratic rights on the job and in the unions. These actions help weaken the union bureaucracy and strengthen rank and file action to win internal democracy. They also serve to intensify demands for effective struggle in defense of the workers interests and to speed the fusion of Negro and white militants into a left wing union force. The general process leads toward a leap from simple union action to formation of a labor party and in doing so improves our chances of recruiting both Negro and white workers into the SWP.

45. Full backing must be given to political work among student youth through close fraternal collaboration between the party and youth organizations. In addition to contact established in campus activity, students and other militants can be reached by way of the peace movement. An effective approach to these elements requires a combination of political firmness and tactical flexibility. We support all demands, limited though they may be, that bring the peace fighters into conflict with Washington's war policy and help generate anti-capitalist sentiments. We support united actions around these demands and oppose efforts to exclude any tendency from the movement. At the same time we combat the efforts of liberals, reformists and pacifists to disorient the peace fighters politically. We undertake to advance our views in a way that will bring the most sympathetic hearing, presenting our program in a patient, reasoned, educational manner. We follow a similar policy in the case of the Cuban defense movement where comparable forces are involved. Ad hoc formations of the kind that arise in a movement of this nature are necessarily limited in capacity. Their struggle potential is of an intermittent character, depending on the degrees of intensity in the imperialist attack on Cuba. Ability to maintain consistent propaganda activity, and to develop it in sufficient depth, is restricted by the heterogeneous political composition of such ad hoc formations. In view of these limitations our support must be realistically attuned to their actual capacity to meet the needs of the day.

46. If we are to build a revolutionary working class party there can be no temporizing where basic class interests are involved, nor can there by any needless tolerance of obstacles to the propagation of our program. Militants moving toward revolutionary positions are already disoriented enough through lack of union intervention on their side in struggles around major social issues. Our role is to serve as a bridge in historic consciousness of the basic vitality and revolutionary power of the working class. We need to explain over and over again how revolutionary leaderships are built by linking together workers with class struggle experience and middle class individuals capable of fully identifying themselves with the workers' cause. Young intellectuals who manifest

that capacity are coming toward and already entering our party. If they recognize the revolutionary capacities of workers in the party, and if the workers understand the worth of intellectuals dedicated to the revolutionary struggle, then the party will be capable of creating valuable new cadres of leadership quality. To help both the young workers and intellectuals in their political development, internal party education should be systematically related to external activity in basic terms of our theory, program, strategy and tactics.

47. For the coming period the SWP will still have to swim against the stream, contending with an unfavorable environment. The principal tasks in this period of transition are to hold firm to our principles and outlook and prepare those points of support which will enable the party to move forward most swiftly and effectively as soon as the anticipated openings in the next stage of the class struggle emerge.

8 Kennedy's War in Vietnam[27]
(*1963*)

Theodore Edwards (Edmund Kovacs)

Like its predecessors, the Kennedy administration continues to support every reactionary or counter-revolutionary ruling clique in the under-developed countries of the world under the guise of fighting 'communism'. Economic and military subsidies to these native oppressors continue to be misrepresented to the American taxpayer as 'aid' to the colonial masses. Whenever such assistance to kings, sheiks, assorted tyrants and puppet rulers fails to keep the colonial peoples in check, the Kennedy administration has shown no hesitancy in resorting to clandestine CIA maneuvers, military shows-of-force, or outright armed intervention.

Its most flagrant intrusion in Asia is the current military operation in South Vietnam. (Twelve thousand US 'advisors' are busily engaged in what the *N.Y. Times* calls 'the secret war'). The *Times* editorial of October 17, 1962 observes that 'a pall of unnecessary secrecy, which far transcends military requirements, has obscured from the public too much of the progress of a war to which we are now fully committed'.

'Deliberate policy restrictions by Washington and by the South Vietnamese government in Saigon' are blamed for this lack of information.

The Soviet Policy

The Western imperialists are not the only international force intervening in Southeast Asia. Since World War II, the Soviet bureaucracy has been applying its interpretation of 'peaceful co-existence' to the Indo-Chinese revolution.

In World War II, the Japanese occupied Indochina, a colony of the French for 80 years. The collapse of Japan in 1945 swept the Communist Party dominated

---

27   Edwards 1963.

Viet Minh movement under Ho Chi Minh into control of virtually the entire country. Under pressure of the Kremlin and of the French CP, however, the Ho Chi Minh government agreed to the incorporation of Vietnam into the 'French Union'. As soon as the French had landed enough troops, they abrogated all accords with Ho and initiated full scale warfare against the Viet Minh.

Under instructions from Moscow, the French Communist deputies voted credits to finance the war in Indochina that was carried on by the various coalition governments in which they participated until they were thrown out of office in May 1947. For nine long years of bloody civil war, the Viet Minh peasant fighters continued to battle the French expeditionary forces, inflicting 172,000 casualties and suffering untold casualties themselves.

Stalin recognized the Ho government – not in 1945 when it had undisputed control – but in 1950 when it was fighting desperately to regain power from the French. The Kremlin's hand, moreover, had been forced by the arrival of the Chinese Communist armies at the borders of Indochina in 1949, at which time Mao Tse-tung recognized the Ho government.

The Viet Minh fighters defeated the French at Dienbienphu in 1954, despite the $5 billion that the French imperialists had spent to get back their Asian empire (plus another $2 billion contributed by the US). At the Geneva negotiations in 1954, the Kremlin once more succeeded in bargaining away much of the gains won in the civil war by the Viet Minh partisans. The Soviets (and the Chinese) agreed to carve up Indochina into Laos, Cambodia, and North and South Vietnam, all to remain 'neutral' in the East-West struggle.

The 1954 Geneva agreements provided also for nation-wide elections in Vietnam in 1956 under the supervision of an International Control Commission (composed of India, Canada, and Poland) to set up a united government for Vietnam. The signatories, including France and Britain, agreed that there should be no foreign bases or foreign troops in any part of Vietnam, limiting the number of foreign advisors to 685 and banning any further shipments of military supplies.

The US government agreed to abide by these agreements. However, Washington broke its word immediately and attempted to replace the French colonialists in trying to contain the Southeast Asian revolution. Laos became a cold-war battleground. The CIA and the State Department spent over half a billion dollars there in the course of seven years, seeking to destroy the Pathet Lao movement by setting up, not a neutral, but a pro-imperialist landlord regime.

In South Vietnam, the US government helped Ngo Dinh Diem to establish his dictatorial rule. Diem refused to carry through the 1956 plebiscite that he would have lost hands down. In spite of constant harassment and expulsions by the

Diem government and pressure from Washington, Western correspondents in Saigon have provided an accurate enough picture of the kind of government that Diem represents.

In an article in *Newsweek* of April 30, 1962, probably written by François Scully, who was later expelled by the Diem government, the following is observed: 'All real power in Vietnam still is concentrated in the hands of Diem and his numerous family. One brother, Ngo Dinh Nhu, is official Advisor to the President; another brother, Can, is governor of Central Vietnam. A third brother, Thuc, is a Roman Catholic Archbishop and Vietnam's ranking prelate; a fourth, Luyen, is the Vietnamese Ambassador to Britain. Nhu's wife, Madame Nhu, a member of parliament, not only controls the palace but wields enormous economic power. Her father is Vietnamese Ambassador to Washington; her mother is the Vietnamese observer at the UN'.

The *Newsweek* correspondent continues: '"I am putting loyalty above competence", says Diem when Americans ask why he does not pick the best men to serve Vietnam. And when anyone suggests economic and social reforms – higher taxes, more land for the peasants, monetary reform – Diem literally looks at the ceiling'.

The writer then asks: 'Can the US really win the fight against the Viet Cong with Diem as its standard-bearer? Many US officials, especially military men, are convinced that it can – and will. Unable to see any realistic alternative to Diem, they take the public position "don't knock our man ... he can win" – a politer version of Franklin D. Roosevelt's legendary verdict on the Nicaraguan dictator Anastasio Somoza: "He's a bastard, but he's our bastard"'.

In another dispatch, written after his expulsion on September 24, 1962, Scully points out that even the most trusted palace officials are searched twice for concealed weapons. The power behind the secret police is a man named Tran Kim Tuyen, whose official title is 'Director of Social Studies'. The power behind Tuyen in turn is Diem's brother Nhu. Scully continues:

> Perhaps the most extraordinary personality in the Ngo dynasty is Ngo Dinh Nhu's wife. Mme. Nhu is a beautiful, gifted and charming woman; she is also grasping, conceited, and obsessed with a drive for power that far surpasses that of even her husband. Like Diem and his brother, Mme. Ngo Dinh Nhu sees the family as a dynasty rather than as an evanescent political force. It is no exaggeration to say that Madame Nhu is the most detested personality in South Vietnam. This is because though Diem is nominally president, Madam Nhu and her husband have the power, and the Vietnamese know and resent it.

Scully observes that: 'Ngo Dinh Nhu's personal brand of nationalism has one aim: to identify the country exclusively with the Ngo family and with the mandarin class into which they were born. Lately, Ngo Dinh Nhu has been making increasing public appearances throughout the country. He travels like a viceroy, and often confuses the southern peasants with his aristocratic, low-keyed Annamese royal-court accent'.

Scully, who lived most of his adult life in Vietnam, reports that one village notable told him after one of these visits: 'If the effect of all this were not so disastrous, it would be hilariously funny'.

Other longtime French residents in Saigon note that the regime of President Diem has much of the same paternalistic, authoritarian and adulatory features as the preceding rule of the French puppet emperors. Like Bao Dai, Diem suggests that he rules by a mandate from heaven.

In reality, the Diem government exists by the grace of the US Diem does not control much more of Vietnam than did the French expeditionary force.

Warren Rogers Jr. in May 1962 reports the following for the *Herald Tribune* News Service: 'At present, the fact is that the Diem regime controls only the major cities and, in general, the China Sea coastline from the 17th Parallel to the northern reaches of the Mekong River delta's swampy rice bowl. All else is either under effective, well-disciplined, government-like control by the Viet Cong, or it is no man's land'.

Peasant Revolution

The precise extent of guerrilla control is a matter of dispute, but all reports agree that the peasant revolution dominates the countryside. The guerrillas of South Vietnam (dubbed Viet Cong, i.e. Viet Communists, by the US military) are the authentic armed force of the Viet peasantry. Igor Oganesoff, in the *Wall Street Journal* of March 20, 1962, estimates that the guerrillas collect money, provisions, recruits and labor from more than half the rural population, instituting land reform in their areas. Denis Warner, in the September 13, 1962, *Reporter*, judges that the 'Viet Cong is a bigger and better armed force than it was a year ago, dominating three-fifths of the land area and slightly less than a third of the population of fourteen million, with access to an estimated two million potential recruits of military age'.

The economic effects of the peasant insurrection are striking. In the *Wall Street Journal* of December 27, 1962, Norman Sklarewitz writes that:

> ... by dominating the countryside for almost six years, the Viet Cong ... has been able to break the flow of food products to the government-held cities and cut off consumer markets for manufactured goods. The Communist strategy of attacking lines of transportation and ambushing truck convoys and supply trains between the rice paddy fields of the Mekong Delta and Saigon has reduced the movement of rice by one-fourth in just two years. Overall rice production has sunk by 500,000 tons in one year.

Sklarewitz points out that in 1960 Vietnam exported $27 million of rice. The 1962 export total will be down to $2 million and Diem will have to receive US-donated rice to feed the city population. The US spent an estimated $200 million in 1962 in direct food and aid grants.

Seeking to crush the revolt in the countryside, the Vietnamese government is pursuing a course of action called (variously) rural reconstruction, province pacification, or the strategic hamlet program. While Diem's brother, Nhu, is overall director, the US government is the prime inspirer and supporter of this project.

The plan for crushing the peasant insurgency is the brain-child of a 45-year-old Scot named Robert G.K. Thompson, former Defense Minister of Malaya. Thompson's system of floodlighted, wire-fenced 'new villages', into which 450,000 Malayan peasants were 'resettled' is credited with helping the British imperialists crush the guerrilla uprising there in a bloody 12-year war that required half a million troops.

Working directly with Diem and his US advisors, Thompson produced a similar but bigger plan for the pacification of South Vietnam. It calls for control of the peasant population by 'resettling' them into a nationwide network of 'strategic hamlets' – a polite term, for concentration or slave-labor camps!

Here is what these settlements are like. Farm families are uprooted, their houses and stores put to the torch, while the people are moved by force into the new fenced in villages. On the doorframes of each hut in the strategic hamlet are nailed census boards giving the names of all occupants. Only those whose names are listed are allowed to work their fields in the morning. Even these are first checked to see that they carry no extra food for the guerrillas. Anyone caught outside the fence after curfew is fair game.

In January 1963, the program was reputed to total 4,077 villages, encompassing 39 percent of the population. It calls for 11,182 'strategic hamlets' by 1964, completing the agglomeration of the South Vietnam peasantry into a series of concentration camps.

In a letter to the *NY Times* on October 22, 1962, Tran Van Tung, a pro-American Vietnamese exile, asks: 'When will America learn that it is always fatal to the cause of freedom and democracy to support a cynical tyrant as the 'only alternative' to Communism?'

Tran concludes that: '... hated and feared by 80 percent of his people, continuing domestic policies that would shame Hitler, Diem stays in power only because of US support'.

Other leaders of the Vietnamese Democratic Party, an anti-Diem bourgeois grouping, appeal to the Kennedy administration in a similar vein. A letter by Nguyen Thau Binh, appearing in the *Los Angeles Times* of December 22, 1962, states that 'the Vietnamese regard the US simply as the latest of their colonial oppressors, since it is the US which keeps Diem in power – all in the name of "anti-Communism"'.

But feudal landlordism, propped up by concentration camps, mass arrests, murders, rigged elections, a censored press, and an autocratic regime, do not deter the Kennedy administration from supporting their man in Saigon. *Newsweek* of September 24, 1962 quotes an unnamed US official in Saigon: 'We're going to win this war, with this government, and as it is'. *Newsweek* adds: 'This is a considered statement of US policy in South Vietnam'.

Kennedy Support

The Kennedy administration has dropped any pretense of 'reforming' Diem's regime. With a sure class instinct, the US monopolists show only contempt for the advice of liberal dreamers on how best to organize 'democratic' counter-revolutions. Recognizing that any 'democratic' middle-ground between revolution and counter-revolution has long since vanished in Southeast Asia, the Kennedy administration has thrown its full weight behind Diem's reign of terror.

The US government spent $2 billion from 1954 to 1961 to prop up Diem. In the past year, the expenditures rose to $400 million a year, or over $1 million a day. In flagrant violation of the 1954 Geneva accord, 12,000 US military personnel now help Diem pursue his war against his own people.

'Kill-Ratio' Experiments

The US military have taken enthusiastically to the Vietnam operation. An article in the *Wall Street Journal* of November 9, 1962 explains how 'Pentagon Experts Use Vietnam War to Test New Tactics, Weapons'. The Pentagon is using Vietnam as a convenient proving ground for assault boats, amphibious personnel carriers, night-vision instruments, wire-lasso guns, squirt-message radios, defoliation sprays, flashlight-operated land mines, pocket flamethrowers, new rapid-fire rifles, napalm-bombing techniques, troop-carrying helicopters, armed helicopters, and other sky cavalry concepts, as well as war dogs to hunt down guerrillas.

The fight against the peasant guerrillas waged with this latest technology is incredibly cruel. Men, women and children are hunted down like wild beasts. Prisoners are habitually tortured and summarily executed, while US advisors watch. Entire villages are incinerated by napalm bombs dropped by US pilots. So are guerrilla hospitals.

The ghouls in the Pentagon who feed the gruesome statistics into their war-games computers report gleefully that the 'kill-ratio' is favorable to the Diem regime. For 1962, the official estimates are 13,000 Diem casualties against 30,000 peasants killed, wounded or captured. US casualties are reported as 30 killed in action.

Despite these New Frontier experiments in military technology, the South Vietnamese guerrillas refuse to be crushed. Guerrilla units, estimated to number 20,000 in April 1962, are now said by the US military to number 23,000 full-time guerrillas (even after 30,000 presumably were killed), plus another 100–200,000 part-time guerrillas.

The Diem government and the Kennedy administration would like to blame the South Vietnamese revolt on Ho Chi Minh. They charge that the guerrillas are being augmented and supplied by North Vietnamese slipping into South Vietnam over the Cambodian and Laotian borders. The role of their own savage repressions in driving the peasantry into armed struggle is glossed over in silence by the stalwart New Frontiersmen and their puppet-autocrat.

Jerry A. Rose, in the May 10, 1962 *Reporter*, points out that 'numerous munitions factories, set up in straw huts, produce a steady flow of crude rifles and pistols, mortars and mines, grenades and bullets for the guerrilla fighters. The materials are purchased on the local market by peasant women; the work is done by the peasant men'.

'Expropriate' US Arms

In addition, the guerrillas capture and use the latest American arms, including non-recoiling artillery. A UPI dispatch from Saigon, dated January 8, 1963, reports: 'US military advisors Tuesday said Communist guerrillas, who have boasted they will win the war with captured American weapons, seized enough new arms in the past week to equip at least two companies'. Other reports say that the guerrillas are capturing 'sampan-loads' of modern American equipment.

On January 2, 1963, at the village of Ap Bac, only 30 miles from Saigon, 200 determined guerrilla fighters with automatic weapons mauled 2,000 Diem troops, killing 100, including three Americans, and downed five US helicopters. The Diem forces outnumbered the guerrillas by 10 to 1 and were supported by planes, artillery and armor. A UPI dispatch from Saigon, dated January 7, 1963, reported that 'angry US advisors charged Sunday that Vietnamese infantrymen refused direct orders to advance during Wednesday's battle at Ap Bac and that an American Army captain was killed while out front pleading with them to attack'.

This moved Hanson W. Baldwin, military expert of the *NY Times*, to observe that 'some helicopter enthusiasts' tended to forget 'that it is men, not machines, that win wars'. He observed further that Diem's troops 'displayed some of the same basic faults they had demonstrated in other operations; they showed little inclination to use their legs and little desire to attack'.

On January 7, 1963, Arthur Krock, his fellow commentator of the *NY Times*, called for 'fundamental administration review of its current policy of military aid in South Vietnam'. He concludes, however, that 'it will be very difficult for the President to find an alternative to the US policy that has proved ineffectual, and trends to deeper and deeper involvement in Southeast Asia'.

No End in Sight

The Kennedy administration shows no disposition to veer from its fatal course. Admiral Harry P. Felt, commander of US forces in the Pacific, said this January that 'the war in South Vietnam is going fine'. He added that the 'South Vietnamese are killing more Viet Cong than the government of South Vietnam is losing in battle' and that 'the kill-ratio is running from three to six in favor of the forces of Premier Ngo Dinh Diem'.

However, Diem's troops are untrustworthy. On November 11, 1961, five paratroop battalions tried unsuccessfully to depose Diem. On February 27, 1962, two Diem pilots, sent on a mission against guerrilla fighters, bombed and strafed the palace of President Diem instead. Afterwards, only US pilots were sent on air strikes.

The Kennedy administration is following a plan of operations decided upon a year or so ago when the decision was made to crush the peasants of South Vietnam at all costs. At that time, the *Wall Street Journal* published a revealing article by Henry Gemmill with the dateline of March 26, 1962. It is headed: US

Leaders Are Determined on Victory, Even If It Means Invading Red Territory. Gemmill writes: 'Determined on victory in South Vietnam, the makers of US policy must be willing to elevate the plane of warfare if low-level fighting isn't producing results ... Suppose, for instance, that Ngo Dinh Diem's government, already lacking in solid support through the countryside, suffers further grave erosion, while the Red guerrillas gain. Suppose, too, that the American public becomes disturbed by slowly mounting casualty lists ...'.

According to Gemmill, 'doctrine now circulating would call for turning to more vigorous war'.

As outlined by the reporter, 'the first move would likely be an ultimatum to Ho Chi Minh that unless hostilities ceased in South Vietnam the war would be carried directly to its source, North Vietnam. If this went unheeded, US bombers would go to work on the airfields, ports, and rail lines of North Vietnam. If army divisions poured in, they'd be thrown into North Vietnam, not South Vietnam'.

The North Vietnamese aid that is successfully smuggled in could account for only a small fraction of the strength of the guerrilla forces. But facts are unimportant when the Cold War blazes up into a hot war against a colonial revolution.

There seems little doubt that the 'National Liberation Front' set up in Hanoi in January 1961 tends to control the political aims and leadership of the South Vietnam guerrilla fighters. There are indications that the North Vietnamese are split in the Moscow-Peking dispute, with Ho Chi Minh inclining towards the Russian and others towards the Chinese views on the tactics and strategy of colonial revolutions.

A captured guerrilla document dated September 25, 1962, published in the *NY Times* (Western Edition), January 20, 1963, would indicate that the Ho government favors a settlement along the lines of the Laotian formula. The document talks of forcing the Americans and Diem to the conference table, where they will be compelled to compromise. It emphasizes that the guerrillas must understand 'transitional steps' on the way to victory.

An end to the blood-bath now drenching the South Vietnam countryside would certainly be a relief to the long-suffering Vietnam peasantry. However, the Indochinese peoples have borne immense sacrifices in their 20-year-long struggle for liberation. Their revolution should not be short-changed again, as it was in 1945 and 1954.

As of now, US imperialism seems little disposed to any kind of compromise. Moreover, its flagrant violations of the 1954 Geneva deal are on record for all to see and learn from. The real face that the Kennedy administration presents to the masses of Asia can be seen in the brutal war it is conducting in South Vietnam without any authorization from the American people.

9 Reunification of the Fourth International[28]
(1963)

Farrell Dobbs and Joseph Hansen

The healing of a ten-year-old division in the ranks of the majority of the Fourth International – the World Party of the Socialist Revolution – which took place at a Reunification Congress held in Italy in June, marks a most encouraging step forward for the movement founded by Leon Trotsky in 1938.

The two groupings of the Fourth International that participated in the reunification were headed by the International Secretariat and the International Committee, the views of the latter being supported in the United States by the Socialist Workers Party. With the fusion, the 'United Secretariat of the Fourth International', representing a joint leadership, was elected to replace the former bodies and to head the reunified movement.

For some years the majority of both sides had felt that the political and organizational differences which appeared in 1953 and which precipitated a split the following year had been largely superseded by events. While substantial differences remained, they were considered to be of secondary importance in face of the necessity and feasibility of combining forces on a world scale on the basis of a principled program. At the Reunification Congress, leaders of both sides stated that they had not changed their views about the past dispute, but all of them agreed on the advisability of deferring attempts at historic assessments and of putting the unsettled differences aside for consideration at a later date after common work and new joint experiences can be expected to have overcome whatever factional feelings remain from the past.

A Principled Unification

A document submitted for the consideration of the world Trotskyist movement by the Political Committee of the Socialist Workers Party, advocating

---

28   Dobbs and Hansen 1963.

early reunification on the basis of sixteen points, was adopted unanimously at the Reunification Congress as a statement of the fundamental principles on which both sides stand. By this action the document became a charter of the reunification.

The three main areas of agreement are outlined as follows:

First of all, in highly condensed form, the document restates the views put forward by Trotsky in the 'Transitional Program' of 1938, explaining the agonizing world crisis of our times as reflecting at bottom a 'prolonged crisis in revolutionary leadership' in face of the need to go forward from capitalism to socialism. The delay of the world socialist revolution is ascribed to the incapacities and betrayals of the traditional working-class leadership; i.e., the trade union, Social Democratic and Stalinist bureaucracies. Strong emphasis is placed on the need for constructing revolutionary-socialist parties, and certain tactical problems in this process, involving membership in existing mass proletarian parties ('entryism'), are noted. A special point reaffirms the principles of democratic centralism.

Trotsky's characterization of the Soviet Union as a workers' state that must be defended and of the Stalinist bureaucracy as a parasitic caste that must be opposed and overthrown is likewise reaffirmed.

Secondly, the analogous analyses made by the Fourth International of the new workers' states which have appeared since Trotsky's death are included. Prominent in this section is the characterization of Cuba as a workers' state.

Thirdly, in the current world political scene, de-Stalinization is recognized as a two-sided development of prime importance, involving welcome concessions to the masses but intended by the bureaucracy to bolster and prolong its own arbitrary rule against the pressures for proletarian democracy. The differences that finally shattered the Stalinist monolith, now most dramatically displayed in the Chinese-Soviet dispute, are held to have been fostered by deep-going revolutionary processes, evident above all in the colonial world.

The prominent role of the peasantry and of guerrilla warfare in the colonial revolution since the end of World War II is noted as an experience that 'must be consciously incorporated into the strategy of building revolutionary Marxist parties in colonial countries'.

This section ends with strong stress on potential developments in the imperialist countries where, it is held, the final decisive battles will occur, determining whether civilization will be reduced to radioactive ruins or go forward to the enduring peace made possible by a socialist reorganization of society.

In addition to the political positions indicated above, the document makes organizational recommendations to be considered at a subsequent congress 'which, without breaching the centralist side of democratic centralism, would remove any doubts that might still remain as to the guarantee of democratic rights contained in the statutes'.

The Reunification Congress adopted three other important documents. Two of them deal with current developments in the Soviet bloc countries and with the Chinese-Soviet dispute. The third one, 'The Dynamics of World Revolution Today', is a study of the dialectical interrelationship of long-range trends in three sectors, the colonial world, the Soviet bloc and the imperialist countries. We are publishing it in this issue of the *International Socialist Review*.

The reunification of the Fourth International was a conscious response to the widening opportunities for building revolutionary-socialist parties. In 1953 the world Trotskyist movement was under heavy pressure from two major unfavorable developments. One was that although the establishment of workers' states in Eastern Europe and the victory of the Chinese Revolution were highly progressive events, an immediate consequence was the temporary strengthening of Stalinism. The other was the quiescence of the class struggle in the United States and the rise of McCarthyism. Today the situation is quite different. The strengthening of the Soviet Union through the proliferation of planned economies and the relative weakening of imperialism finally broke up Stalinist monolithism and gave fresh actuality to the program of Trotskyism in the land of its birth. The colonial revolution has shaken all Asia, Africa and Latin America, bringing the heartening developments in Algeria and placing a workers' state within ninety miles of Florida. In the United States itself, the great citadel of world reaction, social stagnation has been broken with the rise of the Negro struggle in new and dynamic forms.

To the majority of Trotskyists throughout the world it became increasingly self-evident that the continued division of the Fourth International was anachronistic and that vigorous efforts must be made to heal the split so that united forces could be brought to bear in the promising situations developing in all directions. The victory of the Cuban Revolution and the fact that both sides, through parallel analyses, reached virtually identical conclusions concerning its meaning powerfully reinforced the trend toward reunification.

The Opposition to Reunification

While the overwhelming majority of the Trotskyist movement, representing twenty-six countries, have now been united, two minority groupings refused to participate. The holdouts are a faction headed by J. Posadas, located principally in Latin America, which split from the International Secretariat last year, and a minority of the International Committee forces headed by Gerry Healy, a faction based mainly in Britain and France. To justify their opposition to reunification, both groupings have developed political differences with the majority of the world Trotskyist movement and appear rather deliberately to be seeking fresh disputes.

The Posadas tendency held a conference last year in secret from the rest of the Trotskyist movement. The delegates then announced that they had held an 'Extraordinary Conference of the ivth International' and had adopted a 'historical Resolution to be the international Provisional leadership until the Extraordinary World Conference, which this Conference summons'. Since then the faction has called itself the 'ivth International'.

It has published typographical facsimiles of genuine publications of the Fourth International. (Despite the paucity of members, the grouping is impressively energetic about getting out publications). At first glance, so far as the names and mastheads are concerned, these are indistinguishable from the originals; and the counterfeits, which are heavily loaded with articles and speeches that either are signed by Posadas or done in perfect imitation of his verbose and turgid style, have led to some confusion, especially in Latin America.

The main political position distinguishing the Posadas grouping is that it advocates the 'right' of the Soviet Union to 'initiate' nuclear war. The first issue of a newspaper distributed by the faction in England puts it this way:

> *One of the slogans under which the Extraordinary Conference took place was:* THE BOLSHEVIK MILITANT OF THIS EPOCH IS HE WHO IS PREPARED TO FACE THE LAST SETTLEMENT OF ACCOUNTS BETWEEN CAPITALISM AND THE SOCIALIST REVOLUTION AND THE WORKERS' STATES – WHICH WILL BE SETTLED WITHIN THE NUCLEAR WAR – HE WHO IS PREPARED ALSO TO FACE ITS CONSEQUENCES. (Emphasis in original).

In a resolution passed by a 'First Congress of the Revolutionary Workers Party (Trotskyists)' held recently in England, the invitation to join Posadas in preparing for doomsday is explained: The 'permeating of the once-staid British society by violence in every sphere, will find its final expression in a desperate rallying of forces for the final throw'. This will be a 'final military showdown against the workers' states and colonial revolution'. The projected 'cataclysmic reckoning' is described as being at the very heart of all politics today. 'The Third World War is the coming reality, and any failure to point this out with absolute honesty to the workers, preparing them for the dreadful destruction and, at the same time, the decisive opportunity for seizing power which this war before or during it, affords, is treachery to bolshevism and a monstrous betrayal of the class'.

It must be granted that fear of a nuclear world war has a strong basis in current reality. The majority of the Fourth International agree on that and, in fact, the Trotskyist movement has been sounding the alarm since Hiroshima and Nagasaki. The differences with Posadas occur on two points. First, the Fourth International takes a much graver view of the possible consequences of a nuclear war than Posadas does. In the opinion of all other Trotskyists it could well mean the finish of civilization if not all the higher forms of life on our globe. Posadas, in contrast, believes that a 'communist society' could rapidly be constructed on the wreckage. Secondly, Posadas believes that nothing can be done to prevent nuclear war; it should indeed be welcomed as the necessary means to clear away capitalism. The Fourth International, in opposition to this view, is confident that the working class will prove able to avert the disaster in time through socialist revolution.

Posadas does not engage in much discussion on these questions. His method is the simple one of denouncing the 'opportunism', 'capitulation', and 'betrayal' of the 'former Trotskyists – Pablo, Germain, Frank, Cannon, Healy'.

Here is a fair sample of the Posadas view of the majority of the Trotskyist movement: 'Lacking confidence in the immense revolutionary élan of the workers awaiting revolutionary leadership, this clique is in tow to the so-called "left" in the labour and peace movements. They deny the possibility and even the need of open revolutionary sections. They flinch from preparing the workers for war and the seizure of power'.

When Posadas passed his 'historical Resolution', declaring himself 'to be' the leadership of the Fourth International, he could count on forces in a number of Latin-American countries. At the time, he headed the 'Latin-American Bureau', a regional subdivision of the movement, and he had utilized this body in factional preparations for his coup. As it became clear that his revelations about the political death of the parent body scarcely corresponded to the reality, he ran into trouble. The important Bolivian section, for instance, repudiated him and his 'Latin-American Bureau' virtually unanimously. Elsewhere splits in his ranks have occurred. On the other hand some vigorous personal crusading in Europe has won him a few new converts. Likewise, the Cuban Trotskyists remain faithful to the 'Latin-American Bureau', and their newspaper *Voz Proletaria*, which appears regularly in Havana, thus unfortunately presents a rather bizarre image of 'Trotskyism' as it criticizes Castro for his stubborn centrist failure to accept the hard gospel of Saint Posadas about a coming nuclear Apocalypse and how to win redemption by speeding it up.

The Healyite Grouping

The other tendency which has opposed reunification is led by Gerry Healy, the secretary of the Socialist Labour League. Healy, to his credit, does not share the views of Posadas about an inevitable nuclear doomsday that should be speeded up. He does hold with Posadas, however, that the leaders of the majority of the world Trotskyist movement have gone over to 'opportunism' and 'betrayed Trotskyism'. (In the interests of strict accuracy a shading must be noted in this common view. Healy differs with Posadas on one point, holding that the name of Healy should not be included in the list of betrayers).

Healy is of the opinion that the reunification itself is a 'betrayal'. The reasons he advances for this view are that reunification must be *preceded* by a full accounting of the differences of 1953–54, an assessment of responsibility, and corresponding acknowledgments of guilt. Any reunification without these prerequisites, Healy contends, is unprincipled, can only prove ephemeral, and he will have nothing to do with.

It was argued against this that the world Trotskyist movement is not monolithic. Groupings with much deeper differences than opposing views over who was right in a past dispute can coexist and collaborate in the same revolutionary-socialist organization under the rules of democratic centralism. In the Socialist Workers Party, for instance, even a state-capitalist grouping has lived for years without undue friction. Why should not common political positions on the key issues of the day prove to be powerful enough to cement the two sides of the Fourth International despite differences over the past?

The reasonableness of this reply gave Healy trouble. His response was to probe more strenuously for current political differences that would preclude reunification. This search, however, led him to develop some rather far-reaching political differences of his own that finally brought him into grave opposition with the majority of the International Committee as well as the International Secretariat.

These differences became sharpest over estimates and policies in relation to the colonial revolution, above all the Cuban Revolution.

The majority of the world Trotskyist movement long ago came to the conclusion that Cuba is a workers' state and that under Castro's leadership it has entered the road toward socialism; the Cuban Revolution, in fact, being the opening of the socialist revolution in the Western Hemisphere. Even Posadas shares this view. The British and French sectors of the International Committee are virtually alone in holding otherwise. In an article last year, 'Trotskyism Betrayed', the National Committee of the Socialist Labour League maintained the outlandish position that the 'state foundations' in Cuba remain 'capitalist'.

The regime, we are told, 'is a variety of capitalist state power'. Castro, it is argued, 'did not create a qualitatively new and different type of state from the Batista regime'.

Healy is quite serious in thus comparing the revolutionary Cuban government to the Batista regime. He goes even further, listing Castro himself as just another 'Chiang Kai-shek'.

These weird conclusions are derived from a simple-minded sectarian pattern of thought: It is impossible to carry a revolution forward to the successful establishment of a workers' state without the *preceding* construction in every instance of a revolutionary-socialist party. Such a party did not exist in Cuba before the revolution. Therefore, no workers' state was established. Therefore, what exists in Cuba must be capitalist.

It proved quite useless to call Healy's attention to the changes in Cuba's economic, social and political structure successfully carried out under Castro's leadership. To insist on the facts, Healy maintained, is to reveal that you are not a dialectical materialist but an 'empiricist'.

Similar fantasies now determine Healy's policies in many fields. In the Negro struggle in the United States, he concentrates his attacks on the 'clerics', the Muslims and the Socialist Workers Party, which he holds to be 'opportunistic' because it raises partial, transitional slogans. In Algeria, instead of joining in centering fire on the dangerous neocolonialist tendency, he singles out Ben Bella and the Trotskyists as the enemy. In Britain itself the 'fake lefts' are his main target. Everybody to the right of Healy is denounced as a 'betrayer'. In brief, instead of advancing to meet the leftward moving stream in Britain, Healy is taking the opposite direction – towards deeper isolation.

Speaking at the July convention of the Socialist Workers Party on the ultraleft, sectarian, isolationist, anti-international course now being followed by the National Committee of the Socialist Labour League, James P. Cannon, National Chairman of the SWP and the most experienced leader in the world Trotskyist movement, came to the conclusion, 'The SLL is doomed'.

Despite the direction in which Healy was moving, every effort was made to bring the minority of the International Committee into the reunification. They were invited to participate in a preliminary conference of the majority of the International Committee. They were invited to send observers to the Seventh World Congress of the forces of the International Secretariat, and to send observers to the Reunification Congress of the Fourth International. Healy brushed the invitations aside.

He went still further. Instead of seeking friendly relations with the united Fourth International, he publicly attacked both the Reunification Congress and the Socialist Workers Party, using, of course, the epithets of 'betrayal' to which his vocabulary has become more and more reduced. This was the opening of a campaign to further enlarge the already formidable differences which he has developed. To give his attacks more authority, he utilized the name 'International Committee', although the majority of this grouping participated in the Reunification Congress and now constitute part of the united movement. In this, Healy echoed the not-so-novel organizational methods of Posadas.

Doctrinaire Conservatism

The course now being followed by Healy and Posadas and their followers is much to be regretted. Under the democratic centralism which governs the Fourth International, they could have maintained their political views within the organization and sought to win a majority. The fact that they rejected this course is the strongest possible proof either that they are opposed to democratic centralism or that they consider their political differences with the rest of the world Trotskyist movement to be so profound that collaborating in a common organization is excluded in principle.

The two factions combined, however, constitute only a small minority. While they can prove to be a problem in certain areas, they can scarcely affect the progress of the Trotskyist movement as a whole.

It would have been Utopian to hope that the Fourth International could be reunited one hundred percent and at a single stroke. Immense events have occurred since the end of the war and the Trotskyist movement, which is a living movement, suffered its own crises in attempting to meet them on the theoretical and practical level. The Cuban Revolution, coming at the close of a long process (and, we hope, the beginning of a new one), had the effect of precipitating many things.

In the Trotskyist movement, it increased the pressure for reunification and thereby also had the opposite effect of bringing out defects in theoretical understanding and political capacity. The end result was a clarifying process that forced the movement as a whole to review all that it has accomplished, particularly on the theoretical level, since the end of the war. In the intensive internal discussion, the analyses of the character of the state and regime in China, Yugoslavia, and even the East European countries came up. Some switches occurred in these areas, too, as comrades discovered that they hadn't really grasped the previous theoretical work or at least all of its implications. Misunderstandings were cleared up in some cases; masks came off in others. All the various shadings of opinion are now fairly well recorded either publicly or in discussion bulletins available to the membership of the Trotskyist movement. This alone represents a considerable achievement and a big step forward.

Despite the wildness evident in their positions, both the Posadas and Healy factions are doctrinaire. The revolutionary Marxist movement correctly stresses the importance of building a revolutionary-socialist party. Healy converts the principle into an absolute, excluding thereby any variation which reality may present us with. The case of Posadas is not much different. Marxists have long stressed that war has often proved to be a mother of revolutions. Posadas converts this into the dogma that revolution can have no other mother (forgetting Cuba!) and carries it to the absurd conclusion that the most destructive of wars will necessarily have the most progressive consequences.

Thus the leaders of both factions see broad guiding principles as absolute prescriptions. Instead of trying to apply doctrine in an intelligent way as a guide in the infinitely rich reality which the historical process compels the movement to face, they insist on reality conforming to doctrine on pain of nonrecognition.

That these conservative tendencies did not succeed in holding back the majority from a dialectical appreciation of the great new achievements of the colonial revolution, and that they could not halt the process of reunification despite their bitter opposition to it, augurs well for the future of the Fourth International.

The Revolutionary Opportunities

The reunification takes place against a background of unparalleled revolutionary opportunities. Thus, even though the healing of the split does not involve mass parties anywhere in the world, the substantial number of cadres it does bring together can move ahead rather rapidly. In a surprising number of countries they have already established promising beginnings. Where they have known how, in the tradition of Leninism, to adhere firmly to the basic principles of revolutionary socialism and yet adopt flexible tactics – and this is the case with the majority of the world Trotskyist movement – their prestige among vanguard workers and intellectuals is very high. In addition, they enjoy friendly relations with many of the new revolutionary and even socialist-minded currents that have been proliferating as one of the consequences of the rise of the colonial revolution, particularly after the victories in Cuba and Algeria. An upsurge in the class struggle could face these new currents, in association with Trotskyism, with the immediate opportunity to organize mass revolutionary-socialist parties and in some places put them in position to move toward a contest for power.

One of the most favorable sectors for such a turn of events is Latin America. Few days go by that do not bring news of coups or attempted coups, counter coups or attempted counter coups, as Fidel Castro noted in his July 26 speech. The spectacular shuffling of regimes in the recent period in places like Ecuador and Argentina, the downfall of the Trujillo dictatorship in the Dominican Republic and the repeated efforts to similarly bring down Duvalier in neighboring Haiti are but the most visible symptoms of general social unrest reaching from the Rio Grande to Tierra del Fuego. This rise in revolutionary potential on a continental scale is now common knowledge. What is not so commonly known is the reflection of this process in the radical movement.

The Cuban Revolution sent cleavages, sometimes with shattering impact, through all the political formations of the left. The Moscow-Peking dispute compounded the effect. The immediate results were a decline in the prestige, authority and attractive power of the traditional leftist parties, Communist as well as Social Democratic. Within these organizations, leftward moving tendencies developed and totally fresh parallel ones appeared here and there outside the old formations.

The subsidence of the old parties and incipient development of new formations has not proceeded in a simple way. On the contrary, sharp ups and downs show that it is a complex process. But three significant new facts should be noted: First, in places like Brazil and Peru, a tendency has appeared or grown stronger among the peasants to organize along trade-union lines. Secondly, in many areas guerrilla forces have gone into action, seeking quite consciously to follow the example of the Cuban and Chinese fighters. Thirdly, the student youth have repeatedly displayed a strong bent toward action based on independent estimates of what is required nationally. Sometimes the actions have developed on an impressive scale. To discount the priority of opinion in Moscow (or Peking) is a symptom of greatest significance, for it is one of the prime requisites to build national leaderships capable of independent analysis and action.

The weakening of the old Communist and Social Democratic parties in Latin America may seem to be a paradoxical effect of the Cuban Revolution. It may even appear that the Kennedy administration is succeeding in isolating the Cuban Revolution. The truth is that we are witnessing the displacement of bureaucratic roadblocks to revolution. It is part of the preparatory process for the rise of genuinely revolutionary parties. The other part of the preparatory process is the ideological ferment, the testing of ideas, the attempts – sometimes inept – to take the revolutionary initiative, the discussions and the assessment of experiences, and the regroupment and bringing together of revolutionists of widely different origin.

It is obvious that the unification of the major forces of world Trotskyism can help play a catalytic role in the formation of new leaderships in Latin America capable of following judiciously the example which Cuba set in opening the socialist revolution in the Western Hemisphere.

The prospects are hardly less bright in Africa where a whole series of new countries have emerged, through sometimes desperate struggles against imperialism, to take their place in the arena of world politics. Here the greatest hopes and expectations attach to Algeria. Although the newly independent country faces an exceedingly difficult situation inherited from more than a century of colonial slavery and seven and a half years of one of the bloodiest wars in history, its people have resolutely decided to move toward socialism. Already agriculture, Algeria's main industry, has been nationalized in effect and its operation placed under Workers' Council and Workers' Management Committees. The example has not been lost on the rest of Africa and the Middle East, and Algiers is coming to be regarded as the Havana of the African continent and the Arab world.

The struggle against neocolonialism and against imperialism is far from won in Algeria. A polarization of forces has occurred, with the left wing rallying around Ben Bella against the neocolonialists. The Trotskyists in Algeria are very active in this struggle. Trotskyism, in general, has great prestige among broad circles of the Algerian vanguard because of its record in aiding the underground fighters in the most difficult days of their struggle.

In the Far East, the fires touched off by the Chinese Revolution continue to blaze. The Vietnam freedom fighters have put up such a heroic and effective struggle that more and more voices in Washington suggest withdrawing from the dirty war in which Kennedy involved America. The rise of pessimism in Washington is paralleled by increased optimism in the colonial world over the possibilities of a revolutionary outcome in Vietnam. A defeat for imperialism in Vietnam could have immense consequences in Indonesia and Malaya where the political stream continues to flow toward the left.

Trotskyism was at one time a strong force in Vietnam, but the leading Trotskyists were killed by the Japanese imperialists during the occupation or by the Stalinists and the movement has not yet recovered from the ferocious repression. In Asia, at the moment, the Trotskyists are strongest in Ceylon, where they head the labor movement and hold seats in parliament. The Trotskyist movement also has a base in India.

In both lands, where the movement goes back to the struggle for freedom from British imperialism, the Trotskyists strongly urged reunification on a world scale. Their representatives at the Reunification Congress expressed great satisfaction at the success that was recorded there and declared that it would have immediate benefits as well as greatly facilitate building the movement in other areas of the Far East with which they are in touch.

In the Soviet Bloc

The opportunities for the relatively swift development of revolutionary-socialist forces in the colonial world are quite apparent. This is not so in the Soviet Union, the East European countries and China. In these lands, the main task of revolutionary socialism is to establish or to re-establish the proletarian democracy for which Lenin and Trotsky stood. But no organized tendency fighting for this aim is known to exist on any considerable scale. How long can the totalitarian forms of political rule continue to operate without generating an organized movement for the restoration or introduction of Leninist democracy? The fact is that conditions are quite ripe for its appearance, especially in the Soviet Union. *De-Stalinization* constitutes a series of concessions paid out to the masses in a calculated way by the bureaucracy in order to slow down, if not head off, this very tendency. The end effect of de-Stalinization, however, will be to accelerate the drive of the masses for political democracy.

Trotskyism is endemic in the Soviet Union. It can flare suddenly and spread with great speed. This is one of the main reasons why the bureaucracy is so concerned about restricting freedom of thought in the arts and sciences. Implied in the freedom to discuss and engage in abstract art or psychoanalysis or research in genetics is the freedom to discuss and engage in revolutionary-socialist politics.

The thirst for political freedom is quite intense. Any number of signs show it, not the least of them being the immense popularity of Fidel Castro and all the Cuban revolutionists with the Soviet masses.

The difficulty which the bureaucrats experience in keeping Trotskyism buried is ironically evident in their own revival of the subject even if only in the form of accusations. Both Mao and Khrushchev hurl the charge of 'Trotskyism' at each other. While the charge may not stick in either case, it certainly increases the pressure to discuss Trotskyism and to find out what it really stands for.

The first consequences of the collapse of the bureaucratic monolith, so far as direct, immediate gains for the Trotskyist movement were concerned, came among Communist parties outside the Soviet bloc. The revelations at the Twentieth Congress broke down the prohibitions against dangerous thoughts enforced in the Communist parties under Stalin. In the ensuing discussions, some rank and filers and even intellectuals came over to Trotskyism. It became possible in certain parties to discuss Trotskyist views and even to talk with genuine, live Trotskyists with at least the beginnings of objectivity. This process, which is far from concluded – in fact, it has hardly begun in sectors as important as the French Communist Party – put heavy pressure on the world Trotskyist movement to compose its internal differences. The reunification is therefore viewed by both sides as a great gain in the essential work of aiding members of the Communist parties to overcome the evil heritage of Stalinism.

The schism between Moscow and Peking, which is more and more compelling the protagonists to broach the most fundamental questions of revolutionary-socialist perspectives and strategy, inevitably involves Trotskyism to an increasing degree and opens up truly enormous opportunities for its ascendance. These opportunities alone made it the evident duty of Trotskyists to put aside differences of secondary order in order to effectively advance the main principles of the program on which they stand.

In the Capitalist Citadels

In the main centers of world capitalism, the past decades have been particularly difficult for the Trotskyist movement. The combination of prosperity, reactionary political trends and relatively quiescent class struggle, characteristic above all of the United States, but extending to one degree or another throughout world capitalism, compelled the radical movement as a whole to mark time for an unexpectedly prolonged period. That the Trotskyists were able to hold their own and even register a few gains is a tribute to their stamina and to the power of the ideas that inspire them.

The first signs of a shift in the objective situation have now begun to appear. In Europe the new trend was announced by such events as the general strike in Belgium in 1960, the shift to the left in Britain which has placed the Labour Party in position to win the next election, and a series of important strikes in Italy, France and Germany. The underground movement in Spain has been inching ahead as a direct reflection of the growing self-confidence of the Spanish workers, particularly the miners.

The beginning of the change in the United States proved to be spectacular, since it fell to the Negro people to take the lead in breaking the trance that has gripped the country since the rise of the witch-hunt and McCarthyism in 1947. The independent self-action of the Negro people could take no other form but dramatic and often very militant demonstrations if it were to have genuine effect in battering down the violent prejudices that bar the way to equality. It is possible for this movement to now move rapidly into politics where its most effective field of action lies, and this in turn can open up an entire new and brilliant chapter for revolutionary socialism in America.

For the Trotskyist movement in the United States, represented by the Socialist Workers Party, the problem of reunification had no directly national aspect. But the Socialist Workers Party is keenly alive to its international meaning and the benefits to be derived indirectly in its own work from a united world movement. The Canadian Trotskyist movement, represented by the Socialist Educational League, is similarly situated. In both the American and Canadian organizations, the Reunification Congress was hailed as a big step forward.

One of the prime considerations in the minds of those who pressed most strongly for reunification of the Fourth International was the youth. On all continents it is they who are now moving into the center of the revolutionary stage. The series of student demonstrations that swept the globe from Korea to Turkey in the past several years is proof of this. The new generation has displayed its capacities up to this point with the greatest impressiveness in the Cuban Revolution. In Latin America, those most actively concerned about learning from the Cuban experience and applying the lessons are the young people. In the United States it was youth who took the initiative in the staging of demonstrations that touched off the new surge forward in the Negro struggle, and it is they who have provided the main active forces in the picket lines, sit-ins and Freedom Rides that have made headlines internationally.

The tendency of this new generation to begin its revolutionary experience with *deeds* is of the utmost significance. It testifies to the enormous internal pressures in the capitalist system, to the widespread diffusion of the idea of seeking a revolutionary way out, and to the power of the living examples of revolutionary success from the Russia of 1917 to the Cuba of 1959.

The Cuban Revolution was marked by the predominance of action over conscious revolutionary theory; but in its course, as was inevitable, consciousness began asserting its rights and the Cubans themselves turned increasingly to the revolutionary classics in search of the meaning of what they had accomplished. This road leads in the final analysis to Trotskyism, which contains the quintessence of revolutionary-socialist theory. In moving in this direction, the Cubans have blazed a trail for millions of youth around the globe.

A generation of youth armed on a sufficiently wide scale with Trotskyist theory would signify the finish of the capitalist system. With an understanding of why they have rebelled against the social system into which they were born and how they must go about changing that system, the new generation will prove invincible.

May the reunification of the Fourth International help the youth to seize the unique opportunity which is theirs – the successful discharge of the greatest task in the history of humanity, the establishment of world socialism!

10 A Study of the Feminine Mystique[29]
(1964)

Evelyn Reed

The Feminine Mystique, by Betty Friedan, New York: W.W. Norton & Co., 1963. 410pp. $5.95.

The Feminine Mystique is an outstanding sociological study – an overdue challenge to the mercenary mythmakers who have invented the glorified image of the Happy Housewife Heroine and imposed it upon American women.

The author, a mother of three children, analyzes the plight of women like herself who belong to the privileged upper middle strata of American society. Most women have no choice except to be tied to a household or chained to a factory or office job – or both. But the women that Betty Friedan examines are more fortunate. They have access to all the advantages of our culture – education, scholarship, interesting and well-paying professions. And yet most of them have forfeited development of their higher capacities to enroll in the ranks listed as: 'Occupation: housewife'.

Exposed by the author are the realities behind the show-windows of Suburbia where female residents suffer agonies from 'a problem that has no name'. This is their inability to 'adjust' to their narrow, stultifying sphere of existence. She also describes the catastrophic consequences that this debasement of women inflicts upon the whole family. Few escape the pathology flowing from the 'Feminine Mystique'.

Betty Friedan's findings have a wider relevance than the well-to-do housewives she has investigated. These set the pattern of behavior and aspiration for working-class housewives, who mistakenly believe that because middle-class women have all the advantages, they also have all the answers. In this way distorted ideas and values seep down to infect masses of women, including some working women who wonder whether they might not lead a better life as a full-time housewife. This book should help settle their doubts.

---

29   Reed 1964.

Springing Old Trap

The Feminine Mystique is a modernized version of the old formula for domestic enslavement more bluntly expressed as 'Woman's place is in the home'. The new element is the poisoned bait of the Mystique by which women today are voluntarily lured back into the trap that their grandmothers fought to escape from.

Betty Friedan reminds us that in the nineteenth century and in the first decades of the twentieth, progressive middle-class women led an inspiring 'feminist' struggle for women's rights. Out of this rebellion they won the right to higher education, participation in production, professional careers, independent ownership of property and the vote. These reforms were an immense improvement over their previous chatteldom, and could have been a springboard to further advances to full human stature and dignity.

Instead, the Second World War and its aftermath brought about a sweeping setback, characterized by the author as a 'counter-revolution' against women. The call for this retreat was sounded by Farnham & Lundberg's book *Modern Woman: The Lost Sex*, published in 1942. The 'lost' women were the independent ones interested in science, art, politics and engaged in careers beyond the family circle.

In place of intelligent, creative, public-spirited women came the new image of the 'feminine' woman – the empty-headed housewife contented within the 'cozy' walls of a pretty home. As the Mystique gained momentum, domesticity became 'a religion, a pattern by which all women must now live or deny their femininity', writes the author. What began as a trek back to the old corral became a stampede during the prosperity of the 1950s.

To mobilize women behind their own defeat, facts about the pioneer fighters for women's rights were distorted. Although most of the feminist crusaders had husbands, children and homes, they were depicted as 'embittered sex-starved spinsters' incapable of fulfilling their 'femininity' as wives and mothers. Among the unforgivable traits of these spirited women was their enjoyment of participation in the struggle for social change!

Also blacked out of the record was the ultra-reactionary source of this retreat back to the home. It was Hitler in the 1930s who enforced the notorious Three K's for women: *Kinder, Kuche, Kirche* (children, cooking, church). By the 1940s a similar slogan was sold to American women in the disguised, glamorized package of the Feminine Mystique. The author likens the blind docility with which middle-class women accepted their fate to prisoners in Nazi concentration camps, who became unprotesting 'walking corpses' marching to their own doom:

> In a sense that is not as farfetched as it sounds, the women who 'adjust' as housewives, who grow UP wanting to be 'just a housewife', are in as much danger as the millions who walked to their own death in the concentration camps – and the millions more who refused to believe that the concentration camps existed.

True, the barbed wire surrounding the 'comfortable concentration camps' of Suburbia was invisible. What was visible to these victims of 'The American Dream' were the gilded trappings of the standard middle-class home. As a lifetime occupation, however, they were bogged down in domestic trivia requiring the intellectual exertions of an eight-year-old. Even then there was not enough work to occupy their full time. Thus, housework 'expanded to fill the time available', as the inmates squandered their energies in more frantic 'busywork' on meaningless details. Working women can usually polish off in an hour the chores on which fulltime housewives spend six hours and still leave unfinished at dinnertime. 'Even with all the new labor-saving appliances', the author points out, 'the modern American housewife probably spends more time on housework than her grandmother'.

'Like Diogenes with his lamp', Betty Friedan went in search of at least one intelligent, capable woman who felt fulfilled as a full-time housewife. She found none. What she did find, out of a sample test of 28 women in an upper-income community was the following:

> Sixteen out of the 28 were in analysis or analytical psychotherapy. Eighteen were taking tranquilizers; several had tried suicide; and some had been hospitalized for varying periods, for depression or vaguely diagnosed psychotic states. ('You'd be surprised at the number of these happy suburban wives who simply go berserk one night, and run shrieking through the street without any clothes on', said the local doctor, not a psychiatrist, who had been called in, in such emergencies) ... Twelve were engaged in extramarital affairs in fact or in fantasy.

It was this conflict of reality with the widely publicized image of the happy housewife which caused Betty Friedan to break the hypnosis of the Mystique in her own life. Asking the key question: 'What made these women go home again?' she then proceeded to collect the data which explained how the trick was done.

The Brainwashers

A high-powered propaganda machine was put into motion to exalt housewifery and stifle women's desires for something more than a husband, home and children. Beginning with the 'sex directed' educators in the schools and colleges, this campaign has penetrated into every avenue of mass indoctrination. The key word in this technique of thought control – as effective as a blackjack on the skull in a dark alley – is the word 'feminine'.

College girls, terrified lest they lose their 'femininity' through any display of brains or serious study, learn to camouflage their intelligence or obediently empty their minds altogether. Their main preoccupation, fostered by parents and educators alike, is 'the pursuit of a wedding ring'. As one educator put it, college for women was the 'world's best marriage mart'.

Higher education for women was readjusted to fit the new goal; it became a veneer for suburban wifehood. Courses in advanced cooking, in marriage and family adjustment displaced courses in chemistry, physics, etc. Old-fashioned educators, repelled by the 'sophisticated soup' dished up as Liberal Arts courses, were brought into line – or pushed aside. Even such Ivy League colleges as Vassar, Smith, Barnard and others, 'which pioneered higher education for women in America and were noted for their uncompromising intellectual standards', tumbled from their heights. As the spokesman of a famous woman's college put it: 'We are not educating women to be scholars; we are educating them to be wives and mothers'. With commendable irony the girls promptly abbreviated this to 'WAM'.

Summing up the consequences of this deterioration in education, the author writes: 'Sex-directed education segregated recent generations of able American women as surely as separate-but-equal education segregated able American Negroes from the opportunity to realize their full abilities in the mainstream of American life'.

Along with this lowering of educational standards, the age level for marriage took a sharp plunge (often beginning even in the high schools), while the birth rate soared. The fashion for 'WAMism' swept the nation, spearheaded by middle-class women who 'led all the others in the race to have more babies'.

> The average age of first marriage in the last 15 years, has dropped to the youngest in the history of this country, the youngest in any of the countries of the Western world, almost as young as it used to be in the so-called underdeveloped countries ... the annual rate of population increase in the US is among the highest in the world – nearly three times that of the Western European nations, nearly double Japan's, and close on the heels of Africa and India.

Sustaining and extending this redirection of women are the powerful molders of public opinion: editors and writers of the slick magazines for women, newspaper columnists, TV shows, movies, popular novels, pulps, and all the rest. Insidiously and unremittingly they warn women that even yearning to express their intellects and talents would be 'heavily paid for' by the loss of their 'femininity'.

The social sciences: applied sociology, psychology and anthropology are likewise misused to buttress this Feminine Mystique. Even alert and intelligent women find it difficult to question propaganda when it is disguised as science. The more dubious findings of the eminent psychologist, Freud, are perverted and vulgarized to lend authority to the theme that woman's place is in the home. 'For reasons far removed from the life of Freud himself, Freudian thought has become the ideological bulwark of the sexual counter-revolution in America', says Betty Friedan. For example, 'penis envy' became a psychological catch-all; the answer to women's resentment against their inferior status. It was invoked as a bludgeon against such 'unfeminine' demands as freedom and equality with men.

The noted 'functional' anthropologist, Margaret Mead (perhaps unwittingly) has been one of the most influential contributors to the pseudo-scientific campaign propping up the Feminine Mystique. According to this 'major architect' of opinion about women, it is the 'entrances and exits' of the body which are decisive in shaping the individual in society.

Utilizing bits and patches of Freud's teachings, she returned from the South Seas where she charted tribal personality according to literal 'oral' and 'anal' tables, bringing women the good news that in their bodily organs they are, after all, the equals of men. Since women possess that supremely feminine 'entrance', the vagina, the equality of women stems from the fact that for every penis – there is a uterus! She 'equated those assertive, creative, productive aspects of life on which the superstructure of a civilization depends with the penis and defined feminine creativity in terms of the passive receptivity of the uterus', says the author. Thus, 'through her influence, procreation became a cult, a career, to the exclusion of every other kind of creative endeavor'.

Ironically, Margaret Mead did not guide her own life by what she wrote in her books, as Betty Friedan points out. 'She has demonstrated feminine capabilities that go far beyond childbirth; she made her way in a man's world without denying that she was a woman'. But not until recent years has Margaret Mead modified her position and begun to chide women – as well as their over-domesticated husbands – for too much preoccupation with home and family.

However, all these educators, scientists and other molders of public opinion are not independent thinkers. They are themselves molded by the controllers of our economy and directly or indirectly serve their needs. Paramount among these, of course, is the need for expanding sales and greater profits.

The 'Sexual Sell'

Betty Friedan generously says that the 'Sexual Sell' in consumer's goods is not the result of an 'economic conspiracy' by big business. However, she presents ample evidence that the profiteers are the main movers and prime beneficiaries of the immense apparatus generating the drive toward keeping women in the home. Women are the major buyers of things for the home and its inmates. Thus, as the author points out, 'In all the talk of femininity and women's role, one forgets that the real business in America is business'.

To step up the sale of things and more things, through rapidly changing fashions, is the job of the commercial advertising and sales promotion agencies. Women's weaknesses are carefully studied and ruthlessly exploited by the most unscrupulous members of the Madison Avenue brainwashers, the 'manipulators in depth'. Taking advantage of the knowledge that most housewives are restless, unhappy and bored, the 'Depth Boys' have come up with magic formulas promising 'feminine fulfillment' through the purchase of things.

The endlessly 'hungry' women who do not understand that they are really starved for means of expressing their productive, social, cultural and intellectual potential become easy prey for this gigantic sales swindle. Since her own identity as a human being has collapsed, writes Betty Friedan, 'she needs these external trappings to buttress her emptiness of self, to make her feel like somebody'.

One of the chief professional 'motivators', who is paid about a million a year for his services, told the author how cunningly this fraud is perpetrated:

> Properly manipulated (if you are not afraid of that word) American housewives can be given the sense of identity, purpose, creativity, the self realization, even the sexual joy they lack – by the buying of things ...
>
> In a free enterprise economy we have to develop the need for new products. And to do that we have to liberate women to desire these new products ... This can be manipulated. We sell them what they ought to want, speed up the unconscious, move it along ... The manufacturer wants her back into the kitchen – and we show him how to do it the right way. If he tells her all she can be is a wife and mother, she will spit in his face. But we show him how to tell her that it's creative to be in the kitchen. We liberate her need to be creative in the kitchen.

To stimulate the housewife into becoming a passionate thing-buyer, the 'Depth Boys' overstimulate her appetites for food, sex and procreation. Thus the slick magazines feature dramatic full-page color spreads of 'gargantuan vegetables; beets, cucumbers, green peppers, potatoes', not to speak of succulent roasts dripping with gravy and fluffy pies and cakes. In large sized print usually reserved for a first grade primer, foods are 'described like a love affair'. This 'oral' satisfaction requires, in turn, the buying of the right home with a gorgeous kitchen, sometimes decorated with mosaic murals and original paintings, equipped with gleaming electric mixers, red stoves with rounded corners, and all the other paraphernalia and gadgets that subtly tie in status with stomach.

Sexual gratification is likewise promised in glamor ads featuring lipsticks and hair dyes, hi-fashion clothes, perfumes, chrome-plated cars and the like. The sacred joys of procreation demand a great diversity of products from pink and blue, toy-filled nurseries to Dr. Spock's current baby bible. Through some oversight, that bodily 'exit', the anus, is least imaginatively treated; soft toilet tissue is still toilet paper even if it comes in four different colors and white.

If, after all their frenzied purchasing, the results do not stack up with the promises, the housewives are invited to slake their thirst with salt water. They can double and triple their purchases of things, but, as the author points out, women have minds and capacities that food, sex or procreation by themselves cannot satisfy. And those who think that their discontents can be removed by more money, a bigger house, two fireplaces instead of one, three cars, another baby, moving to a better suburb, 'often discover it gets worse'.

The Feminine Mystique plays as big a role in supporting the consumer market as cold-war propaganda does in the domain of producers' goods. Commenting on the explosive sales boom of the Fabulous Fifties, the author writes: 'It would take a clever economist to figure out what would keep our affluent economy going if the housewife market began to fall off, just as an economist would have to figure out what to do if there were no threat of war'. In short, just as the Merchants of Death prosper by exploiting the 'menace of Communism' on foreign fronts, the Merchants of the Mystique get rich by exploiting the 'menace of unfemininity' on the home front.

But the real menace, which lies below the level of general consciousness, is the dehumanization of the American people – a process that affects not only the housewife but sucks the whole family into its vortex.

The Vortex

The purchase of things – even a mountain of junk – fails to produce the Happy Family of Togetherness pictured by the advertisers. On the contrary, family relationships degenerate into relationships among owners of things. There are many millions of impoverished women who are deprived of the necessary things that would make their lives more bearable and fruitful. But among these surfeited middleclass women, the possession of things possesses them – and impoverishes their personalities.

When the wife is reduced to a thing-buyer, the husband becomes a 'thing around the house' who justifies his own frantic activities in the rat-race by claiming it's all necessary for the 'wife and kiddies'. The children, too, become converted into living possessions in a home filled with ornaments of all kinds. Unable to understand, much less articulate, the real source of their resentments, husbands and wives, parents and children, become alienated from one another, often blaming one another for their stunted lives.

Most desperate are those housewives who have abandoned attempts to kill all their time with housework. But they seek for relief in the wrong directions. Some, guided by the all-pervasive exaltation of sex, become the 'sex-seekers' inside or outside of marriage. But the more aggressive they become in the pursuit of sexual bliss, the less they find what they are seeking. Betty Friedan sums up the 'faceless, depersonalized' sex-seeking of today as follows:

> Instead of fulfilling the promise of infinite orgiastic bliss, sex in the America of the feminine mystique is becoming a strangely joyless national compulsion, if not a contemptuous mockery. The sex-glutted novels become increasingly explicit and increasingly dull; the sex kick of the women's magazines has a sickly sadness; the endless flow of manuals describing new sex techniques hint at an endless lack of excitement. This sexual boredom is betrayed by the ever-growing size of the Hollywood starlet's breast, by the sudden emergence of the male phallus as an advertising 'gimmick'. Sex has become depersonalized, seen in terms of these exaggerated symbols.
>
> But of all the strange sexual phenomena that have appeared in the era of the feminine mystique, the most ironic are these – the frustrated sexual hunger of American women has increased, and their conflicts over femininity have intensified, as they have reverted from independent activity in search for their sole fulfillment through their sexual role in the home. And as American women have turned their attention to the exclusive, explicit, and aggressive pursuit of sexual fulfillment, or the acting-out of sexual

fantasy, the sexual disinterest of American men, and their hostility toward women, have also increased ... The sellers, it seems, have sexed the sex out of sex.

Other housewives turn toward their own children as the closest and most malleable means for relieving their dissatisfactions. For the woman who 'lives through her children', mother-love becomes converted into 'smother-love'. Even worse, women who are robbed of normal, adult relationships carry on what amounts to 'love affairs' with their children. The more susceptible young males can be 'virtually destroyed in the process'. Women and boys comprise the majority of patients in the psychiatric clinics.

Girls, brought up under the influence of the Feminine Mystique are likewise vulnerable to becoming emotionally arrested at an infantile level. Those who marry young become the transmission belt for conveying this infantilism to their own children. Betty Friedan calls this 'progressive dehumanization'.

Equally damaging is the parasitism encouraged in the middle-class homes where everything is done for the children, everything supervised for their comfort and pleasure down to the 'curl of their hair'. The advertisers feed this indulgence with sales campaigns directed at the 'gimme' kids. This excessive pampering is imitated by better income working-class parents who are deluded into believing this is giving their own children 'the best'. But in homes where the living is easy, the children tend to grow up soft, passive, lazy and incompetent. Unable to organize a program of serious study and work, and lacking ambition to achieve maturity, they seek to fill up their vacant time with 'kicks'. As the author writes: 'A questionnaire revealed that there was literally nothing these kids felt strongly enough about to die for, as there was nothing they actually did in which they felt really alive. Ideas, the conceptual thought which is uniquely human, were completely absent from their minds or lives'.

This absence of vital purpose, this indifference to human values, was noted by army doctors and psychologists who studied G.I. prisoners of the Korean War. Many of them, unlike their Yankee forebears, lost all resourcefulness, became inert, uncommunicative, did nothing to help their sick comrades, and even cast others out in the snow to die. Such dehumanized behavior, opined one doctor, was 'the result of some new failure in the childhood and adolescent training of our young men'.

Social Connections

Betty Friedan connects all the consequences of the flight back to home and family with the predominant state of conservatism and loss of interest in public affairs and social struggles:

> What happened to women is part of what happened to all of us in the years after the war. We found excuses for not facing the problems we once had the courage to face. The American spirit fell into a strange sleep; men as well as women, scared liberals, disillusioned radicals, conservatives bewildered and frustrated by change – the whole nation stopped growing up. All of us went back to the warm brightness of home ...
>
> It was easier, safer, to think about love and sex than about Communism, McCarthy, and the uncontrolled bomb. It was easier to look for Freudian sexual roots in man's behavior, his ideas, and his wars than to look critically at his society and act constructively to right its wrongs. There was a kind of personal retreat, even on the part of the most farsighted, the most spirited; we lowered our eyes from the horizon, and steadily contemplated our own navels.

This is certainly true. But what is the alternative to total submersion into family life? Betty Friedan's diagnosis of the disease is superior to her remedy for it. She suggests that more serious education and study, together with interesting, well-paying jobs, will open the door of the trap. This is the same kind of limited, individual solution that the feminists formerly proposed – and that subsequently proved so ineffective. Some fortunate women can do what the author has done – turn around, make a 'new life plan' and escape the domestic cage. But the life-plans for the great majority of women are determined for them by forces outside their personal control – the ruling powers.

The sicknesses that Betty Friedan describes with so much penetration and courage are the products of a diseased social organism, in which the rights, welfare and opportunities of human beings are subjected to the dictates of the profiteers. During a capitalist war women can be taken out of their homes by the millions and put to work in the factories. But when they are no longer needed as producers, they are sent back home to become primarily consumers. In both instances, what is decisive is not the needs of women as human beings but the interests of the monopolists. These masters of America shape the lives and livelihoods of womanhood and the whole family according to their own corrupt and corrupting aims.

Woman's destiny cannot be fundamentally transformed until this truth is understood and acted upon. The feminists of the past could achieve their limited reforms within the framework of a still-ascending capitalism. But today it has become dead-end capitalism. It is good but not enough for women to become more social-minded, as Betty Friedan advocates. They should now become socialist-minded, because only a root-and-branch change in the whole venal system can save us all from further dehumanization.

11 The Triple Revolution: Political Implications and Program for Action[30]
(1964)

James P. Cannon

[**Editors' Note:** Cannon's talk was preceded by the following remarks by Asher Harer: 'The speaker for tonight, summarizing the discussion of today, is James P. Cannon, national chairman of the Socialist Workers Party, a founding member of the IWW [Industrial Workers of the World], a founding member of the Communist Party of America, and a founding member of the Socialist Workers Party of America. He has spent many long years in the labor movement as a union organizer and as a socialist agitator, propagandist, teacher, and writer. The title of his presentation tonight is "What Next? Political Implications and a Practical Program of Action That Flows From The Triple Revolution Manifesto". That is certainly a mouth-filling title and what we are about to hear will fill our minds and I'm sure will instruct us in the future'.]

After such a flattering introduction I can hardly wait to hear what I'm going to say. (Laughter). Being an Irishman, I know that it's larded with a lot of blarney. And though we like to hear it, we don't take it too seriously (because we feel we merit at least ten percent of it).

The document under discussion today, which was introduced by Mr. [William] Worthy this morning and which most of you have read, I assume, by now, is, in my opinion, perhaps the most important new contribution to social thought that's been made this year, and perhaps for several years, in this country. It's all the more significant and, in my opinion, all the more effective and useful because of its source. This devastating indictment of the social system as it operates in America today did not come from a group of disgruntled radicals or revolutionists, but from a group of thinkers who wrote it for the benefit of

---

30 Cannon 1994. This talk was given at the West Coast Vacation School of the Socialist Workers Party (in northern California) on September 4, 1964. It was transcribed by Lee DeNoyer from an audiotape of nearly 30 years vintage – a few passages where the words were inaudible have been indicated.

the rulers of this country, calling their attention to some facts which they had digested and analyzed, and explaining to them that something would have to be done far more seriously, of a far more thoroughgoing nature than they had even contemplated yet. The real bosses of the country were so busy counting their extra profits that they had forgotten to ask themselves the old question that the learned politicians used to ask, 'Whither are we drifting?'

The men who were assembled at Santa Barbara, in our own state, in that rich man's town, in plush quarters, had gathered together and, you might say, computerized some of the facts and gave them a terrible looking tape. And just because of its origin in Santa Barbara at the Center for the Study of Democratic Institutions, which is a highly respected subordinate branch of the Fund for the Republic, it has already been widely publicized and its central theme has not been missed by anybody.

Its central theme is that it's necessary to change the value standards of modern society as a result of the multiplied productivity of modern production made possible by automation linked to computers, which they call the cybernetic revolution.

The Triple Revolution Manifesto is a warning from inside their house that if they do not change their standard of values, that if they do not recognize that the people displaced by automation are entitled to compensation sufficient to assure a decent living, they are headed for a crisis of chaos and disorder.

Those are the words of the scholars, not those of a soap box agitator from the IWW. Those are the words of the scholars who are working, and I'm happy to tell you, at the expense of an institution paid for out of funds left by the late Henry Ford. And that proves something to me. That proves that Ford's worth more dead than alive! (Laughter).

Now what should be, radicals, revolutionists, and fighters for the rights of Negroes in the human rights movement, what should we do with this document that has been prepared from the other side of the fence, so to speak? I say we should grasp it with both hands without any further delay and put it to our own uses. And that goes not only for the party that I represent. I think it applies equally to the Negro movement, which has reached a point in its development where it has either got to do some more thinking for itself or appropriate some of the thinking of others, as I'm proposing we do. These others are the signers of the document on the Triple Revolution.

Sectarianism vs. Revolutionary Marxism

It doesn't come easy for American radicals to take ideas from other people. There's a certain traditional conservatism, which goes by the name of sectarianism. By the way, sectarianism is often misunderstood. A lot of people think it means extreme radicalism. I had a talk with Comrade Trotsky once about that. I recalled that Lenin had said that ultra-leftism is just the other side of the coin from opportunism. He [Trotsky] was asking me to stop over in England on the way to the World Congress in '38, where they had four different groups calling themselves Trotskyists, and asked me to see if I could use my good offices to effect a unification among them, at least long enough to have them send a united delegation to the founding congress of the Fourth International. I had been reading some of their literature and I said to Comrade Trotsky, 'You know, I get the impression that all of these groups are afflicted with the traditional sectarian sickness of British radicalism. And it's a *conservative* sectarianism'. And he answered me quite abruptly. He said, 'Well, you know it's very hard to find a *revolutionary* sectarian'.

Why, we used to be so damn radical in this country that before the First World War, about the time of 1912 or 1913, Victor Berger, the reformist socialist from Milwaukee, was elected as the first socialist congressman, and one of his first actions was to introduce a bill for old age pensions. And the left wing of the Socialist Party and the IWW denounced this at the top of their voices as nothing but a damn reform and we wouldn't take anything less than the whole socialist package. Why, even the great Bill Haywood himself wrote an article in the *International Socialist Review* with the heading 'Against Old Age Pensions'. I wouldn't dare to show an article like that to a recipient of Social Security today!

Do you know that the American Federation of Labor under the philosophy of Gompers and later of William Green had a schematic conception that the government should keep out of the relations between the unions and the employers altogether, and that when the terrible crisis of 1929 and the '30s broke out and the demand began to be made for unemployment insurance – by this time by the radicals who had learned a little something – it was officially opposed by William Green, the president of the American Federation of Labor, on the grounds that that would mean government interference in what should be the free play of collective bargaining between helpless unions and all-powerful bosses? I have not yet heard, and I don't think there is one case on record, of a member of the AFL-CIO today who has not only not refused to take his unemployment check, but who's been five minutes late to collect it! I don't think so. We've learned a little, and we've got to learn to take what's good wherever we can find it.

That's one of the things that we learned from Lenin, one of the many things. In 1917 when the Bolsheviks took over the government of Russia, they represented the majority of the working class organized in the soviets, but they needed the support of the peasantry, which was the overwhelming majority of the country. I will just quote directly from a remark made by Trotsky in an article he wrote in 1923. He said, 'Bolshevism began with a program of the restitution of bits of land to the peasants, replaced this program with that of nationalization, and then made the agrarian program of the Social Revolutionists its own in 1917'. The party of the Social Revolutionists was a peasant party, bitterly opposed to the Bolsheviks, and the Bolsheviks took their land program and put it into law as a decree. And the Social Revolutionary politicians hollered bloody murder, 'You're stealing our program!' And Lenin, who with all his other great merits had a sense of humor, answered them. With a straight face, but a twinkle in his eye, he said, 'Did we ever promise that if you had anything good we wouldn't take it?' (Laughter). So that's our precedent, so to speak, for appropriating the program of the Triple Revolution.

Automation, Unemployment, Poverty

Now I think you've been told before, and you've read – if you read anything that's published in this country – that we are the richest country in the world. And you know from all the evidence around you every day, brought to a focus by the two conventions of the Democratic and Republican parties, that we're not only the richest country in the world, but we're also the most conservative country. But this document on the Triple Revolution reminds us what some of us have already known, that there's a terrible instability about this rich and powerful country. A terrible feeling of insecurity and fear on every side. Not only among the poor, not only among the workers who've got jobs, but also among those who've got money and are afraid they're not going to be able to keep it. That's the real motive force behind the Goldwater movement: fear, insecurity. They've got more money than they can count, but they want to make sure that they can keep it all. So they want to abolish the income tax, cut government spending, do away with public welfare, and all the rest that costs money, out of fear for the future.

We had a film here last night or the night before on the results of automation, taken not yesterday, but seven years ago in 1957. It was an hour-long film presided over by Edward R. Murrow, showing scenes of automatic processes in bakeries and other industries, and it showed, I think, two meetings, one a meeting of bakers after he had shown us a bakeshop with loads of dough coming down on two endless rivers of a moving belt, moving from the origin place without human intervention anywhere down to the ovens and then coming up baked as bread. And there was a meeting of union bakers discussing that. Any they were not children; they looked like substantial men of family of 40 and 50. They were discussing, 'What is this going to do for us?' There was one thing that you could see on the faces of all these men who in the prime of life ought to be the picture of confidence and optimism. Fear was on every face. And everyone who spoke up at the meeting wondered, 'What's going to happen to us if we lose our jobs, our seniority, our medical benefits, our pension rights, and so on?' The same thing was repeated in a meeting of auto workers. That was *seven* years ago when the cybernation revolution was just trying out its wings for the first time.

Since then it has moved at an accelerated speed, and you can imagine from the facts and the figures that are given to us by the authors of the Triple Revolution Manifesto how the men in the shops with jobs and seniority rights, how secure they feel and how happy and contented they may be. Then we heard our comrade speak the other day when we were talking about the state of the unions, how the men in his shop at Chevrolet had voted 98 or 99.5 percent to strike. They've got jobs. They're privileged in comparison to the unemployed. They've got seniority. They've got pension rights and medical benefits. And yet they were so dissatisfied that they were angry at the union for calling for a showdown first at Chrysler. They wanted a strike in Chevrolet first. And the Ford workers voted almost exactly by the same percentage to be the first go to out on strike. In this richest country in the world, where they tell us everybody ought to be happy.

Another important document contributing to social thought the past year has been the book written by Michael Harrington, the Social Democrat and former social worker, called *The Other America*, a study of poverty in America. I've been reading that book for the last month, very closely and attentively, and it's a harrowing revelation. Harrowing. He gives the government figures – [backward and forward], upside down, cross-checked, and proved in every other way – that at least 25 percent of the population of this richest country in the world live below the poverty level. That means about 40 or 45 million people in this rich and powerful country, 45 million human beings that America has not provided a decent existence for; the old and the sick, the young and the unemployed.

Now we have the figures on unemployment given to us. We've got two sets of figures. One is the official government set. It says the rate of unemployment is about 5 percent, hovering around that, a little above and below, in a period of boom. And the authors of the Triple Revolution say, not in my language, but in their own polite academic language, 'That's all a damn lie! The rate is not 5 percent; it's closer to 10 percent, because the government figures include only those who are registered and applying for work, and there are at least the same number who have gotten tired of looking for work, have given up and quit. They're not only taken off the payrolls of the factories; they're even taken off the list of the unemployed. They're the forgotten people'. The projection of these figures, from the document on the Triple Revolution, shows that this is going to mount, allowing for what I consider the impossible, allowing the present industrial boom to continue and even go a little higher, that the number of jobs eliminated by cybernation, on the one side, and the oversupply of products of the baby boom of the postwar years coming into the market is going to add anywhere from 2 to 3 million to the unemployed list – *every year*.

This is only 1964. Where are we going to be in 1970, if we live that long? There may be a couple of million more added every year to the unemployment list. The unemployment slag heap, as some call it. And what is far more likely, in view of fact that Europe and Japan are also increasing their productivity through automation and cybernation, and that the world market competition becomes more severe and America can't sell its goods abroad as freely as it has in the postwar years and they run into a recession or a depression, whatever they want to call it, and have to close down some of their production – you're going to have a tremendous reservoir of millions and millions and millions of people without prospect, without hope.

The authors of this document, gentlemen and scholars as they are, go so far as to say that all the talk about creating new jobs is a cruel hoax, that they're not creating new jobs. On the contrary, they are cutting off more jobs all the time.

Now I see this seething mass not as a number of figures in the government statistics, but as a mass of human misery and frustration and desperation and anger that's going to look for some kind of action, some kind of solution, and there you have the raw material ready to hand either for a fascist movement, led by some demagogue who will promise them anything they want, or [for] a revolutionary movement that will offer them a realistic program of struggle to change things fundamentally.

The African-American Struggle

I see in the fact that this development of the productive system at the expense of the employment of workers, which hits the Negroes twice as hard as it hits the whites, and the anger, the protests, and frustration, and even the desperation that rises out of these terrible ghettos. I can see the danger of a *racial* conflict which will be completely destructive all the way around. And I take it to be one of our central tasks as Marxists to strive with all our might to see that the movement of protest takes a different direction: the direction of unity of the oppressed Negroes and the unemployed and oppressed white people in a common battle and not in a racial conflict.

Now, brotherhood has been preached for, I guess, at least two thousand years, but I don't know much brotherhood that's ever been achieved that way. You hear every pompous politician – even including Barry Goldwater – say the way to end the racial conflict is to bring about a change in the hearts of men. Try that on a Kluxer [Ku Klux Klan member] or a cracker. Try changing the heart of people who *profit* by the super-exploitation of the Negro. It doesn't work that way.

But brotherhood has existed in this world. You see it whenever you're out on the picket line. You see brothers who may not like each other very well in the shop, but when they're out on the picket line protecting their jobs and their welfare against scabs, they work together in great shape. The material basis for unity in action, the basis for brotherhood – if you want to extend it to its ultimate extreme – is common interest and common need. When you have that, you got something to go on.

This was illustrated for me very graphically by a story told me by Herbie Hill, the labor secretary of the NAACP. He was down in Birmingham at the time of the big struggles there, investigating particularly the state of the unions, and how the Negroes were represented in the different unions. He said he discovered that the most desegregated union in Birmingham, where the Negroes were employed most freely and on equal terms, was the Brotherhood of Teamsters. He went to see the head business agent and asked him, 'How come that you're different from some other unions here and don't discriminate against Negroes'. He said, 'Well, I'll tell ya, boy', – Now this is not my language, I'm quoting literally – He said, 'We ain't nigger lovers, but when we fight these goddam bosses we need all the muscle we can git. And some of these Black boys have sure got it'.

He told me another story, along the same lines almost, of a big, husky Negro steel worker just coming off a hard day's work, getting on a bus and plopping himself down on the front seat. The bus driver turned to him and said, 'Now listen, boy. Be reasonable. Let's not have any trouble. Go to the back of the bus'. The Negro steel worker just stood up to his full height and looked down at the bus driver and said, 'Boy, let me tell you something. I ain't one of these peace-lovin' Negroes you've been hearin' about'. And the bus driver pushed down the button and the bus rolled on.

The Class Struggle

Now, I say the basis for brotherhood, or at least for cooperation, for alliance, for united action is common interest and common need, and I think that obtains among the great bulk of the white workers, especially the unemployed and the poor and the lower rungs at least of the workers in the unions, and they number many millions.

While this is somewhat of an intrusion on the subject of tomorrow, it's covered in the Triple Revolution as one element of it, the struggle for human rights. I'm a firm believer in the idea, not only a believer, I'm convinced in my knowledge, that all whites are not the same and that there's a great deal of difference between a man who's walking home with his last unemployment check in his pocket and the owner of the plant that laid him off, and a distinction ought to be made between them. There's a common interest with one, and eternal enmity with the other.

It's become rather commonplace nowadays for some people to cross off the American labor movement with its seventeen and a half million members. I just read a piece the other day that just ruled that out of order – they don't count, they're conservative, contented, privileged – they're never going to do anything.

I say those who doubt the capacity of the American workers to play their historic role in the great social struggles yet to come ought to remember or read about the '30s and the '20s. We went through a prolonged boom in the '20s. Throughout the entire postwar period after the First World War, with the exception of a recession in 1921 which was soon overcome, up to 1929 there was a booming economy and the unions actually declined in membership. There wasn't a trace of militancy except in the depressed industries like textiles and some parts of the coal fields. And a lot of people were saying the same thing then, 'You got to write off the working class'.

As a matter of fact, the unions didn't extend into the basic industries at all; they were restricted to only a narrow fringe of skilled craftsmen for the most part. Even in Minneapolis, union building tradesmen had to sit by and see the two biggest downtown buildings going up before their eyes, built by nonunion labor.

It was pretty hard to be a revolutionary communist in those days. It was pretty hard to go up against the general feeling of passivity and against the people continually saying, 'The workers will never do anything; they'll never rise'. Until there came the depression of 1929, I think you've all heard about that. You've probably got scars from it somewhere, either you or your family.

That depression lasted, with slight upturns, for ten years. That depression hit a working class that was not organized in a single one of the basic industries. The only unions they had were company unions. That is, unions organized by the company with their own stooges in charge of them. A cruel hoax that the workers hated worse than no unions at all. The workers were completely unorganized and atomized, and it took them five or six years, and it took an upturn in the economy when a number of them got back into the plants, before they could begin to manifest a little fighting spirit. In the meantime wages had been slashed mercilessly by the bosses.

They went back to jobs at miserable wages and [with] intolerable conditions. And then in 1934 a few things began to happen. There were sporadic strikes around the country which were smashed. The regular formula was to call out a lot of hoodlums, cops, militiamen, detectives whatever they needed ... [several words completely inaudible] ... and they would break the strike. Until the Autolite strike in Toledo in the spring of '34, led by the Musteites, a radical political organization. They were also the leaders of an unemployment movement, the Unemployed Leagues, which they brought into cooperation with the pickets of the plant, and the strike was won by militant action. And then the Minneapolis strikes in '34 ... [and the San Francisco maritime and general strike.] [Tape becomes inaudible again for a sentence or more.] ... which shook this country because these were three American strikes that weren't broken, but were won. And I read the other day in a biography of John L. Lewis by Saul Alinsky, who said that John L. Lewis noticed these three strikes and saw in them a future trend and that influenced him greatly toward throwing his support to the Committee for Industrial Organization that later became the CIO.

And from that beginning mushroomed the uprising of the workers which culminated in the sit-down strikes of '36, '37, '38 – in rubber, steel, auto – and finally in 1941 the organization of the Ford plant and the solid construction of the CIO.

I've always called the rise of the CIO a semi-revolution. If there had been adequate leadership, nobody knows where it might have ended. *I just simply discard the idea that the workers will not move if the squeeze is put on them.*

In the long-drawn-out postwar boom since World War II, propped up by enormous military expenditures and foreign loans and other government spending, you know, the $50-odd billion military budget is the real cushion on which the whole economy rests. If disarmament were declared tomorrow and they stopped spending money for military preparations, there would be the biggest crisis in history.

Now in the light of the material given to us in this document on the Triple Revolution, where they predict chaos and turmoil unless people are provided with compensation when they can't be provided with jobs, I think it's fitting for us, who try to think about social problems and try by our thinking and our actions to influence the course of development, to ask who will spark the next upsurge of the American working class as a whole? My personal opinion is that it will take a somewhat different direction than it did in the '30s. It is quite likely, as a matter of fact, I think almost certain, that it is going to begin with the organization of the unemployed. You can't have ten million people out of work month after month and year after year and then their number increasing one, two, or three million every year without somebody deciding to do something about it.

And the obvious thing will be to organize the unemployed, as attempts were made in the '30s. There was one unemployment council movement led by the Communist Party, there was another big Unemployed League movement led by the Musteites, there was a third unemployed organization led by the Socialist Party people. And here is a peculiar phenomenon that maybe many of you have forgotten or hadn't heard – that many of the young firebrands who went into this unemployed movement were college students who had graduated or dropped out with no place to go, no jobs in sight, who went into the unemployment movement and there, under the direction of the various political organizations, learned how to organize, learned how to talk, learned how to conduct themselves in meetings, learned how to act as leaders. And later when the industrial rise took place in the mid-'30s under the pump priming of the New Deal, when the factories began to open, these same young college boys – many of them, scores and hundreds of them – went into the factories and became the prime movers in the CIO.

The Logic of Black Nationalism

Now I think they'll do something like that again this time: that the unemployment movement of the '30s will be repeated on a greatly magnified scale. I don't see any reason today, right today, why in Harlem and other ghettos, where 50 percent of the teenage youth are unemployed, according to the figures given from many sources, where the rate of unemployment of Negro adults is twice that of the whites, where they live in these overcrowded, rat-infested houses that are ready to fall apart; they're so cramped and miserable that they go out on the streets because it's more comfortable to stand on the street corner than to stay in the house – I can't see any reason why they don't begin right away organizing something more than the mere demand for civil rights, which formally have been granted, while their economic conditions have been deteriorating year by year in the whole period since 1956, since the civil rights movement began to develop following the Montgomery boycott.

This is the terrible, crying, brutal paradox – that the more militant the Negroes have become, the more they have organized, the more they have asserted themselves, and the more legal gains they have made, the worse has become their economic condition, year by year. That's what's behind these flare-ups, which are simply lightning flashes: heat lightning signifying greater storms.

I can't see why they don't start organizing. And I don't see why there should be any conflict between Negroes and whites. The whites have got to recognize once for all that the Negro people are fed up with the traditional system of organizations dominated by white liberals. They want to have their own organizations and they want to have their own leaders. And if they're going to have any cooperation between them and white workers, we've got to recognize that trend and say it's progressive.

I think they make a certain mistake. They've been terribly disillusioned and let down by the white liberals, who are on hand everywhere calling all the shots until trouble starts and then dropping out or saying, 'You're going too far'. They tend to judge, I guess, all white people by the white liberals. But you know Heywood Broun, who got into the labor movement in the '30s and helped a lot, the founder, I guess you could call him, of the Newspaper Guild, a great help to the CIO unions wherever they were in trouble. He gave a definition of a liberal that I think is going to stick forever. He said, 'A liberal is a man who reaches for his hat when the fight starts!'

Now, I think it's a good thing that the Negro people have learned that, and got disillusioned with them [the liberals], and build their own organizations, beginning [with what] I think is the natural, logical, wide open field for them; the unemployment movement. I don't see why they can't organize it from block to block in Harlem.

Labor Bureaucracy vs. Militant Struggle

Here I come to a disagreement with a minor point in the Manifesto on the Triple Revolution. Among the other things they suggest, without realizing what they were doing, they suggested that the trade union leaders should interest themselves in the unemployment question and negotiate for them. I say that's about the worst thing that could happen to the unemployed. All the negotiating that the labor skates will do for the unemployed is to negotiate them out of the plant to make room for the seniority men. That's what they do in every contract.

Every contract that's hailed as a great innovation, beginning with the longshore contract [and going] to the steel contract and other places, is an agreement to safeguard the jobs of seniority men at the expense of the younger, the newer, the poorer.

I saw Reuther on the film – this was seven years ago, the automation film – and he was pontificating in an interview with Ed Murrow about automation. He didn't seem to have a line of worry on his face. He looked well padded, well groomed, his hair all in order with his greasy kid stuff, and he was talking like a business executive. He said, Something has got to be done. Labor, management, and government have got to get together and work out something. That's seven years ago and they haven't worked out anything yet, and they never will.

The unemployed have got to have their own autonomous organizations. And then the question arises immediately – we're going to take a hand in this, I hope – what can be the program of the first unemployment organizations?

I know the workers of America are not ready to hear the full socialist message. And those comrades in our own ranks of a sectarian bent who answer the arguments of the Triple Revolution by saying nothing will do any good but socialism haven't got anything to say to the worker who isn't ready to hear the socialist program. What we have got to find is what Trotsky called a *transitional* program that will correspond to their present understanding and their present acceptance.

I think the program outlined in the Triple Revolution, that everyone is entitled to work or compensation, will be accepted generally by workers both Black and white, if they're unemployed. I don't think you'll find many that are the least bit worried about somebody calling it a dole. This is not a dole. This is *payment* for the fact that you're a citizen of this country and that you've got a life to live. It's not a beggar's dole; it's a human right! And that's the way it's got to be presented. And the demonstrations for jobs are like pounding your face against a stone wall, when you know and they know and everybody knows that there are no jobs.

We've got to say 'Jobs or Compensation'. That's the way it's got to be formulated. And if they answer, 'How can we give you compensation if you don't produce anything?' We say, 'All right, give us jobs'. 'We can't give you jobs'. 'Well, what do you want us to do? We're human beings. We're citizens of this great free country. Now let's have a slice of some of the benefits. You got plenty of money. Take it out of General Motors' profits. Cut 20 million dollars out of your military budget and spend it on maintaining the human rights and human dignity of your unemployed citizens thrown out of your factories. Or let the moon alone for a while and spend 20 million dollars making the earth fit to live on'. (Applause).

The organizers and agitators of the unemployment movement under this transitional program have an irresistible argument that will be accepted by the intelligent workers everywhere and for which the bosses can't give much of an answer. Ever since this document was published nearly six months ago, they have been repeatedly commenting on it, but I have never seen anywhere any serious attempt to refute it. Not even this latest article in *Life* magazine. It's been more widely circulated than you realize. *Advertising Age*, which is an organ of big business, reprinted the thing entirely and even went so far as to provide the type for this pamphlet we have here. The business community has heard all about this, and I think they're waiting to see what the workers are going to do about it, especially the unemployed workers.

Developing a Transitional Program

Now, when I agreed to give this speech last week or ten days ago, I knew that I was going to say that this program should be adopted by our party and by other radical organizations and by the Negro movement. I sense a great stalemate in the Negro movement, that their program is too limited for their needs. They have got to adopt a *social* program. It doesn't do the Negroes huddled in the horrible ghettos much good to tell them, 'I'm fighting like hell to get you the right to vote', which they've had for years in New York. Or the right to desegregate schools, which they know is not going to be done and the right to eat a hamburger in a greasy restaurant. What they want is jobs. They want to make a living, or they want to live somehow.

The trouble with the Negro population of this country is not merely discrimination, although that's terrible; the trouble with them is what George Bernard Shaw said many years ago, 'The trouble with the poor is their poverty, and the trouble with the rich is their uselessness'. (Applause). I think that the Negro organizations have got to turn their attention to developing a *social program*. And I was going to let it go at that, my first thought, until I picked up last week's *Militant*. And after reading that, I must make a slight correction. I had not seen in any organization in the labor movement or the Negro movement or the radical movement anywhere an outright editorial statement supporting the Triple Revolution's program.

Then I picked up last week's *Militant* and here's what I read – under a dateline, of all places, Meridian, Mississippi. 'A freedom school convention assembled here August 6–8. The delegates to the convention, most certainly the first of its kind in Mississippi, or for that matter any state in the South, were teenage Negro freedom school students'. They came to a convention in

Meridian, Mississippi, where the three civil rights fighters were murdered. Following that they assembled in a freedom convention, and what do you think they adopted as one of the resolutions? Just listen to this: 'Among the significant demands raised by the convention were a public works program, on the one hand, and a guaranteed income of at least $3,000 annually for every citizen'. Here in Meridian, Mississippi, teenage Negro children have put themselves at the very head of the entire humanistic movement of America as the first to raise the specific demand for a guaranteed annual income for every citizen.

And further, support to labor was indicated in the following plan: 'We will encourage and support more strikes for better jobs and adequate pay. During the strikes, the employers should be enjoined from having others replace the striking workers'. Now there's a hit and a miss. One, they're for strikes and support of strikes. And they don't specify only strikes involving Negroes; it's strikes involving workers both white and Black. That's a hit. The miss is, in my opinion, where they say, 'The employer should be enjoined from having others replace the striking workers'. That is, they should get a court injunction. I know a better way! (Laughter).

Just get some colored men with muscle from the teamsters union in Birmingham and some Irish Catholics who've forgotten their religion for the moment and put 'em on a picket line! That's the way to keep scabs out of the plant – mass picketing.

But I salute these young teenagers who have adopted for the first time a social program which I am convinced is going to be the transitional program of the entire movement of the disinherited in this country. The transitional program with the demand for either jobs or compensation. And the very fact that they come out in support of strikes without specifying the color of the people involved shows they're reaching out for allies among the white working class. And God knows they need them. Minorities have played great roles in revolutions in the past, but they haven't always won. They've won in those cases where they've recognized the need for allies.

Now everybody knows that the greatest revolution in history was made in Russia in the name of the working class in 1917. But not everybody knows that the total number of industrial workers in Russia in 1917 was less than three million. Three million industrial workers in a sea of peasants, about 150 million at the time. Now how did they overcome this terrible disparity? They didn't do it by fighting the peasants. They did it by seeking an *alliance* with them. They needed allies, and they offered to the peasants, if you come with us in the revolution, you can take that land you're working for the landlord and chase him the hell off of there. The great slogan that they rallied them with was 'Peace! Bread! Land!' – something everybody understood. And when foreign intervention came, and the White Guards tried counterrevolution, and they had to organize a huge army to beat off the invaders from many of the imperialist nations and the White Guards at the same time, they did it with an army primarily of peasants. Because the peasants were given something to fight for: the land, and the promise of peace when they chased off the White Guards, which they did eventually, although it took them four years to do it.

Lenin's genius didn't confine itself to accepting the Social Revolutionaries' land program in order to win the alliance with the peasants. He brought forward his program about the right of nationalities to self-determination. He recognized there's such a thing as a national spirit among the many countries that had been absorbed and assimilated in the old Russian empire. And they proclaimed the right of self-determination. They could decide for themselves whether or not they would come into the Soviet Union. And by the very fact of offering that to them, they made allies out of them. And with such allies, the peasants, the oppressed nationalities, the petty bourgeoisie in the towns, the intellectuals, by offering something to them and inviting them into collaboration, they turned the minority of 3 million workers into a majority that was able to carry through the revolution and to reorganize the whole social system from top to bottom.

Now the demand for jobs or compensation, not a dole, but as they say in Meridian, Mississippi, '$3,000 a year for every citizen who is unemployed', is a *political* demand. It's not to be addressed to some corner supermarket or some used car lot demanding they put on another salesman or two. It's a political demand addressed by mass demonstrations before the political institutions of the country: the city halls, the state capitals, and the national capital in Washington.

I'm not much of a utopian, or given to indulging in mistaking wishes for possibilities, but I can foresee a great mass of unemployed Negroes marching out of Harlem to meet a similar mass of unemployed whites and march together, each under its own leadership, down to the city hall to tell the mayor they want jobs or compensation. I can see great marches up to the capital of the state of New York in Albany and marches to Washington. And out of demonstrations of that kind, not only will there be a great proliferation of militancy and confidence, but there will come a spirit of solidarity based on common interests and common needs that will bind the Negro and white workers together, not in the name of an empty formula, but in the name of necessity, to protect each other.

I can foresee that movement knocking on the doors of the union offices and the union meeting halls and asking the organized workers on the job to lend their support to this demand. And I can see great masses of employed union workers saying, 'That's a damn good idea. I'd like to see that done. I'll vote for it. If I lose my job tomorrow, I'd like to step into a situation where I can get compensation – not merely limited to half pay and unemployment insurance, which runs out in six months and then leaves me hungry – compensation as a matter of right as a citizen'. There's a basis there. I don't say it's going to be realized in one jump, but there's a basis of common interest between the employed and the unemployed. The employed have got nothing whatever to lose by supporting such a thing as that; they can see a mutual benefit in it.

Revolutionary Leadership

What we're looking for, of course, out of all this is where can we get a mass movement started on the way to doing a much more complete job than merely providing compensation? And who will lead it? Who will lead this movement? I say those will lead who can. Those will lead who think. Those will lead who see what's new in the situation and what it portends for the future, and are able to learn and to change and to adapt themselves to new conditions and new possibilities.

I have followed very attentively the evolution of Malcolm X from his previous position after his visit to Africa and his consultation with various leaders there and his own experience: a change from sectarian religious withdrawal from the mass movement to a proposal that all Negro organizations cooperate, to the statement that he's not against white people as such, he's just against the white people that are on his back. [I have noted] his declaration that this is an international struggle, and his trying to enlist the support of the African nations to bring the scandal of discrimination against American Negroes before the United Nations. A man who's capable of learning and changing is capable of learning more and changing more. And that has to apply to us, too. We've got to learn and to change and to hope that, by the exchange of ideas and experiences among all the people who've got bitter grievances against this system, we'll come out with a common program that will bind us all together into a great invincible force.

The transitional program of compensation as a citizen will lead to stronger demands as gains are made. With each advance confidence in the masses will grow and things will begin to be called by their right name, which we don't hear now in this present atmosphere of conservative fear and insecurity. The word social revolution will be uttered and will resound in this country and [be] spoken out loud, and the word socialism, which you hear all over Africa and Asia today, will be heard in the streets of America. It will ring out like the old

Liberty Bell in Philadelphia on the first Fourth of July, and with its clamor proclaim: freedom throughout the land and for all inhabitants thereof.

And the movement rallied around such words as social revolution and socialism will learn to sing again. And that'll be the sign that it's coming alive and that it's young and confident of its future. And wouldn't it be wonderful to be alive and to be young in that day? I think of the words of Wordsworth the poet about the first days of the great French Revolution, which began the change of the world, the downfall of the old outlived feudal system. He said, 'Bliss was it in that dawn to be alive, but to be young was very heaven'.

And I think of the words of another noble poet of the people, I guess the poet that I love above all others – Shelley, the poet who sang of freedom and who exhorted the oppressed everywhere to rise up in unvanquishable numbers and tried to give them confidence. In words that used to be quoted by an old friend of mine in the IWW named Jack White [?; name unclear] who used to wind up his speeches with that note of confidence from Shelley:

> Fear not that the tyrants shall rule forever,
> Nor the priests of the bloody faith.
> They stand on the brink of a mighty river
> Whose waves they have tainted with death.
> It is fed from the springs of a thousand dells.
> About them it rages and foams and swells.
> And their thrones and their scepters I floating see
> Like wrecks on the shores of eternity.

Many thrones and scepters have gone down the river of history since Shelley wrote those noble words, and some are yet to come. The biggest and heaviest and ugliest and most oppressive of all is in this country. And we should not doubt, we should not fear, that this tyrant will rule forever. It will also go down on the river of history and that will be what they call the great day in the morning, and people will really sing on the way to that day, 'Ain't nobody gonna turn me around'.

CHAPTER 4

Challenges of Black Liberation

Paul Le Blanc

The dilemma faced by the socialist movement in the United States since its beginnings was what W.E.B. Du Bois once identified as that facing the world in the entire twentieth century – the racism associated with 'the color line'. We have noted, in the first volume of this documentary trilogy on US Trotskyism, the early uncertainties and limitations afflicting comrades in the Communist League of America and its successors from 1929 through 1939, concluding with a clear anti-racist orientation fashioned collaboratively by C.L.R. James and Leon Trotsky.[1]

This orientation was undergirded by a particular variant of black nationalism: positing the necessity of 'self-determination' in the triple sense of black control of all black liberation struggles, black control of black communities, and (if desired by African Americans) the right to a separate national existence for African Americans. The orientation posited, at the same time, the need for black-white working-class solidarity, and the centrality of the black liberation struggle in overall working class's revolutionary efforts to bring about a socialist society beneficial to all – with full equality among all people, regardless of racial, ethnic of national origin.

We saw in the second volume of this trilogy how that orientation was applied in the 1940s and early 1950s, further developed and articulated by various US Trotskyists, black and white (among the latter George Breitman playing a particularly key role). As the 1950s flowed into the 1960s – particularly with the upsurge of the civil rights movement in the wake of the 1954 Supreme Court decision, Brown v. Board of Education, calling for the desegregation of public schools (with very broad implications for equal citizenship rights throughout the country), powerfully inspired as well by anti-colonial revolutions involving various 'peoples of color' in battle against white racist power structures.[2]

---

1 On Du Bois, see Mullen 2016. For documentary surveys on African American experience and struggle in the United States, see: Grant 1996 and Le Blanc 2017. Essential documents on the Trotsky-James collaboration can be found in Trotsky 1994, and a narrative account is offered in Allen 1983, pp. 227–331.
2 Surveys of the civil rights struggle are provided in: Braden 1965; Branch 1988; Marable 2007.

Analytical reportage on Southern struggles by Lois Saunders and Fred Halstead, and the ambitious theorization on 'How a Minority Can Change Society' by George Breitman, give a vivid sense of multiple strands of this freedom movement. These reflect a distinct trajectory, from the powerful mass initiatives for racial integration associated with Martin Luther King, Jr. and his Southern Christian Leadership Conference (SCLC), to the bold and in some ways more radical push by the Congress of Racial Equality (CORE), the formation of the militant Student Nonviolent Coordinating Committee (SNCC), and the growing influence of black nationalism and Malcolm X. George Breitman was particularly involved, in Detroit, with interactions with a rising wave of African American insurgency associated with the Freedom Now Party. More than most on the Left, he evidenced a keen appreciation of Malcolm X. Shortly after the death of 'our shining black prince' (as Ossie Davis put it in his funeral oration), Breitman edited the first collection of his speeches, *Malcolm X Speaks*, and wrote the influential *The Last Year of Malcolm X: The Evolution of a Revolutionary*.[3]

A complicating factor in the burgeoning civil rights struggle involved a leadership influenced by pacifism (generally disdained by Marxists) and not adhering to the Trotskyists' distinctive revolutionary socialist perspectives. This was true of the leaders of the activist wing of the movement – represented in various ways by A. Philip Randolph and his protégé Bayard Rustin, Martin Luther King of the Southern Christian Leadership Conference (SCLC), James Farmer of the Congress of Racial Equality (CORE), and of a number of younger activists in the Student Nonviolent Coordinating Committee (SNCC). What has until recently been lost sight of (and was generally unacknowledged by US Trotskyists) is the fact that all of these leaders were influenced by radical and socialist perspectives that were explicitly influenced by Marxism. (Particularly influential were followers of the ex-Trotskyist leader Max Shachtman). At the same time, however, in the Cold War atmosphere they were inclined to adopt the protective coloration of 'liberalism', and also they increasingly inclined in the direction of reformism and adaptation to the liberal capitalist politics of the Democratic Party. This would eventually result in a break in which many in SNCC, but also to a significant degree Martin Luther King (contrary to commonly-held Trotskyist attitudes), would be pulled leftward, while Rustin and Randolph would be pulled rightward.[4]

---

3 Context is provided in Le Blanc and Yates 2013. On CORE and SNCC, see Meier and Rudwick 1972, and Carson 1981. Black nationalist currents are traced in: Bracey, Meier, and Rudwick 1970; and Dillard 2010. On Malcolm X, see Breitman 1994 and Breitman 1970.
4 For Randolph and Rustin, see Anderson 1986 and D'Emilio 2003. For King and SCLC, see Gar-

Further complications naturally arose from the incredibly tangled racial dynamics afflicting every level and dimension of US society, and reflected within the Socialist Workers Party as well – most explicitly discussed here in Robert Des Verney's remarkable contribution. Such dynamics had much to do with what came to be known as 'black nationalism', which became particularly important in the urban centers of the North, where the SWP was concentrated.[5]

Dissatisfied with the Trotsky-James synthesis that guided (or failed to guide, depending on one's interpretation) the SWP beginning in 1939, Richard Fraser had for years, inside the party, sharply challenged the validity of the *black nationalism* concept and analysis, calling instead for what he called 'revolutionary integrationism'. In the polemic presented here, he usefully supplements Des Verney's comments on the complex currents and counter-currents within the SWP on this question.[6]

No one labored more diligently than George Breitman to define, develop, argue for, and practically utilize the dominant perspective within the Socialist Workers Party that harmonized black nationalist and socialist perspectives. His efforts are reflected in the SWP's 1963 'Freedom Now' resolution, reproduced here, and put him in a unique position to play a role in the influential though short-lived Freedom Now Party in Detroit, and particularly to connect with and help popularize the ideas of Malcolm X. Major excerpts are presented here from a presentation given in Detroit three weeks after the black leader's death.[7]

---

row 1988. The stories of CORE and SNCC are provided, respectively, by Meier and Rudwick 1972, and Carson 1981. For socialist and Marxist elements in the civil rights struggle, see Le Blanc and Yates 2013.

5 An outstanding collection on black nationalism in the United States can be found in Bracey, Meier and Rudwick 1970. Key texts on the Northern urban dimension of the civil rights and black liberation struggles can be found in Sugre 2008 and Dillard 2010. On Robert Des Verney (1928–95), see Clark and Mailhot 1995.
6 On Fraser, see International Communist League/Spartacists 1994.
7 On Breitman, see Marcus 2005. His key books on Malcolm X are Breitman 1970 and Breitman 1994.

1 The South's Dilemma[8]
(1959)

Lois Saunders

The United States Supreme Court on September 29, 1958 told the South to end its obstruction and to get on with the task of integrating its schools.

It thus set the legal framework within which the continuing battle of the Negroes for equality in educational opportunities must unfold. For the first time the question was posed to the South as a choice between the alternatives of admitting a limited number of Negroes to all-white schools or closing down the schools entirely: integration or no education.

The Court made it clear that henceforth the South must accord the same rights to Negro children as it does to white children. 'The constitutional rights of children not to be discriminated against in school admission on grounds of race or color', stated the unanimous decision, '… can neither be nullified openly and directly by state legislators or state executive or judicial officers, nor nullified indirectly by them through evasive schemes for segregation whether attempted ingeniously or ingenuously'.

In an unusual move, the Court gave advance warning that it would hold unconstitutional any legislation or plan that seeks to subvert its orders. The decision continued:

> State support of segregated schools through any arrangement, management, funds or property cannot be squared with the [Fourteenth] Amendment's command that no state shall deny to any person within its jurisdiction the equal protection of the laws.

This emphatic 'No!' was the Supreme Court's answer to an appeal from Little Rock officials for postponement of the token integration enforced there last year after federal troops put down riots officially inspired by Arkansas Gov. Orval E. Faubus. The request for a two and one-half year delay was a stratagem calculated to nullify the Court's previous rulings and bring integration to a halt.

---

8 Sanders 1959.

Had the Court backed down and granted the delay, it would have meant putting off school desegregation to an indefinite future throughout the South. Little Rock was the symbol and the testing ground, and this was universally recognized. In fact, federal judges in Virginia and elsewhere held up judgments in other school cases pending the Little Rock decision. The granting of the delay there would have been an invitation to racists everywhere to foment riots in the Faubus fashion, and then use the resulting violence and tension as an excuse for preventing court-ordered integration.

Even more was at stake, however, than the fate of integration; the authority of the federal government had been brought into question. By the time school opened in September, the South had gone too far in its defiance to permit the Court to yield to the Little Rock appeal. The South again, as in the period before the Civil War, was asserting the supremacy of the states and accusing the federal government of exceeding its powers by intervening in the matter of race relations. By choosing States Rights as its battle cry, the South threatened the foundations upon which the government is based. Successful defiance of specific federal court orders in one sphere opens the way for defiance elsewhere and weakens the entire governmental structure. Faced with a fundamental challenge to its authority, the Court had no alternative but to insist that its orders be carried out. This was the same issue that a year earlier had impelled the reluctant Pres. Eisenhower to send federal troops into Little Rock.

In the ruling of September 29, already referred to, the Court made it clear that it took a serious view of the challenge to its authority. Chief Justice Earl Warren, who wrote the decision, quoted from two of his predecessors, Chief Justice John Marshall who served from 1801 to 1835, and Charles Evans Hughes who was Chief Justice from 1930 to 1941, to restate the basic concepts of government that have guided the United States throughout its existence.

He quoted Marshall as follows:

> It is emphatically the province and the duty of the judicial department to say what the law is ... If the legislatures of the several states, at will, annul the judgments of the courts of the United States and destroy the rights acquired under those judgments, the Constitution becomes a solemn mockery.

From Hughes, Warren quoted:

> If a governor can nullify a Federal Court order it is manifest that the fiat of a state governor, and not the Constitution of the United States,

would be the supreme law of the land; that the restrictions of the Federal Constitution upon the exercise of state power would be but impotent phrases.

Can It Be Enforced?

In denying the delay sought by Little Rock, the Court spoke out with unmistakable clarity. Yet its order was insufficient to send a single Negro child to. a white school. In the normal course, the Supreme Court has spoken, its decision is final and the disputed issue is settled. This does not apply, however, to cases involving race relations in the South, for these cases reflect a basic clash between antagonistic social forces. Demands of Negroes for equality even in limited spheres can be satisfied only by weakening the Jim Crow structure of society, the system which assures the continued rule of the white supremacists. To settle cases that involve struggles of such sweep, something more than a Supreme Court verdict is required. Some means must be found to enforce the verdict.

This is the essence of the problem. Can the Supreme Court decision be enforced? And if so, how?

Negroes say that the decision can be enforced and that it must be enforced now. They regard it as a monstrous crime against their children that they continue to suffer the degradation and disabilities of segregated, inferior schools in defiance of the clearly enunciated law.

They are right, of course. Justice cries out that their demands be met. Concern for human dignity, for the education of the millions of Negro children growing up in the South, for their modest but intense striving merely to be treated as equals, dictate that the court decision should be enforced.

But like the court ruling itself, such considerations carry little weight with white Southern leaders. Instead of complying, the South insolently defied the Court, challenged the decision and organized systematically to oppose it. Since May 17, 1954, when the Supreme Court handed down its initial school decision holding that segregation in itself equals discrimination and is unconstitutional, the Southern states have passed close to 200 laws to prevent integration in the schools.

They have devised endless delaying tactics; they have organized and activated the White Citizens Councils and the Ku Klux Klan; they have resorted to economic boycott and terror against Negroes who seek their rights, and economic pressure and social ostracism against whites who are unwilling to conform to the Southern dictate and obey its taboos. They have thus sought to organize the totality of white society into the 'massive resistance' policy of which they boast.

The South has made it abundantly clear that it is prepared to use every resource it can muster in defense of segregation. In following this course, it is doing what every ruling class or group has always done and always will do. It is fighting to preserve its own special privileges.

Those in power in the South owe their elevated position to the denial of rights to Negroes. This is true of the US senators and representatives, the state governors, the state and city administrations and the courts. It is also true of the landlords who exploit the sharecroppers and of the manufacturers who benefit from the open-shop, low-wage situation that results from division of the workers along race lines.

This 'way of life' is based upon the myth of Negro inferiority. Segregation is one of the means whereby the myth is perpetuated. Separate and inferior schools are part of the Jim Crow pattern and in turn supplement and reinforce the degrading effects of segregation.

Any gains made by Negroes, no matter how small, tend to destroy the myth. Give the Negro an adequate education, equal opportunities for employment, the right to vote and to hold office, and the myth will explode. Once Negroes acquire equality of status, the arbitrary rule of the white supremacists and the advantages they reap from that rule will come to an end.

Integration – in Ten Centuries

The effectiveness of the South's resistance is reflected in the statistics on school integration. Up to the present time, not a single elementary or high school anywhere in the Deep South has been integrated, and there has been only a trickle of integration in the Middle South. The important gains have occurred in the border states, but even here the process has slowed to a virtual halt.

The first two years following the 1954 Supreme Court decision saw many thousands of youngsters attending mixed schools for the first time – in Washington, D.C.; in Wilmington, Delaware; in Baltimore; in much of Kentucky and most of Missouri.

Then integration bogged down. By the fall term of 1956, some 700 school districts, almost a quarter of the approximately 3,000 in the South, were desegregated. In 1957, only 57 new districts were involved. This September the number of newly desegregated school districts dropped to 12, involving only 307 Negro children.

In the whole state of Tennessee, one of the states of the Mid-South, a total of

117 Negroes were enrolled in formerly all-white classes up to the end of school last spring. If Tennessee were to maintain that rate, it would take about 1,000 years – ten centuries – to integrate its 133,740 Negro students.

The battles now convulsing the South are not being fought over full integration, but over token integration. Only a small number of Negro children in what is called 'integrated situations', that is, school districts where some integration has taken place, are attending formerly white schools. This does not, however, minimize the importance of the present conflicts.

The resistance of the South surprised no one, least of all Negroes who know what it means to feel the lash and the torch of racist rule. Negroes, however, did believe that the federal government was bigger than the South and that, moreover, it spoke with one voice. They assumed that the President 'of all the people' had the power to force the South to obey and the will to use that power. They were to learn otherwise.

The Sage of Burning Tree

The President of the United States enjoys great moral authority. Had Eisenhower spoken out at any time during the past four years in defense of integration, or had he at any time made it clear to Southerners that they must admit Negroes to white schools or suffer the consequences, much of the South's defiance would have crumbled. Those individuals who are prepared to obey the law whether they agree with it or not would have acquiesced. The lawless elements who carry out the reactionary tasks set them by the Faubuses, the Almonds, the Eastlands and the Griffins would think twice before dynamiting a school, or a Negro church or home, or a synagogue, if they would be punished for their actions.

But time and again when Negroes have appealed directly to the President for support, he has been too busy shooting quail in Georgia, or fishing or playing golf to answer their appeal. A singularly glaring incident occurred on October 25 when Eisenhower snubbed 10,000 students who participated in the Youth March on Washington. Leaders of the demonstration had written in advance to request a hearing, but when a small delegation arrived at the White House, Eisenhower was not at home, nor were any of his aides. The delegation went away empty-handed, leaving its prepared statement with a police guard. The President, they learned, had spent the late morning at the Burning Tree Golf Course.

On those few occasions when Eisenhower has mentioned integration, it was to urge Negroes to be patient, repeating the old bromide about how you can't change men's hearts by passing laws. This is the language of the South, spoken by the President of the United States. It begs the question, for Negroes are little concerned about what goes on in the hearts of Southern whites. Let the Southerners hug their hate to themselves as tightly as they like – but also force them to comply with laws that guarantee Negroes their rights.

The farthest Eisenhower has ever gone in his speeches was to deplore the bombing of synagogues after the dynamiting of a Jewish temple in Atlanta in October. When he sent troops to Little Rock in September, 1957, he was careful to explain that he did so only because Faubus had openly defied a federal court order. Even in that tense situation he made it clear that he was not taking sides publicly on the integration issue. Instead of supporting the Negroes in their demand that the law be enforced, Eisenhower has given encouragement to the South in its resistance to the law.

Congress, the third branch of government, could have passed laws increasing the power of the Justice Department, but Congress, like the President, has refrained from taking action to back the Supreme Court ruling. In the Civil Rights bill which it passed in the summer of 1957 – the first such legislation since Reconstruction – Congress carefully extracted from the measure those sections that would have strengthened the enforcement powers of the federal government.

The fact is that, despite appearances, neither the President nor Congress serve the interests of the people. This is true whether those in office belong to the Republican party or the Democratic party. Both parties are controlled by finance capital which has ruled the country ever since it gained ascendancy in the Civil War, and it is, by and large, the interests of Big Business that are served by the lawmakers and the executive. Control of Congress is exercised primarily through a bloc between Southerners and Northern conservatives. Within this bloc, the most stable group is that which comes from the Deep South. Wall Street, despite the fact that its publicists keep assuring us that Marx's theories have been disproved, has a clear understanding of the conflict between its interests and those of the workingman, whether he has a white skin or a black skin. It has, therefore, a profound distrust of any congressmen or senators who show a tendency to 'coddle' labor, including the Negro, for it recognizes that not all the legislators are equally pliant and reliable servants. When Pres. Eisenhower in his campaign speeches prior to the November elections lashed out against what he called the 'radical' wing of the Democratic party, he was not merely indulging in campaign oratory; he was also voicing the apprehensions of the financial rulers of the country.

The strange phenomenon of the Supreme Court enunciating a policy which neither the President nor Congress is prepared to enforce reflects the contradiction faced by Big Business. It is determined to impose its policies through control of the executive and the conservative bloc in Congress. At the same time, it is bedeviled by Negro pressure at home and damaging criticism of American race relations in foreign countries. It is also faced with the changing economy of the South where industrialization is beginning to supplant the plantation in importance, with the resulting increase in the demand for semi-skilled and skilled labor.

To satisfy these conflicting needs, Wall Street finds it convenient to speak with two voices. The Court says proceed with integration; the President counters with an admonition not to proceed too rapidly. With one hand it giveth; with the other it taketh away.

We can expect, therefore, that the extension of Negro rights will be held to a minimum, and that, as a corollary, the gains that Negroes make will be in proportion to the amount of pressure exerted both here and abroad.

'Massive Resistance'

The crisis that has built up in Little Rock and in Virginia and which will develop elsewhere stems in large part from the dual policies of the government described above. Astute politicians like Faubus are emboldened to defy the Supreme Court by the sympathy they find in high places. When the Court this fall issued what amounted to an ultimatum, Faubus replied by putting into operation the 'massive resistance' laws passed by a supine legislature, and proceeded to close the city's high schools. Little Rock's educational system was thrown into chaos. For two months some 3,500 students were deprived of their right to attend classes. Since then makeshift private schools, poorly equipped and inadequately staffed, have been limping along, giving a sketchy education to some of the white students. No provision has been made for the Negroes.

A similar, though somewhat calmer, development took place in Virginia. There Gov. J. Lindsay Almond also closed the schools rather than permit token integration, and they have remained closed. He shut 10,000 white students out of Norfolk schools rather than allow 17 Negroes to attend classes with them. He closed schools in Charlottesville affecting 1,700 white pupils and in Front Royal, where about 1,000 white youngsters were involved. The court had ordered 12 Negroes integrated in Charlottesville, 22 in Front Royal. In Little Rock only six Negro students were ordered admitted to Central High School.

The logic of the elaborate plans the South has worked out during the past four years made the closing of the schools inevitable. Yet this act was decisively different from all those which had preceded it, for now for the first time a segment of the dominant whites was injured just as much as were the Negroes.

Encouraging Signs

As a result, cracks and fissures have appeared in the South's smooth facade of white supremacist. Up to now the division has been along race lines, with divergent views among the white population smothered in a common anti-Negro unity. With the cracking of that unity, the differences that have existed beneath the surface, including class differences, begin to manifest themselves.

Already we are hearing voices that sound strange in the South. When Faubus, after ordering the high schools to remain closed, called for a referendum to decide whether the schools should be kept closed or opened on an integrated basis, white women of Little Rock organized a 'Women's Emergency Committee to Open Our Schools', and conducted a house-to-house campaign to get their neighbors to vote in favor of integration. One member of the committee commented: 'It's ridiculous to try to retain the ways of old granddad in this age of sputniks and missiles'. During the same campaign, 63 of the city's leading lawyers, many of whom number railroads and other large corporations among their clients, took out ads in the daily papers, urging a vote for integration.

In Charlottesville, Virginia, last June, when school closing was threatened but had not yet become a reality, a poll was taken of PTA members at Venable Elementary School, one of those affected by the court order. Of the 305 parents who replied, 177 favored 'limited integration', against 128 who preferred closing the schools rather than admit a few Negro students. When the school was finally closed this fall, the townspeople were split in two. Two committees were formed, one for integration, the other for segregation.

A sizeable section of Virginia's teachers also are prepared to accept integration. At its state convention October 30, the Virginia Educational Association heard an address by Gov. Almond and then voted a resolution asking him to convene the General Assembly and pass laws to reopen the schools. A softening resolution was tabled by a vote of 650 to 151.

The American Federation of Teachers likewise took a fine stand at its convention in Milwaukee and set an example that other unions should copy. The convention refused to reinstate its all-white Chattanooga local and upheld its constitutional provision that prohibits any local from 'limiting its membership on account of race or color'.

It also called upon the federal government to take over and run on an integrated basis all schools that have been closed. This same proposal has appeared in a number of places and gives some evidence of developing into a popular demand.

Another proposal that seems likely to spread is one for 'local option', that is, letting the residents of a city or town ordered to integrate decide by referendum whether they prefer to close the schools or admit Negro children. One such referendum has been held in Norfolk, Virginia. A threat to close schools next year in Atlanta, Georgia, has brought forth a similar demand from the mayor there. Let the people vote on the issue, he urged.

An action that is highly unusual in the South – if, indeed, it has ever occurred before – took place in Norfolk in October when a group of white parents filed a lawsuit against the governor and other state officials asking that the state's segregation laws be ruled unconstitutional and that the six schools that have been shut down be reopened.

The press, too, here and there, is showing signs of shifting its position. On October 5 the *Roanoke (Virginia) Times* commented editorially:

> The program of massive resistance has now come to the bitter and inevitable finality ... [Yielding to the court is onerous] but to deprive Virginia's children, white and colored, of education or to give them a defective education is an even greater evil.

There has occurred, also, a beginning of political activity in favor of integration. In Virginia, a white woman, Dr. Louise O. Wensel, the mother of five children, ran as an independent candidate in the November 4 election against Sen. Harry F. Byrd and his tightly knit, pro-segregation machine. In her campaign, she charged Byrd with using 'dictatorial control' to impose an unconstitutional program of massive resistance. She obtained an unprecedented vote equal to one-third of the total. Her strongest support came from those cities immediately affected by integration orders: Norfolk, 42 per cent; Arlington, 38 per cent; and Charlottesville, 37 per cent. A special referendum two weeks later on November 18 confirmed the election results. In voting on the school issue, 41.2 per cent of Norfolk's citizens preferred accepting integration to keeping the schools closed.

In Houston, Texas, in the November elections, a Negro housewife, Mrs. Charles E. White, upset all expectations and won election to the city's school board, after campaigning on a clear-cut pro-integration platform. She could not have been elected without white votes.

Of special interest among these first voices raised against the monolithic anti-Negro refrain are the voices of the youth. At the height of the agitation in Little Rock this year, a group of teenagers gathered at Hall High School and solemnly drew up a petition asking that the schools be reopened and stating that they had no objection to attending classes with qualified Negroes. In Norfolk, when the schools were closed there, about 100 students gathered in a parking lot near the Northside Junior High School and collected signatures on a petition which stated: 'Not as segregationists or integrationists but as students who want an education we ask you to please keep our schools open'.

In Van Buren, Arkansas, in the western part of the state, a 15-year-old girl, Jessie Angelina Evans, president of the Student Council, put her elders to shame when she stood up before a turbulent school board meeting and asked segregationist parents: 'Have YOU thought what you make those Negro children feel like, running them out of school?' To hostile questions, she replied: 'Negroes have a right to attend school just as much as anybody. If we don't object, why should anybody else?'

These are as yet only scattered voices in a wilderness of reaction, for the most part neither pro-Negro nor pro-integration, merely pro-education. In almost every case those who have spoken out in favor of integration have prefaced their remarks with the accepted ritual of the South: 'I am opposed to integration ... but' or 'I dislike the Supreme Court decision as much as anybody ... but'. Thus the prejudice remains, even while segregation tends to break down in fact – proving again the Marxist theorem that outworn social ideas often persist after the institutions which nourish them have disappeared.

The numbers involved in this incipient opposition to the South's 'massive resistance' are as yet too few to give the needed assistance to the Negroes who, as a minority, must find allies in order to carry their fight to a successful conclusion. The logical alliance is with the labor movement, but the cooperation that exists between Negroes and labor is limited and sporadic.

It would be incorrect to say that the labor movement has done nothing to further Negro demands for equality. The industrial unions formed in the militant thirties, especially in such areas as Detroit, have an excellent record in this regard and have demonstrated what can be done when workers unite. The unions have fallen down miserably, however, where their support is needed most, in the heartland of Jim Crow. In most instances the white workers of the South, instead of mobilizing on behalf of Negro rights, have formed an unnatural alliance with their class enemies against the Negroes, while their national leadership, grown conservative, has buckled under segregationist pressure and has failed even to discipline its own members. (There have been some exceptions. One, already noted, is the American Federation of Teachers; another is the Packinghouse Workers Union).

Insistence on the part of the national union leaders that their locals in the South support the Negro fight for integration would, moreover, bring them into conflict with the politicians of the South and would pose the need for forming a labor party, in opposition to the Democrats as well as the Republicans. Such a perspective runs counter to the intentions of the union leadership which is busy courting the Democrats in the false hope that they can resolve the problems facing the working class by putting in office the political representatives of the capitalists.

Negro leaders have been preoccupied with efforts to steer a course towards victory in the fight against segregation, while at the same time avoiding the horror of a racist massacre, and have shied away from organizing along political lines, even when such a development seemed possible, as in the march on Washington on May 17, 1957, the third anniversary of the Supreme Court decision.

They didn't call the demonstration a March on Washington. Instead, they referred to it as a 'Prayer Pilgrimage', and the choice of name was significant. The leaders did not conceive of the demonstration as an inspiring beginning of a mass movement, national in scope, spearheading the formation of a new political alignment. Had the Rev. Martin Luther King, the acknowledged leader, called upon that demonstration to reject both Democrats and Republicans and take steps, together with white workers, to initiate a new party, he would have set in motion a political force that could eventually have challenged Jim Crow rule. Those in charge of the demonstration chose to contain it within safe limits and channel it into a prayerful supplication, pleading for understanding and love, then dispersing quietly and inconspicuously.

In the main, Negroes have chosen to carry on the fight through legal contests, where they have won singular successes. Both the Negro leaders and the Negro people have given inspiring examples of integrity, courage, devotion and persistence. They demonstrated these qualities in the Montgomery bus boycott where the entire community under the leadership of the Rev. King and the Rev. Ralph D. Abernathy, organized itself to walk for more than a year in order to win the right to 'sit up front'. A heroic example was set also by the 'Little Rock nine' who faced the mob and the bayonets of the state troopers and who then stood up to the jeers and insults and taunts of white students throughout the school term. Their heroism has been matched by that of students in other test cases, and of countless other individuals in every section of the South.

But heroism, even when backed by a Supreme Court decision, has proven insufficient to overcome the entrenched power of the Southern rulers. They maintain their power through political control and it is only through political action that they can be dislodged. In other words, we can expect that the Supreme Court decision will be enforced in the Deep South only when a political realignment has taken place of such proportions as to make possible a successful bid for power by forces in opposition to the white supremacists.

It is for this reason that the rift within the white population of the South brought about by the closing of the schools is of such special significance. Integration in places like Norfolk has become a live political issue instead of merely a dirty word used to inflame passions and instigate violence. There is now activity where before there was dead calm.

It is too soon to predict future developments, but this much can be said: the more Negroes challenge white supremacy, the more the division within the white South will deepen, and the greater will be the opportunity for the liberal forces and the white workers to line up alongside Negroes so that together they can strike a decisive blow against segregation and for equality.

2 The Jackson Freedom Ride[9]
(1962)

Fred Halstead

What later became the Jackson Freedom Ride and Jail-in was originally planned in the New York office of the Congress of Racial Equality as a relatively modest undertaking. It was meant to test a 1955 Supreme Court decision against segregation in interstate transportation facilities.

A group of Negroes and whites left Washington, D.C. May 4, 1961 on a Trailways and a Greyhound bus, planning to take a direct route through seven Southern states to New Orleans. There, on May 17, the anniversary of the 1954 Supreme Court school desegregation decision, a Freedom Rally celebrating the end of the test was planned.

Though the twenty-two original Riders, most of them CORE leaders, were not prepared for what happened in Alabama, they did know they faced danger. In a similar test by CORE in 1947, called the Journey of Reconciliation, racists had threatened a riot, local police had arrested twelve testers and three of the men served thirty-day sentences on a Southern road gang.

But this time the testers clearly had Federal law on their side. James Farmer, CORE national director, wrote President Kennedy and officials of the bus companies, informing them of the planned test. The riders had resolved to test integration of seating, terminal eating facilities and rest rooms. If arrested by local police, they planned to reject bail and serve time in jail in protest.

En route from Washington they tested in Virginia and North Carolina – where sometimes they got served and sometimes they didn't. In Rock Hill, S.C., two Riders were pummeled by attackers but not seriously hurt. In Winnsboro, Henry Thomas, a Negro, and James Peck, a white, were arrested when they sat together at the terminal lunch stand. They were released after a few hours and charges against them dropped.

The Riders had no trouble in Georgia, but when they phoned from Atlanta to Rev. F.L. Shuttlesworth, a militant Negro leader in Birmingham, they were told white racists were expected to mobilize at the station there. Their first hint that

---

9 Halstead 1962.

trouble was even closer came when the driver of the Greyhound bus stopped just outside of Anniston, Alabama and spoke briefly with another Greyhound driver going the other way.

In Anniston, the bus was surrounded by a mob armed with metal bars. Windows were broken and tires slashed before the police arrived and let the bus get out of town. But the mob piled into cars and pursued it.

About six miles out, one of the slashed tires went flat, the bus stopped, and the mob surrounded it. A fire bomb was thrown through a rear window. A newsman took pictures of the burning bus which were to arouse the attention of the world.

> 'It was incredible', said Freedom Rider Albert Bigelow, 'the bus was filled with smoke and outside these hoodlums were shouting "Heil Hitler" and "Sieg Heil".'

All the passengers escaped the fire; but some of the Freedom Riders were beaten as they alighted and the bus was completely destroyed. After police arrived again, the mob dispersed and the injured were treated. The Freedom Riders were taken on to Birmingham by ten volunteer auto drivers mobilized by Rev. Shuttlesworth.

The Trailways bus was running an hour behind the Greyhound. When it reached Anniston – and the news of the bus burning – the ordinary passengers got off, but the Freedom Riders stayed on. They were beaten and forced to the back of the bus by eight attackers who boarded in Anniston and took the front seats. Then the bus drove on to Birmingham. 'For the entire two-hour ride', reported Jim Peck, 'the hoodlums craned their necks to stare at us with looks of hatred'.

Meanwhile at the bus station in Birmingham, a crowd of about thirty 'heavy set men' had been waiting all day. Reporters – both local and national – knew what was coming. The Columbia Broadcasting Company even had its top man, Howard K. Smith, covering the scene. Every child in Birmingham knew that police chief 'Bull' Connors' department was in collusion with the segregationists. CORE and local Negro groups had requested Federal protection.

But the Federal authorities did not provide it.

When the bus arrived, reported Smith,

> the toughs grabbed the passengers into alleys and corridors pounding them with pipes, with key rings and with fists. One passenger was knocked down at my feet by twelve of the hoodlums and his face was beaten and kicked until it was a bloody pulp.

Then the police arrived and the attackers moved down the street where, said Smith, 'I watched some of them discussing their achievements of the day. That took place just under Police Commissioner Connors' window'.

When asked later why he had placed no policemen at the station, Connors said too many were off duty because of the holiday. The date was May 14 – Mother's Day. Federal authorities offered no such excuse, but Attorney General Robert Kennedy promised to safeguard interstate passengers in the future.

The bruised and bandaged Freedom Riders showed up at the bus station the following morning for the next leg of the trip – to Montgomery. Drivers for both companies refused to take them out, and another mob began gathering. They decided to skip the bus trip and fly on to New Orleans to be there in time for the May 17 Rally.

After a harrowing wait of many hours at the airport, during which another large mob gathered and two flights were canceled because of a bomb-scare, the original group of CORE Freedom Riders finally took off, reaching New Orleans shortly after midnight on May 16.

The morning papers carried the story of how the Freedom Ride had been 'stopped' in Birmingham.

But in Nashville, Tennessee, a young Negro woman, a student at Tennessee State who had transferred there from Chicago and had been active in the exceptionally militant Nashville student sit-in movement, decided the Rides would have to go on 'or everything we have worked for is gone'.

She was Diane Nash, a member of the leading committee of the Nashville student movement which had connections with the Nashville Christian Leadership Council and the Student Nonviolent Coordinating Committee.

The NCLC is for Nashville, what the Southern Christian Leadership Conference, headed by Dr. Martin Luther King, is for the South as a whole. The Student Nonviolent Coordinating Committee was at that time simply a coordinating center for student sit-in groups at some 16 Southern Negro campuses. (SNCC now has a permanent office in Atlanta, and is in the forefront of the most militant mass struggles that have broken out in the South since mid-August, 1961. Its leaders are young Negroes, including Diane Nash, who is currently based in Jackson, Mississippi).

The relationship between the Nashville student groups and the NCLC was described by David Halberstam in the June 22, 1961 *Reporter* as follows:

> The Nashville sit-ins, for instance, were started by students, with the Nashville Christian Leadership Council moving in later. 'There was an agreement that the ministers would have some control over the movement and would be consulted', a sympathetic observer has reported, 'but

they had to agree to participate, to sit in, to be on call, to attend emergency meetings – and those kids have daily emergency meetings – to take the same risks and make the same sacrifices the kids did. This was the price for retaining their influence'.

When Diane Nash began rallying the students to carry on the Freedom Ride which the CORE group had just been forced to temporarily abandon, an agent of the Federal Justice Department tried to talk her out of it. Halberstam reports the conversation:

The situation in Alabama was such, he said, that to go in at that point would be dangerous and irresponsible. 'It was like talking to a wall', he remarked later. 'She didn't hear a word I said'.

Following an all-day meeting in Nashville at which it was decided to continue the Ride, the Rev. Kelly Miller Smith of NCLC and ten students, Negro and white, headed for Birmingham. Diane Nash stayed behind, organizing support. Thus began the saga of 'the Nashville Twelve'.

When they reached the Greyhound station in Birmingham, the drivers refused to take buses out to Montgomery, where racist mobs were reported to be organizing. The students refused to leave the station, tying up the bus service. They were arrested there May 17, together with several supporters from Birmingham including the intrepid Rev. Shuttlesworth.

After over twenty-four hours in jail under 'protective custody', several of the group were driven to the Tennessee border in an auto caravan led by Police Commissioner Connors himself, and dumped on the highway. The story is told that they walked across fields to another road, reached a phone and called Diane Nash in Nashville. She drove out, picked them up and they returned – on back roads to avoid police – to Birmingham.

It is a matter of record that they arrived back at the bus station around noon May 19, to the chagrin of all those who wanted the Ride to stop.

Joined by other students arriving from Nashville, they held the station down until Saturday morning, May 20 when the company finally provided a driver. The bus pulled out about 9:00 a.m. with twenty-one Nashville students aboard, under guard of the state highway patrol and officials of the US Justice Department. The breach at Birmingham had been filled.

Attack in Montgomery

The Riders were attacked in Montgomery by a mob of about three hundred whites who injured at least twenty persons before police stopped the riot. Most seriously beaten was Freedom Rider James Zwerg, a Southerner born and raised, and the only white male in the group.

That night was a night of car burnings, bomb threats and racist mobs in Montgomery. It was the night fifteen hundred people were marooned by a racist mob in the Ripley Street Baptist Church at a meeting addressed by Rev. Martin Luther King and James Farmer, who had returned from New Orleans.

It was the night Attorney General Robert Kennedy was finally forced to take specific action and call out the Federal marshals. Alabama's Governor Patterson also called out the state's national guard units. The Nashville students had made it clear that Patterson's former policy of allowing racist mobs to rage, would not stop the Freedom Rides, and that Attorney General Kennedy was not going to be able to sweep the whole problem under the rug.

There followed three days of discussions and planning among all the major organizations involved in the Freedom Rides. Representatives of the NAACP, the SCLC, the Nashville student movement and CORE were there. At a private meeting, dominated by the Nashville students, the decision was made to continue into Mississippi, where Jackson was the next major stop.

The Freedom Ride had been transformed from a test by a single relatively small organization into a massive effort involving – each in its own way – all the major groups in the civil rights struggles, with a general call for volunteers from throughout the country.

On Wednesday, May 24, two Trailways buses pulled out of Montgomery under National Guard escort. Aboard were twenty-seven Freedom Riders, including the Nashville students and three of the original CORE group, James Farmer, Jean Lewis and Henry Thomas.

The buses drove – without a rest stop – straight to Jackson. There, all twenty-seven were arrested, charged not with violating the state's segregation laws, but with a 'breach of the peace' statute. Mississippi's tactic would be to tie the Ride up in the courts. This would require, of course, that the Federal government not take decisive executive action against Mississippi's legal subterfuge.

On the same day, Attorney General Robert Kennedy made his public appeal for a 'cooling off period', asking that the Freedom Rides be abandoned 'until the present state of confusion and danger has passed and an atmosphere of reason and normalcy has been restored'.

The request was denounced by leaders of every civil rights organization involved, including the NAACP. An editorial in the June 1 *Afro-American* summed up the general feeling: 'If there were a series of bank robberies Mr. Kennedy would not dare ask the banks in any given section to close. He would see that they were given protection'.

The first twenty-seven Jackson Riders were convicted May 26, given a six-month suspended sentence and a $200 fine. To work out the fine would take sixty-seven days. Twenty-two Riders, including CORE national director James Farmer, refused to pay. The tactic of the movement would be to crowd the jails.

Thus began the first sustained and massive Jail-in in the United States since the free speech fights of the Industrial Workers of the World a half century ago.

Volunteers came from all parts of the country, passing as a rule through Montgomery from the East and New Orleans from the West. They often stopped briefly en route making contact with local anti-segregation groups – a profound experience.

'The girls I met in the CORE group there [New Orleans] were human beings such as I have never before met in my life. They live and breathe the movement', wrote Freedom Rider Mary Hamilton, in the pamphlet *Freedom Riders Speak For Themselves.*

Most of the Riders were not members of CORE, but volunteered for the occasion. The historic continuity of past social struggles was not insignificant in this more or less spontaneous selection. This reporter, in interviews with over twenty veterans of the Jail-in asked the question: 'What percentage of the Jackson Freedom Riders would you estimate had some sort of radical political background?' The average of the estimates was 50 percent.

Freedom Rider William Mahoney, a Negro student, described some of the types in the September issue of *Liberation*:

> My cellmate, a Negro worker, came because he had been chased home by white toughs once too often ... On my right, in cell 12, was the son of a well-to-do business man who had come because it was his moral duty. His aim was to 'change the hearts of my persecutors through the sympathy and understanding to be gained by nonviolent resistance'. He spoke proudly of his father who had fought hard and 'made it', and was constantly defending North America's economic and political system from the attacks made upon it by myself and the man in the next cell.

About half the 322 persons arrested in Jackson were whites. Of the Negroes, some forty were from Mississippi itself, and many were veterans of the sit-in movement. Most were students or unemployed youngsters just out of school. About sixty of those who did time in jail were women.

After the first few bus and trainloads into Jackson, the Rides became routine and didn't make the headlines. Freedom Rider John Lowry, in a speech at Queens College last October, described one such experience as follows:

> Three of us, Elmer Brown, a Negro and Norma Matzkin and myself, who are white, left the Port Authority bus terminal in New York July 2. Our first sign of segregation was in Raleigh, N.C. where the facilities were integrated, but you could see the shadow of the letters 'white' over the entrance where the sign had been taken down.
>
> From somewhere in South Carolina on, we couldn't get served together, but we didn't make an issue out of it because we had been instructed not to do anything that might interfere with our getting to Montgomery safely, and on time.
>
> We arrived there early on the evening of July 3, were picked up at the station by Tom Gaither, a CORE representative, and driven to the home of Rev. Ralph D. Abernathy, one of the leaders of the famous Montgomery bus protest. We were told not to answer the phone or open the door because the Klan was harassing the house. The next day we attended a picnic at a farm outside town with a lot of local high school kids.
>
> On July 6 five others arrived from the Mid-west to join us for the trip to Jackson. One of them was Ike Reynolds, who had been on the bus that was burned at Anniston.
>
> We had a brief training period, including lectures by Gaither on the theory of non-violence. He emphasized the concept of an 'active state of love' toward those who might torment us. I remember that in the discussions someone substituted the word 'compassion', but Gaither insisted on 'love'.
>
> We also practiced 'socio drama' – a CORE technique of training by enacting a situation that might happen to us. We giggled at this but inwardly we took it seriously. The practice gave us some confidence.
>
> The eight of us went to the bus station in Montgomery, Friday evening, July 7. One, Bill Hansen, was not supposed to identify himself as a Freedom Rider so he could make a telephone call if something happened. But a reporter had been given a list of all eight of us and kept asking 'Where's Hansen?' It produced some tense moments at the station but the reporter finally shut up.
>
> The bus had a police escort out of Montgomery. I remember catching the eye of a white girl on the bus as I entered. She was about 18 and very pretty, and she gave me a big smile. After the word went around among

the passengers that we were Freedom Riders, she turned in her seat and looked daggers at me.

A white man about twenty-five said in a loud voice to Norma: 'I bet you've f–d a nigger too'.

One passenger was particularly cordial to us. He was a Negro and said he had made several trips on buses with Freedom Riders. I don't know if he was an agent of some kind or what, but he gave us the impression that he made it a point to observe these trips.

The bus stopped in Meridan, Mississippi, not far from the Alabama line. The town square was packed with people and police, even policewomen. A big fat cop got aboard and announced: 'This is not a rest stop. Only those with tickets to Meridan can get off here'. Then he yelled out the window: 'We can't do anything. They're sitting segregated'. (We had been told to do this so we wouldn't get arrested before we got to Jackson).

A Negro woman passenger with an infant asked to get off to get milk for the baby. The cop said, 'I'll get it for you', and he did. He didn't charge her for it, just handed it over and got quickly off the bus.

I remember that as the bus pulled out I saw two boys about ten years old, one white, one Negro, on the edge of a fountain in front of the city hall. They were sitting together, talking, obviously friends.

When we stopped at the station in Jackson, the bus driver – who had acted in a matter-of-fact and neutral manner throughout – said simply: 'There are Freedom Riders on this bus. Please let them off first'.

In Prison

They were quietly arrested in the station and sent to the Hinds county jail, then transferred to the maximum security unit at the State Penitentiary at Parchman. When the trucks in which they rode stopped at the prison walls, they could hear the singing of the other Freedom Riders inside. They were stripped, examined, questioned, given light underwear – their only clothes for the entire stay – and locked in cells.

They, and the hundreds of others, submitted to this under the impression that the hand of the Federal government would be forced, that a concrete victory – not just another batch of court test cases or another unenforced ICC ruling – would result. Their hopes in this respect were not to be realized.

On June 16 a group of leaders of the organizations cooperating on the Freedom Rides had visited Attorney General Robert Kennedy at a private conference in Washington. 'There are indications', said the June 17 *New York Times*,

CHALLENGES OF BLACK LIBERATION

'that the Attorney General had told the leaders that he felt the demonstrations started last month had made a point but that nothing further could be gained by continuing the demonstrations'.

The court was imposing stiffer sentences on the Riders. The tactic became, not to work out the fine, but for each Rider to stay as long as he chose, up to the time-limit for appeal – forty days – and then to post bail. CORE's finances were strained to the breaking point.

For the politically naive among the Riders, the implications of the process now unfolding were caught by Eugene V. Rostow in the June 22 *Reporter*: 'For above all, the Freedom Riders bear witness to their faith in law – a faith we must not, dare not betray'.

The faith in the present system of many a young man or woman was sorely tried by the solitary cells, 'wrist breaker' handcuffs and the vaginal searches at Parchman Penitentiary.

But their faith in themselves and in the movement was strengthened and their understanding of the society in which they live deepened. As Freedom Rider Robert Martinson wrote in the Jan. 6 *Nation*: 'The Riders were being trained by experts [prison guards]. How many thousands of young people are receiving similar educations in the South?'

'As for Kennedy's name – among the 'prisoners' it was a dirty word', said Freedom Rider Louise Inghram in *Freedom Riders Speak For Themselves*. She quotes a song they sang to the tune of *Frere Jacques*:

> Brother Bob, Brother Bob,
> Are You Sleeping, Are You Sleeping?
> Freedom Riders waiting, Freedom Riders waiting,
> Enforce the law! Enforce the law!

Performance of Leaders

There was discussion about the leadership of the movement. There was great respect for James Farmer, who spent the full thirty-nine days in jail, but enthusiasm for Martin Luther King and Roy Wilkins was less widespread. Many thought they should have taken the Ride and gone to jail. Then, the argument went, the eyes of the world would have stayed on Jackson, Kennedy would be kept on the spot, and a concrete victory would result.

King is quoted in his own defense in the July 6 *Jet*:

I wanted to go. I don't believe in this business of leaders staying outside of jail. But my advisers on the SCLC board urged me not to. They said, 'you're still under six months' probation for that traffic sentence in Georgia. You'll be in jail eight months – two in Mississippi and six in Georgia. You'll be out of circulation too long and right in the midst of our voter registration drive. People will say you have absolutely no regard for the law, that you are a publicity seeker with a martyr complex. What sort of example could you set going to jail for a traffic offense?' (The unprecedented long probation on the traffic offense was itself part of a concerted harassment by Georgia courts of Rev. King for his civil rights activities).

By the time those arrested first were getting out of jail, the Ride was petering out. Superficially the net result would be a new ICC ruling requiring the removal of segregation signs in all terminals and a set of court cases against Mississippi's legal subterfuge. The more profound effects of the experience were revealed during a mid-August weekend in Jackson.

The court, in an attempt to further strain CORE's finances, ordered 189 of the Riders out on appeal to appear in Jackson on the same day, Monday, August 13, for arraignment.

There was a great feeling of anticipation among them as they arrived in Jackson that weekend, where most of them were put up on the campus of Tougaloo College. In prison, they had talked around walls, but often didn't see each other, so this was their first chance to meet a large group of fellow Freedom Riders face to face.

There was much talk, some argument, some planning. Representatives of the most militant sections of the movement were there talking up plans for future actions.

The mood of the weekend is summed up by what happened at a meeting of the defendants in the college chapel Sunday. The lawyers recommended that the defendants segregate themselves the next day in court to avoid complicating the issue. Objections were so strong a new meeting had to be called and the recommendation rescinded. The next day the courtroom was integrated.

Sunday night there was a mass meeting in the Masonic Temple in honor of the Freedom Riders. Several thousand persons, white and Negro, tried to get in the small hall, and they sat integrated. The first such gathering in Jackson, Mississippi in living memory.

In general, the Negro community of Jackson activated itself around the events of the Jail-in and a viable movement now exists there.

After the arraignment, veterans of the Jail-in went off to various places in the South, where they participated in, and often sparked the rash of militant mass actions which broke out in the South in the latter half of 1961, and which have brought the civil rights movement to the highest point in its history.

Some went to Nashville for more sit-ins. Some went to Monroe, N.C. in response to a call by Robert F. Williams. Some went to Albany, Georgia where over seven hundred demonstrating Negroes were arrested in December, and where a successful bus boycott is now in progress. Some went to McComb, Mississippi on a voters registration project, where they activated the local high-school students in a series of demonstrations – in the heart of the worst Jim Crow area of the country.

One of the original CORE Freedom Riders, B. Elton Cox, helped lead the demonstration of fifteen hundred Southern University Students in Baton Rouge, Louisiana, the aftermath of which is still shaking that campus, the largest Negro university in the country.

Veterans of the Jackson Jail-in helped spark the mass sit-ins on Route 40 and on Maryland's Eastern Shore. Almost everywhere the struggle has taken a turn toward mass action, veterans of the Jackson Jail-in have been there, often in leading roles. A group of them even showed up on a picket line of low-paid hospital workers in New York City this January and played a role in turning the tide toward a victory for the union.

So what was the Jackson Freedom Ride and Jail-in? For the South, it was an event out of which a new cadre of young and militant Negro leaders took the initiative. For the country as a whole, it was a school and a convention for a part of the vanguard of the new generation of American youth, which will not be a silent or a frightened one.

3 How a Minority Can Change Society[10]
(1964)

George Breitman

The year 1963 was the most eventful in the history of the American Negro struggle. As it ended, people all over the country were stopping to assess what had happened, to think over what was done and what was not done, what was accomplished and not accomplished. Clifton DeBerry, the Socialist Workers party candidate for President this year, had an opportunity at the end of 1963 to make a coast-to-coast tour of most big northern cities and to learn something about the current thinking of Negro militants. He told me one of the things he had observed was the difficulty in getting across the idea about how much the Negro people can do even though they are in a minority, about how much they can do on their own, alone and unaided if necessary. He noticed this difficulty in speaking with Negro trade unionists, but not only them. He felt a lot more attention has to be paid to ways of explaining, in a logical, convincing manner, how much a minority is capable of accomplishing. He felt that misunderstanding on this point is one of the reasons why the idea of an all-black political party has not yet caught on with more Negroes.

Why is it so hard for many Negroes, even militant Negroes, to grasp the full potential of determined minority action? I would say there are three reasons:

First, the teaching, the influence, the propaganda of the whole capitalist system from cradle to grave are aimed at brainwashing the people; at convincing them, among other things, that minorities can plead and beg, but cannot do anything significant, cannot accomplish any big changes, until they have the consent of the majority. Above all is this idea burned into the minds and souls of Negroes, whose history is distorted or denied, and who are made to feel not only that they are a minority, but an insignificant minority, who have never amounted to much by themselves and who, without the stern supervision or benign direction of the great white fathers, would hardly know how to flush a toilet. In other words, for Negroes to comprehend how much a minority can do

---

10   Breitman 1964.

they must buck everything drilled into them from the beginning of childhood; they virtually have to make a revolution in their thinking.

There is a certain irony in these things taught by the capitalists because the capitalists are a minority themselves – in fact, a much smaller minority than the Negro people. Yet this capitalist minority controls the whole country, lock, stock and barrel – its wealth, its means of production, its political structure – and therefore is a living refutation of what it tells us about the limits on what a minority can accomplish.

The second reason why it is hard to see the truth about what a minority can do is that the present Negro leadership, almost in its entirety, is enslaved by the ideas promulgated by the capitalist class, repeats and spreads those ideas, and does everything in its power to discourage the mass of the Negro people from taking steps genuinely independent of the white majority.

A third reason is that the radical movement, virtually the whole radical movement with the exception of the Socialist Workers party, although it approaches questions from a different standpoint than that of the ruling capitalist class, has failed to comprehend the essence of this question, and instead of promoting and encouraging both theoretically and practically an understanding of the dynamics and potential of minority action, in some ways even discourages it. An example is their attitude toward the Freedom Now Party. I do not know of a single organization in this country claiming to be Marxist or socialist or communist that supports the Freedom Now Party, except the Socialist Workers Party. The Communist Party, the Socialist Party, the Socialist Labor Party, the Progressive Labor Movement – all are either flatly opposed to, or feel very uneasy, about the development of an all-black political party independent of the power structure and of the two major parties. And if you trace back the causes, you will find them to be most unMarxist, unsocialist and uncommunist failures to grasp the revolutionary implications of the independent struggles of the Negro minority.

I want now to examine some typical arguments by the present Negro leaders against such independent action. When the Freedom Now Party was organized in Michigan a few months ago, the press was very much concerned about it. And every 'big name' Negro who came to Detroit for several weeks thereafter was immediately buttonholed by the press and invited to make some statement on, or rather against, the Freedom Now Party.

One of these was Rev. Martin Luther King, who obliged with the following statement:

> I am opposed to anything or any party that teaches separation of the races because I am for integration. If the party is designed to get more Negroes

interested in politics, fine; otherwise I can see no good that can come from an all-black party. One-tenth of the population will never be able to dominate nine-tenths.

In this statement I think Rev. King is guilty of counterposing 'separation of the races' and 'integration' in a completely false and unwarranted way. The Freedom Now Party does not 'teach the separation of the races'. It recognizes that this is a society where the races are separated in fact, and attempts to utilize the separation that has been imposed by capitalism in order to change society and do away with the discrimination made possible by this imposed separation. King is well aware of this. He is a preacher, the head of a church which happens to be all-black. He does not reject or oppose this church because it is all-black. He knows that there is nothing racist about this church being all-black. It is the result of living in a racist society. And he works through this all-black church and tries to build it, at the same time that he advocates integration and seeks to utilize this all-black organization to promote integration.

Now why can't an all-black party do the same thing that an all-black church does, that is, take advantage of the separation created by this racist society in order to weld together the black victims of racism so that they can work to end racism altogether? Why not? Why is it permissible in King's eyes for Negroes to pray together, but not permissible for them to join together in political action in the way they find most effective for ending their oppression? Shouldn't King, if he is logical and consistent, propose that Negroes give up their all-black churches too because they are not integrated? Posed this way, King could reply, 'But we have an all-black church because it's the only kind available to us'. And the answer of the Freedom Now Party could be, 'Yes, and an all-black political party is the only kind available to us that we think has any chance of solving our problems'. So King is confusing rather than clarifying the real relation between 'separation' and 'integration', which are not necessarily opposites at all, since the formation of all-black organizations and institutions may actually be a means of achieving the goal of 'integration' instead of being in contradiction to that goal.

King's other remark was even more revealing: 'One-tenth of the population will never be able to dominate nine-tenths'. Maybe not, although I've already pointed out that the capitalists, a minority of less than one per cent, dominate the other 99 per cent of us. Anyhow, that's not the issue posed by the Freedom Now Party. It is not the Freedom Now Party's goal for the Negro one-tenth to dominate the white nine-tenths. Just the opposite – its goal is to keep the white nine-tenths from dominating and oppressing the black one-tenth. *How* to do this – that's the real difference between King and the Freedom Now Party. Must the minority adapt itself in its methods and tempo to the prejudiced majority, just because it is a majority, and not do certain things because the majority will not like it? Or, can the minority end the domination of the majority by acting with complete independence from the majority ideologically, organizationally, politically – and *only* by acting independently? King prefers not to discuss this real difference. That's why he misrepresents his opponents' position with irrelevant talk about the inability of one-tenth to dominate nine-tenths.

Randolph's Position

Another noted figure who came to Detroit at the time was. A. Philip Randolph, Vice-President of the AFL-CIO and President of the Negro American Labor Council. He too dutifully came forward with a statement against the Freedom Now Party, from which I'll read just the first two sentences: 'Racial isolation in any form cannot register any influence on American political events. It is completely foreign to the political thoughts and actions of America'.

It could be pointed out that what Randolph calls 'racial isolation', in the form of all-white organizations like the Ku Klux Klan and the White Citizens Council, has registered plenty of influence on American politics. But I think it may be more useful to stress that in his eagerness to damn the Freedom Now Party, Randolph here is really damning himself. By 'racial isolation' he means all-black organization for the purpose of ending the isolation foisted on Negroes by a racist society. Randolph is so blinded factionally that he has forgotten his own role, the thing for which he will probably be best remembered; for it so happens that next to Marcus Garvey and Elijah Muhammad, Randolph is the American Negro leader who did the most in this century for what he now calls 'racial isolation', that is, all-black organization.

The first March on Washington Movement, which Randolph organized in 1941, was all-black, and Randolph was foremost in insisting that it be all-black. Even though it did not materialize in a march, because Randolph yielded to Roosevelt and called it off at the last minute, that first call for a March on Washington in 1941 nevertheless accomplished more than the interracial march that took place last August, because it forced Roosevelt to issue the first FEPC order, which is more than the 1963 march accomplished. Instead of 'isolating' the Negro struggle, I think it can be said that that all-black organization, small and imperfect though it was, did more to influence American life than any interracial movement has done since.

How do you influence the course of events anyway? Is it done by strict adherence to the procedures and forms approved by the forces in power, or by following the rules they lay down? All experience, American as well as 'foreign', testifies to the contrary. As long as you abide by their rules, either in the way you organize or the way you fight, they know they have little to fear from you and pay you little attention. The only valid test for all-black organization is this: does it at this time and under these circumstances help or hinder in mobilizing the masses for uncompromising struggle? It doesn't matter if whites, liberal or conservative, don't like it and call it all kinds of names. What counts is what the black masses think about it. If they think it is good, if it enables them more effectively to organize for struggle, then it can have a shattering impact on present-day American society and politics. Influence can be wielded in more ways than one, and that which helps the masses to organize is most 'influential' in the long run.

I will cite only one more example of the kind of reasoning employed by Negro opponents of independent minority action. Also attacking the Freedom Now Party was Alex Fuller, Vice-President of the Detroit AFL-CIO Council. He said:

> We can continue to make gains only by working with people of good will. It is a serious mistake when minority groups, now on the threshold of making tremendous gains for Negroes ... separate themselves from others who are working for the same objectives ... We cannot afford to separate or isolate ourselves ... We stand on the side of all democratic-thinking people who believe and advocate first-class citizenship for everyone. We cannot do it alone.

Translated, what Alex Fuller means is this: Negroes can't get anywhere, Negroes can't get anything, unless they remain in the Democratic party; therefore they must wait until the Democrats are ready. But the truth is somewhat different. Negroes will never get first-class citizenship in a thousand years so long as their political power remains tucked away in the vest pocket of the Democratic party. If they have to depend on and wait for the Democrats or the Republicans, and similar 'people of good will', their children and their children's children will never know the taste of freedom.

Nobody in his right mind wants to separate 'from others who are working for the same objectives', but it is a lie to pretend that the Democratic party, any more than the Republican Party, has the 'same objectives' as the Negro people.

If that were the case the present massive Negro revolt would have no purpose or meaning. The objective of the major parties is to quiet the Negroes with a few token concessions, while the objective of the Negro people is freedom.

Surely there's a difference here, and it is just this big difference that separates Negroes from Fuller's 'democratic-thinking people'. Negroes want freedom now, and 'democratic-thinking people' want them to have it later. The only way Negroes can prevent 'separation' from the liberals on this issue is to give in to them and let them decide when and where and how much freedom Negroes shall have. That's what Alex Fuller and the other Negro leaders have done and what they want the Negro people to do or keep on doing. But the tendency favoring the Freedom Now party has decided that a hundred years of political dependence on these democratic-thinking people of good will is enough, because such dependence, far from bringing them to 'the threshold of tremendous gains', will lead only to another hundred years of the same. They have made their declaration of political independence, and now they are striking out on their own, determined to use their political power for themselves first, last, and all the time.

Characteristics of Negro Minority

Before proceeding to our examination from a Marxist point of view of how much and not how little a minority can do, I should make clear that I am not talking about just any minority, but about a minority with certain characteristics, certain features, and a certain history. And also, yes, I am talking about a minority of a certain size. Let me get the size question out of the way first.

Obviously, not every minority is big enough to do the things I am talking about. Size is important too. If there were only two or three million Negroes in this country, which is approaching a population of 200 million, they could not accomplish what a minority of 20 million can. But 20 million is a big force, big enough to tear things up, big enough and weighty enough to appreciably affect the course of events. After all, how many countries in the world, not only the new ones in Africa and Asia but also the old ones in Europe and the Americas, have a population of 20 million? Out of more than 100 countries, not more than 25 at the most, so that around three-quarters of the countries in the world are smaller in population than the Negro people of the United States.

Size and relative weight are not the only important factors to be considered. A minority of even 40 million cannot do much if satisfied with its conditions or indifferent and apathetic about them. As important as size, or more important, in deciding what a minority can do are social, economic, political, historical, and psychological factors.

What I am trying to say is that what a minority can do depends on whether or not it is oppressed and exploited because of some minority trait or feature, is separated out by society for special inferior status, is denied equal treatment, opportunity and rights; whether or not it is at the bottom of the social ladder so that when it rises it shakes the whole structure; whether or not it is a part of the most productive and potentially most powerful force in the modern world, the working class, and yet at the same time is denied the full benefits of membership in that class; whether or not the oppressive and exploitative society in which it exists is stable or in crisis, challenged on all sides and therefore no longer able to maintain the *status quo*; whether or not this minority believes that it can take advantage of the crisis of society; whether or not it is affected by and responds to the great tides of change and revolution sweeping the globe and has a sense of kinship and solidarity with the masses rising up and changing the rest of the world; whether or not its oppression tends to knit it together for common action and goals; whether or not it is compact and so situated geographically that it can act with maximum cohesive-ness and impact; whether or not it has learned to see through the brainwashing which the ruling class uses to keep this minority in subjugation; whether or not it has lost patience as well as respect for the majority; whether or not it sees any further reason to continue believing in promises or in gradualism; whether or not it has the capacity to free itself from the influence of conservative leaders who have always held it back and to replace them with more militant and revolutionary leaders; whether or not it realizes it never has made any gains except by fighting for them; whether or not it has the capacity to defend itself against terror and violence; whether or not it is developing a militant and radical consciousness, ideology, philosophy and methodology of its own that can motivate and spark sustained, audacious and independent struggle.

In short, I am talking about characteristics that fit the American Negro people or which they are in the process of acquiring at an extremely rapid rate. Of the many things such a minority can do, I shall now list some, not necessarily in the order of their importance:

What a Minority Can Do

1. It can force serious concessions from the ruling class. Anyone who expects the capitalist class to grant full and genuine equality to the Negro people is going to be sadly disappointed, because equality is simply not compatible with, or

possible under, a social system of the type that we have in the United States today. But that is no reason for Negroes to stop trying to get whatever they can squeeze out of the ruling class until the time comes when it can be deposed. Militant struggle can force the present ruling class to lift some of the existing racial restrictions and barriers in the form of more rights more jobs, better jobs, better schools, better housing, less police brutality, and a greater measure of formal equality before the law. Negroes will not settle for such partial gains and concessions, but they would be fools not to fight for them and take them and utilize them to press for other and more fundamental changes.

2. A minority, properly oriented and led, can go much farther than it has thus far gone to make the present system unworkable and intolerable. Bayard Rustin calls this 'social dislocation' (and warns against its 'limitations'). Rev. Albert Cleage, chairman of the Freedom Now Party in Michigan, calls it 'a strategy of chaos' (and urges its application be expanded). Others give it the name of 'mass civil disobedience'. Whatever you call it, it has barely been utilized in America up to now. It consists of making the system so inconvenient and expensive that white people will be forced to ask themselves whether continued discrimination is worthwhile and whether in their own interest they should not help to do away with it altogether.

It means lying down, interposing your bodies on the airport runways, on the expressways, at the plant gate, at the school entrance, at the bank, at the points of production, and the points of distribution, and the points of transportation, and throwing a monkey wrench into the wheels of the system, attempting to paralyze it, to bring it to a stop. It means saying:

> If we Negroes can't have decent and equal schools, then let's not have any schools. If we can't have jobs and job equality, then let no one be able to work. If we can't vote, then let no one be able to vote. If we can't belong to the unions as equals, then we don't care what happens to the unions.

It means carrying the principle of the sit-down strike, which stops production, much farther and into entirely new areas of social life.

I say that this has hardly been exercised as a full-scale weapon of the Negro minority, but I have no doubt that it will be. Already some members of the Student Non-Violent Coordinating Committee, headed by Diane Nash Bevel, have proposed such action and have had it rejected by moderate leaders like Rev. King, who talks about civil disobedience but is mortally afraid of really unleashing it without restriction on a mass scale. The sit-ins, the lie-ins, the wade-ins, etc., were just a small, faint, preliminary version of what is still to come in a giant size and to the accomplishment of deep social convulsions and conflicts.

To avoid misunderstanding, let me say that what I am talking about here is not pacifism but an all out struggle, which will be the equivalent of a general strike when it reaches full flower. And a general strike usually tends to pose questions about who shall have power in the land.

3. A minority can, merely by carrying through its fight for democratic rights without compromise, help to educate and radicalize the American people, especially the youth in whose hands the future lies. In fact, it is already doing so. You in this audience of young socialists and young radicals know better than anyone else how profoundly your thinking about the whole world has been influenced by the Negro struggle; how their fight for equality enabled you to see through the official myths about 'democracy' and 'the free world', to understand the brute reality of the capitalist power structure, to reach new conclusions about capitalism and socialism. Not only the Cuban revolution, not only the danger of atomic war, but something much closer to home, the Negro revolt, has helped to educate or re-educate you, to shed the blinders of liberalism, and to persuade you to dedicate your lives to the fight for a better world. In this respect you are not so much unique as early, because the deepening struggle of the Negro minority will have similarly healthy effects on other young people and on some of the not completely hopeless older people as well.

4. A minority not only can educate other forces but can set them into motion too. It can stimulate them to fight for their own needs and interests through the power of example as well as the power of pressure. You heard one illustration of the power of example this morning – the report about the rent strike which began among Negroes in Harlem and is now spreading to some white sections of the population in other parts of New York City. Another small but striking example occurred in Detroit last summer. A militant Negro demonstration in front of police headquarters, to protest the police shooting of a young Negro woman in the back, came to the very brink of a physical clash. That was a Saturday, and it was followed two days later, on Monday, by another demonstration at another police station, near which cops had shot a young white man in the back. This second demonstration, involving mainly young whites, *raised the same slogans as the first* and culminated in a pitched battle with the cops after the youths had thrown rocks and bottles at them. Not long ago I noticed a small newspaper item about some airline strike pickets who had been picketing up and down outside the Newark terminal for a long time, with little public attention paid to their grievances. One day they suddenly decided to go inside the terminal and demonstrate there, which was prohibited by an injunction. Quickly arrested, they were asked what had got into them. Their explanation was that they had seen that Negroes were able to get action by sit-ins and by

going places where they weren't supposed to, so they thought it was a good idea to do the same.

These are all small-scale illustrations, but bigger and better ones are in the offing. The rulers of this country are well aware of the stimulation-and-contagion effects of militant Negro struggle. That is one reason why they want to stop it before it goes too far and explains the hasty turnabout that induced the previously indifferent Kennedy administration to suddenly introduce civil rights legislation last year.

5. A determined minority can also divide the majority, can actually split it up at decisive moments and junctures. This, of course, is one of the best ways of reducing the disadvantages of being a numerical minority, because it drastically changes the odds against the minority. The Socialist Workers party's 1963 convention resolution showed how this process has operated historically. If our analysis and theory are correct, this isn't a matter of history only, but of the present and the future. Let me refer briefly to the Civil War as an example of the process which can split the majority.

The Civil War was not just a conflict between abstract and impersonal forces, between Northern capitalism and Southern slavery; it was a struggle between classes and living people. No one played a greater role in stimulating and progressively resolving that conflict than the slaves and ex-slaves. Again and again in the three decades before the Civil War the rulers of the North and the South decided to avoid a final showdown by compromising over the slave question. Great hopes were raised and brilliant reputations were made overnight by these eminently 'reasonable' negotiations and agreements reached over the bargaining table in Congress and then enacted into law. But the slaves were not consulted about these great compromises. They would not have consented to them anyway, because they left the condition of the slave unchanged, that is, intolerable. So the slaves continued their own independent efforts to become free, just as if these great compromise agreements had never existed.

They continued, just as before, or more so, to run away by the thousands and tens of thousands, to commit sabotage and arson, and to engage in various forms of civil disobedience, self-defense and insurrection. These independent actions of the slaves helped to prevent the compromises from working and to stimulate the birth and growth of abolitionism among whites, who threw their weight onto the scales against further compromise. Thus the slaves reopened and widened the gap between the South and the North every time the great compromise statesmen tried to close it.

By acting in every way they could to defend and liberate themselves, the slaves drove a wedge between the slaveholders and those who wanted to compromise with the slaveholders. By acting in self-interest, and alone when they had to, the slaves divided the whites politically and morally and deepened the divisions to the breaking point. That, above everything else, is what made the struggle irrepressible, constantly widened the breach and deepened the division among the whites, and led inexorably to civil warfare. And then, at the crucial moment, after the outbreak of the war the rulers on both sides had tried so hard to avert, the Negroes pressured the northern government into accepting a revolutionary emancipation policy and completed the process by providing what the reluctant Lincoln later admitted was the military balance of power in the war itself. All this happened without a conscious plan, you might say instinctively. Imagine what will happen when the Negro militants absorb this lesson from history and then consciously work out a strategy to fully utilize this process that is set in motion by the elemental desire of the masses to be free!

We can expect, we can be certain, that the deepening of the Negro struggle for equality will have similarly divisive effects on the white majority in our own time. The majority is not homogeneous anyway; it is strained and torn and in conflict over a thousand questions of policy and class interest. A skillful leadership of the Negro minority will know how to pick the right place to drive new wedges, to deepen already existing and potential differences among the whites, to sharpen their conflicts, to set them fighting each other, and, in the process, as the SWP 1963 convention resolution also says, to find mutually beneficial alliances with those classes and forces whose interests are closer to those of the Negroes against those forces that are most hostile to the Negroes.

Under certain conditions, therefore, a minority, just by fighting for its own rights, can divide the majority into two or more minorities locked in combat with each other. This in turn can result in bringing to power a different kind of majority, not based on color, in which the original minority can take a leading part.

Those who confine themselves to scratching the surface can see only the limitations of being a minority, which leads to lamentation, pessimism, and self-induced paralysis or subservience. But when we examine the situation in all of its complex and contradictory reality, probing it deeper and from all sides; when we study majority-minority relations in motion as well as when they are standing still; when we perceive that the majority has problems too, and weaknesses, and many points at which it is vulnerable and susceptible to successful attack, and that these majority problems and weaknesses are becoming more acute than ever before, then we find, not just limitations for the minority, but also infinitely varied and promising openings and opportunities for transforming, transcending, and overcoming limitations.

6. The Negro minority is also in a position to upset the whole political structure of this country – just by 'going it alone' in politics, just by the decisions

Negroes make about how to use their own votes and their own minority political strength. Our 1963 convention resolution explored this question too, before the present Freedom Now party was started, but it bears restatement because it is such an effective refutation of black liberals who contend the Negro is politically impotent and 'destined to fail' if he acts on his own in politics.

Negroes can form their own party. Negroes can run their own candidates against the Democrats and Republicans. Negroes, because they are already a majority in many districts, thanks to the segregated housing system that jams them tightly together in the big city ghettos, can, right now or any time they form their own party, elect dozens of black candidates to Congress from these districts and hundreds of state and local representatives. In this way they can get representatives in public office who will be responsible and accountable to the Negro community instead of to the corrupt major party machines. And since this bloc of black representatives will not be small, it will enable them to hold and wield a certain legislative balance of power and to compel bigger concessions from the power structure than the tokens and crumbs they are now thrown; all of this, you notice, without any drastic change yet in political relations – just by taking advantage of the political and electoral conditions created by segregation, by refusing to vote Democratic or Republican, by voting black. This would mark a real advance at least in the number and quality of Negro representatives in office, but that would be only a part of the result of independent political action.

By forming their own party, Negroes can paralyze the Democratic party and rock the whole political structure to its foundations. Without Negro votes, the bell will toll the doom of the Democratic party. Without Negro votes, the Democratic coalition with the labor movement will be undermined and destroyed. Without Negro votes for that coalition, the unions will be forced to reconsider their political orientation, and this will encourage and strengthen the union forces who will eventually form an independent labor party. Without Negro votes, the present two-party system will pass from the scene and be replaced by something different, out of which Negroes may be able to acquire new and more reliable allies than up to now. And all of this can be accomplished by the simple device of forming a Negro party and running independent Negro candidates. Really, when you think about the potential, you can almost pity the ignorance of those Negro leaders who preach that Negroes are incapable of any political role other than tagging along behind the liberals.

7. The last on my partial list of things the Negro minority can do should be of special interest to another and smaller minority – socialists, white and Negro. I am convinced that if militant Negroes, not yet socialist, are not so concerned with this point now, they will be later, as their continuing political

experience draws it to their attention. At any rate, my point is that the Negro people, although a minority, can, with consistently revolutionary leadership, lead the American working class in the revolution that will abolish capitalism.

We have long held the view that while the Negro struggle is the struggle of an oppressed minority for democratic rights, for equality, it tends, because the masters of this country are both unwilling and unable to grant equality, to become part of the general movement of the exploited and oppressed to abolish capitalism and proceed toward socialism. In this tendency to pass over from democratic to socialist goals, to pass beyond the capitalist framework that now envelops it, the Negro struggle is similar to the colonial struggles, which also take off from democratic aims, such as independence and self-government, but find themselves unable to attain those democratic aims until they wrench the imperialist boot from off their neck. The Chinese call this process the 'uninterrupted revolution', and Leon Trotsky called it 'the permanent revolution'. But that is not what I am discussing here. What I am talking about now is something else – the capacity of the Negro people to lead the working-class revolution to replace capitalism with socialism.

To grasp this idea we must rid our minds of the conception that any social revolution in general or any working-class revolution in particular has to be *led* by a majority. I will try to illustrate this by going back to the first victorious workers' revolution, the Russian revolution of 1917. It was victorious because it had the *support* of a majority of the Russian people. But it was not led by any class, or by any vanguard of a class, that comprised the majority of the population. It was a revolution *supported by the majority*, and it could not have succeeded without that majority support, but it was *led by a party that represented a class that was a minority of the country*.

We call it, and it was, a working-class revolution. But out of 150 million people in Russia in 1917 the workers were a small minority. There were probably no more than 10 million workers, and that included agricultural workers, some of whom were workers only part of the time. Counting their families, they made up about 15 or 16 per cent of the total population. Yet this class, with a proper leadership in the form of Lenin's Bolshevik party, was able to lead a revolution that abolished capitalism in Russia.

This is one of the things that befuddled and ruined the Mensheviks, the Social Democrats, and other white liberals of that day. As they understood Marx's analysis of the conditions needed for social revolution, it could not take place and should not even be attempted until the country was industrialized to the point where the working class was a majority of the population, as in England then or in the United States today. And if it was attempted before the workers were a majority of the population, it was, according to these people, bound to fail. And they were so sure the Russian revolution was not according to either Hoyle or Marx that most of them pitched in and did their utmost to make it fail.

But they misunderstood Marx and Marxism, as fortunately Lenin, Trotsky, and others did not. A socialist revolution can be led by the working class even when the working class is a minority, provided that working-class minority can get an alliance with, and support from, other non-capitalist forces and classes in the country. In Russia this meant an alliance with the peasants, who constituted around seventy-five per cent of the country. The working-class minority was able to lead the Russian revolution and lead it to victory, not only because it took advantage of the crisis of the capitalist class in the war, not only because it had a qualified leadership, but also because it worked out an effective alliance with the most oppressed sections of the peasants. This alliance was designed to meet the most pressing demands of the peasants, but it did not make any concessions to them about the need to throw the capitalists out of power; and it was based, first of all, on the needs and interests of the working class minority, because the workers were the backbone of the revolution, the most revolutionary force in the country, and represented the historic march of social progress.

Now why, in discussing the American revolution of the 1960s and 1970s, have I gone all the way back to 1917 and far-off Russia? I did so because I thought it would throw light on the distinction between the *making* of a revolution and the *leading* of a revolution, on the leading role that a minority can play, on how dogma can blind one to the leading role of a minority, and on how the successful leadership of a working-class revolution by a minority class depends partly on its ability to make alliances with other exploited classes and groups. I know I am not proving anything about America by this reference to Russia, but perhaps it can help us to look at the role of revolutionary minorities in a fresh way.

The working-class revolution has to be led by workers through their independent party, or parties, or councils. That's one of the things Marx taught us. But Marx never said anything about the revolution having to be led by white workers. He only said by workers – by the most revolutionary workers. The Negroes in this country are a racial minority, but that is only one of their aspects. It would be truly fatal to forget their other primary aspect, namely, that in their overwhelming majority they are proletarian in composition. In fact, Negroes are more proletarian than whites in this country. Negroes are an important section of the working class as well as a racial minority. Unless we are blind, we must see that they are at present and will probably remain the most radicalized section of the working class, the section of the working class that has the most to gain and nothing to lose from social revolution. If this is true, then why should it be so hard, when we are discussing what a radical minority of the working class can do, to conceive of the possibility that it may lead the rest of the working class and its allies in the revolution that will abolish capitalism?

As a matter of fact, that is just what Leon Trotsky, who did so much to rescue authentic Marxism for my generation and yours, was trying to teach us twenty-five years ago when we set out to reach a correct and revolutionary analysis of the Negro struggle. Things were different in 1933, before the CIO, and in 1939, long before the current radicalization of the Negro people. But let me read you some things Trotsky told us in the 1930s [2] and see if they do not apply with even greater validity and relevance to the changed conditions of the 1960s. My first quotation is from a discussion in Turkey between Trotsky and an American, thirty-one years ago, at the depth of the depression and before the CIO was formed. English was not Trotsky's native tongue, and his English was not too good, but his ideas were. He was talking, in 1933, about what would happen when a mass radicalization began in America, and he said:

> I believe that by the unheard-of political and theoretical backwardness and the unheard-of economic advance the awakening of the working class will proceed quite rapidly. The old ideological covering will burst, all questions will emerge at once and since the country is so economically mature the adaptation of the political and theoretical to the economic level will be achieved very rapidly. It is then possible that the Negroes will become the most advanced section. We have already a similar example in Russia. The Russians were the European Negroes. It is very possible that the Negroes also through the self-determination will proceed to the proletarian dictatorship in a couple of gigantic strides, ahead of the great bloc of white workers. They will then furnish the vanguard. I am absolutely sure that they will in any case fight better than the white workers. That, however, can happen only if the communist party carries on an uncompromising merciless struggle not against the supposed national prepossessions of the Negroes but against the colossal prejudices of the white workers and gives it no concession whatever.

That was 1933. Six years later, in 1939, Trotsky discussed the Negro struggle with another delegation from the United States, and, touching on the conditions that make workers conservative or radical, he said:

> If the workers' aristocracy is the basis of opportunism, one of the sources of adaptation to capitalist society, then the most oppressed and discriminated against are the most dynamic milieu of the working class. We must

say to the conscious elements of the Negroes that they are convoked by the historic development to become a vanguard of the working class. What serves as a brake on the higher strata? It is the privileges, the comforts that hinder them from becoming revolutionists. It does not exist for the Negroes. What can transform a certain stratum, make it more capable of courage and sacrifice? It is concentrated in the Negroes. If it happens that we in the SWP are not able to find a road to this stratum, then we are not worthy at all. The permanent revolution and all the rest would be only a lie.

Let me repeat just three of those statements now: It is 'possible that *the Negroes will become the most advanced section*'. It is possible that the Negroes '*will proceed to the proletarian dictatorship ... ahead of the great bloc of white workers*'. '*The Negroes are convoked by the historic development to become a vanguard of the working class*'. What Trotsky was trying to get us to understand twenty-five and thirty years ago, it is plain, was the possibility that the Negroes could lead the working-class revolution. Our party tried to understand this and to express it in the very first resolution on the Negro struggle it ever adopted, which made it the first party ever to put this idea forward. Let me read the first two sentences of that resolution, which is reprinted in full in *Documents on the Negro Struggle*, and which was adopted by the Socialist Workers party convention in 1939:

> The American Negroes, for centuries the most oppressed section of American society and the most discriminated against, are potentially the most revolutionary element of the population. They are designated by their whole historical past to be, under adequate leadership, the very vanguard of the proletarian revolution.

So what I have been trying to say, in stating that the black minority can lead the white majority of the working class in the coming social revolution, is not really new, because the Socialist Workers party explicitly stated that concept in a formal convention resolution in 1939, before most of the people in this hall were born.

Then why does it seem new to many of us? Because, I am sorry to say, there can be a big gap between accepting or even repeating an idea in a general way as logically correct, and grasping in all of its concreteness a profound truth that flies in the face of all prevailing opinion and prejudice, absorbing it and making it a part of you, a central part of your thought and your action. There is also a considerable difference between accepting a general proposition that may turn out to be correct at some indefinite future time and accepting it as a possibility, or even a probability, that can have the most far-reaching consequences for you right now or in the near future.

Although in 1939 we accepted the idea that the Negro minority can lead the working-class revolution and readily adopted that as the official position of the Socialist Workers party, the truth is that it was only a surface acceptance and adoption. We were not yet ready, despite what we put in our resolution, to fully understand what Trotsky was trying to get us to see. And six or seven weeks after our 1939 convention adopted this resolution, J.R. Johnson, the chairman of our party's committee on Negro work at that time, who had been under Trotsky's influence the chief author of the resolution, wrote in our paper an article referring to the resolution. Johnson said that while the idea in the resolution was correct, and while 'the place of the Negro is in the very front', nevertheless the formulation in the resolution was an 'overstatement'. Instead of saying that the Negroes are destined to be 'the very vanguard', he wrote, it would have been more correct to say that they are destined to be 'in the very vanguard'. This was a real weakening of the idea Trotsky had tried to persuade us of. Although it left the Socialist Workers party with the most advanced position on the Negro struggle, it was a definite step backward.

But now, with Trotsky long dead, I think we are able to return to that original unweakened idea and see it in an entirely different light – not as an overstatement, but as a cold, hard, factually correct appraisal of a vital possibility that can crucially affect the future of all Americans. Because what Trotsky could not teach us completely we have now been able to learn from the actual development of the Negro struggle itself right before our own eyes these last two or three years. What we were not advanced enough in the 1930s to accept as theory, we are now able to apprehend as concrete current event. Because the fact is that the Negroes are already a vanguard. They are already out in front of most white workers. They are more radicalized than the white workers. They are more ready to fight and sacrifice and die in order to change this system.

And so today many of us, I am sure, will be able to grasp and act on the concept of Negroes as leaders of the workers' revolution not just as a possibility but as a probability. I shall not try, because that is a job for the whole movement, to work out or complete everything that flows from this concept, except to say that much does, and that all of it seems to me a cause for optimism. Nor shall I try here to discuss the kind of alliance I think the Negro vanguard of the working-class revolution will have to effect with the advanced section of the white workers if the revolution is to be led to success, except to say that I do not think it can be an alliance that will make concessions in principle to the white allies of the Negroes, any more than the revolutionary vanguard in Russia sacrificed any principles in their alliance with the peasants. Instead, I shall conclude, with much left hanging, by saying that if the ideas in this talk are correct, if the concepts about what a minority can do will be of practical and theoretical benefit in advancing the Negro struggle for freedom, then what they demonstrate is the validity and even the indispensability of Marxism to Negro revolutionists, whether or not they belong to the Socialist Workers Party.

4 Why White Radicals Are Incapable of Understanding Black Nationalism[11]

(*Excerpts, 1963*)

Robert Vernon (Robert Des Verney)

Introduction

The aim of the present paper is to probe into a specific area of relations between radicals and Negroes which has been given little serious attention: that of why Negroes who are more or less oriented in a nationalist direction cannot understand or agree with what white radicals are saying, and those aspects of the experiences and ways of thinking of most white radicals which block their way to any understanding of how nationalist-oriented Negroes think and feel. White radicals almost invariably have no idea of what they sound like to Negroes, and never hear the nationalist point of view in its full context.

This contribution cannot come near presenting the full picture, and there may be points of importance which escape the author, and which will have to be supplemented. But white radicals are at present in a far worse position. They have virtually no comprehensive contact with the whole range of thinking of Negroes today, and are hampered by their background as American whites in using to best advantage the meager contacts they do have.

It is not the purpose of this article to present a political program, or rounded-out solutions on the Negro struggle or on the class struggle. Because of the manner and tone of presentation, it is necessary to insist here that this article is not intended to be an espousal of separatism or attack on integration, or repudiation of white radicals and white workers. It is rather something of a guided tour of the panorama of black nationalist thinking and experiences, for the benefit of white radicals who never get to see any appreciable fragment of the whole picture and are bound to misinterpret that fragment they do get to see.

---

11   Vernon 1963.

No pretense is made of presenting a balanced and rounded picture of nationalist vs. integrationist orientations. White radicals generally have little trouble sympathizing with and understanding in some depth any efforts in the direction of integration and the individuals and organizations engaged in such efforts. This article attempts to present another (not *the* other) facet of the total picture. No distinction is made between the various tendencies of white radicals, since all of them sound pretty much alike to most Negroes at the present time.

Radical organizations and publications have been making efforts in the direction of a confrontation of their views with those of nationalist-oriented Negroes, reflecting the increased importance and rapid growth of black nationalism in recent years. In most such encounters, however, we witness more hostility and misunderstanding than any meeting of the minds. White radicals are eager to understand, but don't know where to grope for the understanding; Negroes will 'tell off' the white radicals and try to knock them off their high horse of Marxist knowledgeability. Moreover, most nationalist-oriented Negroes are flatly uninterested in communication with any whites, radicals or otherwise. It is no subjective concern of theirs if white radicals don't understand them, they are only interested in enlightening and organizing other Negroes. This article may serve as an elementary introduction to some special features of black nationalism, with due attention paid to the peculiar background of North American white radicals.

The First Questions

> You know, my cousin really digs this freedom ride and sit-in stuff. For a whole year he runnin' around tryin' to get this luncheonette integrated, gettin' arrested and beat on the head. Finally this cat get the place integrated and, you know what? Man, they didn't have nothin' he wanted!
> – adapted from DICK GREGORY

Should nationalism among Negroes, whether in organized or latent form, be regarded by Marxist-oriented radicals as a dangerous rival, a misleading and confusionist force objectively serving the class enemy, an obstacle and roadblock standing in the way of Negro-white unity in the fight against the bosses? Or is it an unavoidable though repulsive phase of growing pains through which some or most Negroes may unfortunately have to pass on their road to the straight and true path of the Marxist revolutionary party of white and black Americans?

Does black nationalism perhaps have anything at all valuable in its own right to contribute which Marxists can appreciate and try to channelize into the 'real' struggle? Or can it serve to any appreciable extent as a dynamo of potential revolutionary energy and a battering ram against the status quo, a valuable adjunct to a revolutionary upsurge directed explicitly against the capitalist system, in fruitful collaboration with a Marxist-led revolutionary movement?

At this stage it is a step forward to even pose the questions lucidly and start to probe for some answers. *Yes* and *no* answers are meaningless; what we need to examine is to what extent and under what sets of conditions would the affirmatives to these questions become valid? And revolutionists want to know not only what the score is, but what avenues of action are open, what can be done to change things, These are the real questions, of far greater importance at the present stage than the more 'basic' programmatic speculation about a far-off eventual hypothetical choice between extremes of complete separation vs. complete integration and assimilation.

The more negative reactions to black nationalism have been almost universal among white radicals of all 57 varieties (not to mention the rest of the white population, which doesn't go for integration either) for a number of reasons. Let us survey some prominent reasons. For three decades now, white radicals have been dedicated to the struggle for integration in the United States, for getting US Negroes full citizenship rights on paper and reality. Most of their contact with Negroes, and all of the contacts they consider fruitful and meaningful, have been with Negroes struggling for integration. Radicals don't understand and are not politically or sociologically equipped to understand the intense need for nationalist identification on the part of Negroes. White radicals cannot advocate nationalist policies even if they see merit in them, because of their delicate position in the American race picture. Black nationalism, once it is in full swing in its influence on individuals or groups of Negroes, eliminates any possibility of whites doing fruitful 'work' in the Negro community.

Nationalism competes with alarming success for the very working class Negroes that radicals are desperate to recruit. The feeling that 'they are taking away from us (and misleading) people who rightfully belong in our party' is readily entertained. Nationalists are too quickly dismissed as a bourgeois movement by radicals, not only in the general sense that any movement not dedicated explicitly to the abolition of capitalism is bourgeois, but specifically because the nationalists (and with them the working class Negroes they attract) advance such ideas as BUY BLACK!, i.e., replacing the white businessmen in the black ghettoes by black businessmen, attempting to set up cockroach-level black business enterprises in the ghettoes. To top it off, black nationalists are not averse to displaying explicit and specific hostility to white radicals they come into contact with.

We shall attempt to discuss all these points.

The Appeal of Nationalism

Radicals, like everyone else, may fall into a rut of becoming hypnotized with familiar words and familiar concepts which have explained things before and should open all doors to be encountered. They must be wary of falling into the habit of only considering the fundamentals, as they are used to seeing them, in an area where they have no 'feel', viewing everything broadly in terms of long-range concepts of a generalized nature, and complacently assuming that, by having examined the 'fundamentals', they are in a position to grapple with what is really important. The white problem in the United States, and the Negroes' response to it, cannot be exhaustively studied by a ritualized treatment of such concepts as capitalism vs. socialism, revolution, peace, integration vs. separation, as such. Habits and outlooks formed thus far in the history of the radical movement, in studying Marx and Lenin, in the discussion and analysis of past revolutions, the US labor movement, the history of radical tendencies in the United States, the colonial revolution, are all valuable and useful, but fail to clarify the obscure subtleties of peculiar complex problems such as this one.

The ultimate program or the definitive decision by any group of black nationalists or organization of black nationalists on the standard familiar problems of statehood, attainment of nationhood by a people, complete separatism as program for action, how to implement such a program, whether or not the program as a whole or this or that aspect of the program is practical, practicable, or consistent, is not of major importance at this time, and should not take up the entire attention of radicals, who are faced with problems of a different nature in their present relations with Negroes. The definitive disposal of these 'basic' questions in some distant future is in fact largely irrelevant to the existence of profound, persistent, and widespread moods of nationalist feeling, total rejection of all aspects of white society that can be recognized as white, including the white radicals, and less intense or explicit expressions of these moods on the part of large and steadily increasing numbers of Negroes who are not necessarily members or followers of any organized nationalist tendency.

White radicals tend to approach the problem of the spectrum of black nationalistic thinking, feeling, and groupings in somewhat the same manner as they would approach the spectrum of white radical political groupings, i.e., as organizations with worked out programs based on some variety of European-tradition analyses of all great political problems facing the world of today, with stringent attempts to appear consistent in the light of the logic of the particular tendency and its traditions of rigid argumentation. But black nationalism is today a turbulent spectrum of moods, currents, and sects, generally with a low political level compared to traditional Marxism, but high compared to the rest of the US population. Most black nationalist organizations and individuals experience no compulsion to work out, at this time, such thought-out and hair-splitting 'answers' to all the great questions facing mankind as radicals do; their memberships are frankly not interested in all the world's problems, but only in the problems of black people and, by extension, colored peoples in general. What the memberships find fascinating and exhilarating about the organizations and their spokesmen and atmosphere is that the black nationalists tell 'the truth' about the white problem and the white world in which they are forced to live, that they express a clear, unambiguous, uncompromising rejection of the whole stinking mess, and, best of all, provide avenues of expression for the dignity, sense of personal and group identification, sense of national belonging which Negroes (and, for that matter, everyone anywhere) need but will find nowhere else in the United States.

Negroes will certainly not find that need fulfilled by white radicals or their organizations. For reasons which we shall examine later, white radicals are totally oblivious to the socio-psychological value of nationalist identification, and its revolutionary potential in the case of Negroes living in the United States. While some radicals may eloquently point out that the nationalist organizations have not answered all the great questions of the day, have not explained how they, realistically expect to carry out their eventual program of a separate state or repatriation 'back' to Africa, and that something they said once is not consistent with what they are saying now, all this is of little or no interest to the nationalists' black audience, especially as the criticism comes from the mouths and pens of whites. Aside from general race suspicion, this audience quite correctly feels that the white critics are out of touch with them.

When white radicals encounter nationalist feeling and proceed to argue against it, they almost invariably turn their Marxist swords on the various impractical and unrealistic aspects of the ultimate nationalist 'program', to whatever extent such programs are delineated. There is no difficulty in logically demolishing the crackpot schemas of back to Africa and separate states for the black man on this continent. Yet this 'Marxist' argumentation is sure to have no effect on the black listener. For no matter how unrealistic and impracticable the millenary program of his nationalist organization is (assuming he even belongs to one), there is no getting around the fact that the black man knows that right now he is here in America and this is certainly NOT his country, he does not

CHALLENGES OF BLACK LIBERATION

feel at home here, the white people all around him in the bus and subway, on the job, are certainly not his people, their values are not his values, their outlook on the world is not his outlook, the mutual relations are cold, strained, and alienated if not downright hostile.

These facts, negative as they are, provide more than enough justification for the existence of nationalist moods and nationalist organizations at the present time. Negroes who join, support, or listen sympathetically to such organizations are not necessarily seriously interested in the ultimate 'programs' espoused by these groups, but respond with sure and certain intuitive political judgment to the fact that these organizations, groups, and individuals are really 'saying something', they are telling 'the truth' about the here and the right now, whatever one may think of their ultimate pie in the sky. They satisfy deep-felt psychological and sociological needs common to people who do not have their own country and need to elaborate their own image to live up to, not somebody else's.

But these needs are remote from the understanding of the white radical, who does have a country. The negative aspects are of little or no interest to the white radical, who lacks any nationalist feeling. In fact, since white nationalism can only be arch-reactionary in the US, the white radical is much better off without it, and lack of it casts no aspersion on him. But by the same token the white radical is at a loss to understand what contribution these undeniable, ever-present negative facts, which bear down on Negroes every moment of the day (in addition to everything else obnoxious in the racist

US which likewise bears down on Negroes every day and which radicals do understand and fight), can make to the complex of nationalist feelings in Negroes. At the present level of political development and nationalist consciousness of Negroes in the US, this negative attraction to nationalism is more than adequate to sustain these moods and organizations. More political clarity, not so much about the ultimate program, but about action to be carried out right now, will be demanded from nationalist leadership as this consciousness develops further under the impact of events.

∴

It is common to dismiss black nationalists (particularly organized black nationalist tendencies) as people engaging in escapism, people withdrawing from the real struggle, who have much less in common with radicals than do integrationists and assimilationists. They are commonly considered nowhere near as practical and realistic in their outlook as are integrationists and assimilationists.

This evaluation is not well grounded. Integrationists, nationalists and white radicals are all unrealistic, each in their own ways. There is some aspect of reality which they fail to see or don't want to see. In some important ways, black nationalists have far more in common with white radicals than most integrationists have. Sometimes the distinction is not clear. Negroes evincing marked nationalist attitudes are engaged in integration struggles, but are not yet interested in joining any nationalist organization or sect.

White radicals certainly do not sound realistic to blacks at this time: they have nothing substantial to offer, the white revolutionary workers they talk about do not exist in any perceptible number, the white-ally working class they speak of does not resemble the white working class all Negroes know from their daily job experience. Integrationists are impractical in the long run, leaving aside any impractical ideas or tactics they have or follow in the present integration struggles, in that their goal is to achieve complete integration into a society which cannot be completely integrated and which is not worth integrating into. Nationalist-oriented people do not object to the integration of public toilets, bus stops, etc., but quite realistically remain unmoved by the idea of being integrated, absorbed and assimilated into the great insipid white morass of these wonderful United States of America.

The possible theoretical contributions white radicals might conceivably make to the struggle are limited severely by their total lack of feeling for, total alienation from any understanding of, the subjective need for identity on the part of Negroes as a people separate and distinct from the surrounding majority of melting-pot whites. White radicals tend to focus too much either on total integration or on total separation as end results of some long-range denouement, training their powerful Marxist telescopes on the distant mountains while wandering off the trail.

What do black nationalists have in common with white radicals? Unlike assimilationists, nationalists take no responsibility for being true-blue Americans and accepting the wonderful American Way of Life. Assimilationist Negroes want desperately to be real true solid Americans 'like everyone else, just give me a chance to prove it'. The self-identification with True American is something assimilationists certainly share with white radicals, who are, in the 'good sense', True Americans par excellence. However, white radicals reject the foreign policy and the state apparatus, and align themselves with forces outside the United States that the US is out to crush or control. In this they share much common ground with the black nationalists, who also reject the foreign policy, aspirations, and alignments of the US along with everything else they reject. Black nationalists are acutely sensitive to nationalist anti-imperialist currents in Africa, to some extent in Asia and Latin America, and take great joy in every piece of evidence of the downfall of 'the white man's power' throughout the world, i.e., any defeat of US imperialism or its allies anywhere in the world.

Nationalist Negroes are outspoken and adamant in their repudiation of the Gandhian turn-the-other-cheek and love-your-enemy philosophies preached by Rev. Martin Luther King and white liberals. This they share with some radicals (the revolutionary ones) and with some integrationists. Much of the popularity of the nationalists rests on just this fact, and this is already understood by most radicals.

Much more basic common ground between white radicals and black nationalists is the social composition of the black nationalists, largely working class (in contrast to the lower middle class orientation and self-image of the integrationist students). The mass following of the black nationalists, particularly of the Black Muslims, is exactly the mass of downtrodden, unskilled proletarians completely alienated from US society that the white radicals need to recruit, in order to build integrated parties solidly rooted on the American scene and containing the human material with which to deal blows to the capitalist system. No matter how radicals interpret the 'program' of a nationalist movement in formal class terms, the class composition of the nationalists' following should never be left out of focus.

But it is hardly the case that the nationalists are taking away from the radicals people whom the radicals would have otherwise won over. Even during the thirties, when radicals did have something meaningful to say to the black masses (namely: here are some white workers en masse and on the move, your allies in the living flesh raring to go and pitch in to help you win), nationalist feelings and nationalist movements were by no means dead and dormant. At the present time, radicals have virtually nothing to say to the black masses that communicates much meaning to them. The radicals 'ain't sayin' nothin''. The people the nationalists (and particularly the Black Muslims) have been reaching have been outside the range of influence and contact of white radicals since the thirties, and many of them were inaccessible even then, while the nationalistic message rings up a resonant response, generates energy and enthusiasm unmatched by any other appeals in many denizens of the ghettoes, the white radical message, even if heard, leaves the same people relatively cold. This general phenomenon, corroborated in dozens of Negro communities by the sweeping spread of the Muslim movement, is a sure indication that the nationalist rejection of white society strikes a deep response among Negroes irrespective of what their attitudes and opinions might be as to the ultimate 'program', if any, implied or stated in the nationalist appeal.

Radicals will more frequently face the problem of dealing with radicalized Negroes having strong nationalist leanings, rather than Negroes actually belonging to or committed to a membership organization, in the immediate future. It is understandably irritating to white radicals, whose organizations must have a sizable Negro membership if they are to thrive and survive and grow roots in the real working class, to see ferment and bitter anti-status quo feeling sprouting up among Negroes all over, and yet to see themselves getting nowhere with recruiting. These nonaffiliated nationalist-minded Negroes seem to be the natural recruiting material for white radical organizations, given their hard-knocks radicalism, total rejection of US society, and combative potential and spirit. The main problem facing radicals is to find a bridge to these people, not to take theoretical potshots at the deficiencies in the separatist 'programs'.

Down South and Up South

The heroic struggle of Negro students in the South is viewed by radicals as the brightest spot in the national picture. This is a struggle which white radicals and white liberals, too, can understand, sympathize with, join in. Concomitantly, the white radicals often draw the conclusion that the nationalists are phonies compared to the freedom riders and sit-in fighters, that the nationalists are withdrawing from the real fight to escape in a never-never land. The integration struggle down South is seen as the model for all Negroes. The Southern front is seen as the central and dominant feature of the entire Negro struggle.

The only thing right about that picture is that the students and other Negroes fighting for integration under severe odds and at great personal risk in the South are indeed heroic and inspiring, and their struggle is certainly the front line in the South today. The comparisons are all wrong. Up North (or Up South, as some Negroes say) is not the same as Down South. The problems of Northern Negroes are not identical to those of Southern Negroes, however much they may have in common.

The 'real' Negro struggle consists of several struggles on different fronts, all interrelated. Southern Negroes have to struggle for the most elementary rights: the right to sit anywhere on a bus, to walk on the sidewalk, to not suffer humiliation in ten thousand segregated ways, to cast a ballot in a meaningless election, to sit at a greasy-spoon lunch counter to get served tasteless food – the list is endless. All this in addition to the problems that Negroes in the North and West of this great land have to cope with. But the focus of attention is different.

The struggles in the South are waged primarily to win aspects of integration which Negroes elsewhere already 'enjoy'. Negroes outside of the South are more immediately interested in higher wages, better living and working conditions, job and educational opportunities, and a lot more. A lot more that is not so readily formulated: a society in which they can feel at home as a people, as humans, identification in their own eyes as part of humanity. Southern Negroes want these things, too, but are immediately occupied with more elementary struggles for which they have fashioned suitable weapons for the moment.

Northern Negroes have always been lukewarm to the awkward efforts of white radicals to transplant Southern issues and methods to the North, where other problems take the forefront. There is no lack of sympathy for the Southern front, but what the radicals have in mind in these efforts is not clear and doesn't register. Urbanized Negroes in the teeming hellholes of Chicago, New York, Philadelphia, Pittsburgh, Detroit don't have to freedom-ride on the bus or subway, they can go to the public beach in most cases, nobody stops them from voting. They can eat in any greasy spoon by legal right. Their kids can go to a token-integrated school where they will be taught decadent white American ideology and effete white American values. A Harlem Negro can take a suite in the Waldorf Astoria if he has the money and wants to splurge it that way (and if he calls in his reservation from some non-Harlem address). It's the Law.

Then why aren't Northern Negroes happy, with those beachheads of integration?

Negroes in the North should seem about due for the melting pot. They have formal and legal status, even more or less the economic status, of previous ghetto immigrants (Irish, Italians, Jews) who have long since been assimilated. So why don't they melt? They have problems, true, but so did the other ethnic groups mentioned. Why this paradox of growing nationalism stronger in the urbanized and integrated North rather than in the totalitarian, segregated South? (Black Muslims are growing pretty fast in the South, too, though).

The bulk of Northern Negroes are economically restricted to rat- and vermin-infested slum tenements and the dirtiest low-paying jobs. But this was true of immigrant groups in the past. As long as they knew some of their brethren had made it to 'success' and had hope for their children rising up in the American world, they didn't lose faith in the American Way. A few became radicals, but lost any interest in 'that nonsense' as the society managed to absorb them. At no time was there a mass rejection of America comparable to what we see among Negroes today.

If Negroes in the North and West were headed straight into the American melting pot, with the unquestioned goal of becoming assimilated as have the various waves of immigrants from Europe, and even Oriental immigrants, then integration, and gradual integration at that, would be on the order of the day, with no serious challenge from any quarter. True, one ethnic group may have a harder time getting into the melting pot than another, but it's all a matter of degree. It would only be a matter of time and grit before significant numbers of Negroes had made it. Nationalism would be at best something to amuse a few old cronies born in the South who never adjusted to Big City life.

Would radicals then be happier, seeing the urban Negro population all solidly in favor of integration and assimilation? Negroes in the North all 'enjoy' to one extent or another the very elemental rights which Negroes in the South are presently struggling for. Yet it is precisely in the urban Negro proletariat that black nationalism finds its most fertile soil. Why should this be a source of distress, annoyance, and chagrin to white radicals who are for fundamental changes and not just assimilation of Negroes into the status quo? The radicals would never have been able to influence these people, and don't know what to say to them anyway.

A radicalization of these masses through a mechanism operating independently, infusing self-confidence, self-expression, powered by the tremendous appeal imparted by nationalist fervor, providing an avenue for the organization into a mass movement of previously politically unorganized and voiceless masses seething with hatred for the status quo – all this should be good reason for optimism among revolutionists. It might not be exactly what they expected, it is certainly not entirely to their liking or understanding, being out of their control; it is far from being an ideal political vehicle for revolutionary change. But it is a thousand times better than the alternative picture of the same tens of thousands of Negroes sitting it out patiently in the illusion of getting their chance to cash in on the American Dream.

The implications of this massive swing toward nationalism are deadly for the prospects of the survival of the American Way. Of course, nationalist sentiment among Negroes, raised to whatever fever pitch, is not going to automatically alter the status quo. But it should be obvious that this is only the beginning of a process, not the end stages. And even at this early stage, the promise of integration into the American Way of Life is empty and insipid to hosts of Negroes.

James Baldwin quotes a friend, who he says is not a nationalist: 'I might consider being integrated into something else, an American society more real and more honest – but *this*? No, thank you, man, who *needs* it?' (*Nobody Knows My Name*).

It is no tragedy, then, that so many Negroes are not wild about more integration and still more. The problem ahead is that nationalist organizations are geared more toward expression of sentiment than toward action. Radicals should put their minds to work to probe out suitable courses of action – for nationalists, left nationalists, as well as integrationists, in collaboration with radicals.

There is a tragi-comic aspect in the spectacle of white radicals moaning that Negroes reject the society that the radicals themselves say history has condemned.

Thinking Black

In the eyes of most Negroes, white radicals appear to be far more attached to US society than black nationalists are. This should come as a surprise to radicals. In the white-radical framework of reasoning, the radical has the truly fundamental approach in explicitly stating a decision for socialism and against capitalism, thus definitively rejecting US class society in a manner matched by no other trend in society in the profundity and sweep of the break with the status quo. Emotionally, however, white radicals are more or less in harmony and even in love with America and with American atmosphere (with American culture, if such a thing can be said to exist) and feel very much at home in the United States – their country. Of course they are intensely interested in reforming this society through some revolutionary change. Their break is with bourgeois society, not with US society, in the sense of the American people and its 'culture'.

Black nationalists, on the other hand, do not feel at all at home in the United States or among their allegedly fellow Americans. No Negroes do, to tell the truth. Just as the society rejects them, black nationalists reject every aspect of that white society which they identify as white. Remember that it is not just the bourgeois class society which rejects Negroes, but the whole of the US society, which is referred to here as 'white society'. Negroes have the choice of trying to turn themselves inside out to live up to this white society and its values or rejecting this society and seeking values of their own.

A dominant culture decides for itself and for 'everybody' what is normal, sane, in good taste; it sets the standards for maturity, intelligence, morality, and human nature.

Those aspects of human behavior which the dominant culture represses or assigns a low value to are looked upon with revulsion and ridicule, and considered a badge of inferiority. The dominant group projects its repressions onto the groups it dominates and despises the latter for not kowtowing to the master group's values. The victimized group may chafe under the 'stereotypes' or may attempt to assert its own values. Assimilationist James Baldwin states the case:

'One had the choice of either "acting just like a nigger" or of *not* "acting just like a nigger" – and only those who have tried it know how impossible it is to tell the difference'. (*Nobody Knows My Name*).

A Negro is nationalist in direct proportion to the extent of his rejection of this white society and his self-identification with Negroes as a distinct people. Black nationalists entertain no hope or interest in improving any aspect of US society, not even through a white people's revolution to come about in some far-off millennium. Black nationalists can find nothing good about the United States and its white people that might interest them: the materialistic TV-crazy chrome-plated-commodity-happy H-bomb-wielding paradise of the white man has nothing to offer Negroes even if the greasy spoons, public toilets, movie houses and public schools were integrated.

The white US has no music worthy of the name, no indigenous culture, no soul, no life, no poetry, no national purpose, no meaningful goals, no desirable friends abroad, no understanding of the world and its people, no genuine fraternal links with other peoples struggling to build a better world, no appreciably large mass of poor white people who appear to offer a reasonable prospect of being allies of the Negroes in the foreseeable future. Even the white-led labor movement and the white US Communist Party are shoddy specimens compared to their counterparts in other countries.

Unlike youth in the newly developing African countries, Negro students have no prospect of studying and making their living in the service of their people, say as engineers, technicians, organizers of industry, statesmen. Liberals and radicals are generally aware of the crushing of incentive in Negro children faced with few prospects of getting decent jobs and opportunities. But the fact of not having a society to grow up into is at least as devastating. A few individual Negroes can achieve American-style 'success', they can have their pictures in *Ebony* as the First Member of the Negro Race to achieve such and such a position pulling down so many thousand dollars a year salary. But this 'success' will be in the service of an alien society and alien people, and measured by the yardsticks of an alien culture.

Unlike Negroes of any persuasion, white radicals along with all other melting-pot whites in the US genuinely feel that this is their country not just in words but deep down in their bones. White radicals seek to identify with the country's alleged revolutionary traditions from way back 200 years ago, and feel they are the realest and truest Americans. For Negroes, nationalist or not, this is self-deception and escapism. Negroes may be physically in America, and their ancestors may have been here longer than some white families, but Negroes are not Americans if that word properly describes the white population. Negroes have never been Americans, perhaps never will be Americans, and do not want to be or become such Americans (i.e., share the empty, cold, materialistic, selfish Madison-Avenue-touted Way of Life).

White radicals have nothing in their experience that equips them to understand this complex of feeling in a real human sense. White radicals know from a distance, and in the abstract, of the powerful attraction of nationalist feeling in other countries, other revolutions. They can glibly quote from great Marxist thinkers on the subject of nationalism and self-determination. In dealing with black nationalism in the US, white radicals attempt to apply their Marxist understanding in a groping, clumsy way, usually contrasting the extreme abstraction of complete all-out assimilationist integrationism into America-as-it-is to the extreme of separatism and 'back' to Africa. White radicals are capable of writing erudite documents replete with excellent quotes from Marx and Lenin pertinent to these two extreme variants, spend much time discussing the history of their faction fights on the subject, note with satisfaction how far their white-radical rivals stray from the correct Marxist approach on the subject, but remain deaf and blind to what Negroes are really concerned about in that area.

Buying Black

Capitalism vs. socialism is not a crucial subjective issue to Negroes at this time. While any trained radical can point to some conceivable danger resulting in some conceivable situation from this ambiguity, radicals are out of their sense of proportion in attaching undue importance to the lack of explicit stands against capitalism per se on the part of Negroes not already recruited to radical parties.

Why should Negroes in the US get worked up against the concept of capitalism as such? What in their experience would favor or hinder such an attitude? And why should their lack of interest in this great Fundamental Question be misinterpreted into some sort of acquiescence in capitalism as such? The answer to the latter question is found in the formalistic and dogmatic approach common in the thinking of many white radicals (and in most people, of course; radicals have no monopoly on rigid and mechanical thinking). Since capitalism vs. socialism is the basic question to the white radical, he is ready to judge and catalog other individuals and tendencies on how they respond to that question. As long as the cataloguing encompasses social entities in the white world which he understands, the white radical categorizes well. Whites could be radically opposed to the status quo only insofar as they take an explicitly anti-capitalist stand.

But Negroes are already a solid phalanx of non-capitalist mass, at the bottom of the social heap and in a state of continual economic depression. There is very little of anything that deserves the name Negro middle class, and no representation in the ruling class whatsoever. There are individual assimilated and ultra-assimilated Negroes in higher echelons of government service, and two (2) Negroes now on the Stock Exchange. But this constitutes no independent social force sharing even a tiny fraction of power with the white ruling class. Black capitalism in the US is nonexistent as a social force, to the point of the concept being ludicrous.

While US Negroes are anything but explicitly pro-capitalist, the confrontation of socialism vs. capitalism as a concept leaves them cold for the most part. This is natural, since what US Negroes face is a hostile white world, with all sections and income levels of the surrounding white world, from the Rockefellers and Kennedys on down to the poor white worker and farmer, arrayed against them in hostility, frigidity, and contempt. In this hostile bloc of all classes, the white capitalist class does not stand out any more sharply than the other whites in its hostility, and may escape being on the mind of non-Marxist-oriented Negroes because of the lack of direct personal contact. No matter what Negroes say or don't say, or think or don't think about US capitalism as such, US capitalism is not and never has been any friend of the Negroes, and the Negroes are no natural friends of US capitalism. White capitalism (the only capitalism in the US) is simply rejected along with the rest of white society.

Now why should black workers be interested in having black-owned businesses prosper? Once the existence of nationalist feeling is known, one should naturally expect some such attitude. But the attitude is irritating to white radicals, rubbing them the wrong way on a fundamental point of doctrine, so that white radicals immediately feel impelled into a stubborn argument with any Negro who argues BUY BLACK! to the detriment of other points on which the white radical and Negro might find substantial common ground. As the white radical pontificates on how capitalism is wrong no matter what the color of the capitalist is, and why separatism is no solution, and the unity of Negro and white workers is what … the Negro (not necessarily nationalist) may be thinking: 'This is a damn shame. This ofay[12] is just against black people having money. He raises hell against capitalism and Wall Street at the top of his lungs right now, but in a couple of years he might forget all that jive and settle down and

---

12   **Editors' Note:** Among many African Americans, the word 'ofay' has been synonymous with *bigoted white* or even *white* in general – being derived from the 'pig-Latin' rendering of the word *foe*.

make him more loot than I will ever see. But it bugs him to see any black man have money and power'.

Negroes can have no experience with black exploiters; even if there are a handful somewhere in the country they are too sparse to constitute a recognizable social phenomenon. The possibility of a black bourgeoisie (in the real sense, not E.F. Frazier's[13]) taking shape in the country is utterly fantastic, no less so than the possibility of Negroes all going back to Africa or taking over a separate territory within the confines of the US, or being integrated completely into capitalist society.

The BUY BLACK! argument aims at making the black ghetto black, i.e. owned and managed and run by blacks.

Running white businesses off the main drag in the ghetto is a popular notion, not at all limited to competing Negro businessmen. In fact, the latter would be horrified if the people among whom the notion is popular ever got going in direct (physical) action to carry out such a Yankee Go Home! program. There would be no businesses at all left, only martial law on the streets. (A 1962 picketing campaign on Harlem's 125th Street against white merchants, many of whom are Jewish, took on anti-Semitic overtones. Supporters of the United African Nationalists chanted 'Black Man Stay, Jew Go Away'. Negro businessmen and community leaders repudiated both this and the picketing tactics).

The popularity of BUY BLACK! is natural. The workers in the ghetto have to take crap from white bosses on the job (and from white workers on the job), see white cops patrolling the streets busy shaking down numbers men and beating heads. They rub elbows with alienated and distant poker-faced whites on the integrated subway or buses. But they don't want to see whites raking in all the money in the ghetto, too, running even the local drug store, bar, soda fountain, clothing shop. This is a constant and grinding irritation. What is important is that the feeling is there, not just that there is no long-range practical program for removing the irritation within the capitalist framework. It is the more acute form of irritation at having to look at white movies, white TV stars, white faces on the advertisements, the sourpusses of white presidents on the dollar bills.

What would an unskilled worker resident of the black ghetto have to lose by resonating enthusiastically to the Muslim rejection of white society coupled with a program of complete separation with dignity (not specified how to carry it out)? The ghetto inhabitant living in the integrated Northern city is already

---

13   **Editors' Note:** A reference to sociologist E. Franklin Frazier's study *Black Bourgeoisie*. In Marxist parlance, *bourgeoisie* often refers not to all businessmen (including small shopkeepers, funeral directors, barbers, etc.), but to the very wealthy and powerful elite that dominates the capitalist economy.

about as integrated as can be achieved by the methods used in the South. Aside from that he is already effectively separated in his residence, social ties, outlook on life, relation to society, job opportunities, freedom and opportunity of expression. The nationalist appeal doesn't threaten to take anything away, and offers something not found anywhere else.

Now would that same unskilled worker stand to lose anything if the nationalist program was, or could be, carried out at this time? Frankly this question is academic. The possibility of carrying out that type of separation program would mean that almost all Negroes were involved in a violently anti-status quo movement, upsetting the stability of the whole country. Long before the situation reached that point, other factors outside the Negro population and even outside the United States would have been brought into play through the interaction with the black revolt and the instability of the power-house of the capitalist world right on its home grounds.

On the other hand, any counter-reform attempt to intensify discrimination or enforce segregation where it does not now exist would encounter ferocious resistance from all Negroes, whatever their orientation. Nationalists are for some kind of separation on terms agreeable to Negroes, not for accepting humiliating and dehumanizing segregation conditions dictated by whites. These are not just words. No membership or following they could attract would tolerate it otherwise.

Take the A-Train

It is obvious from talking to white radicals that most of them have never actually spoken with a black nationalist or listened to them harangue on the street corners in Negro neighborhoods, to their natural audiences. We, therefore, insert here a few brief excerpts of nationalist utterances, limited to New York.

No Black Muslims are quoted since their newspaper is readily available and widely circulated. The book by C. Eric Lincoln[14] also provides interesting quotes.

What is important below is not just what the nationalists are saying, but the fact that in each case the speaker is in rapport with his black audience, which responds wholeheartedly to his remarks.

∴

---

14   **Editors' Note:** This refers to sociologist C. Eric Lincoln's study *Black Muslims in America*.

NY TIMES March 2, 1961, in an unusual article on Harlem nationalists in the wake of the protest at the UN against the murder of Lumumba:

> 'Our ties have to be linked with Africa', said Edward Davis, an unemployed laborer and president of the African Freedom Movement.
>
> 'I'm no Communist ... but when I go to a demonstration and find Communists there, too, I'm glad to see them. That's more reinforcements for us. I'm not for the Communists and I'm not for the capitalists. I'm for black'.
>
> ... at one point, someone interrupted and mumbled what was apparently a defense of America's position on the Congo crisis. Mr. Davis exploded with such fury that everyone in the room was shocked into silence.
>
> 'DAMN THE UNITED STATES', he shouted. Then, in the next breath, he added, 'Excuse me, ladies'. He cast an apologetic glance toward the two women in the crowd ...

∴

A United African Nationalist speaker in Harlem, at Seventh Avenue and 125th Street (summer of 1960):

> ... you know, things are really looking up when you see even these white folks' Neegroes starting to get some sense in their heads, starting to take pride in Africa. Twenty years ago, if you talked to one of these Neegroes, you know, one of these colored folks trying to integrate himself into the white man's world, always trying to get into the white man's face, win his 'love', move into his neighborhood, marry the white man's daughter, go to his school, instead of building up his own neighborhood and looking out for black, if you talked to him about Africa, he'd say: now you get out of my face with that Africa talk, you ain't sending me back to no bush country, with those monkeys jumping all over and a bunch of naked savages running around. But now, even Mr. Neegro is starting to shake off the white man's teachings, starting to take pride in the land of his ancestors. Africa is a rich country, Africa has everything. Iron, copper, gold, diamonds, oil, everything you need to build a great country. But the white man never told us that. He only told us Africa was nothing, nothing but jungle and savages ...
>
> ... Some colored folks, they still act like you're crazy if you talk about Africa. Now why shouldn't black folks want to go back to Africa? Africa's

> our country. Africa can't be such a bad place if those white folks fight so hard to stay there and hang on to the riches they found there! ...
>
> ... wouldn't you all rather live in a black man's country, see a president with a black face, the chief of police with a black face and all the policemen black, go into the bank and see a black face sitting behind the desk? Wouldn't you rather be in a country where you could look at the money and see a smiling black face looking back at you, instead of old George Washington's sour puss? ...

The week of Fidel Castro's stay at the Hotel Theresa in Harlem in September 1960 was an occasion for pronounced manifestations of nationalist sentiment on Harlem streets in the vicinity of the hotel. On September 28, when A. Nunez Jimenez and Juan Almeida took an unannounced stroll through about fourteen or so blocks in the neighborhood, the crowd swirling and snowballing around them ran to some thousands, all of them enthusiastically hailing the Cubans: There is no question that this demonstration was spontaneous. People in windows opening up all along the impromptu route reacted with the same effusiveness. When the two barbudos got back to the Theresa twenty minutes later, the marching crowd had grown to such proportions that the cops became panicky and made desperate efforts on foot and horseback to break it up and disperse it. Some cops were hit by flying objects and a major riot was narrowly averted.

A symptomatic incident shortly before this involved a Negro across the street from the hotel, who had to be physically restrained by by-standers from socking another Negro who had made disparaging remarks against Castro. (The bystanders sympathized with the attacker, but wanted to prevent trouble). The gist of the angry nationalist's remarks, cleaned up for propriety, was:

'... so you're an American, you can't stand Castro talking out against America? Then what the hell you doing here in Harlem, you so damn American? How come you got a black skin like me? Don't come to me with that "American" stuff, I'll go right upside your head! If you're so American, you don't have to live here in Harlem, why don't you go downtown and live with your fellow Americans? ...'.

∴

Now listen to the incisive and lyrical language of one Garveyite speaker on a street corner in Brooklyn's ghetto (early 1961):

> ... this Martin Luther King say you got to love the white man. He say if the white man go upside your head, why you just supposed to turn the other

cheek and love him, make him love you. That's the Christian way. Now *why* you folks want the white man to love you? You know the white man don't love nobody. White man don't even love his own kind. The Jew don't get along with the Eye-talian. The Eye-talian don't like Irish. The Irish, they don't like Pollacks. Pollacks don't like Germans. Germans don't like nobody. But *all* of 'em get together against *you* and *me*! That's no lie! Only thing the white man respect is power. You get you some power, he respect you. He don't have to love you ...

... You ask yourself, why all of a sudden these liberal white folks so eager to have you integrate with them? All this time we is just dirt, they don't want to have nothin' to do with us. Now they say please come in, integrate with us nice white folks, you our black brothers. Why they saying that now? Because they is catching hell, that's why. All over the world, Asia, Africa, Cuba, Japan, everywhere you look, the white man is starting to catch natural hell. Now his house burning clear down to the ground, he want us to help him put out the fire ...

... Lemme ask you folks this. Who loves Russia? You answer me that one now. W-H-O loves Russia? Yeah! Don't NONE of these white folks love Russia! They always talking against the Russians, want to kill them. They hate Russia almost as much as they hate us, and that take a whole LOT of hating!

But they RESPECT Russia. Because Russia got power. White folks don't be messin' roun' with Russia. They fly that U-2 plane over Russia, old Khrushchev start bangin' that shoe, wavin' a H-bomb right in the white man's face. Uncle Sam back down. Uncle Sam know he done went too far this time. He even a-po-lo-gize!! Ain't that somethin'? But he don't have to apologize to no black man. Black man waitin' for the goddam white man to love him. Black man ain't got nothin' behind him, 'cept what he sits on ...

... you know the folks in Africa are fighting against the same damn integration you brainwashed colored folks over here so crazy about. The Frenchman say to the Algerian: What you want independence for. You integrate with us. You is a Frenchman. Algerian, he say: that's a DAMN lie! ...

Blind Spots of White Radicals

An understanding of the gap now separating black nationalists and white radicals must be sought not only in the life of the Negro in a white United States, but also in the history, struggles, attitudes, and life of the white radicals in the peculiar setting of the rich and powerful United States. Particular attention is due to the problem of singling out the factors which contribute to making white radicals insensitive to the dynamics of black nationalism, thus crippling the radical approach and rendering the frantic efforts of white radicals to build a bridge to Negroes largely ineffective.

Estrangement between the white radical vanguard and the Negro masses is, of course, nothing new, and various aspects of it are already clear to radicals who have studied the matter. The white labor movement and the Negro emancipation movement shared very little in common, in the way of conscious collaboration and identification as allies, from the pre-Civil War period until the Thirties. Prior to the decade of the CIO and the moderately successful penetration by the Communist Party of the Negro ghettoes at that time, Negroes had been attached to the Republican Party, had never seen a friend in the white labor movement, in fact usually met a bitter enemy there intent either on driving Negroes out of jobs and keeping them out, or at best callously indifferent. This story is familiar to many radicals, is well documented, and has been discussed. We need only note here that the total picture has obviously never been changed definitively, and that consequently the roots of Negro nationalism run deep and far back in history, regardless of when specific nationalist organizations may have been founded or became attractive to large numbers.

The CP black belt theory and the abstract recognition of the right of the Negro people to demand separation if they so choose have very little if anything to do with the development of black nationalism, and have not constituted any attempt to reach to nationalists on the part of the white radicals. The CP theory is due to the Russian experience on nationalities and self-determination, transplanted blindly onto the American white radical movement. It would not interest nationalists one way or the other, and it is doubtful that the influx of disappointed Negro radicals into the nationalist movement following the Second World War and their disenchantment with the CP had any qualitative effect on the character of black nationalism.

Black nationalism is rooted in the Negro masses, in their conditions of life, in the filth and choking squalor of the slums, in Jim Crow and in the impossibility of their identifying fully with the surrounding white America. Its physiognomy and character contain features, discussed elsewhere in this paper, totally alien to any variety of Americanized radicalism. In any case, white radicals have always been hostile to black nationalism, the new look toward that phenomenon is very recent, and none of their previous activity was ever aimed at reaching to the nationalists.

The word AMERICANIZATION sums up much of the fog separating white radicals and blacks. Americanization has been a very positive achievement of the white radical movement. At the same time it is a major hindrance to their understanding Negroes, or vice versa. Aside from the IWW, many of the early radical movements developed among Russian, German, Jewish, Italian immigrants imbued with socialist sentiments when they arrived at Ellis Island. It was necessary to grow past that stage and transform to a movement which looked American to home-grown American workers, as American as apple pie and Pepsi-Cola. This was definitively achieved by the time the CIO upsurge had started to level off. At the present time all the white radical groups, whether CP, SWP, SP or derivatives thereof, are thoroughly Americanized in their mannerisms, outlook, self-image, and cultural traits.

The membership of the white radical groups consists of real Americans in all respects except for their political views, which do not conform to the reactionary strident chauvinism of the American Century. (In the case of social democrats, who are really liberals rather than radicals, that exception may be disregarded). Being so American, their ability to criticize some aspects of the American personality is blunted. Such cultural features as anti-intellectualism, lack of recognizable indigenous culture, the self-delusions that Americans are the only 'regular folks', free and easy-going, not stuffed shirts, full of pioneer spirit and good-natured sense of humor, fair-minded, to hear the Americans tell it; the almost universal narrow-mindedness, rugged-individualist selfishness, coldness toward fellow human beings throughout all classes of the white American population, the total absence of any inspiring national goals, the poverty and emptiness of American emotional and cultural life, the alienation from all other peoples of the world (except some imperialist and racist countries) – all this is either accepted, escapes critical notice, or is blamed on capitalism per se.

Radicals are fully aware of the politically reactionary aspects of American policies and condemn those aspects of American life which they can pinpoint as direct products of capitalism per se, but are basically in harmony with what passes for American culture, and identify with the American (i.e. white) people. They had better. Their job and goal is to get closer to and fuse with the American workers and people, and this requires being American.

Fortunately, Negroes in the US have never become so Americanized, and fortunately never will be, the way things look. Only the Negroes have any indigenous music, have positive goals to strive for as a people, feel anything resembling warm kinship for other peoples struggling for a better life. Negro masses do not have a higher cultural level or tastes, and may 'enjoy' some of the worst trash in US mass culture, but even so they still miss 'the truth' relating to their own lives which they do not find in that 'culture'. Negroes are also readily receptive to any criticism of that 'culture'. They are not eager to rise to the defense of 'our' American Dream. Such American cultural traits as selfishness, commodity acquisition fever, emotional coldness, more pronounced than in other capitalist countries, make some headway among many Negroes who are trying hard to assimilate to the point of actually becoming Americans, but this Americanism will have a tough time displacing the vitality Negroes have preserved through centuries in the white wilderness.

In November 1960, addressing a meeting in Harlem after returning from Cuba, Robert F. Williams related: '... this white reporter asked me in Habana: How do you feel, Mr. Williams, as an American, when these Cubans yell Cuba Si, Yanquis No? I told him, well, the first thing you have to understand is, I'm not an American! ...'. At this point the entire Harlem audience broke out into unrestrained applause, stamping, and shouting of approval which did not die down for several minutes, and clearly demonstrated that Williams had made another one of those statements, typical of his, which strike deep down, all the way down, in the consciousness of black listeners, the kind of statement that says what the black man has always thought, maybe said in some form on some other occasion.

White radicals presently take on the acrobatic job of being American to American (white) workers while at the same time trying to win over Negro (anti-American) masses, blissfully assuming that the two peoples are basically identical except for a little skin pigmentation, and seem oddly disappointed on finding out that empty American society, which the radicals reject in their own way, is not something all Negroes are just dying to become integrated and immersed into.

This brings us to the overemphasis on integration as an end in itself, the next great stumbling block to the understanding between white radicals and Negroes. The white radical feels most at home with more or less militantly integrationist Negroes, for reasons generally understood. He has great difficulty in understanding or even suspecting the depth of alienation of Negroes from – not just capitalist society in the US, but from American society period. The white radical is not equipped to understand either the black nationalism he sees in organized form or the dynamics and origins of that phenomenon rooted deep in Negro life, and until recently was not even really interested.

At best, white radicals now tend to take a closer look at nationalism as an annoying obstacle and roadblock which has to be studied in order to facilitate the task of eliminating it, so we can all get down to the pleasant job of integrating into the world's one and only unique society known as America, becoming all of us American workers, hand in hand, black and white together seeing eye to eye, to fight the bosses and make our America the great country it was destined to be. If the worst happens, and Negroes actually begin to demand geographical separation or repatriation to Africa as a majority, white radicals will then reluctantly support their right to undertake such an unfortunate and foolish step. That is essentially about all the white radical has had to say on the matter. No serious attempts have been made to probe the possibility of channelizing nationalist sentiment into the battle.

The need to overcome the white chauvinism rampant in the American radical movement prior to the Russian Revolution, the need to fight the proliferation of white chauvinism in the labor movement in general and to eliminate it in new recruits to radicalism, the almost exclusive contact with militant assimilationist Negroes, and the natural lack of affinity for black nationalist thought and feeling all combine to reinforce the fixation on integration as an end in itself.

The fight against white chauvinism has been an indispensable part of the development of the radical movement, and a positive achievement. At the same time, this necessary and valuable fight to eliminate all traces of white chauvinism acted to dull even further any sensitivity white radicals might conceivably have or acquire to the limitations of integration and assimilation as a goal.

Any suggestion that Negroes were 'different' from other Americans had to be stamped out vigorously. Militantly assimilationist Negroes are extremely sensitive to the least implication that they are not exactly the same as 'everyone else'. Jim Crow, blatant American-style racism, and all of its derivatives and sugar-coated liberalized versions adhere strongly to the principle that Negroes are both different and inferior (the corollary to the notion that anyone who is different from an American cannot help but be inferior).

Where Negroes lacked a clear feeling of identification as a people, it is understandable that the circumstances of complete immersion in a white wilderness, with their horizon limited to the United States indefinitely, with no acceptable image to live up to except the white man's, with no independent and developing African States, no Cuban Revolution to be contrasted to the American Dream from which Negroes were being excluded, would lead to a temporary desire to actually be Americans, rather than a striving to achieve some sort of modus vivendi on a basis of equality or peaceful co-existence with this alien people among whom Negroes are interspersed.

A revealing reaction of white liberals and radicals to black nationalists is, very often, the stupidly smug view that nationalists must be Uncle Toms or some variety or modification of Uncle Toms, or that they feel beaten and inferior, simply because they do not aspire to that glorious, sublime state of being an integral part of the great American people.

⁂

The US Communist Party is especially sensitive to petty bourgeois assimilationist pressure, and its tightrope act is most fascinating. On the one hand, the CP is as American as any radicals can get to be, even to the point of waving the Stars and Stripes and singing the Star Spangled Banner. At the same time, they were dragging along, in their ideological baggage, a stillborn black-belt self-determination theory which had nothing whatever to do with any current or section of the Negro community, nationalist or otherwise, accepted solely by those individuals recruited to the CP for other reasons. This Russian-fathered abortion did not sit well with half-Americanized integrationists, inside the CP and outside, and became the butt of much criticism with nothing much positive to show for itself. Red-baiting assimilationists demagogically and maliciously took the CP to task for, of all things, wanting to have Negroes segregated in a separate nation after communism takes over (the die-hard suspicion of Negroes toward all whites, any whites, no matter how friendly they talk, contributed mightily to the pressure). No matter how much the CP tried to soft-pedal the idea, and mollify it down to the quite correct position that while they were not actually advocating such an idea, they would support it if the demand was raised by a majority of Negroes, the CP still had to cringe from attacks by the NAACP (Henry Lee Moon in *Crisis* magazine, for instance) and other assimilationists for even mentioning the terrible and nasty thing. Eventually, in 1959, the CP buried it definitively, washing the stains off its hands, in order to ingratiate themselves still further with assimilationist liberalism – but at the very moment when assimilationists are losing touch with, the Negro people!

Even in the SWP, nervous voices sometimes express anxiety at the very mention of the right of separation as an abstract parenthetical secondary and hypothetical point buried in the SWP resolutions. Since the question of geographic separation is far from being the central issue separating nationalist-oriented Negroes from white radicals, the traces of hysteria on this minor issue give a measure of the magnitude of the lack of communication this article addresses itself to.

⁂

Another important parting of the ways between Negro mind and white radical mind is on the question of the American Worker. Despite whatever evidence to the contrary, the white radical must, in order to survive in this bleak period of political apathy in the labor movement, absolutely must magnify every trace of militancy, trade-union consciousness, strike action, and remind himself over and over again of the glorious history of some active past period of the labor movement, to reassure himself that the American Worker is second to none in militancy and revolutionary potential. It is not enough to dryly state that, through our Marxist knowledge, we know objectively that no matter how quiescent the American (white) worker appears now, conditions will mature which will reactivate the class struggle and bring out the great potential inherent in the American proletariat, that then the great American worker will take the lead in the revolution (or fight for peace) and so forth. In the face of the sneers by liberals, reactionaries, and even the workers themselves, radicals must reinforce this view. The rank-and-file members must also be pepped up emotionally by promoting this image of the American worker second to none, and any grain of truth which can be mustered to sustain the image must be amplified out of all proportion. If the white workers get along with the status quo and are indifferent or hostile to their Negro 'brothers', this must be blamed on other radical tendencies, or on the union leadership, but in no case must the image be questioned.

The net result is that white radicals begin to take on an air of unreality, as if they were in Dreamland or someplace, but certainly not in the United States of America in 1963. A hothouse atmosphere of left-wing optimism has to be generated and sustained if the beleaguered radical groups are to survive, and the temporary divorce from reality is no doubt worth the price.

This glorified image of the white worker strikes almost all Negroes of whatever persuasion, except those already members of the radical groups and, therefore, partaking to some extent of the green-house environment, as out of tune with reality, even an insult to their intelligence. The adverse effect of this kind of talk, offering Negroes the prospect of joining hand in hand with this imaginary revolutionary white proletariat which does not at all resemble the white proletariat the Negro lives in daily contact with, is even more sharply exacerbated, in the case of nationalistic Negroes, in response to the self-satisfied assurance of the radical who has studied Marxism and knows the basic answers.

White political geniuses who claim to have nothing less than a scientific knowledge of society are ready at the drop of a hat to argue why the nationalists are all wrong and impractical in their aims and methods, and give the impression that they have the basically correct program and orientation and only have to improve the way they are carrying out their program, don't even get to first base because they sound so utterly way out on this point, as well as on quite a few others discussed earlier.

It has to be emphasized at this point that Negroes are not reacting with skepticism just because the white workers they know seem politically dead, quiescent, or conservative in their outlook, but often because the white workers are, along with the rest of society, hostile and disgusting chauvinists. The attempts to glorify the white workers' revolutionary future and alleged revolutionary implications of his historic past struggles will in that case spark hostility on the part of the Negro listener who has this salt rubbed into his wounds.

The problem can be minimized when a radical who is not too hung up on Marxist shorthand slogans disemboweled from the rounded-out thought that the slogans summarize, and who tries to make clear he knows what the American scene is now, but is pointing out objective conditions in the making which will change the scene, is trying to communicate with a Negro who is willing to listen. But even then the mere mention of the idea that white workers will someday play revolutionary roles may sound so absurd to the Negro listener that the radical's entire argument will be discredited. If the adept white radical puts the case sensibly enough, forcefully enough, in a properly developed context, and seems to be more lucid and in contact with reality than most white well-wishers Negroes usually come into contact with, there remains the question of the relevance to the black man's problems now of this great upsurge of progressive whites to occur sometime in the indefinite future.

Anyone who succeeds in putting the spotlight on other subtle disparities between the viewpoint of white radicals and Negroes will be doing a great service to the present and future struggle. ...

More Questions to Probe

What aspects of black nationalism offer any leverage for white radicals and Negro radicals in association with white radical organizations? Which aspects of black nationalism, in its endemic form throughout the Negro population and in its organized forms, lend themselves most readily to being channelized into effective action against the status quo, i.e. against US capitalist power and against US imperialism on a world scale, with assistance of white radicals to the extent that the latter are aware of such possibilities and are capable of meshing their actions and theory with the tremendous appeal and dynamism which nationalism is capable of generating?

There is a wide unknown territory here open for probing thought and experimental action. It is no surprise if few or no answers are available, since no one has posed the question seriously.

The questions are worth formulating only with respect to revolutionists. Since both revolutionists and militant Negroes (integrationist or nationalist) are objectively and/or subjectively against the status quo, one can speak of a misunderstanding where the two groups do not communicate. For liberals and those mainly interested in modifying US foreign policy to produce improved relations with the Soviet Union (without otherwise disturbing the status quo), their lack of communication with Negroes is based on a deeper divergence of interests.

One undeniably attractive point about integrationists is that, if they are not too given to red-baiting or fear of radicals, they allow opportunity for radicals to 'do work', to engage in some form of common action with Negroes. By its very nature, black nationalism shuts out almost all avenues of common activity, discussion, or other opportunities for radicals to 'do work'. To date, there has not been much probing by radical organizations, if any probing at all, in the direction of sending Negro members into nationalist organizations or milieus to 'do work'. This might be due to the alienation of the radicals from the nationalists, more likely to the distaste white radicals (and assimilationist Negroes likely to be recruited into white radical parties) feel for the black nationalist orientation, but it is also due to the political intractability of the nationalist groups (singleness of purpose, no room for dissident minorities, religious structure in the case of the Muslims).

The most serious obstacle to such colonization work, however, should any white radical organization be foolish enough to try it, would be the fact that the nationalists would exert a far stronger attraction on the radical Negroes sent in than the latter's parent organization, and the 'colonizers' would be the ones influenced and recruited. Consider the example of Dr. Lonnie Cross, who as Dr. Lonnie X was a key speaker at the 1963 Chicago convention of the Black Muslims.

Integration struggles not encumbered by an insistence on making Negroes over into white Americans of dark skin, and not steeped in the repulsive Gandhian turn-the-other-cheek philosophy, will not interfere with building a bridge to those elements of the Negro population North or South who feel about as integrated legally and formally as they are going to get or care to be, short of some fundamental change in society. Integration in the sense of smashing specific Jim Crow apartheid institutions and broadening educational and job opportunities for Negroes does not constitute an irreconcilable opposite to the nationalist feeling of self-identification as a people not identical to American whites.

Negro radicals may attempt, in some areas, to experiment with riding the nationalist bronco themselves, to see if they can tap some of these resources directly, rather than by liaison with an already established nationalist group.

One obvious arena for work to be anticipated, sought out, or encouraged is any emergence of left nationalist currents, whether independent of existing nationalist organizations or gestating within the confines of such organizations.

Radicals who are good at spotting the shortcomings and illusions besetting nationalist groups might profitably communicate these criticisms, free of the traditional white clumsiness on the question, to such groups, encouraging their leftward development and contributing to their political development on general matters.

If the Black Muslims enter firmly onto the road of political action by and for the black man, with participation in local and national elections, the impact would be close to what revolutionists have always hoped for in a labor party (with the difference that the white-dominated unions have for the present nothing to contribute, except fifth-column activity for the benefit of the Democratic Party and the status quo).

Massive participation in politics by black nationalists would shift the picture in a direction much more amenable to participation by radicals, in its total impact on the national scene, in its reciprocal effect on the nationalists themselves as they grapple with new and vital problems, and in the sense that radicals are more at home with such situations, generally speaking (although there will certainly be some surprises).

The notion of separatism could undergo some interesting modifications as nationalism gains nationwide strength. The black belts are forming, as politically viable black strongholds, not in hinterlands of the deep South, but right in the hearts of the industrial and urban centers. Washington, D.C. now has a Negro majority with no real home rule, in fact with rule by Dixiecrat congressmen. Philadelphia has a huge Negro minority, and could conceivably come under the local control of a well-organized and power-conscious Negro electorate. A continued process of whites diffusing out into the suburbs and Negroes crowding into ghettoes in the center of town, with the ghettoes spreading out through the city, is a phenomenon common throughout the country. These situations are made to order for black nationalist political campaigns, and it is only a matter of time before efforts turn in that direction. The political battle between a Negro-controlled metropolis and a hostile white state capital plus suburbs will be a humdinger.

Legal defense and physical defense against racist violence and frame-up conspiracies are areas of action in which radicals have experience. Some new twists will be introduced if and when the Muslims carry out their promise (threat) to clean up the ghettoes and get rid of white racketeers, criminal elements and lumpen, and any other activities where they begin to encroach on the prerogatives of the white state power (not to mention some of its juiciest revenues).

Nationalist influence spreading in existing labor unions will give radicals a whole new crop of theoretical and tactical problems to play with. The appeal of nationalism to Negro youth down to the teen-age level has not been assessed, and no doubt varies widely across the country. The appeal of nationalism, particularly of the Black Muslims, to Negro women, the role of women in nationalist organizations, which women are attracted to it and which are not, are another set of un-probed questions.

It would be helpful to make a survey of the appeal and strength of nationalist currents across the nation. (This article is based on direct experience limited to New York). It would be worthwhile to know the various groups that exist, their strength and attractiveness relative to the Black Muslims and relative to assimilationist groups, what activities they engage in or seem to be inclined towards, who they appeal to, what areas seem to be open for common action and discussion. The extent of urban concentration of Negroes and out diffusion of whiton to the suburbs, and the chances of Negroes electing militant local candidates, backed by a political powerhouse like the Muslims, could potentially be, are important things to know.

Closer contacts between Negroes and other peoples with whom Negroes have more in common than they have with American whites will be of enormous benefit in developing any aspect of the Negro struggle in the United States. At present, the attention of even the nationalists is too much boxed into a narrow US framework, which limits the goals and the perception of the possibilities. Radicals could be of immense value in this context, promoting, stimulating, and facilitating significant contacts between proletarian Negroes (who would otherwise never get the opportunity) and nonwhite peoples more or less in the same boat and engaged in struggles against the same US imperialism. Indians throughout the Western Hemisphere, Negroes in Latin American countries and in the West Indies, and Africans have a wealth of experience, ideas, violent feelings, and mutual stimulation to share with American Negroes. Such contacts on a reasonably broad scale might have explosive effects, here and elsewhere.

It would be helpful to begin right now in some serious discussion of ways in which US reactionaries might seek to manipulate, head off, or channelize into less harmful (to them) directions any upsurge of nationalism which begins to take on threatening proportions. ...

∴

Difficult as it is to predict the forms which the struggle will take, some long-range predictions about what will definitely not happen can be made. In the long run, integration into the status quo and separation from the status quo are both impractical, impracticable, and even undesirable. At the same time, the status quo is intolerable to Negroes, who are and will continue to be in open rebellion against it along both lines. And the concept of socialism carries no weight as a realistic alternative for the time being. These are the actual boundary conditions within which we shall have to work. The actual struggles which will take place will constitute syntheses of these apparent extremes, until such time as domestic and international events act to channel the struggle explicitly against capitalism per se, and pry the white workers loose from their TV sets. In the meantime, the Negro people in the US are not going to be sitting still, and the relative weight of integrationist and nationalist aims and methods in the struggle will be decided in the heat of battle.

The distance between the black nationalist rejection of what they see as white America and the white radical rejection of what socialists see as bourgeois America is not as great as it used to look.

5 Freedom Now: The New Stage in the Struggle for Negro Emancipation and the Tasks of the SWP[15]
(1963)

Socialist Workers Party

I   'Freedom Now': a New Stage

Under the banner of 'Freedom Now', the Negro struggle for equality has entered a new stage. This is comparable in significance to the change that occurred in the 1830s when a wing of the Abolitionist movement, previously dominated by schemes for piecemeal purchase and deportation of the slaves, raised the explosive demand for immediate and complete emancipation.

The most notable characteristic of this new stage in the Negro struggle is the clear and sharp rejection of gradualism, which is the program, method and perspective of capitalist liberalism. *Freedom Now* is an essentially radical and potentially revolutionary demand. It brings its advocates, regardless of their particular views, into growing conflict with the White House and the Southern Democrats, with the labor leaders as well as the liberals, with Negro as well as white exponents of moderation, compromise and tokenism.

The ruling class of this country cannot grant this demand. Neither can it suppress or sidetrack the movement. That is why a consistent struggle to achieve it will stimulate profound changes not only in race relations but also in class and political relations in the United States.

Freedom Now sentiment is generated from numerous sources: by urbanization, industrialization and migration as a result of which three-fourths of the Negroes live in cities rather than rural areas and one-half outside the South; by inspiration from the colonial revolutions against white imperialist domination in Africa, Asia and Latin America; by the smallness, fewness and slowness of concessions offered to the demand for equality; by the conviction that the rulers of this country will never grant equality voluntarily or without pressure,

---

15   Socialist Workers Party 1963.

and that their difficulties in the cold war make them more vulnerable to pressure; by disappointment in the old-style Negro leaders and the labor bureaucrats. It is spurred by the growth of racial consciousness and solidarity, which flows from common experiences of oppression and is strengthened by historical and contemporary evidence that the Negro must rely on himself first of all if he is to make any progress. This sentiment is bolstered in some circles by a questioning or repudiation of the values of capitalist (white-dominated) society.

The results have been a spread of the Negro struggle into every corner of the country; a sizable increase in the number of active fighters, with the most important new reinforcements coming from the student youth, who are not encumbered by the skepticism, routinism or defeatism of many of their elders and are imparting a new vigor and vibrancy to the struggle; assertions of independence, coupled with heightened self-confidence and growing determination that the Negro will decide his own goals, work out his own tactics and lead his own struggles; more openly expressed feelings of mistrust and suspicion of whites and bitter resentment against paternalism in any form; the raising of new demands and proposals that are unacceptable to most liberals (special consideration or priority for the needs of the Negro to compensate for centuries of oppression and deprivation, adequate and effective Negro representation in all places and at all levels, bloc voting, etc.). This new phase has already witnessed a significant growth of Negro nationalist and separatist sentiment along with the appearance of new national organizations and hundreds of local groups dedicated to equality. This is all part of the ferment, discussion, experimentation, and lively search for ideas, methods, programs and leadership capable of guiding the struggle for equality to victory.

The new period which was definitively ushered in with the Battle of Birmingham in May 1963 has been marked by the following features:

1. The struggle is acquiring an ever greater mass character. It actively involves hundreds of thousands ranging from students and middle class people to the most disinherited and dispossessed of the city ghettoes. They have stepped onto the arena of action as a mass force of constantly growing dimensions and dynamism.
2. Mass action in various forms has now recrossed the Mason-Dixon line. The opening punch was delivered in the fight for jobs at the school construction site in Philadelphia which spread to New York and other places. The dam burst with the turnout of a quarter million Negroes in the June Freedom March in Detroit, the biggest protest demonstration of its kind in this century. From the start the demands in the North are on a higher

socio-economic level than those in the South, striking deeply into the established class structure.

3. The impact of these events has shocked the Kennedy administration, provoked a political crisis in the country and compelled federal, state and local governments to take steps not even remotely contemplated before the upsurge of the Negro revolt. The Kennedy administration does not intend to grant equality. It is anxious to contain and, if possible, buy off the leadership by offering the minimum of concessions to keep the mass movement from moving too fast and far ahead.

4. The top Negro leaders feel even more nervous and unsteady. They are being forced to talk, and in some cases even act, more militantly because they fear the power of the revolt which they did not unloose and cannot control. They also fear that the ruling class upon whom they rely will not grant enough concessions soon enough and that the mass movement will continue to sweep around them and beyond them, dragging them along as they try to slow it down. The profound insecurity of the official leaders, their lack of control over the masses, the emergence of new forces and potential new and bolder leaders are positive signs of an ascending revolt that is becoming more and more radicalized.

5. In the South at this stage the civil rights struggle has some special traits distinguishing it from the rest of the country.

   a. Because of the glaring and intolerable violations of the most elementary democratic rights, Southern freedom-fighters are in a position to expose and dramatize the injustices of Jim Crow, constantly embarrass the federal government and deepen the indignation against segregation not only throughout the United States but throughout the world.

   b. In parts of the South where Negroes are a majority, such moves as the call for the election of a Negro sheriff in Leflore County, Mississippi have a highly explosive character because they directly challenge and endanger the white supremacist structure. Voter registration drives in rural areas where uncompromising Negro candidates might become mayors, judges, or sheriffs could upset the whole balance of power there.

   c. What happens in Mississippi, Alabama and Georgia has immediate repercussions upon the moods of the movement in the North. Any outrage and outbreak of violence, or any outstanding demonstration and achievement in the South, arouses the Negro communities in the rest of the country. Thus the intensification and extension of the struggle in the South is a sharp goad to the national civil rights movement. Conversely, the advances of the Northern struggle, such as the direct actions for jobs, tend to feed back into the South and raise the struggle there to a higher level.

II   The Present Tendencies

The *Freedom Now* forces face the task of uniting into an effective movement and equipping themselves with a program, a philosophy and a perspective. Success in these efforts will depend on correct evaluations of the competing tendencies now in the field, of the intentions of their racist enemies, and of the Negro movement's relations with other sections of the population.

The NAACP was for a long time the dominant civil rights organization. But its relative influence has declined and it is today challenged on all sides. Its leadership, middle class and liberal, relies mainly on legal and legislative action and discourages mass action, initiative and struggle. Afraid of being outflanked and bypassed by more militant organizations, they have attempted to modernize their 'image', but the NAACP remains the chief protagonist and symbol of gradualism. The Negro masses may appreciate it as a legal defense arm and legislative lobby, but they do not feel welcome in it and most do not belong to it.

A pacifist tendency has acquired strength and its leaders prominence since the late 1950s. Its main organizations are the Southern Christian Leadership Conference, headed by Martin Luther King, and the Congress of Racial Equality. Their prestige derives in part from the fact that, unlike the NAACP, they have sanctioned and participated in certain kinds of direct action. But King's pacifism also has the opposite effect of restraining the full unleashing of mass struggle and initiative. He preaches 'love' of the racist enemy and threatens to cancel civil rights struggles whenever the masses display a readiness to defend themselves against racist violence. Although King speaks the rhetoric of *Freedom Now*, it is not accidental that the liberals support him as 'the right kind of Negro leader' while the Kennedy administration feels he can be used to keep the masses from getting out of control.

There is an essential difference between pacifism which preaches no resistance to assaults at all times and at all costs, and a defensive pacifism imposed by an unfavorable relation of forces. The need for organized self-defense against white supremacist gangs and police officials is as yet openly supported only by small groups of Negro militants. The Gandhist-pacifist leaders are ready to rely upon government military force while they repudiate in principle the adoption of self-protective measures by Negroes who are menaced with attacks by Jim Crow elements who are shielded by or may even be part of the state apparatus.

The Student Non-violent Coordinating Committee is a tendency distinct from King and CORE. It originated in the desire of militant students to strike out on a road different from that of the gradualists. It does not preach a binding commitment to Gandhism. For its leaders, nonviolence is rather a tactic than a dogma or principle and one that does not exclude the right of self-defense. SNCC is a vanguard-type movement whose main emphasis is on direct action as a means of organizing the Southern masses for independent struggle.

The Negro American Labor Council was formed to fulfill the indispensable function of leading and coordinating the fight against discrimination in industry and the labor movement. Because of their numbers and strategic position as a link between the labor movement and the Negro community, Negro unionists can play a crucial role in enlisting union support for the independent struggles of the Negro people and Negro support for the unions. But outside of a few cities the NALC has so far failed to recruit many Negro workers into its ranks. Partly this failure is due to the tight bureaucratic grip on the organization by the A. Philip Randolph leadership. The NALC is weakened by the fact that most of its leaders owe their union posts to appointment by the union bureaucracy and are afraid to jeopardize these by undertaking bold actions unacceptable to the Meanys and Reuthers.

The Muslims, headed by Elijah Muhammad, are the most dynamic tendency in the Northern Negro community today. Previously a small, uninfluential religious sect, they have acquired a considerable predominantly working-class membership in the Northern cities, a more substantial following, and the respect of millions of Negroes who are stirred by their forthright denunciation of racial oppression and their determination to free themselves from white domination. Nationalist and separatist, they reject not only gradualism and tokenism, but also the right of their oppressors to control and exploit Negroes. They boldly declare the capacity and right of the Negro people to govern themselves. Important weaknesses include their failure to understand the economic causes of racism and their lack of a program of action enabling them to participate in and influence partial, immediate and transitional struggles of the Negro masses. In the last year the Muslims have begun to overcome their isolation by greater flexibility in their approach toward other Negro organizations. An important and promising step forward was their recent declaration in favor of political action in the form of election campaigns to elect black candidates.

The most radical tendencies with a social or political orientation have been inspired by the example of the Monroe, N.C., movement headed by Robert F. Williams. Monroe has made valuable contributions to the theory and practice of self-defense. However, the movement has been weakened by the persecution, frame-up and exile of its leader.

Significant parts in promoting the struggle against liberalism and gradualism are being played by newly-formed regional and local groups in all parts of the country.

It is from among these groups and currents that the Negro leadership of an effective struggle for equality will be gathered and united. But it is necessary to add that at the present stage none of these tendencies, including the biggest, can claim the affiliation of more than a small percentage of the Negro people. The *Freedom Now* movement is forming, re-forming, learning, developing, preparing, defining and refining. However, the great mass of the Negroes, concentrated in the big ghettos of the North and South, have yet to be heard from.

III   Negro Nationalism Today

General definitions of nationalism are inadequate for understanding and explaining Negro nationalism in the United States today. While it has resemblances to the insurgent nationalism in African countries, and to the nationalism of oppressed minorities in the old Russian Czarist empire, American Negro nationalism also differs from them in certain important respects. Moreover, Negro nationalism is still in an early stage of its development and will surely undergo changes in the future. A definitive analysis will have to wait until Negro nationalism becomes a mass movement and acquires firmer and more fixed features than it now displays. Nevertheless, it is already possible to draw a number of conclusions for guidance.

Capitalism segregates the Negroes, confines them in ghettos, builds walls around them and binds them together in common resentment against racial discrimination, proscription, deprivation and abuse. This is the soil in which Negro nationalism is rooted and grows. It is an outgrowth of these conditions, a reaction against them, a way of resisting and fighting them. In the past the hope that these conditions could be eliminated tended to weaken Negro nationalist sentiment and suspend its activity. However, the belief that these conditions will exist in this country forever, or for another lifetime, serves to nourish, strengthen and activate Negro nationalism.

The intensification of separatist moods among Negroes in the Northern cities expresses a rejection of American class society from top to bottom and a strong desire to break free from the evils of that society. It is their verdict that the present 'American Way of Life' has nothing worthwhile to offer Negroes. In the absence of a revolutionary labor movement or powerful socialist vanguard, the radicalism of the Northern ghetto masses flows through channels of race-consciousness, repudiating US society as the white man's world. The urge to tear loose and separate from the social fabric of US capitalism is not far removed from the urge, under different forms, to abolish that system in revolutionary struggle.

The 1948 convention resolution of the Socialist Workers Party noted the appearance and growth of an embryo Negro 'nation within the nation'. It is still an embryo today, but bigger and more mature. Racial-national sentiments have been fed and stimulated by the mockery of tokenism at home and the successes of colonial revolution abroad. The Negro is keenly aware that as a second-class citizen he is both a citizen and not a citizen. He sees plausibility in the concept of internal or domestic colonialism, which correctly stresses the many similarities between the capitalist treatment of the Negro people in this country and the imperialist treatment of colonial peoples.

But the American Negro people are in a situation with some unique aspects. They are an oppressed minority without a clearly defined geographical, language or cultural basis for differentiation from their oppressors. Negro nationalism is at this point a broad medium for 'self identification', a method of differentiating a racially oppressed minority from its oppressors and of uniting it ideologically and organizationally to free itself from oppression. Negro nationalism plays a function for the Negro people here in many ways like that which class consciousness plays for the working class.

James Baldwin's attempt at a definition of nationalism is a useful one to build on. This author said it means 'that a certain group of people, living in a certain place, has decided to take its political destinies into its own hands'. Applied to the United States, as it was meant to be, this means that large numbers of Negroes have decided, and more are in the process of deciding, that they cannot leave their future in the hands of the white oppressors but must unite with other Negroes and decide for themselves what they want in and from the United States.

This consciousness is the basic feature of Negro nationalism today. It is expressed in various ways – most commonly in the stimulation of racial pride, declarations of independence, the desire for Negro leadership and control of the civil rights struggle, mistrust of whites – and it is present to varying degrees in most Negro tendencies, both integrationist and separationist.

Viewed in this light, Negro nationalism, as it now exists, should not be equated with Negro separatism, the tendency that advocates creation of a separate Negro nation. The two are not the same thing. All separatists are nationalists but not all nationalists are separatists. Nationalism expresses the desire of Negroes to decide their destiny, including, among other things, their attitude toward the question of a separate nation. Nationalists want the right to decide their destiny, and to create an independent movement and other conditions that will make it possible for then to decide their destiny. But so far they have not made a choice in favor of a separate nation.

For many Negroes, nationalism is considered and may prove to be a way of uniting the mass of the Negro people and forcing the rulers of this country to grant them equality inside the United States. They leave open the question of separatism for a future stage, neither rejecting nor endorsing it now.

The first big task of the Negro struggle is the mobilization and unification of the Negro masses in an independent movement to fight for their equality – an indispensable condition for an eventual revolutionary alliance of the working class and the Negro people. Negro nationalism is progressive because it contributes to the creation of such an independent Negro movement. It will remain progressive so long as it fulfills that function, whether the struggle be fought along integrationist or separatist lines.

Revolutionary socialists welcome the growth of such Negro nationalism and give its participants wholehearted collaboration in the fight against our common enemies. For us, Negro nationalism and revolutionary socialism are not only compatible but complementary forces, that should be welded closer together in thought and action. The common sympathy and support for the colonial revolution and hostility to imperialist domination is an important bond between the two movements.

Revolutionary socialists must be ready to learn from militant Negro tendencies and to absorb everything progressive in their spirit and ideas; at the same time it must never be forgotten that we have things to contribute as well as learn. The nationalist tendencies still lack a comprehensive and realistic program to solve the problems of the Negro people, and many nationalists have confused conceptions. Revolutionary socialists must be simultaneously firm and patient in demonstrating that Marxism, properly understood and applied, is valid and relevant for the Negro struggle – firm because of our confidence in the correctness of the socialist program, patient because we know that the logic of the Negro struggle inevitably leads it into socialist channels.

Nationalism itself is an empty vessel which can be filled with vastly different contents. The nationalism of Chiang Kai-shek is the opposite of that of a Chinese Communist revolutionist or a Fidel Castro. Militant Negro nationalists can have wrong ideas and petty-bourgeois illusions. Negro Marxists have to imbue the nationalist sentiments and struggles of their people with a revolutionary, scientific, anti-capitalist content and direction.

They will be greatly aided in this work by the progress of the colonial revolution. The ideas of socialism are being adopted by more and more of the colonial peoples striving for national and social liberation in Africa, Asia and Latin America. This popularity of Marxist and anti-capitalist doctrines, movements and governments among the non-white races will exert an increasing influence upon the vanguard elements of the Negro struggle here which will lend strength to the positions of the SWP.

Negro socialists must bring forward, as an inspiration and guide for American Negroes, the example of Cuba where the overthrow of capitalism through the socialist revolution has uprooted discrimination and established genuine equality and fraternity of black and white citizens ninety miles from the Southern coastal states.

IV   Separatism and a Separate Nation

The theoretical position of revolutionary socialism on Negro separatism was first worked out at the Socialist Workers Party convention in 1939. Now, when Black Muslim influence has made separatism a live political issue among many people, it needs to be restated, adapted to current conditions and made unmistakably clear.

In 1939, we foresaw the possibility that the Negro people, as part of their struggle to end centuries of oppression and exploitation, might some day decide that they want a separate nation, controlled and administered by themselves. We said that if this happened, it would settle the long theoretical dispute about whether or not Negroes are a national minority as well as a racial minority, and that we, as supporters of the right of self-determination, would support the Negro demand for a separate nation and do everything in our power to help them obtain it.

In taking this position we did not become advocates of a separate nation, as the Communist Party used to be, nor do we advocate it now. What we advocate is the right of the Negro people to decide this question themselves. All we commit ourselves to do is support their fight to achieve whatever *they* decide they want, whether it be equality through integration or equality through segregation, or both.

It appeared to us in 1939 that the mass of the Negro people had not yet expressed themselves on this point, or had not expressed themselves definitely. Nine years later, in the resolution adopted at our 1948 convention, we noted that the growing 'feeling of racial and national solidarity among the Negro people thus far aims solely at acquiring enough force and momentum to break down the barriers that exclude Negroes from American society, showing few signs of aiming at national separatism'. It was clear that the vast majority of the Negroes were integrationist in the sense that they favored abolition of each and every discriminatory and segregationist device and institution in this country. But we did not take that to mean that the Negro masses had reached a conclusive position for or against separatism. We felt both in 1939 and 1948 that the question was still 'open' – that the Negro people might make a different decision about separatism in the future.

By 1963 the situation has changed considerably, but not decisively. On the one hand, the Muslims, the strongest advocates of separatism, have made serious organizational gains and growth of their general influence has been even greater. On the other hand, more Negroes than ever before are actively engaged in assaulting the Jim Crow barriers. If such activity makes them integrationists, it is necessary to point out that a profound division of feeling agitates many Negro integrationists. They have mixed feelings of attraction and repulsion in relation to the Muslims.

In general, Negro thought and discussion about separatism and related questions is much more intense than 15 or 24 years ago. But the mass of the Negro people have not yet taken any settled stand on these questions, and we must still await their definitive decision.

Until the Negro masses decide, the SWP neither advocates nor opposes a separate nation. We defend the right of the Negro people to make such a decision. This means we defend the rights of separatists to meet, speak, write and circulate their views and be free from government or vigilante assaults and frameups. It means refuting the slander that the Muslims and other separatists are 'counterparts' of the White Citizens Councils and the Ku Klux Klan. It means counteracting the widespread but mistaken notion that separation, freely chosen by Negroes, is 'equivalent' to segregation imposed by white supremacists.

Our attitude toward separatists, including the Muslims, is a friendly one. We recognize that the mere existence of the Muslims has had healthy effects, pushing rival Negro tendencies to the left and thereby imparting an impetus to even purely integrationist battles. We note with interest that, far from being a hardened sect, the Muslims have shown capacity during the last year to change in a direction that better serves the interests of all Negroes. However, they have still to develop a program of action for the struggles now taking place.

Where we differ with them, we differ in a friendly way, and we seek collaboration with them on mutually acceptable projects. We make it plain that we are not opposed to separation, if that should be the will of the Negro masses. Instead of attacking separatism as 'utopian', we seek to point out the revolutionary implication of the mass struggle for it and urge its advocates to develop radical methods, tactics and programs as the only way to achieve it.

If the Negro people should decide they want to separate, we would openly come out in favor of granting them separation. At the same time we would continue to fight before, during and after any separation which might take place, to abolish all racial inequalities and the cause of such inequalities in the United States. In that sense, we are and will remain integrationists, whatever else happens. We are convinced that the revolutionary struggle for socialism and the establishment of a socialist government will eliminate the basic causes of racial antagonism, and create the conditions for equality and integration of all in a new type of living together.

v   The Capitalist Orientation

The future of the Negro struggle depends first of all on what Negroes do about it. It depends on what their allies do – or do not do – about it. And it also depends on what their enemies do about it.

The ruling rich are the foremost enemy of the Negro people. The capitalist class introduced the system of racial oppression in this country, first in the form of slavery; they continued it under other forms after slavery was abolished; and they maintain it today. The rich initiated and have continued racial oppression because it was and is a convenience in the exploitation of labor, a source of super-profit, and a method for dividing the labor force and disrupting its efforts to unite against its exploiters.

That the responsibility for racial oppression rests on the capitalist class is not at all contradicted by the fact that other sections of the population, including the working class, are infected to one degree or another with race prejudices and poisons. If this were not so, Jim Crow could never have existed. But the capitalist system injected these prejudices into the white workers and reinforced them by granting the white workers concessions and privileges at the expense of the Negroes. The chief responsibility belongs on the capitalists, not on the workers who go along with racial discrimination and who are themselves victims as well as beneficiaries of racism. It is necessary to ceaselessly combat racist prejudices and practices of the workers too. Yet we must keep in mind that it is not the workers but the capitalists who have the political and economic power in this country and who control the propaganda-information-education-police apparatuses. It is an incontrovertible fact that the capitalists have used their power to perpetuate rather than abolish racial oppression.

Gradualists, even when forced to admit these historical facts, answer that things are different now or soon will be. They claim that steady and substantial progress has been made in recent years; that the gains already made indicate that this progress will continue indefinitely until it results in the total eradication of the color line; and that this process will be accelerated by the government because of its propaganda needs in the cold war. The evidence does not support these claims.

Progress is actually slow, small and uneven. Moreover, in some areas there is retrogression rather than progress. Average Negro family income in 1962 was 54 percent of average white family income whereas ten years before it had been 57 percent. While the incomes of both groups rose during this decade, that of the whites rose more, and so the income gap has been growing greater, not smaller. The rate of unemployment among Negroes has been around twice that among whites since the end of World War II, which is a greater disproportion than existed during the depression of the 1930s. During recessions the gap grows bigger, reaching a rate 2½ and 3 times that of whites.

Negro children still receive an average of 3½ years less schooling than white children. The proportion of dilapidated housing occupied by Negroes is more than five times as big as that occupied by whites. On an average, Negroes still die seven years sooner than whites; discrimination from the cradle to the grave costs the Negro this much of his life span. There is still not a state in the country where a Negro may not be subjected at any time to humiliation, abuse, or worse.

The real trend is exemplified by the school situation in the South since the Supreme Court decision in 1954. Its restricted application is deliberately obscured since schools are classified as 'desegregated' if one or a handful of Negroes is admitted. The fact is that after nine years less than 8 percent of Southern Negro children attend the same school as whites. At this rate it will take another century before the Southern school system is open to Negroes.

Where small gains have actually been made, their benefits have not been equally distributed. Some Negroes have been able to obtain jobs in areas previously closed to them (professional, clerical, white collar) and to attain the income and status of the Negro middle class (which is proportionately smaller, more insecure and less well paid than the white middle class). At the other pole, conditions of large numbers of Negroes have deteriorated badly because of unemployment and automation. Negro workers are hardest hit by the effects of automation. Overall, the gains of the more fortunate minority of Negroes are more than offset by the increasingly chronic poverty and deprivation imposed on the majority of the Negro people.

Studying the present trends in the light of the past, revolutionary socialists conclude that racial oppression can be abolished in the United States only if the present capitalist profit system is eliminated and replaced by a system based on production for use. Critics of this position reply that history has provided examples of capitalist countries relatively free of racism. Therefore, they conclude, racism is not an indispensable component of all capitalist societies and so American capitalism can be rid of this feature without necessarily abolishing capitalism itself.

Such thinking is misleading because it is based solely on generalities. The SWP conclusion is based on a *concrete* analysis of the nature and contradictions of the specific capitalist structure in the United States. This has had a history different from other capitalist countries, out of which specific economic and political relations developed, out of which specific interests, needs and institutions arose and still *flourish*. This particular capitalism, the American, may be forced to modify some of the features of its race system. But the ruling class will never willingly abolish it because it has too much of a stake in its maintenance, because it knows that attempts to uproot it in the South would inevitably give birth to a regional political revolution that would tend to become transformed into a social revolution.

American capitalism is not just tarred with racism. Its very roots are inextricably intertwined with racial oppression and it knows that pulling up the latter would endanger the former. To be sure, Jim Crow genuinely embarrasses the American ruling class in its foreign relations and diplomatic maneuvers. But it would rather go on being embarrassed than to risk the consequences of any serious effort to get rid of the cause of the embarrassment.

There is no evidence in anything happening now that the capitalists or their government intend to eradicate racial oppression in our time. Even their spokesmen who deplore the situation do not believe it will be eliminated in this century. Their real perspective is not to abolish racism, but modify it, reform it, remove some of its secondary features, repeal the laws that make segregation mandatory – and to do this little at a pace so slow it will extend over several generations in a way acceptable to the Southern white supremacists.

At the very most, the capitalist goal is to establish throughout the country relations between the races like those that now exist in the North – where formal segregation is not sanctioned or is even prohibited by law, but where the rankest segregation and inequality exist in practice. They hope that this gradual process of reform will enable them to claim abroad that American democracy is improving race relations at home; that it will avert explosions in the South that could spread to the North; and that it will contain Negro discontent and rebelliousness at home.

They are also prepared to grant additional posts and concessions to a thin layer of the Negro middle class in the hope of using them to restrain the Negro people as a whole. Where they cannot buy off opponents, they will use harassment, intimidation and persecution to suppress and break up Negro groups which refuse to submit to the capitalist power structure. The best American capitalism holds out for the mass of the Negro people is not the prospect of equality in this generation or the next, but the promise that *formal* inequality may be removed some time in the remote future.

VI   The Labor Movement and the Negro Struggle

Historically, it has been shown that the more radical and democratic the leadership of organized labor is, the more it seeks to wipe out racial barriers and integrate Negro workers in the unions, to solidarize itself with the Negro people as an oppressed minority and to promote a fighting labor-Negro alliance against their common enemies.

The opposite is also true. When conservative or liberal-sounding bureaucrats dominate the labor movement, their main concern is the preservation and expansion of their own privileges and powers. They do everything they can to avoid fighting the capitalists about anything; they subordinate and betray the interests of the union rank and file, the unorganized workers and all other oppressed groups; and they are indifferent or hostile to the Negro struggle for equality.

The role of the labor movement is one of the crucial differences between the 1930s and the 1960s, and it bears directly on the present moods and activities in the Negro community.

The youth of today find it hard to appreciate how profoundly the rise of the CIO affected race relations. It brought about the 20th century's first major progressive shakeup and reversal in these relations. Until then, discrimination and segregation had been growing worse and harsher in every area, including the old AFL unions, which had always turned their backs on the Negroes. Then, with the coming of the CIO, for the first time in many decades, the Negro worker saw a powerful hand held out to him and an invitation extended to enter the house of labor, or at least one floor. Despite previous painful and discouraging experiences with whites, the Negro workers rallied magnificently to the new industrial unions and played a key role in smashing the open shop in basic industry. No other group was more loyal or devoted.

This was not because the CIO, even in its best days, fulfilled all its obligations to Negroes. But, unlike every other major force, it welcomed the Negro. This held out the promise that the growing unfavorable trend of race relations in the country could be reversed. Although the Negroes never won complete equality in the unions, through their own efforts and with the aid of the CIO they did gain a strong foothold in the unions and industry, from which they could exert leverage for further gains. Before the stagnation of the labor movement set in during the late 1940s the Negroes had reached their present imposing numbers inside organized labor (1½ million). Equally important, the CIO, by its very existence, served as a shield behind which the Negro community as a whole was able to consolidate its forces, develop new and more independent demands, and lay the ground for the struggles of today and tomorrow.

Much has changed in the last quarter century. With the aid of the government and the employers, the labor bureaucrats have house-broken most of the unions and decimated or destroyed radical influence in them. Militant oppositional groups, which were usually the Negro's closest ally inside the unions, are now absent or impotent. The labor movement has been on the defensive for years. The capitalist-minded bureaucrats are guided by class collaboration, not class struggle. In practice, this means not fighting the employers but seeking deals with them – sometimes to preserve the conditions of the older, more privileged, higher seniority workers and always at the expense of the weaker and most exploited workers, of whom the Negroes and other minorities form a large part.

The bureaucrats pledged to eliminate racism when the AFL and CIO merged in 1955. But, as with every other progressive task, they have given only lip service to this pledge. They even blame the rank and file union members, rather than themselves, for its non-fulfillment. They simply cannot understand why the Negroes are demanding more from the labor movement than they did when they first joined it in the 1930s. Some labor bureaucrats harbor racial prejudices, and all of them, like their liberal friends, are guilty of paternalism. When the Meanys and Reuthers instruct the Negroes to take it easy and wait, and this doesn't work, they react to the demand for equality with outright hostility or tokenism. Their only real interest in Negroes is collecting their dues and keeping them tied to the Democratic Party.

Inside the unions some Negro members have become discouraged or demoralized and abandoned the fight against the bureaucracy, as some white militants have done. Negroes outside the unions confuse the labor bureaucracy with the labor movement as such. They fail to recognize that millions of white workers have reason to hate the bureaucrats too and will seize the first chance they get to throw the bureaucrats off the backs of all the workers, white and black.

Some Negro nationalists are disposed to declare the unions 'dead' and write them off. They disregard the fact that on the surface the labor movement appeared to be even deader in the late 1920s and early 1930s, not long before the upsurge of industrial unionism. Also evident is a tendency to counterpose independent Negro organization to a labor-Negro alliance, as though these two things were in contradiction, and even to reject the desirability and possibility of a militant labor-Negro alliance. The mobilization and merger of the forces needed to eliminate racism are considerably complicated by these feelings and beliefs, for which the labor bureaucracy must be held primarily responsible.

However, the consequences of the default of the union leadership have not all been negative. Awareness that the labor bureaucracy cannot be counted on to defend the Negro workers or the Negro people has strengthened the desire of Negro workers for their own means of defense and advancement inside the labor movement. This is reflected in the formation of the Negro American Labor Council and in the hundreds of formal or informal Negro caucuses or clubs inside local unions. Outside the labor movement it has been a big factor in stimulating nationalist sentiment and activity, and generally strengthening the feelings of self-reliance and the trend toward independent action and struggle.

Unlike capital, labor has been and is capable of playing differing roles in relation to the Negro struggle, depending on which forces are at the head of the unions. Revolutionary-socialists recognize that the labor movement in the grip of its conservative and capitalist-minded bureaucracy is increasingly remote from the rank and file and is shamefully defaulting on its responsibilities to the Negro people.

But the unions don't belong to the bureaucrats, who have usurped the power they hold and betray the ranks they are supposed to represent. As happened after the 1920s, we anticipate that the union movement will be transformed and radicalized again, and at a higher level than in the 1930s, by the effects on the working class of the crises and contradictions of capitalism and the failure of non-radical methods to solve the problems of automation, unemployment, speedup, inflation, insecurity and the war danger.

The coming radicalization of the labor movement will be accompanied by and accomplished through the creation of a left wing in the unions. This cannot be some vaguely 'progressive' formation interested mainly in winning union offices, but a group that will be distinguished by class struggle policies, an independent labor party orientation, and active support for the Negro struggle inside and outside the unions. Militant Negroes will contribute to this big change both by forming their own groups in the unions and helping to build and be part of a left wing, or closely connected with it. To abstain from either of these tasks would be to insure the continued dominance of the labor bureaucracy, at the expense of the living conditions and rights of 1½ million Negro union members, 6½ million other Negro workers who want to be union members, and the Negro people as a whole.

VII Independent Political Action

The Negro struggle is above all a political struggle – that is, its solution requires political action. The coming labor-Negro alliance will operate in many areas and through many forms, but above all it will be a political alliance. And yet it is precisely in the field of politics that up to now practically all tendencies in the Negro movement are weakest and *least independent*, both in theory and practice.

Some tendencies ignore politics, but politics do not ignore them. The effect of political abstention is to leave the monopoly of political power in the hands of capitalist parties and demagogic politicians who use that power against the Negro people. Others recognize the importance of politics and participate in politics – but only in the two major parties that are opposed to Negro equality. Among politically active Negroes are some whose main interest is in electing Negroes to office. But these are repeatedly frustrated because the Negro Democrats or Republicans whom they help elect usually turn out to be captives and apologists for the corrupt capitalist political machines rather than consistent spokesmen for the Negro people.

Most current tendencies reflect, to one degree or another, the desire of the Negro masses to determine their own destiny – to have their own organizations, their own leaders, their own strategy, tactics and programs. But few of these tendencies have expressed a similarly independent spirit in the vital field of politics by breaking with the parties of their oppressors and organizing to challenge their political monopoly. Yet such a break and such a challenge are implicit in everything that has happened up to now. It is contradictory and self-defeating to talk about *Freedom Now* while accepting the right of the white supremacists and gradualists to jointly wield the political power of this country.

The idea of a Negro party, a civil rights party or an equal rights party, is not a new one. Representative Adam Clayton Powell has talked about it on and off during recent years. *Liberator*, the Liberation Committee for Africa magazine, wrote about the need for an 'Afro-American political party' during the 1962 election campaign. More recently Elijah Muhammad, leader of the Muslims, has advocated that Negroes run and elect their own candidates to public office because 'there will be no real freedom for the so-called Negro in America until he elects his own political leaders and his own candidates'. William Worthy has spoken along similar lines.

The basis for such a party already exists. Millions of Negroes are concentrated in the big cities of the country, North and South. United in a party of their own, they are so situated geographically that they could sweep the elections in dozens of congressional districts. They could send a bigger bloc of Negroes to

Washington than they did in Reconstruction days and elect a sizable body of state and city legislators who would for the first time be beholden to no one but the Negro community. Both nationally and locally they could hold the legislative balance of power and be in a position to compel bigger concessions from the dominant parties. More fundamentally, with a party of their own Negroes could take a lead in undermining and changing the whole power structure.

The immense implications of such an independent Negro course in politics illustrate graphically the truth of the revolutionary-socialist analysis that the independent Negro struggle tends to stimulate, spur and shake up the major forces in the country. The creation of a Negro party running its own candidates would rock the whole political structure to its foundations. It would throw the Democratic Party into a crisis. Without the majority of Negro votes which it now gets, it could never again hope to hold national power. The only place it could go would be down. Organized labor would be faced with an excruciating dilemma too. Its coalition with the Democrats is justified on the ground that the Democrats can 'win'. But when it becomes plain that they cannot win, the unions would be forced to reconsider their whole political policy. Advocates of a labor break with the old parties would get a bigger and better hearing from the ranks. Thus the creation of a Negro party would benefit not only the Negro but his present and potential allies.

The Socialist Workers Party contends that racism, like unemployment, exploitation and war, can be abolished in this country only by independent political action aimed at taking control of the government out of the hands of the capitalists and their parties. As a step in this direction, we have long advocated that the unions break from the Democratic Party and form an independent labor party that would seek to politically unite workers, farmers and Negroes and elect their representatives to office. In addition, and for the same reason, we have also endorsed and supported representatives of the Negro community whenever they have run for office independently of and in opposition to the old parties, even when they were not socialists.

Extending this policy in the light of current developments, we publicly express our readiness to support and collaborate with any Negro party or *Freedom Now Party* that runs candidates of its own in opposition to the capitalist parties and seeks to elect representatives whose primary allegiance will be to the Negro community. Our support of such a party in no way conflicts with our own independent socialist political campaigning or with our continued advocacy of a labor party. On the contrary, we believe that a Negro party, a socialist party, and a labor party would find much in common from the very beginning, would work together for common ends, and would tend in the course of common activity to establish close organizational ties or even merge into a single or federated party. Revolutionary socialists don't care whether capitalism and racism are abolished by a single party or by a combination of parties, just so long as they are abolished.

VIII   Strategy of the Negro Struggle

In previous convention resolutions, the SWP predicted that the Negro movement would precede and outpace the labor and anti-capitalist movements. This prediction was based on the fact that while the Negro community is predominantly proletarian, the Negro people are more than just another more heavily exploited section of the working class, and the Negro movement is more than just a part of the general working-class movement.

As an oppressed minority, the history of the Negroes is different, their position in society is special, their consciousness is influenced by racial, national and international as well as class factors, and they have developed their own standards, their own methods of action and their own forms of struggle. Although they are a minority numerically, they are a compact minority, knitted together by capitalist segregation in the ghetto and by a common sense of resentment against injustice, and they often play a role disproportionate to their numbers, a vanguard role. This prediction has been strikingly confirmed by recent events, which sees the Negroes in motion and out front while the labor movement is standing still and lagging behind.

Previous SWP resolutions have also analyzed the special factors tending to radicalize the Negro movement. The Negro struggle is the struggle of an oppressed minority for democratic rights, for equality. But because the American capitalist class will not grant equality, it tends to merge with the wider struggle for the abolition of capitalism, for socialism. Under the banner of democratic rights, the Negroes learn to reject the myths about American democratic capitalism, and through their own experiences in fighting for democracy they reach deeply radical conclusions, frequently ahead of other sections of the potentially anti-capitalist forces. This analysis has also been verified and validated by recent developments which find the Negro movement becoming radicalized, rejecting gradualism and passing beyond liberalism, which is still the dominant ideology of the labor movement.

These disparities between the Negroes' growing activity and radicalization and labor's relative inactivity and conservatism have at this stage raised a number of complicated problems. In addition, they have produced some questioning and even rejection in certain nationalist circles about a third aspect of the SWP's traditional analysis of the Negro struggle, expressed in the following perspective: while the labor and Negro movements march along their own paths, they do march to a common destination, and the freedom of the Negroes from oppression and of the workers from exploitation can be achieved only through the victory of their common struggle against capitalism.

Our differences with such nationalists do not concern the facts. We both agree that a gap has appeared between the Negro movement and the labor movement and that present relations between them are strained or cool. We disagree over the meaning of these facts, their significance for the future, what to do about them. Since the relations between these two movements are the key to the future of this country, and through it of the world, they deserve the most sober appraisal and searching study.

The fact that the tempos of development of the two movements are uneven is neither new nor really surprising. Since their origins and histories are different, they have rarely marched in step. At the present time it is not the Negro movement that is laggard or out of step but organized labor. The complications occur, not because Negro radicalization is premature or unwarranted, but because labor radicalization has been retarded and is long overdue.

Faced with the disparity of development between the two movements and the frictions generated by it, the liberals do not prod the labor leaders to hurry up, go ahead, initiate a new course. They tell the Negroes to slow down and wait. The union leaders and Negro gradualists offer the same advice. And even some radicals and ex-radicals do the same in effect when they exaggerate the dangers of Negroes 'going it alone'.

But the Negro movement will not wait, should not wait, and should push ahead with an expansion of its independent action. To do anything else would set back the Negro cause for many years. We say this without the slightest modification of our fundamental view that the Negroes cannot win their goal of equality in this country without an alliance with the working class.

Although Negro independence and radicalization may not produce large-scale common action with organized labor under present circumstances, it will hasten common action eventually. In previous SWP resolutions, we explained that because the Negroes are doubly exploited, their struggles have exceptional effects on the social and political life of this country. Their fight for simple democratic rights tends to upset the status quo. Their special demands introduce unsettling elements into the consciousness of the working class as a whole, disturbing the relations between the classes and inside the classes. Their independent action serves to spur, stimulate, awaken, excite, inspire, divide, unite, and set into motion other, bigger forces.

Correctly appraised, the independent course of the Negro movement, and even its essentially nationalist aspects, does not signify a permanent and principled repudiation of a labor-Negro alliance. What militant Negroes object to is any alliance based on subordination or gradualism in which the Negroes are merely a junior partner supplying manpower but having little to say about the policies and tempo pursued by the team. What they want is an alliance that will include *Freedom Now* as one of its main demands and in which the Negroes will have an equal voice in setting policy.

There is no inconsistency, in logic or practice, between organizing or reorganizing the Negro movement along independent lines and achieving alliances with other sections of the population. Many Negroes view doing the first job as an indispensable condition for successfully doing the second. They believe – correctly, in our opinion – that they must first unite, shape and orient their own movement. Only then will they be able to bring about an alliance of equals, where they can be reasonably sure that their demands and needs cannot be neglected or betrayed by their allies. This does not mean that they cannot begin forging links with the most progressive elements in the labor movement even now. But they feel that if any temporary conflict arises between these two tasks priority should be given to the imperative need of creating an independent Negro movement.

The strategy of the Negro struggle in the coming period can be expected, if our analysis of the past and the present is correct, to follow the course of uniting, dividing and uniting.

Numerically, Negroes are today about one-ninth of the population. (One-fifth at the time of the American Revolution, one-seventh at the time of the Civil War). For some, this is a reason or pretext for the feeling that there is nothing much Negroes can do until the white majority changes its racial attitudes; Negroes can only follow, not lead. This is just another way of saying that the Negroes must – wait.

Revolutionary socialists emphatically reject this approach. Our analysis has demonstrated that the Negro has a vanguard role to play, that his independent struggle will set other currents into motion, and that the worst thing he can do is wait. This is one of the telling differences between a revolutionary approach and a liberal approach, however the latter may be dressed up. Being a minority is not a reason for waiting, but a reason for developing a course of action and program that takes this fact into account and finds ways of overcoming it.

Throughout American history militant Negroes have always understood that their progress depends on their own readiness and ability to struggle. The tactics of today's struggle are necessarily different in this country than in countries like South Africa or Angola or Kenya, where black people are the great majority, and where simple majority rule can mean an end to racial oppression. But here, as in Africa, the liberation of the Negro people requires that the Negroes organize themselves independently, and control their own struggle, and not permit it to be subordinated to any other consideration or interest.

This means that the Negroes must achieve the maximum unity of their own forces – organizational unity, in a strong and disciplined nationwide movement or congress of organizations, and ideological unity, based on defeating, exposing and isolating gradualism and other tendencies emanating from their white oppressors. This phase of the process is now beginning.

Having united their own forces, the independent Negro movement will then probably undertake the tasks of division and alliance. It will seek ways to split the white majority so that the Negro disadvantage of being a numerical minority can be compensated for by division and conflict on the other side.

That has happened at earlier crucial points in American history. When the whites became divided between revolutionists and Tories in the American Revolution, the Negroes allied themselves with the former, and were able to gain emancipation from slavery in many Northern states. In the first half of the 19th century the independent struggles of the Negroes – slave insurrections, mass escapes via the Underground Railway, sabotage, etc. – helped to widen the breach between the North and South and prepare the way for the Civil War. In the Civil War itself the Negroes threw their weight on the Northern side, pressured the North into accepting an emancipation policy, and provided the military balance of power. In the 1930s, when a division among the whites occurred along classic class lines, the Negroes drove in the wedge by giving overwhelming support to the CIO, helping to batter down the open shop and effect their own entry into the labor movement.

In each of these cases, the process of social division was accompanied by or led to a process of social and political alliance in action. That is how we see the future too. United, the Negro people through their independent struggle will help to divide the white population – between those who most benefit from racism and those whose interests are really damaged by racism. In the process of this struggle, the Negroes will both seek and find alliances. The major one will be with an insurgent working class, and especially with its most anti-capitalist forces.

The general alliance between the labor movement and the Negro fighters for liberation can be prepared for and preceded by the cementing of firm working unity between the vanguard of the Negro struggle and the socialist vanguard of the working class represented by the Socialist Workers Party. This is the primary task of the SWP in the present period of the *Freedom Now* movement.

IX The Role and Tasks of the Socialist Workers Party

The role of the Socialist Workers Party is to assemble and programmatically equip the forces that will lead the coming American revolution to abolish capitalism and racism. This function is indispensable because American capitalism is so powerful and racism is so deeply rooted in it. If the SWP did not exist it would be necessary to form another organization to carry out this function, which no other existing political party, big or small, now aspires to fulfill.

The SWP operates in an arena wider than the Negro struggle, narrowly considered. For militant Negroes concerned first and foremost with the Negro struggle, this may at first appear as a disadvantage or liability. It is neither.

The SWP agrees that the first task of Negroes is to organize themselves independently. But the Negro movement does not and cannot exist in isolation from other forces and conflicts at home and abroad. The broader perspective and concern of the SWP with the totality of social struggle is an invaluable asset. Its revolutionary activity in the labor and other mass movements provides a means of enlisting allies and neutralizing potential enemies of the Negro movement in both its present formative and its future stages, and of connecting the class struggle with the Negro struggle in such a way as to strengthen both.

The SWP seeks to equip both revolutionary whites and Negroes with the best set of scientific tools yet devised to change society – Marxism. Drawn from and fusing the lessons of American and world experiences, Marxism is constantly enriched, refined and rendered more effective by the experience of new struggles. It illuminates the causes of racism and points to the method for eradicating them. The SWP has long sought to 'Americanize' Marxism (that is, to apply it to American conditions and use American conditions to modernize and expand Marxism itself). In order to accomplish this, it must now also work to 'Afro-Americanize' Marxism (that is, apply it to the specific conditions of the Negro people and use the experience of their struggle to further concretize and enrich Marxism).

The SWP believes and acts on the belief that the working class cannot achieve its aims without the Negro people achieving theirs. The American revolution for a socialist democracy cannot succeed unless it is based on an equal and mutually acceptable partnership between the working class and the Negro people. It is this belief, deeply ingrained and expressed in the SWP's program and practice, rather than any written or verbal assurances or pledges, which affords an objective basis for regarding the SWP as different from other organizations most of whose members are white.

Its unblemished record in the class struggle and the Negro struggle during hot wars and cold, its uncompromising attitude toward capitalism and all its agencies and ideas, have earned the SWP the right not to be considered as just another party, or even just another radical party. Unlike the Communist Party, the SWP has never called on Negroes to subordinate, suspend or give up their struggle for any other interest or cause, national or international. Unlike the Socialist Party, the SWP has never urged Negroes to support any of the political parties of their oppressors, and its opposition to gradualism in the Negro struggle is matched by its opposition to that same policy in all other fields. Unlike the Socialist Labor Party, the SWP does not belittle, stand aside from and turn its back on the immediate and partial struggles of the Negroes, but views them as a necessary and hopeful link to future, more fundamental struggles and participates in them actively and wholeheartedly. White or black, those who understand the need for a revolutionary-socialist party will find the genuine article in the SWP.

The present tasks of the SWP in connection with the Negro struggle for liberation are:

1. To better educate the entire membership; give ourselves a deeper and more sensitive understanding of the feelings, aspirations and needs of the Negro people; become more closely acquainted with their history, their current tendencies and organizations, the obstacles they face; above all, absorb, steep ourselves in the revolutionary character of their struggle, so that it becomes and remains a central feature of our work at all times. In this way we can inoculate ourselves against paternalism and other conscious or unconscious manifestations of the racial pressures that capitalist society brings to bear on everyone, even within the revolutionary party dedicated to ending capitalism.

2. To provide, through the party leadership, permanent help, guidance, coordination, encouragement and expansion of our work in the Negro struggle.

3. To devote more attention, energies and forces to the Negro struggle.
   a. While our white members cannot aspire to leadership of Negro organizations, they can play important auxiliary roles there when permitted to join and can help our Negro members when not permitted to join. Their direct participation in the struggle is doubly important in branches where we have few or no Negro members, since this is one way of contacting and recruiting Negro members. White members have the duty to fight against racism wherever they are and can greatly promote the party's work by fulfilling this duty. White members in the unions have the vital tasks of combating inequality on the job and at the hiring gate, supporting battles for Negro representation at all levels of union leadership, helping

to build a left wing unequivocally committed to aiding the Negro struggle, working for labor collaboration with existing Negro movements and wherever possible persuading the unions to initiate such collaboration.
    b. Just as most workers in the party are expected to work in their unions and most students to work in campus organizations, so most of our Negro members will belong to Negro organizations, which they seek to build along militant lines. They work to unite the Negro community around a *Freedom Now* program. They join and help to promote independent Negro electoral activities. If members of unions, they help to form Negro groups and a broad left wing in the unions, and whether union members or not they propose collaboration between the labor and Negro movements whenever feasible. Negro Marxists have irreplaceable functions to perform in the struggle of their people. They serve as a two-way channel of communication between the movements of the Negro masses and the conscious struggle for a Socialist America: (1) In the Negro community they popularize the ideas and proposals of revolutionary socialism. With the help of Marxist methods, they exercise their rights, as Negroes, to help form the ideology of their race, including its attitudes toward integration and separation. (2) In the SWP they strive to equip themselves for the role of revolutionary leadership in the mass movements and remain alert to see that the party as a whole understands and pays the necessary attention to the problems of the Negro struggle.
4. To expand and strengthen the party's Negro cadre and forces in the Negro organizations and the civil rights movements, by:
    a. Recruiting revolutionary Negroes and helping to train them for leadership in the party and mass movements.
    b. Bringing more of our present Negro membership into the party leadership at all levels.
    c. Widening our contacts among individual Negro radicals and collaborating with them closely and fraternally if they decide to form radical or socialist groups of their own.
    d. Recruiting revolutionary whites, especially youth, like the Freedom Riders who are already engaged in courageous struggles for civil rights.
5. To develop, in collaboration with other Negro militants, a series of demands and proposals which will connect the needs of the struggle at its present stage with its ultimate aims. The proposals for a thirty-hour week

at forty-hours pay and a *Freedom Now* party should figure prominently in such a program today.
6. To expand and improve the party press's treatment of the Negro struggle and expand the circulation of our literature among Negro militants.

The seriousness with which we apply ourselves to these tasks will be a test of our capacity as a revolutionary party.

6 Revolutionary Integrationism[16]
(*Excerpts, 1963*)

Richard Kirk (Richard S. Fraser)

Preface

The Black Revolt in the South is objectively on the threshold of still another new stage in its development: a stage of political organization for revolution – organization for a show-down struggle against the police-state and for a new democratic political system.

Southern Negro militants, young and old, have sustained a courageous struggle for the past ten years. After the high points of Montgomery, where working class leaders pushed the ministers into the foreground, and Little Rock, officially led by the NAACP while an armed community waited, the movement tended to recede. Restless over the inaction of the clergy and NAACP, the youth then entered the scene, bringing to life struggles all over the South. Sometimes with small numbers, but with indomitable spirit, they catapulted the morale of the movement and shamed their elders into motion.

The movement as a whole operated generally within the confines of reformism, i.e. the attempt to change the racial climate of the South by reform. While the youth, in SNCC, never considered themselves bound to reformism in principle and are politically unprejudiced and open-minded, they have not challenged the theory of reformism.

The Robert Williams movement in Monroe did. It synthesized the activism of the youth, the proletarian ranks and behind-the-scenes proletarian leadership of Montgomery, and the mass aggressiveness later displayed so dramatically in Birmingham. Williams was the first to publically project a radical ideology, a bold and revolutionary strategy, and a proud internationalism.

The three streams of the civil rights movement – youth, the church, and the working masses – converged in Birmingham, with the ministers fronting. Birmingham was to be the culminating effort, the key battle, of the ten-year struggle,

---

16   Kirk 1963.

designed to break the back of segregation in the South. The Negroes fought heroically. They shook the country and the world. They emerged with honor and with new strength – but with no concessions obtained. All agreements made by the Birmingham petty-bourgeoisie were nullified by the overwhelming pressure of the southern police-state.

For the participants, this only confirms what they already know or feel – *that there is no possibility of winning Freedom Now through pressure-attempts to reform the totalitarian police-state.*

The preachers placed ultimate faith in the federal government, which has failed in all of its promises, and here failed again. Kennedy's man in Birmingham failed miserably in his 'arbitration' operation and the Brothers Kennedy stood glaringly exposed as fakers. The Reverends, in turn, lost much prestige in the process. And who gained stature? Robert Williams. A figure like Leroi Jones, a *northern* intellectual in Birmingham as a reporter, assured his audiences of street demonstrators that their experience proved the validity of the concepts of Robert Williams.

Birmingham represented the failure and exposure of reformism in the South; but it also and simultaneously represented a great leap forward in organization, experience and awareness. The mood, the pace, the tremendous dynamic of the demonstrations and reminiscent of great strikes and insurrections; observers and participants reporting back are tremendously stirred by the complex phenomenon they witnessed: an elated but disappointed community soberly evaluating its overwhelming experience.

The militant Negroes of the south are now groping for the handle of a new weapon. They know or sense what it is, but they hesitate to articulate it. The essence of it is:

1. *There must be a new leadership, radical and bold.*
2. *It must be prepared to lead a revolution, because the whole police-state system must be destroyed.*
3. *A political struggle, requiring a new political party, is the only vehicle.*

Being a one-to-four minority in the South, however, dims the prospect of Negroes overthrowing the police-state alone. Consequently, they will realize that they must so fashion their strategy as to break through the racist wall separating them from the white workers. They must persuade the southern white workers and poor farmers to see the identity of political interest between white workers and Negroes and the common class interest which crosses the color-line. Together, they will forge a merged struggle for democratic rights – for race equality, civil liberties and the rights of labor. As it develops its revolutionary perspective, the southern civil rights movement will orient toward an alliance with a revived northern labor movement. Only northern labor has the power to paralyze the ability of the government to intervene against the southern revolution.

And since the southern Negro movement cannot wait until northern labor sheds its passivity and bureaucratic leadership, it must proceed to shake up and spur northern labor into life. Southern Negroes will thus profoundly stimulate the northern giant into recovering its capacity for struggle.

⁂

Geographically separated, facing two complementary but different forms of capitalist rule, and responding with diverse tactics and levels of consciousness, the southern movement and the movement 'Up South' and West are still bound together by mutual experience, solidarity, and exploding racial consciousness born of frustration too long endured.

Militant currents emerging from the seething ghettos of the North and West recognizing the blind alley of reformism, ignored by the labor bureaucracy, and suspicious or uncertain of the ability of socialist organizations to understand and/or adapt themselves to the needs of the Negro struggle, have long been grappling with the problem of the *nationwide crisis of leadership in the movement.*

As a consequence of this crisis, they are experimenting with local and regional levers of upsetting the status quo, and are prepared for more massive and radical assaults upon white supremacy as conditions ripen.

The vacuum produced by the long hiatus of the reformist leaders found poignant expression in the rise of the Black Muslims. As a fiery propaganda sect, they spurred the reformist leaders by unmasking their accommodation to white domination and by agitating the entire country with their pithy truths about race relations in the US.

The doctrine of separatism, however, orients this movement away from the physical struggle against racial discrimination into contemptuous abstentionism. They substitute for combat a classical Utopian attempt to build up an independent Negro economy in the US.

The Muslim movement is a contradiction: articulate and defiant – superstitious and backward. It is a transitional phenomenon which will cease to exert its appeal when a more rational and internally consistent movement develops in the Negro community to fulfill the demand for truth, audacity, a goal, and uncorrupted leadership.

From where is such a leadership to come? The Negro movement in the North is extremely complex and its dynamics invariably produce a multitude of leadership sources. A number of militant, race conscious, independent and determined organizations have already appeared in northern cities, headed by new, younger leaders who are developing swiftly and might well become part of the future national leadership.

The impact of the Southern struggle is stirring vast new layers, the broad church section especially.

Many older militants and independent radicals are invigorated by events and ready to return to action.

A new powerful force among the artists and intellectuals is heralded by the appearance of individuals like Baldwin, Worthy, Hansberry, etc.

The Negroes of the North have been ready for a basic social change for decades, and we should expect to find streams of leadership flowing from every walk of life, every institution, every city, every class! Above all, as the revolutionary perspective is increasingly projected, the relatively privileged Negro trade unionists will come boldly forward again.

⁂

The accelerating Black Revolt represents the most significant revolutionary development of our time, the most fertile field for the growth and flowering of socialist ideas, the most dynamic spur to the working class as a whole and the finest source of new radical leadership.

The SWP must be oriented to take advantage of the opportunities this situation offers. Given solid ideological footing and a deliberate sensitivity and flexibility, the party can enhance its image and make giant strides in and with the Negro movement ...

Part I: the Coming Southern Revolution

... A dialectical interdependence links the Southern Labor Party, southern unionism, and the left wing in northern unions.

In a police-state, simple mass action (picket line, mass meeting, boycott, etc.) is not enough to win any democratic rights, including union recognition. Local tactics must be geared to the real nature of the oppressor, to inter-racial working class solidarity, and to active assistance by the northern Negro and labor movements. This is the historical difference between union organizing in the 30s and union organizing in the 60s; the former demanded class struggle in a bourgeois democratic environment; today what is needed is political struggle against the iron heel of a brutal totalitarian state apparatus, the southern wing of US capitalism.

The very backwardness of the Dixie sector grips the more advanced northern labor movement by the throat, choking and stifling it; to survive, the north must break this stranglehold. Defense of the southern movement is the opening wedge in this struggle for self-preservation.

Part II: the North: the Prolonged Crisis of Leadership and the Quest for Program

The Reformist Leadership. Whereas the southern movement is characterized by mass activism and the beginnings of ideological probing, the northern sector is only just becoming, by reflex, a mass movement, despite its rare advanced level of political consciousness. The South is proceeding swiftly and classically from action to thought; the more complex North has been studying programs and parties for 30 years and its passivity syndrome was the outcome of this frustrating search.

Uncertainty, accommodation, cynicism, or blind rage are not programs for action; they cannot mobilize. Only a call and a tactic – strike! boycott! sit-in! – can do that. The main 'call' up north by Negro leaders before the Till Case and Montgomery was the NAACP's deadening 'take it to court' refrain.

Reformism's decrepitude, only just unveiled down south, has been an acknowledged fact in the North so long that it's generally accepted as a joke, like bad bus service.

Working class Negroes in the North, living amidst poverty and injustice, are generally conscious of the need for fundamental social change and have been for decades. Their economic position and their rejection by white society have rendered them immune to the American myth of a progressive, stable and benevolent capitalism supplying plenty for all. In the truth of their lives they find the truth about American society.

This radical awareness, while undirected toward a specific means of social change, has expressed itself in an overwhelming response to every opportunity to demonstrate in breadth against the status quo: Through the old Communist Party, the CIO, the March on Washington Movement, the wartime struggles, the SWP, the racial wars in Harlem and Detroit, the Progressive Party, the Harlem reception of Castro, the pro-Lumumba demonstration, etc.

Consciousness has kept pace with reality. But in the absence of a leadership adequate to the task, decades of disappointment and disgust resulted. Where matured objective conditions and mass consciousness exist without a leadership prepared to advance the struggle to higher levels, all elements of a crisis of leadership are present. The entire movement, denied the logic of its own dynamic, tends to degenerate.

What is the source of this protracted crisis?

The struggle against racial discrimination has centered around the demand for integration. The official leaders of the integration movement have come from the middle class professionals. The inability of this leadership to express the needs of the masses and to develop an effective strategy is lodged in the contradictory position of the middle class in general, compounded by the peculiarities imposed by the race system.

The ghetto petty-bourgeoisie – the self-employed and the professionals – feed on the masses and often despise and fear them: at the same time, they are brutally rejected by white society and identified with their 'inferiors'. On the one hand, they enjoy a racial monopoly of certain businesses and occupations, thereby profiting from segregation: on the other hand, the flagrant gap between their living standard and their social status outside the ghetto is a source of daily humiliation and resentment against racism. A conflict therefore exists between their class and racial interests. By turns cynical, conciliatory or enraged, they still exert a basically conservative pressure upon the leaders of the integration movement, intensifying their hostility toward fundamental change and their habit of compromise and tokenism.

A less conservative but still restrictive pressure on the leadership stems from a section of the new middle class of professionals and semi-professionals who are the main beneficiaries of integration struggles. With good jobs in the white world (government, education, public institutions, and the white-collar sector of industry), this group sees individual assimilation as the goal. Theirs is 'the desire to achieve acceptance in American life by conforming to the ideals, values, and patterns of behavior of white Americans' (E. Franklin Frazier). But the desire can rarely be realized. Revolving in a restricted circle of fellow Negro professionals and white liberals, they, too, are ambivalent. In limbo between two worlds, and unsure of their identity, they have no mass influence.

The leadership of the integration movement comes mainly from these two sectors and reflects their political schizophrenia. Pushed hard today by the ranks and by national pressures into tough talk and sometimes frenetic activism, they still more or less zealously guard their pro-capitalist respectability and conformism. The failure of the middle class leadership to inspire and advance the movement is caused by reformism. The old-style leaders can provide no solution to the elementary demands of the southern struggle and they lock up the northern movement in capitalist politics.

There is no class-race conflict in the Negro worker. The struggles for civil rights and working class solidarity are complementary and equal parts of the drive of the entire working class for emancipation.

Worker-leaders, however, have been rendered cautious by events. Unions, paralyzed by bureaucracy and government, remain essentially unmoved by civil rights struggles, whether inside or outside the unions. Negro working class loaders within the unions become conservatized and intimidated by the class collaborationist passivity of the unions and by the shakiness of their own privileged jobs and higher incomes (relative to the community norm). At the present moment they provide no alternative leadership to that of the middle class.

From the early 30s to 1950, the cream of Negro militants, numbering many thousands, dedicated themselves to leading the Negro movement toward socialism, first through the Communist Party and after 1941, through the SWP. But neither party was able to demonstrate convincingly its capacity to apply Marxism to the Negro struggle. This failure of theory and practice forced Negroes to seek solutions elsewhere or caged them in doctrinaire formulas. No substantial Marxist leadership was built, and the desire of socialist Negroes to lead the Negro movement in a militant anti-capitalist direction was blunted.

∴

The contradictory and demoralizing co-existence of a reformist leadership with militant ranks has caused a certain revulsion-reflex against the principle of integration. Negroes are increasingly attracted to newly revived doctrines of separatism. But here, too, they are finding a leadership basically reformist and arbitrary, oriented elsewhere than the field of struggle.

Is there no alternative to reformist-conformist integration versus a black homeland? This 30-year old dilemma can only be answered by Marxist analysis. What do logic, history and sociology provide in the analysis of the Integration-Nationalism-Separatism complex?

Nationalism

A Nation, according to orthodox definition, is a people united by an exclusive geography and a common heritage, language, history and mode of production, all comprising a distinctive culture.

Nationalism had long been attained by the powerful nations of western Europe when the developing Russian revolution revealed a new aspect of the National Question over a hundred small oppressed nations and pre-national tribal peoples discovered or re-discovered national aspirations long throttled by Great Russian chauvinism and newly liberated by the economic crisis and the Bolshevik slogan of self-determination.

These deep-seated national aspirations became a huge revolutionary centrifugal force, aiding in the destruction of the Czarist empire and the capitalist regime which followed making it possible for the Russian proletariat to win and hold the power.

Long before the Revolution itself, Lenin oriented the Bolsheviks toward these backward, even primitive, agrarian peoples with an analysis of the whole problem of the National Question and the role of Self-Determination. This analysis became a new body of Marxist theory, guiding socialists in the task of trying to awaken latent nationalist drives for the struggle against capitalism,

∴

US Negroes obviously do not fit into the classical definition of a Nation. But it is contended that they nevertheless are a potential nation, that they may *become* a Nation if and when they achieve a national consciousness. And what constitutes a national consciousness? Apparently, 'a certain group of people, living in a certain place, has decided to take its political destinies into its own hands'. So at that point where Negroes fight in their own way for their own goals and with their own leaders, they apparently become transformed. They metamorphose from a race into a Nation, the Negro question turns into the National Question, and the fate of the Negro suddenly becomes determined not by his own history in America but by the laws of national development deduced from the plight of small backward nations under the Czarist empire, who collectively constituted the majority of the population of the empire.

That Negroes are a potential 'Nation' is an unproved assumption. That Negroes constitute a 'Nation' or an 'incipient Nation' or an 'emerging Nation' or even a 'Nation within a Nation' requires concrete analysis, rarely supplied.

For instance:

1. If Negroes are not a classic nation, what particular aspects of nationalism in their condition make for the possible emergence of a national consciousness? ('Oppression' is no answer).
2. Granting, for argument's sake, that some concrete nationalist factors do apply, producing similarities, why is the Right of Self-Determination the correct slogan? Might it just as logically not be correct given the differences? What is decisive here?
3. How can a classic nationally-oppressed group directing its own destiny be equated to any oppressed group fighting for freedom? May a national-

consciousness someday be achieved by child-laborers, women, atheists, migratory workers, aged pensioners and sharecroppers?
4. The Bolsheviks directed European nationalism into serving the Revolution. Precisely how and why is Negro Separatism progressive and anti-capitalist?
5. Why does the relatively advanced and exploding Negro struggle need the type of slogan designed to raise the consciousness of a very backward agrarian European or Eurasian tribal people?
6. If a dormant nationalism will awaken under conditions of self-awareness and crisis, how explain the rejection of separatism by Negroes over a 300-year period of revolutions, revolts, wars, upheavals, etc.?

Answers to questions like the above are almost invariably based on abstractions from international experience, and not on the powerful realities and extraordinary history of the Negro in the US. Marxists tend to minimize the voluminous works of Negro scholars who investigated and dissected the Negro question, but their opinions are weighty and must be considered.

Race and Segregation

These Negro scholars (O.C. Cox, E.F. Frazier, James W. Johnson, Alain Locke, etc.) consistently maintain that the Negro question is a unique race question, that the kind of oppression suffered by Negroes in the US is unique in history, that never before on earth has a group been persecuted purely because of skin color, i.e. race.

What is race? It is not a valid biological category. *It is a social relation.* It arose out of capitalist necessity to justify the slave trade and human chattel slavery to a western world simultaneously discovering the inalienable rights of man and social justice. Thus the fictions of race superiority-inferiority and the non-human nature of Negroes were invented.

In the southern United States with its unlimited expanse of virgin land, slavery took firm root. Initiated by mercantile capitalists, the southern slave system became more powerful than they, producing an independent ruling class which eventually ruled the US itself.

The pervasive economic and political power of the slaveowners disfigured American society from the outset by imposing upon the entire nation the ideology of white supremacy, the hypocrisy and irrationality of race and race relations, and a tolerance of the horrors of chattel slavery.

After the Civil War and Reconstruction had destroyed the old slaveowning class, northern capital, from both economic and political motives, betrayed its promises and created a revised, capitalist form of race relations, based upon many of the traditions and social relations of slavery. Segregation took the place of the chattel as the main prop.

An analysis of this tortuous history reveals that race, i.e. race relations, is a peculiar and *independent* category of social relations. Race stands in relation to historically necessary social categories – class, nationality, caste – as irrational.

Social relations deriving from class, nation, etc. may be unjust, oppressive, reactionary. Still, these categories have a material foundation in modes of production and play progressive roles during certain historical periods (the class struggle is 'the motive force of history').

Race exploitation, on the other hand, has no necessary relation to any mode of production. A system of exploitation and discrimination, revolving around the axis of skin color, arbitrary and perverted: it serves no progressive function whatsoever. It has caused all of American society to become organized around race relations, and, therefore, around prejudice. The race consciousness of white workers supersedes even their class consciousness, dulling their minds, doubling the obstacles for Negroes, preventing the organization of the proletariat as a class.

Because of the utter irrationality of race as a reason for social partition, segregation is absolutely required for the perpetuation of racial exploitation and because of this interdependence of segregation and discrimination, the Negro movement for nearly two centuries has directed its main line of struggle against segregation, against that barrier which prevents Americans from becoming a whole people, from becoming themselves.

∴

Can't we, nevertheless, *call* the Negro question a National question because of some similarities? Not without denying its unique character. The Negro question is not merely different than the National question, but diametrically opposed to it.

(1) *Segregation* is no factor whatsoever of National oppression. On the contrary, forced assimilation is the rule and mode of oppression.
(2) In oppressed Nations, the bourgeoisie tends toward assimilation with the oppressor: among Negroes, the bourgeoisie (the small but rich capitalist class) is the only consistently pro-segregation class.
(3) Separatist movements among oppressed Nations are almost universally progressive and liberating in philosophy and ideology, attacking concretely the institutions and practices of the National oppressor. Negro separatist movements have all accommodated to the form of oppression –

segregation. They accept and cater to the irrational concept of *race* as a scientifically legitimate biological category that justified social division. Some separatist movements have been militant, but within the framework of retrogressive concepts. Other separatist movements objectively capitulated to white supremacy on almost every score.

(4) The historic drive of oppressed nations is towards separatism: the historic drive of the Negroes is against separatism and segregation.

(5) For an oppressed nation to become integrated is a reactionary concession to the status quo, a defeat: integration for Negroes is *revolutionary*, because American capitalism incorporates segregation in its fundamental structure and cannot survive without it.

(6) Potential and pre-nations, once aroused, have no difficulty in perceiving a qualitative difference of identity in themselves and their oppressor. Negroes are Americans in nationality according to all basic criteria, and recognize only the unfair white-imposed color line as the difference between them and whites.

Among the oldest non-native inhabitants of this country, the Negro has contributed a huge share to its wealth, progress and world pre-eminence. He has played heroic and sometimes decisive roles in all of the historically important events. His life is inextricably involved with whites. Precisely because this is his homeland, prejudice and discrimination are infuriating. He has no other home. His Afro-Americanism doesn't indicate a previous nationality, for a continent is not a nation, and his culture and customs are not those of any African nations. Indeed, he knows not *where* in Africa his ancestors lived, and often feels strange with Africans (and vice versa). His affinity for Africa is racial and *inter*nationalist.

Africans themselves are Pan-Africans first and nationals second. In defiance of the laws of European national development, the African revolution pushed *national sovereignty* into the background of its independence struggles almost from the beginning. In Kenya, for example, the Kikuyu gave their first military-defensive organizations not national but continental designations, such as 'The African Fighting Forces' and 'Defense Council of the Whole of Africa, Kenya Branch'. *Africa for Africans* is the central rallying slogan of the revolutions there! The strictly national aspirations of the peoples of Black Africa (scores of nations and incipient nations, most of which had few or no relations with each other historically) has long been superseded by consciousness, deriving from the added burden of racial oppression under colonialism. What is commonly called African 'Nationalism' is more accurately described as African Internationalism.

On every score, the Negro question stands by itself as a unique phenomenon among exploited minorities, demanding independent analysis based on the key factors of race and segregation. To lump it together with its opposite, with European nationalism, obscures its character and its goals. ...

The predominance of Garveyism in the Negro community proved transitory; rent by internal contradictions and crises, it evaporated as soon as realistic instead of romantic avenues of resistance to racial discrimination opened up. This occurred in 1925 when the organization of the Brotherhood of Sleeping Car Porters was achieved, merging Negro socialist leadership with the proletarian struggle.

In alliance with the NAACP, these new working class leaders undertook a campaign for jobs in Harlem, popularizing labor unionism and paving the way for later Negro entrance into the main stream of working class struggle: the CIO.

There have been minor separatist movements such as that for a *49th State* (in the early thirties). This was an attempt by the Negro bourgeoisie to turn the movement away from integration opportunities offered by interracial trade unionism. It never received popular support, nor have others until recently.

The only two separatist movements since 1800 (Colonization and Garveyism) which attracted a mass support were *transitional vehicles* to higher stages of struggle which repudiated separatism. They both served a function in the Negro movement, but never represented an important historical objective of Negroes. Rather, they were a mode of existence after demoralization and/or the closing of mas-s avenues of struggle. In both cases when doors of struggle opened, separatism, always born of demoralization, disappeared.

The Black Muslims are the latest major separatist movement, resulting somewhat from the isolation of the Negroes from the labor movement, but more specifically from the closing of the doors of struggle by the bankrupt northern reformist leaders.

The Muslims' anti-conformist and anti-reformist posture strikes a responsive chord among the most exploited sections of the unrepresented Negro workers. Their ruthless unmasking of race reality in the US through blistering blitzkrieg attacks on whites and on the discredited Negro gradualists and opportunists reflects and deepens the wisdom of their audiences on this score. Through their businesses and schools, the Muslims train men for jobs and women for domestic virtue; they rehabilitate former habitués of police court and prison and offset degeneration among the demoralized and backward. They project, like Garvey, an economic program for black business, both cooperative and private, within the ghetto, heightening race consciousness and community solidarity through this program. Even at worst, such proposals do bring more money into the Negro community, through jobs and surplus value, and the community needs both.

But, like all previous separatists, the Muslims are ambiguous; they embody retrogressive as well as progressive ideas, Utopian as well as rational objectives.

Their organization is militaristic and autocratic. Their schools preach a doctrine of defensive racism, absolute male supremacy, anti-Semitism, descent from Allah, and cosmic vengeance. Their call for an independent state opens no channel for struggle against oppression. Their concept of black business as a cure-all is Utopianism in classical form.

Many analysts have noted the 'pathetic' aspect of the Muslims – their wild reach for a glamorous identity. This is a by-product of the post World War II trend among some Negro intellectuals to disdain the study of Negro history and culture, equating it with the segregationists' glorification of Uncle Tom. Negro leaders, subsequently, not only had no program but no historical race-identity and race-tradition to offer. The Muslims had both. An old program – but a new God and a new invented identity, which imparted to some of the poorest Negroes a new sense of security and solidarity.

So once again, in the absence of a realistic and inspiring program of action, mysticism, razzle-dazzle and speak-bitterness became the mode of existence for sections of the most oppressed.

Much more serious, however, is their sectarian abstention from struggle, as graphically revealed in Birmingham. Amid the greatest mass actions in the modern South, they scoffed from the sidelines. After the demonstrations subsided and the results were in, they did a brisk business in memberships on the following basis: they wrote off the tremendous mass experience, from which such rich lessons are being learned, as a dismal defeat proving the folly of struggle.

Incapable of fundamentally advancing the struggle, they actually retard it in their own way, no less than the Wilkinses and Kings ...

Black Nationalism of White Radicals and the Question of Self-Determination

Until the complete Stalinization of the Comintern, the radical movement in the US was vaguely integrationist ...

But Garvey's mass support in the 1920s was very impressive. Stalin sent a Comintern representative to the 1929 Jamaica convention of the Garvey movement to debate the question 'Should Negroes join the Comintern?' (instead of Garvey's organization). Garvey won.

That same year ushered in the 'Third Period' of international Stalinism, characterized by an anti-reality adventuristic program which took form on the Negro question in the imperative slogan of 'Self-Determination for the Black Belt'. Not only was the now-obvious independent and special nature of the struggle equated to nationalism, but separation was proclaimed as the only revolutionary course.

White Communists promptly undertook a search for some historical foundation to this theory, seeking to discover national peculiarities of the Negroes and trying dutifully to uncover separatist trends which would verify the prognosis of Negroes constituting an incipient Nation needing only to have their consciousness and will to struggle awakened in order to discover that what they really wanted all along was a separate territory, independent government and racial exclusiveness.

The research yielded meager results; its continuity was, moreover, regularly disrupted by the twists of Kremlin policy which alternately injected Self-Determination during leftish periods and withdrew it during ultra-rightist swings. Communist militants thereafter came to identify Self-Determination with 'real Leninism' and with Foster, while Integration was associated with 'social-democratic reformism' and Earl Browder.

The Trotskyist leadership (apparently with the exception of at least Oehler) took the position that not a national but a racial question was involved and that the struggle for civil rights, not racial autonomy, was the militant anti-capitalist direction of motion.

From the meager documentary material available, it would appear that while they didn't have a fully worked out position, they had basically correct political instincts on this question, and these were brought before Trotsky in 1933.

Trotsky, suspicious of a political organization in a bi-racial country composed exclusively of the dominant race, defended the basic nationalist line of the CP (1933 Conversations). He stated that while his knowledge of the US Negro question was too inadequate for a decisive opinion, he felt in the American attitude a similarity to that of Rosa Luxemburg and the reformist Social Democrats on the issue of the Eastern European nationalities.

The only thing he urgently proposed, however, was an immediate and thorough discussion of the question in the Communist League of America, but apparently no such discussion was held. American Trotskyism on the Negro question grew over into its opposite: from integration to Nationalism. This process was crystallized in the 1939 Resolution, committing the SWP to Nationalism and the Right of Self-Determination.

So from 1929 on, as the modern integration movement gained steam, no radical parties could see or understand the revolutionary implications of integration. The specter of nationalism and its corollary principle of self-determination hovered constantly over the Negro question, with confusing results ...

Part III: the SWP and the Negro Struggle

... While the above is somewhat oversimplified, it provides a starting point: what are the various tendencies in the party on the Negro question?

There are at least six more or less distinct areas of opinion, not all clearly defined, and some overlapping. Nevertheless, they reflect most of the attitudes in the civil rights movement and on the 'left'.

(1) *Black Nationalism for White Radicals*. This broad tendency, discussed previously, holds (a) that integration ultimately is reformist and Social Democratic, and the demand for a separate state is the only revolutionary demand: or (b) that either road may validly be chosen when the decision is made; or even (c) that the Negro question is a national question, but integration will be chosen.

Ironically, hardly had the ink dried on the 1939 Nationalist Resolution when there occurred an influx of militant integrationist Negroes into the party. Under the combined pressure of these workers and the integrationist movement of the 40s, comrades adhering to Nationalism generally restrained their views, never advancing them publically and rarely privately. Consequently, until 1948, scores of new comrades in the party never dreamed that self-determination was the official line and never even heard of it.

Negroes sensed something strange and ambiguous and assumed it was prejudice. Tortuously expressing itself in policy, tactics and social relations over the years, it played its part in the alienation of almost an entire generation of Negro revolutionaries.

(2) *The Negro Question as an Appendage of Trade Unionism*. This is not so much a theory of the Negro Question as an unbalanced emphasis on trade unionism, an over-identification of unions with the working class and a myopia about non-unionistic facets of the class struggle.

Not a formal doctrine, it is a prejudice in favor of trade unionism, giving rise to the feeling that the Negro struggle, though independent organizationally, is tactically dependent upon the labor movement for virtually every move or advance – something like the Russian proletariat-and-peasantry relation.

In this connection, Daniel Guerin may be pardoned for dissociating himself (*Negroes on the March*) from SWP maritime policy. On the West Coast, the white Deck and Engine departments were equated to the proletariat while the largely Negro Stewards Department was considered dependent, and destined to follow the decisive proletariat. This is an a-typical example but illustrates the extremes to which this ideology may lead.

When unions are dormant, however, and the Negro movement is obviously in motion, Negro dependence is promptly shifted from unions to the Colonial Revolution or some other more 'decisive' category.

Another characteristic of this tendency is its assumption that the Negro movement is similar enough to the labor movement for the general laws of trade union development to apply.

For example: From the early '40s until quite recently, a fetishism of the NAACP existed around the idea that the NAACP was the ordained organization of Negro struggle and to organize anything outside it would approximate the *dual unionism* of the CP's ultra-left period.

Because of this arbitrary subordination of the Negro movement to a trade union principle, our Negro cadre was imprisoned in this orientation for years, unable even to probe the possibilities of independent, militant, and working class Negro organization. Many Negro comrades finally contrived their escape from this policy and from the party as well.

All party unionists are not of this opinion, and non-trade unionists may hold it. There are no rules in this tendency about what other theories its adherents may subscribe to. Some believe in integration, others adhere to extreme nationalism, etc. Both Nationalism and Trade Union Primacy entail the danger of reinforcing the prejudices of white workers, the former by indicating a probable and endorsable segregated socialism, the latter by ascribing a dependent and subordinate role to the Negro struggle.

(3) *Economic Determinism*. The vanishing idea that the needs of production (skilled labor, etc.) require the capitalist class to do something drastic about the south.

(4) *The Activists*. These include most of the Negroes in the party. They feel detached or skeptical about the theoretical discussion; the party has been discussing for years and nothing has changed very much. They are anxious for the party to collectively devise a means of intervening more effectively than has been the case, and they expect the party leadership to take the lead in achieving this.

They are generally dissatisfied with party grasp of and performance in the Negro movement, considering it inadequate: while they play their role in the transmission-link operation, informing the party of developing moods and groupings, they feel that no reciprocal levers for effective intervention are given them in exchange.

Outside the party they must cope daily with the hostile white world: inside the party, many resent having to criticize, complain or push, believing that awareness of the need for a better orientation and climate should be the entire party's responsibility and concern.

Some deduce that no meaningful interrelation of party and Negro movement is currently objectively possible, and more fuel is added to the flame of separatism.

(5) *The Official Compromise Resolutions*. Here, the differences among all recognized tendencies are usually softened and then 'unified'. The party is offered some integration, a great deal of nationalism, just enough separatism, much trade unionism, plenty of self-determination, a pledge of increased activism, a great deal of theoretical neutralism and an over-all injunction to wait-and-see.

Inasmuch as this type of resolution, speech, and article determines and expresses party theory over the years, it may be said that in terms of a guide to action, we have no fundamental theory at all.

(6) *Revolutionary Integration* – the viewpoint expressed in this Resolution, i.e. the Negro Question is a unique racial (not national) question, with a movement marked by Integration (not Self-Determination) as its logical and historical motive force and goal, thereby producing a struggle that is necessarily transitional to socialism and a revolutionary vanguard for the entire working class. ...

When the SWP recognizes the Negro struggle as the core of US politics and labor, it will understand both the proletariat and the Negro a little better. ...

7   Malcolm X: The Man and His Ideas[17]

(*Excerpts, 1965*)

George Breitman

[**Editors' Note:** The speech was delivered at the Friday night forum in Detroit on March 5, 1965.]

It is still painful to speak of the death of Malcolm X. It is probably too soon to appraise him adequately. It will take time before we can do him justice, before we can see him in his full stature. It is painful because with him gone, we momentarily feel smaller, weaker, more vulnerable.

Our sense of loss was for his family, for the movement he was building, for the Negro people, for the revolutionary cause as a whole. There is something in us that cries out against the fact that he was cut down in his prime, still a young man, before he had made his full contributions to the struggle, before he had accomplished everything he was capable of accomplishing for human emancipation.

I was still a young man 25 years ago when another great revolutionary was assassinated – Leon Trotsky. Perhaps I did not fully realize his leadership, advice and political wisdom would be missed, and probably I was under the influence of the belief common among young people that to show certain kinds of strong emotion is a sign of weakness. Anyhow, I did not cry when Trotsky was killed, and I could not help crying when Malcolm was killed.

It was not because I considered Malcolm the greater of the two men. One reason for the difference was the realization that Malcolm, at the age of 39, was still in the process of reaching his full height, still in the process of working out his program, still in the early stage of building a new movement – whereas Trotsky, at the age of 59, had already reached full maturity, had already worked out his main ideas and his program, and left behind him the solid foundations of a movement that could not be destroyed by war, by persecution from both the Allied and Axis Powers, or by cold war reaction and witch hunts.

---

17   Breitman 1965a.

But while it is painful to speak of Malcolm, and not yet possible to see him in full perspective, we are able even now to begin to make an appraisal of his ideas, and of how he came to the ideas that constitute his heritage. When we do this, we must try to put emotion aside, or to bring it under control. That is what Malcolm urged when he spoke here in Detroit three weeks ago – that we learn to think clearly about the struggle and the ways the power structure seeks to curb and sidetrack the struggle; that we think clearly and rely on reason and learn how to see through trickery.

Malcolm Little's mother was born as the result of her mother's rape by a white man in the West Indies. When Malcolm was four, the house where he and his family lived was burned down by Ku Kluxers. When he was six, his father met a violent death, and he and his family always believed he had been lynched.

The family was broken up. Young Malcolm lived in state institutions and boarding home. He got high marks in the grade school in Mason, Michigan. Then, at the age of 15, he became a dropout. He went to live with his sister in Boston, and went to work at the kinds of jobs available to Negro youth – shoeshine boy, soda jerk, hotel busboy, member of a dining car crew on trains traveling to New York, restaurant waiter in Harlem. There he drifted into the degrading life of the underworld – gambling, drugs, hustling, burglary. You can find it all described in his autobiography, which will be published soon, up to and including his arrest for burglary, conviction, and sentencing to 10 years in prison. That was in 1946, when he was not quite 21 years old, the age of many of you in this audience.

Law of the Jungle

What were his ideas then? That life is a jungle, where the fiercest survive – by fleecing the weak and defenseless; where each man looks out for Number 1, which can only be done by accepting the jungle code. 'The main thing you got to remember is that everything in the world is a hustle', he was told by the friend who helped him get his first job.

Although his father had been an admirer of Marcus Garvey, feelings of race pride did not exist in the young man in the zoot suit. He tried to straighten his hair in emulation of white men who, as he later said, had taught him what he knew and instilled in him the values of racist white society. I think you can find thousands of youngsters in today's ghetto like the 21-year-old Malcolm Little in 1946.

Prison is hell. Prison is also a place where you can think, where some important decisions have been made. Eugene V. Debs, after who this meeting hall is named, was converted to socialism while he was in prison in 1895. Prison is where Malcolm underwent a conversion that literally transformed his whole life.

By letters and visits from members of his family, he was introduced to the Nation of Islam, headed by Elijah Muhammad. This American religious sect, popularly known as the Black Muslims, worships Allah as god, and practices some ritual of the orthodox Muslim religion, with certain variations of its own, especially in the sphere of race.

It teaches that original man, when the world was a paradise, was black, and that the white man is a degenerate and inferior offshoot, destined to rule the world for 6,000 years and then be destroyed. The 6,000-year period is now ending, and black people can save themselves from the coming catastrophe only by withdrawing, by separating from the white man and following Muhammad, the Messenger of Allah.

From a scientific standpoint, Black Muslim mythology is no more and no less fantastic or bizarre than other religions. But the Black Muslims are a *movement* as well as a religious group, providing a kind of haven and hope and salvation for outcasts, encouragement at self-reform, brotherhood and solidarity against a cruel and oppressive world.

I am not going to go into detail about the Black Muslims; you can find plenty about it in writing. The point is that Malcolm experienced a genuine religious conversion in prison, believing that Elijah Muhammad was a holy man, and that the Nation of Islam provided a path of salvation not only for him, but for his people.

While in prison, this drop-out after the eight grade began to educate himself and learn how to speak and debate, so that he could participate more effectively in the movement after he got out. Not know how else to proceed, he started with a dictionary, copying all words in a table beginning with 'A' that might be helpful. He was astonished to find so many 'A' words, filling a tablet with them alone. He went through to 'Z', and then he writes, 'for the first time I could pick up a book and actually understand what the book was saying'. The story speaks volumes about the quality of education in Michigan – and in the US.

From then until he left prison, he spent all the time he could in the prison library, 'picking up some more books'. Within a few years he was to become the most respected debater in the country, taking on one and all – politicians, college professors, journalists, anyone, black or white, bold enough to meet him.

There are tremendous reservoirs of talent and even genius locked up in the black ghettos and white slums, among the masses – which can be set free and put to work when the acquire hope and purpose.

Organizing Ability

After six years in prison, when Malcolm was 27, he won parole by getting a job with his oldest brother, Wilfred, as a furniture salesman in the Detroit ghetto. That was the spring of 1952. Later that year he traveled to Chicago to hear Elijah Muhammad, and he met him. He was accepted into the movement and given the name of Malcolm X. He volunteered his organizing services in Detroit, and did so well he was made assistant minister of the Detroit mosque after the membership had tripled.

At the end of 1953 he went to Chicago to live with Muhammad and be trained by him for some nine months. Muhammad sent him to Philadelphia, which had no mosque; in less than three months a mosque had been formed. He was obviously a man of unusual talent, energy and devotion. Muhammad picked him to head the movement in New York, and he went back to Harlem in 1954, before he was 30 years old. In a few short years, his work helped to transform the Black Muslims from a virtually unnoticed to a nationally very well known organization; and he himself had become one of the country's most noted figures, one of the most desired speakers on the nation's campuses, and the object of admiration by the nation's most militant youth.

Before proceeding chronologically, I want to say a few words about Malcolm s a public speaker. I am not an expert in this field, and hope somebody who is will make a study of it. There is certainly plenty of material, thanks to the fact that many of his talks were taped and are readily available.

His speaking style was unique – plain, direct like an arrow, devoid of flowery trimming. He used metaphors and figures of speech that were lean and simple, rooted in the ordinary daily experience of his audience. He knew what the masses think and how they feel, their strengths and weaknesses. He reached right into their minds and hearts without wasting a word; and he never tried to flatter them. Despite an extraordinary ability to move and arouse his listeners, his main appeal was to reason, not to emotion.

This is true even about speeches in which he was presenting ideas that he abandoned in the last year such as the last great speech he made as a Black Muslim – his speech to the Grassroots Conference in Detroit in November 1963 ... It is won of his best speeches, although I repeat it does not reflect his thinking at the end, and is worth listening and re-listening to, because of the qualities I have been trying to pinpoint. And because his main appeal was to reason, he was the very opposite of a demagogue, the very opposite of what the kept press called him.

It was also a style very different from Elijah Muhammad's. I don't mean only that Malcolm commanded the weapons of wit and humor, which are alien to

Muhammad. Muhammad's appeal was to faith, authority (divine authority), to the hereafter; Malcolm's appeal was to reason, to logic; it dealt with the real and the present, even when he was expounding Muhammad's line. To be able to listen to Muhammad for any length of time, you had to be a believer, convinced in advance, while Malcolm seemed to achieve his greatest success with non-Muslims.

These few remarks about Malcolm as a speaker are admitted inadequate. I make them only in the hope of interesting someone more qualified than I to study and write about it. I only wanted to convey the idea that there rarely has been a man in America better able to communicate ideas to the most oppressed people; and that this was not just a matter of technique, which can be learned and applied in any situation by almost anybody, but that it was a rare case of a man in closest communion with the oppressed, able to speak to them because he spoke for them, because he identified himself with them, an authentic expression of their yearning for freedom, a true product of their growth in the same way that Lenin was a product of the Russian people.

Split with Muhammad

We come now to the second period of Malcolm's life, 1963, and the split with Muhammad, which was consummated in March 1964. The year 1963 was a year of stirring and movement in the Negro struggle, with hundreds and thousands in the streets; the year when the struggle moved from the South to the Northern ghettos, where the Black Muslims were strongest. It was not yet a revolution, but a prelude to revolutionary struggles. This was a situation that sharpened a dilemma and then produced a crisis in the Black Muslims.

By their militant stance they had helped push other Negro organizations to the left. This was their positive contribution. But they were on the sidelines of the struggle, not participants. They talked in angry tones but did nothing when non-Muslim Negroes were under attack. They were separated not only from whites but from Negro militants.

Among the members, younger and less conservative than in the pre-Malcolm period, signs could be detected of a desire to get into the battle, to pass from propaganda to action. Muhammad tried to allay the ferment; one example was his call, at the organization's national convention in February 1963, for independent black political action. But he soon pulled back from this and other moves that might have drawn the Black Muslims out of their abstentionism. When the Freedom Now Party was started six months later, he refused to endorse it or let the members join.

The occasion for the split was a remark made by Malcolm after Kennedy's death in November 1963, followed by Muhammad's silencing of Malcolm, with a virtual suspension that was humiliating. But this was only the occasion, not the cause. The basic factor behind the split was the growth of militancy and mass action in the Negro community, and the different ways in which the two main tendencies in the Black Muslims wanted to respond to the masses knocking on the doors of their mosques.

There is an instructive relation between the way Malcolm came into the Black Muslims and the way he left. He turned to them from a state of isolation, not only the physical isolation of prison, but an alienation from society generally and from his own people as well. His years in the Black Muslims had been good for the organization, and they were good for him. He had travelled all over the country as Muhammad's chief troubleshooter, and he knew the ghetto nationally as no one else did. His vision had broadened, his interests had widened.

He entered the Black Muslims because he was alone and lost, and he left, you could say, because now he was in closest touch with the Negro people, attuned to their needs and wants more than the Black Muslims were or wanted him to be; because he was becoming the spokesman of a growing multitude looking for a new road; because he had found a new role, or because a new role had been thrust upon him, which his whole life's experience told him he had to accept, however difficult it would be.

It could not have been an easy decision. Consider the circumstances: 38 years old, a wife and several dependent children; a secure post, relatively well paid, home provided, car provided, expenses; great prestige; a position in an organization second in authority to a man in his late sixties who was not in good health. Some men in his place would have taken the easy way – keep quiet, do as you are told, stay out of the line of fire, mend your fences, and wait. That's the American way – in business, in government, church, fraternal, and labor circles.

Essence of the Change

But Malcolm x was not that kind of man. He had been disturbed to see that Muhammad and some of his ministers were, like other preachers of puritanism, not living in accord with the strict puritanical code they prescribed for ran-and-file Black Muslims. He tried to overlook things like this – his eyes were mainly turned to the outside world of the broad Negro struggle. He was not the only minister who knew that new, bolder and more active policies were needed if the Black Muslims were to fulfill their real responsibilities to the

Negro people. But the other ministers who recognized the need for change – they played it safe. They weren't Malcolm x.

Malcolm had what can be called a second rebirth early in 1964 when he decided his place was with the Negro masses more than with Muhammad's organization. As a Black Muslim leader, he had rejected corrupt American society. Now he passed from merely rejecting it (a negative, passive position) to rebelling against it and organizing to change it (a positive, active position). That was the essence of the change.

Some ultra-leftists in the Negro community did not understand this and talked condescendingly about Malcolm becoming 'weak' or 'soft'. But the American ruling class and its spokesmen understood what was happening, and they were more hostile to him after the split than before. And they had greater reason to hate and fear him after he set out to build a new movement. That is why, as George Novack puts it, he 'was crucified by the paid press long before he was martyred by the assassin's bullets'.

We have heard the expression, 'the new Malcolm x'. It is appropriate in some ways, misleading in others. Some of his ideas did change starting last March, but others did not. Let us at least mention those that did not change before examining those that did:
– That Negroes can get their freedom only by fighting for it;
– That the government is a racist government and is not going to grant freedom;
– That gradualism, the program of the liberalism, white and black, is not the road to equality;
– That Uncle Toms must be exposed and opposed;
– That Negroes must rely on themselves and control their own struggle;
– That Negroes must determine their own strategy and tactics;
– That Negroes must select their own leaders.

These are ideas that Malcolm believed in before he left the Black Muslims and that he still believed the day he died. ...

[Political Perspectives]

In approaching the immensely difficult and exhausting job of building a new movement, in opposition to new as well as old enemies – a task which radicals should best be able to understand and sympathize with – Malcolm showed from the start that he did not want merely a replica of the Black Muslim structure plus some modifications in policy. He wanted a different kind of organization, with a different kind of relation between leaders and ranks.

The Black Muslims built everything around a mystique of leadership and faith in and submission to a divine, all-wise chief. That Malcolm wanted something radically different could be seen from the statement at his first press conference after the split. He denied that he was 'expert in any particular field'. He called for help in the form of ideas and suggestions from all quarters, especially students, white or black.

He note only accepted advice, but sought it. He not only invited criticism, but welcomed it. I am aware of one such case personally. I never met Malcolm or saw him in person, but I wrote many articles about him, most of them supporting and defending him. It was typical of him, I think, that the only one of these articles bout which he sent me a message of appreciation was one that was most critical of some implications in a speech he made.

When he read something useful or pertinent to the problems of his organization, he would go out of his way to get copies for his fellow leaders so that they could read and thing about it and develop informed and collective attitudes. On the day he was killed, he was scheduled to present for discussion his ideas on the program of the Organization of Afro-American Unity. It is plan that he was trying to develop a far more democratic organization and a far more collective leadership than the Black Muslims ever dreamed of. ...

Malcolm believed in black unity after as well as before the split. But as a Black Muslim, when he meant and had to mean was black unity under the leadership and control of Muhammad, and with unquestioning acceptance of his religious dogmas and discipline. The kind of black unity Malcolm sought after the split was the unity of all Negroes, whatever their religions, whatever their philosophies, so long as they were ready to fight for freedom ...

In the area of political action Malcolm was also far ahead of the Black Muslims. That didn't take much doing, since they abstain from politics. He favored Negroes organizing politically and running and electing their own candidate, and driving out of office black stooges of the major parties. He participated in a Harlem conference on independent political action before his death.

But his position on politics was largely general. He said he found some good in that the Freedom Now Party was doing, and while he was in Africa last summer, he briefly gave consideration to an offer that he run on the Michigan FNP ticket for the US Senate; he decided instead to remain in Africa longer. However, he never affiliated with the FNP, for reasons not discussed publicly; maybe he thought the FNP was premature or launched without sufficient groundwork on too narrow a basis.

While his thinking on politics was still in a process of development, and uncompleted, there was nothing general or tentative about his attitude to the capitalist parties and the two-party system. To him they were both enemies of the Negro people, currently as well as historically, and neither merited an iota of support from Negroes. ... In terms of the political spectrum, he stood on the radical side, although he had not reached strong conclusions about how to organize independent black political power. ...

At his first press conference last March, Malcolm had this to say on the question of alliances: 'Whites can help us but they can't join us. There can be no black-white unity until there is first some black unity. There can be no workers' solidarity until there is first some racial solidarity. We cannot think of uniting with others until we have first united among ourselves'.

This, as I pointed out at the time, is not the statement of man claiming that black and white working-class solidarity is unnecessary, or that it is impossible. On the contrary, it is the statement of man explaining one of the conditions through which workers' solidarity may be achieved on a broad and durable basis. And if I may quote myself for one more sentence, I noted: 'Revolutionary socialists will certainly agree [with Malcolm] that a meaningful and mutually beneficial labor-Negro alliance will not be forged until the Negro people are organized independently and strongly enough, numerically and ideologically, to assure that their interests cannot be subordinated or sold out by the other partner or partners in any alliance'.

... When he spoke at a Militant Labor Forum in New York last May, he said: 'In my recent travels into the African countries and others, it was impressed upon me the importance of having a working unity among all peoples, black as well as white. But the only way this is going to be brought about is the Negroes have to be in unity first'.

So far as I have been able to learn, that remained Malcolm's position to the end. He was not opposed to alliances with other forces, including labor, provided they were the right kinds of alliances and provided the Negro part of the alliance was independently organized, so that it could guard against betrayal by being able to pull out of any alliance that went bad ...

[Socialism and Black Nationalism]

Next let us consider briefly Malcolm's attitudes to capitalism and socialism. In an interview with the *Young Socialist* he stated: 'It is impossible for capitalism to survive, primarily because the system of capitalism needs some blood to suck. Capitalism used to be like an eagle, but now it's more like a vulture and can only such the blood of the helpless. As the nations of the work free themselves, then capitalism has less and less victims, less to suck, and it becomes weaker and weaker. It's only a matter of time in my opinion before it will collapse completely'. Marxism might question whether capitalism will collapse, or have to be collapsed, but who can question that in his last months Malcolm was taking an unequivocally anti-capitalist position?

Malcolm did not learn about socialism by reading Marx, but he managed to learn about it anyway. He learned about it from the colonial revolution, especially its pro-socialist contingent. He had discussions with Castro and Che Guevara and Algerian socialists and socialists in Ghana, Guinea, Zanzibar, and elsewhere, including the United States. When he was asked last May at the Militant Labor Forum what kind of political system he wanted, he said:

> I don't know. But I'm flexible. As was stated earlier, all of the countries that are emerging today from under the shackles of colonialism are turning toward socialism. I don't think it's an accident. Most of the countries that were colonial powers were capitalist countries and the last bulwark of capitalism today is America and it's impossible for a white person today to believe in capitalism and not believe in racism. You can't have capitalism without racism. And if you find a person without racism and you happen to get that person into conversation and they have a philosophy that makes you sure they don't have this racism in their outlook, usually they're socialists or their political philosophy is socialism ...

Let us now conclude this discussion of Malcolm's ideas during this last year of his life by examining his positions on black nationalism and separatism. This is important because some political opponents of Malcolm are already circulating distorted stories about him, alleging that he was on the verge of quitting his movement, going over to his opponents, etc. ...

Black nationalism and separatism are not the same thing, though unfortunately they are often confused. Separatism is a tendency favoring the withdrawal of Negroes into a separate black nation, either in America or in Africa. Black nationalism is a tendency for Negroes to unite as a group, as a people, in organizations that are Negro-led and Negro-controlled, and sometimes all-black, in order to fight for their freedom. Black nationalism, as it now exists, does not imply any position on the question of a separate nation in the future, for or against. So you can be a black nationalist without being a separatist, although all separatists are black nationalists. ...

When Malcolm X was a Black Muslim, he was of course a separatist. At his first press conference after leaving the Black Muslims last March, he said he was out to build a black nationalist movement, and the major stress was on black nationalism. But he also had a few words to say about separatism. He said he still thought separation was 'the best solution'; previously he would have said the *only* solution. 'But', he continued, 'separation back to Africa is still a long-range program, and while it is yet to materialize, 22 million of our people who are still here in America need better food, clothing, housing, education, and jobs *right now*' (his emphasis).

At the time I took this to be a declaration of his intention to build a black nationalist movement that would attempt to unite the Negro people in a fight for immediate needs, while at the same time continuing to hold up separation as a nation as an ultimate objective, and to make propaganda for it accordingly. But I was obviously wrong, because after that statement last March I cannot find any place where Malcolm advocated a separate nation. And on May 21, a few hours after returning from his first trip to Africa, when he was asked at a press conference if he thought Negroes should return to Africa, he said he thought they should stay and fight in the United States for what is rightfully theirs. ...

What about his position on black nationalism? Everyone called him a nationalist, friend and foe, and there was no question about it until a few weeks ago. Then he was asked, in the *Young Socialist* interview, 'How do you define black nationalism, with which you have been identified?'

He began by saying, 'I used to define black nationalism as the idea that the black man should control the economy of his community, the politics of his community, and so forth'. That is, he used to define it in the traditional way, as I tried to do a few minutes ago.

The second paragraph of Malcolm's reply ... relates a discussion he had with a white Algerian revolutionary he met in Ghana last May who sought to convince Malcolm that his self-designation as a black nationalist tended to alienate people 'who were true revolutionaries dedicated to overturning the system of exploitation that exists on this earth by any means necessary'. His third and final paragraph was:

> So, I had to do a lot of thinking and reappraising of my definition of black nationalism. Can we sum up the solution to the problems confronting our people as black nationalism? And if you notice, I haven't been using the expression for several months. But I still would be hard pressed to give a specific definition of the overall philosophy which I think is necessary for the liberation of the black people in this country.

Please notice: He was reappraising his *definition* of black nationalism and wondering if it can be *summed up* as the solution; he had stopped using the term, but he had not yet been able to find another definition for the philosophy necessary for black liberation. Now let me offer what I think is the explanation for all this.

Malcolm had been a black nationalist – it was a starting point for all his thinking, the source of his strength and dynamism. And he remained a black nationalist to his last hour, however uncertain he was about what to *call* himself or the program he was trying to formulate. It would be a bad mistake to mix up what he was with what he thought might be a better name for what he was.

The most urgent need of the Negro people is still the mobilization and unification of the Negro masses into an independent movement to fight for their freedom. Black nationalism is still highly progressive because it contribute to that process and to the creation of that kind of movement. But black nationalism is a means, not an end; it is a means, but not the only means; it is probably an indispensible means toward the solution, but it is not the whole solution. It helps to build an independent movement, but it does not necessarily provide the program that will lead such a movement to victory. ...

As he discussed with people in Africa, in the Near East, at the United Nations, and in the United States, as he studied and thought and learned, he began to become a black nationalist plus. Plus what? I have already given you many quotations from his speeches and interviews showing that as he studied the economy, the nature of the political and social system of American capitalism, as he developed greater and keener understanding of how this system functions and how the ruling class rules and how racism is a component and instrument of that rule, he came more and more to the conclusion that not only must the Negro control his own community, but radical changes have to be made in society as a whole if the Negroes are to achieve their freedom.

Black nationalism, yes. But the solution cannot be *summed up* as only black nationalism. Needed is black nationalism plus the transformation of the entire society. Whatever difficulty Malcolm my have had in finding the right name, what he was becoming was black nationalist plus revolutionist. ...

Malcolm's uncertainty about the right name arises from the fact that he was doing something new – he was on the road to a synthesis of black nationalism and socialism that would be fitting for the scene and acceptable to the masses in the black ghetto. He did not complete the synthesis before he was murdered ...

But the stunning blow to the struggle does not destroy the struggle. Malcolm will not easily be replaced. But he will be replaced. The capitalist system breeds not only racism but rebels against racism, especially among the youth. Malcolm cannot be replaced overnight, but meanwhile we all can and should strive harder, work harder, fight harder, unite more closely to try to fill the gap left by this man we loved, and give help and encouragement to those destined to replace him.

CHAPTER 5

Divergences and Consolidations

Paul Le Blanc

After the 1953 exit of the substantial group around Bert Cochran, a significant leadership shift was effected within the SWP. James P. Cannon formally stepped down from leadership of the SWP, retiring (or semi-retiring) from the party center in New York to Los Angeles. The two central leaders were now Farrell Dobbs and Tom Kerry, although Murry Weiss and Myra Tanner Weiss – with particularly close ties with Cannon – also had significant influence. While this had potential for the generation of dissension and divergence, such things came most dramatically from other quarters.

In the 1950s, a significant oppositional current developed in the Socialist Workers Party, led by Sam Ballan (generally known by his party name: Sam Marcy) and Vincent Copeland in the Buffalo branch of the SWP. They saw the world divided into two camps – bourgeois and proletarian – that were engaged in a Global Class War. The Soviet Union and other countries ruled by Communist Party dictatorships were seen as dominant elements in the proletarian camp, and despite increasingly diluted Trotskyist criticisms, this 'Global Class War' tendency gave full public support to these dictatorships, including in situations in which popular uprisings within their own countries challenged them. This included support for the 1956 military invasion of Hungary by the Soviet Union, which brutally repressed the popular revolution against the dictatorship there.

This tendency remained in the SWP as 'disciplined and loyal members', while ideologically constituting 'in effect a party within a party', Marcy later reminisced. Excerpts from Marcy's 'The Global Class War' of 1953 and from Copeland's 1956–57 document 'China, Hungary, and the Marxist Method' give a sense of their perspectives. Marcy and his co-thinkers finally left in 1959 to establish the Workers World Party. 'We based our conceptions on those developed by Marx, Engels and Lenin', Marcy emphasized in 1996, adding that 'Trotsky contributed much to explaining the era that followed Lenin's death', but that all of the organized Trotskyist tendencies 'had become violently anti-Soviet and anti-socialist, as shown by their hostility to the USSR as it existed, to the socialist countries of Eastern Europe, and above all to the People's Republic of China'.[1]

---

1 Thomas 1998; Griswald 1998; Marcy 1996. On Vincent Copeland, see Lambert 1993.

In the early 1960s a very different oppositional group crystallized around Tim Wohlforth and James Robertson, attracting support among a substantial segment of the recently recruited young activists who had been helping to build the Young Socialist Alliance of which they were key leaders. Claiming to represent Trotskyist orthodoxy, they opposed what they saw as uncritical supportiveness by the SWP majority for the Cuban Revolution, rejected the SWP's support to black nationalism (preferring the 'revolutionary integration' position of Richard Fraser), and flatly opposed the rapprochement with the 'Pabloite' sector of the Fourth International led by Ernest Mandel (whose 'party' name was Germain).

A sharp division soon ruptured this opposition. Robertson and others around him viewed the SWP as no longer revolutionary, but instead as 'centrist', veering toward opportunist reformism; they sought to bide their time, recruiting to and building up their faction before the inevitable split. Wohlforth and those around him chose to follow the leadership of the British group, the Socialist Labour League (later renamed the Workers Revolutionary Party), headed by Gerry Healy. The SWP had been formally aligned with this group, and with a French group headed by Pierre Lambert, from 1953 until 1963. Wohlforth's current was instructed to remain in the SWP and seek to win a majority, rejecting any appearance of the disloyalty. This divergence is reflected in the documents 'The Centrism of the SWP' and 'Call for the Reorganization of the Minority Tendency'. The Robertson group was soon expelled from the SWP for disloyalty, and the Wohlforth group was also rapidly forced out – resulting, respectively, in the Spartacist League and the Workers League (which many years later took the name Socialist Equality Party).[2]

A key issue in this divergence was the SWP majority response to the Cuban Revolution – which they argued was a revolutionary overturn of both imperialist domination and capitalist property relations, in the interest of the great majority of the Cuban people, a living embodiment of Trotsky's theory of permanent revolution: democratic revolution spilling over into socialist revolution. The fact that this was led by revolutionaries who were not Trotskyists was a theoretical-political 'deal breaker' for the young oppositionists, who insisted that genuine Trotskyism does not allow for such a development, and that the SWP majority was capitulating to the 'Pabloism' that it had opposed in the 1950s factional dispute in the Fourth International.

---

2 Useful accounts of all of this can be found in Alexander 1991, pp. 864–6, 917–33, and Wohlforth 1994, pp. 76–151. More on each group is available at the websites of each: Spartacist League – http://www.icl-fi.org/directory/slus.html, and Socialist Equality Party – http://www.socialequality.com/about (both accessed 23 June 2016).

Other dissident and semi-dissident currents (including some who shared the majority position on the Cuban Revolution) were also pushed to the side, as the Kerry-Dobbs leadership sought to enforce greater unity and stability. Most prominent among the marginalized were those associated Murry and Myra Tanner Weiss, who had, in fact, not sought to organize an ideologically distinct 'opposition'. Another current *was* developing a distinctive set of political positions, led by Richard Kirk and Clara Kaye (Richard and Clara Fraser), influential leaders of the Seattle branch. Advancing the perspective of 'revolutionary integrationism', and placing special emphasis on feminism, their tendency was marked by a positive attitude toward Maoism, and by calls for a 'creative' rather than a 'routine' approach to politics. The Frasers – who would soon split away to form the Freedom Socialist Party – offered a critique of and alternative to the SWP leadership in the document 'Radical Laborism Versus Bolshevik Leadership'.[3] Dobbs, with support from George Novack and the full backing of Kerry, produced a document codifying their own approach, which became the official position of the SWP – 'The Organizational Character of the Socialist Workers Party'.

---

3 Online material regarding Richard Fraser is provided at: https://www.marxists.org/history/etol/document/icl-spartacists/prs3-fraser/ (accessed 23 June 2016). For Clara Fraser and the Freedom Socialist Party, see: https://www.marxists.org/archive/fraser/index.htm, and http://www.socialism.com/drupal-6.8/home (both accessed 23 June 2016).

1 The Global Class War and Destiny of American Labor[4]

(*Excerpts, 1953*)

Sam Marcy (Sam Ballan)

Is There an Independent Destiny for the American Working Class?

I propose to discuss in this article what I believe to be the basic and underlying issues in the current discussion. The first one is: Is there an independent destiny tor the American proletariat? The second one is: What is the historical fate of Stalinism in the new epoch of global class war, and how does this affect the task of the American vanguard, the SWP?

Let us consider the first issue. Is it possible for the American proletariat to carve out tor itself an independent destiny, an independent road toward socialism separate and apart from Europe and Asia? Is it possible to strike out on an entirely new path, which will lead to the broad highway of the American Revolution? After all, is it not true that the American working class is still virgin soil and really has no allegiance to any political party in the sense that the Europeans, or the Asians, or the Latin Americans have? Is it not possible to start from a new beginning, brush aside the Stalinists as well as the debris of the various socialist sects and begin anew, dig deeper and deeper into the trade unions and conduct the struggles there in the spirit of the independent class politics of Lenin? If we divorce ourselves from the fate of Europe and Asia, will we not get the ear of the workers more readily? If the workers hate Stalinism and Russia, be it for good or for bad reasons, of what concern is it to us if they will follow us on *our* path to socialism?

In Europe and Asia there is a complex – or contradictory combination – of revolution and reaction. Such is the situation in Russia, Eastern Europe and China. Is it not far better to disregard the whole complexity? Why take the onus of Europe's curses on own back? Why carry a burden which is not necessary, and certainly not acceptable, to the American workers today and perhaps not

---

4 Marcy 1953.

even adaptable to the American scene? Will we gain more by linking up our fate with the revolutions of the East and of Europe, or by withdrawing from them? Does what is described as the revolutionary complex in Europe and Asia hinder or help us? Is the revolutionary reality of Europe and Asia a magnet through which we can draw the most advanced elements into our party, or is this revolutionary reality not overshadowed and outweighed by the dark specter of Stalinism? Will we gain more by drawing upon the revolutionary reality in Europe and Asia, or will we lose more as a result of the terrific obstacles which Stalinism puts in our way as a bar to the American worker?

I have raised this series of questions in a particularly sharp manner because I think it has a close relevance to the present discussion. I have raised these questions because I have felt for a long time that sooner or later the process of uneven development in the revolutionization of the world proletariat would place these questions on the agenda in the American party. This would happen because of the tardiness in the radicalization of the American working class and the fact that the revolutionary center of gravity is still in the East. The revolutionary center of gravity has been moving with giant strides, but thus far, further and further East, so that by now it has fully in its grip not only the continent of Asia, but Africa and the Middle East. The tidal wave of world revolution abroad is in sharp contrast to the reactionary trend that has dominated this country for several years now. That is why the above series of questions must be put on the agenda and fully examined.

Let us begin with the most, elementary question. Is the American proletariat an independent social entity? Obviously the answer is no. But let us pursue it a little further with the aid of a quotation from Lenin.

The Link in the Chain

Lenin wrote: 'The whole of political life is an endless chain composed of an infinite number of links. The whole art of the politician consists in finding and taking firm hold of the link that it is most difficult to take from you, the most important at the given moment and the one which best guarantees to you the possession of the whole chain'.

Lenin's reference to the link and the chain offers an almost perfect analogy of the relationship between the American proletariat and the world-wide proletariat. The American proletariat, is the link, the world proletariat is the chain. The American proletariat is historically the most important and decisive link for the fate of the whole chain. But – and this is of the greatest importance – the link is indissolubly connected und intertwined with the whole chain. Separate the link from the chain and neither the link nor the chain exists. If the American proletariat were a social entity not connected with the chain, then we could consider the question of an independent destiny. But the American proletariat is an inseparable and completely inter-dependent link, not merely of the world proletariat, but of an entire global class camp. Unless we view the American working class in this light, we cannot see it in proper historical perspective, nor can we analyze the course of its ultimate destiny. In order to fully answer the questions posed, it is absolutely necessary to consider the new world setting.

I have introduced in the above paragraph the conception of the global class camp, the camp of which the American working class is an indispensable and key part, whose fate, let me repeat, is completely tied up with it. The conception of our class camp is different today from any other period in the history of, the working class. There was a period in the history of the working class when its camp was confined almost exclusively to the exploited proletariat. That was in the period prior to the October Revolution when it had relatively few allies among the oppressed masses in the colonies and dependent countries when the latter slept the sleep of centuries. Of course they were always allies in a social sense but not politically articulate. In the epoch that saw the rise of the victorious revolution in the USSR headed by Lenin and Trotsky, the Soviet Union was at the head of the camp of the exploited which already included millions of awakened colonial masses. In the epoch of Stalinist degeneration and the consequent isolation of the Soviet Union, the isolated workers state introduced a monstrous distortion, mutilation, and atomization within the camp of the world proletariat. In the present epoch our class camp is not only constituted differently because it is a new historical period, but because it has a number of characteristics which distinguish it from the previous epoch.

In What Manner Is Our Class Camp Different Than in the Previous Epoch?

In the first place, the camp of the proletariat today, unlike the previous epoch, has the bulk of the oppressed peoples in the colonies and dependent countries within its camp as allies. The mass of peasants, semi- and non-proletarian elements of the backward countries, which in previous epochs were the reserve of imperialist reaction, can now be regarded not merely in a social but in a political sense as well, as having been attracted to and daily becoming more and more part and parcel of the camp of the proletariat. The revolutionary ferment all over the colonial world is testimony to this fact. Our class camp is numerically much larger, much more politically conscious than in all previous epochs. The second characteristic of our class camp is that it has state allies, states where the working class, if not in a political sense, then certainly in a social and historical sense, hold ruling power. The third characteristic of our camp, as differentiated from the Stalinist epoch proper, is that the deformity and mutilation introduced by the Stalinist leadership at the head of this camp is now on the threshold of its exit from the historical scene; whether this be a matter of months, or a few years is not of great moment. What is of great moment is that the conditions for its existence are slipping from under its feet. The fourth characteristic of our class camp is that the new state allies, China and Eastern Europe, by their very existence, have so thoroughly undermined the foundations of the imperialist structure that it can virtually be said that the world relationship of forces has been definitely and irretrievably turned in favor of our camp. However, this turn in the relationship of forces does not automatically decide the fate of our camp. But merely sets the stage for the inevitable struggle.

Our camp, the camp of the exploited, is still characterized by the same deficiencies which have characterized the exploited, the oppressed and subjugated classes in all previous historical epochs. It lacks, first and foremost, at its head, a leadership willing, capable and ready to insure victory in the unfolding conflict with imperialism. As in all previous historical epochs, the exploited classes are still blinded by the class enemy's poisonous ideology of sectionalism and narrow-mindedness, the purveyors of which are the labor lieutenants of capitalism and the Stalinist bureaucracy. Our camp needs unity but in large part is characterized instead by totalitarianism. It needs revolutionary internationalism but instead is consistently being injected with the chauvinism of imperialism or the no less virulent chauvinism of the Moscow oligarchy. The entire class camp with all its shortcomings, with all its dire failings, with all the terrible handicaps of treacherous leadership, is nevertheless moving onward, not consistently, not uniformly, not everywhere with the same tempestuous revolutionary sweep, but it is moving steadily and invading the fortresses of imperialism. Our class camp, it becomes plainer every day, constitutes an invincible and wholly viable social formation. The struggle that it is conducting is many-sided. It fights its battles not only economically and politically but, as is now evident, with military means.

The Global Class War

Actually, there has been a global war on ever since Korea. The bourgeoisie has long been aware of this, and its most authoritative representatives are applying the conception of the global war with every new turn of the situation. Let us examine this war before we resume our main point, the relationship of the American proletariat to the entire class camp.

On May 4, 1953, the *New York Times*, in an editorial on the crisis in Indo-China, wrote: 'Thus what might seem at first glance to be a small jungle war in the hinterland of a little and obscure state in the interior of Southeast Asia comes into perspective as part of a great global conflict that is both physical and ideological. It cannot be divorced from other developments in that conflict. It must be seen, therefore, in (this) light ...'.

Thus we see from this authoritative organ of the bug bourgeoisie that they regard the war from an exclusively global viewpoint, and the bourgeoisie has so regarded it for quite a long time. Of course, the bourgeoisie does not in so many words characterize the global struggle as a global class war. Why should it? The bourgeoisie must always mask the class character of its predatory war in the interests of duping the masses.

I believe I was the first one to show that the global war was in reality a global *class* war. I did this in a memorandum submitted as material for a pre-convention discussion entitled 'Memorandum on the Unfolding War' on October 29, 1950. ... In this memorandum I stated:

> The fact that the opening phase of the war [in Korea] may manifest itself (or rather conceal itself), even if only initially and temporarily, as a war between nations, should not in the slightest degree obscure its clearcut *class* character. *It is not a war between the nations but a war between the classes* ... in this war the geographical boundaries are *social boundaries*, the battle formations are class formations, and the world line of demarcation is the line rigidly drawn by the *socialist* interests of the world proletariat. Every worker must know his place as well as his duty.

We must now come back to the elementary generalization made earlier to the effect that the American proletariat is not an independent social entity but, on the contrary, an unbreakable link in the class chain. It must share its fate and its destiny, and since its role is enormous and decisive within the camp, all the heavier are its responsibilities to the camp. ...

'The Road to Peace'

Now let us see how far the line of our party has been in accord with the conception of the emergence of two irreconcilable class camps in global conflict for hegemony over society. Let us examine Comrade Cannon's pamphlet, *The Road to Peace According to Lenin and According to Stalin*. Comrade Cannon's pamphlet was not written in some by-gone era of peaceful development. It was published in 195 in the midst of the era of the global class war. The author's point of departure is *not* the existing world of social relationships. True enough, there is a passage where Comrade Cannon makes allusion to 'the class struggle of the workers merging with the colonial revolutions in common struggle against imperialism', but he does not indicate that this concrete world we are living in is torn by two irreconcilable class camps whose struggle has already broken out in military warfare, where the casualties are already counted in the millions, where the fighting is on opposite sides of the class barricades.

But Comrade Cannon's pamphlet, as the subtitle indicates, is 'according to Lenin and according to Stalin'. It is the road to peace according to Lenin that we are interested in. The road to peace, as Lenin taught us, is through ruthless and implacable class war. The war in Korea is a class war. It has to be waged in that manner. Nowhere in his pamphlet does Comrade Cannon ever characterize the war as a class war. One has to infer it or guess it. Nor does he view it as part of a general class war. Comrade Cannon points out that according to Lenin, war in the epoch of imperialism is inevitable. That is true, and it is also good criticism of the perfidious Stalinist theory of co-existence. But it is not sufficient criticism of Stalin's road to peace to say that co-existence is a delusion, and that war is inevitable. It must also be shown that we, the Leninists, are for the road to peace in this *concrete* global class war through the vigorous, unrelenting and energetic *prosecution of the war*. Our road to peace is fighting the war to a finish through the *combined* efforts of the exploited and oppressed in our camp. This also is not shown in Comrade Cannon's pamphlet. The American proletariat is not depicted as an inseparable detachment of one army in one class camp whose aim is *overall* victory over the class enemy. Furthermore, Comrade Cannon does not deal with Korea as a case of the class war. He does not see the battlefield in Korea as a picket line or one of a series of world picket lines demarcating the socialist interests of the global class struggle. In effect, he does not deal with the war from a thoroughly revolutionary internationalist point of view. ...

The Defense of the USSR

It has been traditional in our movement to include a section on the unconditional defense of the USSR in any document or popular pamphlet which deals with war. Comrade Cannon's pamphlet, dealing precisely with this question, the question of war, in order to continue this tradition, should contain such a section. But all that we can find in Comrade Cannon's pamphlet is a bare reference to the 'heritage of October'. No one except a party member could possibly infer from this isolated phrase that our movement is for the unconditional defense of the USSR.

Such a section – on the defense or the USSR – is all the more necessary, particularly because Comrade Cannon goes into such detail in his descriptions of the monstrous crimes of Stalinism. Where one deals in such meticulous detail with the degeneration of the Soviet state and Stalinism, it is all the more important to make crystal clear our defensist position on the USSR. I am not for splashing all over the pages of the *Militant* blaring headlines of unconditional defense of the USSR. But every worker who is thinking at all about politics sooner or later approaches us with this question: 'Where do you stand on Russia?'

The Soviet Union is a contradictory phenomenon. It is a revolutionary social system with a counter-revolutionary leadership. Comrade Cannon expounds on the concentration camps, frame-ups, etc. What he says is true. But this truth alone is insufficient.

There was a time when we were practically the only group in the labor movement consistently explaining this truth from the revolutionary point of view. But today the bourgeoisie has seized upon this aspect of the Soviet state and broadcast it to the four corners of the earth. Today this is practically all the American worker hears. It is drummed into his ears day in and day out by the tremendous capitalist apparatus of radio, television, the press and the pulpit. He identifies the reactionary aspect of the Soviet Union with the entire social system, just as the capitalist class wants him to do. Hence it is all the more obligatory to emphasize the other side of the Soviet Union, its class character, its new social system. It is necessary to explain that it is a living, viable workers' state, an historic gain of the working class, a conquest to be defended. ...

2 China, Hungary, and the Marxist Method[5]
(*Excerpt, 1956*)

V. Grey (Vincent Copeland)

Our Position

We condemn the first Soviet military intervention against the unarmed demonstration on October 23. But recognizing that the consequent nation-wide uprising was swiftly turned into a restorationist movement, we should support the second entry of the Red Army and its overthrow of the Nagy regime.

We should call for an Independent Soviet Hungary *allied to and equal to the Soviet Union*. This is integral to our call for the political revolution to regenerate the Soviet State under the banner of world revolution. 'The overthrow of the bureaucracy presupposes the preservation of state property and planned economy'. – Trotsky, *In Defense of Marxism*. The overthrow of the Hungarian bureaucracy must presuppose the preservation of state property and planned economy in both Hungary and the Soviet Union.

We should strongly reiterate our defense of the Soviet Union against imperialism, and our subordination of the task of overthrowing the bureaucracy to this defense. We should arm the advanced workers ideologically for the coming great conflict, which Hungary may have brought closer! In the long run, the bureaucracy cannot successfully defend the Soviet Union itself, not to mention Hungary. Only genuine proletarian revolutionists can do so.

The great lesson of the half-blind Hungarian counter-revolution is the necessity for the Marxist party. The Chinese revolution proved that there could be the possibility (after 24 years of armed struggle) of one class defeating another class without a Marxist leadership. Hungary has proved that the substitution of the bureaucratic leadership by a revolutionary leadership *within the same class* cannot be accomplished without the Marxist party.

The bourgeoisie says the Hungarian revolution 'will not have been in vain'. By this they mean that genuine communism has had a historic set-back. It is

---

5 Grey 1957, p. 25.

hard to deny that this is so. But if the proletarian vanguard learns all the lessons of Hungary and learns them thoroughly, it will prepare itself to lead the whole class in the next inevitable leap forward. This leap will come earlier and extend farther than the bourgeoisie now imagine on the basis of their estimate of Hungary. But our estimate is more profound than theirs. In the deeper sense, the Hungarian uprising, counter-revolutionary though it proved to be, is a training ground for proletarian revolutionaries. It will be studied and debated for a long time. Its lessons will be deeply pondered and well learned. The more clearly the proletarian vanguard assimilates the lessons of Hungary and the reasons for it – the more surely 'it will not have been in vain'.

3 Summary for Minority on World Movement[6]
(*Excerpts, 1962*)

Tim Wohlforth

... To me the central question which we have been discussing in one form or another is the role of the working class in the revolutionary process. It is our contention, our feelings that there is a tendency on the part of the majority in its international resolution, in its approach toward Cuba, in its current Political Committee draft, to see other forces substituting for the role of the working class. I mention here the working class and not the party. I think we were a little off previously in emphasizing simply the party. It is not – our dispute is not simply over the necessity of the party anymore but more basically over the necessity of the class in the conscious form, whether or not that takes the precise form of the party. That to me is the difference. This flows from an empiricist outlook on the part of the majority which I went into and which will have to be gone into much more thoroughly and much more competently than it has been done here in a literary discussion.

Secondly, on the question of Cuba. ... Now I can't go into a detailed analysis of the current Cuban development but I want to say a few things because I think they're very important. I've been reading the material I get (the Speeches of Fidel Castro, etc.) and I've been watching the developments in relation to Escalante and other current developments in Cuba. My own opinion and attitude – I feel that Castro will go down as one of the most remarkable figures in history. I feel that he is an extremely sincere revolutionist. I feel he fulfills every criterion established in the international resolution for a revolutionist. I feel that if the Cuban revolution had to depend on any one individual it would be difficult to find a better one for it to depend on. The whole crisis of Cuba today, the crisis of its future – not so much of its present (though it is already beginning to show up) – is whether or not the individual, the greatest individual can replace the working class. That is the crisis. ...

---

6 Wohlforth 1962.

I was attacked by Joe six months, a year ago, at the last plenum for just talking about disaster, disaster, disaster – danger, danger, danger. That was because I raised the threat of Stalinism. I mentioned that there was a danger of Stalinism in Cuba. This danger exists and it still exists. And the danger of Stalinism isn't the danger of an individual. We know what it is. It is the danger of the isolation of the revolution, of the lack of working class control over the governmental apparatus. It is that element of consciousness of the necessity of working class control which Fidel does not yet have and at least our approach should be to point that out and carry out a campaign to do that. So that's my analysis of Cuba. It may be wrong. It may be crazy, but that is my analysis.

Now you say, have events vindicated your analysis. I would say that events have fundamentally not really vindicated any analysis yet because the thing is still in process. If the governmental apparatus, without the creation of real workers control as a result of the struggle of the working class itself – should this apparatus prove capable of leading Cuba onto a new course of an undeformed workers revolution, then we will have to reevaluate our whole analysis, reevaluate our whole concept of working class rule. We will go back and reevaluate Debs' ideas that only the working class can rule for the working class, that only the workers can rule in their own name. We will have to reevaluate that and recognize that a benevolent bureaucracy that is pro-working class can substitute as the rulers of an undeformed workers state. That I do not see. But, if that happens, we will change our position. We will have to. But in the meantime your position is not vindicated. Our position is not vindicated. We both have different analyses of an unfolding event.

Similarly no position was vindicated in Yugoslavia for several years – two or three years. We can go into the Yugoslav question. It's related. I want to make it very clear what my position is on Yugoslavia in 1948 and 1950. That is that Yugoslavia was a deformed workers state at the time that it broke from Stalin. The only possible way you can understand Yugoslav developments is to recognize this. And the Yugoslav bureaucracy could not reform itself. Why? Because we do not look upon leaders of a bureaucracy simply as individuals. They represent the interests of a social caste which must be overthrown by revolution precisely because social castes as castes do not reform themselves just like classes do not reform themselves. This is Trotsky's position. Does it apply to Yugoslavia? I say it does. Therefore we could say emphatically that it was impossible for Yugoslavia to have become an undeformed workers state, to evolve that way, except through the intervention in a revolutionary capacity of the masses.

The perspective of the International at that time was all wrong because it did not orient toward the independent intervention of the masses in Yugoslavia.

The events proved that it was wrong. If it had evolved in another way you would have a basis today to say that Cuba, Cuba too will evolve into an undeformed revolution without the intervention of the masses. You would be correct in your line today.

But it didn't, so at least you ought to put a question mark over the application of the identical method today – as if we had not gone through an experience and as if Pabloism had not been completely repudiated by history itself.

The question of Stalinism happens to be one of the most important questions that has come up today. The concept that Yugoslavia carried through a political revolution, Yugoslavia which is today a deformed workers state where a political revolution must be carried through; the concept that Mao's China carried through a political revolution where today it is a deformed workers state where a political revolution must be carried through is a gross distortion of the theory of the political revolution. Gross distortion of that theory.

Secondly, some comrades here seem to be saying that the question of political revolution is an open one. They are saying that it is possible that you will need an insurrection, but it is also possible that the bureaucracy will reform itself. This is a defensive position if you want to argue it. It has a name and its name is Deutscherism and we know its Deutscherism. If you think Deutscher is a simple advocate of reform, that he doesn't believe that it is possible for a revolutionary overturn, then you haven't read Deutscher. Read his best, don't read his worst. Read his *Russia in Transition*. This is what he says. He says it's possible that you're going to have to have a revolutionary overthrow but it is also possible the bureaucracy may evolve in a different way. That's Deutscherism. Deutscherism is identical to exactly what Weiss and Deck wrote in that article and what in an even more open and blatant way Myra defended at this meeting and what Dave defended in relationship to Yugoslavia. That's Deutscherism. That we have struggled against and that is not our view. That is not the Trotskyist attitude toward Stalinism, And we ought to make that clear, we ought to clear up these concepts. That's our task.

Changing nature of Pabloism. What can you say? The problem is simple. It is this. It is simple in this sense. The problem is not the question of the changing Pabloism but of the changing SWP. I don't claim that there is no political basis for the regroupment of the SWP majority and the Pabloites. I think there is a strong political basis because the SWP majority has adopted the essential views of the Pabloites. Now I don't have to argue with you about this. All you have to do is what I did in my document. Some day when you have a spare evening, go back and read the views of the party at the time of the Open Letter and read what you're saying now. It's a different line. That's all I have to say. Now maybe you were right to change your line but it's a different line and if there is a new world reality which requires a change in line it can't be the whole past 15 years. It's got to be the period since 1953. It's got to be the period after China, after Yugoslavia, when we said, despite these events, we still maintain this particular line as against Stalinist conciliationism which we analyzed in the document 'Against Pabloite Revisionism' – 50 or 60 pages in detail – accusing the Pabloites of the identical formulations and identical views that can be found in the 1961 International Resolution. There has been an evolution. The evolution has been in that direction. ...

Now on the question of reunification, Comrade Alvin raises the analogy of the 1903 period, the 1928 period, the period when he said essentially Lenin and Trotsky were defending a new program. That's not true. They were defending an old program. In those periods, the periods of the organization of a party and the period after 1928, Lenin and Trotsky were essentially trying under different conditions to coalesce together the revolutionary forces, the revolutionary Marxist forces as against all the other tendencies and trends. These were periods of turmoil and confusion within the international movement. In both cases turmoil within an international movement which adhered to a common – so-called common – Marxist outlook. In 1903 it was a matter of assembling the real Marxists from the phonies. In 1928 it was assembling the real revolutionary communists. That was the problem in both cases. Periods when it was necessary to carry on a dual process of pulling in forces – and they did it in those periods – and breaking from centrists.

That's essentially the problem today. Anyone who holds that we have today a theoretically cohesive – theoretically and politically cohesive – international doesn't know what they're talking about. Our problem today is precisely to coalesce the essential Trotskyist forces on an international basis. This coalescence must be done through the two processes of the pulling together of every sincere revolutionary element in the Trotskyist movement and a struggle against every centrist and revisionist element within the Trotskyist movement. If there weren't such revisionist elements how come there was the split in 1953 to begin with? That is essentially the dual process.

The party majority has proposed only one of these two processes. No longer is there a question of struggle. It is only a matter of figuring out organizational formula to pull everyone into. Into what? And around what program? The central Trotskyist program? Well what is the central Trotskyist program? That has to be defined, has to be defined in a political and ideological struggle. That is what is under discussion today in the international. Not simply how we can get people together but around what do we get them together. And, that is why the discussion of organizational formula has already gone over into the question of political program.

Now my own feeling is this. What we need and what we're going to have is a full and thorough international discussion aimed at precisely this: defining the Trotskyist program and around that basis reunifying and pulling together the international. Now it goes without question that this will be a very complex, a very long process.

Our position is this: we feel that the Socialist Workers Party is adopting a political outlook.an international outlook, which is in contradiction to its traditions, and to its own methods of work in this country. That's our opinion. We may be wrong. We believe this. This is our opinion. Flowing from that opinion, it is our conviction that with future developments in the US especially and internationally our outlook will be verified. In which case, in our opinion, the whole business of a minority-majority division will no longer be necessary. It is this approach and this attitude that we take. Perhaps – of course you think we're dogmatic and sectarians and will never recognize reality – but perhaps as these developments occur in this country and internationally your outlook will be vindicated in which case believe it or not we may even change our minds though it is difficult for you to conceive of that idea

Now I think I have posed several questions, several historical happenings which if they do occur will mean that, as far as we are concerned, a fundamental change in our whole outlook: One would be to be shown in reality that the Stalinist bureaucracy can be reformed. This would require a new orientation and we would have to abandon ours. To be shown in other words that other forces outside of the working class with its own consciousness, its own actions, in its own capacity, and with its own party can make revolutionary change of a fundamental socialist nature in our society. Then we would change our outlook. I don't think that that outlook is going to be vindicated and people who see in Cuba a vindication of that outlook had better remember what they say today, next year. You can also remember what we say. We'll see what happens.

4 The Centrism of the SWP[7]
(1962)

James Robertson

1   The Decisive Importance of the Nature of the Party

The American Minority has been nurtured in the SWP and is a tendency within the party. The SWP (and youth) continue to loom large as a shaping influence upon the minority. How the SWP is analysed and summed up determines a) the tasks of the minority which are carried out within and through the SWP, b) the nature, scope, and very existence of the minority groupings, flowing from our conclusions about the stat and direction of development of the party. Thus the question of the nature of the SWP is of *decisive and central* importance to our perspective and tasks.

It would be an error to view the 'nature of the party' as some kind of a priori or external label to be applied to the SWP. To know the nature of the SWP is to know how the party is moving and will move in response to events, opportunities and challenges in the class struggle and in relation to the aim of the Socialist Revolution.

It is possible to perceive the broad outlines of the party's political shape even under conditions of relative quiescence. It must be our continual responsibility to do this, checking our expectations against results, so as to properly orient our tasks. To do otherwise would render our entire role directionless and random, at the mercy of chance impressions and momentary situations.

2   Some Relevant Party History (a Sketch of Highlights Since 1940)

a. The American Trotskyists took a stunning double blow in 1940. Over half of the movement broke away and a few months later Leon Trotsky was murdered.

---

[7] Robertson 1964.

Among those breaking away from the movement (40% of the party and 80% of the youth) were most of the party's writers. Theorists, as well as a whole political generation who had made up the youth leadership. The party lost nothing in the way of intransigence and solidity through these blows as was shown by its resolute role in the Smith Act trial and the upsurge in the working class trade-union struggles during 1943–47 out of which issued Cannon's affirmation, 'The Coming American Revolution'. However, a theoretical sterility and blunting of political alertness took place and was never made good. All these circumstances underline the recent statement of the British SLL that the SWP had made no political contribution to the world movement since 1940 (in 'Trotskyism Betrayed' by SLL-NC, July 21, 1962).

b. The response of the SWP to the Tito-Stalin split marked the opening of a period in the party's existence which was concluded with end of the regroupment period. (The response to the Cuban revolution is on a new and different plane). It was a period in which, when opportunities opened up somewhere, the party typically would initially respond in a revolutionary manner. Failing to get sufficient results, it would begin to water down its approach, enthuse over dubious elements and press hard against the limits of formal revolutionary doctrine. Then a halt would be called, cooling off took place, and its 'historic opportunity' or 'hero' of only yesterday, though perhaps unchanged, became completely passé.

The eulogistic and shameful scrabble after 'comrade' Tito in 1949–50 was a reaction to disappointments in the reversal of the trade-union struggle, a sharp decline in the party's size and influence, all in the context of the growing witch-hunt, which started Cochran-Clarke's restlessness to break out of the revolutionary movement.

Similar reactions set in internationally in the Fourth International; but it was not until the Cochran group in the United States was ready to break overtly with Revolutionary Marxism that the then US majority recoiled and led a world split which arrested the rightward drift in the party for a time. Yet, the split was weak and defensive for the following reasons:

1. It placed organizational over political issues. The split of the FI was simply announced in the pages of the *Militant* as a reaction to the world center's support of the Cochran-Clarke group. It was not fought out to a culmination and rupture, thus catching the SWP's co-thinkers by surprise and unprepared and left the neutrals perplexed and inside the FI.
2. It placed national over international considerations, as was in addition shown by the SWP's endorsement of the expulsion of the French majority by the Pablo center in 1952. (See *SWP International Discussion Bulletin* of November 1952, 'Documents on the Crisis of the PCI (French Section

of the FI). This took place only a year prior to the SWP's own break with Pablo.

Immediately in 1954, at Weiss' instigation, the party was made to undergo the strange experience of the anti-McCarthy campaign in which McCarthy was dished up as a full-blown fascist who had to be fought in the streets by the trade-unionists. This qualitative over-statement of McCarthy's role was accompanied by an agitational campaign in the very depth of a period of terrible isolation, reaction, and passivity, while the *Militant*, week after week, shredded and reduced to a parody the Trotskyist understanding of fascism.

Then in 1956–58 came the series of regroupment activities growing out of the Stalinist crisis which began with the adoption of the excellent SWP 'Statement on Socialist Regroupment' and which correctly facilitated the SWP's involvement in open forum discussions. It also facilitated and encouraged the winning-over of a left-wing from the liquidating Shachtmanite YSL [Young Socialist League]. Soon however the impatient attempt at a pay-off at any price led to flattery in the *Militant* of the Gatesites [a faction and then split-away from the Communist Party led by John Gates] who were heading for the Democratic Party and to an adaptation to the *National Guardian*, as in the building of Guardian supporter clubs. Then came the treatment of the ISP [Independent Socialist Party] with an approach of robbery principles. Only the intransigence of anti-Trotskyist elements saved the SWP from being a partner to a common electoral New York state slate which would have placed the SWP in the compromising position of being in an electoral block for propaganda. The feverish assertion in the PC draft resolution of March 1959 that regroupment was bigger and better than ever, came just when the regroupment period had palpably come to an end. But then J.P. Cannon called a halt and that was that. The party was contained rather formally within nominally principled limits.

3   The Present Political Positions of the SWP (i.e. the 'Auto-Catalytic' or 'Chain-Reaction' Breakaway of the SWP from the Programmatic Fundaments of Revolutionary Marxism)

Revolutionary parties are not immune to errors (e.g. the Bolsheviks' 'revolutionary democratic dictatorship of the proletariat and peasantry'). *However*, the further and clearer the departure from the politics of a consistently class-struggle character, the stronger the restorative (correcting) force within the party.

But, after an incubation period of some years (see point 2) the party, *unclearly* over the youth, *openly* on the Cuban Revolution (i.e. the permanent revolution), and *grossly* over Pabloism and the Fourth International (i.e. internationalism) has not merely broken with Leninism, but has overtly replaced it with something else. What has been in recent years a tendency to give an opportunist twist in practice to attempts of the party to seize on opportunities, until a halt was called by restorative forces within the party (characteristically J.P. Cannon), has *changed to an overt breakaway* from Marxism with the party's response to the Cuban revolution, so that the accumulated opportunist forces and appetites within the party were not only unleashed but outright encouraged by Cannon's initiative in attacking the SLL. With the response to the Cuban revolution, the variance between words and deeds has become qualitative. The dominant motives and practice today are a clash of attempts to recruit dubious human material at the expense of revolutionary principles, opposed by the fear that any recruitment efforts might alienate the 'friendly' leadership groupings of whatever organization the majority can locate (i.e. July 26, Local 1199, SNCC, etc.).[8]

4   The Degenerative Process – The SWP as a Centrist Party

Centrism is a catch-all word to describe any of those organizations which in Lenin's words are 'revolutionary in words, opportunist in deeds'.

The SWP in particular has fallen victim to *degenerative processes* similar to those which overtook the pre-World War I German Social Democracy and Lenin's Bolsheviks, so that the party stands today:

a. in opposition to the most essential aims of the Trotskyist movement for a major part of the globe in the declared dispensability of a revolutionary proletarian party to lead the colonial masses to victory (victory as opposed to the stalemate of the deformed workers' states of the still more illusory 'victories' that do not transcend entanglements of capitalist imperialism);

b. internationally no longer for a world party, a Fourth International as the self-organized, international vanguard of the working class; instead the SWP seeks a limited unity of mutual amnesty with other centrists in order to form both an 'international publicity agency for assorted "leftward-moving" bureaucracies' and to retain an organizational fig leaf to cover

---

8   **Editors' Note:** July 26 refers to pro-Castro elements in Cuba and among Cuban-Americans in the US Local 1199 refers to a left-wing trade union, concentrated in New York City, of hospital and health care workers. SNCC refers to the radical civil rights group, Student Nonviolent Coordinating Committee.

their break with the essential substance of proletarian internationalism – the struggle to build a world party of the workers.

Given these profound differences with Revolutionary Marxism, it is to belabor the obvious to insist *merely* upon the centrist character of the SWP. On the contrary, it is critically important, in accepting the characterization of the SWP, not to be swept away and into a split perspective as though centrism equaled some kind of political leprosy. To quote a 'Letter to Ed' of 18 October 1961 which deals with this question:

> In the past few years the party has begun to react to opportunities by turning each one into a cycle of opportunism until the given opening is exhausted. Each time a selection takes place, some – notably the Weiss group – get worse and move toward liquidationism, but others react and are impelled in a leftward direction. This process has just begun, if one stops to view the SWP historically. There are two roads open. Either each wave of oppositionals will let themselves get washed out of the party, making it even harder for succeeding left-wingers, or each opportunist venture into fresh fields will augment the revolutionary Marxists with additional forces.

5 The SWP as a Rightward-Moving Centrist Party

Centrism is a phrase which covers a multitude of sins. As Trotsky put it: 'Speaking formally and descriptively, centrism is composed of all those trends within the proletariat and on its periphery which are distributed between reformism and Marxism and which most often represent various stages of evolution from reformism to Marxism and vice versa'.

The SWP falls short of being a left-centrist party, that is, one of those organizations or groupings (often moving left from the social democrats or out of the CP) which genuinely desires and seeks to work for the socialist revolution but suffers some internal limitation in the form of ideological or organizational baggage which it is unable to transcend in practice. (E.g. the Workers Party USA, 1941–46; the Austrian Revolutionary Socialists, 1934–38; the left-wing of the POUM at various times).

The SWP's practical excursions into activity bear not *merely* the stamp of being mistaken or inhibited in some way from a revolutionary standpoint, but in addition have become opportunist in intent. The theoretical or political 'explanations' are just that, not guides to revolutionary action, rather 'covers' – rationalizations to maintain a revolutionary rhetoric. Comrade Mage's recent

'Critical Notes on the Political Committee Draft 'Problems of the Fourth International and the Next Steps'' is nothing but a political exposé of a whole series of such rationalizations.

The disease of the SWP is degenerative in character and some insight and guidance can be gained for us by comparison with the CPUSA which was undergoing a degenerative process in the period 1924–34. However, it is important to keep in mind the quite different circumstances and mechanism in the case of the SWP.

The SWP in its leadership has become a very old party. From 1928 to the present – 34 years – it has been led by the same continuous and little changing body of personnel. Thus it is the most long-lived, ostensibly revolutionary, organization in history. Its current National Committee must have one of the highest average ages of any communist movement ever.

While the leadership is old, many of the leading rank and file party stalwarts at the local branch level are middle-aged and comfortably well off – skilled workers with many years seniority and homeowners to boot. Most extreme, but no means unique in this respect, is one of the two largest party branches, Los Angeles.

6 General and Long-Term Conclusions re the SWP

The divisions within the SWP are irreconcilable since they reflect differences which are and will ultimately be reducible to the difference between reform vs. revolution. It is a strong temptation in politics to succumb to impatience and seek to artificially accelerate what is deemed inevitable in the long run into an immediately posed issue. The break of the SP with Marxism has taken place over 'foreign' issues about which many subjectively revolutionary members are insensitive and unaroused.

The process of clarification within the SWP will not be complete until the party has to face up to major class struggles within the United States. From now until such a time the role of the revolutionary Marxists within the party must be that of an aggressive, political polarizing force.

The fundamental task of the minority must be to win unambiguously the mantle of Trotskyism, of recognition as the revolutionary Marxist party within this country.

5 Call for the Reorganization of the Minority Tendency[9]
(*1962*)

Tim Wohlforth et al.

1. The tendency expresses its general political agreement with the tendency of the International Committee which has agreement around the 1961 International Perspectives Resolution presented by the Socialist Labour League. It must, therefore, begin fro the standpoint of its responsibilities towards the political struggles of this tendency in relation to the construction of the revolutionary party in the United States.

The tendency recognizes that the building of the SWP as a revolutionary party depends on and derives from its adherence to the revolutionary international perspective and approach.

2. The tendency must pay particular attention to the development of a perspective for work in the United States and the Negro movement. The main political work of the tendency within the party will be to patiently explain the nature of Pabloite revisionism and liquidationism as a method, and its relation to the problem of developing a concretely revolutionary perspective for work in the trade union and Negro movement.

3. The tendency must recognize that the SWP is the main instrument for the realization of socialism in the U.S. There is no other organization outside the party which can decisively aid the struggle for socialism at the present time. Our comrades must therefore work as loyal party members; contribute to all aspects of the work, literary and practical, taking part in all the party's electoral activity and sub drives [i.e. campaigns to secure subscriptions to the *Militant*] and accepting the administrative decisions of the leadership even though we might be very much against them.

Members of the tendency must recognize that the SWP is their party and they must speak as people who are responsible for their party. The difficulties of the party must not be exploited in a factional way. These must be seen as

---

9   Wohlforth et al. 1963, pp. 44–5.

the overhead price for lack of political clarification. Since the responsibility for this clarification now rests squarely on the shoulders of the tendency, to make factional capital out of the party's difficulties would be nothing more than shelving that task which is the main purpose for the existence of the tendency.

The tendency must not make premature characterizations of the leadership of the SWP except of those, such as Weiss and Swabeck, who have clearly revealed their Pabloism in theory and practice.

The center group which is, of course, the majority cannot be described as a finished tendency in the same way as the Pabloites. To be sure there are elements of centrism in its thinking and activity, but these do not predominate. To characterize the SWP as a finished centrist tendency is to give up the political battle before it has begun.

We must believe that by common work and political discussion it will be possible to win a majority of the party to adopt a correct line on Pabloism and for the building of the revolutionary party in the United States.

4. The present tendency shall dissolve and shall re-establish itself on the basis of the preceding points.

5. Only those comrades who accept this outlook can be considered part of the tendency.

6 Radical Laborism Versus Bolshevik Leadership[10]
(*Excerpts, 1965*)

Richard Kirk and Clara Kaye (Richard Fraser and Clara Fraser)

Character of the Present Leadership

Thirteen years have elapsed since the fight with the Cochranites.

Until 1961, the stewardship of the SWP was nominally held jointly by the current regime and the Weiss group leaders. With the elimination of the Weiss group, the Dobbs-Kerry group entrenched itself and established a political monopoly of the leadership.

What are the principal achievements of the existing leadership since consolidating themselves?

1. The withdrawal from Cuba defense work and from trips to Cuba designed to break the travel ban.
2. The reduction of the once-independent youth to a chattel of the SWP National Office, and the prolonged insulation of these youth from the ferment around them in the general student movement.
3. The removal of all political-minority representation on the Political Committee; the avowed intention of destroying all minority formations, pockets and opinions in the party at large; and the tidal wave of expulsions on ephemeral grounds and in an unprecedentedly compulsive manner.
4. Recurrent disasters in our relations with the northern Black struggle and an absolute self-segregation from the southern struggle that is indefensible, especially on the incredible organizational grounds of 'no forces available'.
5. Rejection of obvious and principled opportunities to enlarge the party through serious fusion, regroupment or united front tactics.
6. Chronic organizational and political intimidation of all party advocates of the emancipation of women.

---

10   Kirk and Kaye 1965.

7. Ignominious default in regaining ideological hegemony over the radical movement, rationalized away by the canard of an absence of qualified personnel to accomplish this.
8. Refusal to assume organizational initiative of any kind in any mass movement, and the corollary of elevating basic organizational tasks of the party (fund-raising, subscription drives, paper sales) to the plane of political crusades, thereby reducing party life to internal maintenance plus election campaigns.

It is time to inquire into the nature of a leadership which has basically undermined the interventionist and democratic traditions of the party, and yet appears before the party with complacency and with an Organizational Resolution that validates everything it has done and then proceeds to shake the big stick at the remaining party dissidents.

What is Wrong with the Regime?

An analysis of it history and modus operandi leads inescapably to the conclusion that the present leadership is *Radical Laborite* in character and not Bolshevik.

It is Laborite because it believes that socialist politics on an extended scale will develop exclusively through the medium of a labor party based on the unions. It is Radical because of the powerful residue of the traditions of revolutionary socialism in the party.

In its social origin, the regime derives from the militant AFL unionism of the '30s, and its vision does not basically project beyond the trade union upsurge of the distant future that will lead to the labor party. This myopia lends an antipolitical cast to its view of reality.

Not typical syndicalists, nor anti-party in the Cochranite sense, the regime nevertheless does not intervene decisively in the *real political life of the time* so long as the arenas of struggle and motion remain outside the labor movement and sometimes opposed to it. The regime permits participation in other movements (in a grudging response to pressure from party branches in the field) but the 'participation' proposed by the center is a follow-the-leader adaptation to the prevailing winds of whichever movement strikes its fancy at a given time. When controversy develops, as it must, within these movements, the word is usually, 'Get out!'

The rigidly unionistic framework of the regime's long-range strategy results not only in non-intervention but in a deep-rooted, anti-theoretical habit.

As a consequence of the single-minded unionistic-laboristic blueprint for revolution, the party has become increasingly constricted, rigid, conservative and turned-inward. This produces, in turn, deepening errors of theory, program, strategy and tactics in those areas demanding the greatest familiarity and precision of evaluation: the colonial revolution, youth, the peace movement, the Black struggle, the labor movement, women's emancipation and revolutionary regroupment.

The chief characteristics of the Radical Laborites, then, are fourfold: they are non-interventionist, contemptuous of theory, union-bound in strategical orientation, and politically unstable in their reactions to any given juncture.

Non-interventionist

Exclusively focusing on the strategic variant of the labor party, the leadership is generally impervious and insensitive toward non-unionistic facets of the class struggle, and where it must evaluate the radical developments of any stage, it is inconsistent and ambivalent, apparently disinterested in fundamental (rather than reportorial) conjunctural analyses and the tactical shifts (other than inspection tours) indicated by conjunctural changes.

The regime recognizes struggles other than large union upheavals for general propaganda purposes only. Somewhat like the Socialist Labor Party clinging to its fetish of Socialist Industrial Unionism and riding out a half-century with election campaigns and journalistic commentary, the SWP seems resigned to a pattern of reporting and general socialist education.

The vital problems and needs of the newly developing vanguard groups in the country are treated superficially; except for correctly urging them to independent political action, the *Militant* has no more advice for them than the *National Guardian*, which approves them all, or the *Weekly People*, which is contemptuous of them all.

What should Malcolm X have done? What should the Student Non-Violent Coordinating Committee and the Mississippi Freedom Democratic Party do? Students for a Democratic Society? Progressive Labor Party? What next for the campus teach-ins? What program for women? Doesn't anybody have to do anything before the unions move? Evidently not. Evidently no current development involves urgent *political* problems, demanding direct intervention, initiative and agitation by the SWP.

Today's real and potential mass movements are considered interesting but secondary and subordinate phenomena, and their groping leaders are viewed by the SWP with an uncritical blindness which sometimes borders on adulation, or with excessive political suspicion and competitive organizational mistrust.

Compounding the error, the regime also neglects probes into the unions, preferring to wait until the time is more patently promising. Comrades working in unionized shops are instructed *not* to appear as 'union politicians' but to concentrate on recruiting to the party. Not only is this a false polarization of interdependent activities, but the logic involved would force the party not to conduct election campaigns on pain of being labeled 'Establishment Politicians' – an accusation frequently made against us which we constantly have to explain.

And today we must explain it again to the party leadership: wherever we are, we are revolutionary politicians working within extant structures in order to either change their policies or overthrow the structures themselves. If it is tactical to work within the framework of the *bourgeois state* via election campaigns, how downright sectarian it is to fear the guilt-by-association charge engendered by working within the framework of the degenerated class organs of the proletariat – the union movement!

We are not spectators of the internal union processes from within the unions; wherever our organizational participation in the union provides us a rostrum for principled propaganda and agitation, we would be foolish to abjure it.

It is significant that the Political Resolution stresses our 'propagandistic' nature and tasks, while the Organizational Resolution mentions the multitudinous areas of participation and intervention supposedly characteristic of our party and evidently supposed to be maintained. But this is a liturgical chant only. Business will proceed as usual, and intervention will be cooled off and discouraged wherever possible. The present projected 'intervention' in the youth antiwar movement, for instance, will produce as few lasting results and political continuity as did our participation in Fair Play for Cuba Committee, Committee to Aid the Monroe Defendants, Freedom Now Party, etc., because the orientation to mass work is either politically wrong or tactically superficial.

Anti-theoretical

Coming forward in the struggle against the petty-bourgeois intellectual opposition in 1941, and helping to defeat it, the present Dobbs-Kerry leadership gradually converted our suspicion of middleclass intellectuals into a rejection of all theoreticians in politics.

The Dobbs-Kerry regime tolerates 'theory' on foreign affairs which do not deeply concern it – China, Cuba, the International – and on questions of abstract philosophy, which are not troublesome as long as they remain abstract.

But any encroachment upon its domestic territory by a minority viewpoint is promptly labeled – intellectual! The word has become synonymous with 'oppositional' and with 'petty-bourgeois' and is used as an insult.

The dialectical interconnections of the Leninist concept of worker-Bolshevik, Marxist-intellectual, organizer-theoretician, etc., have been summarily split in two by the regime with the separate parts reassembled into new units. Theory/ideology is now the exclusive function of the regime, while the ranks and the organizers are expected to work at sub drives, fund drives, forums and campus activities, period. Naturally, this 'leave the thinking to us' law results in very little thought by anyone at all.

Minorities are answered not with logical political disputation, but with muddying distortion and fabrication of the issues, invective and personal-organizational attacks. Political arguments used to be serious and educational experiences for the entire party membership; today, any consistent or persistent theoretical, strategic or tactical difference provokes a reflex characteristic of the labor officialdom, echoing its intolerance, prejudices and sewer terminology.

Contempt for theory breeds an inability to tolerate criticism, and both traits are expressed in the anti-intellectualism of the radical laborites.

Neo-economist

The Dobbs-Kerry leadership is the second major negative tendency closely associated with labor unionism to appear in the SWP in the postwar period.

Between the present leadership and the Cochranites an obvious affinity existed, marked by the reluctance and tardiness of the Dobbs-Kerry break with Cochran. However, an important difference exists between these two factions.

The Minneapolis Teamsters Union and the Sailors Union of the Pacific (and Marine Firemen) were the first two mass labor bases won by the SWP and they produced the present leadership of the party.

These unions, not as socially and politically advanced in terms of overall program and ideology as the newer CIO unions, were nevertheless extremely militant in their pursuit of job benefits and resistance against government intervention into the unions.

They were therefore among the first objectives of the employer-government drive to housebreak the labor movement. The Teamsters came under fire immediately before World War II and the Sailors Union of the Pacific shortly after the war. The hierarchies of these unions joined forces with the bosses and the state to drive out the radicals, and the struggles which ensued forced a sharp and decisive break between the SWP and these unions, cutting off the present SWP leadership from its base of mass support.

The Cochranites, on the other hand, were still more or less firmly entrenched, mainly in the United Auto Workers, in 1951. They were propelled away from the party because they had a mass milieu and mass base to lean on and escape into as the witch hunt became general.

Centrist?

Of recent years, several opponents of the Dobbs-Kerry leadership both within and outside the party have characterized the majority as Centrist. The prevalence of this term requires an evaluation of the regime with respect to a definition of the word.

The Dobbs-Kerry regime does reveal definite political deviations from revolutionary criteria.

1 *The Regime Certainly Flirts with Reformism in Three Areas*
Their approach to the Black question is reformist, as most glaringly revealed in the curious proposition that All-Black political action is the solution to the race question in the North while 'Troops to the South' will raise the political level of Blacks there.

Secondly, the party regime has substituted the '30 hours work for 40 hours pay' slogan for Trotsky's sliding scale of wages and hours, instead of connecting them. While 30–40 is an important demand to press, and may obviously have positive consequences, it still does not, by itself, necessarily constitute a bridge from reformist to revolutionary consciousness. On the contrary, it may become a means of strengthening reformism at a given stage. And in sectors of the economy undergoing automation, the 30–40 slogan doesn't scratch the surface of the vast unemployment problem.

Thirdly, the very barrenness of the Political Committee's current Political Resolution, void of either conjunctural analysis or revolutionary perspective, holds the door open to further flirtations with reformism.

2 *The Political Reflex of the Leadership to Critical Events and Shifts is Demonstrably Non-revolutionary*
Forceful intervention by comrades Cannon and Graham was needed to rectify the hands-off, Third Camp policy adopted at the outbreak of the Korean War.

The political line during the Cuban missile crisis was at best ambivalent and at worst bordered on joining the anti-Soviet hysteria, only from the 'left'.

The regime betrays an obsession with 'security' (as in the Cuba trips) which more often than not attempts to mask an unsure policy. Their unseemly concern with respectability occasionally veers toward panic, as evinced after the Kennedy assassination, revealing marked instability, impressionism and legalistic defensiveness. The *reductio ad absurdum* of this approach was performed by the Young Socialist Alliance leadership when it issued national mimeographed instructions to its convention delegates, including married couples, forbidding them to 'shack up' with each other because of 'security'.

3   *The Disinterest in and Hostility towards Any Movement for Women's Emancipation Reveals Another Facet of the Basically Non-Bolshevik Outlook of the Present Leadership*

All right. Do all these enumerated weaknesses add up to centrism?

Trotsky defined centrism as *an unstable political formation in motion between reformism and Bolshevism.*

The course of motion in centrism is to be found largely in external social forces which exert both reformist and revolutionary pressures. But the one thing which clearly characterizes the SWP leadership is its ability to insulate itself from all external pressures by means of a rigid sectarianism.

Isolated from *both* the reformist and revolutionary pressures exerted by the mass movements, it is subject to the direct pressure of the capitalist class, with no counter-pressure from the mass movements.

The effects of this pressure have been thus far insufficient to cause *motion* in the SWP; rather, a certain stagnation grips the party and its leadership.

If and when the SWP majority relates itself to the existing mass movements, and permits itself to feel and react to the contradictory and alternating pressures generated there, its true and definitive political character will emerge. Life will show whether the present indefinite state of the core of the majority signifies centrism. Everyone, in fact, will be tested under these conditions.

Meanwhile, we do not yet see that the political designation of centrism has an important bearing on the problem of party leadership in the SWP today. More important at this moment and decisive for the future are its sectarianism, self-insulation, irrational suspicion of new vanguard formations – particularly anything emanating from the CP milieu or the South – and insensitivity to the problems and struggles of the most oppressed.

These traits derive not so much from centrist faults as from a Laborite-Economist reflex operating in the period of a *degenerating* labor movement.

Actually the regime has not changed very much in the past two decades. Vast changes in the objective situation have simply exposed another side of its character.

Strategy of the Holding Operation

This is a state of suspended animation which freezes program and cements the cadre in a decades-long cliffhanging position until the resurgence of organized labor – the main question – is at hand. Then, the party is supposed to drop down to *terra firma* and move in. The present 'tightened-up' propagandistic activism is only a new form of the basic holding operation, designed to make it palatable to energetic youth.

This self-paralysis and self-segregation, this marking time and treading water, is constantly being disturbed by the pressure of changes, turns and crises provided by everyday events. The economy gyrates in abrupt swings and cycles, social relations shift, and political repercussions accumulate; the rhythm of revolutionary politics, like that of life, is the rhythm of the seesaw. But the regime will not be provoked into altering its freeze-in; it equates programmatic firmness with the posture of the spectator and tries to modulate and modify the significance of every development to fit its own long-range timetable.

Its perspective and schedule, however, based on a concept of relatively uneventful evolution, leave no room for relating to the leaps and twists of the real political world. The regime hopes to see a growth in the party from small to big to bigger, and then, someday, on to Power. Unfortunately, such a smooth and predictable progression is not in the nature of things, as the German Social Democracy came to learn. Behind the welfare state facade of US capitalism lie a voracious imperialism, the Mississippi police state, the Vietnam War, etc., all producing cataclysmic reactions. It is possible to keep one's head and balance only if the chronic imbalance and inbred surprises of the system are appreciated and anticipated as the norm. But the party is rocked and disoriented at virtually every new and unexpected juncture because it is not geared to dialectics, materialism or political flexibility.

The very nature of monopoly capital dictates the swift sequence of widely varying conjunctures. A fixed program that does not grow, and a petrified long-range strategy that persists no matter what, are results of contempt for the changing winds of reality. The SWP today has asserted its superiority over the basic laws of political motion: it promises that hanging on, hanging tough, waiting it out and letting the struggle *come to us*, is sufficient for eventual victory.

In a revolutionary period, we expect the masses to intervene in their own destiny. We expect a revolutionary party, however, to be doing this *all the time*.

7 The Organizational Character of the Socialist Workers Party[11]
(*Excerpts, 1965*)

Farrell Dobbs and George Novack

I   **Preamble**

Differences over our organizational principles and practices have arisen periodically in the development of our party. It has been our experience that in periods of sharp internal political dispute there often arises, as a corollary, a conflict over our basic concepts of democratic centralism, expressed either implicitly or explicitly. In such cases it becomes the responsibility of the party leadership to restate and reaffirm the concepts which govern our organizational forms and procedures.

At the founding convention of the SWP in 1938, after the split from the 'all-inclusive' Socialist Party, cognizance was first taken of the need to codify the basic Leninist concepts of democratic centralism. This was done in the form of a resolution adopted by the convention. The action was intended to serve a double purpose: (1) To effect a codification of our organizational concepts to bring them into line with the revolutionary principles embodied in the program of the founding convention. (2) To cement the fusion of the left wing split-off from the SP with the Trotskyist cadres who comprised the most homogeneous Marxist tendency in the newly fanned party by making available to the ranks a clarifying statement of our Leninist views on party organization.

The Leninist concept of democratic centralism was subsequently challenged, most notably in the struggle with the Burnham-Shachtman opposition in 1939–40 and in the Cochranite split of 1953. On each occasion, the party reaffirmed its basic organizational principles and amplified them to ward off and defeat the specific challenges to our concepts of democratic centralism.

In the recent political dispute which culminated in the expulsion by the National Committee plenum of the leaders of the Robertson faction for disloyalty we noted: (1) The existence of a considerable number of younger com-

---

11   Socialist Workers Party National Committee 1965.

rades who, because they joined our ranks after 1953, were relatively unfamiliar with the past disputes in the party over the 'organization' question, did not have available the documents of those disputes and were only vaguely acquainted with our basic concept of democratic centralism. (This category does not include the disloyal Robertsonite leaders who consider themselves 'experts' on this score.) (2) The existence of various individuals and tendencies who spoke as defenders of the Robertsonites against the disciplinary action taken by the plenary session of the party leadership for their blatant disloyalty to the party. It is contended that such disciplinary action constituted a 'violation' of our concepts of democratic centralism. In the course of the discussion representatives and defenders of the Robertson group advanced views which the party leadership, in its overwhelming majority, consider at variance with our basic concepts of party organization and procedure. It thus becomes imperative to clarify, once again, the Leninist concept of democratic centralism to remove whatever confusion has arisen on this score and to amplify, in the light of the current controversy, our basic ideas on party organization.

To this end, the December 1963 plenum of the National Committee designated a drafting commission composed of comrades Cannon, Warde and Dobbs, to submit a draft codifying our fundamental views on democratic centralism as they have evolved out of past controversies and introducing such amplifications as are indicated by the conflicting views manifested in the current discussion.

II Record of Party Struggle for Its Organizational Principles

The organizational structure and practices of a Marxist party are not immutable. They are derived from the major tasks to be accomplished at a given stage of the class struggle. The need for an ideologically homogeneous and democratically centralized organization flows from the perspective and actuality of deepening social crisis and sharpening class conflict which makes imperative the revolutionary solution of basic social problems. The anticipation and active preparation of such revolutionary developments in the United States has determined the kind of party our movement has set out to build from its birth.

Its organization form is intended to serve the central aims set forth in our program of abolishing capitalism and reorganizing America on a socialist basic. Only a combat party of the Leninist type is capable of organizing and leading the working class and its allies to the conquest of power in the main fortress of world imperialism. Confronted as the people are by the most powerful and ruthless ruling class in the world, the party of the American revolution must be conceived and constructed as a cohesive and disciplined combat organization. That is why our party has sought to base itself on the tested and proven Leninist rules of organization, summed up in the concept of democratic centralism.

Democratic centralism is a dialectical concept which does not lend itself to rigid definition and application regardless of time, place and circumstance. Our party has forged its own specific form of the Leninist concept in the heat of struggle under concrete American conditions. The party's organizational principles are an integral part of its living history. These clearly-defined and well-established principles are ready to be taught to young revolutionaries coming into our ranks and to be defended against attempts to water them down and thereby corrode the revolutionary fabric of the party.

As a combat organization the party strives for political homogeneity in the sense that admission to its ranks requires fundamental agreement with its program and principles. For similar reasons unconditional loyalty and disciplined conduct are required as a condition of membership. To safeguard party unity in debating and deciding policy, a conscious effort is made to teach comrades to argue out problems on the basis of principles and to act always from the standpoint of principle. Along these lines the party has developed in a free and democratic internal atmosphere. All individuals and tendencies have a full chance to contribute to the development of the party and to the shaping of its leading cadres.

The party is guided by the concept of democratic centralism in regulating both its public activity and its internal affairs. Full rights are accorded to minorities as conditioned by the democratic principle of majority rule. Minority views may be presented in internal discussion at the proper time and in an appropriate manner as determined by the party. Once a decision has been made on disputed issues the minority is subordinated to the majority. Between conventions authority becomes centralized and the party confronts the outside world with a single policy, that of the majority. All members are required to subordinate themselves to the policies and decisions of the party. Official party bodies determine what is correct procedure, and no individual or group can arrogate that right.

Through these democratic-centralist practices the party maintains its role as a revolutionary vanguard. Its character as a combat organization is safeguarded. Unity in action is preserved. Firmness of political line is assured and the party is enabled to maintain its principles unadulterated.

Relation of Organization to Politics

Building a Leninist-type party entails uncommon difficulties because of this country's position as the powerhouse of world capitalist reaction. Alien class pressures bear down upon the party with enormous force in a hostile political environment. At times these pressures generate centrifugal currents in our ranks. Ideas, moods and motivations at odds with our program and traditions penetrate the party's internal life. Those affected tend to translate their own nervousness into exaggerated criticism of the party and begin to develop basic differences with the party line.

The seemingly abstract relation of organization to politics then becomes very real, because those who develop basic political differences also develop an urge to throw off restrictions imposed upon them by the party's organizational concepts. They become antagonistic to democratic centralism. Attempts are made to undermine the party's homogeneity and make it amorphous; to render it diffuse in class composition, identity and outlook; to revise its principles; to weaken its discipline and unity in action; and to debase the meaning of party membership.

Party building therefore involves a continuous process of cadre selection. While striving constantly to attract new forces, we also find it necessary from time to time to part company with those in our ranks who become disoriented. In the struggle for our principles the party creates stable cadres educated against both opportunism and sectarianism. Through long experience the party has learned to be on the alert for signs of opportunist tendencies toward capitulation to alien class pressures and to mobilize for struggle against them. Similarly the party is schooled to oppose sectarian abstentionism and ultra-left adventures designed to leap over objective difficulties. While combatting both opportunism and sectarianism, the party educates its cadres to shape their course along the basic lines of the Transitional Program adopted by the Trotskyist movement in 1938.

Transitional Program

Central to the Transitional Program is recognition that mankind's crisis in the struggle for socialism is primarily a crisis of revolutionary leadership. It is the aim of the Trotskyist movement to build a combat organization capable of filling the leadership void. To do so the party can countenance neither opportunist adaptation to the status quo nor sectarian abstention from living struggle at its prevailing level of development. The party intervenes in the daily struggle with transitional demands stemming from today's conditions and today's consciousness within sections of the mass movement. All these demands are aimed toward leading the masses to one final conclusion: the conquest of power by the working class.

Only a tightly-knit combat party can meet these revolutionary tasks. In the struggle to build such a party cadre selection goes on as a constant molecular process. New individuals are attached to the movement and some already in our ranks drop away. The proportions between these two categories vary with the ups and downs of external political trends. At given conjunctures the process may pass beyond individual selection and involve organized groups. In a political upturn a leap in party growth may be accomplished through a principled unification with other forces who are moving toward Trotskyist positions. Or at another stage an organized group may split away from the party from either sectarian or opportunist motives. Thus unifications and splits are alike methods of building the party, each representing a concentrated form of expression of the continuous process of cadre selection.

The SWP had its origins in the break of the Trotskyist Left Opposition from the Communist Party when the latter succumbed to Stalinist degeneration in the Twenties. Starting with such cadres as could be salvaged from the CP, the pioneer Trotskyists reached out for new forces turning revolutionary in the labor radicalization of the Thirties. Some reinforcements were secured through individual recruitment, but the main gains were registered through unifications with the American Workers Party in 1934 and soon thereafter with the left wing of the Socialist Party. No less decisive in shaping the viable Trotskyist cadres of the Thirties was the 1935 split of the sectarians in our ranks who opposed the unifications.

Petty-Bourgeois Opposition

The founding of the SWP in 1938 marked the completion of such unifications as were possible under the given conditions. Adverse political trends were already developing as the labor radicalization subsided; and when World War II began in 1939 the party was plunged into a deep internal crisis. The petty-bourgeois wing of the party quickly capitulated to the pressures of bourgeois public opinion which bore down heavily upon the movement as the ruling class prepared for American entry into the war. An organized opposition, led by Burnham, Shachtman and Ahern, began a vicious fight to overthrow the party's program and principles.

Their first panicky impulse was to rush to the mimeograph machines and issue a call for the masses to rise in spontaneous opposition to war. Their next step was to renounce the Trotskyist position of unconditional defense of the Soviet Union against imperialist attack. Through Burnham they questioned many of the principles of Marxism. Through Shachtman they began to replace Trotsky's definition of the Soviet Union under Stalin as a degenerated workers' state with the false theory of bureaucratic collectivism.

In a frenzy to free themselves from party discipline the petty-bourgeois opposition opened an all-out attack on democratic centralism. They demanded the 'right' to publish their own public organ. To grant their demand would have destroyed the centralist character of the party; it would have meant the creation of dual party structures and a complete breakdown of discipline. That, of course, was precisely what the petty-bourgeois opposition wanted, as they demonstrated when they split from the party upon being defeated at the 1940 convention.

The same convention reaffirmed the Leninist character of the party in its resolution on 'The Organizational Conclusions of the Present Discussion'. Dealing specifically with the opposition's demands, the resolution reaffirmed and made more explicit the party's unconditional right to control the public activity of all its members. After the split the party published a book by Comrade Cannon, *The Struggle for a Proletarian Party*, in which the organizational lessons of the 1939–40 internal struggle are documented and analyzed. The book constitutes a valuable guide to young revolutionists eager to learn the Leninist principles of organization.

American Theses

Cleansed of the petty-bourgeois defectors from Trotskyism the party stood firm throughout the war. In the 1944–46 labor upsurge it was able to win many new rebels to its ranks, thereby recouping the losses experienced in the 1940 split. With a confidence tempered in the fires of adversity, the party charted its post-war perspectives through the American Theses adopted at the 1946 convention.

With revolutionary advances abroad confronted by the military interventions of US imperialism, the Theses assert, the role of America in the world is decisive. The showdown battles for the communist future of mankind will be fought in this country. A socialist victory here, merging with the world revolutionary forces, will put an end to the outlived capitalist system as a whole.

As against all petty-bourgeois skeptics, the Theses affirm the capacity of the American working class to fulfill its historic role as an organic part of the world revolutionary process. US capitalism is heading toward a deep social and political crisis that will precipitate an unparalleled mass radicalization. The working class will acquire political class consciousness and organization in a sweeping movement similar to the rise of the CIO. Given the decisive leadership of a revolutionary vanguard party, labor and its allies will move toward the conquest of political power.

It is to fill precisely that vanguard leadership role that the SWP has shaped its political course and organizational structure, following the example of the Bolshevik party of Lenin and Trotsky. The SWP has hammered out its revolutionary program in ideological battles and it defends that program against every kind of revisionist assault upon it. The party has assembled a strong core of professional leadership which it strives to expand in order to strengthen party work and maintain leadership continuity. It aims to train its cadres in the irreconcilable spirit of a combat party of revolution, a party aspiring to lead the workers to victory in a struggle for political power.

Pessimism and Impressionism

The party's capacity to uphold the perspectives of the American Theses was soon to be put to the test under worsening objective conditions. A reactionary atmosphere of cold war and witch-hunt replaced the favorable climate of the labor upsurge in the mid-Forties. A new minority opposition, born of petty-bourgeois pessimism and impressionism, developed within the party under the leadership of Cochran. It was an unprincipled combination, divided as to whether political hope should be placed in self-reform of the Soviet bureaucracy, or in the miracle of an American union bureaucracy turned militant. What held the combination together, until they split from the SWP, was their common loss of faith in the revolutionary capacity of the working class. They denied that anybody could build a party capable of smashing the bureaucratic obstacles within the labor movement and leading the masses toward the conquest of power.

As always happens when basic political differences arise, the Cochranites began a campaign to undermine the party's democratic-centralist principles. Their attack centered on an attempt to subvert the principle of majority rule by imposing a minority veto of majority decisions. At the May 1953 plenum, in the middle of the internal struggle, the National Committee responded with a resolution reaffirming the organizational principles laid down by the 1938 and 1940 party conventions. The resolution also contained a third section rejecting the Cochranite attempt to set up 'dual power' in the leadership and specifically affirming the application of majority rule through official party bodies. Soon thereafter the Cochranites went on a sit-down strike against the party which led to their suspension in November 1953 and later to their formal expulsion. In the political conflict a big majority of the membership rebuffed the Cochranite attack on the Transitional Program and American Theses.

Leaving aside similar experiences of lesser degree, such are the landmarks of internal struggle through which the party has worked out and maintained its organizational cohesion. Despite extremely-prolonged objective adversities, all revisionist attacks have been fought off. The party remains firmly committed to its vanguard aim of leading the American workers and their allies to the conquest of political power. Battle-tested cadres have been developed and a vital core of professional leadership created. The party's basic principles as a combat organization have been clearly established: firmness in political line; unity in action; disciplined conduct in all internal party affairs; unconditional loyalty to the party.

New Attack on Principles

Today the party faces yet another attack on its organizational principles which comes as a reflex to the appearance of new political differences. Toward the end of the Fifties an unusually protracted internal discussion began, centered on the Chinese question, Negro Struggle, Cuban question and reunification of the world movement. Minority groupings took form around one and another issue. A factional atmosphere was soon generated inside the party, especially by a minority combination made up of the Robertson-Mage-White and Wohlforth-Philips groups.

It was plain from the outset that the Robertson-Wohlforth combination had the idea that middle class intellectuals must take over American Trotskyism and set it straight. They began with factional sorties in the youth around several issues. Later they linked themselves with the Healy faction of the Socialist Labor League in a declaration of war on the SWP policies and leadership. They opposed party policy on such key issues as world unification, Cuba, Algeria, the Negro Struggle. In the name of 'proletarian' intervention in the mass movement they advanced a hodgepodge of sectarian abstentionism and harebrained adventurism. In general they showed the usual traits of the rootless petty-bourgeois radical caught up in frenzied self-delusion.

In the fall of 1962 the combination split into the Robertson-Mage-White and Wohlforth-Philips components, apparently in a dispute over tactics in their factional attempt to overturn the party's program and principles. They entered the 1963 pre-convention discussion as rival factions but without any significant differences in political line. As the discussion proceeded they took pot-shots at one another that helped to reveal the depth of their hostility toward the party majority; an outstanding example was the Wohlforth faction's revelations about anti-party documents secretly circulated by the Robertsonites. At the party convention both factions were defeated politically by an overwhelming majority, and both were excluded from representation on the incoming National Committee because their loyalty to the party was in question.

Expulsion of Robertsonites

After the convention the Political Committee requested a Control Commission investigation into the Wohlforthite charges concerning the anti-party attitude of the Robertson faction. The Commission obtained copies of documents by Robertson, Ireland and Harper that had been circulated behind the back of the party. Its findings were reported to the Political Committee for action as provided by the party constitution.

These Robertsonite documents constituted a declaration of unending war on the party which was characterized as 'right-centrist'. Policies were outlined for that amounted to a factional raid on the party. In practice it meant double recruitment, first to the tight faction, then formally to the party, on the basis of the faction's own program and methods; indoctrination of contacts against the party program, convention decisions and organizational principles before they applied for party membership. They ridiculed the idea of party patriotism and sneered at the concept of party loyalty as a 'religion'. Faction discipline was put before the party discipline in their party-wrecking expedition.

Because of their disloyalty, in word and deed, the Political Committee suspended from membership Robertson, Mage and White as leaders responsible for the factional disloyalty; also Harper and Ireland for their complicity in the secret documents. Further disciplinary action was referred to the National Committee. The December 1963 plenum approved the PC action and expelled the five from the party.

The disciplinary action against the Robertsonites has been assailed by all organized minorities within the party and by some individual members. It has been contended from one and another quarter that party loyalty is only an idea; that disciplinary measures can be taken only upon specific proof of overt acts of indiscipline; that the party leadership has introduced new organizational concepts in an effort to settle political differences by suppressing the right of organized dissent; that the leadership is trying to make the party monolithic in the Stalinist manner.

Party Loyalty

Not one of those assertions and accusations contains an iota of truth. To begin with, loyalty is far more than an abstract idea; it is a standard of political conduct. The party's whole democratic-centralist structure is founded on the rock of organizational loyalty. Without loyal members the party, as a voluntary organization, would have no basis upon which to maintain the necessary discipline in carrying out its revolutionary tasks. Disloyal people don't believe in the party, they won't pitch in selflessly to help build it, and they will resist and evade discipline. That is why the organizational resolution adopted at the SH-P's founding convention specified that unconditional loyalty to the party is required of every member.

Brushing aside that specific provision of party law, an attempt is made to brand unconstitutional the disciplinary procedure against the Robertsonites which hinges on the issue of party loyalty. It is charged that the trial procedures under Article VIII of the party constitution have been violated. The charge is unfounded as it ignores the fact that Article VIII covers procedures in handling disciplinary matters originating at the branch level. When the National Control Commission acts, however, its procedures are governed entirely by Article VI of the party constitution, and the provisions of the latter article were followed to the letter in the Robertson case.

Another charge is directed at the Control Commission itself, which is alleged to have exceeded its authority in demanding and 'presuming to evaluate' the Robertsonite secret documents. Again the charge is utterly without foundation. Article VI authorizes the Control Commission to investigate 'any individual or circumstance', and it obligates party members 'to furnish the Control Commission or its authorized representatives with any information they may require'. As to its alleged 'presumption' in evaluating the Robertsonite documents, Article VI provides that the Control Commission 'shall present its findings and *recommendations* to the Political Committee for action'. (Emphasis added).

Acting strictly within its constitutional authority, the Control Commission obtained the documents in question. Upon examination it found that they manifested a hostile and disloyal attitude toward the party, and it said so in its report to the Political Committee. Taking the same view, the Political Committee suspended from membership those held primarily responsible for the documents. The plenum approved the Political Committee action, and it expelled from the party those the Political Committee had suspended.

An Anti-party Faction

Although the action against the Robertsonites was unique in one respect: the form of the evidence involved, it had its precedent and justification in the loyalty issue over which they were expelled. Usually an anti-party faction tries to conceal its divisive aims until it is ready to split, and its disruptive course must be exposed through its disloyal acts. The Robertsonites seemed to think, however, that they could get away with their secret circulation of anti-party documents, using them in their factional raid on the party, until they themselves decided the time had come for an open split. Although given every opportunity to repudiate the documents and affirm their loyalty to the party, not one of them did so. They seemed to believe the party would have to submit to their wrecking operation until and unless specific acts of disloyalty could be proved against them.

The plenum transcript on the subject shows that disloyal acts were indeed committed by the Robertsonites, but that is beside the point. With or without proof of specific acts, the party had the right, and its leadership the duty, to stop the self-indicted factional raiders who were out to wreck our movement. Any doubts on that score should have been definitively resolved by their attitude and actions since the expulsions in peddling malicious gossip to the capitalist press as part of their attempt to smear the SWP publicly.

Some opponents of the disciplinary action have argued, however, that in principle anyone can advocate anything he pleases within the party; and the policy followed in the Robertsonite case has been likened to capitalist use of thought-control measures. The argument is false on both counts. The SWP is a voluntary organization which individuals or groups are free to join or leave as they agree or disagree with its program, aims and activities. But they are not free to accept or reject the imposition of governmental authority. If they resist the regulations governing society as laid down by the state power, they are not simply told they will have to depart and organize a rival party of their own; they are threatened with jail. That is why governmental attempts to proscribe views are anti-democratic; and it is idiotic to accuse the SWP of aping the capitalist government in the Robertson case.

Basis of Party's Existence

As a voluntary and revolutionary organization the SWP has the right to define the basis for its existence. The party exercises that prerogative by putting distinct limits on the right of advocacy within its ranks, as determined by majority decision through the official bodies, acting in compliance with the party's program, principles and convention decisions. Disloyal people not only cannot advocate anything they please within the party; they cannot be allowed to carry on their advocacy behind the back of the party. Those who don't want to comply with the party's democratically-decided definition of the basis for its existence have the right to withdraw from the organization and form one of their own.

It has also been claimed that the leadership, while acting in the name of striving for relative internal homogeneity, is actually trying to make the party monolithic. To lightly make so grave a charge is irresponsible, because it infers a Stalinist form of degeneration within the SWP; and the charge is baseless. Monolithism means the suppression of all political dissent and the imposition of rigid political conformity by a dictatorial bureaucracy. It is a Stalinist corruption of Leninism which our Trotskyist party rejects and combats. We are guided by the Leninist concept of relative internal homogeneity based on loyal adherence to the party's program and principles and voluntary acceptance of its discipline. These qualities enable the party to maintain internal stability and to function dynamically in its public activity, even though conjunctural political differences arise. Ample room is provided for the expression of dissident views, even major ones of serious import. The right to organize tendencies and factions is safeguarded. All the leadership demands is that every member be loyal to the party's program and principles and be disciplined.

Factionalism and Party Unity

A properly conducted discussion of internal political differences contributes to the good and welfare of the party. It facilitates the hammering out of a correct political line and it helps to educate the membership. These benefits derive from the discussion provided that every comrade hears all points of view and the whole party is drawn into the thinking about the questions in dispute. In that way the membership as a whole can intervene in disputes, settle them in an orderly way by majority decision and get on with the party work. This method has been followed by American Trotskyism throughout its history and has resulted in an effective clarification of all controversial issues.

Concentration on private discussions of disputed issues, on the other hand, tends to give the comrades involved a one-sided view and warps their capacity for objective political judgment.

Inexperienced comrades especially are made the target of such lop-sided discussion methods. The aim is to line them up quickly in a closed caucus, and prejudice their thinking before they have heard an open party debate. When dissident views are introduced into the party in that manner groupings tend to form and harden, and the dissenting views tend to assert themselves in disruptive fashion, before the party as a whole has had a chance to face and act on the issues in dispute.

A relatively homogeneous party should be able to resolve episodic differences without resort to factionalism. Even when comrades have differences of a serious nature over one or another particular aspect of party policy it does not follow that they should rush to form a faction. Objectivity requires that they do no more than form an ideological tendency which confines its activities to a principled collective effort to argue for a change in the given policy; and the tendency should present its views openly before the whole party in a responsible and disciplined manner.

A tight-knit faction, however, is qualitatively different from an ideological tendency. It tends to become in effect a party within the party, with its own program and its own discipline. Such a formation cannot be justified politically unless its organizers consider their differences so fundamental that they must conduct a showdown fight for control of the party. Factionalism means war inside the party, and it entails the possibility and danger of a split.

For these reasons internal party disputes should be conducted in an objective way, both to safeguard party unity and to educate the membership in principled politics. Comrades should not be hasty to organize internal groupings. When the party has made its decision on the issues in dispute, groupings formed during the polemical struggle should dissolve into the party as a whole.

Regulation of Internal Affairs

Temporary groupings that arise out of conjunctural political differences should not be perpetuated regardless of principled considerations indicating the need for their dissolution. If they are, it indicates that narrow group interests have been put ahead of basic party interests. A danger arises that such permanent formations may degenerate into unprincipled cliques bound together by personal associations; and their existence may drive others into counterformations. An atmosphere of aimless, endless internal conflict is generated that could tear the party to pieces.

It is precisely to safeguard itself from such harmful consequences of factional anarchy that the party exercises the right to regulate its internal affairs. While a decision is being reached, comrades holding dissident views receive all normal minority rights, including the right of organized dissent. After a party decision has been made the democratic rights of the majority take precedence. All members are required to accept the majority decision and help to carry it out. Comrades holding minority opinions are not disqualified from serving the party in any capacity; nor are they asked to give up their dissident views. They must simply await a new opportunity to present their views when internal discussion is again formally authorized.

Comrades opposed to expulsion of the Robertsonites disregarded the significance of the expression of party opinion at the July 1963 convention. An exceedingly long preparatory discussion had been held. Minorities received most of the space in an unprecedented volume of internal bulletins. During pre-convention discussion in the branches, and at the convention itself, minority reporters got generous time allotments. Democracy in action, as represented by the convention vote, showed a very strong majority, while the dissenting groups taken as a whole constituted only a weak minority. Through that decisive test of the relation of forces, the convention firmly decided the issues in dispute. The discussion was terminated for the time being; and all comrades were expected to pitch into party activity on the basis of the convention decisions.

Thought and Action

It shows disrespect for the opinions of the party membership when dissident comrades seek to proceed as though the convention vote meant nothing. To contend that differences have arisen in new forms, as has been said, is simply a pretext for continuing discussion of issues decided by the convention. Equally deceptive are the arguments that party comrades are thinking people who don't want to be reduced to simply doing organization chores, and that polemical discussions will liven up an otherwise dull branch meeting.

Without critical political think and rethinking one could not be a revolutionist. But there must be alternative periods for emphasis upon thought and action. The party is not a perpetual discussion circle whose chief function is to provide a forum where free-thinkers can express themselves whenever and however they please. Ours is a disciplined party of action. We discuss in order to arrive at a policy to serve as a guide for collective action and we decide in order to act as a united body with a single purpose. Those who say they find it impossible to function in such a party really mean they don't want to do much except talk. They are not serious militants worthy of a workers party.

Considering all the facts, it is ridiculous to charge the leadership with introducing new organizational concepts intended to suppress organized dissent. If new concepts have been introduced within the party, and they have, they don't come from the leadership; they come from those who challenge the elementary obligation of the party leadership to defend the integrity of the party against a wrecking operation. Although the present minorities have varying political differences with the majority and between themselves, they appear to hold a common wrong view on the question of internal party discipline.

The disloyal Robertsonites are defended on the grounds of alleged minority rights. It is claimed that an organized minority has the unconditional right to determine its own conduct inside the party. Discipline is held to apply only to public activity. Official party bodies are allegedly without right or power to regulate a minority's activities in organizing itself and presenting its political views.

To grant such demands for special license to organized minorities would strip the party of the right to regulate its internal affairs and would undermine its whole democratic-centralist structure. The democratic principle of majority rule would be overturned; discipline in public activity would be confounded; and all semblance of political homogeneity would be lost. The party would become converted into an all-inclusive federation of autonomous factions; it would degenerate into a political jungle where perpetual factional warfare prevailed.

Party of American Revolution

It is foolish to imagine that the coming American revolution can be led by a party honeycombed with political kibbitzers, professional 'democrats' who disdain the rights of the majority and factional hooligans. In this country the masses and their socialist spokesmen face the most vicious ruling class. At home its government deals with social protest through legal and extra-legal thugs armed with clubs, tear gas, fire hoses, cattle prods, dogs, guns and bayonets. The ruling class made America the shame of the world as the first and only nation to use atomic weapons against other human beings. The rulers of this country unleash brutal military interventions against anti-capitalist rebels abroad; and they repeatedly go to the brink of nuclear war in their efforts to turn back the world revolutionary tide.

To go up against such a ruling class labor and its allies need the leadership of a cohesive and disciplined combat party. If our party is to meet that need it must once again beat back disintegrating factors which threaten and undermine its revolutionary vitality. The membership must be educated and reeducated in principled Trotskyist politics and the Leninist principles of democratic centralism. The party must tighten up against internal disruption, demand responsible conduct from every member, enforce discipline and require unconditional loyalty to the organization. While scrupulously protecting the normal democratic rights of minorities, the democratic principle of majority rule must be no less rigorously enforced. Only in that way can we approach our revolutionary tasks as *one* party with *one* program.

Again, and once again, comrades must be taught that party patriotism is part of revolutionary consciousness. Disloyalty and indiscipline must be looked upon as crimes that bring punishment. A party that aims to lead the most decisive revolution of our time must have members who believe in it, who want to help build it, and who are quick to defend it. People of that caliber must in turn have the kind of a party to which they can confidently dedicate their life and their hope for the socialist future.

III   Codification of Organizational Principles

From the whole experience of more than a century of working class struggle throughout the world we have derived the Leninist principles of organization, namely, democratic centralism. The same body of experience has demonstrated that there are no absolute guarantees for the preservation of the principle of democratic centralism, and no rigid formula that can be set down in advance, *a priori*, for its application under any and all circumstances. Proceeding from certain fundamental conceptions, the problem of applying the principle of democratic centralism correctly under different conditions and stages of development of the struggle can be solved only in relation to the concrete situation, in the course of the tests and experience through which the movement passes, and on the basis of the most fruitful and healthy inter-relationship of the leading bodies of the party and its rank and file.

Basing itself on the specific experiences and needs of American Trotskyism up to that time, the 1938 founding convention of the Socialist Workers Party defined our organizational principles in a resolution 'On the Internal Situation and the Character of the Party'.

Soon thereafter a minority faction, led by Burnham, Shachtman and Abern, demanded the right to publish a dual public organ which would have amounted to freeing them from party control over their public activities. In rejecting the minority demand the 1940 party convention reaffirmed the 1938 resolution and extended the definition of principles in a resolution on 'The Organizational Conclusions of the Present Discussion'. Later on a minority faction headed by Cochran demanded a dual leadership authority in the form of veto powers within official party bodies intended to obstruct the carrying out of majority decisions. The Cochranite demand was rejected by the May 1953 plenum of the National Committee. The plenum adopted a resolution, 'On the Organizational Principles of the Party', which reaffirmed the 1938 and 1940 resolutions and further extended the definition of our democratic-centralist norms.

At present our organizational principles are again under attack, this time in the form of a demand for dual disciplinary standards under which organized minorities would have the unconditional right to set their own norms of conduct inside the party. The demand is rejected as in violation of the Leninist principles defined in the 1938, 1940, and 1953 resolutions. In accordance with those resolutions which are hereby reaffirmed, and in view of the new problems that have arisen, the party's organizational principles are further defined and codified as follows:

Character of the Party

The Socialist Workers Party, as a revolutionary workers' party, is based on the doctrines of scientific socialism as embodied in the principle works of Marx, Engels, Lenin and Trotsky and incorporated in the basic documents and resolutions of the first four congresses of the Communist International; and as embodied in the Transitional Program, the American Theses and other programmatic documents of the Trotskyist movement. The party's aim is the organization of the working class in the struggle for power and the transformation of the existing social order. All of its activities, its methods and its internal regime are subordinated to this aim and are designed to serve it.

The Bolshevik party of Lenin set an unparalleled example for the building of the vanguard party capable of leading the working class to the conquest of power. The SWP, as a combat organization, which aims at achieving power in this country, models its organization forms and methods after those of Russian

Bolshevism, adapting them, naturally, to the experience of recent years and to concrete American conditions.

We reject the contention of social democrats, skeptics and capitulators disillusioned in the Russian revolution and its aftermath, that there is an inevitable and organic connection between Bolshevism and Stalinism. This reactionary revision of Marxism is a capitulation to democratic imperialism. It is capable of producing only demoralization and defeat in the critical times of war and revolution. Tendencies which advance skeptical criticisms of Bolshevism express their petty-bourgeois composition and their dependence on bourgeois public opinion. The petty-bourgeois is a natural transmission belt carrying the theories of reaction into the organizations of the working class.

Those who seek to identify Bolshevism with Stalinism concern themselves with a search for absolute guarantees against the Stalinist degeneration of the party and the future socialist power. We reject this demand for iron-clad insurance as completely undialectical and unrealistic. Our party, in the first instance, is concerned with the struggle for state power, and therefore with creating a party organization capable of leading the proletarian struggle to this goal. There are no constitutional guarantees which can prevent degeneration. Only the victorious revolution can provide the necessary preconditions for preventing the degeneration of the party and the future state power of the working people. If the party fails to carry through and extend the revolution the degeneration of the party is inevitable.

Insofar as any guarantees are possible against the degeneration of the proletarian party, these can be obtained only by educating the party in firm adherence to principles and by a merciless struggle against any personal and unprincipled clique combinations within the party. The history of the movement in this country amply reveals that such clique, with its utter disregard for principles, can become the repository for alien class influences and agents of enemy organizations seeking to disrupt the movement from within. The SWP condemns cliquism as hostile to the spirit and methods of Bolshevik organizations.

Revolutionary Centralism

From the foregoing it follows that the party seeks to include in its ranks all revolutionary and class conscious militants; from the labor, civil rights and student movements – all opponents of capitalism – who are prepared to stand on the Trotskyist program and to be active in building the movement in a disciplined manner. The revolutionary Marxian party rejects, not only the arbitrariness and bureaucratism of the Communist Party, but also the spurious and deceptive 'all-inclusiveness' of the social-democratic variety, which is a sham and a fraud. Experience has proved conclusively that this 'all-inclusiveness' paralyzes the party in general and the revolutionary left wing in particular, suppressing and bureaucratically hounding the latter while giving free rein to the right-wing to commit the greatest crimes in the name of socialism and the party. The SWP seeks to be inclusive only in this sense: that it accepts into its ranks those who accept its program and principles; and that it denies admission to those who reject its program and principles.

To overthrow the most powerful capitalist ruling class in the world, the SWP must be organized as a combat party on strong centralist lines. The resolution adopted at the founding convention gave a correct interpretation of the principles of democratic centralism. Its emphasis was placed on the democratic aspects of this principle. The party leadership has faithfully preserved the democratic rights of the membership since the founding convention. It has granted the widest latitude of discussion to all dissenting groups and individuals. The duty of the National Committee is to execute the decisions of the convention, arrived at after the most thorough and democratic discussion, and to permit no infringement upon them.

Conditions, both external and in the internal development of the party, demand that steps now be taken towards knitting the party together, towards tightening up its activities and centralizing its organization structure. For the work of penetrating into the mass movement, for the heavy struggles to come against capitalism, it is imperative that a maximum of loyalty be required of every leader and every member; that a maximum of activity be required commensurate with the given situation of each comrade; that a strict adherence to discipline be demanded and enforced.

The struggle for power organized and led by the revolutionary party is the most ruthless and irreconcilable struggle in all history. A loosely-knit, heterogeneous, undisciplined, untrained organization is utterly incapable of accomplishing such world-historical tasks as the proletariat and the revolutionary party are confronted with in the present era. This is all the more emphatically true in the light of the singularly difficult position of our party and the extraordinary persecution to which it is subject. From this follows the party's unconditional demand upon all its members for complete discipline in all public activities and actions of the organization.

Leadership and centralized direction are indispensable prerequisites for any sustained and disciplined action, especially in the party that sets itself the aim of leading the collective efforts of the proletariat in its struggle against capitalism. Without a strong and firm National Committee and its subordinate bodies, having the power to act promptly and effectively in the name of the party and to supervise, coordinate and direct all its activities without exception, the very idea of a revolutionary party is a meaningless jest.

Membership Rights and Obligations

Only a self-acting and critical-minded membership is capable of forging and consolidating such a party and of solving its problems by collective thought, discussion and experience. From this follows the need of assuring the widest party democracy in the ranks of the organization. Party membership confers the fullest freedom of discussion, debate and criticism inside the ranks of the party, limited only by such decisions and provisions as are made by the party itself or by bodies to which it assigns this function. Affiliation to the party confers upon each member the right of being democratically represented at all policy-making assemblies of the party (from branch to national convention), and the right of the final and decisive vote in determining the program, policies and leadership of the party.

With party rights, the membership has also certain definite obligations. The theoretical and political character of the party is determined by its program which demarcates the revolutionary Marxist party from all other parties, groups and tendencies in the working class. The first obligation of party membership is loyal acceptance of the program of the party and regular affiliation to one of the basic units of the party. The party requires of every member the acceptance of its discipline and the carrying on of his activity in accordance with the program of the party, with the decisions adopted by its conventions, and with the policies formulated and directed by the party leadership.

Party membership implies the obligation of one hundred per cent loyalty to the organization, the rejection of all agents of other, hostile groups in its ranks and intolerance of divided loyalties in general. Membership in the party necessitates responsible activity in the organization, as established by the proper unit and under the direction of the party; it necessitates the fulfillment of all the tasks which the party assigns to each member. Party membership implies the obligation upon every member to contribute materially to the support of the organization in accordance with his means.

Rights of Party as a Whole

The rights of each individual member, as set forth above, do not imply that the membership as a whole, namely, the party itself, does not possess rights of its own. The party as a whole has the right to demand that its work be not disrupted and disorganized, and has the right to take all the measures which it finds necessary to assure its regular and normal functioning. The rights of any individual member are distinctly secondary to the rights of the party membership as a whole. Party democracy means not only the most scrupulous protection of the rights of a given minority, but also the protection of the majority. A dissenting minority has the right to organize itself, but the conduct of organized minorities, just as that of every individual member, must be subject to regulation by official party bodies.

The party is therefore entitled to organize its internal discussion and to determine the forms and limits. All inner-party discussion must be organized from the point of view that the party is not a discussion club, which debates interminably on any and all questions at any and all times without arriving at a binding decision enabling the organization to act, but from the point of view that we are a disciplined party of revolutionary action.

The party must be cleansed of the discussion club atmosphere, of an irresponsible attitude toward assignments, of a cynical, smart-aleck disrespect for the organization. To maintain party unity and make common political work possible, the majority must have the unconditional right to decide all issues in dispute; every member must accept the decisions unconditionally and help carry them out. Official party bodies must determine correct procedure, both in public activity and in the regulation of internal affairs, on the basis of the party's principles and statutes.

Discipline

The party in general not only has the right, therefore, to organize the discussion in accordance with the requirements of the situation, but the lower units of the party must be given the right in the interests of the struggle against the disruption and disorganization of the party's work, to call irresponsible individuals to order, and, if need be, to eject them from the ranks.

The decisions of the national party convention are binding on all party members without exception and they conclude the discussion on all disputed questions upon which a decision has been taken. Any party member violating the decisions of the convention, or attempting to revive discussion in regard to them without formal authorization of the party, puts himself thereby in opposition to the party and forfeits his right to membership. All party organizations are authorized and instructed to take any measures necessary to enforce this rule.

Press

The party press is the decisive public agitational and propagandist expression of the organization. The policies of the press are formulated on the basis of the resolution of the conventions of the party, and decisions of the National Committee not in conflict with such resolutions. Control of the press is lodged directly in the hands of the National Committee by the convention of the party. The duty of the editors is loyally to interpret the decisions of the convention in the press.

The opening of the party press to discussion of a point of view contrary to that of the official leadership of the party or of its programmatic convention decisions must be controlled by the National Committee which is obligated to regulate discussion of this character in such a way as to give decisive emphasis to the party line. It is the right and duty of the National Committee to veto any demand for public discussion if it deems such discussion harmful to the best interests of the party.

Proletarianizing the Party

The working class is the only class in modern society that is progressive and truly revolutionary. Only the working class is capable of saving humanity from barbarism. Only a revolutionary party can lead the proletariat to the realization of this historic mission. To achieve power, the revolutionary party must be deeply rooted among the workers, it must be composed predominantly of workers and enjoy the respect and confidence of the workers.

Without such a composition it is impossible to build a programmatically firm and disciplined organization which can accomplish these grandiose tasks. A party of non-workers is necessarily subject to all the reactionary influences of skepticism, cynicism, soul-sickness and capitulatory despair transmitted to it through its petty-bourgeois environment.

To transform the SWP into a proletarian party of action, particularly in the present period of reaction, it is not enough to continue propagandistic activities in the hope that by an automatic process workers will flock to the banner of the party. It is necessary, on the contrary, to make a concerted, determined and systematic effort, consciously directed by the leading committees of the party, to spread out into all sectors of the mass movement – civil rights organizations which are becoming radicalized and in which workers predominate; labor organizations within industry and among the unemployed; campuses where an increasing number of students are turning toward socialist ideas.

Central to all mass work must be the sinking of party roots into mass organizations and the recruitment of workers and students, black and white, into the party. At the same time students must be taught that they can transform the Trotskyist program from the pages of books and pamphlets into living reality for themselves and for the party only by integrating themselves in the workers' movement and breaking irrevocably from alien class influences. They must wholly and selflessly identify themselves with the working class through its vanguard party. Unless they follow this road they are in constant danger of slipping back into apathy and pessimism and thus be lost for the revolutionary movement.

Party activity must be organized on the basis of campaigns which are realistically adjusted to the demands and direction of the mass movement. These campaigns must not be sucked out of the thumb of some functionary in a party office, but must arise as a result of the connections of the party with the mass movement and the indicated direction of the masses in specific situations.

All party agitation campaigns, especially in the next period, must be directed primarily at those mass organizations in which we are attempting to gain a foothold and attract members. General agitation addressed to the working class as a whole or the public in general must be related to those specific aims.

The press must gear its agitation into the activity conducted among specific sectors of the mass movement so as to transform the party paper from a literary organ into a political organizer. The integration of the party into the mass movement, and the transformation of the party into a proletarian organization, are indispensable for the progress of the party.

Responsibilities of Leadership

To build the combat organization capable of leading the masses to power, the party must have as its general staff a corps of professional revolutionists who devote their entire life to the direction and the building of the party and its influence in the mass movement. Membership in the leading staff of the party, the National Committee must be made contingent on a complete subordination of the life of the candidate to the party. All members of the National Committee must be prepared to devote full-time activities to party work at the demand of the National Committee.

The party demands the greatest sacrifices of its members. Only a leadership selected from among those who demonstrate in the struggle the qualities of singleness of purpose, unconditional loyalty to the party and revolutionary firmness of character, can inspire the membership with the spirit of unswerving devotion required for victory.

The party leadership must, from time to time, be infused with new blood, primarily from among the younger party activists. Comrades who show promise and ability through activity in the mass movement should be elevated to the leading committees of the party in order to establish a more direct connection between the leading committee and the mass movement, and in order to train those engaged in mass work for the tasks of party direction itself.

The leadership of the party must be under the control of the membership, its policies must always be open to criticism, discussion and rectification by the rank and file within properly established forms and limits, and the leading bodies themselves subject to formal recall or alteration. The membership of the party has the right to demand and expect the greatest responsibility from the leaders precisely because of the position they occupy in the movement. The selection of comrades to the positions of leadership means the conferring of an extraordinary responsibility. The warrant for this position must be proved, not once, but continuously by the leadership itself. It is under obligation to set the highest example of responsibility, devotion, sacrifice and complete identification with the party itself and its daily life and action. It must display the ability to defend its policies before the membership of the party, and to defend the line of the party and the party as a whole before the working class in general.

Sustained party activity, not broken or disrupted by abrupt and disorienting changes, presupposes not only a continuity of tradition and a systematic development of party policy, but also the continuity of leadership. It is an important sign of a serious and firmly constituted party, of a party really engaged in productive work in the class struggle, that it raises from its ranks cadres of more or less able leading comrades, tested for their qualities of endurance and trustworthiness, and that it thus insures a certain stability and continuity of leadership by such a cadre.

Continuity of leadership does not, however, signify the automatic self-perpetuation of leadership. Constant renewal of its ranks by means of additions and, when necessary, replacements, is the only assurance the party has that its leadership will not succumb to the effects of dry-rot, that it will not be burdened with dead-wood, that it will avoid the corrosion of conservatism and dilettantism, that it will not be the object of conflict between the older elements and the younger, that the old and basic cadre will be refreshed by new blood, that the leadership as a whole will not become purely bureaucratic 'committee men' remote from the real life of the party and the activities of the rank and file.

Role of Official Bodies

As provided by the party constitution, the National Committee directs all the work of the party, decides all questions of policy in accord with the decisions of the national convention, appoints subordinate officers and sub-committees, including the Political Committee, and in general constitutes, between national conventions, the functioning central authority of the party.

The Political Committee, appointed by the plenum, functions as the central authority of the party between plenums of the National Committee and is authorized to speak and act in its name. It shall be optional with the Political Committee whether or not it will conduct a poll of the National Committee before acting on any question before it, except that such a poll shall be taken upon the request of any National Committee member for a plenary meeting of the National Committee. The Political Committee is obliged to comply with the decision of the majority of the full National Committee in such a poll.

All party organs, institutions and bodies, including the party locals and branches, shall be under the supervision of the Political Committee, acting for the National Committee. All party units and individual party members are required to comply with any directives of the Political Committee between plenums of the National Committee, pending appeal to the plenum.

As provided by the party constitution, Local Executive Committees shall direct the activities of the Locals and act with full power for the Locals between city conventions. Branch Executive Committees, on the other hand, as provided by the party constitution, shall be subordinate to the Branch membership.

In accordance with the principle of democratic centralism, minorities shall have the right to present their views in all internal party discussions. The plenum, and between its sessions, the Political Committee, has the right and duty to lay down rules for the regulation of the discussion, to see that it is fairly conducted as has invariably been the case in the past, and to see that it does not disrupt the orderly functioning of the party in all its activities.

The principle of majority rule shall apply with full force and effect in all party bodies and in all party activities.

CHAPTER 6

Debates and Interventions

Paul Le Blanc

Items in this chapter give a sense of other issues on which there were divergent opinions debated within the Socialist Workers Party.

One dispute arose in regard to Isaac Deutscher, whose writings had a powerful impact through the 1950s and 1960s. A Polish Trotskyist in the 1930s who had considered the 1938 formation of the Fourth International to be premature and a sectarian mistake, he reinvented himself in the 1940s, when – as an ex-Trotskyist and refugee in Britain – he became fluent in English and achieved international prominence as a journalist. His focus was international events, with a specialty on Eastern Europe and the USSR, but in 1949 he produced a massive, scholarly biography of Joseph Stalin. Deutscher wrote as a sophisticated Marxist, with a strong Trotskyist influence but a decidedly independent bent. His well-researched portrait of Stalin offered a detailed, nuanced, and illuminating account of the revolutionary movement and struggles through which Stalin was shaped, of Stalin's own climb to power, and of the subsequent policies he advanced, with attention to what Deutscher considered not only the bad and the ugly, but also the good.

Specifically, Deutscher saw Stalin – despite his brutality and national narrowness, despite his distortions of Marxism and suppression of an inner-party democracy that had been the norm in the time of Lenin, despite the vicious and murderous quality of many of his policies – as having played a largely progressive role in overseeing and helping advance the industrialization and modernization of the USSR, which could provide the basis for a future socialist society. Deutscher believed such socialism would necessarily require genuine democracy and freedom of expression, with a humanism absent from Stalin's personality and practices, but that this might be achieved through political reform, even self-reform, of the existing bureaucratic rule. He saw the Stalinist bureaucracy and the bureaucratic dictatorship as continuing to represent – in highly distorted and often destructive form, to be sure – some of the original revolutionary aspirations of the 1917 revolution, and that the foreign policy of the USSR in the Cold War had progressive qualities as well, as a counterbalance to US imperialism and as a force often inclined, for its own systemic reasons, to deploy Soviet military forces or to aid various anti-colonial and national liberation struggles, in order to make more and more of the world non-capitalist.¹

This corresponded to the orientation in the Fourth International represented by Michel Pablo, and Deutscher's work had consequently been targeted for polemical assault, including by none other than James P. Cannon himself – 'Trotsky or Deutscher? On the New Revisionism and Its Theoretical Source'. As the factional struggle receded into the past, and as Deutscher produced the first and then the second volume of his monumental biography of Trotsky – *The Prophet Armed* and *The Prophet Unarmed* – the attitude toward Deutscher began to shift, with Joseph Hansen repeating some of the criticisms while at the same time acknowledging virtues in Deutscher's account.² But with the publication of the final volume, *The Prophet Outcast,* Hansen offered the fairly laudatory review presented here – which, as we can see, generated a sharp criticism from George Breitman, with a rejoinder in which Hansen stuck to his guns.³

Far more contentious was an ongoing debate around the Chinese Revolution of 1949, and particularly around the subsequent regime and policies under the leadership of Mao Zedong (most commonly before the 1970s spelled Mao Tse-tung) and his comrades in the Chinese Communist Party. After the disastrous destruction of what had been a very substantial Chinese Communist movement in 1927 (due to its leadership reluctantly following directives of the Stalin-Bukharin leadership of the Communist International), Mao and other survivors fled to and regrouped in China's rural hinterlands. Here they eventually built up a powerful peasant base, fighting against Japanese invaders as well as the corrupt right-wing Nationalist dictatorship of Chiang Kai-shek. The popular support that had by the end of the Second World War enabled them to win a civil war against the Nationalists, declaring the People's Republic of China in 1949. The Chinese Trotskyists, some of whom had been top leaders of the Communist Party up to 1927, were either imprisoned or forced into exile with the establishment of Mao's regime, and they themselves were sharply divided on how to interpret and respond to events. There were also differences among US Trotskyists.⁴

---

1   Deutscher 1967. For Deutscher's journalism, see Deutscher 1970. For some background material, see: Horowitz 1971; Deutscher 1968; Caute 2013.
2   Cannon 1954; Hansen 1960. George Breitman's two-part polemic on the Stalin biography (1949), and his five-part critique of the first of Deutscher's Trotsky volumes (1954), each part taking up a full page in the *Militant,* can be found in the George Breitman Internet Archive at: https://www.marxists.org/history/etol/writers/breitman/index.htm (accessed 22 June 2016).
3   The three volumes have been combined into a single-volume edition – Deutscher 2015.
4   The 1927 massacre of Communists in China is the focal point of one of the twentieth cen-

There was general support in the SWP for the 1949 revolution. This was seen as a mass insurgency of the country's impoverished peasant majority, led by well-organized Chinese Communists who viewed themselves, more or less, as a stand-in for the Chinese working class. But the explicitly Stalinist ideology of Mao and the Chinese Communist Party was viewed differently by different US Trotskyists. Since Stalinism was seen as essentially counter-revolutionary and authoritarian, Mao and his comrades were viewed very critically and with deep suspicion by some. For similar reasons, some concluded that because they were leaders of a popular and successful revolution, Mao and his comrades could not be seen as genuinely Stalinist, nor as flat-out authoritarians. A number of different currents (though in all cases minority currents) advanced such a perspective within the SWP, from the 'global class war' tendency around Sam Marcy to those associated with Richard Fraser and Clara Fraser in Seattle.

The case for thoroughgoing support for Maoism was persistently articulated – over a number of years – by two veteran Trotskyists, Arne Swabeck and Frank Glass (using the name John Liang) – mostly in SWP internal discussion bulletins. One of their most complete analyses, before they parted ways over secondary analytical differences, is presented here. In 'Maoism and the Neo-Stalin Cult', SWP leader Tom Kerry articulated a thoroughgoing critique of this general approach, taking on as well the growing influence of Maoism on the US Left in the 1960s, and advancing a more orthodox understanding of the Trotskyist position.[5]

---

tury's great novels, Malraux 1934, and a classic left-wing journalistic account is available in Isaacs 2010, corroborated by a pioneering history in Schwartz 1951, and by Trotsky's analyses, gathered in Evans and Block 1976. Two divergent currents in Chinese Trotskyism can be found in Peng Shu-tse 1980 and Wang Fan-hsi 1991, with further explorations in Benton 2016. On the revolutionary struggle led by Mao and his comrades, see Snow 1994, and Belden 1970. For popularly written accounts of post-revolution China, see Snow 1962 and Karnow 1972. Historic overviews are provided by Fairbank and Goldman 2006, and – more succinctly – from a Marxist perspective with a focus on Mao's revolution, by Rousset 2009.

5 On the rising tide of Maoism within the US Left in this period, see Elbaum 2002. South African-born Frank Glass (1901–88) had several names, including Cecil Glass, Li Fu-jen, and John Liang, and – becoming a Communist in 1921 and a Trotskyist in 1928–29 – he was at different times a leading member of the South African and Chinese Trotskyist movements, before coming to the United States in 1941. More information on him can be found in Lovell 2000, pp. 302–4, and Hirson 2003. Danish-born Arne Swabeck (1890–1986) moved to the United States in 1916, became involved in the Socialist Party and Industrial Workers of the World, was a founding and leading member of the US Communist movement, then a founding and leading member of US Trotskyism. Expelled from the SWP for organizational infractions in 1967, he briefly joined the then-Maoist Progressive Labor Party, and later the socialist new left group New American Movement. For more on him, see Phelps 2002; also see James P. Cannon's affectionate tribute in Cannon 1953.

Not long after the publication of his polemic, Kerry and Dobbs initiated disciplinary proceedings against Swabeck for violating organizational discipline. This would finally culminate in his expulsion. His disagreement with this approach contributed to a series of interventions by James P. Cannon, with which this chapter concludes.

Differences were noted between what some had called 'the Cannon regime' and that of Dobbs and Kerry. 'With Cannon there was *political* leadership', commented Morris Lewit who (under the party name 'Stein' remained in the central leadership throughout the 1950s). 'With Dobbs and Kerry it was minutiae. You know, neither of them brought political grasp'. Dobbs, a veteran of the Teamsters struggles in the Midwest, had been pushed into the position of national secretary, although in Lewit's view, 'he wasn't prepared for this kind of job. He was really green ... I was sorry for him ... He was a trade union man who never had a chance to participate in a political discussion in a branch, which for us was novel'. Kerry was far more politically oriented than Dobbs, in Lewit's opinion, but he also had a problematical side. 'Tom was a fighter, a factionalist', in Morris's opinion. 'He had to be restrained all the time'.[6]

There was some concern about creating an appropriate balance within the SWP's central leadership. In part through Cannon's pressure from afar, Lewit, with Dobbs, Kerry, and Murry Weiss, served on a four-person Secretariat that functioned between meetings of the Political Committee. Unlike the others, he wasn't on staff, and his job prevented him from reading all of the materials to be discussed and from engaging in certain preliminary discussions. Yet he made his own distinctive contributions: 'I'd have to knock down some of their ideas, you know, that were not very mature'. In 1960, devastating health issues removed both Lewit and Weiss from their leadership positions – with Weiss a combined stroke and mental breakdown, with Lewit an undiagnosed potassium deficiency.[7]

That Cannon was dissatisfied over the resulting predominance of the Dobbs-Kerry leadership is reported in the recollections of a younger comrade who got to know him, Leslie Evans. Cannon complained to him about what he perceived as a routinist and ingrown orientation, and that the SWP 'has become intolerant of differences of opinion'. Cannon also objected to the notion of simply getting rid of comrades considered to be problematical: 'The party is a voluntary organization. You can't hire and fire in the party. If you lose an experienced person

---

6 Le Blanc and Smith 2000, pp. 289, 290.
7 Le Blanc and Smith 2000, p. 290.

you can't go out on the street and hire a replacement. You have to conserve what you have'.[8] George Breitman reports:

> When the PC decided to submit a resolution on organizational principles to the 1965 convention, it chose a committee of Dobbs, George Novack, and Cannon to prepare a draft. Dobbs wrote it and Novack edited it. A copy was sent to Cannon, who sent it back without comment. He thought the draft was poorly written and too ambiguous on certain key points, but did not undertake to amend or redraft it. He did not attend the 1965 convention, which adopted the resolution by a vote of 51 to 8.[9]

It was also at this convention that a new element was drawn into the SWP's central leadership, a youthful activist layer around a relatively recent recruit named Jack Barnes, ostensibly following the lead of Dobbs and Kerry, capable and creative in his own right, and perceived as being absolutely loyal to the Trotskyist program. But there was an aspect of the Dobbs and Kerry approach to that program that Morris Lewit saw as problematical, with its stress on centralized discipline and expulsions: 'That's what happened with the Barnes clique: super-disciplinarians. I blame the party leadership for going along with them. And then it came to them, and *they* were kicked out'.[10]

Lewit is here linking realities of the 1960s with developments of the 1980s, when the Barnes leadership carried out a super-centralist purge that eliminated many 'old-timers' (including Tom Kerry himself) and simply abandoned the SWP's historic program in what turned out to be a relatively transient and distorted 'Castroist' orientation. It could be argued that this problematically telescopes different aspects of a more complex reality. A younger participant, Barry Sheppard (a one-time ally but ultimately an opponent of Barnes) remembers the 1965 SWP convention and the 1965 organizational resolution in very positive terms,[11] and emphasizes what he sees as the very positive qualities of the Dobbs-Kerry team:

> Farrell's main strength was shown in assembling a team. This team worked together, and no one was a star. ... The rule was to encourage everyone to do the best they could, not to discourage. Farrell also was a kind of watchdog over our program, together with Tom. This helped us keep our

---

8   Evans 2009, pp. 155, 163.
9   Breitman 1986.
10   Le Blanc and Smith 2000, p. 291.
11   For Sheppard's very positive account of 1965 events, see Sheppard 2005, pp. 142–55.

Marxist bearings as we navigated new waters. ... Farrell was able to play this role because of his political and moral leadership. He was absolutely incorruptible. He never had an exaggerated view of himself, and was able to learn from others and encourage them to make contributions. ... Bringing this team together and making it function as a thinking machine was no small task. ... Farrell Dobbs, together with James P. Cannon, Tom Kerry and other party leaders of Farrell's generation ... kept the party together through the difficult days of the [Cold War anti-Communist] witch-hunt. The Dobbs team was able to recruit a new layer of young people as that became possible in the mid-1950s, and especially in the 1960s. They were able to educate us, and give us room to develop and demonstrate our own leadership capabilities, and to gradually take over the reins. The transition in leadership became complete in the early 1970s.[12]

At the same time, many others associated with the SWP experience as it unfolded in the 1970s and 1980s have found resonance in the kinds of things Cannon was trying to communicate in the 1960s, which are presented here.

These documents were originally gathered together by George Breitman and issued by a group of former SWP members, the Fourth Internationalist Tendency, as a pamphlet entitled 'Don't Strangle the Party'.[13]

---

12 Sheppard 2005, pp. 221–2.
13 More on the Fourth Internationalist Tendency is available at: https://www.marxists.org/history/etol/document/fit.htm (accessed 22 June 2016).

1 Deutscher on Trotsky[14]

(1964)

Joseph Hansen

The Prophet Outcast by Isaac Deutscher. New York: Oxford University Press, 1963, 543pp. $9.50.

The final volume of the trilogy tells the story of Trotsky in banishment from the workers' state which he, together with Lenin, had founded. It describes the great intellectual contributions made by this giant revolutionist in these years, his final political battles, and the bitter personal tragedies that befell him before he was slain by Stalin's emissary. The volume was obviously not an easy one for the biographer. The central issues of our time, in which Trotsky stood as the continuator of Marx, Engels and Lenin, are still with us, have grown in acuteness in fact, and it is impossible to deal with Trotsky without also dealing with these. To talk about Trotsky means to talk about the capitalist system in its period of decay and violent resistance to social and economic change, about reviving the proletarian democracy destroyed by the reactionary bureaucratic caste that appeared in the Soviet Union, about the as yet unresolved problem of creating a leadership capable of leading humanity forward to a new and better order.

No matter how Deutscher chose to handle these topics, what he said was bound to be controversial. An additional hazard was that the Trotsky of these years was the Trotsky most familiar to the present generation, the man who still exists in living memory and whose image seemed to become engraved on all who met him, if only briefly.

The biographer met these challenges very well indeed. As in the previous volumes, he remains scrupulous toward facts,[15] seeks the truth, and does not

---

14   Hansen 1964.
15   **Footnote by Hansen:** Even such a biased reviewer as Carleton Beals was reduced to pointing to the listing of 'Almazar', a right-wing general involved in Trotsky's political break with Diego Rivera, as 'proof' of Deutscher's 'pseudo-scholarship'. 'No such general has ever existed or been a presidential candidate', Carleton Beals assures us in the October

hide his own views and predilections. The disagreements one may have with him thus center on points in which his judgment and political views affect the final portrait he offers of Trotsky. The merit of the biographical material he has assembled can be questioned by no one, unless ill will enters in. It is a precious contribution to knowledge of Trotsky, his ideas, and the character of the time he lived in.

The general plan of the volume is the same as the two previous ones. Deutscher presents summaries of Trotsky's main writings during the years under consideration, plus excerpts to give the reader a taste of the original. These are nearly always well chosen and constitute a valuable part of the book. But since, unlike the earlier years, most of the original sources are readily available, the biographer has legitimately reduced the proportion of anthology to the necessities of historical narrative.

Conscientious work in the Trotsky archives at Harvard has enabled Deutscher to present new material of the greatest interest. He was particularly fortunate to obtain the special permission of Natalia Trotsky before her death to examine family correspondence. The revelation thus provided of the family life of the Trotskys, particularly when it was caught up most tensely and tragically in the tempestuous public struggles of the final years, adds a new dimension to the image of Trotsky hitherto available to the public. Deutscher even permits us to glimpse over his shoulder a few lines related to Trotsky's love-life with Natalia, words written only for her. Finally, Deutscher has interviewed many people who met Trotsky or who worked closely with him. From their reports he has selected what he felt he needed or had room for.

Out of these rich and varied sources a picture of Trotsky emerges that is the most life-like of the three volumes, although, to be completely frank, the finished portrait does not quite catch Trotsky, in my opinion, at least as he was

---

issue of *The Independent*. 'Such is Deutscher's notable scholarship'. Beals, evidently emotionally upset by the passing reference in the biography to his strange role in the Dewey Commission, displays such ill will that he does not even offer to make the necessary correction about the Mexican general. The name should be spelled Almazan. The petulance of Beals, of course, could be due to Deutscher's 'pseudo-scholarship' in another unfortunate matter: 'Deutscher does not even spell my name correctly. His account is a sham, and a distortion. Save your money'. (Deutscher spelled the name of His Royal Highness 'Carlton'). Beals' own pseudo-scholarship in relation to Mexico showed up, however, when he failed to note the most obvious error in Deutscher's biography. In the photographs facing page 480, the caption reads: 'Two views of the "little fortress" at Coyoacan'. The top view is of the home owned by Frida Kahlo where Trotsky first stayed after coming to Coyoacan. The bottom view is of the house which Trotsky had to buy after the break with Diego Rivera.

known to his closest collaborators in the final years, and calls attention rather too much to the biographer. I will return to this.

∴

Deutscher considers the Prinkipo period, from 1929 to 1933, to be by far the most productive and fruitful of Trotsky's final years. He devotes half the volume to it. Trotsky's literary production at Prinkipo was indeed enormous and of the highest quality: the three-volume *History of the Russian Revolution*; an autobiography, *My Life*; a series of profound and stirring articles on the most crucial issue of the day – the rise of Nazism; continuation of his current appreciations of developments in the Soviet Union, the only original Marxist contribution on this subject at the time; occasional writings of first-rate importance on such topics as the beginning of the Spanish revolution; and a wide correspondence on an international scale related to the task of reconstructing the revolutionary-socialist movement.

Deutscher does an excellent job of inventorying and assessing these treasures. His praise of Trotsky as a historian is especially warm and appreciative.

> Like Thucydides, Dante, Machiavelli, Heine, Marx, Herzen, and other thinkers and poets, Trotsky attained his full eminence as a writer only in exile, during the few Prinkipo years. Posterity will remember him as the historian of the October Revolution as well as its leader. No other Bolshevik has or could have produced so great and splendid an account of events of 1917; and none of the many writers of the anti-Bolshevik parties has presented any worthy counterpart to it.

Deutscher does not hesitate to estimate it as the greatest work of its kind:

> His historical writing is dialectical as is hardly any other such work produced by the Marxist school of thought since Marx, from whom he derives his method and style. To Marx's minor historical works, *The Class Struggle in France*, *The 18th Brumaire of Louis Bonaparte*, and *The Civil War In France*, Trotsky's *History* stands as the large mural painting stands to the miniature. Whereas Marx towers above the disciple in the power of his abstract thought and gothic imagination, the disciple is superior as epic artist, especially as master of the graphic portrayal of masses and individuals in action. His socio-political analysis and artistic vision are in such concord that there is no trace of any divergence. His thought and his imagination take flight together. He expounds his theory of revolution with

the tension and the *élan* of narrative; and his narrative takes depth from his ideas. His scenes, portraits, and dialogues, sensuous in their reality, are inwardly illumined by his conception of the historical process.

Trotsky's autobiography, in Deutscher's opinion, is less satisfactory because of a certain unevenness. One can agree with Deutscher in this without sharing the reasons he offers for finding the latter part of the book not up to what can be expected from Trotsky at his best. Deutscher holds that Trotsky's explanation of the struggle with Stalin is defective. Trotsky 'does not go to the root of the matter and he leaves Stalin's ascendancy only half explained'. Deutscher feels that Trotsky pictures Stalin as too much villain and that he 'virtually ignores the intrinsic connexion between the suppression by Bolshevism of all parties and its self-suppression, of which Stalin was the supreme agent'. The flaw, in Deutscher's view, is thus due to faulty political vision – a considerable weakness in the man whom Deutscher otherwise views as a supreme political genius. However, Trotsky was quite familiar with the theory for which Deutscher argues, concerning the alleged organic connection between Bolshevism and Stalinism. He specifically rejected it on more than one occasion, and with arguments that I find still convincing.

Trotsky's defective political insight, if such it is, is not peculiar to *My Life*; it is common to everything he wrote, touching this subject, in his final years. What really gives the autobiography its unevenness is the shift away from personal material. The first chapters are on the level of great autobiographical literature. The latter parts shift to political polemic. Excellent as this may be in its own right, it clashes increasingly with the autobiographical form in which it is cast. In contrast to his openness in the first parts in offering absorbing intimate material, Trotsky, in the final parts, becomes more and more reticent.

The reasons for this are perfectly understandable and, in fact, do Trotsky credit. His primary interest was not psychological self-revelation but political action. He remained to the end of his life a leader who necessarily subordinated all other considerations to the interests of the political wars he was engaged in. Deutscher, one must agree, is right in saying about the autobiography that 'if he had not written it in 1929, or shortly thereafter, he might not have written it at all'.

In unity of form and content, Deutscher's biography contrasts favorably with the final sections of *My Life*. As we follow Trotsky's thought and the course of his political battles, we participate at the same time in his personal fortunes. We catch some of the pleasures, the more common emotional stress and the searing tragedies. We get to know something of Zina, the daughter who suffered a nervous breakdown under Stalin's persecution, who resisted psychoanalytic treatment and who finally committed suicide. Leon Sedov, the devoted son comes to life for us – Leon, who had such a close political and personal relationship with his father that he became the receptacle for explosive paternal tensions that could find no other safety valve and which Leon could not understand but only brood over in the final days before his own death at the hands of the implacable common foe. Natalia emerges as a granite figure. To Deutscher she is the heroine of the epic and all who read this biography are bound to share his admiration for her. She was truly of the stature required to share to the end the fortunes of the prophet outcast.

As the titles of the trilogy indicate: *The Prophet Armed*, *The Prophet Unarmed*, and *The Prophet Outcast*, Trotsky's capacity to see into the future was, for Deutscher, his most irresistible gift. He cites examples of Trotsky's almost uncanny accuracy. Two of them in the final volume will undoubtedly impress everyone who reads them. The first one, on the grand level of the international class struggle, illustrates the contrast between Trotsky's clear vision of the meaning of the rise of Hitler and the blindness of the Stalinists, represented in this case by Thaelmann: As late as September 1932, a few months before Hitler became Chancellor, Thaelmann, at a session of the Comintern Executive, still repeated what Münzenberg had said:

> In his pamphlet on how National Socialism is to be defeated, Trotsky gives one answer only, and it is this: the German Communist Party must join hands with the Social Democratic Party ... This, according to Trotsky, is the only way in which the German working class can save itself from fascism. Either, says he, the Communist party makes common cause with the Social Democrats, or the German working class is lost for ten or twenty years. This is the theory of an utterly bankrupt Fascist and counter-revolutionary. This is indeed the worst, the most dangerous, and the most criminal theory that Trotsky has construed in these last years of his counter-revolutionary propaganda.

'One of the decisive moments in history is approaching', Trotsky rejoined,

> ... when the Comintern as a revolutionary factor may be wiped off the political map for an entire historic epoch. Let blind men and cowards refuse to notice this. Let slanderers and hired scribblers accuse us of being in league with the counter-revolution. Has not counter-revolution become anything ... that interferes with the digestion of communist bureaucrats ... nothing must be concealed, nothing belittled. We must tell

the advanced workers as loudly as we can: After the 'third period' of recklessness and boasting the fourth period of panic and capitulation has set in.

In an almost desperate effort to arouse the communists, Trotsky put into words the whole power of his conviction and gave them once again the ring of an alarm bell:

> Workers-communists! There are hundreds of thousands, there are millions of you ... If fascism comes to power it will ride like a terrific tank over your skulls and spines. Your salvation lies in merciless struggle. Only a fighting unity with social democratic workers can bring victory. Make haste, communist workers, you have very little time to lose.

The second example is Trotsky's admonition of Trygve Lie, who later became head of the United Nations. The then Minister of Justice in the Norwegian government put Trotsky under house arrest, barred him from answering the charges in the infamous 1936 Moscow frame-up trial, and even cut him off from correspondence. Lie attempted to force Trotsky to sign a shameful agreement not to make any statements referring to the Moscow frame-up trial, in which Trotsky and his son were principal victims, and to submit the mail, telegrams and telephone calls of himself, his wife and secretaries to censorship. 'Twenty years later eye-witnesses of the scene still remembered the flashes of scorn in Trotsky's eyes and the thunder of his voice as he refused to comply'. He leveled a series of damaging questions at Trygve Lie.

> At this point Trotsky raised his voice so that it resounded through the halls and corridors of the Ministry: 'This is your first act of surrender to Nazism in your own country. You will pay for this. You think yourselves secure and free to deal with a political exile as you please. But the day is near – remember this! – the day is near when the Nazis will drive you from your country, all of you together with your *Pantoffel-Minister-President*'. Trygve Lie shrugged at this odd piece of soothsaying. Yet after less than four years the same government had indeed to flee from Norway before the Nazi invasion; and as the Ministers and their aged King Haakon stood on the coast, huddled together and waiting anxiously for a boat that was to take them to England, they recalled with awe Trotsky's words as a prophet's curse come true.

∴

There is justification in singling out this aspect, in emphasizing Trotsky as *prophet*. It helps create interest in what he had to offer the world. Nevertheless, a certain amount of reduction occurs. At worst, the image, with its undue connotation of extra-sensory intuitive powers, tends to obscure the image of Trotsky as scientist. It contributes to an imbalance in the portrait. Before coming to that, however, it is perhaps advisable to say something about Deutscher's differences with Trotsky, which come to the fore in this volume.

Throughout the biography Deutscher stresses the continuity of Marxist thought represented by Trotsky, evaluates to the best of his ability what Trotsky added to the body of Marxist literature and offers accurate and readable presentations of Trotsky's special contributions. In previous volumes he considered Trotsky's theory of permanent revolution, his brilliant work in the field of literary criticism, his outstanding role in the 1905 and 1917 revolutions, his program for the first workers' state as it stood isolated in the twenties, his opening of the struggle against Stalinism. In this volume, Deutscher calls special attention to Trotsky's analysis of the nature of fascism and how to fight it – an addition to Marxism that is little appreciated today, primarily because of the unending campaign of slander against Trotsky.

Most of Trotsky's followers would add to this list, and even put it in the top rank of his achievements, the analysis of the Soviet Union as a degenerated workers' state, particularly Trotsky's estimate of the roots and nature of Stalinism. Deutscher has strong reservations on this. He feels that Trotsky, while making the fundamental contribution, did not see altogether clearly on the subject:

> *The Revolution Betrayed* occupies a special place in Trotsky's literary work. It is the last book he managed to complete and in a sense, his political testament. In it he gave his final analysis of Soviet society and a survey of its history up to the middle of the Stalin era. His most complex book, it combines all the weakness and the strength of his thought. It contains many new and original reflections on socialism, on the difficulties with which proletarian revolution has to grapple, and on the role of a bureaucracy in a workers' state. He also surveyed the international position of the Soviet Union before the Second World War and tried to pierce the future with daring and partly erroneous forecasts. The book is a profound theoretical treatise and a tract for the time; a creative restatement of classical Marxist views; and the manifesto of the 'new Trotskyism' calling for revolution in the Soviet Union. Trotsky appears here in all his capacities; as detached and rigorously objective thinker; as leader of a defeated Opposition; and as passionate pamphleteer and polemicist. The

polemicist's contribution forms the more esoteric part of the work and tends to overshadow the objective and analytical argument. Because of the wealth of its ideas and its imaginative force, this has been one of the seminal books of this century, as instructive as confusing, and destined to be put to adventitious use more often than any other piece of political writing. Even its title was to become one of the shibboleths of our time.

Deutscher follows with a summary of the book which is quite good. (However, 'Stalinist state' for 'Stalinist regime' in a 'workers' state' is scarcely a happy condensation). He finds himself in agreement with Trotsky's program against bureaucratism and for proletarian democracy and considers it still relevant 'over a quarter of a century after its formulation'. Then he indicates one of his main disagreements with Trotsky:

> From the tenor of *The Revolution Betrayed* it is clear that he saw no chance of any reform from above; and there was indeed no chance of it in his lifetime and for the rest of the Stalin era. But during that time there was no chance in the Soviet Union of any political revolution either. This was a period of deadlock: it was impossible either to cut or to untie the Gordian knots of Stalinism. Any programme of change whether revolutionary or reformist, was illusory. This could not prevent a fighter like Trotsky from searching for a way out. But he was searching within a vicious circle, which only world-shaking events began to breach many years later. And when that happened the Soviet Union moved away from Stalinism through reform from above in the first instance. What forced the reform was precisely the factors on which Trotsky had banked: economic progress, the cultural rise of the masses, and the end of Soviet isolation. The break with Stalinism could only be piecemeal, because at the end of the Stalin era there existed and could exist no political force capable and willing to act in a revolutionary manner. Moreover, throughout the first decade after Stalin there did not emerge 'from below' any autonomous and articulate mass movement even for reform. Since Stalinism had become an anachronism, nationally and internationally, and a break with it had become an historic necessity for the Soviet Union, the ruling group itself had to take the initiative of the break. Thus, by an irony of history Stalin's epigones began the liquidation of Stalinism and thereby carried out, *malgre eux memes*, parts of Trotsky's political testament.

But can they continue this work and complete it? Or is a political revolution still necessary? On the face of it, the chances of revolution are still as slender as they were in Trotsky's days, whereas the possibilities of reform are far more real.[16]

In *The Prophet Outcast* Deutscher still holds that 'continuous reform' is more likely than 'a revolutionary explosion'. However, he agrees that this can be only a tentative conclusion. There can be 'little or no certitude'. He says finally, 'At any rate, the present writer prefers to leave the final judgment on Trotsky's idea of a political revolution to a historian of the next generation'.

It is not my intention to get into a dispute at this time with Deutscher on 'self-reform' or 'political revolution', a complicated question. I will only indicate the central issue. The *immediacy* of a political revolution is not at stake – the disagreement is not about that. What is involved in *principle* is the character of the ruling *caste* in the Soviet Union. In Trotsky's view it was not just a bureaucracy but something more, somewhat like a class in its rapacity and its need to monopolize power but lacking the economic roots and economic stability of a true class. Will such a social formation, out of self-volition, eventually offer the masses effective forms of proletarian democracy? Trotsky held the view that the answer was no, since the effective operation of proletarian democracy would signify liquidation of the bureaucracy as a social formation enjoying special privileges, A negative answer, in turn, implied that political revolution was the only means left to the masses to intervene in their own rule.

---

16   **Footnote by Hansen:** In connection with this, Deutscher refers in a footnote to an attack on his views leveled by James P. Cannon in 1954. Perhaps it is opportune to attempt to clear this up. Some harsh and even unjustified things were said of Deutscher. At the time, Deutscher's theory about the possibility of the self-reform of the Stalinist bureaucracy figured in an internal crisis of the Socialist Workers Party. A sector of the cadres and leaders were strongly influenced by Deutscher's theory. A split occurred and some of them capitulated to Stalinism. The crisis was not confined to the SWP but affected other sectors of the world Trotskyist movement. To many Trotskyists, Deutscher's position appeared as an alternative program which could prove to be a bridge to Stalinism. It was therefore viewed with hostility. It turned out, however, that Deutscher was not interested in recruiting from the Trotskyist movement or in organizing a sect of his own, still less a cult. This spoke strongly in his favor. After the Hungarian uprising another phenomenon soon became noticeable to the Trotskyist movement. Many members of Communist parties, shaken by the events, began reading forbidden literature. Not prepared to touch the works of the devil himself, Deutscher's writings appeared less 'counter-revolutionary' to them. Having begun dipping into Trotskyism in this way, they thirsted for more. Through Deutscher, some of them eventually found their way to Trotskyism. Deutscher's position under these circumstances proved to be a bridge from Stalinism to Trotskyism. Trotskyists could not be against that kind of public facility. They therefore began undertaking their own self-reform – in relation to Deutscher.

This did not necessarily mean a 'violent explosion', although it would certainly signify a thoroughgoing shakeup undertaken at the initiative of the masses.

None of the concessions granted by Stalin's heirs up to now have affected the political monopoly held by the bureaucratic caste. Trotsky's conclusions would thus seem to have received corroboration from the pattern of the reforms themselves.

From the viewpoint of the world Trotskyist movement, Deutscher's agreement on the validity of Trotsky's program establishes the possibility in principle of practical collaboration with him, even though action, so far as he is concerned, might never go beyond working for 'continuous reform'. Since advocates of 'continuous reform' and political revolution have the same end in view – the establishment of proletarian democracy in the workers' states – a rather wide basis for co-operation exists. To this it can be added that it will doubtless be in the process of seeking to obtain reforms of increasing importance that the Soviet masses will eventually prove in life who saw most clearly and who suffered to some degree from illusions as to the means by which Stalin's alteration of the political structure will eventually be rectified.

∴

In addition to inability to prophesy correctly how the workers' state would be regenerated, Deutscher holds that Trotsky failed to forecast correctly the pattern which the world revolution actually took in the postwar period. I would not deny that there is an element of truth in the latter assertion. The specific pattern of the Chinese Revolution – organization of the peasantry into armies and their advance from the countryside to the city – offers the most spectacular example of a mode foreseen by no one. The Cuban Revolution offered powerful confirmation of what could be deduced in the case of China – that there is much still to be learned about potentialities in the revolutionary process, in particular about the increasing role of revolutionists of action (foreseen by Trotsky) in contrast to the earlier predominance of the pioneers of theory.

To say that these revolutions deviated from the pattern forecast by classical Marxism does not bring us to the heart of the matter, however. The October Revolution in its time likewise deviated from the forecasts of classical Marxism (Trotsky's theory of permanent revolution was not yet part of 'classical' Marxism), yet in the final balancing of accounts the October Revolution offered the most powerful confirmation of classical Marxism. The problems in theory offered by China and Cuba are not qualitatively different. What they point to is the importance of the method to be used in approaching them. This was already indicated by Trotsky – if not as prophet, then as scientist.

In a postscript, Deutscher offers some contributions in relation to this. What he says is interesting but not exactly new to the Trotskyist movement, which has been discussing these questions since the downfall of capitalism in eastern Europe.

∴

In passing, Deutscher notes certain physical characteristics of Trotsky. The likeness grows to photographic accuracy. (Photography always misses somewhat). This is all the more notable since Deutscher never happened to meet Trotsky and had to rely on the impressions of others besides, of course, the written record.

The portrait as a work of art, one must also agree, is quite good. A reservation, however, must be registered. Deutscher's preoccupation with accounting for the apparent discrepancies between Trotsky's program of political revolution in the USSR and the actual post-Stalin concessions; Trotsky's program of socialist revolution in the industrially advanced countries and the actual advance of the world revolution in the colonial sector; Trotsky's program for rebuilding the revolutionary-socialist movement and the actual organizational weakness to this day of the Fourth International; lead him, in my opinion, to miss something very important. I am not interested here in debating these questions, but in considering how Deutscher's positions affect his finished portrait.

Trotsky was enormously attractive to not a few intellectuals. His power of prediction, his range of intellect and culture showed his mind without the slightest doubt to be one of the greatest the West has produced.

To follow Trotsky's thought in all its ramifications is an absorbing study, as Deutscher's biography proves. It is a challenge to measure Trotsky's theory against the historical reality. The temptation can even be strong to vie with the master by attempting a better construction where it may seem he went wrong. This is perfectly legitimate and one cannot quarrel with such ambitions. They can prove to be productive. A trap does exist, however. The very subtlety, range and depth of Trotsky's thought and the quantity of his productions, which make him so magnetic to intellectuals, can lead one to overlook Trotsky's essential simplicity.

In working closely with Trotsky, one soon noted an extraordinary combination of qualities: enormous energy, unbelievably quick perception and rapport, extraordinary memory, and the mobilization of these gifts in a most efficient and businesslike way. Mobilized for what? A very simple task – the establishment of planned economy in place of the anarchic relations of capitalism. This was the elementary chore which this genius set for himself as a youth when he decided to choose Marxism as his field. It was the job to which he stuck steadily through the years. He was still working at it when he was struck down.

If you wish to question the wisdom of how Trotsky directed his genius, as Deutscher does in the instance of his seeking to build a new international, it would seem in order to begin by questioning the wisdom of this primary decision.

A case can be made out concerning the abysmal waste of taking humanity's very greatest intellects and compelling them to become occupied with bringing order into our way of organizing the production and distribution of food, clothing, housing and taking care of the rest of our basic social needs. Trotsky's answer to that is that we do not choose the time we are born into. Our problem as individuals in finding our niche is to grasp the main tasks facing mankind, and, as members of the human race, do what we can to help accomplish them. From Trotsky's viewpoint this also offers a human being the greatest possible satisfaction.

All the rest follows, including the burning importance which Trotsky placed upon organization of the Fourth International.

But like all great men Trotsky had his foibles! Of course. But having granted this can we in all consistency maintain that the biographers of great men, including the biographer of Trotsky, are free from them? If we concede to Deutscher the saving grace of having his own foibles, perhaps it will not be considered out of order to suggest that one of them was failure to see the importance of probing deeply into the meaning of the kind of human relations that Trotsky advocated, sought, instigated, enjoyed, and participated in organizing, above all at the close of his life, in the light of his enormous experience and when he was at the very height of his intellectual powers. To bring the inner Trotsky into full light, he must be seen, I would judge, in the setting of his active pursuit of these human relations and as they fitted into his own great guiding purpose in life.

Our biographer's usually keen insight deserts him at this crucial point, and in place of all the threads falling satisfyingly into place to disclose the coherence of Trotsky's intelligence and will, the threads fray out into loose ends. Deutscher shows his prophet with eyes growing dim.

How such a clear-sighted genius could fail so lamentably to see things which Deutscher considers obvious remains an unresolved contradiction in the biography. Deutscher seems to sense this. He grants that Trotsky remained unfailingly optimistic about revolutionary perspectives to the very end; yet he suggests that doubts had begun to creep in. He makes much of Trotsky's argument in the factional struggle that broke out in the Socialist Workers party in 1939 that if the working class proved incapable of meeting its historic obligation then Burnham's anti-Marxist theory of 'bureaucratic collectivism' would prove to be the wave of the future, socialism a mere Utopia and all of Marxism wrong. He suggests that Trotsky at bottom discounted the movement he had founded: 'his real last will and testament' contains 'not a single mention of the Fourth International'. Deutscher bears down rather heavily on the theme:

> Thus at the close of his days Trotsky interrogated himself about the meaning and the purpose of all his life and struggle and indeed of all the struggles of several generations of fighters, communists, and socialists. Was a whole century of revolutionary endeavour crumbling into dust? Again and again he returned to the fact that the workers had not overthrown capitalism anywhere outside Russia. Again and again he surveyed the long and dismal sequence of defeats which the revolution had suffered between the two world wars. And he saw himself driven to the conclusion that if major new failures were to be added to this record, then the whole historic perspective drawn by Marxism would indeed come under question.

I think that Deutscher is wrong in believing that Trotsky 'interrogated himself'. He was answering the interrogations of others, and with the most powerful arguments at his command. Trotsky was as hard as diamond and completely flawless in his view of the long-range course of history. What did Trotsky really do 'again and again?' He posed the alternative facing mankind: barbarism or socialism. He did not hesitate to pick up the arguments raised by those who had really begun to doubt and to sicken of the struggle. He spun them to logical absurdity and exposed their theoretical bankruptcy – *their* bankruptcy.

Commenting on the 'overemphatic and hyperbolic' argument which Trotsky leveled against Burnham, Deutscher comments: 'Perhaps only Marxists could sense fully the tragic solemnity which these words had in Trotsky's mouth'. It is true that this was the way they sounded to some of the leaders of the opposing faction, but they hardly sounded that way to Trotsky or his closest collaborators.

We can perhaps better appreciate Trotsky's meaning by considering the same basic alternative which he posed as it stands today, almost a quarter of a century later. If the acuteness of the alternative had grown less, *without the action of the working class*, then the founding of the Fourth International would have turned out to be a Utopian project because its aim – the mobilization of the working class to avert barbarism – proved to be not necessary. Or if we faced the opposite situation – an actual perspective of centuries of barbarism, the project likewise would have proved to have been Utopian. What is the truth?

Neither situation holds. The alternative is still posed, but the delay in determining its outcome has enormously increased its acuteness.

The alternative, socialism or barbarism, has become the alternative, socialism or nuclear ruin. Physicists now tell us – Trotsky's followers only repeat it – that war with atomic weapons can signify the suicide of mankind and even the destruction of all the higher forms of life. Trotsky's picture of the possibility of a barbarism in which mankind would have to crawl painfully forward on all fours is idyllic compared to the 'tragic solemnity' of the picture now facing us – a barren planet in which life itself might have to crawl up again from the amoeba or, if lucky, some of the lower vertebrates.

Does this mean that we must abandon hope or that there is room for more doubt than in Trotsky's last years before the outbreak of World War II? On the contrary! The need for socialism is posed all the more imperatively.

This leads us directly to the point of sharpest difference with Deutscher. Who is to be credited with this 'success' in intensifying the acuteness of the historic dilemma facing the world? The Second and Third Internationals! The life-and-death importance of Trotsky's final efforts to construct a new international has received sufficient confirmation we should think.

A pure pragmatist will demand, 'All right, where are the revolutions in the West?' The question lacks the intended force because it leaves out the great postwar upsurge, especially in Italy and France, a phenomenon which Deutscher does not consider although it is surely relevant in any discussion of Trotsky's forecasts. Is another upsurge, of even greater potential power, ruled out? In questions relating to the decline of a system and the rise of a new one, sufficient range must be taken; exactly how much range is not easily determined even by a genius like Trotsky.

Deutscher is so concerned to prove the hopelessness of Trotsky's project of rebuilding the world-wide revolutionary socialist movement that he puts in question a different thesis which he proffers; namely, that Stalin was much more capable than Trotsky estimated him to be. Stalin, as Deutscher proves, was infinitely afraid of the Fourth International. He displayed an obsession over it. Was this merely paranoia, the counterpart to Trotsky's grotesque foible, or did the capable Stalin have a certain amount of reason in his efforts to exorcise the phantom? Why Stalin's extraordinary concern over the sectarian squabbles and impotent goings-on of Trotsky's followers? (Other rulers, too, have shown strange disinclination to accept the view that the Trotskyist movement can be dismissed as a 'failure').

It is hard to know exactly what Deutscher thinks Trotsky and his run-of-the-mill followers should have done in the years when they were fighting the spread of fascism, struggling against Stalinism and the reformism of the Social

Democracy, warning of the danger of World War II, posing the historic dilemma facing mankind and seeking to build a revolutionary-socialist leadership.

Trotsky's work in collaboration with the 'vulgar' followers who rallied to his program provides one of the best keys to a deeper understanding of his character. Deutscher is grievously blind to this. If you view Trotsky primarily as a prophet, as Deutscher does, this blind spot becomes understandable. It is not easy for a prophet to transfer his gifts; it is even quite a foible to try it. If you look at Trotsky just a bit differently, however, his efforts come into better focus. Let me resort to analogy. In an epidemic it is necessary for a physician to take a leading part in the community defense, utilizing his special knowledge to help organize, with whatever means are available, a campaign to stem the epidemic and eventually eliminate the possibility of its recurrence. In his novel *La Peste*, Camus offers us the figure of Dr. Bernard Rieux, who finally succeeded in mobilizing his home town against the disease first noticed in the abnormal behavior of the rat population. The team assembled by Dr. Rieux learned a great deal about bubonic plague and how to meet it at the risk and even cost of their own lives. Dr. Rieux, a genuine humanist, offers his highest tribute to these comrades and collaborators in the fearful work they had to undertake together. A certain symbolism is evident in this remarkable novel. The perceptiveness displayed by Camus in the case of his main figure is instructive and well worth pondering.

Deutscher condemns the human material Trotsky had to work with, implying that this was one of the basic reasons for the 'failure' of the Fourth International. He feels that the human material which Lenin and Trotsky had at their disposal before the October Revolution was better. In the West, particularly, the quality was poor.

The question, however, is not that simple. As the Spanish Revolution – to name an outstanding instance – proved, the raw human material was adequate to the task at hand. The cadres that came to Trotskyism at the time were far from being the worst fighters, the least self-sacrificing, or the least intelligent. The Stalinists, anyway, feared them to an uncommon degree and with good cause because they were of the same rebel type that staffed the ranks of the Communist parties, men and women who were loyal to those parties by mistake, because they had not yet had time or opportunity to understand the difference between the Soviet state and its Stalinist regime.

The tempo of developments, which in general favored the swift growth of Trotskyism, particularly in relation to the Communist parties, turned against the movement in two supreme instances, the outbreak of war and the victory of the Soviet Union. The first event temporarily deferred everything, laying the foundation, of course, for explosive developments later on. The second, a completely progressive outcome, had the contradictory effect of temporarily strengthening Stalinism (as the Trotskyist movement clearly saw at the time) while preparing even more certain conditions for its ultimate liquidation (as the Trotskyist movement predicted).

In any case, on the exceedingly difficult, complex and challenging problem of building a revolutionary-socialist movement, Trotsky and Deutscher are of different schools. Deutscher's deep skepticism was not to be found in Trotsky, not a trace of it. On the other hand, Trotsky was thoroughly familiar with the skeptical attitude, considered it without foundation objectively, held it to be a deadly danger and did his best to immunize his youthful followers against this disease.

Having said this, we can grant that the Trotskyist movement did have many difficulties, had its share of temperamental personalities who exercised undue weight in the small organization and who no doubt offered the great teacher problems of little novelty or intrinsic interest. Trotsky's attitude toward his pupils, for his movement was also a training ground, was one of infinite patience. And, we repeat, while he could be acidly ironic he never displayed skepticism, if we may make exception of his well-known reservations concerning followers of petty-bourgeois origin, especially the 'intellectual' variety, a subtlety in Trotsky's thought which Deutscher does not examine, since he dismisses the whole subject.

The strangest part is that Deutscher shows the highest regard for Trotsky's followers in the Soviet Union who were butchered by Stalin down to the last man and woman he could lay hands on. Deutscher also indicates Trotsky's feelings toward them. But the emotion Trotsky felt for his Russian followers was not qualitatively different from the warmth he displayed toward all who shared the vicissitudes of the struggle with him, his comrades in China, the rest of Asia, in Latin America, in Africa, in Western Europe, in Canada and the United States.

Trotsky's feelings could not be much different towards them because they, too, to the best of their abilities, were fighting the plagues of fascism, Stalinism, 'democratic' witch-hunting and the approaching war. They too shared with him the conviction that what is required to right things in this foul time we live in is basically rather simple. In short Trotsky and his followers, many of them at least, understood each other.

Instead of this unity, Deutscher presents a grotesque mismatch between Trotsky and his followers. And instead of the unity of Trotsky's Marxist outlook and his action in founding the Fourth International, Deutscher presents an irrational contradiction between the lucid vision of a prophet and the ludicrous bungling of a dabbler in petty sectarian politics. In studying the finishing touches to the portrait, where we have been led to expect a standard worthy of the subject, we suddenly become overly aware of the artist. We notice the brush in his hand and hear him arguing his special points of difference with the subject.

Just the same, the portrait is good enough so that looking at Trotsky on Deutscher's canvas, we suspect the Old Man of winking at us over the gesticulating brush. 'We have always had trouble with our artists. Let us not ask too much from them, but take gratefully what they can give'.

2 Exchange of Views on Deutscher Biography[17]
(1964)

George Breitman and Joseph Hansen

Editor:

I strongly disagree with Joseph Hansen's review of the final volume of Isaac Deutscher's biography of Trotsky. Although Comrade Hansen lists many of the points on which Deutscher is wrong and misleading, and answers some of them, he is on the whole too soft, too conciliatory. An example of what I object to is his footnote about Deutscher's reference in *The Prophet Outcast* to an attack on his views by James P. Cannon in 1954. Hansen attempts to 'clear this up' in the following way: 'Some harsh and even unjustified things were said of Deutscher'. His explanation is that 'at the time Deutscher's theory about the possibility of the self-reform of the Stalinist bureaucracy figured in an internal crisis of the Socialist Workers Party'. A minority, which eventually split away, was strongly influenced by Deutscher's theory.

'To many Trotskyists, Deutscher's position appeared as an alternative program which could be a bridge to Stalinism. It therefore was viewed with hostility. It turned out, however, that Deutscher was not interested in recruiting from the Trotskyist movement or in organizing a sect of his own, still less a cult. This spoke strongly in his favor'.

After the Hungarian uprising, Hansen continues, 'another phenomenon' became noticeable. Many Communist Party members, still afraid to read Trotsky's writings, began to read Deutscher. 'Having begun dipping into Trotskyism in this way, they thirsted for more. Through Deutscher, some of them eventually found their way to Trotskyism'. Thus Deutscher's position proved to be 'a bridge *from* Stalinism to Trotskyism. Trotskyists could not be against that kind of public facility. They therefore began undertaking their own self-reform – in relation to Deutscher'.

---

17   Breitman and Hansen 1964.

Deutscher and the Cochranites

But it is simply not true that 'harsh things' said about Deutscher in our press can be attributed to the undoubted fact that the Cochranite minority of the Socialist Workers Party embraced Deutscher's views in 1953. That embrace and its consequences were the main reason why Cannon attacked Deutscher's position at that time, as he himself pointed out (*Fourth International*, Winter 1954), but harsh things had been written about Deutscher long before then. In 1949, when his Stalin biography appeared, I wrote two articles in *The Militant* sharply condemning it, despite its positive features, for its false analysis of the Stalinist bureaucracy as fundamentally progressive. This had nothing whatever to do with any internal situation in the SWP.

In 1953, *The Militant* printed two more articles by me on the development of Deutscher's ideas after Stalin's death (in *Russia: What Next?*). By this time Deutscherism was an internal issue, but I would have written exactly the same criticism if it hadn't been. In the spring of 1954, when the first volume of Deutscher's Trotsky biography appeared, the Cochranites had broken with revolutionary Marxism completely and were no longer of interest to me. But *The Militant* printed six more articles by me on the pernicious errors and distortions of Deutscher. They were harsh, all right, but I cannot find anything unjustified in them, even ten years later; and I see that I correctly predicted then just what position Deutscher would take now in the final volume on the formation of the Fourth International.

Hansen now makes it appear that our common hostility to Deutscher 10 and 15 years ago was based on a belief that he was interested in 'recruiting' Trotskyists to a sect or cult of his own. This was never my opinion at that time, nor did I hear of anyone expressing such an idea until, after the publication of the second volume of the biography in 1959 Hansen began to revise his attitude toward Deutscher. It never occurred to me 10 years ago because, on the face of it, Deutscher was essentially a commentator and bystander. He could not have any interest in recruiting anybody to any organization because he thought and thinks organization is useless or harmful. All he was interested in doing was refuting Trotsky's *ideas*, while praising Trotsky was a genius and prophet.

What Deutscher wanted to recruit members of the Fourth International to was not another organization but to the conception that it was a waste of time to build such organizations. Personally, I think it would speak more 'strongly in his favor' if he had tried to build an organization to put his ideas into effect, as Trotsky did. In this connection, I do not understand why Hansen finds it 'hard to know exactly what Deutscher thinks' Trotsky and his followers should have been doing. Everything Deutscher writes testifies to his belief that Trotsky and his supporters should have been writing against fascism, Stalinism, imperialism, etc., and that's all. Analysis and propaganda, yes; building a revolutionary party or international, no.

I also have serious reservations about Hansen's contention that 'through Deutscher, some of them (Communist Party members) eventually found their way to Trotskyism'. It is true that some of them found an introduction to Trotsky's ideas in Deutscher, but in a distorted form. To find 'their way to Trotskyism', they would have had to go around or over Deutscher, not through him, and, in this country at least, few did. For most of them, Deutscher served as a stopping point; as a justification for breaking with Stalinism, but also as a justification for rejecting Trotsky's conclusion on what to do.

For most readers of the Trotsky biography, I believe, the conclusion will be that Trotsky was a great man but that 'Trotskyism' is Utopian and impractical. As a 'public facility', Deutscher is more like a detour or dead end than a bridge, and I not only could be against that kind of facility, but am. If this is what led Hansen to 'reform' his attitude to Deutscher, I would recommend that he take another and closer look at where this facility has led most readers.

Finally, I question the use of Hansen's analogy of Deutscher's biography of Trotsky with a portrait that might be painted of Trotsky by an artist. ('Let us not ask too much from them (artists), but take gratefully what they can give'). If Deutscher gives a portrait, that is only incidental. His is a *political* biography, that is, political analysis, not art (however well Deutscher writes). Perhaps Hansen's review would have been better if he had treated it primarily as false political analysis rather than as a work of art marred by the obtrusiveness of a gesticulating brush.

George Breitman
Detroit, Michigan

Reply by Joseph Hansen

If I understand Comrade Breitman correctly, it is *his opinion* that the third volume of the biography calls for an attack on the political and theoretical views of Isaac Deutscher – not only an attack, but a 'harsh' one; and that any other way of proceeding signifies an unjustifiable concession. I disagree, of course.

The immediate problem, it appears to me, is to decide whether Deutscher's biography of Trotsky, especially the third volume, is in over-all balance, an asset to the world Trotskyist movement or not. Comrade Breitman fails to state his opinion on this.

The question could scarcely arise, of course, if it were not for Deutscher's handling of Trotsky's relation to the Fourth International and his depreciation of the movement and its members. There is, I am well aware, anger in the Fourth International over this aspect of the third volume, particularly among young comrades who see with clear vision the historic import of Trotsky's work in founding the movement. But then anger is not the best counselor in politics.

The truth is, in my opinion, that the biography is a valuable, even monumental contribution, but that it has flaws. These stem from Deutscher's own theories which he frankly states. For the Trotskyist movement, a first review, it appears to me, should indicate in what way and to what degree the flaws affect the portrait that is offered of Trotsky, but that it should leave no doubt on the main point – that the biography as a whole is a very positive contribution. This is what I sought to do in the review.

Importance of the Biography

If I may venture a prediction, Trotskyists throughout the world will give this biography a prominent place in their bookstores and literature racks and advise contacts to read it. They will also indicate their differences with the biographer, particularly on the question of the Fourth International, undoubtedly engage with him in further polemics, and suggest that those who are interested will find it fruitful to consult other writings, not least of all Trotsky's own works. And this attitude, I am sure, will prove sound.

Comrade Breitman and I obviously disagree on the possible effect of Deutscher's biography on the growth of the Trotskyist movement. No doubt a good many readers, in the United States 'at least' – under present political conditions – will accept Deutscher's estimate of the Fourth International uncritically. But I do not believe that this will hold to the same degree elsewhere, or that it will hold in the United States with a rise in the class struggle. If I judge the biography correctly, it will provide rebel youth with a sufficient appreciation of Trotsky to want more; to arouse interest in going to original sources; and, as the question of constructing a revolutionary party grows still more acute, they will be less and less inclined to pay attention to what Deutscher thinks should or should not have been done in 1938.

The possible influence of the biography must be judged on a wider basis than is provided by the United States. Countries like Italy and Japan where Deutscher is widely read should at least be brought in, not to mention some of the workers states where his writings have become known and where they constitute a first introduction to Trotsky.

∴

On a couple of specific points related to the footnote which Comrade Breitman questions:

I made the statement, with specific reference to an article written by James P. Cannon in 1954, 'Some harsh and even unjustified things were said of Deutscher'. Taking issue with this statement, Comrade Breitman defends the 'harsh' things which James P. Cannon said in his article of 1954 and widens the defense to include things said by Breitman in many articles beginning in 1949. I do not understand why Comrade Breitman feels it necessary to take in so much territory unless he feels something fundamental is involved.

But this is not the case, as I think can be shown without great difficulty. First of all, as to my failure to use a 'harsh' tone in considering Deutscher's views. I see no factional fight in the Fourth International today which involves Deutscher's views *in the way some of us thought they were involved in 1953–54*, a feeling which I am convinced was reflected in Comrade Cannon's article of 1954. Am I mistaken in this estimate of the situation in the Fourth International today? I do not think so.

Secondly, on Comrade Cannon's article as an expression of Trotskyist programmatic positions – I think that it stands up well if it is borne in mind that the harsh tone was due to special circumstances. But, thirdly, I believe that it must be admitted that the article included some 'unjustified' statements. These were not deliberate, since Cannon's standard in the sharpest conflict – it long ago became even his style – is to maintain scrupulous fairness toward an opponent even if he feels that political harshness is demanded in a situation. Inaccurate information was involved in the 'unjustified' remarks. My footnote was intended as a rectification for the record since Deutscher had called attention to it in the biography.

Possible Deutscher Cult?

Comrade Breitman considers that I am mistaken in the view that there was a fear in the Socialist Workers Party during the faction fight with the Cochranites that a sect or cult might form around 'Deutscherism'.

'This was never my opinion at that time', Comrade Breitman writes, 'nor did I hear of anyone expressing such an idea until, after the publication of the second volume of the biography in 1959, Hansen began to revise his attitude toward Deutscher'.

All I can say to this is that it was my own opinion at the time that the danger existed. I came to this opinion in the New York local where the fight first flared up in an acute way and where I had some influence from the beginning in shaping its development and final outcome. At the time I was under the impression that others shared this opinion, especially those involved in the brunt of the struggle in New York. Evidently Comrade Breitman neither shared this view nor heard about it at that time. As to the change in my views on this specific point, it began in 1955 – not 1959 – and was due in part to what happened in the faction fight and to new evidence which by 1958 had become definitive in my mind. This involved no change on basic political and theoretical questions; I saw certain individuals and tactical questions differently.

I still think it speaks in Deutscher's favor that he did not respond to any overtures or opportunities to sponsor a sect based on his special views. I am looking at this from the standpoint of the political interests of the Trotskyist movement. On the other hand, I share Comrade Breitman's view that Deutscher's depreciation of the launching of the Fourth International and the effort to build it has nothing in common with Trotskyism. I sought to voice this in the review: 'Deutscher's deep skepticism was not to be found in Trotsky, not a trace of it. On the other hand, Trotsky was thoroughly familiar with the skeptical attitude, considered it without foundation objectively, held it to be a deadly danger and did his best to immunize his youthful followers against this disease'.

This is 'too soft, too conciliatory?' All right, but the political position is evident, isn't it?

As for the objection about considering the portrait of Trotsky created by the biographer, I fail to get it. What's a biography for if not to give us a portrait as well as a history? Is art necessarily at war with politics? How apt Deutscher is when he says of Trotsky's *History of the Russian Revolution*: 'Whereas Marx towers above the disciple in the power of his abstract thought and gothic imagination, the disciple is superior as epic artist, especially as master of the graphic portrayal of masses and individuals in action. His socio-political analysis and artistic vision are in such concord that there is no trace of any divergence'.

Trotsky as 'epic artist!' Well, why not? And in the same way it is perfectly legitimate and proper to apply the same criterion to the work of his biographer and ask how well he meets it. I think that on the whole, he did very well; save that when it came to Trotsky and the Fourth International his 'artistic vision' failed him.

3 The Chinese Revolution – Its Character and Development[18]
(1962)

Arne Swabeck and John Liang (Frank Glass)

I

The third Chinese revolution, initiated in 1949 by the overthrow of the Kuomintang regime, reproduced the dynamics of the 1917 Russian revolution on the vast scale of Asia. The new China became a powerhouse, extending the revolution to North Korea and North Viet Nam. It sparked colonial revolts in Southeast Asia that swept through the Middle East and into Africa. The revolution ended the political isolation of the Soviet Union, upset the capitalist world equilibrium and altered the relationship of world forces to the advantage of the nascent socialist order.

The second Chinese revolution of 1925–27 had been defeated primarily because of the opportunist, class-collaborationist policy which Stalin imposed on the Chinese Communist Party (CCP). The CCP was subordinated to the Kuomintang, and the workers and the peasantry to the bourgeoisie. The resurgence of 1947–49 triumphed when the CCP, retaining its political independence, engaged in a struggle for power by revolutionary means, and proved itself an adequate instrument for the historic task.

II

Between the defeated revolution of 1925–27 and the revolutionary triumph of 1947–49 lay the protracted period of civil war and struggle to repel the Japanese imperialist invaders. After Chiang Kai-shek's forces, defeated in frontal warfare, had retreated to the West, a predominantly peasant army, operating in the countryside, under CCP leadership, continued the struggle. Peasants who could

---

18   Swabeck and Liang 1962.

not otherwise have been mobilized rallied in support of the party policy that combined the fight against the invaders with the struggle against oppressive landlordism. Once mobilized, the peasantry proved to be an invincible force.

In the anti-Japanese war the CCP and its guerrilla armies gained the initiative and leadership. The party's forces grew swiftly. This determined to whom the victory would belong in the subsequently renewed civil war and struggle for power. Though the party leaders for a time entertained illusions about a coalition government, which did not and could not materialize, they did not repeat the Stalinist policy of subordinating their party to the Kuomintang. In the 'Anti-Japanese United Front', the CCP leaders maintained the independence of their party. When the revolutionary tide rose towards its peak, Stalin continued to give official recognition to the Chiang Kai-shek government, but the CCP set a course toward the conquest of power.

III

From the revolutionary victory came the People's Republic of China. The CCP leaders characterized the new order as the People's Democratic Dictatorship. With it re-emerged the old political formula, the 'bloc of four classes', which in 1927 had served to conceal the subordination of the Communist Party to the Kuomintang. But it appeared this time in an entirely different situation. The 'bloc of four classes' now became a political formula for the subordination of the national bourgeoisie and the petty-bourgeoisie to the alliance of workers and peasants, under the leadership of the working class. The 'compradore' or 'bureaucratic' capitalists, who were interlocked with the foreign imperialists and native landlords and had controlled the state power and monopolized economic life – these had been vanquished together with the Chiang Kai-shek regime.

IV

A revolution is a process, not an event. This simple axiom has been most clearly demonstrated in China. After the victory of 1949, which overthrew the Kuomintang regime, expelled the imperialists and created the premises of national unification, the revolution progressed to successively higher levels. The new regime set out first to wrest all capital from the bourgeoisie and centralize the means of production in the hands of the state. Alongside of these measures there took place a step-by-step reorganization of agriculture.

The properties of the 'compradore' capitalists, together with all Kuomintang state-owned enterprises, were confiscated. By 1952, the major part of industry, the banks, all the railways and most of the coastal and Yangtse shipping had become state property. Private enterprise remaining in the hands of the national bourgeoisie (medium and small capitalists) was encouraged to develop under government control. Unlike the young Russian Soviet Republic, where civil war necessitated total nationalization in order to secure militarily the power of the working class, China could afford to take more time. China's civil war had already been won. Capitalist ownership was allowed to operate under control of the new workers' state as a means of facilitating the restoration of a broken-down economy.

V

Meanwhile, the program of land reform proved a powerful engine of social change and economic progress. The peasants themselves had swung into action. They abolished landlordism, distributed the land to those who worked it and brought the countryside into the mainstream of social revolution. This was elemental democracy – not the democracy of a debating society, but of great masses of the people in their everyday life.

With the basic premises of land reform and economic reconstruction thus assured, the CCP put forward its general line of transition to a socialist-type economy. Where private enterprises of the national bourgeoisie operated under government control, they were now to be converted gradually from capitalist ownership to ownership by the whole people, a 'step by step abolition of systems of exploitation and the building of a socialist society'. The transition was to be effected by means of 'control exercised by administrative organs of state, the leadership given by state-owned economy, and supervision by the workers'.

VI

In 1953 the first Five Year Plan was launched. Industrialization now became a prime objective. But the contradiction between the individual, small peasant economy and the needs of socialist industrialization came quickly to the fore. Though land reform was completed, the primitive farming techniques on fragmented holdings led to a new class differentiation in the countryside. Poor, middle and rich peasants reappeared. This promoted the growth of capitalist tendencies and undermined socialist planning. There arose an imperative need for rural reorganization. Industrialization required large-scale agriculture, the amalgamation of midget peasant plots into more efficient farm units. The Peking government accelerated the development of the agricultural producers co-operatives. But while collectivization alone could not notably elevate the technical level of agriculture, it was essential as a foundation for technical and cultural progress.

VII

Like industry, agriculture had to be subjected to state planning so that the production of food supplies and industrial crops could be regulated and agricultural surpluses made available to help supply capital for industrialization. In its turn, the real material basis for socialism could be provided only by a machine-building industry capable of the technical reorganization of agriculture. The interdependence of these two major sectors of the economy necessitated their simultaneous development. Collectivized agriculture furnished food and raw materials for the rapidly growing urban and industrial areas, while industry provided better tools and sane mechanical implements to help elevate the technical level of agriculture. The alliance between workers and peasants was thereby strengthened.

Collectivization unfolded through a series of steps in which each new stage followed logically from the one preceding. These carried the peasantry from the early mutual aid teams, through the simple producers' co-operatives, to the socialist type cooperatives and finally the Communes, set up in 1958. Each stage provided sufficient time for verification and development to prove its progressively increasing value to the peasant, to agriculture and to society.

VIII

From the beginning the poor peasants were encouraged to take the lead in this profoundly revolutionary advance. It was they who formed the backbone of the peasants' associations. They received government loans, and, together with the lower middle peasants, they were relied upon to fight the rich peasants and spearhead the socialist reorganization; they remained firmly in the vanguard through its various stages. No rich peasants or former landlords were allowed to join the cooperatives until these were solidly established. Concretely, these measures illustrate the Peking policy of support to the poor peasants in building the alliance with the middle peasants. Not Stalin's policy was followed, but

Lenin's, namely: 'To succeed in achieving an alliance with the middle peasants – without for one minute renouncing the struggle against the kulak and always solidly supporting ourselves on the poor peasants'.

An important reason tor the success in transforming Chinese agricultural relations lies in the methods pursued by the Peking regime. They stand in sharp contrast to Stalin's collectivization, forced through by police terror against ferocious peasant resistance. Stalin's measures brought the Soviet Union to the brink of disaster. The CCP leaders used the methods of persuasion in order to enlist voluntary peasant cooperation.

A party directive, adopted December 1953, declared: '... they [the cooperatives] represent a transitional form through which the peasants can be induced to advance naturally and willingly to socialism'. It stressed as a 'basic principle' that the development 'should be voluntary on the part of the peasants ... compulsion and commandism and expropriating the peasants' means of production are criminal acts ... blind, rash adventurism is totally wrong'.

Mao Tse-tung characterized this rural reorganization as 'spreading the very essence of socialism, that is, making the principle of linking the collective interest with the individual interest the touchstone by which all words and. deeds are judged'.

IX

Some pressure from above to achieve the rural reorganization may have been exerted through state control of supply and marketing. But actual coercion is unnecessary where people willingly cooperate. The fact is that initiative from below, from the peasants themselves, was constantly outrunning government expectations. Skeptical peasants were left alone until they saw the more effective work with better returns and then came along. Thus over and above the economic gains, there was human advance.

The greatest assurance to the peasants was the right to manage their own affairs. The democratic control established at the outset, when the peasants dealt harshly with the landlords, was continued. It is maintained in the rural people's communes. These are self-governing politico-economic units. Each commune plans and carries out its own public works, its own agricultural, industrial, commercial, housing, medical, welfare and other activities – even including military training. While government administration and commune management are integrated, the communes are governed by elected councils in which all but former landlords have the right to vote.

X

Advances from the smaller cooperatives to the rural people's communes provided that broader field required for the fullest mobilization of labor in order to raise agricultural production and carry out large-scale projects like conservation, irrigation and reforestation. Together with such large undertakings, the small and medium-sized industrial plants, promoted by the regime and sprouted by the communes, furnished correctives to the chronic underemployment for the rural population. Surplus labor in the country found employment without migrating to the cities.

The rural industrial enterprises, sustained by local resources and supplying tools and materials for local needs, help fill the time gap until nationalized industry can provide the more complex implements of farm mechanization. More important, in these enterprises some of the agricultural labor force acquires technical skills indispensable to the growth of industrialization.

Above all, the communes have destroyed the outworn social and family relations that impeded progress. Opening up a broad road leading away from medieval barbarism to modern civilization, they have rescued great masses from the scourge of hunger, while assuring productive increases in farming and the completion of vital public works. This economic and social yardstick is for historical materialists the basic measure of progress.

XI

The peasants entered the cooperative labor force of the communes as wage workers. A social transformation of profoundly deep-going consequences thus occurred in the countryside. Transcending the achievements of the original land reform which destroyed feudal land relationships, this transformation signified the disappearance of the peasantry as a property-owning class.

The preponderant role of the workers' state in all phases of economic life, the nationalized property relations, state planning and industrialization, together with the elimination of private proprietorship in land and the launching of the communes – all these factors provide the foundation for the socialist structure of the new China. On this foundation a new culture is arising – a new age of science and technology, of the development of the arts, the banishment of ignorance and oppression, and the narrowing of the age-old cultural gulf between city and country.

XII

Marxists have generally assumed that the peasantry because of its intermediate and dependent social position, its cultural backwardness and its individualistic proprietary characteristics, is unable to play any leading independent political role. 'But Marxism', as Trotsky once observed, 'never ascribed an absolute and immutable character to its estimation of the peasantry as a non-socialist class ... The very nature of the peasantry is altered under altered conditions'. Trotsky noted the great possibilities discovered by the Bolshevik regime for influencing the peasantry and for re-educating it, and he added the significant remark: 'History has not yet plumbed to the bottom the limits of these possibilities'.

The Chinese revolution has probed deeply into these possibilities. In the civil war and anti-Japanese struggle the peasants played a political role independent of the landlords and the bourgeoisie. In fact, the Chinese Red Army, the revolutionary military power designed and assembled by the CCP, was overwhelmingly peasant.

As early as 1927, in his 'Report on an Investigation into the Peasant Movement in Hunan', Mao Tse-tung predicted: 'In a very short time in China's central, southern and northern provinces, several hundred million peasants will rise like a tornado or tempest, a force so extraordinarily swift and violent that no power, however great, will be able to suppress it. They will break all trammels that now bind them and rush forward along the road to liberation ...'.

The CCP accepted this estimate. It organized and it led the peasant uprising. A communist-led peasantry became the predominant force of the revolution. History showed once again that every social revolution creates its own unique forms and methods of expression, of struggle and of development.

XIII

While the peasants became the great battering ram, the CCP did not overlook the leading role of the working class and the importance of struggle in the cities. Shortly after Mao Tse-tung made his prediction about the peasant rising, he wrote a letter on behalf of the Front Committee to the party center, April 1929, in which he declared: 'Proletarian leadership is the sole key to the victory of the revolution ... It is therefore a mistake to abandon the struggle in the cities ... For the revolution in a semi-colonial China will fail only if the peasant struggle is deprived of the leadership of the workers'.

This conception of working class hegemony in the revolution was reaffirmed at the national party conference held in Yenan in 1937. Explaining that China would reach the stage of socialism only by going through that of bourgeois democratic revolution, Mao insisted that this 'bourgeois democratic revolution can be completed not under the leadership of the bourgeoisie, but only under the leadership of the proletariat'.

A declaration by Mao Tse-tung stated this policy of the CCP more explicitly, in June 1949, as the party prepared to take full state power:

> The leadership of the working class is necessary because it is the most far-sighted, just, unselfish and richly endowed with revolutionary thoroughness. Without its leadership the revolution is bound to fail, and with the leadership of the working class the revolution is victorious. In the era of imperialism. no other class in any country can lead to revolutionary victory.

XIV

To carry this concept into practice the party adopted a resolution stating that, henceforth, 'The center of gravity of the work of the party must be placed in the cities'. As the cities were liberated from Kuomintang rule, workers joined the CCP in large numbers. In 1950 it was decided to halt peasant recruitment and concentrate exclusively on recruitment of workers.

From this point onward the workers were considered the key factor in the constellation of political power; they were treated accordingly and they acted accordingly. China's ability to industrialize depended in large measure on their discipline and initiative. Special steps were taken to provide educational facilities for them and their children and to keep the ladder to technical, intellectual, political and managerial advancement open. A system of workers' participation in the administration of production was set up in all state enterprises under 'the leadership of management'. Simultaneously, the peasants were advancing step by step toward the socialist transformation of agricultural relations. Abundant labor power available in urban and rural areas was converted into the capital of China's socialist future.

XV

The energy, ingenuity and inspiration unleashed by the revolution promoted a socialist consciousness among the masses. They not only welcomed, but they demanded, and themselves undertook, the most decisive shake-up and abolition of capitalist property in city and village. In its forward surge, the ma.es movement exerted pressure and checked party tendencies toward class conciliation. The CCP not only rode, but as its policies show, tried to guide the revolutionary wave, with which it was compelled to keep pace. This reciprocal relationship between party and class has been a decisive feature of the Chinese revolution. The CCP, by its leadership of the revolution, from the overthrow of the Kuomintang through all the subsequent stages of social transformation, played and still plays a revolutionary role. This being so, we cannot continue to assert that the revolution was 'deformed' by CCP leadership and that the state which emerged from the revolution is a 'deformed workers' state'.

XVI

Every social revolution creates its own forms of state power, suited to its particular tasks and to the conditions of its development. China is no exception. To slap the label 'Stalinist' on the Peking regime because it arose from a revolution led by the CCP would amount to endowing Stalinism with a quality of permanence it does not possess. This parasitic growth originated and developed in a period of revolutionary retreat. It could not arise out of conditions of revolutionary advance.

Relations between the Peking regime and the people have been determined by the process of revolution – above all, by the continuous revolutionary advance. The class foundation for this relationship has been the alliance of workers and peasants under the leadership of the workers. The Peking government bases itself, first and foremost, on the working class and is supported by an overwhelming majority of the population.

XVII

When assuming state power the CCP leaders maintained their view that the Chinese revolution would be consummated in two stages – the bourgeois-democratic and the socialist. The first task of the new state was to carry through the historically belated bourgeois-democratic revolution: overthrow of the Kuomintang, expulsion of the imperialists, national unification, land reform. This democratic stage grew logically and without pause into the socialist stage, affirming in life the 'permanency' of the revolution.

XVIII

The Peking government is a highly centralized regime and as such displays bureaucratic tendencies – arbitrariness and commandism. But there is not in China a BUREAUCRACY such as developed in the Soviet Union under Stalin, a hardened social formation of a parasitic character, consuming an inordinate share of the national product, standing above the people – a social formation of the type that crystallized in the Soviet Union in a period of revolutionary retreat. China is a workers state with 'bureaucratic distortions' in the sense that Lenin applied this definition to the Soviet state during its formative years.

The CCP leaders always closely identified themselves with the people and proved responsive to the needs and demands of the masses. In the planning and promotion of a new social order there was and there is collaboration between government and people. The democratic tendency also appears in the armed defense of the revolution. Peking did not hesitate to arm the people and establish a militia in which millions of young men and women serve on a basis of equality. The same democratic tendency occurs in the rural communes, self-governing socio-economic units. In industry, the workers take part in the formulation and execution of productive plans and have unions to defend their interests. Thus the relationship between government and people is similar to that in Cuba, where we hold the Castro regime to be democratic although 'lacking as yet the forms of democratic rule'.

XIX

Our party's 1955 resolution ('The Third Chinese Revolution and Its Aftermath') had one positive merit: It designated China a workers state, obligating the party to defend this state against imperialist intervention and internal counter-revolution. In all other important respects the resolution has been proved invalid, particularly in its prediction of an inevitable collision between the Peking regime and the peasantry.

A turn is imperative. The program and slogan of the political revolution, which flowed from our false conception of the Peking regime as 'Stalinist', must be discarded in favor of critical support to the regime and backing for its basic policies, both domestic and international. This does not exclude, but rather implies, criticism of all bureaucratic manifestations and stress on the need for democratization in every phase of government and society, to be achieved by peaceful reform, not by the overthrow of the Peking government.

XX

In the ideological dispute between Peking and Moscow we must also take a stand on the side of Peking. This dispute arises directly out of the uninterrupted revolutionary advance in China, contrasted with the bureaucratic conservatism of the Kremlin rulers. The Peking-Moscow dispute has material roots that go back to the beginning of the Peking regime in 1949. Among them we may note: (1) The reluctance of the Kremlin to return or make restitution for industrial machinery looted from Manchuria in the closing days of World War II; (2) Soviet tardiness in withdrawing its occupation forces from Port Arthur and Dairen; (3) Kremlin failure to give maximum economic aid to China – still a cause of strained relations. The CCP justifiably demands that aid to revolutionary China should be given precedence over aid to former imperialist colonies now ruled by their national bourgeoisie.

The material conflicts between Peking and Moscow lead directly into the ideological dispute and serve to illuminate it. While the guidelines of Moscow policy are those of bureaucratic conservatism, those of Peking conform closely with the principles of revolutionary internationalism.

XXI

The needs and interests of the continually developing Chinese revolution cannot be adjusted to the Kremlin policy of peaceful co-existence with imperialism. This is a major factor in the conflict between Peking and Moscow. China's position in Asia, where it is surrounded by the undeveloped world of which it is a part, dictates the necessity of extending the revolution. Peking's foreign policy has therefore included consistent and active support to revolutionary struggles by colonial peoples, especially in Southeast Asia and Korea, but even as far away as Algeria and Cuba. This cuts across the efforts of the Kremlin to reach a peaceful modus vivendi with imperialism, above all with the United States.

In the ensuing controversy, the CCP leaders have advanced Marxist-Leninist positions on vital political questions: (1) The role of imperialism and the struggle against imperialist war; (2) the revolutionary or the parliamentary road to workers' power. Other contested questions flow directly from these two.

XXII

Without specifically naming the Kremlin rulers, the CCP rejected their contention that since Lenin's time there have been important changes that have outmoded his views on imperialism and war. 'On the contrary', says the CCP, these changes 'have more clearly confirmed the truths revealed by Lenin'. They continue: 'We believe in the absolute correctness of Lenin's thinking: War is an inevitable outcome of systems of exploitation and the imperialist system is the source of modern wars. Until the imperialist system and the exploiting classes come to an end, wars of one kind or another will still occur'. Therefore, 'Marxist-Leninists must expose the absurdities of the imperialists and modern revisionists on these questions, eradicate their influence among the masses, awaken those they have temporarily hoodwinked and further the revolutionary will of the masses'.

Regarding an alleged 'peaceful' road to socialism, the CCP speaks in equally clear terms. It takes issue with the declaration of the Twentieth Congress of the CPSU to the effect that the increasing strength of the Soviet sector opens up possibilities of achieving socialism throughout the world by new 'forms', including the conversion of parliament 'from an organ of bourgeois democracy into an instrument of genuine popular will'. This, say the Chinese, is 'precisely what divides Marxists from revisionists'. And they add: 'The capitalist-imperialist system surely will not crumble of itself. It will be overthrown by the proletarian revolution within the imperialist country concerned, and the national revolutions in the colonies and semi-colonies'.

Hence, 'contrary to the modern revisionists who seek to paralyze the revolutionary will of the people by empty talk about peaceful transition to socialism ... the proletariat must never allow itself to one-sidedly and groundlessly base its thinking, policy and its whole work on the assumption that the bourgeoisie is willing to accept peaceful transformation. It must at the same time prepare for alternatives: one for the peaceful development of the revolution and the other for the non-peaceful development of the revolution. Whether the transition will be carried out through armed uprising or by peaceful means is a question that is fundamentally ... determined only by the relative strength of class forces in that country in a given period'.

XXIII

The stand of China's leaders is a development of great significance. It tends to accelerate the process of breaking bureaucratic rule in the Soviet Union by its challenge to the monolithic authority of the Kremlin bosses and its reassertion of the principles of socialist internationalism. Peking's policy has already borne fruit: it compelled the Kremlin to identify the Soviet Union with the Algerian independence movement, despite Moscow's policy of peaceful co-existence with French imperialism.

Peking's stand is proving a stimulus to the revolutionary re-orientation of communist-minded workers in the capitalist world as they reject the opportunism of the Kremlin and seek anew the path to the socialist revolution. We must not dismiss this ideological dispute as a mere quarrel between two groups of Stalinist bureaucrats. That would mean misreading all the signs and excluding ourselves from an important development. Instead we should take sides in the dispute, supporting the positions taken by Peking.

4 Maoism and the Neo-Stalin Cult[19]
(1964)

Tom Kerry

With the publication of the recent Chinese indictment entitled: *The Leaders of the CPSU are the Greatest Splitters of Our Times*, the split between Peking and Moscow becomes definitive. The full text of the statement is published in the Feb. 7 issue of *Peking Review*. The text goes beyond the title by characterizing the Khrushchev leadership as the greatest splitters of *all* time, by asserting that 'the leaders of the CPSU are the greatest of all revisionists as well as the greatest of all sectarians and splitters known to history'.

The statement purports to be a historical review of splits and splitters from the time of Marx and Engels up to the present day. Its central thesis had been previously projected in a speech by Chou Yang, vice-director of the Propaganda Department of the CPC Central Committee, delivered on Oct. 26, 1963 to a scientific gathering at the Chinese Academy of Sciences. To wit: That 'revisionism' arose to plague Marx and Engels at the very dawn of the socialist movement. So it was at the beginning and so it will continue to the very end.

Chou Yang argues that inasmuch as every thesis must have its antithesis, the promulgation of the Marxist revolutionary doctrine [thesis] inevitably gave rise to its opposite [antithesis] revisionism. Not only were the founders of scientific socialism fated to combat revisionism but Lenin too, in his day, was compelled to enter the lists against the revisionists. And, according to the dialectic of Chou, such was the fate not only of Marx, Engels and Lenin, but 'of Stalin too'.

> 'This phenomenon may seem strange', Chou Yang opines. 'How can certain people who had previously been supporters of revolutionary scientific socialism degenerate into counter-revolutionary anti-scientific revisionists? Yet it is not at all strange. Everything tends to divide itself in two. Theories are no exception, and they also tend to divide. Wherever there is a revolutionary scientific doctrine, its antithesis, a counter-revo-

---

19   Kerry 1964.

lutionary, anti-scientific doctrine, is bound to arise in the course of the development of that doctrine. As modern society is divided into classes and as the difference between progressive and backward groups will continue far into the future, the emergence of antitheses is inevitable'.

With all due apologies to Chou, a nagging question still persists in thrusting its way to the fore: What is the criteria for determining who is and who is not a 'Marxist-Leninist?' Chou has a ready answer. The Khrushchev leadership has repudiated Stalin. 'To repudiate Stalin completely', Chou affirms, 'is in fact to negate Marxism-Leninism, which Stalin defended and developed'.

According to the Maoist schema of historical development the split was inevitable from the beginning. However, it is still necessary to fix the exact moment in time and the precise issue which signaled the dialectical transformation of Khrushchevite Marxism-Leninism into its opposite, revisionism. The time and issue are pinpointed in comment number two on the *Open Letter of the Central Committee of the CPSU*, entitled *On the Question of Stalin* (Sept. 13, 1963). It reads as follows:

> Stalin died in 1953; three years later the leaders of the CPSU violently attacked him at the 20th Congress, and eight years after his death they again did so at the 22nd Congress, removing and burning his remains. In repeating their violent attacks on Stalin, the leaders of the CPSU aimed at erasing the indelible influence of this great proletarian revolutionary among the people of the Soviet Union and throughout the world, and at paving the way for negating Marxism-Leninism, which Stalin had defended and developed, and for the all-out application of a revisionist line. *Their revisionist line began exactly with the 20th Congress* and became fully systematized at the 22nd Congress. *The facts have shown ever more clearly that their revision of the Marxist-Leninist theories on imperialism, war and peace, proletarian revolution and the dictatorship of the proletariat, revolution in the colonies and semi-colonies, the proletarian party, etc., is inseparably connected with their complete negation of Stalin.* (My emphasis).

The aspect of the Sino-Soviet dispute about which this article is especially concerned is the attempt to revive, regenerate and reconstitute the 'Stalin cult' on a world scale. The working class of all countries – I repeat, *all countries* – have paid a heavy price for the virus of Stalinism that has for so long poisoned the wellspring of Marxist thought and revolutionary socialist action. Millions of worker-militants who flocked to the liberating banner of Leninism in the aftermath of the Bolshevik-led Russian October revolution were corrupted, debauched and cruelly betrayed when the Stalin faction seized the power, strangled the workers' and peasants' Soviets, emasculated Lenin's party and extended its malignant sway over the international communist movement.

To begin with, it is a gross exaggeration to assert that the heirs of Stalin now occupying the Kremlin have 'completely negated Stalin'. For their own reasons and their own interests they have been constrained to lift but one tiny corner of the veil that has for too long shrouded the countless crimes committed by the genial butcher who defiled the name of Lenin and besmirched the proud banner of Bolshevism. Stalin was no Marxist-Leninist. He was a murderer of Marxist-Leninists – including some thousands of devoted Stalinists. The Chinese do a great disservice to their own cause in the struggle against the Khrushchev brand of 'revisionism' and to the regeneration of Bolshevik-Leninism by attempting to lead a movement *back to Stalin*. For nothing in the revisionist views today advocated by Khrushchev were not at one time or another in the past promoted and advocated by Stalin.

∴

There is today a growing mood of discontent and opposition to the flagrantly opportunist policies and practices of the Khrushchev leadership being manifested in Communist party formations throughout the world. A number of splits have already taken place and more are looming on the horizon. The questions raised by the Sino-Soviet dispute have been an important ingredient in this ferment. In their Feb. 7 document, Peking openly calls for an extension of these splits and encourages, promotes and supports the 'schismatics'.

The back-to-Stalin gambit is designed to channelize the opposition to Kremlin 'revisionism' within strictly defined limits governed by the needs and interests of the Maoist bureaucracy; to circumvent untrammeled discussion of the many basic issues raised in the dispute by insisting on establishing and maintaining the hierarchical order of progression – Marx-Engels-Lenin-Stalin-Mao. If successful it can only serve to substitute a Mao cult of infallibility for the now defunct Stalin cult in which all disputed questions of Marxist-Leninist theory and practice will be subject to the *ipse dixit* of the cult leader.

This tendency is already to be observed in the groups that have split off from the various Communist parties and embraced Maoism. In this country, for example, a small group which split from the American Communist party several years ago, after coyly flirting with Maoism for a period, has finally plumped for Peking as against Moscow. It modestly calls itself the Progressive Labor Movement. In the recently published winter issue of its magazine, *Marxist-*

Leninist Quarterly, there appears a programmatic statement by the National Coordinating Committee of PLM which purports to meet the need of the American working class for a 'revolutionary theory'.

We are informed in an editorial note that: 'During the past year the Progressive Labor Movement has been discussing the [Sino-Soviet] debate concerning correct Marxist-Leninist theory for our movement and for the international movement'.

We are availing ourselves of this opportunity to comment on those aspects of the 'debate' that concern us here: Stalin and Stalinism. In making their Great Leap from Moscow to Peking the leaders of PLM faithfully parrot the Maoist line on the merits and demerits of Stalin. Along with Peking they flay Khrushchev for downgrading Stalin in his 20th Congress speech because: 'It did not place both his enormous contributions and his serious errors in their actual historical context, but offered instead a subjective, crude, total negation of a great Marxist-Leninist and proletarian revolutionist'.

In an almost verbatim paraphrase of the Chinese statement *On the Question of Stalin*, the PLM article draws a balance sheet of Stalin's assets and liabilities and concludes that on balance, Stalin's contributions are 'primary' and his errors, 'secondary'. What precisely were these errors?

> In the matter of Party and government organization, Stalin did not *fully apply* proletarian democratic centralism. He was *in some instances* guilty of abrogating it. There was a great development of centralism without the absolutely essential corresponding growth of proletarian democracy. This *appears to have fostered* an inordinate growth of bureaucracy which *often resulted* in reliance on administrative *'diktat'* rather than the *full participation* of the party membership and people in making and carrying out policy. (Emphasis added to underscore the method of introducing qualifying phrases intended to minimize Stalin's 'errors').

But let's continue – the worst is yet to come! The PLM statement then plunges into a learned dissertation on 'contradictions', lifted bodily from Mao, to explain why Stalin fell into the 'error' of presiding over the monstrous frame-up trials and purges which converted the Soviet Union into a veritable chamber of horrors.

> 'Stalin', we are informed, 'erred in confusing two types of contradictions which are different in nature. Thus, he did not differentiate between contradictions involving the Party and the people on the one hand and the enemy on the other, and contradictions within the Party and among the

people. Consequently, he did not employ different methods in handling these different types of contradictions. Stalin was right to suppress the counter-revolutionaries. If he had not he would have been derelict in his defense of the Soviet State. Thus, many counter-revolutionaries deserving punishment were duly punished. But, because contradictions within the Party and among the people were not recognized as something totally different, something natural and even essential to the Party's theoretical growth and development, no Communist method of principled inner-Party struggle, proceeding from unity through struggle to a higher unity, was developed. *Many innocent people, or people with differences which could have been worked out in the course of principled ideological struggle, were wrongly killed*. (My emphasis).

Unfortunately, people who were 'wrongly killed' are just as dead as those killed 'rightly'. When Stalin was alive *all* were indiscriminately dubbed 'counter-revolutionary' and summarily executed. Those who now deplore such 'secondary errors' were among the first to applaud Stalin's frightful atrocities as evidence of his not being 'derelict in defense of the Soviet State'.

Who now is to decide which were the innocent and which the guilty? Who is to judge? As an aftermath of Khrushchev's 20th Congress speech on the Stalin cult a few of the 'wrongly killed' were 'rehabilitated' and a few of Stalin's crimes were disclosed. A few more rehabilitations and disclosures at the 22nd Congress. Instead of pressing for a full disclosure of all the facts of Stalin's crimes and the rehabilitation of all of Stalin's victims, the Maoists demand that Khrushchev call a halt to the 'attack on Stalin'.

∴

Under compulsion to settle accounts with their own Stalinist past, the authors of the PLM statement, present us with a bowdlerized condensation of the history of the American Communist party. We are informed that the CPUSA was cursed with 'revisionism' from its very inception. We are further enlightened by the assertion that the one golden era of the American CP was the period following the expulsion of the Lovestoneite leadership in 1929 encompassing the early years of the Great Depression. In the entire history of the CP one doughty warrior against 'revisionism' is singled out for special commendation: William Z. Foster.

To buttress this contention a companion piece to the PLM statement appears in the winter issue of *Marxist-Leninist Quarterly*, a eulogy of Foster on the occasion of the 80th anniversary of his birth, written by one Fred Carlisle. The PLM message to the American working class urging the need for a 'revolutionary theory' is thus simplified: On the international arena: Back to Stalin. On the American scene: Back to Foster!

Before proceeding further we must comment on the outrageous jargon that is the hallmark of Stalinism and which has now been spiced by the turbid Maoism of the Chinese. Words which had previously been endowed with a precise definition in the Marxist vocabulary have been transformed into verbal abstractions capable, as the occasion demands, of being invested with the most diverse meanings. The term 'revisionism' is a case in point. To Marxists, revisionism has been associated with the name of its most prominent advocate, Eduard Bernstein, author of a book entitled *Evolutionary Socialism*. Bernstein's attempt to divest Marxism of its revolutionary content was designed to provide theoretical justification for the adaptation to capitalist parliamentarism of the right-wing bureaucracy, especially the trade-union bureaucrats, who became a power in the Second (Socialist) International during the prolonged period of imperialist expansion and 'prosperity' in the latter part of the 19th century up to the outbreak of World War I.

The classic manifestation of revisionism was known as Millerandism, after Alexandre Millerand, a French lawyer and socialist deputy in parliament who in 1898 accepted an appointment as Minister of Commerce in the cabinet of the capitalist government. Millerandism became synonymous with parliamentary coalitionism. Millerand was the first Socialist to accept a ministerial portfolio in a capitalist government. His action engendered heated debate in the socialist movement of that time, which was divided into right, left and center. The left wing rejected coalitionism as a betrayal of socialism. The right wing chided Millerand only because he had not consulted the party. The center (Kautsky) introduced a motion at the International Congress held in Paris, in 1900, typical of centrist straddling, 'allowing that socialists might, as an exceptional measure of a temporary kind, enter a bourgeois government, but implicitly condemning Millerand by saying that such action must be approved by the party'.

This compromise paved the way for the later coalition policy of the Social Democracy during and after the outbreak of the First World War. The lessons of the struggle in the Second International against coalitionism constituted an important ingredient influencing Lenin's views on the nature of the revolutionary socialist party. Later, with the formation of the Third (Communist) International, a conscious and deliberate barrier was erected against the infiltration of reformist socialist and centrist muddleheads by the imposition at the Second Congress in 1920 of the 21 conditions for affiliation.

The People's Front Variety

In the hey-day of Stalinism, coalitionism was dignified by the name 'people's front' and was consecrated as the official policy of all sections of the Communist International at the Seventh World Congress in 1935.

Lenin considered coalitionism a betrayal of socialism and fought against it the whole of his political life. To him it was the epitome of revisionism and he wrote his polemical work, *State and Revolution*, as a refutation of the parliamentary cretinism of the coalitionists, and in the process elaborated and refined the revolutionary essence of Marxism. Upon his return to Russia in April 1917, Lenin threatened to split with those Bolsheviks, including Stalin, who favored participation with the Mensheviks in the coalition government established after the February revolution.

One question: Do the Marxist-Leninists of PLM consider people's frontism, the most odious form of coalitionism, as revisionist? They don't say! However, they do extol William Z. Foster as the 'best' of the fighters against the 'revisionism' of the American CP; Foster, who preached and practiced people's front coalition politics to the day of his death. And what of Mao? Can they find anywhere in his voluminous writings a forthright condemnation of people's frontism? I don't think so!

In China, coalitionism was first imposed by Stalin in the revolution of 1926–27. It there took the form of the Stalin-Bukharin formula of 'the bloc of four classes', under which the Chinese Communist party was subordinated to the rule of Chiang Kai-shek's Kuomintang. Under this formula, the Chinese workers and peasants were first disarmed and then butchered by the troops of Stalin's erstwhile ally, Chiang Kai-shek. As a result of this experience, Chen Tu-hsiu, then leader of the CPC, broke with Stalinism along with a number of other prominent leaders. All of whom were expelled from the Stalintern as 'counter-revolutionists'.

It was only after the Seventh World Congress of the CI enthroned the People's Front as the prevailing 'universal truth' of Marxism-Leninism that Mao Tse-tung was elevated to the position of party leader.

The Dialectic of Revisionism

According to the Maoist dialectic in which everything, including theory, divides in two – not three or four but exactly in two – the tendencies in the world socialist movement are neatly separated into two compartments: revisionism and Marxist-Leninism. Revisionism is elevated to the status of an abstract category in which the term assumes a generic character in which is subsumed all that is not accorded the sovereign title of Marxism-Leninism. Reformism, sectarianism, dogmatism, opportunism, ultra-leftism, each or all are included or may be inferred in the general term. What is revisionism today can become Marxist-Leninism tomorrow and vice versa. It has become, par excellence, a cult term. Only the initiates who are privy to the thought of the cult leader can be sure of what it means at any given moment. Instead of a precise word defining a specific tendency it has been transformed into an epithet to smite those bold or foolhardy enough to question or disagree with the latest revelation of the 'leader'.

From time to time differences of interpretation may arise between even the most devoted disciples that might lead to serious doctrinal disputations. The system cries out for a final arbiter around whom must be draped the aura of infallibility. Just as the Catholic Church requires its pope to interpret holy scripture, so does every bureaucratic formation in the labor movement require its 'pope' to resolve disputes that arise as a result of the inevitable conflict of interest between individuals and groups within the bureaucracy. To submit such disputes to the democratic process of discussion and action by the masses would endanger the existence of the bureaucracy as a whole. The bureaucrats fear this course as the devil fears holy water. With the hothouse growth of the Soviet bureaucracy after Lenin's death, Stalin was elevated to the position of supreme arbiter of the parvenu bureaucratic caste and invested with the divine afflatus of infallibility.

In this sense the Chinese are correct in twitting Khrushchev about his indiscretion in seeking to place sole blame on Stalin for the crimes committed during his reign. There is, however, method to Khrushchev's madness. His condemnation of the 'cult of the personality' is calculated to absolve the bureaucracy of all responsibility for Stalin's crimes. His task is greatly facilitated by the fact that once the supreme arbiter is firmly ensconced upon this lofty perch the illusion is created that the 'personality' has achieved complete independence from the bureaucratic machine that created him and that it is the man who manipulates and rules over the machine instead of the other way around. Khrushchev attacks the 'cult of the personality' in order to conceal the ugly visage of the 'cult' of the bureaucracy which continues to rule as before.

∴

Let us scrutinize, in the light of this brief historical review, the tendentious analysis of the Marxist-Leninists of PLM of what went wrong with the American CP, when it happened and what to do about it. 'From the earliest days of the communist movement in the United States to the present', we are informed, 'revisionism and its political manifestation, class collaboration, has been the chronic weakness'.

Not so. While the PLM theoreticians are prone to use the term 'revisionism' in the generic sense indicated above, in this instance they define its concrete political manifestation as 'class collaboration'. In the 'earliest days' of the American CP class collaboration was decidedly *not* its 'chronic weakness'. In the period following the Russian revolution of 1917 the dividing line between the various tendencies in the socialist movement on an international scale was their attitude toward the October revolution.

The revisionists who preached and practiced the doctrine of class collaboration were solidly lined up in hostile antagonism to the Bolshevik revolution. The earliest CP's, both in this country and abroad, were formed almost without exception out of splits over this question in the various parties of the Social Democracy. In this country the several Communist parties were established as a result of a split in the American Socialist party led by the left wing. The left wing split-off from the SP, together with the foreign language federations, comprised the cadres of communism which then split into contending parties each seeking recognition from the Communist International.

Disease of Ultra-Leftism

The basic weakness was not class collaboration but ultra-leftism. The tendency toward ultra-leftism was not at all peculiar to this country but was a malady that afflicted a number of the early communist groups in Europe. In fact, it was precisely against this disease that Lenin polemicized in his now famous pamphlet: *Ultra-Leftism: An Infantile Disorder*. Class collaborationists were not welcome in the Communist International of Lenin's and Trotsky's day.

But let's proceed with our perusal of the PLM statement for a clue to this bowdlerized version of history. 'After the expulsion [in 1929] of Lovestone', we are told, 'the party developed a militant pragmatic approach which appealed to workers during the depression and produced a mass base for the CP'.

In the article by Carlisle, eulogizing Foster, we are instructed that: 'During the 1929–33 years of deepest crisis', the American CP 'came closer to being a correct Marxist-Leninist program for the US than anything that had been developed during the past 70 years'.

This is incredible! The years singled out for special approbation by PLM encompass what has gone down in history as the 'Third Period'. The Sixth World Congress of the CI was held in 1928 under the aegis of the Stalin-Bukharin bloc.

Bukharin headed the right-wing tendency in the CPSU which included such prominent leaders as Tomsky and Rykov. For the whole period prior to 1928 the Stalin bureaucracy proceeded on the Bukharin formula of a casual romp to socialism in which 'socialism' would be established 'at a snail's pace'. The slogan at the time was: Kulak enrich thyself! The Left Opposition, under the leadership of Leon Trotsky, had repeatedly warned that the differentiation among the peasantry in the villages under the Stalin-Bukharin policy was strengthening the grip of the Kulak (rich peasants) on the peasant economy and solidifying their political control over the middle and poor peasantry.

The program of the Left Opposition presented an extensive criticism of the Stalin-Bukharin line and elaborated an alternative program of planned industrialization in the economic sphere and a restoration of workers' democracy in the Soviets and the party. Needless to say, the program of the Left Opposition was suppressed and the adherents of the opposition were slandered, expelled, jailed, and, in Trotsky's case, exiled from the Soviet Union. This did not forestall the development of the crisis predicted by the Left Opposition. It erupted soon after the Sixth Congress when the Kulaks engineered a strike against the Soviet government which threatened to starve the cities into submission and brought the Soviet regime to the very brink of disaster.

Recoiling in panic from the specter of capitalist restoration spearheaded by the Kulaks, Stalin responded with a sharp turn to the left. In startling contrast to the previous line, Stalin decreed the immediate liquidation of the Kulaks, the 'forced march' to collectivization and the first of his series of five-year plans of rapid industrialization. These edicts were carried out in an atmosphere of virtual civil war. The Stalin-Bukharin program adopted at the Sixth Congress was quickly jettisoned.

Stalin broke with Bukharin, who was retired in disgrace, and proceeded to purge the Bukharinists from their positions of leadership in the various sections of the Comintern. In this country Jay Lovestone was tagged as the scapegoat because he was identified with the Bukharin line. Although commanding a majority at the March 1929 convention of the American CP, Lovestone was summoned to Moscow where he was detained while the Stalin machine engineered a switch in leadership. Characteristic of Stalin's machinations, Foster, who was then the most prominent leader of the CP, was sidetracked, and a political nonentity by the name of Earl Browder was tagged as leader of the CP. Being absolutely dependent on Moscow for his authority, Browder was considered a more pliable instrument of Stalinist manipulation and Foster was shunted aside. Foster never forgave Browder for this humiliation.

To buttress his 'left turn' in the Soviet Union, Stalin proclaimed the advent of the 'Third Period' which was to herald the end of capitalism on a world scale. In the world outside the Soviet Union the tactics of the Third Period rested on the twin pillars of the theory of 'social fascism' and the 'united front from below'.

The theory and practice of 'social fascism' was a patent absurdity. Lenin had previously characterized the reformist Social Democrats as social chauvinists, or social patriots, etc. His intention thereby was to pillory the reformists as socialist in words, but national chauvinists in deed; or socialist in word, but bourgeois patriots in deed. But what could the epithet 'social fascism' mean? That the Social Democrats were socialist in word and fascist in deed? But the Hitlerite fascists aimed at destroying the Social Democrats by smashing the independent unions upon which they were based, and made no bones about it. Germany was the major arena in which the battle was to be fought out. According to the theory of 'social fascism', the Social Democracy, which commanded the support of the majority of the German working class, was the 'main enemy'.

The Third Period tactic of the 'united front from below' was another of Stalin's unique contributions which wreaked havoc in the world labor movement. The tactic of the united front was worked out and codified at the Third World Congress of the CI which convened in Moscow from June 22 to July 12, 1921. Contrary to the hopes and expectations of the Bolsheviks, the post-war wave of revolutionary actions subsided after a number of serious defeats. The slogan advanced after the October revolution of the 'conquest of power', was amended because of the change in the objective situation. The Comintern modification was summed up in the slogan 'the conquest of the masses'. That is, to win for the Communist parties the allegiance of a decisive section of the working class in preparation for the next revolutionary wave.

The Social Democrats still commanded the support of a considerable section of the European working class. The tactic of the united front was designed to unite the workers in action against capitalist reaction and for the defense of their interests. The tactic was devised to compel the leaders of the Social Democracy to enter united front actions on concrete issues in defense of the interests of the working class as a whole. In the process of such actions it was considered that the non-communist workers would be won over to the Communist parties as they became convinced of the treacherous nature of their reformist leaders. To forestall the expected attempt of the Social Democrats to limit and derail the united front actions, it was insisted that each organization maintain its independence. As Lenin phrased it: We march separately but strike together.

Stalin took this concept and gave it his own twist – which converted it into its opposite. If the Social Democracy and fascism were 'twins', as he insisted, a united front agreement with the leaders became impossible. To get around this dilemma Stalin concocted the 'united front from below'. That is, the workers adhering to the parties of the Social Democracy were called upon to break with their leaders and join in actions organized and led by the Communist parties. But if they were prepared to go that far, why bother about applying the circuitous tactic of the united front? It didn't make sense. The result was that there was no united front at all. On the contrary, in the name of the 'united front from below' the Stalinists preceded to split the labor movement down the middle.

American Version of Third Period

In this country, and others, the Third Period lunacy became a hideous caricature. Worker militants, members of the Communist party together with their supporters, were yanked out of the existing trade unions and herded into pure 'revolutionary' paper organizations under the leadership of the CP acting through the front of the Trade Union Unity League. The trade-union bureaucrats were tickled pink. At one fell swoop they had gotten rid of their most militant opposition elements. Needless to say, the paper unions of the TUUL were 100 per cent 'revolutionary' – and 100 per cent impotent.

In this country the Third Period idiocy made little difference one way or another. It was in Germany, the key to the whole international situation, that it exacted a heavy toll. By splitting the organized German working class, the 'theory' of social fascism and the tactic of the 'united front from below', paved the way for Hitler's march to power. So complete was the demoralization of the German workers that Hitler's hordes seized the power *without a struggle*.

The victory of Hitler in Germany marked the end of the so-called Third Period. It led to a sharp rightward swing in which the 'united front from below' was transmuted into the 'people's front' at the Seventh World Congress of the CI in 1935. If anything, the 'people's front' line was an even crasser mutilation of Lenin's united front tactic.

Third Period Stalinism can be aptly characterized as 'infantile leftism' gone berserk. And it is this aberration that PLM now advocates as a model for building a 'new' Marxist-Leninist revolutionary communist movement in this country. This, they contend, was the 'heroic' period of the American CP. This view goes far to explain the pronounced tendency toward irresponsible adventurism which characterizes their activity. You can never give birth to a movement – progressive or otherwise – by propounding and following a course of infantile leftism, but you can spawn a numerous crop of victims, which is just about what the Stalinist Third Period line accomplished.

The PLM statement, cited above, attributes the development by the American CP of its Third Period line to 'militant' pragmatism. I must confess that the distinction between 'militant' pragmatism and the non-militant variety, as philosophical categories, eludes me. The implication is that under the leadership of Foster, the American CP arrived at their line independent of the Kremlin. Unfortunately for the authors of the statement, Foster says otherwise. In his *History of the Communist Party*, published in 1952, Foster relates that during a discussion in the CI on the 'American question', following the March 1929 convention, Stalin criticized both the majority [Lovestone] and the minority [Foster] for their 'fundamental error in exaggerating the specific features of American imperialism'.

> 'It would be wrong', the Kremlin sage observed, 'to ignore the specific peculiarities of American capitalism. The Communist Party in its work must take them into account. But', he quickly added, 'it would be still more wrong to base the activities of the Communist Party on these specific features, since the foundation of the activities of every Communist Party, including the American Communist Party, on which it must base itself, must be the general features of capitalism, which are the same for all countries, and not its specific features in any given country'.

Under this formula, Stalin cemented his monolithic control over all sections of the CI. Policy originated in Moscow. And woe betide those who pleaded 'specific peculiarities' to warrant an exception being made for their own section. From then on every twist and turn in Kremlin policy was religiously echoed in every section throughout the world, special national 'peculiarities' to the contrary notwithstanding. Foster got the message. When it came to twisting in conformity with the latest edict from Stalin he was without a peer. This earned for him in the radical movement the appellation, William 'Zig-zag' Foster. This is the peerless fighter against 'revisionism' whom the PLM statement commends to: 'Young radicals [who] can learn from and emulate the devotion to the working class and socialism of such outstanding communists as William Z. Foster'.

Page from CP History

In his panegyric on Foster the self-avowed Marxist-Leninist, Fred Carlisle, explains that the main authority upon whom he relies for an evaluation of Foster is Foster himself. He neglects to add that whole sections of his eulogy were lifted bodily from Foster's *History of the Communist Party*, for which the original author is not credited. 'Foster's historical analyses of these struggles', Carlisle affirms, 'are quite helpful, being more accurate and objective than other available sources'. Irony itself stands disarmed before such monumental naïveté. At any rate, among the many examples of Carlisle's historical scholarship, we select one which raises an important question – Lenin's concept of democratic centralism as contrasted with that of Stalin-Foster.

> 'In 1928', we are enlightened, 'James P. Cannon was expelled form the CP for supporting Trotsky's left-deviationist doctrine. Upon his return from the sixth world congress of the Comintern, which had turned down an appeal from Trotsky in exile, Cannon began clandestinely distributing Trotskyite materials. Though Cannon had been a member of their group, Foster and Bittelman preferred the charges against him of disseminating Trotskyite propaganda, advocating withdrawal from existing trade unions, abandoning the united front and fomenting disruption. Eventually about 100 of Cannon's followers were also expelled and, under Cannon's leadership, formed an opposition league which later became the Socialist Workers Party, affiliated to the Fourth International'.

The charge of 'clandestinely' circulating 'Trotskyite materials', is supposed to convey the impression that Cannon was engaged in some sneaky, underhanded, criminal activity, warranting the most drastic penalty. Precisely what was the nature of this contraband which the sly Cannon was 'clandestinely' distributing to leaders and members of the American CP? The slander that it consisted of 'propaganda advocating withdrawal from, the existing trade unions', and 'abandoning the united front', etc., characteristic of the Stalin-Foster Third Period insanity, is downright ludicrous. The 'materials' actually consisted of Trotsky's article, *Criticism of the Draft Program*, which had been presented for the consideration of the delegates to the Sixth World Congress and which they were bureaucratically deprived of reading because it was suppressed by the Stalin-Bukharin machine. The article, which came into Cannon's possession through accident, was later published serially in the first issues of *The Militant*, then the American organ of the Left Opposition.

Does our learned historian even bother to ask himself the question *why* Cannon found it necessary to distribute such materials 'clandestinely?' Cannon was a member of the top political committee of the CP; he had gone to Moscow as a delegate of the American CP to the sixth congress. Wasn't he entitled to submit whatever materials he possessed pertinent to the decisions of that congress in a discussion presumably called for that express purpose? But, no! By that time the Stalin *pogrom* against Trotskyism raged throughout the communist movement. Trotsky's views were distorted, mutilated, or suppressed by the Stalin bureaucracy. The most effective theoretical weapon in the arsenal of the bureaucracy was the mailed fist – and they wielded it with abandon. And all of this, of course, in the name of 'democratic centralism'.

A Deadly Affliction

As he did with so many of Lenin's contributions, Stalin twisted the Leninist concept of democratic centralism into its opposite, bureaucratic centralism. Under Lenin's concept of democratic centralism, as practiced in his lifetime, all a minority was obliged to do was to *accept* the decisions of the majority after democratic discussion and debate, leaving to the unfolding events to determine who was right and who wrong. Stalin gave this concept just one little twist and converted it into bureaucratic law that a minority must *agree* with the majority.

It is a psychological impossibility to expunge from one's head views, opinions, and thoughts which might be at variance with the views, opinions, and thoughts of others. The practice of bureaucratic centralism inevitably led to the obscene spectacle of individuals driven to public confession of their 'errors' in order to avoid summary expulsion or worse. All of this was embellished and dignified under the heading of 'self-criticism' which, as practiced by Stalinism, could be more accurately defined as self-flagellation.

Trotsky once aptly characterized Stalinism as 'the syphilis of the labor movement'. To urge upon the American workers a return to Stalin-Foster is to counsel a course which could only induce an aggravated case of *locomotor ataxia*. And that is one affliction we would not wish on our worst enemies.

5 Don't Strangle the Party[20]
(1966–67)

James P. Cannon

[**Editors' Note:** These concluding items – unpublished in Cannon's lifetime – were gathered together, with introductory editorial comments and footnotes, by George Breitman, and published as a pamphlet by the Fourth Internationalist Tendency in 1983.]

1   Don't Try to Enforce a Nonexistent Law

February 8, 1966
For NC Majority Only
To the Secretariat

Dear Comrades:

I feel rather uneasy about the circular letter from Tom [Kerry] dated Jan. 28, enclosing a copy of Larry T[rainor]'s letter of Jan. 15 and Arne [Swabeck]'s letter of January 7 addressed to Larry and his letter of Dec. 14 addressed to Rosemary and Doug [Gordon], and also the circular of Al A. announcing his decision to join the PLP [Progressive Labor Party] (which I had already seen locally).

The Swabeck letter and the [Clara] Kaye document, which I had previously received, make serious criticisms of the party and youth actions at the Washington Thanksgiving Conference,[21] and make a number of other serious, and even fundamental, criticisms of party policy and action in general.

---

20   Cannon 1983.
21   **Footnote by Breitman:** An antiwar convention and demonstration at the White House were held in Washington, D.C., Nov. 25–28, 1965, under the sponsorship of the National Coordinating Committee to End the War in Vietnam. The convention was marked by heated controversy between radical and liberal forces, which led to disputes over antiwar policy inside the SWP. Cannon's views about the conference, given in a December 1965 speech in Los Angeles, were published in *International Socialist Review*, October 1974, and

The problem, as I see it, is how to deal effectively with these challenges and how to aid the education of the party and the youth in the process – in the light of our tradition and experience over a period of more than thirty-seven years since the Left Opposition in this country began its work under the guidance of Trotsky. One might well include the first ten years of American communism before that, from which I, at least, learned and remember a lot from doing things the wrong way.

Larry's letter of Jan. 15 suggesting disciplinary action, and Tom's letter of Jan. 28 informing us that the Political Committee has put the question of discipline on the plenum agenda, are, in my opinion, the wrong way.

Probably the hardest lesson I had to learn from Trotsky, after ten years of bad schooling through the Communist Party faction fights, was to let organizational questions wait until the political questions at issue were fully clarified, not only in the National Committee but also in the ranks of the party. It is no exaggeration, but the full and final truth, that our party owes its very existence today to the fact that some of us learned this hard lesson and learned also how to apply it in practice.

From that point of view, in my opinion, the impending plenum should be conceived of as a school for the education and clarification of the party on the political issues involved in the new disputes, most of which grew out of earlier disputes with some new trimmings and absurdities.

This aim will be best served if the attacks and criticisms are answered point by point in an atmosphere free from poisonous personal recriminations and venomous threats of organization discipline. Our young comrades need above all to *learn*; and this is the best, in fact the only way, for them to learn what they need to know about the new disputes. They don't know it all yet. The fact that some of them probably think they already know everything, only makes it more advisable to turn the plenum sessions into a school with questions and answers freely and patiently passed back and forth.

The classic example for all time, in this matter of conducting political disputes for the education of the cadres, is set forth in the two books which grew out of the fundamental conflict with the petty-bourgeois opposition in 1939–40.[22] I think these books, twenty-six years after, are still fresh and alive because

---

reprinted in the *Education for Socialists Bulletin*, 'Revolutionary Strategy in the Antiwar Movement', April 1975, pp. 12–17.

22 **Footnote by Breitman:** *In Defense of Marxism* by Leon Trotsky and *The Struggle for a Proletarian Party* by Cannon (Pathfinder Press, 1973 and 1972) answer the positions of the minority group in the SWP, led by Max Shachtman, Martin Abern, and James Burnham, which split away in 1940 after a bitter factional struggle.

they attempt to answer and clarify all important questions involved in the dispute, and leave discipline and organizational measures aside for later consideration.

Compared to the systematic, organized violation of normal disciplinary regulations and procedures committed by the petty-bourgeois opposition in that fight, the irregularities of Kirk [Richard Fraser] and Swabeck resemble juvenile pranks. Nevertheless, Trotsky insisted from the beginning that all proposals, or even talk or threats, of disciplinary action be left aside until the political disputes were clarified and settled. The party was reborn and reeducated in that historic struggle, and equipped to stand up in the hard days that were to follow, precisely because that policy was followed.

As for disciplinary action suggested in Larry's letter, and at least intimated in the action of the Political Committee in putting this matter on the agenda of the plenum – I don't even think we have much of a case in the present instance. Are we going to discipline two members of the National Committee for circulating their criticisms outside the committee itself? There is absolutely no party law or precedent for such action, and we will run into all kinds of trouble in the party ranks, and the International, if we try this kind of experiment for the first time.

We have always thought proper and responsible procedure required that party leaders confine their differences and criticisms within the National Committee until a full discussion could be had at a plenum, and a discussion in the party formally authorized. But it never worked with irresponsible people and it never will; and this kind of trouble can't be cured by discipline.

In the first five years of the Left Opposition, Shachtman and Abern took every dispute in the committee, large or small, into the New York Branch – with unlimited discussion and denunciation of the committee majority by an assorted collection of articulate screwballs who would make the present critics of the party policy, from one end of the country to the other, appear in comparison as well mannered pupils in a Sunday School. There was nothing to do about it but fight it out. Any kind of disciplinary action would have provoked a split which couldn't be explained and justified before the radical public.

To my recollection, there has never been a time in our thirty-seven-year history when a critical opposition waited very long to circulate their ideas outside the committee ranks, despite our explanation that such conduct was improper and irresponsible. We educated and hardened our cadre over the years and decades by meeting all critics and opponents *politically* and educating those who were educable.

I will add to the previously cited examples of the fight with the petty-bourgeois opposition two minor examples.

1. Right after our trial in Minneapolis in 1941 the well-known [Grandizo] Munis blasted our conduct at the trial as lacking in 'proud valor', capitulating to legalism, and all other crimes and dirty tricks. I answered Munis by taking up his criticisms point by point and answering them without equivocation or evasion. Munis's letter and my answer, some of you will remember, was published in a pamphlet on 'Defense Policy in the Minneapolis Trial', so that all party members and others who might be interested could hear both sides and judge for themselves.

That pamphlet was published twenty-four years ago, and I personally have never since heard a peep out of anybody in criticism of our conduct at the trial. On the contrary, my testimony 'Socialism On Trial' has been printed and reprinted a number of times in a number of editions and, as I understand it, has always been the most popular pamphlet of the party.[23]

2. I notice that the YSA has just recently published, in an internal discussion bulletin, my two speeches at the 1948 plenum on the Wallace Progressive Party and our 1948 election campaign.[24] The circumstances surrounding these speeches have pertinence to the impending plenum.

No sooner had the Wallace candidacy been announced on a Progressive Party ticket than Swabeck in Chicago, consulting with himself, decided that this was the long-awaited labor party and that we had to jump into it with both feet. Without waiting for the plenum, or even for the Political Committee, to discuss the question and formulate a position, he hastily lined up [Mike] Bartell and Manny Trbovitch and the local executive committee and from that, quick as a wink, the entire Chicago Branch to support the candidacy of Wallace and get into the Progressive Party on the ground floor. There was also strong sympathy for this policy in Los Angeles, Buffalo, Youngstown, and other branches of the party. The discussion at the plenum should be studied in light of these circumstances.

My two speeches were devoted, from beginning to end, to a political analysis of the problem and a point by point answer to every objection raised by Swabeck and other critics. It is worth noting, by those who are willing to learn from past experiences, that Swabeck's irresponsible action and violation of what Larry refers to as 'committee discipline' were not mentioned once.

---

23   **Footnote by Breitman:** Pathfinder Press's 1973 edition of *Socialism on Trial*, Cannon's testimony at the 1941 Minneapolis trial, also contains 'Defense Policy in the Minneapolis Trial' as an appendix.

24   **Footnote by Breitman:** Cannon's two speeches at the SWP NC plenum in February 1948, analyzing the new Progressive Party led by Henry Wallace and proposing that the SWP run its first presidential campaign that year, are reprinted in the Education for Socialists Bulletin, 'Aspects of Socialist Election Policy', March 1971, pp. 21–34.

There was a reason for the omission, although such conduct was just as much an irritation then as now. The reason for the omission was that we wanted to devote all attention at the plenum to the fundamental political problems involved and the political lessons to be learned from the dispute. My speeches, as well as remarks of other comrades at the plenum, had the result of convincing the great majority present and even shaking the confidence of the opponents in their own position. By the time we got to the national convention a few months later, the party was solidly united and convinced that the nomination of our own ticket in 1948 was the correct thing to do.

Committee 'discipline' follows from conviction and a sense of responsibility; it cannot be imposed by party law or threats. I have said before that in more than thirty-seven years of our independent history we have never tried to enforce such discipline. There was such a law, however, or at least a mutual understanding to this effect, in the Communist Party during the period of my incubation there. But what was the result in practice?

Formally, all discussion and happenings in the Political Committee and in the plenum were secrets sealed with seven seals. In practice before any meeting was twenty-four hours old the partisans of the different factions had full reports on secret 'onion skin' paper circulated throughout the party. Even the ultra-discipline of the Communist Party never disciplined anybody for these surreptitious operations.

It would be too bad if the SWP suddenly decided to get tougher than the Communist Party and try to enforce a nonexistent law – which can't be enforced without creating all kinds of discontent and disruption, to say nothing of blurring the serious political disputes which have to be discussed and clarified for the education of the party ranks.

I would like copies of this letter to be made available to National Committee members who received Tom's letter of Jan. 28.

Fraternally,
James P. Cannon

2 Reasons for the Survival of the SWP and for Its New Vitality in the 1960s

The party that we represent here had its origin thirty-eight years ago next month when I and Martin Abern and Max Shachtman, all members of the National Committee of the Communist Party, were expelled because we insisted upon supporting Trotsky and the Russian Opposition in the international discussion. It seems remarkable, in view of the death rate of organizations that we have noted over the years, that this party still shows signs of youth. That is the hallmark of a living movement: its capacity to attract the young. Many attempts at creating different kinds of radical organizations have foundered, withered away, over that problem. The old-timers stuck around but new blood didn't come in. The organizations, one by one, either died or just withered away on the vine (which is probably a worse fate than death).

In my opinion, there are certain reasons for the survival of our movement and for the indications of a new surge of vitality in it. I'll enumerate some of the more important reasons which account for this.

Internationalism and the SWP

First of all, and above all, we recognized thirty-eight years ago that in the modern world it is impossible to organize a revolutionary party in one country. All the problems of the different nations of the world are so intertwined today that they cannot be solved with a national policy alone. The latest to experience the truth of that dictum is Lyndon B. Johnson. He's trying to solve the problems of American foreign policy with Texas-style arm-twisting politics. It does not work. We decided we would be internationalists first, last, and all the time, and that we would not try to build a purely American party with American ideas – because American ideas are very scarce in the realm of creative politics. By becoming part of an international movement, and thereby participating in international *collaboration*, and getting the benefit of the ideas and experiences of others in other countries – as well as contributing our ideas to them – that we would have a better chance to create a viable revolutionary movement in this country.

I think that holds true today more than ever. A party that is not internationalist is out of date very sadly and is doomed utterly. I don't know if our younger comrades have fully assimilated that basic, fundamental first idea or not. I have the impression at times that they understand it rather perfunctorily, take it for granted, rather than understand it in its essence: that internationalism means, above all, *international collaboration*. The affairs, the difficulties, the disputes of every party in the Fourth International must be our concern – as our problems must be their concern. It's not only our right but our *duty* to participate in all the discussions that arise throughout the International, as well as it is their right and their duty to take part in our discussions and disputes.

Our Revolutionary Continuity

The second reason that I would give for the durability of this party of ours is the fact that we did not pretend to have a new revelation. We were not these 'men from nowhere' whom you see running around the campuses and other places today saying, 'We've got to start from scratch. Everything that happened in the past is out the window'. On the contrary, we solemnly based ourselves on the *continuity* of the revolutionary movement. On being expelled from the Communist Party, we did not become anticommunist. On the contrary, we said we are the true representatives of the best traditions of the Communist Party. If you read current literature, you'll see that we are the only ones who defend the first ten years of American communism. The official leaders of the Communist Party don't want to talk about it at all. Yet those were ten rich and fruitful years which we had *behind us* when we started the Trotskyist movement in this country. Before that, some of us had about ten years of experience in the IWW and Socialist Party, and in various class struggle activities around the country. We said that we were the heirs of the IWW and the Socialist Party – all that was good and valid and revolutionary in them. We honor the Knights of Labor and the Haymarket martyrs. We're not Johnny-come-latelys at all. We're *continuators*.

We even go back further than that. We go back to the 'Communist Manifesto' of 1848, and to Marx and Engels, the authors of that document, and their other writings. We go back to the Paris Commune of 1871 and the Russian Revolution of 1917. We go back to Lenin and Trotsky, and to the struggle of the Left Opposition in the Russian Soviet party and in the Comintern.

We said, 'We are the *continuators*'. And we really were. We were in dead earnest about it and we were very active from the very beginning. This is one of the marks of a group, however, small, that has confidence in itself. We engaged in polemics against all other pretenders to leadership of the American working class: first of all the Stalinists, and the reformist Social Democrats, and the labor skates, and anybody else who had some quack medicine to cure the troubles of working people. Polemics are the mark of a revolutionary party. A party that is 'too nice' to engage in what some call 'bickering', 'criticizing', is too damn nice to live very long in the whirlpool of politics.

Politics is even worse than baseball, in that respect. Leo Durocher, who had a bad reputation but who carried the New York Giants to a championship of the National League and then to the world championship over the Cleveland Indians, explained this fact in the title of an article he wrote, 'Nice Guys Finish Last'. That's true in politics as well as in baseball.

If we disagree with other people, we have to say so! We have to make it clear *why* we disagree so that inquiring young people, looking for an organization to represent their aspirations and ideals, will know the difference between one party and another. Nothing is worse than muddying up differences when they concern fundamental questions.

Working-Class Orientation

Another reason for the survival of our movement through the early hard period was our *orientation*. Being Marxists, our orientation was always toward the working class and to the working-class organizations. It never entered our minds in those days to think you could overthrow capitalism over the head of the working class. Marxism had taught us that the great service capitalism has rendered to humanity has been to increase the productivity of society and, at the same time, to create a working class which would have the interest and the power to overthrow capitalism. In creating this million-headed wage-working class, Marx said: capitalism has created its own gravediggers. We saw it as the task of revolutionists to orient our activity, our agitation, and our propaganda to the working class of this country.

Putting Theory into Action

Another reason for our exceptional durability was that we did not merely study the books and learn the formulas. Many people have done that – and that's all they've done, and they might as well have stayed home. Trotsky remarked more than once, in the early days, about some people who play with ideas in our international movement. He said: they have understood all the formulas and they can repeat them by rote, but they haven't got them in their flesh and blood, so it doesn't count. When you get the formulas of Marxism in your flesh and blood that means you have an *irresistible* impulse and drive *to put theory into action.*

As Engels said to the sectarian socialists in the United States in the nineteenth century: our theory is not a dogma but a guide to action. One who studies the theory of Marxism and doesn't do anything to try to put it into action among the working class might as well have stayed in bed. We were not that type. We came out of the experiences of the past, but we were activists as well as students of Marxism.

The Capacity to Learn

One more reason for our survival: one factor working in our favor was our *modesty*. Modesty is the precondition for learning. If you know it all to start with, you can't learn any more. We were brought to the painful realization in 1928 that there were a lot of things we didn't know – after all of our experiences and study. New problems and new complications which had arisen in the Soviet Union and in the international movement required that we *go to school again*. And to go to school with the best teachers: the leaders of the Russian Revolution. After twenty years of experience in the American movement and in the Comintern we put ourselves to school and tried to learn from the great leaders who had made the only successful revolution in the history of the working class.

We had to learn, also, how to *think* – and to take time to think. We believed in a party of disciplined action but disciplined activity alone does not characterize only the revolutionist. Other groups, such as the fascists, have that quality. The Stalinists have disciplined action. Disciplined action directed by clear thinking distinguishes the revolutionary Marxist party. Thinking is a form of action. In the early days of our movement we had a great deal of discussion – not all of it pleasant to hear, but out of which came some clarification. We had to learn to be patient and listen and, out of the discussion, to formulate our policy and our program.

Those were the qualities of our movement in the first years of our almost total isolation that enabled us to survive. We had confidence in the American working class and we oriented toward it. When the American working class began to move in the mid-thirties, we had formulated our program of action, and we were in the midst of the class, and we began to grow – in some years, we grew rather rapidly.

Internal Democracy within the SWP

Not the least of our reasons for remaining alive for thirty-eight years, and growing a little, and now being in a position to capitalize on new opportunities, was the flexible democracy of our party. We never tried to settle differences of opinion by suppression. Free discussion – not every day in the week but at stated regular times, with full guarantees for the minority – is a necessary condition for the health and strength of an organization such as ours.

There's no guarantee that factionalism won't get out of hand. I don't want to be an advocate of factionalism – unless anybody picks on me and runs the party the wrong way and doesn't want to give me a chance to protest about it! The general experience of the international movement has shown that excesses of factionalism can be very dangerous and destructive to a party. In my book, *The First Ten Years of American Communism*,[25] I put all the necessary emphasis on the negative side of the factional struggles which became unprincipled. But on the other hand, if a party can live year after year without any factional disturbances, it may not be a sign of *health* – it may be a sign that the party's *asleep*; that it's not a real live party. In a live party, you have differences, differences of appraisal, and so on. But that's a sign of life.

The New Left of the 1960s

You have now a new phenomenon in the American radical movement which I hear is called 'The New Left'. This is a broad title given to an assemblage of people who state they don't like the situation the way it is and something ought to be done about it – but we mustn't take anything from the experiences of the past; nothing from the 'Old Left' or any of its ideas or traditions are any good. What's the future going to be? 'Well, that's not so clear either. Let's think about that'. What do you do now? 'I don't know. Something ought to be done'. That's a fair description of this amorphous New Left which is written about so much and with which we have to contend.

We know where we come from. We intend to maintain our continuity. We know that we are part of the world, and that we have to belong to an international movement and get the benefits of association and discussion with cothinkers throughout the world. We have a definite orientation whereas the New Left says the working class is dead. The working class was crossed off by the wiseacres in the twenties. There was a long boom in the 1920s. The workers not only didn't gain any victories, they lost ground. The trade unions actually declined in number. In all the basic industries, where you now see great flourishing industrial unions – the auto workers, aircraft, steel, rubber, electrical, transportation, maritime – the unions did not exist, just a scattering here and there. There were company unions in all these big basic industries, run by the bosses' stooges. The workers were entitled to belong to these company unions as long as they did what the stooges told them to do. It took a semi-revolutionary uprising in the mid-thirties to break that up and install real unions.

---

25   **Footnote by Breitman:** Reprinted by Pathfinder Press, 1973.

There were a lot of wiseacres who crossed off the American working class and said, 'That's Marx's fundamental mistake. He thinks the working class can make a revolution and emancipate itself. And he's dead wrong! Just look at them!' They didn't say who would make the revolution if the workers didn't do it – just like the New Leftists today don't give us any precise description of what power will transform society.

People who said such things in the 1920s were proved to be wrong, and those who say the same things about the working class today will be proved to be wrong. We will maintain our orientation toward the working class and to its organized section in particular. I hope that our party and our youth movement will not only continue but will intensify and develop its capacity for polemics against all pretenders to leadership of the coming radicalization of the American workers.

Above all, I hope our party and our youth movement will continue to learn and to grow. That's the condition for survival as a revolutionary party. I don't merely get impatient with Johnny-come-latelys who just arrived from nowhere and announce that they know it all, I get impatient even with old-timers who think they have nothing more to learn. The world is changing. New problems arise, new complexities, new complications confront the revolutionary movement at every step. The condition for effective political leadership is that the leaders themselves continue to learn and to grow. That means: not to lose their modesty altogether.

The Importance of the Individual

I'd like to add one more point. The question is raised very often, 'What can one person do?' The urgency of the situation in the world is pretty widely recognized outside of our ranks. The urgency of the whole social problem has been magnified a million times by the development of nuclear weapons, and by the capacity of these inventions and discoveries to destroy all life on earth. Not merely a single city like Hiroshima or Nagasaki, but capable of destroying all life on earth. And it's in the hands of reckless and irresponsible people. It's got to be taken away from them, and it cannot be done otherwise except by revolution.

What can one single person do in this terribly urgent situation? I heard a program on television a short while ago: an interview with Bertrand Russell, the British philosopher, former pacifist, fighter against nuclear war. He's not a revolutionary Marxist but is an absolutely dedicated opponent of nuclear war and a prophet of the calamity such a war will bring. He was asked, 'What are the chances, in your opinion, of preventing a nuclear war that might destroy all life on earth?' He said, 'The odds are four-to-six against us'. He was then asked, 'How would you raise the odds of being able to prevent a nuclear war?' He answered, 'I don't know anything to do except keep on fighting to try to change the odds'.

Now suppose as a result of all the protests and the activity of ourselves and other people, we change the odds to fifty-fifty. Then you have a scale, evenly balanced, where just a feather can tip it one way or another. If a situation such as that exists – which, in my opinion, is just about the state of affairs in the world today – one person's activity in the revolutionary movement might make the difference.

3   A Trend in the Wrong Direction

November 12, 1966
Copies to:
Ed Shaw, New York
Jean Simon, Cleveland
Reba Hansen
New York, N.Y.

Dear Reba:

This answers your letter of November 2 with which you enclosed a copy of Jean Simon's letter of October 12. I was surprised and concerned by Jean's proposals to change the constitutional provisions providing for an independent Control Commission elected by the convention, and making it a mere subcommittee of the NC, which would mean in effect a subcommittee of the PC. This would be the *de facto* liquidation of the Control Commission as it was originally conceived.

As far as I can see all the new moves and proposals to monkey with the Constitution which has served the party so well in the past, with the aim of 'tightening' centralization, represent a trend in the wrong direction at the present time. The party (and the YSA) is too 'tight' already, and if we go much further along this line we can run the risk of strangling the party to death.

As I recall it, the proposal to establish a Control Commission, separately elected by the convention, originated at the Plenum and Active Workers' Conference in the fall of 1940, following the assassination of the Old Man. The assassin, as you will recall, gained access to the household in Coyoacan through his relations with a party member.[26] The Political Committee was then, as it

---

26   **Footnote by Breitman:** Leon Trotsky, 'the Old Man', was assassinated in Mexico in August

always will be if it functions properly, too busy with political and organizational problems to take time for investigations and security checks on individuals.

It was agreed that we need a special body to take care of this work, to investigate rumors and charges and present its findings and recommendations to the National Committee.

If party security was one side of the functions of the Control Commission, the other side – no less important – was to provide the maximum assurance that any individual party member, accused or rumored to be unworthy of party membership, could be assured of the fullest investigation and a fair hearing or trial. It was thought that this double purpose could best be served by a body separately elected by the convention, and composed of members of long standing, especially respected by the party for their fairness as well as their devotion.

I can recall instances where the Control Commission served the party well in both aspects of this dual function. In one case a member of the seamen's fraction was expelled by the Los Angeles Branch after charges were brought against him by two members of the National Committee of that time. The expelled member appealed to the National Committee and the case was turned over to the Control Commission for investigation. The Control Commission, on which as I recall Dobbs was then the PC representative, investigated the whole case, found that the charges lacked substantial proof and recommended the reinstatement of the expelled member. This was done.

In another case, a rumor circulated by the Shachtmanites and others outside the party against the integrity of a National Office secretarial worker was thoroughly investigated by the Control Commission which, after taking stenographic testimony from all available sources, declared the rumors unfounded and cleared the accused party member to continue her work. There were other cases in which charges were found after investigation to be substantiated and appropriate action recommended.

All these experiences speak convincingly of the need for a separate Control Commission of highly respected comrades to make thorough investigations of every case, without being influenced by personal or partisan prejudice, or pressure from any source, and whose sole function is to examine each case from all sides fairly and justly and report its findings and recommendations. This is the best way, not only to protect the security of the party, but also to respect the rights of the accused in every case.

1940 by an agent of the Soviet secret police who pretended to be a sympathizer of the Fourth International.

As far as I know, the only criticism that can properly be made of the Control Commission in recent times is that it has not always functioned in this way with all its members participating, either by presence or correspondence, in all proceedings – and convincing the party that its investigation was thorough and that its findings and recommendations were fair and just.

⁂

It should be pointed out also that the idea of a Control Commission separately constituted by the convention didn't really originate with us. Like almost everything else we know about the party organizational principles and functions, it came from the Russian Bolsheviks. The Russian party had a separate Control Commission. It might also be pointed out that after the revolution the new government established courts. It provided also for independent trade unions which, as Lenin pointed out in one of the controversies, had the duty even to defend the rights of its members against the government. Of course, all that was changed later when all power was concentrated in the party secretariat, and all the presumably independent institutions were converted into rubber stamps. But we don't want to move in that direction. The forms and methods of the Lenin-Trotsky time are a better guide for us.

⁂

I am particularly concerned about any possible proposal to weaken the constitutional provision about the absolute right of suspended or expelled members to appeal to the convention. That is clearly and plainly a provision to protect every party member against possible abuse of authority by the National Committee. It should not be abrogated or diluted just to show that we are so damn revolutionary that we make no concessions to 'bourgeois concepts of checks and balances'. The well-known Bill of Rights is a check and balance which I hope will be incorporated, in large part at least, in the Constitution of the Workers Republic in this country. Our constitutional provision for the right of appeal is also a 'check and balance'. It can help to recommend our party to revolutionary workers as a genuinely democratic organization which guarantees rights as well as imposing responsibilities, and thus make it more appealing to them.

I believe that these considerations have more weight now than ever before in the thirty-eight-year history of our party. In the present political climate and with the present changing composition of the party, democratic centralism must be applied flexibly. At least ninety percent of the emphasis should be placed on the democratic side and not on any crackpot schemes to 'streamline' the party to the point where questions are unwelcomed and criticism and discussion stifled. That is a prescription to kill the party before it gets a chance to show how it can handle and assimilate an expanding membership of new young people, who don't know it all to start with, but have to learn and grow in the course of explication and discussion in a free, democratic atmosphere.

Trotsky once remarked in a polemic against Stalinism that even in the period of the Civil War discussion in the party was 'boiling like a spring'. Those words and others like it written by Trotsky, in his first attack against Stalinism in *The New Course*, ought to be explained now once again to the new young recruits in our party. And the best way to explain such decisive things is to practice what we preach.

Yours fraternally,
James P. Cannon

4 The SWP's Great Tradition

June 27, 1967
To the Political Committee, New York, New York

Dear Comrades:

I am opposed to the motion adopted by the Political Committee recommending the immediate suspension of Comrade Swabeck.

As you have been previously informed, I favor a different approach to the problem raised by Swabeck's letter to [Gerry] Healy. I explained my views to Art Sharon during his brief visit here, and I presume that he communicated it to you. Also, Joel [Britton] showed me a copy of his letter to the National Office in which he reported the discussion which took place at a meeting of the NC members here.

I consider it rather unfortunate that these divergent views were not incorporated in the PC minutes of the meeting which decided to recommend the suspension of Swabeck – so that the other members of the National Committee would have a chance to consider and discuss them before casting their vote on the ballot sent to them together with the PC minutes.

My approach to the problem can be briefly summarized as follows:

1. Since Swabeck's letter to Healy deals with two questions of great world importance – Chinese developments and our policy and tactics in the struggle against the Vietnam war – which are now properly up for discussion in the international movement as well as in our party, any action of a disciplinary

nature which we may propose should be closely coordinated with international comrades, particularly the comrades in England, and carried out in agreement with them.

2. Since we are just now opening up our preconvention discussion, where the questions raised by Swabeck will properly have their place on the agenda, it would be rather awkward to begin the discussion by suspending the one articulate critic of the party's positions and actions. A more effective procedure, in my opinion, should be simply to publish Swabeck's letters (to Healy and Dobbs) with comprehensive and detailed answers.

If past experience is any guide, the education of the new generations of the party and the consolidation of party opinion would be better served by this procedure. Examples in favor of this subordination of disciplinary measures to the bigger aims of political education have been richly documented in the published records of the fight against the petty-bourgeois opposition in 1939–40, and in the internal discussion bulletins dealing with the Goldman-Morrow affair in 1944–56.[27]

3. In the course of discussion, during a number of years of opposition to party policy, Swabeck has managed to isolate himself to the point where the immediate effect of the party's reaction to this new provocation will not be very great one way or the other. But the long-range effect on the political education of the party, and its preparation to cope with old problems in new forms, can be very great indeed.

It is most important that our party members, and the international movement, see the leadership once again in continuation of its great tradition – acting with cool deliberation to serve our larger political aims without personal favoritism or hostility.

Fraternally,
James P. Cannon

---

27   **Footnote by Breitman:** Cannon's letters and speeches about the oppositional group in the SWP led by Felix Morrow and Albert Goldman are printed in his books *Letters from Prison* and *The Struggle for Socialism in the 'American Century'* (Pathfinder Press, 1973 and 1977).

CHAPTER 7

History and Theory

Bryan Palmer and Paul Le Blanc

Articles throughout the various sections of these volumes are steeped in 'history and theory'. Some of what is presented here could have been included in previous chapters. For example, Grace Carlson's critique of racist ideology and William Gorman's study of W.E.B. Du Bois are related to materials in chapters dealing with racism and anti-racism, Myra Tanner Weiss's critique of Sternberg grew out of the factional struggle in the Fourth International, Joyce Cowley's article on the history of women who fought for the right to vote could be placed with other 'new stirrings' materials, etc. In the same vein, various contributions in chapters throughout these volumes could be legitimately placed here. The Trotskyist movement was like that – history and theory infused its origins as Trotsky and many others throughout the world grappled with what had gone wrong with 'the revolution betrayed'. With the founding of the Fourth International and its American section, the Socialist Workers Party, discussions of history and theory were never separable from political discussions of the current time and prescriptions for the future.

At the same time, there is something to be said for highlighting the sustained attention given to matters of history and theory in the US Trotskyist movement – particularly the breadth and diversity represented here. For as the premier capitalist nation in a global system ordered by an accumulative regime driven by the quest for profit, the United States exhibited trends in its development that could be discerned throughout the advanced political economies of the world. But it also had its peculiarities. How all of this factored into understanding the dynamics of revolutionary possibility were of central importance to those struggling to create alternatives to the far-reaching regime of acquisitive individualism.

In the years stretching from the 1920s to the 1960s, capitalism gave rise to the destructive crises of the Great Depression, the rise of fascism, world war, and imperialist aggressions that unleashed deepening colonialist deformations. American history, replete with the complexities of a colonial past that had unleashed an early movement of national liberation, was complicated by the subsequent ambiguities of class struggle that took place within a history scarred by chattel slavery's long legacy of racial divides and intense regional differentiations. As a case study of revolutions made, unmade, and remade, the

United States was a unique configuration of the general development of capitalism, complicated by the kinds of specific particularities that distinguished one national context from another.

George Novack (under the name William F. Warde) was one of dissident Marxism's most accomplished theoreticians. Active in the Trotskyist defense of civil liberties, Novack worked closely with John Dewey, a proponent of American pragmatism in the fields of philosophy, education, and political theory, being centrally involved in the 1937 International Inquiry into the Moscow Trials that Dewey chaired and that vindicated Leon Trotsky in the face of Stalinist depictions of the founder of the Left Opposition as a counter-revolutionary guilty of innumerable crimes.[1] Novack continued this labour and civil liberties work, so vital to dissident Marxism's development, by leading the campaign to defend those prosecuted under the Smith Act in the 1940s. He kicked off this practical building of a coalition dedicated to exonerating and freeing those charged and later convicted in the state trials reaching from 1941–43 with a historical account of just how integral revolutionary thought was to the entire history of the United States (see 'The Right to Revolution' in the 'History and Theory' chapter of Volume 1 of this documentary trilogy). Jailing people for espousing revolution, Novack argued, flew directly in the face of what the United States was about.

This did not, of course, mean that revolutionary ideas always triumphed, or that there were not historical occurrences of shameful bigotry and violent suppression of peoples and their entitlements that were central to American history. 'Progress' in the United States came with considerable costs, as Novack explained in his pioneering Marxist analysis of the Native American experience, in which racist genocide was exposed as central to the triumph of American capitalism. Compromised somewhat by the limited understandings of the time in which this essay was written, Novack's sensitivity to the ways in which the 'First Nations' of the United States were brutally suppressed as part of the preconditions of capitalist development, was nonetheless testimony to the basic insights of Marxist analysis (Document 5).

As Novack (again, writing as Warde) would later suggest in a 1957 pamphlet, 'The Irregular Movement of History: The Marxist Law of the Combined and Uneven Development of Society', the dialectics of historical development revealed how the path of humanity's advancement was disfigured by episodes

---

[1] Novack had earlier produced a key philosophical text on dialectics (Novack 1969), later producing another on materialism (Novack 1965a), while grappling with challenges posed by existentialism (Novack 1965b), and would later produce a Marxist critique of Dewey and pragmatism (Novack 1975).

of shockingly destructive and inhumane expropriation, suppression, and subordination.[2] Marx, for instance, referred to this history being written 'in the annals of mankind in letters of blood and fire'.[3]

One expression of this dialectical orientation was Novack's response to C. Wright Mills, the outstanding sociologist, radical gadfly, and dissident public intellectual. Mills, rooted in the classical sociological tradition but strongly influenced by Marx and Trotsky, was moving decidedly to the left over the course of the late 1950s and early 1960s, and had close connections to the dissident communism of the first British New Left of E.P. Thompson, John Saville, and others who founded the journal, *The New Reasoner*, which would later merge with *Universities & Left Review*, giving birth to the *New Left Review*. The Texan-born Columbia University professor produced a series of outstanding books defining key aspects of US society, reorienting the American intellectual scene. *The New Men of Power: America's Labor Leaders* (1948) dealt with the dynamics of the labor movement in the late 1940s; *White Collar: The American Middle Classes* (1951) examined the phenomenal growth of white-collar 'professionals' in the labour force of the 1940s and 1950s; and *The Power Elite* (1956) demonstrated that – far from being a democracy – the United States of the 1950s was dominated by three immensely powerful and interlocking elites, centered in business corporations, the higher levels of government, and the military. In *The Sociological Imagination* (1959) Mills offered a critique of and radical agenda for the social sciences. Two influential interventions into US political discourse – *The Causes of World War III* (1958), demolishing standard Cold War myths, and Mills's sympathetic account of a revolutionary challenge to the United States, *Listen Yankee! The Revolution in Cuba* (1960) – gave his contribution a special edge, and set the stage for his last publication, *The Marxists* (1962). Published posthumously, Mills's mass market paperback introduced unfamiliar readers to revolutionary historical materialist writings from Marx to Mao, and eased the way for a soon-to-be American New Left to eventually be open-minded and receptive to Marxism. Mills, at the young age of 45, succumbed to heart failure. He never managed to experience the full impact of his impressive scholarly and political labors, and his premature and untimely death in 1962 robbed American intellectual life of one of its most stimulating, wide-ranging, and provocative minds.[4]

Novack met with Mills, admired him, and reviewed his last work, offering a critical but balanced appreciation of the radical sociologist's contribution.

---

2 Warde 1957.
3 Marx 1972, p. 715.
4 For a recent assessment of C. Wright Mills, see Aronowitz 2012.

The comments in the lengthy letter entitled 'Intellectuals and Revolution' by James P. Cannon, the 'grand old man of American Trotskyism' (dismissed by many as being little more than a sectarian and anti-intellectual faction fighter), is noteworthy for what it reveals in its quite thoughtful and appreciative comments about Mills. What separated Novack and Cannon from Mills was not a disdain for intellectuals and their contribution, and the value Novack and Cannon place on genuine intellectual rigor and its importance is evident in their engagement with the radical sociologist. Rather, both Novack and Cannon saw Mills's accomplishments as considerable, and his development as important and promising. They differed from Mills in their conception of what Marxism was and, above all else, in the possibility of an American revolution and the role to be played in that revolution by the working class.

These issues are central in the development of Harry Braverman, a member of the Socialist Workers Party who wrote a number of significant articles on US history for the Trotskyist press under the party *nom de plume*, Harry Frankel. Frankel's sophisticated analysis of American society at the time of Andrew Jackson tackled the importance of class fissures in the United States of the pre-Civil War era at a time when the academic historiography on Jackson and the popular mobilizations of his era highlighted the conventional wisdoms of contemporary 1940s US political and social mythologies of classlessness.[5]

Frankel/Braverman would later become a leader of the Cochran faction. After splitting from the SWP, he would edit the journal *American Socialist* for much of the remainder of the 1950s. He would also play an important role at Grove Press, which published George Lavan Weissman's influential collection *Che Guevara Speaks: Selected Speeches and Writings* (1968), as well as a similar edited volume by George Breitman that provided one of the first collections of the talks and statements of Malcolm X. Subsequently, in the 1970s, as managing director of Monthly Review Press and a major contributor to *Monthly Review*, Braverman produced a classic Marxist analysis of the labor process under capitalism, *Labor and Monopoly Capital: The Degradation of Work in the Twentieth Century* (1974). This best-selling and widely-read book popularized appreciation of the impact of so-called 'scientific management' and its architect, Frederick Winslow Taylor, in disciplining workers, subordinating them to managerial initiatives. The book also carried on the intellectual labors of C. Wright Mills, outlining how the work of white-collar workers was being proletarianized.[6]

5　Subsequent histories would place increased emphasis on the Workingmen's parties and movements of Jackson's time. See, for instance, Hugins 1960, Pessen 1967, and Wilentz 1984.
6　See Palmer 1999, pp. 33–46.

United States history thus served as an entry point for many American Trotskyists into issues of theory and politics and their contributions were, as the case of Harry Frankel/Braverman indicates, to be long-lasting. The clear and stirring explication on the life and ideas of heroic American revolutionary Tom Paine, written by Jean Tussey (using the pen-name Jean Simon), was but one example of how history opened out into understandings of the present, and of the necessity of struggling to realize socialism (Document 7). A lifelong trade union activist and organizer, Tussey/Simon later produced the highly popular edited collection *Eugene V. Debs Speaks* (1972). 'Women Who Won the Right to Vote' by Joyce Cowley, a prominent figure in the Socialist Workers Party of the 1950s, would be widely distributed and read by young (and older) US feminists of the 1960s and 1970s, contributing to the development of the women's liberation movement during those decades.

The historic problem of 'the color-line' identified by W.E.B. Du Bois, and its various ramifications, is the focal point for considerable attention by a number of contributions in these volumes (most influentially from C.L.R. James and George Breitman), but in this section we present two major pieces. One is a lengthy and early work by Grace Carlson, 'The Myth of Racial Superiority'. Carlson – a leading activist in Minneapolis, a Smith Act defendant, and an SWP Vice Presidential candidate – provides the most sustained examination of the topic to appear in the Trotskyist press up to that time. The other contribution presented here is William Gorman's thoughtful and capable survey, 'W.E.B. Du Bois and His Work'. Gorman was a prominent member of the Johnson-Forest tendency, whose members provided many insights and works of value, deepening anti-racist sensibilities and activism within the Trotskyist movement.

Polemics and factional struggles within the Trotskyist movement have often been depicted as the ultimate example of sterile self-destructiveness on the Left. A contrary view is that polemical interventions are clearly necessary when there are serious differences among revolutionaries. Such disagreements cannot simply be papered over, and forceful exchanges that clarify important differences in perspective and program, strategies and tactics necessarily involve spirited debate and argument. Polemics can thus provide an opportunity to clarify important points of theory that will be crucial for orienting activists in practical struggles.

Contributions presented here (reflecting the factional dispute which tore apart the Fourth International in 1953) by Myra Tanner Weiss and George Breitman are of this kind. Tanner Weiss takes sharp issue with a prominent Marxist theorist, Fritz Sternberg, who had earlier been friendly to Trotskyists, but evolved in a reformist direction. In a critical review of Sternberg's *Capitalism and Socialism on Trial*, Tanner Weiss defends Marx from the common charge that he simplistically envisioned some inevitable decline of working-class incomes and living standards – an important question for Marxist activists in the relatively affluent 1950s. Similarly, a sharply critical examination of the optimistic forecast by Isaac Deutscher that the Soviet elite would be capable of reforming itself to eventually usher in a socialist democracy provides an opportunity for Breitman's clear and cogent presentation of Trotsky's analysis of the Stalinist bureaucratic caste and the nature of its hold over the Soviet political economy. Contrary to Deutscher's arguments, Trotsky's analysis stresses the need for a political revolution if the USSR is actually to move forward to socialism.

While George Novack has been commonly cited as the SWP's authority on questions of philosophy, there were in fact a number of comrades who grappled intelligently with questions in this sphere. The multi-lingual Joseph Vanzler, better known in Trotskyist circles as John G. Wright, or 'Usick', was described by Cannon as 'our most learned man'.[7] He provides in this chapter an erudite but clear discussion of the ideas of Ludwig Feuerbach, whose materialist and humanist theorizations helped pave the way for the emergence of Marxism, and which were absorbed – to a significant degree – into the methodology and substance of what Marx and Engels termed 'scientific socialism'.

Particularly relevant for the 'neoliberal' era of the late twentieth and early twenty-first centuries is Joseph Hansen's contribution to this section. A scathing review of the classic neoliberal work by Friedrich A. Hayek, *The Road to Serfdom* (1944), it gives special attention to the logical and historical flaws, and to the class bias, permeating this much-heralded defense of laissez-faire capitalism. Attentive readers who have suffered the consequences of neoliberal policies in recent decades may find Hansen's pointed critical discussion illuminating.

Taken together, in all of their diversity and with whatever limitations might be perceived in what they present, these contributions (simply a few among many that could be provided) indicate a remarkable intellectual vibrancy in the tradition reflected in this documentary trilogy on US Trotskyism.

---

7 See his essay 'Joseph Vanzler', in Cannon 1973a, p. 361.

1 The Myth of Racial Superiority[8]
(1944)

Grace Carlson

History will record the fact that in the 'enlightened' twentieth century more millions of human beings were enslaved by the colonial systems of the powerful capitalist 'democracies' than at any previous epoch. Only in the future socialist society will the full record of capitalist violence, hypocrisy and deceit be revealed. Then, socialist historians will paint a picture of French, English and American imperialist rulers of our day, holding down helpless masses of colonial peoples with one hand, while grasping in the other a copy of the Declaration of Independence, the Magna Carta, or the Declaration of the Rights of Man.

Of the approximately two billion people inhabiting the earth today, only one third are white peoples of European descent, but they keep the other two thirds – the brown, black and yellow peoples – in colonial subjection. 'All men are created equal', 'Liberty, Equality, Fraternity', 'Equal rights for all' – the political slogans which helped the eighteenth century capitalists seize power from the feudal lords have long been collecting dust in national archives. But equalitarian mottoes did not obtain for the white capitalist rulers of the democracies the rich lands and poorly paid labor of the colored peoples of the world which they needed so desperately. Bloody and brutal imperialistic offensives had to be launched in Asia, Africa, and a hundred other regions so that capitalist 'democracy' could function. The myth of white racial superiority was evolved as a vindication of these crimes. (Hitler's vicious persecution of the Jewish people, which he attempts to justify on the basis of the superiority of the 'Aryans', or more particularly, the Nordics, to all other sections of the white race, is simply an application of this theory of white superiority to one segment of the white race).

---

8   Carlson 1944. This article has been slightly edited and abridged.

The Lie of Racial Superiority

The idea of racial superiority was not a twentieth century invention. Conquerors of all ages had recourse to this convenient theory, not only in order to excuse crimes committed against those whom they enslaved, but even more in order to set one group of subject peoples against another. 'Divide et impera' (divide and rule) is the classical expression of this policy used so successfully by the Roman tyrants against the conquered tribes of northern Europe and Britain. How much more successful have been the descendants of those former subject peoples, the English, French and German imperialist rulers of today, in 'dividing and ruling'! For not only has the technique of empire-building been vastly simplified by modern scientific developments, but the population of the globe has increased so tremendously since the days of imperial Rome that, whereas the 'world-conquering' Caesars dominated only scores of millions of colonials, the twentieth century capitalist lords of the earth rule over nearly a billion people!

In his book, *Heredity and Politics*, the English biologist, J.B.S. Haldane writes, 'The earliest statement of that doctrine [racial superiority] known to me is found in the Book of Genesis where the curse on the children of Ham is related. It is worthy of note that if this attribution of priority is accurate, the doctrine of racial superiority is originally a Jewish doctrine, although it is now being used against the Jews in Central Europe'.

According to the Biblical story, Ham, the legendary ancestor of the Negro people, was condemned by the curse of his father, Noah, to be a 'servant of servants' to his brothers, Shem and Japheth. It is interesting to note that anti-abolitionists in the United States found refuge in the 'word of God' many centuries later. An entire volume, *The Bible Defense of Slavery*, was published in Kentucky in 1852 by one such figure, Josiah Priest, as an attempted justification for the continued enslavement of the Negro people.

The dubious historical distinction of having best phrased the doctrine of 'white supremacy' goes to the English poet, Rudyard Kipling, a staunch supporter of imperial Britain's policies in the colonial countries. In his poem, 'The White Man's Burden', Kipling wrote in 1899:

> Take up the White Man's burden
> Send forth the best ye breed –
> Go bind your sons to exile
> To serve your captive's need;
> To wait in heavy harness
> On fluttered folk and wild –

Your new-caught, sullen peoples,
Half-devil and half-child.

The Ancient Civilizations

But the theory and even the expression of the false concept that one race is inherently superior to others did not always have the one-sided character of the 'superior' white race vs. the 'inferior' colored peoples. Haldane quotes a contemptuous reference made by the writer, Said of Toledo, about the Anglo-Saxon inhabitants of northern and central Europe, 'They are of cold temperament and never reach maturity. They are of great stature and of a white color. But they lack all sharpness of wit and penetration of intellect'.

Said of Toledo wrote in the eighth century when the Moors – of mixed Negroid and Semitic extraction – had conquered all of Spain which thus became part of the great Arab empire that stretched all across Northern Africa and Asia Minor. At a time when the future exponents of 'white supremacy' were still immersed in the superstitiousness and intellectual backwardness of Europe's Dark Ages, these highly cultured colored peoples were making great strides in the mathematical, medical and physical sciences, as well as in the arts.

The great historic pasts of others of today's so-called inferior peoples can also be cited in refutation of the false doctrine of 'white supremacy'. The average white student of history knows little about the early Dravidian civilization in India; the Chinese culture of several centuries before Christ, and more notably of the 7th, 8th and 9th centuries A.D.; the advanced civilization of the Mayan and Aztec Indians in Mexico and Central America over a thousand years ago, and so on.

If little is known by white students of the great cultural achievements of the early peoples of India, China, Mexico and other regions, characterized today as 'backward', still less is known of the remarkable history of the black peoples of Ethiopia. In *Black Folk, Then and Now*, a scholarly work modestly designated by its author W.E.B. Du Bois as 'an essay in the history and sociology of the Negro race', there is a wealth of information about the Black Kingdom.

> Research in the Nile Valley and study of the records establish the fact that ancient Ethiopia in what is now the Anglo-Egyptian Sudan was the seat of one of the oldest and greatest of the world's civilizations. The golden age of this culture dates from the middle of the Eighth Century before Christ to the middle of the Fourth Century after Christ. But its

beginnings go back to the dawn of history, four or five thousand years before Christ and in a way Ethiopian history parallels that of ancient Egypt.

A reasonable interpretation of historical evidence would show the history of the Nile Valley was something as follows: Negro tribes migrated down the Nile, slowly penetrating what le now modern Egypt. They there gradually came in contact and mingled with whites from the north and Semites from the east. Stimulated to an unusual degree by this contact of the three primitive stocks of mankind, the resulting culture of Egypt was gradually developed.

What Do Conquests Prove?

Why then have modern historians been silent about the high cultural attainments of the black peoples of ancient Ethiopia, glowing accounts of which have been preserved in the writings of such Greek and Roman historians as Homer (ninth century B.C.), Herodotus (fifth century B.C.), Pliny (first century A.D.), and Ptolemy (second century A.D.)? Why have the role of Negro blood and ancient Negro culture been denied their proper place in the historical explanations of the development of Egyptian civilization? Because, as Professor DuBois correctly points out, the needs of the white slave traders of the 16th, 17th and 18th century Europe and the United States made it necessary to distort and hide all favorable facts and interpretations of the history of the black peoples. DuBois writes:

> The whole attitude of the world was changed to fit this new economic reorganization. Black Africa, which had been a revered example to ancient Greece and the recognized contender with imperial Rome, became a thing beneath the contempt of modern Europe and America. All history, all science was changed to fit this new condition. Africa had no history. Wherever there was history in Africa or civilization, it was of white origin; and the fact that it was civilization proved that it was white. If black Pharaohs sat on the throne of Egypt they were really not black men but dark white men. Ethiopia, land of the blacks was described as a land of the whites ... If at any time, anywhere there was evidence in Africa of the human soul and the same striving of spirit, and the same build of body found elsewhere in the world, it was all due to something non-African and not to the inherent genius of the Negro race.

The fact that a race has been conquered and held in subjection is no proof that it has an inferior culture to that of the conqueror. Still less does the fact of conquest prove the biological inferiority or superiority of peoples. When the Nazi 'blitzkrieg' swept over a dozen countries of Europe in 1939–41, Hitler's sociologists and historians hailed the victories as conclusive proof of the inherent superiority of the Teutonic branch of the so-called Aryan race. Now, the armies of Hitler are in retreat. Does this fact then offer proof of the inherent inferiority of the Germans? Both aspects of this false racial theory will be dismissed by Marxists and an explanation sought in the social and economic factors involved in the situation. The highly efficient productive system of Nazi Germany, closely geared to a modern and radical type of war machine, continued victorious in Europe until it came into conflict with the war machine of the still more advanced American system of production, which had far greater resources in material and manpower. This basically important economic factor, coupled with the great social weight of the superior morale and resistance of the workers and soldiers of the Soviet Union, swung the balance against the Nazi 'invincibles'.

As in this short term historical demonstration of the fallacy of one strongly held belief in racial superiority, so has history offered a thousand other long-term illustrations of the reversal of the roles of the dominant and the subject peoples, of the conquerors and the enslaved.

Neither the testimony of written history nor the extensive research findings of archaeologists, paleontologists and anthropologists offer grounds for a belief in the innate superiority of the white race. The period in which the white race has dominated all of the other races of the earth – a few hundred years at the most – measures only a relatively short span of recorded historical time. It is but an infinitesimal portion of geological time.

Nature experimented for millions of years in the production of organisms capable of adapting themselves to their environment, or as in the case of man, the highest type of organism, capable of changing his physical environment and developing mutually protective relations with other members of his species. ...

The Pre-history of Modern Man

In the age-long evolutionary process from 'amoeba to man', living organisms were forced to adapt themselves to cataclysmic planetary changes. Not until somewhere around 10,000 B.C. did the geography of the world become similar to that of the world today. In the millions of preceding years, geological and geographical change was the rule. Enormous internal activity created constantly changing patterns on the earth's surface – mountain ranges were thrust up or rearranged; continental outlines shifted; some continents disappeared into the earth's seas; the depth of the seas was increased in one millennium, decreased in another. ...

The Neanderthalers – so-called because the fossil remains and primitive tools of this 'almost-human' species were first found at Neanderthal, Germany – were dominant on this earth 250,000 years ago. Thousands of years later, they were exterminated either by the ancestors of modern man or by freezing and starvation during one of the glacial periods. Superior in cranial capacity to the early types of modern man, the Neanderthal man had a certain definite inferiority of body structure. He could not turn his head from side to side or look upward, nor could he oppose his finger to his thumb as modern man can. Such physical characteristics, possessed by modern man's ancestors, had real 'survival value'. ...

Unscientific Criteria

The new types of early man, with widely varying physical characteristics, which evolved in response to tremendous environmental changes, represent the original 'pure' races. From these 'pure' races, the several modern races and national types have been formed by a complex process of interbreeding, selection, and other changes flowing from differences of environment, nutrition, etc. But it is impossible now to speak of 'pure' races. Anthropologists tell us that there were probably no 'pure' races left after the great human migrations and general mixing of the races that occurred at the time of the last glacial period, 18,000 years ago, when most of Europe and a great part of North America were covered with ice.

Evidence for the truth of this statement lies not only in the fact that fossil remains of various racial types have been found all over the world, but that among the living 'races' there are no clean-cut scientific differentiations. Racial classification has become, therefore, a very confused and arbitrary matter. Some anthropologists classify the peoples of the world on the basis of skin color and come out with three, five or seven 'distinct' races. Others use hair texture, cephalic index width of head length of head or a combination of all three of these indices (skin color, hair texture, skull structure), and in this way derive anywhere from two to 17 main races. ...

The classification sanctioned today by a great many anthropologists, i.e., three main races: the Negroid or 'black'; the Mongoloid or 'Yellow-brown'; and the Caucasian or 'white', can be used for practical purposes, but it must be understood that there is a tremendous overlapping between the races on physical characteristics, even on skin color. Just to give one example, the African Bushman or Hottentot member of the 'black' race is far lighter than many swarthy Spanish or Italian 'whites'. Long-headed (dolichocephalic) and round-headed (brachyceplkatic) types are found in all three races. ...

Race politicians who like to give a scientific coloration to their propaganda attempt to show that the Negro is lowest on the scale of evolutionary development, the Mongolian, slightly higher, with the Caucasian at the peak. Considerable 'evidence' is brought forth to prove that the Negro has more primitive physical characteristics, i.e., that he is not so far removed from the anthropoid apes.

Dr. Otto Klineberg, Columbia University's expert on race psychology, has marshalled an impressive array of facts to contradict this pseudo-scientific claim.

'The Negro is by no means the most ape-like of the three races', he writes in his book, *Race Differences*.

> The ape, for example, has practically no lips and the thick everted lips of the Negro may therefore be regarded as the most human and most advanced; in this respect, the Mongolian is closest to the Anthropoid, and the Caucasian intermediate. In the hairiness of the face and body, the Caucasian, and particularly the North European [Nordic] resembles the ape most closely ... the Negro is next and the Mongolian farthest removed. In hair texture, the Caucasian is again closest; the Mongolian is intermediate, while the frizzly hair of the Negro is the least ape-like of the three. In the length of his arms, the Negro may seem to be the most closely related to the gorilla and the other great apes, but it is only fair to note also that in the length of his legs, he is the farthest removed. The hierarchy will entirely depend on the features which are singled out for observation ...

Attempts to create distinct subdivisions of the white race on the basis of physical characteristics result in still more confusion. The most fashionable division is into the Nordics – tall, long-headed, blue-eyed blonds; Alpines – medium height, round-headed, blue or brown-eyed brunettes; Mediterraneans – short, long-headed, dark-eyed brunettes. ('Latin', 'Aryan', 'Semitic' are terms descriptive of basic languages not of physical types. To speak of 'Latin', 'Aryan' and 'Semitic' races is therefore completely misleading). Klineberg says very correctly, '"Unclassifiable" or "mixed" types are very definitely in the majority and there are large regions in which 'pure' racial types are very rare exceptions'.

The 'Intelligence Test'

... 'Race' is, in fact, a political concept which has no precise anthropological definition. Because the concept of 'superior' and 'inferior' races has been an extremely useful weapon in the hands of the ruling classes, it has persisted despite numerous scientific demonstrations of its falsity. When all other proof has failed, the die-hard Nordic theorists and the devout believers in white supremacy cover up their own unscientific positions by referring to the results of intelligence testing among the various 'races'. They point to the undeniable fact that, on the average, Negroes rate lower than whites on intelligence tests; Mexicans and Indians also score lower than whites while 'Nordics' have higher scores than South Europeans. These facts are pointed to triumphantly as irrefutable scientific proof of the superiority of the 'white' race over the colored races, and of the 'Nordics' over all other sections of the white race.

When the French psychologist, Alfred Binet, the 'father of intelligence tests', issued the first set of mental tests in 1905, he, like all other psychologists, believed that these tests measured sheer native intelligence and were completely uninfluenced by environmental factors. If this were true, the problem of determining the relative abilities of the various races would indeed be comparatively simple. But as data from intelligence test studies accumulated during the past four decades, psychologists have been forced to conclude that the presence or absence of educational and cultural opportunities in the given environment exerts a tremendous influence on the individual's test performance. ...

Effects of Poverty on IQ

... Klineberg presents considerable evidence to show that Negro groups, that have had the benefit of a fairly adequate environment, score higher than 'whites' who have lived in a poverty-stricken environment. Most significant is the report that in the First World War test scores of Negro soldiers from the northern states (Ohio, Pennsylvania, New York, Illinois) exceeded the Army Alpha intelligence test scores of 'whites' from such southern states as Mississippi, Kentucky, Arkansas, and Georgia.

The homes and general environmental conditions of the Mexican and Indian people and of immigrant workers, especially the Italian and South European workers, are almost as poverty-stricken as those of the Negroes. That members of these most bestially exploited groups receive lower scores on intelligence tests than those who come from environments which provide richer cultural opportunities proves only that intelligence tests are not valid tests of *native* ability.

Dr. Paul Witty found the average IQ of children from the homes of professional people to be 116; from semi-skilled laborers, 105; and from day laborers, 92. ... The well-known positive relationship between socio-economic status and intelligence formerly led psychologists to conclude that poor people were poor because they were unintelligent! Statements such as the following, made by Stanford University's Professor L.M. Terman, the author of *The Terman Revision of the Binet-Simon Intelligence Test* were accepted uncritically only fifteen years ago: 'Our data', said the Professor, 'show that individuals of the various social classes present differences in early childhood – a fact which strongly suggests that the causal factor lies in original endowment rather than in environmental influences'.

An even more graphic expression of the same cynical 'upper-class' point of view was given by Dr. Leta Hollingsworth: 'Individuals of surpassing intelligence, as measured by intelligence tests, create national wealth, determine the state of industry, advance science and make general culture possible'.

Other Factors in IQ Testing

But even these dyed-in-the-wool hereditarians have had to modify their opinions as evidence accumulated of the improvement in IQ of children of feeble-minded parents who have been placed in average or superior foster homes; of great increases in the IQs of children who attended a superior type of school; of marked changes in the IQs of Negro children brought to New York City from southern communities, etc. The conclusions reached by Dr. Walter Neff in a critical survey of the studies dealing with the relationship between socio-economic status and intelligence are accepted by most psychologists today (very reluctantly by some, to be sure):

> All of these facts taken together lead to a conclusion which we feel is forced and inescapable. Just as Klineberg has shown that the standard intelligence tests are inadequate instruments for measuring the native ability of different races, so do we find that these tests cannot be used for measuring the capacity of different social levels within our society ... All the summarized studies tend to show that low cultural environment tends to depress IQ approximately to the degree agreed to as characteristic of laborers' children and that a high environment raises IQ correspondingly. All, then, of the twenty point average difference found to exist between

children of the lowest and highest status may be accounted for entirely in environmental terms ...

Not only does the lack of homogeneity in social, economic and educational status make comparisons of intelligence test performances of the white and colored races very difficult, but differences in motivation also complicate an interpretation of the test results. For a full exposition of this aspect of the problem as well as of the whole question of race differences, Klineberg's book on the subject should be studied. It is possible here to cite only a few of the examples which Klineberg gives to prove that members of different racial groups are not equally interested in intelligence tests, and therefore do not compete with equal energy.

1. Testers working among the Dakota Indians found great difficulty in securing answers to their questions because 'it is considered bad form to answer a question in the presence of someone else who does not know the answers'.
2. Australian aborigines, accustomed to group thinking and to a group solution of problems could not comprehend why they should work on a test problem alone. The experimenter, Porteus, relates the great bewilderment manifested by members of a tribe, of which he had just been made a member, at the fact that he would not help them solve the problems of the performance test.
3. A study of Negro and white girls in a Pennsylvania reformatory showed that Negro girls quickly lost interest in the test procedure. 'They are suspicious as to the value of the task', writes the experimenter, Baldwin. Anyone familiar with the pattern of segregation and discrimination against the Negro people could add that the Negro girls were also very probably suspicious of the psychologist who was asking them so many questions.

Similarly, differences in culture, or, as Klineberg defines it, 'those attitudes and experiences which an individual receives from the society of which he is a member' have a determining effect on test performance. Here again, it is possible to give only a few of the illustrations which Klineberg has brought together to show that because of differing cultural backgrounds, two equally intelligent individuals from different racial groups would give very different answers to intelligence test questions.

1. On the Army Alpha test (given to the soldiers in the First World War) one question reads, 'Why should all parents be made to send their children to school?' The 'correct' answer is that 'school prepares the child for later life'. The experience of many American Indians, however, has been that

schooling completely un-fitted their children for life on the reservation. So they gave the 'wrong' answer.
2. A picture completion test, part of the Army Beta (a performance test) requires that the subject draw in the missing chimney of a house. One Sicilian child drew in a crucifix, because 'his particular experience had taught him that no house was complete without one'. Similar facts may be adduced to any number.

Although it is an undeniable fact that heredity sets certain limits for mental development, thoughtful scholars after weighing all the evidence have concluded that these limits are very broad and that individuals of every race have tremendous possibilities for mental development if given richer environmental opportunities.

Food and Intelligence

So simple a thing as an adequate diet can constitute a richer environmental opportunity for the ill-fed children of the poor. A New York physician, Dr. A. Newton Kugelmass, reported at a meeting of the American Association on Mental Deficiency in the spring of 1943, that the intelligence of small children can be increased as much as 18 points in IQ by proper diet. His conclusion was based on a study of the intelligence test results of 182 children, who were malnourished at the time of their first test, but better nourished when the second test was given. Children who were well nourished when both tests were given showed no such mental improvement. ...

From all this we Trotskyists draw the following conclusion: In order that an equal opportunity may be had by all peoples for adequate food, decent clothing, proper shelter, full and rich educational and cultural stimulation, the capitalist system which breeds poverty, misery, race discrimination, war, fascism, and a host of other attendant evils must be abolished. The white and colored workers of the 'democracies' must break down the barriers of racial segregation which the capitalist rulers have erected between them. Together with the millions of colonial peoples, they can destroy this decadent social system and with it the capitalist-inspired myth of racial and national superiority.

In the new international socialist world which must and will be built, not racial segregation and discrimination, but widespread interracial mixing and collaboration will be the rule. A new stage of evolutionary development will have been reached; a new unified world race, created. Man, the highest product of the century-long evolutionary process, will have then succeeded, in the words of the great social scientist-revolutionist Leon Trotsky, in ending 'the tyranny of man over man'.

2 Hayek Pleads for Capitalism[9]
(*1945*)

Joseph Hansen

Hayek dedicates his *Road to Serfdom* (1945), 'To the socialists of all parties'. Despite this dedication, which one might believe should have limited its reading public to the left wing political movement, the book has achieved popularity among circles long notorious for their hostility to socialism. *The New York Times*, for instance, praises its 'rigor of reasoning', its 'remorseless logic', its 'impressive authority', and judges it to be nothing less than 'one of the most important books of our time'. Apparently agreeing with the verdict of the *Times*, local Chambers of Commerce are reported to be ordering the *Road to Serfdom* in wholesale lots.

Hayek's message 'to the socialists of all parties' in fact boils down to nothing but a variation of the ancient theme of Big Business that capitalism is superior to socialism. Hayek's sudden vogue among reactionary circles undoubtedly is due to the apparent effectiveness with which he makes out a case for the familiar Chamber of Commerce arguments against socialism.

It must be admitted that Hayek's presentation is somewhat unusual compared to that of most professional red-baiters and defenders of capitalism. Hayek selects his audience and limits his objectives. To understand the purpose of Hayek's arguments, which in themselves are exceedingly weak and easily answered, it is first necessary to visualize the type of individual he addresses. It is not the class-conscious worker, still less the Marxist. He directs his propaganda to that section of the petty bourgeoisie which inclines toward socialism as the only means of ending the continual wars and depressions of capitalism. He attempts to block their further progress toward active participation in the socialist movement and to provide them with a bridge leading toward reaction. The book can thus be classified as a kind of transition propaganda that hopes to take the radical petty bourgeois step by step from a mood of doubt to rejection of socialism and outright support of capitalism.

---

9   Hansen 1945.

Beginning of the Transition

The author early establishes his authority as an economist and successful professor; but he does not lean heavily on this authority until later when he comes to the crucial issues upon which his entire argumentation rests. In his opening he prefers to flatter the intelligence of his reader, speaking in the style of a logician and seeking common grounds of interest. In the preface he implies that he too was a socialist 'as a young man'. He is still an idealist with 'certain ultimate values'. He is self-sacrificing, having painfully carried out his 'duty' to speak out despite 'every possible reason for not writing or publishing this book'.

In the introduction Hayek seeks additional emotional ties with his reader. To believe in socialism, it seems, is not an uncommon error. It is only too human. Moreover it arises from the best of intentions. 'If we take the people whose views influence developments, they are now in the democracies in some measure all socialists. If it is no longer fashionable to emphasize that "we are all socialists now", this is so merely because the fact is too obvious'.

The learned professor's assertions bristle with falsehoods. Socialism, for instance, is not a common belief of our generation, at least not in America, the mightiest stronghold of capitalism. It is still promulgated only by the vanguard of the proletariat. The people 'whose views influence developments' are not 'all socialists'. This does not concern Hayek however. He is making an emotional appeal to the petty bourgeois sickened over the growth of Stalinism, confused by its superficial resemblance to Nazism, despairing over the apparent weakness of genuine Marxism and swept from his feet by the tidal waves of bourgeois war propaganda. The professor's primary aim, as we shall see again and again, is the establishment of emotional rapport with his reader in order to convert him into an enemy of socialism. 'Is it not possible', he continues, 'that if the people whose convictions now give it an irresistible momentum began to see what only a few yet apprehend, they would recoil in horror and abandon the quest which for half a century has engaged so many people of good will?' Observe the neat rationalization the professor provides for abandoning the 'quest': 'Is there a greater tragedy imaginable than that, in our endeavor consciously to shape our future in accordance with high ideals, we should in fact unwittingly produce the very opposite of what we have been striving for?'

Most petty bourgeois who have begun to regret their socialist youth, we presume will hasten to agree with the professor that no greater tragedy is imaginable. Nevertheless, a soul sick petty bourgeois, who has not yet completely freed himself from the last traces of Marxism, might ask for convincing evidence that this tragedy, so difficult to imagine, is applicable to socialism. Hayek aims to provide such 'evidence'.

'Sincere idealists', explains Hayek, have sought socialism in order to bring greater freedom. But instead of bringing greater freedom, 'socialism means slavery'. As proof, Hayek quotes capitalist political thinkers of last century's 'liberal' school to which he claims adherence and cites as confirmation of their warnings against the danger of socialism the instances of Nazi Germany and Fascist Italy, not forgetting of course to point his finger likewise at the Stalinist regime in the Soviet Union.

'But fascism and socialism are polar opposites!' might exclaim the reader in surprise. 'It does not at all follow that what is true of fascism or degenerate Stalinism likewise holds for socialism'.

The logical professor of bourgeois economy replies imperturbably: 'It is probably preferable to describe the methods which can be used for a great variety of ends as collectivism and to regard socialism as a species of that genus. Yet, although to most socialists only one species of collectivism will represent true socialism, it must always be remembered that socialism is a species of collectivism and that therefore everything which is true of collectivism as such must apply also to socialism'.

This is what the *New York Times* admires as 'rigor of reasoning' and 'remorseless logic'. We can agree that it is logic of a kind – the logic characteristic of bourgeois thought in its period of utter decay. How well this logic reflects reality can be seen by any one able to read the press. Fascists and Nazis hunt down socialists in order to murder them. In the 'democracies' the men who 'influence developments' are now preparing to drown the rising European socialist revolution in blood. In Hayek's logic, however, movements in absolute contradiction to each other are amalgamated and pronounced one and the same.

For a petty bourgeois in retreat Hayek's method of thought is 'probably preferable'. Once accepted, all else follows 'remorselessly', including the overthrow of Marxism.

Hayek, of course, is not original in his logic. He simply states more baldly the assumption at the bottom of the whole school which maintains Nazism and Marxism are twins; that Nazi Germany and Soviet Russia are species of one genus; that Stalinists and Nazis are both representatives of a new class hitherto unknown and unforeseen in history. Hayek's method is characteristic of the petty bourgeois approach to this subject. Its appeal to petty bourgeois renegades from socialism has been demonstrated again and again, one of the most prominent recent instances being that of James Burnham, whom Hayek mentions favorably in a foot note.

Where his purposes require it, our bourgeois pundit not only amalgamates the unamalgamable, he divides the indivisible. This gives his logic a symmetry that should please the petty bourgeois eye. The petty bourgeois renegades from socialism have long pondered the question of means and ends in order to construct a suitable rationalization to cover their base retreat. Hayek does not overlook this powerful instrument of bourgeois propaganda. 'All the consequences with which we shall be concerned in this book', he declares, 'follow from the methods of collectivism irrespective of the ends for which they are used'. Thus does Hayek drive an axe between means and ends. In dialectic logic on the contrary, means and ends reciprocate, are in mutual dependence. A revolutionary takes as his end the building of a political party of the working class so that it can become the means to reach a new end, the dictatorship of the proletariat, which in turn becomes the means to inaugurate the socialist society of peace and plenty. Hayek's logic, however, makes an arbitrary abstraction of 'means', amputates it from 'ends' and opens it up like an empty sack in which he can place whatever content he requires to 'prove' his thesis.

Only a soul-sick petty bourgeois, unable to think clearly, could be taken in by logic as 'remorseless' as this. But it is precisely such individuals Hayek addresses, and the efficacy of arbitrarily separating ends from means in driving the petty bourgeoisie from Marxism has been demonstrated many times over. I do not know of an exception among the renegades from Marxism who has not passed through the stage of sweating over 'means and ends'. It is now a standardized argument in bourgeois propaganda.

Hayek deals quite concretely with the dangers, terrors and horrors of socialist means. Among his major exhibits is planning. This spokesman of the capitalist order holds that planning leads to the very opposite of what it sets out to accomplish. Instead of a means of achieving greater freedom, planning in the eyes of the professor becomes the means leading to slavery and chaos. Under the fascists freedom was lost, but the fascists are only one species of collectivism of which the socialists are another, therefore freedom would be lost under the socialists just as much as under the fascists. Or to drop more deeply with Hayek into the logical abyss: Since ends (by this Hayek implies good or bad intentions) have nothing to do with what happens from the use of certain means, and since planning is inherently a bad means, no matter who uses it evil results will follow; but planning is characteristic of socialism, therefore
...

The facts are so well known one is astonished that even the most delirious petty bourgeois could bring himself to accept such 'reasoning'. The fascists in both Germany and Italy used 'planning' to crush the working class, drive down the standard of living, intensify exploitation and unite the capitalist class in a bid for world power through imperialist war. This 'end' had nothing to do with good or bad intentions. The capitalist class utilized fascist 'planning' in order to preserve its rule.

Socialist planning, on the other hand, begins with the expropriation of capitalist property, the expansion of the productive machinery, the raising of the standard of living and the balancing of the economy through correlation of its various sections by means of a general plan. Planning in this case too has nothing to do with good or bad intentions. It is the means the working class must utilize to preserve itself from utter disintegration. At the same time it becomes the means to end the class struggle. Under fascism the class struggle continues; under socialism the classes eventually disappear.

It is not necessary to be a Marxist to see the fallacy in Hayek's analysis of planning. Anyone who understands the class struggle, as do the capitalists, can see that the result of planning is not implicit in planning in and of itself as a means, but is implicit in what class does the 'planning' and for what end. The class struggle in the *Road to Serfdom*, however, receives scant notice. 'Remorseless logic' and 'rigor of reasoning' replace the brutal facts of life in capitalist society. This rejection of class analysis is characteristic of petty bourgeois thought.

The petty bourgeois wants to exorcise the class struggle; he is sick of it. Hence Hayek's argumentation, if it is to achieve its purpose, must inevitably follow the traditional pattern of petty bourgeois thought.

Hayek still has left the task of providing his reader with an arsenal of rationalizations 'proving' the inherent evils of planning. This he accomplishes with a horror show. Human nature, it seems, is so constituted common agreement cannot possibly be reached on all the vast complexity of small details in the general plan; some regions would feel slighted and pained because they did not receive development of their resources equal to that of regions more favorably situated; authority would have to be delegated to a central body; this central body would rule arbitrarily; hence individual freedom would vanish. Thus any petty bourgeois, terrified at the prospect of losing his individual 'freedom', can see that there is no 'greater tragedy imaginable' than planning.

The Horror of Horrors

Hayek does not consider any of the teachings of the Marxists on the subject of planned society. He does not even consider the views of Leon Trotsky, author of the plans in the Soviet Union which enabled that backward country to accomplish in less than a quarter of a century the economic development of hundreds of years of capitalism. Thus he presents a highly distorted picture of what planning is like in both theory and practice. First he divides up the planned economy among countries which would be at each other's throats instead of positing a united world economy in which national boundaries no longer existed. Secondly, he envisages the continued existence of class divisions which would lead to internecine conflicts over planning within each isolated country. Thirdly, he insists on an economy of scarcity which would give rise to group struggles over the division of the national income. Hayek counts upon his readers to accept these omissions and distortions. Apparently the learned professor believes his audience to be completely unfamiliar with the literature dealing with planned economy.

Another means of achieving socialism, the building of a proletarian party, is likewise considered objectionable by our idealistic moralist. The subject naturally holds considerable interest for the bourgeois propagandist since the proletarian party constitutes the means whereby the working class will eventually dispose of capitalist anarchy. Moreover it is precisely in relation to the proletarian party that the sick petty bourgeois experiences most acutely his emotions of revulsion and his urge to flee. The building of the proletarian party is the crucial political problem of the day not only for the working class, but also, from the opposite side, the capitalist class. That is why the capitalists utilize every means to attack, hamper, prevent the building of such a party and to crush it with force and violence if necessary when it does appear. Hayek too places the question of the revolutionary party high on his agenda.

Pursuing his 'remorseless logic' he again amalgamates polar opposites: 'In Germany and Italy the Nazis and Fascists did, indeed, not have much to invent. The usages of the new political movements which pervaded all aspects of life had in both countries already been introduced by the socialists. The idea of a political party which embraces all activities of the individual from the cradle to the grave, which claims to guide his views on everything, and which delights in making all problems questions of party Weltanschauung, was first put into practice by the socialists'.

Now it is true that socialism approaches all the problems of society from the viewpoint of the historic interests of the working class. From their opposing side the bourgeois statesmen do the same for the capitalist class. But what Hayek infers, namely, that fascist 'usages' were introduced 'by the socialists', is not true. The 'usages' of fascism are much older than the socialist movement. If one wishes to know, the real parallel can be found among the practices of any outlived oppressing class or caste in the periods when its rule was threatened by the oppressed. In the tradition of the Inquisition, fascism continues 'usages' that are extremely ancient. To identify Nazism and socialism is not at all different from identifying the victims of the Inquisition with their persecutors. Nevertheless Hayek coolly declares: 'The relative ease with which a young communist could be converted into a Nazi or vice versa was generally known in

Germany ...'. The only distinction Hayek makes between the Nazis and the anti-Nazis of Germany is to call the latter the 'old' socialists and the Nazis their spawn, the 'new' socialists. Their struggle is represented simply as a factional squabble in which the more dynamic won out.

Hayek assures his petty bourgeois audience that a socialist party 'is not likely to be formed by the best but rather by the worst elements of any society'. As solemnly as a witch doctor probing for 'reasons' in the entrails of a chicken, the learned economist lists three 'causes' for the attraction of the worst elements to socialism.

First, 'if we wish to find a high degree of uniformity and similarity of outlook, we have to descend to the regions of lower moral and intellectual standards where the more primitive and 'common' instincts and tastes prevail ... If a numerous group is needed ... it will be those who form the 'mass' in the derogatory sense of the term, the least original and independent, who will be able to put the weight of their numbers behind their particular ideals'. This will be recognized as the theme song of many a renegade from Marxism who ends up as a slavish supporter of the present order. Nevertheless, like the famed song of the Lorelei it seems to exercise a fatal attraction on these petty bourgeois mariners.

Secondly, such 'elements', in the lofty Hayek's aristocratic opinion, require a 'potential dictator'. This dictator 'will be able to obtain the support of all the docile and gullible, who have no strong convictions of their own but are prepared to accept a ready-made system of values if it is only drummed into their ears sufficiently loudly and frequently. It will be those whose vague and imperfectly formed ideas are easily swayed and whose passions and emotions are readily aroused who will thus swell the ranks of the totalitarian party'. All this of course places a somewhat somber shadow on Hayek's earlier pronouncements about the high idealism of socialists, his own erstwhile socialism and the good intentions of those of socialist views who 'influence the development of events'. Nevertheless such propaganda undoubtedly has an emotional effect upon the petty bourgeois in process of rejecting socialism, uneasy over the 'discrimination between members and non-members of closed groups'. Hayek's purpose is to formulate and give expression to the mood of such an individual turning away from the proletarian party with its discipline, its singleness of purpose, its strenuous activity, its great demands on courage and indomitability in the face of world reaction's powerful opposition.

Hayek's third 'cause' does not rise above the level of the rest of his remorseless logic. 'It seems to be almost a law of human nature that it is easier for people to agree on a negative program – on the hatred of an enemy, on the envy of those better off – than on any positive task'. Socialism thus being negative appeals to negative natures in strict accordance with the law of human nature emphasized by Hayek to the exclusion of its correlative, that people under the pressure of events will unite on positive programs that sometimes completely reshape society. Hayek makes out the program of socialism to be simply destructive; it does no more than single out 'Jews' and those better off, such as 'Kulaks' and capitalists for attack. Hayek utters these poisonous slanders with the most 'impressive authority' possible to a bourgeois professor. That he expects his readers to accept such garbage is an interesting indication of the low opinion bourgeois propagandists hold for the petty bourgeoisie and their knowledge of the program of socialism.

Personal Integrity and the Party

Hayek apparently has carefully studied the typical pattern of retreat from socialism followed by such renegades as Eastman, Lyons, Burnham, etc., for he caps his tale of horrors about the proletarian party with a lurid description of what happens to the moral character of its members. 'The principle that the end justifies the means is in individualist ethics regarded as the denial of all morals. In collectivist ethics it becomes necessarily the supreme rule; there is literally nothing which the consistent collectivist must not be prepared to do ... no act which his conscience must prevent him from committing ...'.

Hayek seems to have forgotten the party attracted only the 'worst elements' who presumably would lack the 'conscience' that has now suddenly come into prominence. However, this is a mere bagatelle. When you open all the stops some of the chords are bound to sound discordant. The volume makes up for the lack of harmony.

The sensitive soul of the petty bourgeois in retreat must undoubtedly shrink at the thought of how close he came to sinking in the morass of the socialist movement when he reads Hayek's description of the 'typical German'. Yes, by strange coincidence, as the Allied armies neared their goal in Germany, Hayek's description of the typical socialist became, in fact, that of the 'typical German'.

Hayek's amalgamation of Nazis and socialists does not permit his reader to distinguish just whom he refers to in any particular asseveration. His intention, however, is clearly to utilize all means available in his remorseless logic, no matter how despicable, in order to draw an evil picture of the socialist movement. Thus he declares:

> Since it is the supreme leader who alone determines the ends, his instruments must have no moral convictions of their own. They must, above all,

be unreservedly committed to the person of the leader; but next to this the most important thing is that they should be completely unprincipled and literally capable of everything. They must have no ideals of their own which they want to realize; no ideas about right or wrong which might interfere with the intentions of the leader.

Hayek emphasizes this point so strongly it would seem that bourgeois propagandists who have made a study of this field of their work believe it to be an unusually effective argument:

> The general intellectual climate which this produces, the spirit of complete cynicism as regards truth which it engenders, the loss of the sense of even the meaning of truth, the disappearance of the spirit of independent inquiry and of the belief in the power of rational conviction, the way in which differences of opinion in every branch of knowledge become political issues to be decided by authority, are all things which one must personally experience – no short description can convey their extent. Perhaps the most alarming fact is that contempt for intellectual liberty is not a thing which arises only once the totalitarian system is established but one which can be found everywhere among intellectuals who have embraced a collectivist faith and who are acclaimed as intellectual leaders even in countries still under a liberal regime.

Once again it is to be noted that Hayek does not specify that these evils are peculiar to Nazism and to Stalinism, but on the contrary he incorporates socialism in his amalgam. Apparently he trusts the profound ignorance – or wishful thinking – of his petty bourgeois audience to act as fertile soil for such denigrations. As is well known, in the history of independent thought, of rebellion against the most colossal forces of oppression, the titans stand in the socialist movement. What figures in Hayek's pale sickly world can reach the shoe tops of men like Marx, Engels, Luxemburg, Liebknecht, Debs, Lenin, Trotsky, or for that matter the shoe tops of any rank and filer of the socialist movement who stands against the stream?

Possibility of Plenty

Thus far the 'rigor of reasoning' of our economic witch doctor has 'proved' that planning leads to slavery, that a proletarian party attracts the worst elements, and that socialist morals lead 'of necessity' to those 'features of totalitarian regimes which horrify us'. This would seem enough to arm sufficiently the most wavering of the circle to which Hayek appeals. The professor, however, is aware that he must cross another hurdle.

In the final analysis the whole possibility for socialism in our epoch rests on the feasibility of enormously increasing the productivity of world society. Marxism has determined how this can be done through the efficient utilization of present resources, transport and factories, the elimination of unemployment, the cessation of war, the ending of economic chaos through rational planning and the early expansion of the productive system through the intensive application of science. Many surveys have been made of the possibilities of plenty; the most conservative revealing grandiose perspectives if no more were done than to run the existing machines at full capacity. The experience of war production has opened the eyes of every worker to the potentialities of the modern factory. He needs only imagine peace time goods in place of the present destructive products that are being poured out to get an inkling of what could be done under a truly rational system.

Our representative of capitalist economy, however, attempts to persuade his petty bourgeois reader to the contrary on this crucial point:

> In their wishful belief that there is really no longer an economic problem people have been confirmed by irresponsible talk about 'potential plenty' – which, if it were a fact, would indeed mean that there is no economic problem which makes the choice inevitable. But although this snare has served socialist propaganda under various names as long as socialism has existed, it is still as palpably untrue as it was when it was first used over a hundred years ago. In all this time not one of the many people who have used it has produced a workable plan of how production could be increased so as to abolish even in western Europe what we regard as poverty – not to speak of the world as a whole. The reader may take it that whoever talks about potential plenty is either dishonest or does not know what he is talking about.

Elsewhere, Hayek speaks about the 'familiar cliches and baseless generalizations about "potential plenty"' ... and the 'carefully fostered belief in the irrationality of our economic system ... the false assertions about "potential plenty"'. We will skip the untruth about no 'workable plan' having been produced for Western Europe or the world to increase production, and confine ourselves to consideration of Hayek's principal point about the 'myth' of potential plenty. In view of the surveys that have been made, the practical experience of the Soviet Union, and the evidence of war production, an intelligent worker would expect at least an attempt by the bourgeois economist to prove his brazen assertions. But Hayek is not writing for the 'worst elements' such as intelligent workers. Proof that humanity can never achieve economic plenty? Hayek offers none. Doubtless he calculates that the petty bourgeois to whom he is appealing will be satisfied by the publisher's declaration on the jacket that Hayek is a 'world-famous economist', former 'Director of the Austrian Institute for Economic Research and Lecturer in Economics at the University of Vienna', at present 'a member of the faculty of the London School of Economics'. In the words of the New York Times this is 'impressive authority'. Only in the 'regions of lower moral and intellectual standards where the most primitive and 'common' instincts and tastes prevail' do you find elements capable of demanding proof from such a distinguished bourgeois professor. Hayek simply evades discussing the basic assumption upon which his entire argumentation rests. It would be hard to find a more contemptuous way of dismissing the intelligence of Hayek's petty bourgeois audience.

Having established in his remorseless manner that potential plenty is only a 'myth', Hayek proceeds to the next link of his logic. It concerns the 'inevitability' of socialism, another breathing point in the flight of petty bourgeois radicals from socialism. If economic plenty is unrealizable it follows that socialism is not inevitable. Full planning is an inevitable stage of economic development only in the event that such abundance is produced no basis is left for the formation of selfish groups such as castes, classes. So long as scarcity prevails, ruthless struggle for the major share endures. When this drive wheel comes to a halt, however, then rational planning of world society not only becomes feasible, but inevitable.

For the benefit of a petty bourgeois brooding remorsefully over 'inevitability', Hayek propounds a different view. Man 'knows of no laws which history must obey', he states flatly in his introduction. 'No development is inevitable'. This view constitutes the utter breakdown of science, the denial of the possibility of determining the course of development of any phenomena.

The truth is, Hayek announces triumphantly that 'planning' is not inevitable. 'The conviction that this trend is inevitable is characteristically based on familiar economic fallacies – the presumed necessity of the general growth of monopolies in consequence of technological developments, the alleged 'potential plenty', and all the other popular catchwords ...'.

Are you sure the 'growth of monopolies in consequence of technological developments' isn't a manifestation of the organic tendencies of capitalist economy might ask the petty bourgeois reader, hoping to have his last doubts removed. Absolutely, assures the comforting professor. 'Competition' is being eliminated not by organic changes inherent in the capitalist economic system, but as the 'result of deliberate policy'.

The growth of statism, however, which seems to be what Hayek means by 'deliberate policy', is not an indication of lawlessness and lack of inevitability in economic and political developments. On the contrary it is irrefutable proof that the means of production have become so vast, complex and highly socialized that the irresistible tendency is to bring in the general controls of society, i.e. government. This can occur under the domination of an exploiting class, which simply exacerbates the class struggle, temporarily resolving it in bloody conflict as in Germany, or under the domination of the majority who establish the dictatorship of the proletariat and begin the elimination of class divisions and the development of planning in the interests of the new society as a whole.

In Hayek's opinion all that is required to prevent planning from becoming inevitable is to change government policy. Hayek's petty bourgeois audience should feel comforted over this moth-eaten assumption that the government is not the executive instrument of the ruling class but an independent force above the classes which can be persuaded to restore 'competition' by changing policies without halting 'technological changes'.

Besides attacking socialism head on, Hayek counterposes a Utopia in order to leave his petty bourgeois client with a positive program. The Utopia he advocates is nothing less than 'competitive' society.

Competitive Utopia is quite hazy. The classes are never clearly outlined. We don't know whether they even exist in this snug realm. It seems to consist of small merchants, artisans and farmers all competing with fairly equal resources on the market, all competing according to the Rule of Law, i.e., fixed rules of the game set down in advance so that only 'luck' and 'enterprise' shall determine who will be the most successful. Hayek labels such a system one of 'freedom' and claims it would be the most moral of possible worlds, one where his 'certain ultimate values' would find greatest expression. Foggy as is this Utopia, at least the content of its 'freedom' is clear, this 'freedom' Hayek has been pounding into the ears of his petty bourgeois reader from the beginning of the *Road to Serfdom*. It is the freedom to buy, the freedom to sell, the freedom to exploit, the freedom to make a profit, and the freedom to wage an occasional war. It is the kind of freedom Hayek wants instead of the 'slavery' of planned economy. He believes correct government policy can achieve it.

Competitive Utopia resembles more than anything the free world the corner grocer day dreams about when the chain store across the street takes away his customers with a special sale. In brief it is a petty bourgeois Utopia. Professor Hayek hopes it will appeal to the petty bourgeois radical who reads the *Road to Serfdom* and thus furnish him with an ideal to fight for in place of the united world order of socialism.

Unfortunately it is a reactionary Utopia, as can easily be proved from Hayek's own proclamations. 'What our generation has forgotten is that the system of private property is the most important guaranty of freedom, not only for those who own property, but scarcely less for those who do not'. Competitive Utopia is thus based on private property, i.e., single individuals owning, controlling and exploiting the national resources and economic system. Private property is the cornerstone of capitalism.

This system, as is only too well known, does not stand still but develops glaring inequalities. Hayek justifies inequalities: 'In a system of free enterprise chances are not equal, since such a system is necessarily based on private property and (though perhaps not with the same necessity) on inheritance, with the differences in opportunity which these create'. Thus the snug little realm of Competitive Utopia has already grown into a very real murderous capitalist society in which 60 families can and do constitute, with Hayek's permission, a ruling oligarchy. Listen to this panegyric, worthy of the pen of Henry Ford: 'Money is one of the greatest instruments of freedom ever invented by man. It is money which in existing society opens an astounding range of choice to the poor man …'. Still further, 'who will deny that a world in which the wealthy are powerful is still a better world than one in which only the already powerful can acquire wealth?'

Competitive Utopia even has its unemployed. Hayek feels considerable sympathy for these unfortunates and thinks something should be done for them, in fact he even proposes a solution for unemployment which should have a familiar ring to those who have never suffered unemployment in Competitive Utopia but know its rigors under America's 60 families. Our 'world famous' economist believes, for instances, that 'those who can no longer be employed at the relatively high wages they have earned during the war must be allowed to remain unemployed until they are willing to accept work at a relatively lower wage'. This solution would undoubtedly satisfy Hayek's 'ultimate moral values', the freedom of the lucky to offer what wages they wish and the freedom of the unlucky unemployed to starve.

Competitive Utopia is not quite as rosy as its author pretends. It even has its emergencies when it appears both freedom and competition may be temporarily suspended in order of course to preserve freedom and competition. 'The only exception to the rule that a free society must not be subjected to a single purpose', declares our humanitarian, 'is war and other temporary disasters'. By 'disasters' we presume he refers to strikes, unemployed demonstrations, and proletarian uprisings.

Hayek and Imperialist War

Having brought his petty bourgeois convert to embrace the principle of private property, Hayek carries through his transition to support of the present order, no doubt hoping his convert will trustingly follow. In passing he attacks the trusts – how can you appeal to the petty bourgeoisie without a demagogic attack on the trusts? – but this does not swerve him from his main purpose, that is, to win support for the Second World War which is being waged by some very real trusts far removed from petty bourgeois Utopias. He does the job boldly, not hesitating to state his purpose in the opening sections of his book: 'There is an even more pressing reason why at this time we should seriously endeavor to understand the forces which have created National Socialism: that this will enable us to understand our enemy and the issue at stake between us. It cannot be denied that there is yet little recognition of the positive ideals for which we are fighting'.

Perfidious purpose is apparent in amalgamating Hitler's National Socialism with proletarian revolution. It is ideological preparation for the crushing of the European workers under guise their revolution is in reality simply a new form of Hitler's movement. Hayek even lays the basis for Allied persecution of the Jews: 'We should never forget that the anti-Semitism of Hitler has driven from his country, or turned into his enemies, many people who in every respect are confirmed totalitarians of the German type'. In other words, don't permit the fact that anti-Nazis have been bitterly persecuted by Hitler lull you into handling them in any other way than Hitler did. In Hayek's logic they are simply another species of collectivism, twins of Nazism! Hayek tries to reinforce this ideology by demagogic assertions about 'former socialists who have become Nazis'. This demagogy is strangely coincident with inspired stories in the Allied press about Nazis going underground and disguising themselves as socialists.

As part of his support of the Allied imperialists, Hayek justifies the war time measures restricting the freedom he moralizes over. 'In wartime ... of course, even free and open criticism is necessarily restricted'. This has been the position of petty bourgeois 'liberalism' since the outbreak of the war. It is characteristic of the servility of the petty bourgeois mind before imperialism as soon as the master raises his whip.

Hayek, however, carries his servility to extreme ends, leaving the road open for support of a Third World War of imperialism in preference to socialism which would forever eliminate wars.

'As is true with respect to other great evils, the measures by which war might be made altogether impossible for the future may well be worse than even war itself'. This perspective of unending wars is quite in accordance with Hayek's 'rigor of reasoning' since the imperialist rivalries that lead to World War simply carry 'competition' to its logical conclusion.

Thus we arrive at the true appreciation of Hayek's work, his economics, his logic and his science – it is war propaganda; war propaganda especially aimed at the socialist movement. All the arguments about means and ends, morals, independent thinking, the impossibility of planning, the inevitability of economic inequality, the possibility of 'freedom' under capitalism are seen to be a bridge leading to support of the imperialists in their war for profits, markets and colonies. It is crassly apparent in Hayek's book. Nevertheless the *New York Times* and the Chamber of Commerce expect the petty bourgeoisie will swallow it as 'one of the most important books of our times'.

How far does Hayek wish to take his readers in support of the dying order of capitalism? He swears again and again and again that he is opposed to fascism. However, in rejecting socialism and in amalgamating it with fascism, Hayek opens the road to reaction. An invariable characteristic of petty bourgeois thought is its oscillation between the poles of socialism and fascism. If it rejects socialism, it seems almost a political law it must advance in the direction of fascism by whatever name it may be called. A critical eye can detect phrases in the *Road to Serfdom* which could well appear in *Social Justice*, organ of the fascist demagogue Father Coughlin. Like Coughlin, Hayek attacks both capital and labor: 'When capital and labor in an industry agree on some policy of restriction and thus exploit the consumers, there is usually no difficulty about the division of the spoils'.

Another sentence indicates the tendency: 'By destroying competition in industry after industry, this policy puts the consumer at the mercy of the joint monopolist action of capitalists and workers in the best organized industries'. The direction of thought is still more explicit in the following observation: 'The recent growth of monopoly is largely the result of a deliberate collaboration of organized capital and organized labor where the privileged groups of labor share in the monopoly profits at the expense of the community and particularly at the expense of the poorest, those employed in the less-well-organized industries and the unemployed'. The fascist demagogue promises to 'free' the 'little man' from both the trusts and the 'labor czars'. Hayek's 'liberal principles' even envisage an 'active' state that would not permit 'the use of violence, for example, by strike pickets'. He does not mention what this active state would do about the violence of capitalists who precipitate strikes.

In scientific politics such ideas as these are classified as part of the intellectual preparation of the petty bourgeoisie for fascism. Fascist demagogy drums into the ears of its dupes that labor and capital are equally enemies of the 'little man' although the actual blows of fascism are always directed against the labor movement.

The professor himself seems to have been thinking along lines he does not completely reveal in his book. He states enigmatically: 'If I had to live under a Fascist system, I have no doubt that I would rather live under one run by Englishmen or Americans than under one run by anybody else'.

Even in his ostensible campaign against totalitarianism as a whole the worthy professor has his national preferences which he states well in advance of all eventualities. Just in case fascism does come to power in Britain or America, Professor Hayek makes clear he has already run up the white flag and will be able to get along without making trouble.

How popular Hayek's propaganda will prove among the petty bourgeoisie of America is not yet clear. His support of the war with all its filth, blood and unholy profits will not add to the attractiveness of the *Road to Serfdom* among those layers of the petty bourgeoisie beginning to feel sick at the stomach over the millions of casualties, the colossal destruction and the astronomical costs. Its arguments against socialism, however, may well influence those who have already shifted away from the socialist camp under the impact of the war propaganda. Their vague emotions and confused thoughts are here formulated in what the *New York Times* terms a 'remarkably fine' English style.

Among class-conscious workers, however, the book will be listed as another of the series that began about the time of Roosevelt's 'Quarantine the Aggressors' speech, when the war preparations got seriously under way, munitions orders were placed by the government with the big bourgeoisie and the petty bourgeois intellectuals began their retreat from the camp of Marxism.

3 Three Conceptions of Jacksonianism[10]
(1947)

Harry Frankel (Harry Braverman)

... Jacksonianism [a period in United States history reaching from the election of Andrew Jackson to the presidency in 1828 into the 1850s – B.P.] represented the continuation of the rule of the Southern slaveholding class in national politics, with modifications traceable to a specific relation of class forces. Among the specific circumstances were: the divisions within the planters, the growth in specific weight of the small farming petty-bourgeoisie and the industrial proletariat, and the eruption of these two classes to the political scene in the form of a clamorous mass electorate. These were circumstances which modified the technique of slaveholding rule, but did not *overthrow* it.

This Marxist view is counterposed to the views of bourgeois historians, who see the Jackson period as a time of 'popular revolution'. We shall here consider the theories of two schools of American historians. The first is the famous 'frontier' school which views Jacksonianism as a democratic effect of the frontier upon national politics. The second and more recent school considers Jacksonianism to be an expression of the rule of farmers and workers in Washington. The best known exponent of this view is Charles A. Beard, and it is endorsed by most of the modern liberal historians.

Sectionalism as an Historical Method

Let us turn first to the frontier theory. In 1893 Frederick Jackson Turner read to a gathering of the American Historical Association a paper entitled, *The Significance of the Frontier in American History*. The main ideas of this essay were later expanded by Turner into a series of articles and books dealing with various phases of the frontier and its fancied effects on the national development of the United States. What was his theory? 'The existence of an area of free land',

---

10   Frankel 1947. This article has been slightly edited and abridged.

he wrote, 'its continuous recession, and the advance of American settlement westward, explain American development'. Or as he stated in another article: for 200 years 'westward expansion was the most important single process in American history'. And what was the effect of the frontier? Turner's answer is plain. 'This at least is clear: American democracy is fundamentally the outcome of the experiences of the American people in dealing with the West'. That the Western land areas were decisive in American history, and that their chief result was 'democracy' – this is the heart of Turner's thesis. Turner's writings deal mainly with the Jackson period. It was at that time that the West 'came into its own, conquered national power, and had its greatest effect in the furtherance of 'democracy''.

The Turner school thus starts with a geographical abstraction: the frontier. History is presumed to be based primarily upon a conflict, not of class but of sectional interests. This conception has sunk deep roots in American academic thought. It is a commonplace to refer to the Civil War as a conflict between the 'North' and the 'South', instead of more precisely designating it as a clash of slaveholding and bourgeois economy. Even bias and prejudice are often given sectional labels. Historians boast that their work is free, not only of class prejudice, but of 'sectional bias'. This terminology has become a substitute for thinking for writers of American history. Partly, this has been the result of the inadequate theoretical equipment of the historians, and partly too it has stemmed from a reluctance to adopt Marxist terminology. Thus 'section' has become a cowardly-confused pseudonym for class in the language of American historical writing.

There is a certain plausibility in this sectional approach. It resides in the fact that, in early United States history, economic classes were largely concentrated in geographical regions. The 'South' thus meant the planters, the 'North' the bourgeoisie, and the 'West' the small farmers. In this manner many historians were able to give class analyses in sectional terminology. But to substitute an imperfect concept for a more precise one cannot fail to bring eventual theoretical disaster.

This is the fate of the Turner school, which carried out the sectional approach to its furthest limits by elevating one section to omnipotence. The 'frontier' is a geographical abstraction based upon a shifting region. Its significance can only be appreciated when analyzed in class terms. A specific frontier at a specific time has a class structure differing from that of the same frontier at another time, or another section of the frontier at the same time. The Illinois farmer had more in common with the Massachusetts or Vermont farmer than with his fellow 'frontiersman', the planter further south. If he didn't know this, the Civil War taught it to him, and should have taught it to the historian as well.

By understanding this outstanding flaw in the sectional method, its non-class approach, we come to grips with the inherent weakness of the frontier school. A study of the frontier and of the chief class which inhabited it, the small farmers, is sufficient to convince a Marxist that this section could never take independent control of the state power. The agrarian petty-bourgeoisie, geographically and economically diffused, holding no key position in the national economy, plays an impotent role when it attempts to take an independent course. F.L. Paxson, the chief disciple of the Turner method, in a series of lectures entitled *When the West Is Gone* unintentionally makes this plain. He points out that every frontier 'revolt' up to Bryan and the Populists was a success. Why then was the last wave a failure? 'Something had happened', he says, 'to break the course of normal American thought and action'.

What Paxson fails to grasp is that in every previous movement, the farmer had served as an auxiliary to a predominant social class. The farmer fought in 1776 for the planters and for capitalists against England; in Jefferson's and Jackson's time for the planter against the capitalist, and in the Civil War for the capitalist against the planter. In Bryan's day he was allied with no predominant social class, and alone the farmer could not, nor can he ever, take the state power.

Let us consider Turner's thesis from still another aspect. The existence of the vast western lands fathered, in his view, democratic institutions in the United States. There is no denying a certain element of truth in this. To a degree, which has been greatly exaggerated, the eastern masses drew independence from the western farming opportunities. To a degree, the large class of western farmers helped break down open aristocratic rule. Yet there is another side to the coin which American sectionalist historians have sedulously avoided revealing. And this is – the far greater significance of the western lands for the plantation oligarchy. For that class the existence of a western reserve was economically decisive, because without room to expand the Cotton Kingdom was doomed. The vast land reserves facilitated more than any other single factor the growth of the plantation system after 1800. Considered in this light, the open west made possible the barbaric atavism of an expanding chattel slave system in the 19th century! Shall we disregard the armies of slaves thus created, as the Jacksonian 'democrats' of that day did? Those who talk of the exemplary democracy of the Jackson period do just that.

So much for the special aspects of the Turner frontier school. To its more general conceptions which it shares with other liberal historical theories, we shall return later. Let us consider now the more recent trend of thought concerning the Jackson period among modern historians.

Jacksonianism: Farmer-Labor or Planter Rule?

The impact of Marxism has visibly affected historical thought in every country of the globe. In the United States, where class struggles have been conducted in such open and undisguised forms, this impact could not fail to produce important results. Thus for over forty years there has flourished a school of historians whose chief occupation has been to borrow for their own use some of the tenets of Marxism, while always denying their debt to Marxism, reserving as a matter of fact, envenomed shafts for the consistent and avowed Marxists. Charles A. Beard is the most prominent representative of this group; Vernon L. Parrington, Arthur M. Schlesinger Sr. and Jr., and Louis Hacker are other prominent figures.

The approach of the Beard-type historians to the Jackson period begins with a modification of the Turner school. The 'frontier', they realize, is not so omnipotent as its proponents believe. Rather they turn to a class analysis. Arthur M. Schlesinger Jr., in a recently (1945) published survey, *The Age of Jackson*, makes this clear in his comment: 'It seems clear now that more can be understood about Jacksonian democracy if it is regarded as a problem not of sections, but of classes'. This is a promising beginning, but in the end he completes the circle and returns to the traditional conceptions. For Jacksonianism is viewed by these historians as well, as a popular revolution crowned by the rule of the masses.

We need hardly go further than the chapter heading in Beard's *The Rise of American Civilization*, which characterizes Jacksonianism as A Triumphant Farmer-Labor Party. Subsequent references in his book speak of 'the labor and agrarian democracy', 'the farmer-labor democracy', and so forth. Arthur M. Schlesinger Jr. constructed his entire above-mentioned book around this idea, that the Jackson government was a worker-farmer conquest. Thus common to both the Beard and Turner theories, is the illusory notion of the revolutionary transfer of state power in the Jackson period to the popular masses. To these misconceptions must be counterposed the Marxist understanding of the first sixty years of the Nineteenth Century as a period of uninterrupted, if at times modified, hegemony of the slave oligarchy in national affairs.

If the conception that under Jackson the popular masses seized power were true, it would represent an important social revolution in the United States. (If revolutions were as simple in reality as they are in the minds of these people, the task of revolutionists would be light indeed). We must ask, why did the slaveholder South yield so readily to being dispossessed from political power for which it was to fight tooth and claw thirty years later? Were these impetuous historians to stop and ponder this question before venturing to speak so rashly of 'revolution' they could find but one reply in accord with historical fact. It is this, that the Jacksonian Democratic Party in power did not lay its hands on a single prerogative or institution of the planting class. On the contrary, it protected, strengthened and aided that class, while conducting an offensive to weaken the bourgeois enemy of the planters in the North.

But the historian may protest that the workers and farmers got a hearing in Washington from the Jackson administrations. What of the protection of the land interests of the farmers? The ten-hour laws? The mechanics lien laws? The progress made, especially by the workers, is beyond dispute. First of all, however, it must be understood that such concessions did not directly endanger the planting class, and, for that reason, they could countenance reforms which gained for them national electoral support. Let us recall how John Randolph, planter spokesman in Congress, challenged the bourgeoisie: 'Northern gentlemen think to govern us by our black slaves, but let me tell them, we intend to govern them by their white slaves'.

Workingmen's Parties

Not one of our 'enlightened' historians thinks to suggest that the gains of labor in this period might have resulted primarily from the increasing power and the independent activity and pressure of the workers' organizations. The period just preceding Jackson and during his administrations saw a huge growth of the trade unions and political movement of the workers. Unions were organized in many trades of the growing industrial system. Workingmen's parties were organized in a number of states, and workingmen's newspapers mushroomed. A spreading strike movement in the industrial areas, despite the vicious court rulings on 'conspiracy' charges, testified to the militancy of the movement. Could not such a movement be expected to wring gains from the bourgeoisie independently of Jackson?

A very instructive case is related by the socialist historian Gustavus Myers in his *History of Tammany Hall*. Tammany was the Jackson arm in New York City. In 1829 a Workingmen's Party was organized, inspired chiefly by Robert Dale Owen, son of the famous Utopian Socialist. It propagated the typical workingmen's program of that day: opposition to the 'feudal land monopoly' and to capitalist banks, in favor of a system of free education, and so forth. In the first election in which the new party put a ticket in the field, it polled 6,000 votes as against 11,000 by the established Tammany machine, and elected Ebenezer Ford to the Assembly. Tammany fought the Workingmen's Party bitterly, with every weapon in its well-stocked arsenal. As part of its campaign, it sponsored a piece of reform legislation designed to win the workers back to Tammany. This was the origin of the Mechanics Lien Law in New York State which has come down to us as a gift of the Jacksonians!

The early Workingmen's Parties were eventually assimilated into the Democratic Party and their independent struggle was subordinated to national Jacksonian politics. Arthur M. Schlesinger describes this process with a gleeful air. To those for whom sycophancy is the ideal policy for the labor movement it was a step forward. After all, what can the workers accomplish as an independent force? They should be happy to attach themselves to any Jackson (or Roosevelt) who might throw them an occasional favor.

Marxists have an altogether different conception of the role of the labor movement. We are bound to criticize an alliance which was a severe setback to the labor movement. For the workers to abandon the construction of independent organizations in order to submerge themselves in the Democratic Party was to break the line of organizational continuity so indispensable for the eventual construction of a national labor movement of power and independence. To those who point to the 'reforms' achieved in this period, we reply that at bottom they were the result of the show of power of the workers. An independent policy, designed to take advantage of the division between the planters and the capitalists, would have secured far bigger and more lasting gains. Of course, our criticism here is not of the weak and inexperienced labor movement of that day, but of those 'liberal' historians and modern sycophants who would erect this policy of subservience into an ideal standard for the working class.

The miseducation of the workers by their leaders in the Jackson period left a deep scar on the labor movement. The workers, instead of being in the forefront of the Abolitionist movement, their rightful place, were in the planter controlled Democratic Party. Whoever touched the foul slavocracy was defiled with its filth. The anti-Abolitionist and chauvinist poison among the workers stems from this period of miseducation. Northern Jacksonian 'democracy' must bear the blame for this.

Jacksonian Reforms

Our enlightened historians bring forward another 'proof' of the democracy of Jacksonianism. All the democratic reformers, they tell us, all the 'radical' opponents of 'privilege' and 'monopoly' were in the Democratic Party. The radical ferment of the period was expressed through Jacksonianism. That is their argument. And it is true that much of the agrarian radicalism, petty-bourgeois reformism and proletarian discontent found its expression in the Jacksonian Party. But here again we must proceed with care, and sift out the kernel of truth from the husk of phrases.

The planting class since Jefferson's day had worked out an elaborate ideology with which to justify their rule and their struggle against the capitalist class. Men like Jefferson, John Taylor, John C. Calhoun and certain Jacksonian leaders demonstrate this. Their conception of an ideal society was a basically agricultural economy which they could dominate with ease. An extensive polemical literature was developed against bourgeois ideology placing the 'producing classes' on one side of a struggle against the 'non-producing classes'. It would of course be a mistake to suppose that the planters saw themselves for what they really were: the most parasitic class of the nation. By an ideological sleight-of-hand whose chief attainment was an absolute disregard of the slaves who were the actual producers, the planters converted themselves into the primary producing class of the South and the nation! Violent declamations against the capitalist thief who steals from the producer the fruit of his toil conjured up visions of the planter and his family in their immaculate white clothes, picking cotton all day in the hot sun, month in and month out, only to be robbed of the fruit of their toil by Northern parasites. So spoke the worst thief of all, the slaveholder. And he saw nothing false in his fantastic ideology, so accustomed was he to think of the labor of his slaves as unquestionably 'his own' as though he had performed it himself.

The democratic agitation of the Northern Jacksonians followed these same lines. It pointed out many valuable truths about the capitalist class, and had certain indubitable progressive results. But it suffered from an unpardonable defect – that of defending the slave economy. This defect gave it a generally reactionary cast in the national sphere. The apologist-historians protest that slavery was concentrated in the South, and the democratic agitation in the North had to fight the main enemy. They point to a certain type of Abolitionist whose misleading role it was to make the sins of slavery an excuse for the sins of capitalism. Here too there is a certain grain of truth. Yet what of the Southern Jacksonians? Did they expose and combat slavery? On the contrary, they helped to tighten the noose around the black man's neck. The question should not be posed sectionally to begin with, for Jacksonianism was a national movement. Had it been truly 'democratic', it would have condemned both slave and capitalist exploitation, and fought first of all against the slave system.

Jacksonianism and Abolitionism

The Abolition question, as a matter of fact, is the touchstone of Jacksonianism. It seems difficult to understand how a national movement committed to forthright democratic agitation could have avoided the issue of slavery, or even stood altogether on the reactionary side. Difficult to comprehend, that is, if one does not grasp the fact of slaveholder hegemony in the Democratic Party. It is amazing how many different types of reformers made up the Northern wing of the Democratic Party. It was a reform association with one law: you must leave the issue of human slavery strictly alone! Abolitionism was, as A.M. Schlesinger Jr. mentions in passing, the 'untouchable' of the Democratic Party. In *The Age of Jackson* he writes:

> The Jacksonians in the thirties were bitterly critical of Abolitionists. The outcry against slavery, they felt, distracted attention from the vital economic question of Bank and currency while at the same time it menaced the Southern alliance so necessary for the success of the reform program (!!). A good deal of Jacksonian energy, indeed, was expended in showing how the abolition movement was a conservative plot ... Ely Moore [a union leader who became a Democratic Congressman] spoke for much of labor in his charge that the Whigs planned to destroy the power of the Northern working classes by freeing the Negro 'to compete with the Northern white man in the labor market' ... From reformers like Fanny Wright and Albert Brisbane to party leaders like Jackson and Van Buren, the liberal movement united in denouncing the Abolitionists.

Here, from the mouth of a modern apologist, we have a fair sample of the Alice-in-Wonderland reasoning of the Jacksonian 'radicals'. An alliance with slaveholders is made to 'reform' society, and it must not be endangered by chatter against human slavery!

A Democrat who took his democracy seriously, and extended it to the Negro slaves had no place in this 'Democratic' party. There is an instructive case. William Leggett, one of the ablest journalists of the New York Tammany organization in 1835 attacked an order issued by Amos Kendall, Jackson's Postmaster General (and incidentally radical-in-chief of the Democratic Party!), which barred Abolitionist literature from free national circulation through the mails. In return Leggett was promptly excommunicated from the Party and ruthlessly cast aside. He was pursued to the grave for his heresy, and afterwards Tammany Hall had the ironical temerity to honor his memory with a bust in the same room in which he had been read out of the party.

The issue of slavery was the key to the real nature of Jacksonianism, as it was to become the key to all parties, issues and men. The uncompromising defense of slavery by Jacksonian 'democrats' marks the movement as a planter dominated upsurge. The custom of historians to ignore this, or to give it only passing reference without halting or modifying their paeans to Jacksonian 'democracy' brings them close to dishonesty. They cannot sidestep the issue by pointing to numerous Jacksonians of the North who later became free-soil advocates. That belongs to a later period, when the workers and farmer pawns of the slavocracy were torn away by the developments preceding Civil War. Pro-slavery stamps Jacksonianism with an indelible mark.

As a last defense against the conception of Jacksonianism as a planter power, the historians of the Turner and Beard schools point to the fact that the majority of large planters were for a time supporters of Whig policies against Jackson. Here too there is a germ of an idea, but again it must be separated from the false interpretation placed upon it.

Division among the Planters

... [L]arge planters, particularly of the eastern region ... had grown accustomed to ruling through an alliance with and concessions to the Northern capitalists. When conditions make it difficult or impossible for a class to continue in its previous path, a conservative section of that class tends always to stand in the way of the necessary turn. The Whig planters wanted to continue to rule 'in the old way'. A sharp-eyed historian of the South has perceived the nature of this split in the planting class. William E. Dodd writes in his book, *The Cotton Kingdom*:

> Still there were differences ... The larger planters and justices of the older counties everywhere tended to follow Clay, while the smaller planters, the rising business men, liked the rougher Jackson way. Besides, Jackson could carry the West, and the votes of the West were necessary to any aggressive national policy. *But these differences were the differences of older and younger groups, not the differences of social irreconcilables.* Consequently, though each party twitted the other on occasion with being disloyal to slavery, in any great crisis they were almost certain to unite, for whatever happened, the planters felt that they must control the cotton kingdom. (Our emphasis).

Marxists see the Jackson period as a period of continued planter rule, modified in its external aspects by changing class alignments, and attaching to itself a pseudo-democratic movement of petty-bourgeois reformers who drew behind them large urban and agrarian masses. There can be no 'return to Jackson'. Although Jackson fought the capitalists, he fought them as a representative of the slaveowning class. There cannot be a return to Jackson any more than there can be a return to slavery.

What of the 'modern significance of Jacksonian Democracy' of which the liberals speak so glibly? Jackson and his party did represent a new departure, a new tradition in American politics. They represented the adaptation of the ruling class to the mass movements of workers and farmers. Every essential element of modern party usage stems from Jackson's time. Extended suffrage, party nominating conventions, publication of the popular vote, choice of Presidential electors by popular vote, elective judiciary and so forth, first began to predominate in his period. Likewise the spoils system in national politics, corrupt political machines, and ward heeling politicians, candidates without principles, and demagogic campaigns. The Jackson managers in the campaign of 1828 'cleverly' concealed Jackson's stand on every important issue in national affairs, stressing only his rough western virtues. Little did they realize that they were making a stick to break their own backs. Twelve years later the Whigs had the same 'brilliant' idea, and put into the field a candidate who could out-drink, out-fight and out-log-cabin Jackson's party, and he carried the country. Thus was developed the modern mode of *class rule concealed behind the appeal to the common man*. In a way it was a political 'revolution' – in methods.

Utterly false is the attempt to find a 'modern significance' for Jacksonianism in the phrases and slogans of that movement without regard to its class foundation. Such an attempt leaves the modern liberal with nothing to build on but ... phrases. But phrases are powerless against capitalism now as they were powerless against slavery then. Only the movements of social classes have the power to change society. If Jacksonianism has any 'modern significance' it is this: only by allying themselves with an economically predominant class on the road to power can the urban and agrarian petty-bourgeois masses break the capitalist chains that bind them. That modern class, which is the gravedigger of capitalism, is the proletariat. Marxists will work to build the power of this class and to gain for it allies from other classes. We leave empty-headed liberals to celebrate the reactionary subservience of the popular movement to the slaveholding class a century ago, as they celebrated the subservience of the popular movement to the capitalist-Roosevelt demagogy more recently.

4   A Suppressed Chapter in the History of American Capitalism: The Destruction of Indian Communal Democracy[11]
(*1949*)

William F. Warde (George Novack)

The capitalist rulers of the United States mounted the power through a series of violent struggles against precapitalist social forces. The first of these upheavals took place at the dawn of modern American history with the invasion of the Western hemisphere by the nations of Western Europe and the conquest of the aboriginal inhabitants. The uprooting of the Indians played a significant part in clearing the way for bourgeois supremacy on this continent.

However, the pages of the most learned historians contain little recognition and less understanding of this connection between the overthrow of Indian tribalism and the development of bourgeois society in America. As a rule, they regard the ousting and obliteration of the natives simply as an incident in the spread of the white man over the continent. They may condemn the treatment of the Indians as a lamentable blot on the historical record, but they do not see that it has any important bearing upon the formation of the United States.

This conventional view of Indian-white relations is shared by conservative and liberal writers alike. In their classic liberal interpretation of *The Rise of American Civilization*, Charles and Mary Beard, for example, utterly fail to grasp the social significance of the wars against the Indians, making only scanty disconnected references to them.

President Conant of Harvard has just supplied an instructive illustration of how far the Indian conquest has faded from the consciousness of bourgeois thinkers. During a speech at the *N.Y. Herald Tribune* Forum in October 1948 Conant stated: 'In the first place, this nation, unlike most others, has not evolved from a state founded on a military conquest. As a consequence we have nowhere in our tradition the idea of an aristocracy descended from the

---

11   Warde 1949a and Warde 1949b. This article has been slightly edited and abridged.

conquerors and entitled to rule by right of birth. On the contrary, we have developed our greatness in a period in which a fluid society overran a rich and empty continent ...'.

Conant's speech summoned American educators to demonstrate in theoretical questions what American capitalism must prove in practice – the superiority of bourgeois ideas and methods over the 'alien importations' of the 'philosophy based on the writings of Marx, Engels and Lenin'. The Harvard president insisted that 'not words, but facts' must be the weapons to convince the youth and defeat Marxism. The passage we have cited will hardly promote that purpose, for it contains two serious misstatements of fact about early American history.

In the first place, contrary to Conant's assertion, the bourgeois structure of this nation did 'evolve from a state founded on a military conquest'. It was the conquest of the Indian tribes, not to speak of wars against the Spanish, Dutch and French, which gave England and her colonists mastery of North America.

Secondly, although North America in colonial times was far more thinly populated than Europe or Asia, it was scarcely 'empty' of inhabitants. In order to occupy and overrun the continent, the pioneers first had to 'empty' the land of its original possessors. The founders of Harvard could tell its present head many tales of the difficulties involved in this task.

What are the reasons for this extraordinary blind spot of the bourgeois historians and those who, like Conant, push to the extreme their preconceptions of our national origins?

There is, first of all, the weight of tradition. Historians continue to treat the Indians with the same disdain and lack of comprehension that their forefathers manifested in real life. The pioneers looked upon the Indians as little more than obnoxious obstacles in the path of their advancement who had to be cleared away by any means and at all costs. The English colonists rid their settlements of Indians as ruthlessly as they cleared the lands of trees and wild animals. They placed the Indian 'varmints' and 'serpents' on the same level as wild beasts. In early New England bounties were paid for Indian scalps as today they are awarded for the tails of predatory animals.

What Their Attitude Is

The contemporary professors do not know how to fit the Indians, and the facts of their dispossession and disappearance, into their schemes of interpretation any more than the pioneers were able to absorb them into bourgeois society. The government's final solution of the Indian problem has been to segregate the survivors in reservations, an American equivalent of the European concentration camps and the African compounds. The historians dispose of the Indians by also setting them off to one side, in a special category completely detached from the main course of American historical development.

Indeed, because of their unconscious and narrow class outlook, the bourgeois historians, on the whole, are hardly aware that the fate of the Indians presents any problem. They assume that private property must be the normal foundation of any 'good' society. And so, the annihilation of Indian collectivism by the white conquerors for the sake of private property seems so much in the nature of things as to require no explanation.

But there is more involved than inertia or indifference. Freud has explained individual lapses of memory by an unconscious wish to hide from what is shameful, fearful, socially unacceptable. Where a social lapse of memory occurs, a similar mechanism and similar motives for suppression are often at work, especially where representatives of ruling classes engage in. systematic forgetfulness. That is the case here. The abominable treatment of the Indians is extremely unpleasant to contemplate, and equally unpleasant to explain.

At the bottom of their censorship lies the bourgeois attitude toward the communal character of Indian life. The bourgeois mind finds communism in any form so contrary to its values, so abhorrent and abnormal, that it recoils from its manifestations and instinctively strives to bury recollections of their existence. In any event, the run-of-the-mill historian feels little impulse to examine and explain primitive communism although it was the cradle of humanity and, in particular, formed a starting point of modern American history.

Even contemporary writers sympathetic to the Indians, such as Oliver LaFarge, go out of their way to deny that the basic institutions of the Indians can be termed 'communistic' even while offering evidence to the contrary. 'The source of life, the land and its products, they (the Indians) owned in common', writes LaFarge in *As Long as the Grass Shall Grow*: 'Loose talkers have called this Communism. It is not'. Here is a striking example of how deep anti-communist prejudice runs.

Class calculation reinforces this tendency toward suppression. An understanding of the customs of the Indians and the reasons for their extinction may raise doubts about the eternity of private property and the standards of bourgeois life. Such knowledge spread among an enlightened people may be dangerous to the ruling ideas of the ruling class. Does it not indicate that, at least so far as the past is concerned, communism is not quite so alien to American soil as it is pictured by the witch-hunters?

Thus the expunging of the real facts about the Indians from historical memory today is no more accidental than was their physical elimination yesterday.

Both have their ultimate source in the promotion of the material interests of the owners of private property and the champions of free enterprise.

Economic Causes behind Clash of Indian Tribalism and European Civilization

Modern American society did not originate on unencumbered soil in the pure and painless way pictured by Harvard's President Conant. It arose from the disintegration and ruin of two ancient societies: European feudalism and primitive American communism. Its birth was attended by two violent social conflicts. One was the struggle between the feudal order and the rising forces of capitalism in the Old World. The other was the collision between Indian tribalism and European civilization, which resulted in the breakup of the Indian way of life as a prelude to the establishment of the bourgeois regime in North America.

The historians center their attention on the first process, and it is easy to understand why. Modern American society is the offspring of European civilization; its foundations rest upon a whole series of 'alien importations' from across the Atlantic.

The contributions of the Indians in the making of modern America were not on the same scale and belonged to a different order. But this is no warrant for discounting them as a negligible factor in the peculiar evolution of the American nation. Cast in the minor role of a villainous opposition, the Indian has nevertheless played an important part in the first acts of our national development. For several centuries American events were conditioned by the struggle against the Indian tribes. The European civilization transplanted to the New World grew at the direct expense of Indian life. Let us see why this was so.

In the Indian and the European, ancient society and modern civilization confronted each other and engaged in an unequal test of strength. Over thousands of years the Indians had worked out ways and means of living admirably suited to the North American wilderness.

The Indian Community

The North American Indians were organized in hundreds of thinly dispersed tribes, numbering from a few score to a few thousand people, bound together by ties of blood kinship. Each of these tiny tribes constituted a self-sufficing economic unit. They were far more directly and firmly attached to their natural habitats than to one another. The split-up bands had little unity of action or power of resistance against enemies like the white man They were easily pitted against one another, since, despite an identity of social structure and institutions, they had no strong bonds of mutual interest.

The sparseness and separation of the Indian population resulted from their method of producing the necessities of life. Although there was considerable diversity of conditions from tribe to tribe and from region to region, their basic economic features were remarkably uniform. Except along the seashores, most of the North American tribes lived mainly by hunting wild animals such as the deer and buffalo. Fishing, fowling, berry-picking and farming were important but accessory sources of subsistence. Every type of social organization has laws of population and population growth corresponding to its mode of production. It has been estimated that three square miles of hunting ground were required to sustain each Indian. This imposed narrow limits on the size of the Indian population. Each tribe had to occupy sizable areas to support its members. The Iroquois sometimes travelled hundreds of miles on their hunting expeditions.

The segmentation of the Indians into hundreds of petty tribal units and their slow but persistent expansion over the entire Western World had arisen from the inability of foraging and hunting economy to sustain many people on a given area. This was likewise the main cause for the warfare between neighboring tribes and for the Indians' unyielding defense of their hunting and fishing grounds against invaders. ...

The only ways to overcome the restrictions inherent in hunting economy were through the development of stock-raising or agriculture, a shift from food *collecting* to food *producing*. But unlike the Asiatics and Europeans, the Indians of North America domesticated no animals except the dog and the turkey. They had no horses, cattle, swine or sheep.

The Indians (that is, the Indian women who did the work) proved to be outstanding agriculturists. They had domesticated over forty useful plants, among them maize, tobacco, potatoes, tomatoes, peanuts, beans and others that then and later had considerable economic importance. Agriculture based on maize production gave birth to the various grades of Village Indians and made possible the more concentrated populations and brilliant achievements of Maya and Aztec cultures.

But Indian progress in agriculture became stymied by insurmountable technological barriers. The Indians derived their meat and clothing from wild game, not from tamed and tended animals. They did not invent the wheel or the axle; they did not know iron or how to smelt it. Their implements were mostly made of stone, wood, bone and fiber. Without draft animals and iron, it was impossible to develop the plow or even an efficient and durable hoe. ...

The whites, however, bore with them all the means for advanced agriculture accumulated since the invention of the animal-drawn plow. These improved implements and methods of cultivation were the stepping stones by which Europe had approached capitalism. But along with superior tools and techniques of production the Europeans brought their correspondingly different property forms and relations.

Although the Indians possessed personal property, they were unfamiliar with private property in the means of production, or even in the distribution of the means of subsistence. They carried on their principal activities: hunting, fishing, cultivating, home-making and warfare, in a collective manner. The product of their labors was more or less equally shared among all members of the tribe.

The Indians and the Land

Above all, the North American Indians knew no such thing as private property in land which is the basis of all other kinds of private ownership in the means of production ... The very idea that ancestral lands from which they drew their sustenance could be taken from the people, become air article of commerce, and be bought and sold was inconceivable, fantastic and abhorrent to the Indian. Even when Indians were given money or goods for a title to their lands, they could not believe that this transaction involved the right to deprive them of their use forever.

'The earth is like fire and water, that cannot be sold', said the Omahas. The Shawnee chief Tecumseh, who sought to combine all the Indians from Canada to Florida against the encroachment of the whites upon their hunting grounds, exclaimed: 'Sell land! As well sell air and water. The Great Spirit gave them in common to all'.

... The intruders looked upon the new-found lands and their occupants through the eyes of a civilization founded on opposite premises. To them it was natural to convert everything into private property and thereby exclude the rest of humanity from its use and enjoyment. The conquerors maintained that whatever existed in the New World, or came out of it, was to be vested either in an individual or a power separate and distinct from the community or towering above it, like the monarchy, the state or the church.

The Outlook of the Europeans

They did not exempt human beings from this process. The invaders seized not only the land but its inhabitants and sought, wherever they could, to convert the Indians into their private possessions as chattel-slaves.

Those who were driven across the Atlantic by religious and political persecution were a minority. For the majority, the lust for aggrandizement and the greed for personal gain were among the prime passions actuating the Europeans. It was these material motives, more powerful than wind or wave, that propelled the first Europeans overseas and then inevitably brought them into collision with the aboriginal inhabitants.

The conquerors came as robbers and enslavers; they stayed as colonizers and traders. America had belonged to the Indian tribes both by hereditary right and by life-and-death need to maintain themselves and perpetuate their kind upon the tribal territories. But the tribes wanted to hold the land for different purposes and on different terms than the whites. The Europeans aimed to acquire the land for themselves or for some sovereign or noble who held title for their country. The newcomers needed land, not simply for hunting, trapping and fishing, but for extensive agriculture, for lumbering, for settlements and trading centers, for commerce and manufacture – in a phrase, for private exploitation on an expanding scale.

Thus, regardless of their wishes, the Indians and Europeans were sharply counterposed to each other by virtue of their contradictory economic needs and aims. The Indian could maintain his economy with its primitive communistic institutions and customs, its crude division of labor between the sexes and its tribal ties of blood kinship only by keeping the white men at bay. The newcomers could plant their settlements and expand their economic activities only by pressing upon the Indian tribes and snatching their territories. This antagonism, flowing from their diametrically opposing systems of production, governed the dealings between red men and white from their first contacts.

The ways and means by which the natives were enslaved, dispossessed and exterminated cannot be set forth here in detail. The pattern of robbery, violence, debauchery and trickery was fixed by the Spaniards as early as the landings of Columbus. In their lust for gold Columbus and his men depopulated Hispaniola. Through overwork, abuse, starvation, despair and disease, the original population of the island dwindled from 300,000 in 1492 to an actual count of 60,000 in 1508. Only a remnant of 500 survived by 1548.

The Overthrow of the Indians

The same story was repeated on the mainland of North America time and again during the next four hundred years by the Dutch, English, French and Americans. The Indian wars in New England demonstrated how ruthless and irreconcilable was the conflict between the opposing social forces. While the first colonists in Massachusetts were busy securing a foothold, Indian neighbors established friendly, and helpful ties with them. They gave the Pilgrims food in time of distress, taught them how to raise maize and tobacco and how to cope with the forest and its wild life.

But the divines who enjoined the Puritans not to covet their neighbor's wives taught otherwise about the Indian hunting grounds. These religious and political leaders insisted that all land not actually occupied and cultivated belonged, not to the Indians, but to the Massachusetts Bay Colony which they controlled. Roger Williams was tried and banished from Massachusetts in 1635 because he declared that the 'Natives are the true owners' of the land. His heretical views on the land question were condemned as no less dangerous than his unorthodox religious opinions.

The New England colonists annexed the tribal lands by waging wars of extermination against the natives over the next eighty years, beginning with the Pequot war in the Connecticut Valley in 1643 and concluding with the expulsion of the Abenakis from the Maine and New Hampshire coasts in 1722. The fiercest of these conflicts, King Philip's War (1675–1678), was directly provoked by the struggle over the land. The increase in white population in the Connecticut Valley from 22,500 in 1640 to 52,000 in 1675 whetted the land hunger of the settlers at the same time that it threatened to engulf the Indian hunting grounds ...

This combat to the death continued until the last frontier was settled and the choicest lands seized. 'The roster of massacres of Indian men, women and children extends from the Great Swamp Massacre of 1696 in Rhode Island, through the killing of the friendly Christian Indians at Wyoming, Pennsylvania, when the republic was young, on through the friendly Aravaipas of Arizona, the winter camp of the Colorado Cheyennes, to the final dreadful spectacle of Wounded Knee in the year 1890', writes Oliver LaFarge. That is how America was taken from the Indians.

The Transformation of Indian Life

Before the white conquerors eradicated Indian society, the Indians passed through an intermediate stage in which their customary relations were considerably altered. The acquisition of horses and firearms from the Europeans opened up the prairies to the Indians in the interior by enabling them to range far more widely and effectively in hunting buffalo and deer. But the ensuing changes in the lives of the Plains tribes were accomplished by their independent efforts without direct intervention by the whites and within the framework of their ancient institutions.

The fur trade with the whites had quite different and damaging effects upon Indian life. The fur trade early became one of the most profitable and far-flung branches of commerce between North America and Europe. The fur factors, hunters and trappers served as agents of the rich merchants and big chartered monopolies ... and acted as advance scouts of capitalist civilization.

The Indians were first drawn into the orbit of capitalist commerce largely through extension of the fur trade. In the course of time the fur-trading tribes embraced all the North American Indians except those in the extreme South and Southwest. The growing interchange of products between the tribes and traders upset the relatively stable Indian existence.

At first this exchange of goods lifted the living standards and increased the wealth and population of the Indians. An iron ax was better than a stone hatchet; a rifle better than a bow and arrow. But, as the fur trade expanded, its evil consequences more and more asserted themselves. The call for ever-larger quantities of furs and skins by the wealthy classes here and abroad led to the rapid destruction of fur-bearing animals who reproduced too slowly to meet this demand.

Indians without contact with [white] civilization were careful not to slaughter more animals than were needed for personal consumption. But once they trapped and hunted for the market, other incentives came into play. These drove the tribes whose hunting and fishing grounds approached exhaustion into bitter competition with adjoining tribes for control of the available supply.

The new conditions produced bloody clashes between competing tribes as well as with the white men who sought possession of the hunting grounds for their own reasons. In trade and war, occupations which are not always easily distinguishable, the role of firearms proved decisive. The Indians could not manufacture or repair firearms, or make powder. They had to bargain with the white men for these and the other indispensable means of production and destruction upon which their lives and livelihoods came to depend ...

Various Indian tribes sought to defend themselves and their hunting grounds from relentless encroachment of the colonists by confederation or by allying themselves with one great power against another. They leagued with the French against the British, the British against the French, the Spanish against the British and the King against the Patriots. Later some Southern tribes were to attach themselves to the Confederacy against the Union.

A Hopeless Struggle

Although the Indians fought with unexampled courage and tenacity, neither heroic sacrifices nor unequal and unstable alliances could save them. They lacked the numbers, the organization and above all the productive capacity for carrying on sustained warfare. ... Neither singly nor in combination could the natives do more than delay the onward march of their white adversaries. Their history is essentially a record of one long retreat across the continent under the onslaught of the conquerors.

The French had more harmonious relations with the Indians than the English, primarily because of differences in their economic aims and activities. Except for the Quebec *habitants*, the French were mainly engaged in hunting and trading; they did not covet the Indian lands but sought to maintain favorable trade relations with the tribes. ...

Behind the English hunters and traders swarmed the solid ranks of colonizers, farmers, planters, speculators and landlords who wanted the Indian hunting grounds for their own property.

This contrast was emphasized by Duquesne when he tried to win the Iroquois from their friendship with Britain. The Frenchman told them: 'Are you ignorant of the difference between the king of England and the king of France? Go see the forts our king has established and you will see that you can still hunt under their very walls. They have been placed for your advantage in places which you frequent. The English, on the contrary, are no sooner in possession of a place than the game is driven away. The forest falls before them as they advance and the soil is laid bare, so that you can scarce find the wherewithal to erect shelter for the night'.

The incompatibility of the hunting economy with advancing agriculture also became a major source of division between the American colonists and the English government. King George's proclamation of 1763 forbade loyal governors to grant land or titles beyond the Alleghenies or private persons to buy land from the Indians. This Quebec Act, designed to monopolize the fur trade for the English and contain colonial settlement on the coastal side of the Allegheny Mountains, imparted a powerful stimulant to colonial revolt.

The height of the onslaught against the Indians was attained when the capitalists took complete command of the government. The three decades following the Civil War have been correctly called by the historian Bancroft 'the history of aboriginal extermination'. The Civil War generals turned from battle against the slaveholders to consummate the conquest of the Indians in the West. General Halleck urged that the Apaches 'be hunted and exterminated' and General Sheridan uttered his notorious remark, 'There are no good Indians but dead Indians'. The attitude toward the Indians was bluntly expressed by the Commissioner of Indian Affairs in his report to Congress in 1870: 'When treating with savage men as with savage beasts, no question of national honor can arise. Whether to fight, to run away, or to employ a ruse, is only a question of expediency'.

Capitalist civilization could not stop halfway at reconstructing Indian life and subordinating it to its needs. With the expansion of settlement, the colonists kept pushing the red men westward, hemming in their living space, violating agreements with them, taking over more and more of their territories. The late Nineteenth Century witnessed the final mopping-up operations by which the Indians were deprived of their lives, their lands and their independence. The few hundred thousand survivors were then imprisoned in reservations under government guard.

Defrauding the Vanquished

Victimization of the Indians did not cease even after they had been reduced to an impotent remnant on the reservations. Lands which had not been seized by force were thereafter stolen by fraud. Through the land allotment system the Bureau of Indian Affairs generously gave a small piece of the tribal lands to each Indian, declared the remainder 'surplus', and sold or allotted it to the whites. Thus the last of the communal lands, with some exceptions, were broken up and absorbed into the system of private property and free enterprise.

The insuperable opposition between the two social systems was equally evident on the side of the Indians in their determination to preserve their established ways. There were no lack of attempts, for example, to enslave the natives. But they defended their freedom as fiercely as their lands. The Indians could not suffer servitude. Such a condition was repugnant to their habits, feelings and productive activities.

The Indian warriors resisted to the death any reversal in their status and occupations, sickened in captivity, refused to reproduce and died off. They could not be broken on the wheel of slave agriculture.

It has always been a difficult and protracted job to reshape human material molded by one social system into the labor conditions of another, especially when this involves a degradation in status. Moreover, as the experience of the

Spaniards with the Indians below the Rio Grande testifies, it is easier to transform cultivators of the soil into slaves than to subjugate hunting peoples.

The same attachment to their roving hunting life which induced the Indians to oppose enslavement led them to reject and withstand assimilation while so many other races were being mixed in the great American melting pot. The Indian tribe was indissolubly united with its home territory. The areas which provided food, clothing and shelter formed the center and circumference of their actions, emotions and thoughts. Their religious ideas and ceremonies were bound up with the places associated with their ancestors. To sever the Indians from these lands was to shatter the foundation of their lives.

The Indians either had to remain aloof from white civilization or else remake themselves from top to bottom in the image of their enemy. The latter course involved forfeiting their cherished traditions and traits and converting themselves and their children into human beings of a strange and different type. This leap across the ages could be taken by scattered individuals but not by whole, tribal communities.

The Fate of the Cherokees

Even where they attempted to absorb civilization bit by bit, the white men did not permit the Indians to avoid corruption or extinction. The Indians found that they could not borrow part of the alien culture without swallowing the rest, the evil with the good; they could not modify their communal culture with the attributes of civilization and preserve its foundations intact. The most conclusive proof was given by the fate of the Cherokees, one of the 'five civilized tribes'. The Cherokees, who inhabited the Southern Alleghenies and were one of the largest tribes in the United States, went the furthest in acquiring the ways of the white man. In the early decades of the Nineteenth Century, the Cherokees transformed themselves into flourishing and skillful stock-raisers, farmers, traders and even slave-owners. They amassed considerable wealth, created an alphabet and formed a government modeled upon that of the United States.

However, they took these steps without discarding communal ownership of the lands which had been guaranteed to them forever in 1798 by the Federal government. Thus the Cherokee Nation stood out like an irritating foreign body within Southern society. The Southern whites were resolved to bring the Cherokees under the sway of private property in land and the centralized state power. Under their pressure Federal troops forced the Cherokees from their homes and deported them en masse. Their lands were distributed by lottery to the whites.

Even after the Cherokees resettled on the Indian Territory in Oklahoma, they could not keep undisturbed possession of their lands and customs. The Bureau of Indian Affairs inflicted the vicious 'land allotment' system upon them whereby the tribal territories were cut into individual lots and placed upon the free market. The government changed the mode of inheritance along with the system of landholding by decreeing that property should henceforth descend through the father's offspring instead of the mother's.

This capped the process of despoiling the tribe of its lands and its rights and overthrowing the basic ancestral institutions of the community. Private property, patrilinear inheritance and the centralized oppressive state displaced communal property, the matriarchal family and tribal democracy. The American Ethnology Bureau reported in 1883 that the Cherokees 'felt that they were, as a nation, being slowly but surely compressed within the contracting coils of the giant anaconda of civilization; yet they held to the vain hope that a spirit of justice and mercy would be born of their helpless condition which would finally prevail in their favor'.

Their hope was vain. 'The giant anaconda of civilization' crushed its prey and swallowed it. By such food has American capitalism grown to its present strength and stature. ...

The bearers of capitalism introduced on North American soil the cleavages and conflicts between master and slave, exploiters and exploited, idlers and toilers, rich and poor which have flourished ever since. Alongside the degradation and suppression of the Indians by the whites there developed profound antagonisms between diverse sections of the new society.

Since the planting of the first colonies, white America has never been without privileged possessing classes at its head. In colonial days the masses were dominated by aristocrats of birth and money; after the War of Independence, by Northern capitalists and Southern slaveholders; since the Civil War, by millionaires and billionaires. These ruling minorities have all elevated themselves above the common people – not to speak of outcasts like foreign immigrants, Negroes, Latin Americans and Orientals – and subordinated to their narrow class interests whatever democratic institutions the people have acquired.

This darker side, of the social transformation wrought by the impact of European civilization upon ancient America is usually passed by in silence, or at least slurred over without explanation, by bourgeois historians. Yet the emergence of class stratifications formed one of the essential lines of demarcation between Indian collectivism and white society.

Fountainspring of White Supremacy

... The disdain of the Anglo-Saxon conqueror can be discerned in [the] dismissal of the existence and struggles of the Indians. What is this but an unconscious – and thereby all the more meaningful – evidence of that racial arrogance and antipathy which induces white scholars to disparage the real role of the colored races in American history? This comes from that white-supremacy prejudice which American palefaces have for centuries aimed not only against the red races but against the black and yellow.

Bourgeois scholars distort and deny the distinguishing traits of tribal equalitarianism, the truly democratic nature of Indian institutions and of the whole net of social relations stemming from primitive communism just as they suppress the motives for the destruction of this system. Both cast discredit on the bourgeois past.

Despite their backwardness in other respects, far more genuine democracy prevailed among the Indians than among their successors. Village and camp were administered by elected councils of elders. The tribes discussed and decided all important issues in common. Military leaders and sachems were chosen for outstanding talents and deeds, not for their wealth and birth. Even where chieftainship was hereditary, the chiefs could not exercise arbitrary authority or command obedience without consent of the community. Military service was voluntary. The Indians knew no such coercive institutions of modern civilization as police, jails, courts, taxes, conscript or standing armies.

The equalitarianism and primitive humanism of Indian relations surpassed the proudest claims of bourgeois society. Mutual assistance was the watchword of the community. The tribe cared for all the aged, infirm, sick and young. Hospitality was a sacred obligation, and the Indian was considerably more generous toward the needy and the stranger than the bourgeois who scorned him as inferior. So paramount was this law of hospitality that even an enemy who came without threats had to be given food and shelter.

William Bartram, the naturalist, noted in 1791 that the Creeks had a common granary made up of voluntary contributions: '... to which every citizen has the right of free and equal access when his own private stores are consumed, to serve as a surplus to fly to for succor, to assist neighboring towns whose crops may have failed, accommodate strangers and travelers, afford provisions or supplies when they go forth on hostile expeditions, etc. ....'.

In his description of *The Indians of the United States*, Clark Wissler, Dean of the Scientific Staff of the American Museum of Natural History and an outstanding authority on Indian life, writes that the Indian 'was not really a communist, but he was liberal with food. So long as he had food, he was expected to share it'. This is a typical effort to obscure the communist character of Indian customs. The bourgeois scientist cannot refrain from trying to convert the Indian into a philanthropic 'liberal', whereas the habit of sharing possessions with others was an integral aspect of their primitive communist mode of life.

Anyone in the tribe, for example, could borrow without permission the belongings of another – and return them without thanks. There were no debtors or creditors where private property and money were absent. William Penn wrote: 'Give them a fine gun, coat or any other thing, it may pass twenty hands before it sticks ... Wealth circulateth like the blood, all parts partake, and ... none shall want what another hath'.

How this tribal solidarity was broken up by civilization can be seen from the following petition by the Mohegan Indians to the Connecticut State Assembly in 1789:

> Yes, the Times have turned everything Upside down ... In Times past our Fore-Fathers lived in Peace, Love and great harmony, and had everything in Great plenty ... They had no Contention about their lands, it lay in Common to them all, and they had but one large dish and they Could all eat together in Peace and Love – But alas, it is not so now, all our Fishing, Hunting and Fowling is entirely gone, And we have now begun to Work on our Land, Keep Cattle, Horses and Hogs And we Build Houses and fence in Lots, And now we plainly See that one Dish and one Fire will not do any longer for us – Some few that are Stronger than others and they will keep off the poor, weake, the halt and the Blind, and will take the Dish to themselves ... poor Widows and Orphans must be pushed to one side and there they must Set a Craying, Starving and die.

This pathetic petition concludes with a plea 'That our Dish of Suckuttush may be equally divided amongst us', if it had to be divided.

To this day the traditions of communal equality are so ingrained among Indians uncontaminated by civilization that they put capitalist society to shame. Recently when oil was found on lands allotted to Jecarilla Indians in northern New Mexico, the individual owners could have legally insisted upon taking the entire income for themselves. This would have meant riches for a few and nothing for the others. However, after deliberation in council, all the Indians made over their mineral rights to the tribe so that whatever was gained should be applied to the good of the whole people. How remote are these 'backward' Apaches from the standards of bourgeois 'moralists'.

Perplexing Christian Double Standards

The Indians found incomprehensible many traits of the whites: their disregard of pledges considered inviolate by the native; their fondness for indoor life; their intolerance of other people's ways; their lust for material possessions and money, etc. As primitive hunters and warriors, the Indians were accustomed to slay not only wild game but rivals who interfered with their essential activities ... These customs were justified and sanctified by their religious beliefs. But they could not understand the duplicity of Christians who preached peace and good-will and yet waged relentless war upon them.

The Indian was repelled by the inhumanity displayed by members of the same white community toward each other, the heartless egotism which flowed from class society and bourgeois anarchy. There was greater equality in work and play, in distribution and enjoyment of goods, in social intercourse and status among the Indians than among the whites. Every member of the tribe shared alike in good times or in bad, in feast or in famine, in war as in peace; no one went hungry while a few had more than enough to eat. ...

This spirit of equality extended to women, children and even to those war captives adopted into the clan and tribe. Women not only stood on an equal footing, but sometimes exercised superior authority. The Indian elder's rarely abused or whipped their children. There was no servant class – and therefore no masters.

The forms of society which displaced Indian tribalism surpassed it in a great many respects – but, we repeat, they were never more equalitarian. The American natives lacked many things known to the white man, but they did not suffer from a ruling aristocracy of birth or wealth. The institution of aristocracy in general is bound up with the growth of property and the concentration of wealth in private hands – and, these were indeed 'alien importations' of white civilization.

[Property's Price]

The contrast between the contending cultures was most sharply expressed in, their attitudes toward the acquisition of private wealth. The passion for property had hardly awakened among the Indians. On the other hand, the quest for riches was the most powerful driving force of the new society, the principal source of its evils and the most conspicuous trait of its outstanding representatives.

The precious metals were the quintessence of wealth, prestige and power in

Europe and the Holy Grail of the pioneer explorers in the 'Age of Geographical Discovery'. In a letter written to Ferdinand and Isabella from Jamaica in 1503, Columbus rhapsodized: 'Gold is a wonderful thing! Whoever owns it is lord of all he wants. With gold it is even possible to open for souls a way to paradise!'

Imagine his astonishment when the Haitians, who used the metal for ornament but not for money, freely handed over gold to the Spaniards in exchange for trinkets. This served only to inflame their greed. After stripping the natives of the gold they possessed, Columbus and his men drove them to forced labor for more. But the Caribbeans did not yield their liberty as readily as their gold.

> These chattel slaves were worked to death. So terrible was their life that they were driven to mass suicide, to mass infanticide, to mass abstinence from sexual life in order that children should not be born into horror. Lethal epidemics followed upon the will to die. The murders and desolations exceeded those of the most pitiless tyrants of earlier history; nor have they been surpassed since.
>
> *Indians of the Americas,* by JOHN COLLIER, p. 57

The Aztec chief Tauhtile thought that 'the Spaniards were troubled with a disease of the heart, for which gold was the specific remedy'. What this naive Aztec diagnosed as a 'disease' was really the normal mode of behavior of the white invaders. As the subsequent conquests of Mexico and Peru demonstrated, nothing sufficed to quench their thirst for the precious metals.

Although Sir Walter Raleigh and other English colonizers hoped to emulate Cortez and the Pizarros, they found no ancient civilizations on the North Atlantic coasts to plunder. Their conquest of the Indians, although inspired by similar sordid motives, was conducted along somewhat different lines. The traders cheated and debauched the natives; the settlers seized their hunting grounds and massacred the tribes; the governments incited one band of Indians against another while destroying the rights and freedom of all! This despoiling of the Indians by the whites dominates the entire historical record, from the first settlements in Virginia to the recent attempt by the Montana Power and Light Company to deprive the Flathead Indians of their territorial rights.

Belonging as they did to incompatible levels of social existence, both the Indians and whites found it impossible to reach any mutual understanding for any length of time. The Indians, baffled by the behavior of these strange creatures from another world, could not fathom their motives. Not only the Aztecs but the North American tribes had to pass through many cruel experiences before they realized how implacable were the aggressions of the whites – and then it was too late. They may be excused for their lack of comprehension.

But the same cannot be said of bourgeois historians of our own day who still fail to understand them after the fact.

The founders of the capitalist regime in North America had a double mission to perform. One was to subdue or eliminate whatever precapitalist social forms and forces existed or sprang up on the continent. The other was to construct the material requirements for bourgeois civilization. The destructive and creative aspects of this process went hand in hand. The extirpation of the Indian tribes was needed to clear the ground for the foundations of the projected new society.

The overthrow of the Indians had contradictory effects upon the subsequent development of American life. The installation of private property in land and the widening exchange of agricultural products at home and in the world market provided the economic basis and incentives for the rapid growth of colonization, agriculture, commerce, craftsmanship, cities and the accumulation of wealth. These conditions fashioned and fostered the virile native forces which prepared and carried through the second great upheaval in American history, the colonists' revolt against England.

The rise of the English colonies in North America and their successful strivings for unhampered development form one of the most celebrated chapters in modern history. But an all-sided review of the process must note that a price was paid for these achievements, especially in the sphere of social relations.

5   W.E.B. Du Bois and His Work[12]
(1950)

William Gorman

As he approaches eighty-two, no higher tribute can be paid William Edward Burghardt Du Bois than that it is impossible to seriously consider the Negro in America without being confronted by his name at every turn. Journalist, research scholar, sociologist, historian, novelist, pamphleteer, educator – his evolution intertwines so completely with that of the Negro people since the Civil War that his individual portrait is the collective portrait of the Negro intelligentsia in twentieth-century America. Du Bois is not unaware of this. His autobiography, *Dusk of Dawn*, is appropriately subtitled *An Autobiography of a Race Concept*. We propose to relate the successive stages of Du Bois' conceptions not only to the clash of American capital and labor in general, but also to Du Bois' more direct relationship to petty-bourgeois liberalism on the one hand, and the struggles of the Negro masses on the other.

Du Bois was educated at Harvard and at Berlin. In Berlin, as he himself relates, he was influenced by the 'professorial socialism' of the German universities, a part of that emasculation of Marxism associated with the name of Edward Bernstein. This had a permanent effect on his thought.

When he returned to the United States, strikes, unemployment marches and the meteoric rise of the Populist Party were sweeping the country. The radical American intelligentsia expressed a growing disbelief in that mythology which declared free enterprise, chosen by fate to remake and rule America as the crowning triumph of American history. The presumed natural basis of the plutocrat's rule, individualistic adaptation of Darwinism, Herbert Spencer's 'Survival of the Fittest', proved vulnerable to the class conflicts produced by the very growth of capital. After the defeat of the Populists in the election of 1896, the scene shifted to the hard-pressed middle classes of the cities. Social work and an ameliorative sociology made their appearance hand in hand. With the

---

12   Gorman 1950.

'controlled experiment' as method and 'moral welfare of society' as principle, this early twentieth century critical intelligence appropriated the method of the natural sciences to bolster evolutionary reformism.

Du Bois as Sociologist

In *An American Dilemma* Myrdal declares 'it is merely a historical accident' that Du Bois' sociological writings of the early 1900's 'sound so much more modern than white writings'. The reason for this, says Myrdal, is that:

> The Negro writers constantly have proceeded on the assumption, later formulated by Du Bois, that '... the Negro in America and in general is an average and ordinary human being ...'. This assumption is now, but was not a couple of decades ago, the assumption of white writers ... It is mainly this historical accident why, for example, Du Bois' study of the Philadelphia Negro community published in the nineties stands out even today as a valuable contribution, while white authors ... have been compelled to retreat from the writings of earlier decades.

Myrdal misstates the whole case. Not only is Du Bois' sociology of the Negro superior to similar works by white authors of that period; there is no single body of American sociology on any subject during that period which, for seriousness, thoroughness and extensiveness, can compare with Du Bois' *Philadelphia Negro* and his annual Atlanta studies on the Negro as farmer, artisan, business man, etc.

It was because of the *objective conditions* of the Negro that Du Bois, intellectually a product of this period, seized upon sociology with such inherent belief and urgency. If the new theme of the social sciences – indeed their very creation – was premised upon the recognition of individuals as being constituent parts of a social entity, such compact communities as the Negro Ghetto and Black Belt were crying for study. Despite its affinity for reform, the prevailing theory of Social Darwinism did not refute the ideology of racism. The Negro was outside its vision. Du Bois therefore extended the whole range of social inquiry in America.

Another work of this period was Du Bois' *Suppression of the African Slave Trade*. Written fully fifteen years before Charles Beard's *An Economic Interpretation of the Constitution of the United States*, this is one of the pioneer applications in the United States of economic analysis to historic phenomena. 'The development of Southern slavery has heretofore been viewed so exclusively from the social and ethical standpoint that we are apt to forget its close and indissoluble connection with the cotton market'.

The Du Bois-Washington Dispute

Frederick Douglass preceded Booker T. Washington in pressing forward the need for industrial training for Negroes. Du Bois himself applauded Washington's famous Atlanta speech in 1895 for segregated equality. In the subsequent decade developments within the Negro and non-Negro world began to play havoc with this program. The Negro migrations northward speeded the growth of the Ghetto. These highly urban concentrations of misery marked both the beginning of the Negro's migration into industry and the birth of a professional class far removed from the Southern hinterland. Outside the Ghetto the radicalization of the middle classes and of labor was evidenced by hundreds of thousands of socialist votes in the 1904 elections. The heretofore excluded unskilled workers were finding expression in the new Industrial Workers of the World.

The futility of Washington's philosophy was becoming evident even in the rural South. According to him, the education of the Negro sharecropper and tenant farmer in scientific agriculture would be the means of creating an independent Negro peasantry equal to the white rural middle classes in America. But precisely the scientific revolution in agriculture, the rationalized exploitation of the soil, the growth of capital investment in farming, increases the pauperization of the small agricultural producer. The expansion of capitalism, therefore, strengthened the remnants of feudalism on the Southern countryside. Du Bois, both as acute sociologist and sensitive observer of the Negro's fate, recorded some of his impressions in *Souls of Black Folk*. Moreover, he engaged in a thorough study of an Alabama Negro farm area in 1906 at the behest of the United States Commissioner of Labor. It was paid for, but never published, on the grounds that it 'touched on political matters'. No wonder – for by 1910 official statistics reported 75.3 per cent of the Southern Negro farmers were tenants and sharecroppers.

Not Du Bois, but Monroe Trotter and his *Boston Guardian* began the attack on Booker T. Washington. Du Bois was at this time preoccupied with sociology, with placing the facts at the disposal of the powers that be. But Washington's setting up of a Negro 'ghost government' at Tuskegee to control the Negroes on behalf of capital provoked increasing opposition from the new Negro intelligentsia, Du Bois included. The Atlanta riot in 1906 and the Tuskegee dictatorship ripped apart Du Bois' belief that the Negro was 'a concrete group of living beings artificially set off by themselves and capable of almost laboratory experiments'.

The Talented Tenth and Its Program

Du Bois conceived that the intense political activity in the United States between 1892 and 1912 placed the Negro electorate in a decisive position. To parliamentary democracy he attributed a miraculous power: '... with the right to vote goes everything; freedom, manhood, the honor of your wives, the chastity of your daughters, the right to work, and the chance to rise ...'. Hand in hand with these miraculous powers of the ballot went his conception of a Talented Tenth which would uplift the illiterate and poverty-stricken Negro mass to the level of an advanced world.

In Du Bois' *Philadelphia Negro* (1899), this conception is already established. He writes that the Negro upper class 'forms the realized idea of the group'. And Du Bois finds his precedent: after a series of riots and repressions culminating in 1840, the Philadelphia Negroes were in a desperate situation. New European immigrants were pressing them against the wall economically. 'It was at this time that there arose to prominence and power as remarkable a trade guild as ever ruled a medieval city. It took complete leadership of the bewildered group of Negroes and led them steadily onto a degree of affluence, culture and respect such as has probably never been surpassed in the history of the Negro in America'.

This leadership, according to Du Bois, consisted of southern house servants who evolved into a caterers' guild in Philadelphia. Such a narrow craft conception of leadership was possible in the Nineteenth Century, but was out of step with reality at the beginning of the industrial Twentieth.

The fetishism of education, which has always been strong in the US, experienced a very particular revival at the turn of the century. Around this time John Dewey's notion of applied scientific intelligence was brought forward to revolutionize formal schooling. The classroom was to be a model society, and worse, society was considered a model classroom. According to Dewey, Veblen, Parrington, Beard, leadership of the offensive against monopoly capitalism was now to emanate from the Academy.

Du Bois' Talented Tenth was no mere imitation of this doctrine of Progressivism, but a natural exaggeration rooted in the extreme conditions of Negro life. In order to insure the most painless integration of the Negro into industry, Booker T. Washington had emphasized manual labor training. The Negro intelligentsia's attack on Washington, and implicitly on Andrew Carnegie and other industrialists supporting the Tuskegee idea, was the self-defense of their very being.

The most obvious characteristic of the Negro upper class, then even more than now, is that it parallels the white middle class rather than the capitalist rulers who control production. As a result, the educational level of the Negro professional is far higher than his occupational or income level. One result of this excruciating disparity is self-consciousness, self-idealization, an ideological yearning and reaching out to a future of higher status and social achievement. The Negro intelligentsia in Northern cities was excluded from serving bourgeois society. It was isolated from the Negro majority living on the Southern countryside. It was also isolated from the Negroes in the urban Ghetto. Thus the notion of a Talented Tenth with a historical mission and exalted function was felt necessary to fill this painful vacuum in Negro and Negro-American class relations.

Du Bois' *Souls of Black Folk*, a product of this period, is widely celebrated to this day. The isolation of the Negro intelligentsia lent a stylistic power and passion – yet tempered and lyrical – to these essays. North and South, the post-Civil War counter-revolution was the supreme fact in American Negro life. Lynching was an open wound – between 1885 and 1894 the murder of seventeen hundred Negroes was a tragically accurate index to the degree of Southern barbarism. Du Bois on the fate of the Southern Negro peasantry reads like the writings of the great Russian intellectuals isolated in a backward, peasant sub-continent and jailed in the vast darkness of Czarism, prior to the rise of the Russian proletariat.

However deep its historical roots, the Talented Tenth remains a conception of limiting, restraining and subordinating the Negro masses. Pleading for higher education of the Negro, Du Bois warned that only in this way could 'demagogic' leadership of the Negro masses be avoided. No sooner did there arise a Negro proletariat, integrated into American labor by the mechanism of capitalist production, than the Du Bois-Washington dispute was altogether transcended. The Talented Tenth did not serve to release and guide these new energies, it fettered them; it substituted solidarity with liberal reformism for the specifically new forces and independent activities of the Negro masses.

From Sociology to History

In *The German Ideology* Marx explains that the German bourgeoisie, having arrived late on the world scene, failed to destroy feudal vestiges, to achieve national unification or foreign conquest, and succeeded in triumphing only in the 'shadow world' of ideas. With due respect for all differences, a similar generalization might be made of the post-Civil War Negro. Nowhere in America was the gap between actuality and need so great. The very existence of the Negro Ghetto and landless peasantry necessitated a vision of their negation through the destruction of that society which nurtured serfdom and a Ghetto existence. If Du Bois programmatically was confined more or less to the limits set by white petty-bourgeois liberalism, he could far transcend these limits in his historical works. His speech on Reconstruction before the American Historical Association in 1909, *John Brown*, and finally *Black Reconstruction* – each provided a greater sensation for an ever growing audience. Myrdal and others today can appropriate Du Bois' sociology but not his history.

His transition from sociology to history was not a mere transition in modes of thought or personal interest; it formed part of the blood and anguish of Du Bois' contemporaneity. The conflict with Booker T. Washington had deepened against Du Bois' own will. The 1906 Atlanta riot cast doubt upon the purposes and effects of his sociological investigations. The insurgency of the Negro intelligentsia required not only a symbolic visit to John Brown's grave, but an ideological pilgrimage to the Negro and the nation on the eve of Civil War.

Here were no controlled experiments conducted by a Talented Tenth. 'Most Americans ... had heard of Douglass, they knew of fugitive slaves, but of *the living organized struggling group that made both these phenomena possible* they had no conception'. (My italics). But John Brown knew better than anyone else that he embodied the insurrectionary spirit of the slave mass and was thereby essentially a Negro creation. Because of that same insight Du Bois could declare with such clarity that the Second American Revolution was inevitable. Slavery 'had to die by revolution and not by milder means. And these men knew and they had known it for a hundred years. Yet they shrank and trembled. From round about this white and blinding path ... flew equivocations, lies, thievings and red murders'. Some pages later, Du Bois appropriately asks, 'Was John Brown an episode or an eternal truth?'

Du Bois' version of John Brown was heavily hit by Oswald Garrison Villard, editor of the *Nation* and heir-apparent to Abolition, who was soon to head the new-born NAACP. In Villard's volume on Brown, Harper's Ferry is reduced to an episode. Villard re-appropriated Brown for the glory of American morality in general and the Northern conscience in particular – and, with magnificent inconsistency, even to Villard's own pacifism. Petty-bourgeois liberalism, panic-stricken by the depression of 1907, but safely confined to Teddy Roosevelt and Woodrow Wilson, wildly applauded Villard's volume.

In reaching the heights of his historical conceptions on the Civil War, Du Bois did not abandon either his directed Darwinism or Talented Tenth. Against the clamor about racial inter-marriage, Du Bois in the final chapter of John Brown can only answer: 'The thoughtful selection of the schools and laboratory is the ideal of future marriage ... we can substitute a civilized human selection of husbands and wives which shall insure the survival of the fittest'. If John Brown demonstrates, through history, the inevitability of social revolution, then a sociology subordinated to biological evolution demonstrates for Du Bois that 'Revolution is not a test of capacity; it is always a loss and lowering of ideals'. The *Nation*'s reviewer slammed the book, but complimented the last chapter.

Du Bois will carry this fear of mass upheaval, this fixed conception of a specialized function for a specialized Talented Tenth, over into *Black Reconstruction*, but there it will take a different form, more befitting the time and theme of its writing.

Early Years of the NAACP

The white liberals and quasi-socialists who sponsored the NAACP fancied themselves of direct Abolitionist lineage. This was a delusion: the Abolitionists were revolutionary, their descendants were reformists. Du Bois, the only Negro in the NAACP leadership, suffered as a consequence.

Although the Abolitionists had attempted to dominate the Negroes within their ranks, this was possible in individual cases, not with the mass. The white Abolitionists, consciously or otherwise, were forced to base themselves upon the rebellious and fugitive slaves. Nat Turner made Garrison famous in the 1830's; Frederick Douglass and the Underground Railroad kept the movement from disintegrating in the 1840's; the battles over the return of fugitive slaves together with John Brown's attempted slave insurrection made Abolition a burning issue during the 1850's.

The Talented Tenth of Du Bois' day, however, was in a different position. It could be dominated – and was – because it was isolated from the Negro masses.

Garrison avoided political activity entirely out of exaggerated fear of being contaminated by the slave power. Oswald Garrison Villard and others immediately plunged the new-born NAACP into the misadventure of supporting the pro-Southern Democrat, Woodrow Wilson! Thus twentieth-century liberalism was incorporating the Negro in its futile protests against the encroachment of the monopolies.

Yet even in this unpropitious environment Du Bois found a means of expression. The sponsors of the NAACP had limited their plans mainly to legal action and enlisting the big names of liberalism. Du Bois, almost completely on his own, emphasized the need for a Negro magazine. *The Crisis* proved to be a great success, reaching over a hundred thousand's circulation in less than ten years. Monroe Trotter's *Boston Guardian* had by its militant policy prepared the Negro public years in advance for their protests against Booker T. Washington's Boston speech in 1905. J. Max Barber's militant *Voice of the Negro*, published in the South, had reached a phenomenal 17,000 circulation when the Atlanta riot drove the editor out of town. The Negro migrations North provided a ready-made audience, while the revolutionary implications of the Negro struggle were an immediate stimulus to bold and effective propaganda. At the height of *The Crisis* success, the government tried to ban it from the mails.

World War I, which destroyed the world of Booker T. Washington, made precarious the world of W.E.B. Du Bois. Du Bois recognized this wistfully. 'The Races Congress, held in July 1911 in London, would have marked an epoch in the cultural history of the world, if it had not been followed so quickly by the World War'. (*Dusk of Dawn*).

The Tuskegee machine expired even before Booker T. Washington's death in 1915. The Negro petty-bourgeoisie was solidifying the alliance with its white counterpart. The Negro working class was yet to be reinforced by the hundreds of thousands soon to enter war industries. Meanwhile the strains in the economy were not acute. The Socialist Party, like its sister parties in Europe, had mellowed; membership in the IWW was declared incompatible with membership in the Socialist Party. More than ever Debs' radicalism seemed an individual phenomenon. Samuel Gompers was happily wedded to capital in the National Civic Federation.

The 'Amenia Conference' in 1915, which gathered together former supporters as well as opponents of Booker T. Washington, prided itself in a resolution 'that its members had arrived at a virtual unanimity of opinion in regard to certain principles and that a more or less definite result may be expected from its deliberations'. What definite result? 'In 1916 we found ourselves politically helpless. We had no choice'. Moreover, when America entered the war it was the pressure of a typical petty-bourgeois, Joel Spingarn, that overrode Du Bois' doubts about supporting the war. Spingarn was only one of that layer of quasi-socialist intellectuals – Charles Edward Russell, W.E. Walling, Mary White Ovington, John Dewey – all founders of the NAACP who enlisted Progressivism, Socialism, the Negro and the proletariat behind the war-making of Woodrow Wilson.

It remains impossible for Du Bois, even retrospectively, to correctly evaluate what happened. In tribute to Spingarn he writes: 'It was mainly due to his advice and influence, that I became during the World War nearer to feeling myself a real and full American than ever before or since'.

Yet at the same time he can say: 'I am less sure now than ten of the soundness of this war attitude ... I do not know. I am puzzled ... In my effort to reconstruct in memory the fight of the NAACP during the World War, I have difficulty in thinking clearly'. (*Dusk of Dawn*).

The failure of Du Bois' scientific rationality in the face of imperialist war was only a more extreme form of the bankruptcy of American liberalism before the same phenomenon.

Du Bois and Garveyism

Paternalistic liberalism was exploded by the Negro masses through two fundamental social developments: the proletarianization during wartime and the colonial revolts throughout the world of color. The craft-corrupted AFL locked out the Negro and all unskilled workers from organization and class expression. The response of the Negro masses to industrial society was projected onto the scale of open colonial revolt outside America. As a consequence, the British and French rulers of Africa considered Garveyism as the black variant of international Bolshevism.

Out of this racial solidarity of the Negro masses was born a hatred for that minority, mainly mulatto, who were most distant from them and closest to reigning bourgeois society. For its attempted integration into – and imitativeness of – its counterpart in bourgeois society, the Talented Tenth was placed under a sustained assault by the aroused Negro masses.

An incidental irony of this whole conflict was that Du Bois reached Africa; few Garveyites did. The Garvey movement, attempting to reconstruct a new free Africa through the American Negro, actually reconstructed a new, freer American Negro through Africa as a symbol and conception. Du Bois, intent on 'practicality', proceeded to the task of internationalizing a Talented Tenth. President Coolidge appointed him Envoy-Extraordinary to Liberia in 1924. Through his own energies Du Bois had organized the Pan-African Congress earlier. The third Pan-African Congress made connections with Harold Laski, Ramsay MacDonald and Beatrice Webb. But Du Bois was only internationalizing the dilemmas of his own position in America.

His project died because the imperialists saw in Du Bois merely the lighter shadow of Garveyism while the Garveyists saw in Du Bois merely subservience to imperialism. At home Du Bois found 'the board of Directors of the NAACP not particularly interested. The older liberalism among the white people did not envisage Africa and the colored peoples of the world'.

The negative side of 'Back-to-Africa' was developing in the United States. It was the 'Jazz Age' and the Negro was in vogue. The white intellectuals came to admire the Negro as a *primitive*; this was *their* image of the Negro's contribution. William Lloyd Garrison admonished the Negroes not to smoke, drink or swear, and thus make themselves worthy of the approval of white society. A century later Carl Van Vechten told the Negro to sing, dance and play to be worth the attention of a middle-class Bohemia.

Du Bois saw a new function of the Talented Tenth in the encouragement and guidance of Negro cultural expression as a bridge to the sympathy and support of enlightened white liberalism. The task was to resist the growing conception of the Negro as a child of Nature. It was precisely over this problem that Du Bois clashed with Langston Hughes and others who considered him 'old-guard' and 'upper-crust'. (Langston Hughes: *The Big Sea*).

Darkwater, Du Bois' own work of that period, is no longer tempered and lyrical; it is harsh and shrill. The 'unreasonable' capitalists and imperialists on one side, and the 'unreasonable' Garveyites on the other, make for alternate pages of pleading and threatening which tend to cancel each other out. In one essay, Work and Wealth, Du Bois effectively delineates the role of the craft union leadership faced with the mass influx of unskilled Negro workers, a situation which brought on the St. Louis riot of 1919. This and one or two other essays are minor triumphs of Du Bois as social analyst and historian during the years which marked the emergence of the Negro mass movement.

Black Reconstruction and the New Deal

The main theme of *Black Reconstruction*, published in 1935, is not that 'the Negro is an average, an ordinary human being'. Indeed the critics of Du Bois' volume attacked him for not limiting himself to proving that alone. Du Bois had dealt with Reconstruction a number of times previously, but this was a new stage. "The emancipation of man is the emancipation of labor, and the emancipation of labor is the freeing of that basic majority of workers who are yellow, brown and black'. Du Bois was now seeking an historical anticipation of the modern proletariat in the Civil War Negro. His very errors and exaggerations tend to underscore the extent of his effort to incorporate the Negro into modern proletarian history.

In the totality of style, passion, historical sweep, prodigious research, and boldness of interpretation, Du Bois here far outdistances his contemporaries, the Beards and the Schlesingers. A great work of this kind is always a climax of historical accumulation. Everything was poured into its writing: the slave system, the slave insurrections, the murder of Abolitionists, fugitive slave rescues, the last letters of John Brown, the Civil War, the intervention of Marx's International Workingmen's Association, the Year of Jubilee, the Black Codes, Ku Klux Klan terrorism, post-Reconstruction peonage, the monstrous crimes of world imperialism, southern lynching, northern labor chauvinism, World War, the crash of 1929, the pauperization of the Negro masses and intelligentsia both, Italy's assault on Ethiopia, the rise of industrial unionism, new waves of Southern terror, the threat of another world war.

In the chapter entitled The General Strike, Du Bois presents the Negroes' physical movement from the Underground Railroad to the mass enlistment in the Union Army, not as the flight of a broken people, but as a purposeful weakening and paralysis of Southern economy, as the necessary prelude to its fundamental reconstruction. This was part of a larger conception that the Negro in the South was not simply a long-suffering but essentially a revolutionary laboring class which attempted 'prematurely' to remake Southern society in its own image through land seizures and government based upon mass political participation. And if the prosperity of European imperialism was built on the massacre of the Paris Communards, America's rise as a participant and leader in world plunder was built on the unbridled deceit and terror which broke Black Reconstruction in the South.

This bold, new conception startled the bourgeois historical writers, petty-bourgeois radicals and Negro intellectuals. Characteristically the liberals of the *Nation* and *New Republic* with the Stalinists of the *New Masses*, just then plunging up to their necks into liberal-capitalist Popular Frontism, conducted a united assault upon Du Bois' history. The Stalinists launched James Allen's *Reconstruction: the Battle for Democracy*, as a substitute. Their attack on *Black Reconstruction* in a more concealed fashion has continued up to this day.

Having gone so far to the left (even ultra-left) in assaying the Radical state governments of the post-Civil War period as a 'dictatorship of the proletariat', Du Bois asserts that they were sponsored through self-interest by the Northern dictatorship of industrial and finance capital. The critics latched on to this obvious incongruity and tried to shake the whole book apart with it. But in this incongruity Du Bois is maintaining his principle of the *guardianship of the masses* by the professorial chair, the test-tube laboratory, private or government philanthropy, or an entrenched intellectual caste. The history of the revolutionary Negro elicits from him an accurate, forceful expression. But immediately there comes to the surface at the same time the classical fears of the highly trained intellectual: it is precisely in revolutionary times that the masses seem most untutored, undisciplined, capable of creating only incessant 'violence and dislocation of human civilization' (*Dusk of Dawn*), rather than a new social order, a new way of living, a new stage of thought.

If Du Bois reached a more advanced position than Dewey, Beard, Parrington and the other intellectuals produced by the Progressive Era, it is because the Negro as a whole was not and could not have been incorporated into that era. But in his fundamental inability to comprehend the role of the modern proletariat – Negro and white – and embrace all of its capacities and potential, Du Bois demonstrates that, despite the highly radical coloration of his later beliefs, he remains fixed in the prejudices of the protest movement of small-farmer Populism and urban middle class Progressivism between 1885 and 1915.

Program for the Thirties

The violence of this contradiction in Du Bois has propelled him to strange places programmatically. Characteristically, in 1918, a year after the Russian Revolution, Du Bois organized the 'Negro Cooperative Guild'. During the worldwide economic crisis of the nineteen thirties, Du Bois developed a full-blown program for a planned Negro economy. Of course this was, in a way, an expression of his justified suspicions that New Deal planning would affect little change in the Negro's economic status. But Du Bois' solution is again adaptation to new conditions for the functioning and fulfillment of the Talented Tenth.

In explaining his program, Du Bois reveals the real lack in his theoretical equipment. Writing in *The Crisis* on the Negro's relation to Marxism, Du Bois frankly identifies his planned Negro economy with pre-Marxian Utopianism. Strong on sociology and history, there is a general lack of economics in Du Bois' writings. Thus, when the Negro was being proletarianized on the largest scale, Du Bois could write: 'The American Negro is primarily a consumer in the sense that his place and power in the industrial process is low and small ... I see this chance for planning in the role which the Negro plays as consumer. In the future reorganization of industry the consumer as against the producer is going to become the key man'.

Here is revealed the vast gap between Du Bois and Marxism, which sees the consumer and consumption as functions of production.

When Du Bois broke with the NAACP in 1935, he spoke very critically of the fate that had overtaken the Talented Tenth, which had sought to integrate itself individually into bourgeois society rather than lead the Negro masses. But without their self-identification with the perspective of mass social revolution, no other fate was possible. Indicative of this was the replacement by a first rate lobbyist, Walter White, for the first-rate theoretician and propagandist who had left the leadership of the NAACP.

And when Du Bois called a Conference on 'Economic Planning and the Negro' in 1940 in Atlanta, the attendant Negro intelligentsia contained a large sprinkling of economic planners, not of a separate Negro economy, but for the New Deal, for the dominant, capitalist economy! In the same year as this conference of planners, a hundred thousand Negroes pledged themselves to a March on Washington, which could have delivered a deadly blow to the pretensions of New Dealism. Never was Du Bois so isolated from the actual living mass movement as he was after detailing the heroic efforts of the lowliest slave masses during Black Reconstruction, to create a new society. This paradox has run the full course of Du Bois' life.

Present Sympathy with Stalinism

The current affiliation of Du Bois adds a great deal to Stalinism. It adds nothing to Du Bois. For the time being his hostility to American imperialism for its long betrayal of the Negroes finds a congenial refuge in Stalinism. There he can find embodied in a single movement the two ideals which have dominated his life work in regard to the Negroes: the conception of the Talented Tenth and the urge toward international revolt. Stalinism operates on a world scale. And it approaches and manipulates the masses like an elite convinced of their backwardness and incapacity; hence the necessity to dictate, plan and administer for them from the heights of superior knowledge and wisdom.

This pitiable political decline has been accompanied by a total loss of theoretical moorings. Reviewing Myrdal's *American Dilemma* in 1944, Du Bois gave it unqualified approval. A year later, Du Bois wrote that the problem of a 'harsh' or 'soft' peace with Germany was the same as the problem of reconstructing the South after the Civil War! Writing in the *Negro Digest* of February 1950 in defense of Paul Robeson, he says: 'The American Civil War was not fought to free the slaves and if it accomplished this partially, a wiser nation could have done more by peace than by murder and destruction'. Du Bois thus lands smack in the middle of that conservative American historiography which has been trying to prove for nearly a hundred years that the Civil War was not an irrepressible conflict, but could have been avoided, if only there had been less 'fanaticism' on the part of both slavery and anti-slavery! What then becomes of Du Bois' *John Brown* and at least seventy-five per cent of all Negro historical works?

Du Bois continues '... our New Deal was socialism pure and simple and it must be restored ...'. Are there any serious thinkers today, from Republicans to Stalinists, who believe *both* in the first and the second halves of this preposterous proposition? Amidst the greatest successes of the New Deal, Du Bois could write that the rebuilding of America in the modern world, 'whether it comes now or a century later, will and must go back to ... Reconstruction in the United States ... for slaves black, brown, yellow and white under a dictatorship of the proletariat'. Four years later Du Bois, facing the united hostility of the pseudo-radical intellectuals on this, question, insisted on repeating his exaggerated formulations that the flight of the slaves, the 'general strike' was followed by a 'dictatorship of black labor' during Reconstruction (*Black Folk, Then and Now*, 1939). Today, in the face of atomic war, imperialist counter-revolution, and universal chaos and crisis, Du Bois has nothing to counterpose but New Deal 'Socialism pure and simple!'

Contribution to Revolutionary Perspective

The present generation of Negro intellectuals has one immense advantage over Du Bois. The last generation of social experience has been more permeated with the dynamics of the class struggle out of which the future will be created than all of Du Bois' eighty-two years. Yet his earlier sociological writings, his *Black Reconstruction*, and even *Souls of Black Folk* are imperishable. Such successes are dependent upon self-identification with the movement and sentiments of the broad masses, and recognition, even though limited, of the insurgence of those generally considered the most powerless and retarded – the Negro millions in America.

Du Bois wrote early in the century '... the Negro is a sort, of seventh son, born with a veil and gifted with second sight in this American world'. Convulsive decades in human history have filled this intuitive observation with pressing reality. Speaking to the Association of Negro History in 1939, W.T. Fontaine pointed out that the Negro intelligentsia is 'not at all a *socially unattached intelligentsia*. (His emphasis). Consequently, *Black Reconstruction* by Du Bois is in its very inception an indictment of the democratic-liberal way of life ... The mind of the Negro scholar today ... presents a configuration generally antithetical to democratic-liberal concepts, thought patterns and techniques ... The subtle casts of an old world view shall be broken, and time transformed by might of mind and hand, shall yet yield the black man's contribution'.

Whenever he was inspired by the Negro masses, Du Bois has made notable contributions to the breaking of the traditional molds of American thought. His work is restricted to the Negro question only in origin and theme; its full implications belong to the search for a new way of life for the whole American people by the best representatives of American thought in our time.

6 Tom Paine – Revolutionist[13]
(1952)

Jean Simon (Jean Tussey)

Thomas Paine was born on Jan. 29, 1737. On Jan. 10, 1776, his historic call for the American revolution, *Common Sense*, was published. Both of these events nowadays receive passing notice. But for those who seek to understand the dynamics of the revolutionary process in America and the role outstanding individuals played in that process, Tom Paine deserves a much larger place than the official hero-makers give him.

Most history books, if they mention Paine at all, merely note the undeniable fact that *Common Sense* was an important contribution to the preparation of the public mind for the open revolt against England. Few attempt to explain what went into the making of the man and why he was able to leave his indelible mark on American history.

Early Background

Tom Paine was born in Thetford, England, the son of a Quaker staymaker (corset maker), a handicraft of the same category as shoemaking or tailoring in that day; his mother was a conservative Church of England member. So from his earliest childhood Paine's critical approach to religion was stimulated, by the differences in his own home.

An only child, he was sent for six or seven years to a local grammar school which differed from most in that it provided some education in history and science. He left school at the age of 13 to be taught staymaking. He ran away to sea after five years, was brought back home by his father before he could actually leave the country, but ran away again, this time to spend a brief period on a privateer.

---

13   Simon 1952.

During the rest of his early life in England he supported himself by working from time to time as an exciseman, as a staymaker and as a teacher.

Philosophical Influence

In London in 1757 he attended philosophical lectures at night. The lecturer was A. Ferguson, author of the *History of Civil Society* (1750), which is quoted favorably by Marx in *Capital*. Marx refers to Ferguson as Adam Smith's predecessor and an economist who had a keen appreciation of the harmful effects of the development of capitalist manufacture on the worker. Ferguson undoubtedly influenced Paine's philosophical and political-economic thinking, as expressed in his later writings.

Paine also participated in philosophical debates in a club that met at the White Hart Tavern in Lewes, where he was stationed as an exciseman, or government tax inspector, in 1768.

In 1772 he acted as spokesman for the excisemen seeking an increase in pay. He wrote a tract called The Case of the Officers of the Excise which cited the discrepancy between their nominal salary and their real wages, described the scope and effects of poverty, and urged the government in its own self-interest to raise wages in order to guarantee the honesty and loyalty of its employees by removing temptations.

Spokesman in a Wage Struggle

Subsidized by the contributions of the excisemen, Paine published the report and spent some time in London lobbying It Parliament. The net result of his negotiations was no raise for the men, and the spotting of Paine as a 'troublemaker' to be removed at the first opportunity.

While in London, Paine met Benjamin Franklin, who was there on behalf of the colonies, made a favorable impression and later received a letter of recommendation from him to friends in Philadelphia.

When Paine was finally removed from his government job, for being 'absent without leave', he settled his financial accounts by selling the property of a small shop he and his wife and maintained, separated from his wife, and left for Philadelphia, where he arrived November 30, 1774, with Franklin's letter of introduction.

In Revolutionary America

By January 1775 he was editor of the *Pennsylvania Magazine*, and actively interested in the colonial cause. The issue of independence had not yet been set forth positively by the revolutionary leaders, who still functioned on the basis of demands for reforms.

The first clear-cut call to the masses to break with England and monarchy, to give up the 'patchwork' of reform and embark on the revolutionary course of independence, was issued in Paine's *Common Sense*, published in January 1776. With this Paine took his place as the chief propagandist of the American Revolution.

The pamphlet was written in simple, direct language, devoid of all obscure historical, biblical and other learned references and allusions so common in the literary style of the day. It was a powerful appeal to every segment of the population to join in a broad united front to win complete freedom from England and embark on a career as an independent nation.

A biographer of Thomas Paine has called *Common Sense* 'This pamphlet, whose effect has never been paralleled in literary history ...'. The passage of 60 years since this comment was written has seen great mass socialist movements and a response to Marxist pamphlets far overshadowing Paine. Nevertheless, the effect of Paine's great tract has still never been paralleled by anything in the literary history of the United States.

Program of the Revolution

We must recall that when Paine penned *Common Sense*, the full program of the Revolution had not as yet been given to the people. The Revolutionary War was under way, and the people were in effect fighting for independence, but without as yet realizing it. No one, not even Samuel Adams himself, had as yet put forward the full revolutionary program; not openly at any rate. All minds were weighed down by the incubus of past centuries: monarchy, empire, feudal servitude, all the untouchables of bygone days clouded the minds of the living.

Into this atmosphere, Thomas Paine flung his remarkable pamphlet, which advocated, at one stroke, independence, republicanism, equalitarian democracy, and intercolonial unity! The Revolution was thenceforward armed with a program, or, to put the matter precisely, the program that was in the minds and private conversation of most radicals became the public property of the revolution.

Paine's great literary gift sparkles from every page of *Common Sense*. He stirred the workers and farmers of colonial times with his blunt and unceremonious comments, such as this: 'In England a King hath little more to do than to make war and give away places (jobs); which, in plain terms, is to impoverish the nation and set it together by the ears. A pretty business indeed for a man to be allowed eight hundred thousand sterling a year for, and worshiped into the bargain! Of more worth is one honest man to society, and in the sight of God, than all the crowned ruffians that ever lived'.

In similar blunt terms, he made out the case for completing the Revolution by independence. 'Everything that is right or reasonable pleads for separation. The blood of the slain, the weeping voice of nature cries, "TIS TIME TO PART"'. These words sank into the consciousness of the new nation, and prepared the way for the Declaration of Independence, which followed in six months.

Indicative of how popular Paine's arguments were, *Common Sense* immediately became a best seller. About one hundred thousand copies were sold within the first six months after its publication. Since there was no copyright law, several pirated editions were also widely sold, so that the total distribution of the pamphlet is estimated at at least three hundred thousand – and this at a time when the population was less than three million!

Paine and the Crisis

Paine's other major literary contributions to the American revolution were the *Crisis* papers, issued periodically throughout the war. Aimed at maintaining the morale of the soldiers and the colonial forces, they reported on the events in the war, polemicized against the British and American Tories appealed to the British people, and exuded revolutionary optimism despite defeats.

It is difficult to measure the effect of any particular document, but the circumstances surrounding the issuance of the first *Crisis* pamphlet give some indication of the basis for the comment of Joel Barlow, a contemporary American poet who served as minister to France under Madison. 'The great American cause owed as much to the pen of Paine as to the sword of Washington', Barlow wrote.

Morale was at a low ebb when Paine started the *Crisis* series. From August to December 1776, the Americans had suffered defeats, retreats and desertions. Congress had fled to Baltimore. Washington's freezing soldiers were retreating across New Jersey. Paine, who was accompanying them, gauged the mood and the need correctly, when, without false optimism, he wrote the now famous lines:

> These are the times that try men's souls: The summer soldier and the sunshine patriot will, in this crisis, shrink from the service of his country; but be that stands it NOW, deserves the love and thanks of man and woman. Tyranny, like hell, is not easily conquered; yet we have this consolation with us, that the harder the conflict, the more glorious the triumph.

Washington had the pamphlet read aloud to every army detachment. A few nights later the army made the icy crossing of the Delaware that has been immortalized in painting and story, and won the victory at Trenton that began to turn the tide.

Paine as Man of Action

Acknowledgments of the tremendous role played by Paine in mobilizing sentiment for the revolution have been plentiful from his enemies as well as his friends, and from all the leaders of the colonial struggle as well as historians since. But few give a rounded picture of his activity in the revolution.

In July 1776 Paine joined the Army as volunteer secretary to General Roberdeau, commander of the Flying Camp, an outfit that moved quickly to trouble spots where it was needed. From there Paine went to the army of General Nathaniel Greene as volunteer aide-de-camp.

In January 1777 Paine was appointed secretary of a commission to treat with the Indians in eastern Pennsylvania. His activities in Pennsylvania and around the Continental Congress continued throughout the war, and were by no means limited to legal and official bodies. He served, for example on the Committee of Inspection, a price control committee formed at a mass meeting in Philadelphia on May 27, 1779, to deal with merchants, innkeepers and others engaging in war-profiteering at the expense of the public. As W.E. Woodward puts it in his biography of Paine: 'The committee had no legal standing, but it proposed to accomplish its ends by popular pressure; or by force, if necessary'.

In April 1776 he was elected secretary of the Committee on Foreign Affairs, formerly the Committee on Secret Correspondence, but was induced to resign on January 9, 1779, after he had exposed what he considered shady dealings in some of the secret diplomacy of individuals involved in securing French aid for the revolution.

When Philadelphia was about to be attacked by the British in September 1777, Paine was convinced the city could be saved if the citizens were called out, fully informed on the military situation, and mobilized to build barricades and prepare for street-fighting.

Paine went to General Mifflin, who was then in the city, with his proposal, asking Mifflin, in his own words, 'if two or three thousand men could be mustered up whether we might depend on him to command them, for without someone to lead, nothing could be done. He declined that part, not being then very well, but promised what assistance he could. A few hours after this the alarm happened. I went directly to General Mifflin but he had set off, and nothing was done. I cannot help being of the opinion that the city might have been saved ...'.

His Selflessness

In 1779 Paine's chronic poverty was in a particularly acute stage, but within six months of his election as clerk of the Pennsylvania Assembly in November, he contributed $500 of his annual salary to head a subscription list for the relief of the Army. The funds raised were used to establish the Bank of Pennsylvania to provide for the Army's needs.

Paine resigned his post in November 1780 and went on a mission to France, seeking aid for the colonies. He returned in August with 2,500,000 livres, but Paine was so broke that he had to borrow ferry passage across the Delaware on his way home.

Upon the conclusion of the war Paine spent most of his time at his home in Bordentown, N.J., working on his inventions. A typical product of the spirit of scientific inquiry of his age, he was preoccupied after the revolution with the development of his idea for an iron bridge planned for the Schuylkill River at Philadelphia. He also worked on a planing machine, a new type of crane, an improved carriage wheel, and smokeless candles. He corresponded with Franklin, who encouraged him to continue.

A Permanent Radical

Paine left for France with his model bridge on April 26, 1787. When he returned to America fifteen years later, revolutionary sentiment had so far abated that he was much too radical for his former colleagues and he was now a pariah where he had been a hero. He still had some friends, but persons were publicly discriminated against for holding to his views. Jefferson, however, invited him to stay for a while at the Executive Mansion, and he did.

An attempt to murder Paine was made at his New Rochelle home on Christmas Eve 1804. Though he suspected Christopher Derrick, a local laborer, this revolutionist who exalted objectivity and abhorred personal vindictiveness refused to press charges.

In January 1805 Paine went to New York City to live. He and his admirers continued to he victimized for his views. When he went to vote in New Rochelle on Election Day, 1806, the witch-hunters of his time, got in their final blow: they charged that the man who had lived for nothing but the American cause and the spreading of its principles to Europe was an alien, and denied him the ballot.

When Paine died on June 8, 1809, after prolonged illness, at 59 Grove St., New York City, he had been reduced to almost complete friendlessness, so that the only attendants at his funeral in New Rochelle were a Quaker watchmaker, friends from France – Mrs. Bonnevine and her two sons – and two Negro pallbearers.

Revolutionary Concept of World Scope

The significance of the man and his ideas remain, but they cannot be fully appreciated on the basis of his role in the American Revolution alone. Paine was not a narrow patriot in the modern sense. He was a principled revolutionist first, and when he went to France, and then England, after American independence was established, he continued to champion the struggles against the ancient order in those countries as whole-heartedly as he had the American cause. 'Where liberty is not there is my country', he is said to have declaimed at his departure from America.

During his stay in England he was the guest of Edmund Burke and other Whig leaders for a period, while they were trying to court favorable trade relations with America. But their friendship cooled when they found him unsympathetic to their proposals.

Paine arrived in Paris in 1789 when the French Revolution was underway. Lafayette gave Paine the key to the Bastille as a token of esteem for George Washington, symbol of the American Revolution.

When the French Revolution was viciously attacked and the divine right of kings upheld by Burke in his *Reflections*, published in 1790, Paine took up his pen again in defense of revolution, and wrote an answer, Part I of *The Rights of Man*. It was approved by the English Society for Promoting Constitutional Knowledge, and other democratic groups; but created a considerable controversy not only in England, but in America as well. Jefferson, Madison and Randolph commended it, and Jefferson sent it to an American printer.

Activity in French Revolution

In July 1791 Paine was a prime mover in the organization of the Republican Society which aimed at the overthrow of monarchy and establishment of a French Republic. At the time, many who were later to become Jacobins were still hesitant about advocating the abolition of monarchy, but the Republican Society placarded Paris with a manifesto written by Paine demanding the abdication of the king and elimination of the office.

In November of the same year, back in London, Paine was guest of honor at the annual dinner of the Revolution Society formed to commemorate the English Revolution of 1688. There he made a speech toasting 'The Revolution of the World' – the first man to raise that slogan, according to some historians. His remarks were noted and added to the dossier of the British government's preparations to arrest him for sedition.

Part II of *The Rights of Man* was a continuation of the attack on monarchy and aristocracy, and was dedicated to Lafayette. Its publication early in 1792 evoked a veritable lynch campaign against Paine in England. Burke's supporters instigated public protest meetings, book-burnings of The Rights of Man, and the distribution of medallions bearing slogans like 'The End of Pain', 'The Wrongs of Man', and 'We dance; Paine swings'. Paine's publisher was arrested for printing seditious literature, and the legal sale of the book was stopped by royal proclamation. Black market sales continued.

Paine fought the attack on his writings, distributing free copies of *The Rights of Man* and encouraging his supporters to stand up for his ideas at meetings called to incite feeling against them.

Meanwhile the book was translated into French and acclaimed in that country. In August 1792 the French Assembly conferred the honorary title of Citizen on him, and four departments elected him to represent them in the National Convention. Consequently, when the English issued a warrant for his arrest, he left for France. He was found guilty of high treason in England in his absence.

In France, Paine participated in the Convention with the Girondists. He was selected October 11 to help draft the constitution but he incurred popular disfavor when he attempted to save the life of the king by urging banishment instead of death, and was eventually expelled from the Convention in December 1793.

While awaiting the next turn of events in the Revolution, he completed his *Age of Reason*, an attack on the Bible and organized religion and an exposition of his Deist views.

Paine was arrested by order of a Committee of Public Safety in January 1794. Through the machinations of the American representative in France at the time, his old enemy, the arch-conservative Gouverneur Morris, Paine was disclaimed as an American citizen and kept in prison: Only when Morris was finally recalled at the request of the French, and replaced with James Monroe, was Paine released.

He remained in France, living with Monroe while completing Part II of the *Age of Reason*. Later, when he was living with the editor and publisher, Nicolas Bonneville, Paine was approached by Bonaparte on the prospect of leading a liberating army in an invasion of England. The project did not materialize, but seven years later, in 1804, Paine wrote a letter 'To The People of England on the Invasion of England' in which he still fancied the idea, which was again being discussed, 'as the intention of the expedition was to give the people of England an opportunity of forming a government for themselves, and thereby bring about peace'.

The world revolutionist had considerable difficulty in getting back to America, since Britain ruled the seas and he was a marked man. In March 1801, Jefferson, then president, wrote Paine that a frigate would pick him up. Jefferson was attacked for this in America, and Paine declined the offer to save his friend further difficulties on this score. When the war between England and France ended, so that French ships were no longer liable to attack, Paine sailed for the United States, arriving October 30, 1802.

His active personal participation in the British and French revolutionary movements was at an end, but he continued to write pamphlets and letters, such as the letter to the English people mentioned above, and a series of 'Letters to the Citizens of the United States', attacking the Federalists.

Paine was reviled by his contemporary opponents, misrepresented by writers who repeated their slanders later, and has been inadequately or falsely depicted also by the modern liberals who have claimed to 'rehabilitate' him.

Of his contemporaries, the British opponents of American independence would, under ordinary circumstances, be the least important since their bias is clear. But many of Paine's anti-democratic attackers on this side of the Atlantic could find nothing better to base their slanders on than the interested political hack jobs written by professional propagandists of the British Crown, and therefore it is necessary to trace such slanders to their source.

Two of the earliest hatchet jobs done on Paine, were biographies written by Francis Oldys, A.M., who was actually George Chalmers, a London government clerk, and James Cheetham, an Englishman who came to America to edit an anti-democratic newspaper. Chalmers' book was published in the heat of the controversy between Burke and Paine over the French Revolution.

But Paine's revolutionary ideas made him the butt of equally vicious attack in America. John Adams, for example, labeled him 'the filthy Tom Paine', an epithet that has been continued through modern times.

The New England Palladium called Paine a 'lying, drunken, brutal infidel, who rejoiced in the opportunity of basking and wallowing in the confusion, bloodshed, rapine, and murder in which his soul delights'.

More recent examples of how the early slanders affected his reputation are the fact that Paine's name was voted down for the Hall of Fame, where other Revolutionary leaders are honored; Theodore Roosevelt referred to him as a 'filthy little atheist', and as late as 1942 the Fairmount Park Commission of Philadelphia refused to permit the erection of a statue of Paine because of his 'reputed religious views'.

Paine has not fared so well at the hands of the school of 'objective historians' or the liberals who have attempted to 'rehabilitate' him, either.

Curtis P. Nettels of Cornell University, in *The Roots of American Civilization* (1946) stigmatizes Paine as a 'restless English adventurer in radicalism and idealism', and credits *Common Sense*, the most important single piece of literature for independence in the arsenal of the radicals of 1776, as having been 'written in a rough, vigorous, flamboyant style that drove home with fierce blows the necessity of independence'.

W.E. Woodward, in *Tom Paine: America's Godfather*, (1945) finds it necessary to deprive him of lasting significance by stating that 'Paine was not a radical within the meaning of that term as it is used today. He was an individualist'.

John C. Miller, in *Triumph of Freedom, 1775–1783*, (1948) says that Paine reversed his line of criticism of the French government before the revolution in that country, accepting a bribe in the form of an offer to serve as paid propagandist for France in America. (Paine answered that old slander himself). Miller adds that Paine's irreligion was so bad that Sam Adams had to rebuke him for contributing to the 'depravity of the younger generation'.

James Truslow Adams, in *The History of New England, 1691–1776* (1941), repeats the condescending characterization of *Common Sense*: 'Crude and coarse as it was, it was written in words of power'.

Probably the best of the liberal treatments of Paine is that of Charles Beard in *The Rise of American Civilization*, which, though sketchily, gives some indication of Paine's principled consistency as an outstanding product of his times, as one who played an important part in helping shape revolutionary thinking, and as a courageous fighter whose plebian insight gave his writing a force that none of the superficial or apologetic defenders of the propertied classes could equal.

Paine was in the vanguard of the progressive bourgeois revolution of his day influenced by the classical political economists such as Ferguson and Adam Smith, and the natural rights philosophy, he was well equipped to attack and refute the apologists for the status quo like Burke.

In *The Rights of Man* and other works, Paine expressed the same logic and concreteness in his approach to labor as on other questions. 'Several laws are in existence for regulating and limiting workmen's wages', he wrote. 'Why not leave them as free to make their own bargains, as lawmakers are to let their farms and houses'.

Paine opposed monarchy, slavery, poverty, organized religion and the Bible, and the unequal status of women. He was an advocate of universal education, reform of criminal law, pensions far the aged and other social security measures, reduction of armaments and universal peace.

But Paine was no meek pacifist: in writing on his proposal for reduction of armaments, he said that if others should refuse to disarm, he would take up his musket and thank God for giving him the strength to do so. Moreover his enlistment in the colonial army and his whole life of revolutionary activity belie the picture some historians paint of him as a Quaker pacifist.

The explanation for the popularity of his writings, their broad mass appeal, is undoubtedly to be found in the fact that of all the American revolutionary leaders and writers, he was one who by his origin, background and way of life represented the plebian masses and consequently could consistently give more content to the democratic slogans and ideas of the time.

His popularity with the masses was based on his democratic convictions. Sam Adams, the chief organizer of the First American Revolution, also drew his chief strength from reliance on the masses. That Paine was in contact with and worked closely with Adams is indicated in the following quotation from a letter to Adams dated Jan. 1, 1803:

> I am obliged to you for your affectionate remembrance of what you style my services in awakening the public mind to a declaration of independence, and supporting it after it was declared. I also, like you, have often looked back on those times, and have thought that if independence had not been declared at the time it was, the public mind could not have been brought up to it afterwards.
>
> It will immediately occur to you, who were so intimately acquainted with the situation of things at that time, that I allude to the black times of Seventy-six; for though I know, and you my friend also know, they were no other than the natural consequences of the military blunders of that campaign, the country might have viewed there as proceeding from a natural inability to support its cause against the enemy, and have sunk under the despondency of that misconceived idea. This was the impression against which it was necessary that the country should be strongly animated.

Paine's view of himself and the revolution was clearly stated in another article. 'I had no thought of independence or of arms' (upon arriving in America), he wrote. 'The world could not then have persuaded me that I should be either a soldier or an author. If I had any talents for either, they were buried in me, and might ever have continued so, had not the necessity of the times dragged and driven them into action'.

But Paine's talents as a soldier and author were based on still another quality: he was a revolutionary thinker, honest, courageous, and prepared to go to the root of things. As he put it: 'When precedents fail to assist us, we must return to the first principles of things for information, and think as if we were the first men that thought'. That was Tom Paine, revolutionist.

7 How Stalinism Will Be Ended[14]
(1953)

George Breitman

In his funeral speech over Stalin, Premier Malenkov pledged that he would continue Stalin's policies. But Isaac Deutscher (in his new book, *Russia: What Next?*) does not believe this is likely, except with regard to economic-social policy (planning, nationalization, etc.).

As evidence that the new regime has struck out on a non-Stalinist path, Deutscher points to steps it took in its first weeks – re-organization of the party and government machinery, the amnesty, the promise to reform the penal cone, reversal of the doctors' frame-up, price cuts, criticism of one-man autocracy, appeals for collective leadership, etc.

Now these acts do represent departures from some of the rigid bureaucratic practices associated with Stalin, and they are so viewed by the Soviet people. But do they mean that the Malenkov regime has instituted a decisive break with Stalinism?

Deutscher seems to think so although he states this view cautiously. He recognizes that the government was more or less forced, after Stalin's death ... to conciliate the Soviet people with measures to satisfy some of their aspirations and to keep them hoping for more concessions. He even writes: 'As one analyzes Malenkov's first moves, one can almost hear him pleading in the inner circle of the Kremlin: Better to abolish the worst features of Stalinism from above than to wait until they are abolished from below'.

In other words, one of the basic motivations for the new measures is a fear that the Soviet people may move to overthrow the dictatorship, and a desire to head it off. But when these measures are viewed in this light, doesn't it become clear that they are designed not to weaken the dictatorship but to strengthen it?

A dictatorship cleansed of some of its more repressive and irrational features might secure a broader base of support or tolerance than it did under

---

14   Breitman 1953.

Stalin, especially during the first stages, when the people are hopeful of change and the regime has a desperate need to consolidate its position. But it would remain a dictatorship just the same, wouldn't it?

Sees Tug of War

Deutscher, however, tends to stress only one side of the reasons for the new measures. That is because it is convenient for his theory, which amounts roughly to something like this: 'A tug of war has been going on inside the bureaucracy for some years. One section wants to 'liberalize' and 'rationalize'. Stalinism: at home, it wants to offer some concessions to the people to keep them from getting out of hand; abroad, it wants to offer some limited concessions to the imperialists in order to avert war, which it thinks can be postponed for a relatively long time'.

Their opponents, Deutscher continues, are the die-hard Stalinists, who draw their strength from the political police (bitterly against any changes in the status quo at home) and from the army (whose leaders think war is inevitable and refuse to yield any concessions that might be of strategic value to the imperialists in the coming war). He views the doctor's frame-up as a plot by the police, perhaps in collusion with the army, to weaken the reform forces.

Deutscher thinks the 'liberalizers', in the form of the Malenkov regime, now have the upper hand. He admits that Malenkov, because of his Stalinist training, may not want to go too far; that he does not want to destroy the police, but only to tame and control them; that he may reverse his path, or be overthrown by the die-hards, if the masses get out of hand or if there is a war; etc. But on the whole he suggests that the Malenkov regime represents the beginning of the reform of the Soviet bureaucracy.

Three Variants

In his view, there are three variants:
1. A 'relapse into Stalinism', with the police back in the saddle. If this happens, he doesn't think it would last long because the same factors that have been working to undermine Stalinism in recent years would operate to end its revival. Even if the police should unite with the generals to take over power, he believes this would mean a military dictatorship rather than the traditional form of Stalinism.

2. Military dictatorship. Deutscher thinks this is possible because of the generals' demand for a tough policy in foreign affairs. He does not consider it probable unless the Malenkov regime proves unable to keep the people in line, and does not believe it would mean the restoration of capitalism.
3. 'Democratic regeneration'. He sees this, on balance, as the most likely variant. He assumes that Malenkov wants to go at least part of the way in this direction, and that the masses would support his moves and give his regime the necessary stability within which it could initiate a return to proletarian democracy

How Will It End?

Some of Deutscher's arguments in support of this view are based on speculation pure and simple, which we can neither accept nor reject at this time. But we must reject his major conclusion, which flows from fatal defects in his analysis of Stalinism.

We agree that even while Stalin was alive the base of Stalinism was being undermined by Soviet economic and cultural progress and the spread of revolution throughout the world. We agree that the new regime, whatever its wishes, cannot rule in the same way that Stalin did. We agree that the end of Stalinism has begun (but not, as Deutscher implies in some places, that Stalinism is now a thing of the past). We also agree that the only real alternative to Stalinism in the Soviet Union is workers' democracy. But we emphatically disagree with the contention that the end of Stalinism is going to come about as a result of a self-reform of the Soviet bureaucracy.

Nature of Bureaucracy

What Deutscher doesn't understand and slurs over is the nature of the Soviet bureaucracy as a special social stratum, a caste, whose interests clash with those of the workers and peasants. The bureaucracy did not usurp its privileges merely to enhance its prestige: it has material interests at stake which it will fight to the death to preserve against the workers and peasants who want a reduction of inequality in the sphere of consumption.

Consequently a harmonious reconciliation between the bureaucracy and the masses is not the easy possibility, even probability, that Deutscher airily assumes it to be. The bureaucrats are not going to relinquish their caste privileges until they have been defeated decisively by the working class.

This is not to deny that the downfall of the Soviet bureaucracy may be preceded by a split in its ranks, with one section perhaps going over to the people. But that is not the same thing as expecting a reform of the bureaucracy to lead to 'an orderly winding up of Stalinism and a gradual democratic evolution'.

Another thing Deutscher doesn't understand or accept is the Marxist analysis of the present state form in the Soviet Union as a Bonapartist dictatorship. Although Deutscher is acquainted with this analysis, first worked out by Trotsky, he acts as if he isn't, and he doesn't counterpose any other analysis. But he shows that he rejects it by defining Bonapartism almost exclusively as a purely military dictatorship, and talks about it only as a future danger.

This makes it easier for him to spin his theory about the approaching metamorphosis of the dictatorship into its opposite. But the Malenkov regime's concessions to the people don't change its character as a Bonapartist dictatorship; they only indicate that the dictatorship has been weakened. A weakened Bonapartist dictatorship, even when it waves the banner of 'liberalization', is still a Bonapartist dictatorship. And Bonapartist dictatorships generally have to be overthrown.

What Trotsky Sought

Deutscher's illusions and runaway speculations even lead him to write:

> In the 1930's Trotsky advocated a 'limited political revolution' against Stalinism. He saw it not as a full-fledged social upheaval but as an 'administrative operation' directed against the chiefs of the political police and a small clique terrorizing the nation. As so often, Trotsky was tragically ahead of his time and prophetic in his vision of the future, although he could not imagine that Stalin's closest associates would act in accordance with his scheme. What Malenkov's government is carrying out now is precisely the 'limited revolution' envisaged by Trotsky.

This is a flagrant distortion of Trotsky's views on the regeneration of the Soviet Union. We don't know which article of Trotsky Deutscher is citing, or when it was written. The Stalin regime had not yet reached its fully totalitarian form in the early 30's, when Trotsky thought it was still possible to reform the Comintern; it was not until the mid-30's that Trotsky rounded out his analysis of Soviet political Bonapartism and the measures required to get rid of it.

A Political Revolution

But Deutscher knows that toward the end of Trotsky's life, and especially after the Moscow Trial purges, he never tired of advocating an 'unlimited' political revolution against Stalinism. The revolution Trotsky advocated was of course not directed against the social system in the Soviet Union, which he defended to the end. What he worked for was a political revolution – against social inequality and political repression, for the regeneration of Soviet democracy and the legalization of Soviet parties.

In fact Trotsky went so far, in the 1938 Transitional Program, as to call on the workers 'to drive the bureaucracy and the new aristocracy out of the Soviets' in the same sense that capitalist representatives were excluded from the original Soviets.

Anybody who equates such a revolution, which the bureaucracy would fight tooth and nail, with the 'liberalization' measures taken by Malenkov and Co., is losing touch with reality or adapting himself to Soviet Bonapartism. In neither case can he render any service to the fight for Soviet democracy.

Socialist Regeneration

The reality is this: The Soviet dictatorship is in the throes of a deep crisis. As a result, the bureaucracy has offered certain concessions to the workers to keep them from moving on their own. Instead of satisfying the workers for long, these concessions will encourage them to press for new demands (the East German political strike was a preview of what is going to happen in the Soviet bloc as a whole). The crisis will produce further divisions and conflicts among the bureaucracy which the workers will be able to use for their own purposes. War may delay the process, but cannot abolish it. The Soviet Bonapartist dictatorship is doomed, as Trotsky predicted it would be doomed, by the spread of world revolution, and it will be replaced by the democratic power of the Soviet working class. The change will take place through a political revolution against the Kremlin regime, not through its reform. There is no other way to the socialist regeneration of the Soviet Union.

8 Sternberg vs. Karl Marx[15]
(1954)

Myra Tanner (Myra Tanner Weiss)

Revision of the basic program and theories of Marxism invariably begins with a softening attitude toward its enemies. Such was the case with the Pabloite faction in the Fourth International. This faction is marked by theoretical and political conciliation to Stalinism. [It has] revised the basic Trotskyist concepts in favor of a species of neo-Stalinism, which bears remarkable resemblance to the theories of Isaac Deutscher, a petty-bourgeois advocate of the theory of the self-reform of the Stalinist bureaucracy.

... [T]he anti-Marxist social-democrat, Fritz Sternberg, also received a friendly reception from the Pabloites. But Sternberg, whose position can be seen in the title of one of his recent books: *How to Stop the Russians Without War*, is now a US State Department 'socialist' – a petty-bourgeois theorist for the American and British labor bureaucracy, of the 'enlightened' Stalinophobe variety.

The conciliatory attitude of the Pabloites toward Deutscher, a Stalinophile, and Sternberg, a Stalinophobe, is not so strong a paradox as it might seem at first appearance. To 'junk the old Trotskyism' means to junk the whole body of Marxist theory. In this enterprise, Sternberg, the Stalinophobe, as well as Deutscher the Stalinophile, are natural allies. Petty-bourgeois revisionism in the ranks of the revolutionary movement cannot begin with a crass anti-Marxist program. It develops its revisionist doctrines piecemeal. It begins by displaying receptivity to 'new' alien ideologies. Step by step it empties the 'old' program of its content. The first problem of revisionism is to overcome Marxist orthodoxy. It tackles this problem by a combination of growing hostility to the representatives of orthodoxy, matched by increasing friendliness to the theoretical and political opponents of Marxism.

In a letter to the Editorial Board of *Fourth International* in September, 1952, I criticized the treatment accorded Sternberg by Harry Frankel, one of the lead-

---

15 Tanner 1954. This article has been slightly edited and abridged.

ers of the American Pabloites. I was fully aware that I was also taking issue with Pablo, who concluded his review of Sternberg's book, *Capitalism and Socialism on Trial*, with: 'Such as it is, and read critically by revolutionary Marxists, this work constitutes – thanks to its abundant and serious documentation and to its methodical presentation of facts – *a precious working tool which facilitates a better understanding of the future of our epoch*'. (*Quatrieme Internationale*, Feb.–March, 1952. My emphasis).

George Clarke, the leading American disciple of the Pablo cult, summarized our differences at a meeting of the Political Committee of the Socialist Workers Party Sept. 9, 1952, as follows: 'There are two different conceptions involved here as to how to handle this book. The conception we have used and I think the committee should maintain that, is to view this book as an aid to the study of Marxism and the understanding of American imperialism with a necessary critique of those ideas clearly stated (!) to be in opposition to Marxism. Or, on the contrary, to warn against this book as being a renegade's book and belonging in the arsenal of anti-Marxist literature'. Thus it is clear: the Pabloites wanted to give Sternberg a 'critical' but friendly reception. Sternberg, to them, is not a 'renegade' or an enemy to be 'warned against'.

Pablo begins his review with the following paragraph: 'In a thick volume of about 600 pages, Fritz Sternberg, former (?) Social Democrat and former German Communist, living in the United States since before the war, has summarized the conclusions of thirty years of work. His book is a grand mural of the evolution of capitalism from its beginnings until today'.

Let us take a look at this 'grand mural' to see if Sternberg is aiding Marxists or if Pablo is merely providing Sternberg with a left face.

1   Slows Down Tempo of Capitalist Development

To make the history of capitalist development fit the Social Democratic program of 'critical' support to capitalism, to justify its continued existence, Sternberg slows down the tempo of capitalist accumulation. By identifying capitalism with industrialization or the urbanization of the population, he puts the capitalist conquest of the world into the future. In the opening section of the first chapter, in contradiction to its title 'Capitalism Becomes the Dominant Form of Production', Sternberg says:

> At the beginning of this big period of development (1850–1914) capitalism was an island in a pre-capitalist world, but at its end it had become the dominant form of production for almost one-third of the world's popula-

> tion. However, even at the end of this big period of capitalist expansion the majority of the world's population still did not produce under capitalist conditions. Capitalism embraced the vast majority of the population of Great Britain, the United States and the western parts of the continent of Europe. But even at this peak point of its development, pre-capitalist – chiefly feudalist – forms of production still dominated in Eastern Europe, Asia and Africa. In this period of capitalist expansion, in which capitalism demonstrated its economic superiority over pre-capitalist methods of production, it was generally assumed that the advance of capitalism would continue, until in the end the majority of the world's population would be living and producing under capitalist conditions. This did not come about.
>
> *Capitalism and Socialism on Trial*, p. 20

At the very point, 1914, where Lenin placed the culmination of the growth of capitalism and the beginning of its decline, Sternberg has two-thirds of the world's population yet to be absorbed in capitalist production. How is this great divergence of views possible?

If capitalism is synonymous with industrialization then obviously the colonial world is not capitalist. However, long before imperialism had developed in the industrialized capitalist nations, commercial capitalism had destroyed the pre-capitalist economic life of the colonial peoples. The penetration of capitalist England into India, for example, transformed the colonial Indian labor product into commodities. The old self-sufficient way of life was destroyed. Production for exchange supplanted production for consumption with exchange of only the surplus labor product.

Industrialization did not immediately follow this capitalist transformation. Capitalism does not automatically spell industries. On the contrary, as Sternberg points out elsewhere in his book, British penetration into India brought with it a diminution of the urban population. The trade of artisans, the highly developed handicraft industries of India were destroyed and a landless peasantry was created. This made it all the easier for industrialized power to develop a world division of labor which has been so profitable to the imperialists that several wars and more to come have been fought for its maintenance.

However, if the colonies were non-capitalist then, by the same criterion they are non-capitalist today. Capitalism can still expand to these areas if the imperialists would only be reasonable, thinks Sternberg. In Part III of his book he blames the capitalist stagnation between the two world wars on the 'errors' of the capitalists:

> Quite clearly tremendous possibilities were present here (in China), and if, despite the halt in industrial development in the colonial empires (China was not legally a colony) a process of industrialization had gone on in China, say at more or less Russian tempo (what a big word that 'if' – M.T.), world capitalism would have found a gigantic market to help it out of its difficulties. The tremendous possibilities were not taken advantage of.
>
>   Ibid., p. 223

Sternberg scolds the capitalists for missing a chance to make more profit. But the capitalist knows better than Sternberg where, when and how to invest his capital for the biggest grab. The capitalists are not interested in helping the colonies meet their own need for industrial products. Not only markets would be lost (a demand for means of production would be only temporary) but more competitors would arise. And most important, a source of cheap raw materials would be gone.

In the inter-imperialist competition, possession of cheap sources of raw material constitutes a big advantage. The rate of profit which serves as an absolute limit to the rate of accumulation, varies inversely with the price of raw materials. Furthermore, with the growth of capitalism comes an ever-increasing demand for raw materials. The role played by this part of the means of production in the determination of the rate of profit constantly increases.

Thus Sternberg's 'grand mural' depicts capitalism as a 'youthful' system, with new frontiers to conquer if only the capitalists would realize it. He can try to convince the workers that it is realistic to confine their struggle to pressure on the imperialists to follow a non-imperialist foreign policy.

2   Rejects Lenin's Theory of Imperialism

We can see the same end served of class conciliation in Sternberg's attack on Lenin's theory of imperialism. He attacks Lenin's conceptions by separating monopoly capitalism from imperialism. In a section titled 'Imperialism Not the Same As Monopoly Capitalism' Sternberg says: 'The imperialist drive of Great Britain and France began decades before there was any considerable monopolist concentration. On the other hand, of course, monopolist concentration was already predominant in the United States before the question of imperialist expansion began to play any noteworthy role there'. (Ibid., p. 146).

We can assume that Sternberg read Lenin's book, *Imperialism*. It is listed in the bibliography. Then why this shabby argument? Lenin never claimed that colonial conquest began with monopoly capitalism. Lenin's point of departure was the appearance of a new stage in the internal structure of industrial capital. The laws of capitalist accumulation, disclosed by Marx, had resulted in the domination of finance capital over industrial capital and the growth of monopoly. With this internal transformation, world capitalism *assumed a new character – imperialism* ...

Lenin showed how the export of capital, monopolization, and international cartelization supplanted commercial-relations of the pre-monopoly period with imperialist domination of the colonial world.

Sternberg's fraudulent representation of Lenin's theory of imperialism serves to obscure the specific monopoly-capitalist, exploitive relation between imperialism and the colonial people. Sternberg says:

> To a very considerable extent colonial empires had already been carved out before the opening of the nineteenth century – that is to say, at a time before the development of modern industrial capitalism – but it was not until the second half of the nineteenth century that they began to assume their main function as exporters of foodstuffs and raw materials to the metropolitan centres and as markets for the industrial products of the latter.
>
>   Ibid., p. 45

The colonies from the beginning, insofar as trade instead of plunder was developed, 'assumed' this function that Sternberg wants to place in the second half of the last century. The first American revolution of 1776 was fought primarily in order to stop 'assuming this function'. By the end of the 19th century this function was developed into a fixed division of labor as a result of the direct domination of colonial production by foreign capital.

If one confines his treatment of imperialist-colonial relations to the commercial level, the exploitation of the colonies is obscured, and this is what Sternberg, as an apologist for imperialism, does. On the market all men and countries appear as free and equal.

Sternberg tells us that the colonies 'exported foodstuffs and raw material to pay far the imports of industrial products from the metropolitan centers'. This is typical of Sternberg's formulations. They had to 'pay for' their purchases like all honest men. Only, behind this lovely world of equal exchange is the hot and sweating world of production where inequality and subjugation exist. It is here that the imperialists squeeze an extra lush rate of profit out of the blood and bones of the colonial people.

In the pre-imperialist stage of relations between industrialized and colonial countries, the colonial people produced raw materials for the industrial nations. The latter manufactured the raw materials into finished goods. The colonial countries may have sold the raw materials at value, but they also had to pay for the production cost and profit of the manufactured goods as well as transportation of the goods both ways. But this was not bad enough for the colonies, nor good enough for the industrialized nations. When the latter began to export their capital the colonial people were subjected to capital-labor exploitation in the production of raw materials as well as the earlier commercial disadvantages.

Sternberg wants to dissociate monopoly and imperialism in order to transform imperialist-colonial relations from necessary and inevitable relations under capitalism into a question of state policy to which alternatives can be posed. However, Lenin's answer to Kautsky on the concept of imperialism as a state policy is still sufficient to answer Sternberg:

> Kautsky detaches the policy of imperialism from its economics, speaks of annexations as being a policy 'preferred' by finance capital, and opposes to it another bourgeois policy which he alleges to be possible on the same basis of finance capital. It would follow that monopolies in economics are compatible with methods which are neither monopolistic, nor violent, nor annexationist, in politics. It would follow that the territorial division of the world, which was completed precisely during the period of finance capital and which represents the main feature of the present peculiar forms of rivalry between the greatest capitalist states, is compatible with a non-imperialist policy. The result is a slurring-over and a blunting of the most profound contradictions of the newest stage of capitalism, instead of an exposure of their depth. The result is bourgeois reformism instead of Marxism.
> *Imperialism*, p. 84

3   Theory of the Crisis

Pablo says of Sternberg: 'Influenced by his Social Democratic past, it frequently occurs to him to "criticize" Marx, Lenin, Bolshevism with arguments ... which damage the *scientific solidity* and the *objectivity* of several portions of his work'. (My emphasis). I agree that if it only 'frequently occurs' to Sternberg to attack Marxism, the 'scientific solidity' of the work might be only 'damaged'. But in addition to identifying with capitalism only its more progressive features of industrialization, and rejecting Lenin's theory of imperialism, Sternberg rejects the Marxist conception of the crisis, an ever-present feature of the capitalist system and today, a dominating one. If the other matters only 'damaged' the 'scientific solidity' of the work, surely this would destroy it.

Sternberg's theory of the crisis is the well-worn vulgar theory of under-consumption. This is made clear in his contrast of capitalist crises with pre-capitalist crises. According to Sternberg, before capitalism we had crises of under-production. Now we have crises of under-consumption. This 'profound' contribution is even presented to us in a diagram on page 48 and 49. It is based on the entirely superficial observation that the hunger that stalked the land from time to time in pre-capitalist society was evidence of natural or social disasters that interfered with production. Thus, crises of under-production. Under capitalism, under-consumption follows peak production. Hence, crises of under-consumption. This doesn't bring us one jot closer to understanding the obscure reasons for interruption of production. We are left with the tautology that under-consumption causes under-consumption. Furthermore, he attributes this nonsense to Marx.

In periods of prosperity, commodities are consumed. The fact that workers under-consume is beside the point. The capitalists, whether in productive consumption or in individual consumption, are glad to compensate for this deficiency. As Marx put the problem:

> But if one were to attempt to clothe this tautology (i.e., the idea that crises are caused by a lack of paying consumers) with a semblance of a profounder justification by saying that the working class receive too small a portion of their own product, and the evil would be remedied by giving them a larger share of it, or raising their wages, we should reply that crises are precisely always preceded by a period in which wages rise generally and the working class actually get a larger share of the annual product intended for consumption. From the point of view of the advocates of 'simple' (!) common sense, such a period should rather remove a crisis. It seems, then, that capitalist production comprises certain conditions which are independent of good or bad will and permit the working class to enjoy that relative prosperity only momentarily, and at that always as a harbinger of a coming crisis.
>
> *Capital*, Vol. II, p. 476

The 'certain conditions' referred to by Marx are analyzed by him in Volume III of *Capital*. The continuously changing organic composition of capital results in the tendency of the rate of profit to fall. Sternberg once tried to explain economic phenomena with the use of this theory. His earlier German economic work, while not fully Marxist, still represented an attempt at serious Marxist analysis. But in his contemporary work you will not find a single analysis based on Marx's theory of the crisis.

Along with the American labor bureaucracy, Sternberg belongs to the left-Keynesian school of economic theory. The trade-union officialdom, wishing to see a prolonged future for itself, thinks that all that is necessary to save capitalism is to raise wages. And they can't see why the capitalists, for their own sake, can't agree. If this theory were correct, the workers could never hope to escape from the exploitation of the capitalists. As production increased, living standards could also increase and everyone would get richer. While it might not be right for the capitalists to remain idle while everyone else worked, still things wouldn't be too bad.

But the history of capitalism, as well as Marxist theory, has proved that this is not the case, nor can it be. A wage increase is a precipitating factor in the development of the crisis. Increases in wages will always act to decrease the rate of surplus value, which in turn accelerates the tendency of the rate of profit to fall. When other factors that could compensate are closed off, the crisis cannot be allayed. The under-consumption theory of Sternberg and the labor bureaucrats suits their wishful thinking but it doesn't change the reality.

4   Polarization of Wealth

The polarization of wealth, the result of the accumulation of capital, is of cardinal importance. It is the cause of the intensification of the class struggle, the guarantee of the proletarian struggle for power, and the premise for Marx's theory of the inevitability of socialism. Marx's formulation of this tendency as a law of capitalist society is one of the main targets of all his opponents. They don't want to admit that hand in hand with the accumulation of capital at one pole goes the impoverishment of the masses at the other.

Sternberg tries to refute this with figures that show an increase in the real wages of the working class in the period of the expansion of capitalism, roughly 1850 to 1914. To make it appear that he is battling Marx, Sternberg misrepresents Marx's position. He shows that the average income increased during this period. Then he triumphantly says:

> Now of course the 'average income' could also increase if the rich got richer and the poor grew poorer and poorer – if 'the accumulation of capital' on the one hand was matched by an 'accumulation of misery' on the other. In other words, the 'average income' could increase, whilst at the

same time the broad masses of the people, and the working class in particular, grew more and more impoverished. But, in fact, this did not happen.
>> Op. cit., p. 27

Then comes the statistical proof. Real wages increased: 'If we take the level of real wages in 1913 as 100, then wages in Great Britain stood at 57 in 1850, but by 1855 they had risen to 63, and further increases, with setbacks, followed until the end of the century: 1860, 64; 1865, 67; 1870, 70; 1875, 89; 1880, 90; 1895, 88 and 1900, 100'. (Ibid., p. 27).

Very neatly done. You see the rich can get richer and the poor can get richer, too. Both profits and wages can increase, as Sternberg likes to point out several times in his book. (This is true; but *other things being equal*, wages and profits can increase or decrease only at the expense of each other).

But wait a minute! Marx never said accumulation excluded an increase in real wages. What he did say was that *exploitation* increased with accumulation. 'The result is', Marx said, 'that, in proportion as capital accumulates, the condition of the worker, *be his wages high or low*, necessarily grows worse ... Thanks to the working of this law, poverty grows as the accumulation of capital grows. The accumulation of wealth at one pole of society involves a simultaneous accumulation of poverty, labor torment, slavery, ignorance, brutalization, and moral degradation, at the opposite pole – where dwells the class that produces its own product in the form of capital'. (*Capital*, Everyman edition, p. 714. My emphasis).

Relative to the wealth produced, wages did fall. Elsewhere in the book, Sternberg supplies the statistics that prove Marx was right even in this period of greatest expansion of capitalism. Wages in Great Britain increased from an index of 64 to 100. In that same period, industrial production, according to Sternberg, increased from 34 to 100. In other words industrial production increased 194% while wages increased only 56%. It would seem that the workers were getting a smaller and smaller part of the wealth they produced.

Later on Sternberg will explain to us that the increase in real wages in the period of imperialist expansion was made possible by the super-exploitation of the colonies. But Sternberg does not, then, correct his 'refutation' of Marx's law of polarization of wealth, which like all economic laws applies most concretely in the most general phenomenon, i.e., world economy. On a world scale the law of polarization of wealth was confirmed even in this period of capitalist expansion.

Since 1914, the law of polarization has been confirmed absolutely even in the industrialized countries. The working class must include in the calculation of its standard of living the periods of unemployment as well as the years of labor. For Europe that means nine years of soldier's pay plus years of unemployment between the wars. American labor too must calculate its pay with war and depressions included.

Since Marx's time the law of polarization of wealth has been tragically demonstrated: (1) Between the classes within the nations. (2) Between the colonial and industrialized nations. (3) Between debtor and creditor imperialist nations.

Marx's description of future reality almost a century ago was more accurate than Sternberg's description of past and present reality. 'Mass degradation' is not a matter of a few industrial cities during the period of the rise of capitalism. Today it is the degradation, pauperization, and mass extermination of the people on whole continents. Fascism, with its tens of millions of victims, imperialist wars, with the decimation of whole populations, have written Marx's theory of polarization into the living history of our own epoch.

Bernstein's revisionist attack on Marx's theory of polarization of wealth and poverty had some semblance of superficial reality during the period of uninterrupted capitalist growth. But Sternberg's rationalizations are merely crude Social Democratic apologies for a diseased and senile capitalism.

5   The Revision of History

The re-writing of economic history requires the re-writing of political history. With the softening of the crisis, comes the slowing down and softening of the class struggle. In a section, 'Socialism Underestimated Capitalist Strength', Sternberg tells us that increased living standards of the working class had so softened the class struggle that the 'capitalist system revealed itself to be much stronger than socialists had thought, and although it was badly shaken, it was still strong enough to survive the period between two world wars'. (Op. cit., p. 153).

Capitalism did not survive the interim between the two world wars because of inner strength. Sternberg's 'grand mural' of capitalism paints the mortal crisis of the post-World War I period in rosy colors. Actually it was a period of revolutionary storm in which capitalism survived only because of the treachery of the Social Democratic and Stalinist leaders of the workers organizations.

Out of the war grew the revolutionary crisis that brought the Russian workers to power under the leadership of the Bolshevik Party. Sternberg says, '… the spark of the Russian November revolution did not cause any sympathetic conflagration elsewhere'. (p. 171). And on page 191 he says: 'There was no German revolution'.

This is a lie.

In 1918 the revolution swept the Kaiser from power and brought German capitalism to the brink of the grave. The workers of Germany rallied to their socialist organizations and trade unions in the hope of a revolutionary victory. They were betrayed by Social Democratic leaders of the Noske, Scheidemann stripe. And now they are betrayed by the Social Democratic historian, Sternberg, who would efface the German revolution with a stroke of his pen: 'Thus the war was ended, as it had been begun, from above and not from below'. (p. 189).

The German revolution involved the strongest proletarian force in the entire history of the working class up to that time. As the victory in Russia was the positive confirmation of Lenin's theory of the need for a revolutionary party, so Germany's defeat furnished irrefutable negative proof of the correctness of his views.

By saying 'there was no revolution in Germany', Sternberg is relieved of the odious task of explaining its defeat under Social Democratic leadership. It is much easier just to deny it ever took place. He is then able to turn against Lenin who led the only successful revolution and denounce him as a splitter. '... the bolshevists deliberately perpetuated the disruption of the German working class'. (p. 302). What infamy! On the trail of the Social Democrats lay tragic defeat, incalculable suffering, and eventually Hitler's concentration camps. If the workers were to win their freedom they had to follow an entirely different road. Lenin was a splitter. But in order to break with the capitalists one had to break with their lackeys as well.

6   Capitalist Decline

In Pablo's haste to embrace the anti-Marxist, Fritz Sternberg, he misrepresents Sternberg's views so as to make them a little more palatable to Trotskyists. Pablo says:

> Among the most interesting aspects, and also the most positive (!) of his work, one must consider the last chapters which treat of the changes produced by the second world war, the present situation, and its perspectives ... He sees in a 'united socialist Europe' the best way of preventing the war and of facilitating the socialist evolution of all mankind. But he is afraid that Washington and Moscow would try to prevent such an eventuality even by war.

Now what can be wrong with that? Put in this abstract form Sternberg indeed appears to be an ally. But if Sternberg's views are presented more concretely, and therefore, accurately, we have an entirely different picture. Sternberg is for a united *capitalist* Europe, with capitalist state planning along the lines of England, which will 'evolve' toward socialism, under the initial protection of US militarism.

Sternberg says, 'As far as the situation in Europe is concerned, the danger of war will decline, only if Europe finds a progressive solution – and today that means a democratic socialist solution – to its crisis'. (p. 564). And further, 'If such a federation came about, and were protected from Russian military attack', after a while it would be secure and in a position to compete successfully with Russia for the allegiance of the working class. The pattern is set by England: 'after the second world war, for the first time in Great Britain and for the first time in the history of any big power, the political party of the working people obtained an absolute majority of the seats in parliament and proceeded to carry out a program which aimed at a socialist transformation of the British economic and social system on the basis of political democracy'.

Sternberg confuses capitalist planning with socialist planning in order to justify to the working class a non-revolutionary perspective. Pablo helps him in this by passing on Steinberg's 'socialist' demagogy as good coin.

By 1914, world economy had reached the peak of the primary curve of the development of capitalism. Further accumulation and expansion would take place but, except for a brief decade in the United States, it would occur only with the direct subsidizing of large sectors of industry by the State. 'Free enterprise', even in its monopolized form, was dead. The process of accumulation was no longer self-propelling. The historic need for socialism asserted itself, even when the proletariat failed to take power, by the fact that 'planning' became a necessity even for the capitalist state.

This 'planning', however, has nothing in common with socialist planning. In the essence of the matter, the capitalist state plan is dictated by the laws of capitalist economy, not by the needs of society. This is a greater difference than may be apparent at first. All plans are the work of man's brain. But the laws of capitalist economy operate beyond man's control and dominate him as long as capitalism exists. The need which the plan must serve therefore is a blind unconscious force. For this reason there can be no real planning. In socialist economy the plan is freed from capitalist economic laws. The socialist plan is based solely on society's needs. ...

7   Conclusions

In my letter criticizing the treatment accorded Sternberg's work by the Pabloites, I said: 'The early part of the book is devoted to "refuting" Marx's law of accumulation ...'. To this Harry Frankel replied:

> Comrade Tanner apparently refers to Part I of the book, which does contain such an effort. But the inaccuracy here is the word 'devoted!' I fear that comrades who read the book may now skip this part on the strength of Comrade Tanner's remark if it remains uncorrected. Part I, covering the period up to the first world war, is about 120 pages long. Of this section, only a few scattered pages are 'devoted' to the attacks on Marx, Engels and Lenin, while over a hundred pages give a very good statistical review of the rise of capitalism from 1848 to 1914.

Let me remove from the discussion the question of statistics and whether the book should be read or not. Statistics are always valuable to Marxists whether compiled by Sternberg or the US Department of Commerce. But the *selection* of statistics always serves the theoretical views of the economist. Sternberg's statistics are on the whole drawn from the surface phenomena of the market, and deal with results rather than causes. Lenin in his book *Imperialism* presents statistically the internal changes in industrial capital that operated as a cause for the phenomena that Sternberg only describes. By divorcing the result from its cause Sternberg draws a false picture of the result. Thus, describing capitalist expansion up to World War I we get an avoidable crisis instead of an inevitable one; a 'stable' capitalism just on the eve of its world collapse, etc.

The Pabloites, by painting up Sternberg's book, assist him in this attack on Marxism. Frankel, for example, tells us that 'only a few scattered pages are devoted to the attacks on Marx, Engels and Lenin'. Clarke calls it an 'aid to the study of Marxism'. And Pablo, the head of the cult, calls it a 'precious working tool'.

It is not true that Sternberg explicitly polemicizes with Marxists in 'only a few scattered pages'. The underlying method and the whole edifice is built on reformist anti-Marxist theories. Sternberg doesn't consciously 'refute' Marx's law of polarization in a few pages and then write 100 pages unconsciously showing how this law is demonstrated as the essential trend of capitalism in its 100-year history. Sternberg doesn't consciously 'refute' Lenin's theory of imperialism, which explained the first major result of the laws of accumulation and then unconsciously demonstrate that imperialism is a necessary outgrowth of capitalist accumulation. Sternberg doesn't even bother to refute explicitly

Marx's theory of the crisis, but every chapter of his book flows from the anti-Marxist, reformist theory of production-consumption relations.

Moreover, I haven't taken up his attacks on the 'errors' of Marx and Engels on such questions as revolutionary optimism, colonial development, capitalist agriculture, the theory of the inevitability of socialism; nor his anti-Marxist view on the class nature of the Soviet Union, his Menshevik attack on the Bolshevik 'dictatorship of the party', and his characterization of Lenin as a 'modest dictator'. I haven't answered his jingoistic support of 'democratic' imperialism in the Second World War and his Rooseveltian 'New Dealism'; nor his miserable cover-up of the Moscow Trials; and a host of other questions. I have dealt only with theoretical and political fallacies in Sternberg's work that are sufficiently fundamental to establish that the book has no real claim to 'scientific solidity' and 'objectivity'.

For Pablo, the break with Trotskyism meant that a new atmosphere had to be created. Defenders of Marx against Sternberg, Deutscher and all other revisionists had to be denounced in advance as sectarian, doctrinaire or as Cochran called it, 'Talmudic'. Marx, Engels, Lenin and Trotsky are old-fashioned, outmoded by the 'new reality'. Pablo's haste to dump the orthodox doctrines of Marxism is so great that he refers contemptuously in quotes to the Marxist classics.

We orthodox Trotskyists see in the new reality the confirmation of Marxist theory. For us the validity of the theoretical system of Marx, Engels, Lenin and Trotsky is demonstrated in the *essential* line of historic development.

Revisionist Pabloism ... disoriented by the 'new reality', becomes receptive to alien anti-Marxist currents flowing from the circles of reformist petty-bourgeois radicalism of both Stalinophobe and Stalinophile varieties.

9 Women Who Won the Right to Vote[16]
(1955)

Joyce Cowley

Women got the vote in the United States in 1920. The amendment to the Constitution granting women that right was the climax of a struggle it hat began almost a hundred years earlier. Suffrage leaders were ridiculed and persecuted while they were alive. Today they are either forgotten or contemptuously referred to as disappointed old maids who hated men. This concept of the woman's rights movement as a war against men by sexually frustrated women is even accepted by some modern psychiatrists. But it is historically inaccurate and a great injustice to a number of truly remarkable women.

The status of women in society began to change with the breakdown of feudalism and the rise of capitalism. In the sixteenth and seventeenth centuries in England, women first entered trades. They were frequently partners in the husband's business; widows and daughters carried on the family business. There are records of women pawnbrokers, stationers, booksellers, contractors and even shipowners. In the seventeenth century there were three women to every man in the woolen industry and many women were employed in the silk industry. They also worked in the fields and the agricultural labor of women was an important factor in the new American colonies.

The 'woman question' was discussed as early as the Elizabethan period but this talk did not develop into an organized movement. It was in 1792 that Mary Wollstonecraft wrote the *Vindication of the Rights of Woman* which, historically, marks the conscious beginning of the struggle for woman's rights. This book was a direct reflection of Mary Wollstonecraft's sympathies with the French and American revolutions, a demand that woman's rights be included in the rights of man for which the revolutionists were fighting.

It was in America, not England, that the woman question first developed into an organized movement rather than a subject of discussion in literary circles. This reflects the more advanced position of women in the American colon-

---

16   Cowley 1955.

ies, which was strikingly different from that of women in Europe. The laws of the colonies, modeled on those of England, gave women few legal rights. But the realities of pioneer life, particularly the scarcity of women and the appreciation of their skills, meant that they actually had a great deal of responsibility, engaged in numerous occupations that were supposedly 'masculine' and consequently enjoyed rights and privileges, and a degree of freedom, unknown to women in England.

The Puritan concept of work further influenced the general attitude towards women's activities. In their moral code, work was something you could never get too much of and they did not disapprove of women working, on the contrary they encouraged it. It made no difference whether the woman was married or not; the more she worked the better, and the less likely she was to succumb to the temptations of the devil.

In the colonial period women could vote, and sometimes did vote, as the right to vote was based on ownership of property and not on sex. They were gradually disfranchised by laws prohibiting women from voting – in Virginia in 1699, New York 1777, Massachusetts 1780, New Hampshire 1784 and New Jersey 1807.

At that time men engaged in agriculture and women in home manufacture. Women made most of the products used by the colonists that were not imported. The preponderance of women in the earliest factories in the United States is due largely to the fact that their work was transferred from the home to the factory. This was particularly true of the first major industry, the spinning and weaving of cotton, and accounts for the prominent role of women in early labor struggles, especially the fight of cotton-mill workers for the ten-hour day.

The woman's rights movement, however, did not grow out of the trade-union struggles of women. It was never closely associated with trade-union activities nor particularly interested in the problems of working women. This may seem contradictory unless you keep in mind that the woman's movement was primarily a fight for legal, not economic rights. The legal battle of the suffragists has been won, but in the Twentieth century women still face severe discrimination in wages and job opportunities.

The woman's rights movement *did* spring directly from the abolitionist movement. Every prominent fighter for woman's rights was *first* an abolitionist; and the two movements were closely allied for fifty years, although the 'woman question' frequently caused division in the abolitionist ranks, as the Negro cause became more respectable and more popular than that of women.

Just how did the anti-slavery movement give birth to the struggle for woman's rights? There is a simple explanation for what may seem at first a surprising evolution. Women who started out to plead for the slave found they were not allowed to plead. They were ridiculed when they appeared on a speakers' platform, they were not accepted as delegates when they attended anti-slavery conventions. Within a short time, most of the women prominent in abolitionist circles spoke up for their own rights, too, although a formal organization advocating complete legal equality and suffrage was not formed for another twenty years.

The Early Leaders

A number of misconceptions about the pioneers for woman's rights are prevalent. In the first place, it is assumed that they were all women – women united in a war against men. The truth is *men* were in the forefront of the struggle for woman's rights, notably such spokesmen as William Lloyd Garrison, Frederick Douglass and Wendell Phillips. They were attacked even more viciously than the women and labeled 'hermaphrodites' and 'Aunt Nancy men'.

Furthermore, none of the women in this movement were exclusively preoccupied with sex equality and women's problems. They were, as I said, invariably abolitionists and frequently advocated a great many other reforms – the Utopian variety of socialism, trade unions, atheism, temperance, free love, birth control and easier divorce. Many of these causes were not too popular in the early part of the last century and this accounts to some extent for the common opinion that these women were freaks and probably immoral.

It is not true that most of the feminist leaders were either libertines or embittered virgins. With the exception of Susan B. Anthony, the best known – Lucretia Mott, Elizabeth Cady Stanton, Lucy Stone, Carrie Chapman Catt – were happily married. Mrs. Mott and Mrs. Stanton, founders of the movement, were mothers of large families. They did not marry weak husbands who were dominated by their crusading wives. The husbands were generally men of outstanding ability and achievement, enthusiastic supporters of the woman's cause. The only reason they were to some extent overshadowed by their wives was that the unusual activities of the wives attracted a good deal of attention.

Frances Wright was probably the first woman to speak publicly in this country and to advocate woman's rights. She was Scotch, coming to America in 1818. Brilliant and courageous, she was also one of the extremists, exactly the type who were slandered and laughed at but never ignored. Among numerous other activities, she founded a colony primarily intended to set an example of how to free slaves and give them economic independence. But she was an opponent of marriage and her colony became more famous for its open repudiation of this institution than for any service to the Negro cause.

Opposition to marriage was common among the early advocates of freedom for women. They saw in it – quite correctly, in my opinion – an institution designed for the subjugation of their sex. In those days a married woman had no right to own property, her wages belonged to her husband and so did her children. The simplest way to avoid these evils was to stay single.

In spite of their audacity, these women frequently surrendered to local pressure. Mary Wollstonecraft gave birth to one illegitimate child; but when she became pregnant a second time by another lover, she found the struggle too difficult and married him. Frances Wright and her sister both married for the same reason – they were pregnant.

The sex question explains a lot about the notoriety associated with the first feminist leaders. As the movement grew and became more respectable, it attempted to dissociate itself from advocacy of 'free love', but was never completely successful.

About the same time that Frances Wright founded her well-publicized colony, Lucretia Mott became a Quaker minister. She is one of the most striking personalities in the woman's rights movement. Of unusual intellect and breadth of vision, she studied intensively and was an active lecturer and organizer for fifty years. She supported trade unions when they were almost unknown and generally illegal, which was rare among abolitionist leaders, who seemed to think there was some kind of conflict between the two movements. She also raised six children and apparently enjoyed domestic activities like cooking and sewing, although you wonder as you read her biography how she found time for them.

She was at the meeting held in Philadelphia in 1833 where the first anti-slavery group was organized and from which the American Anti-Slavery Society developed. Although she spoke several times during the convention and played an influential role, it did not occur to her to sign the Declaration that was adopted. Samuel May, in his reminiscences, wrote: 'Men were so blind, so obtuse, they did not recognize the women guests as members of the convention'.

Lucretia's next step was to form a Women's Anti-Slavery Society, but the women were so ignorant of parliamentary procedure that they found it necessary to get a man to chair the meeting – James McCrummel, an educated Negro. The brazen conduct of women in forming this society was attacked by clergymen as an 'act of flagrant sedition against God'. While women were clothing and feeding the Negro on his way to Canada, 'clergymen huddled in churches and wrung their hands, forecasting the doom of the American home and the good old traditions'.

Five years after the Women's Anti-Slavery Society was organized, it held a convention in Pennsylvania Hall, a public building recently dedicated to 'liberty and the rights of man'. While the delegates conducted their business, a mob surrounded the hall. Stones were thrown at the windows, breaking pane after pane, and vitriol was hurled through the gaping holes, while a cry rose, 'Burn the hall!' Two or three hours after the women vacated the hall, it went up in flames.

That night Philadelphia was in an uproar. The mayor wanted to stop abolitionist activities and police protection was non-existent. The mob headed for the home of James and Lucretia Mott. There was a period of tense waiting inside the house while the yells and turmoil in the street grew closer. But as the minutes passed, the noise seemed to recede and gradually fade into the distance. The next day they learned that a friend had joined the mob and when they were within a block of the house, he flourished a stick and cried: 'On to the Motts!' then led them up a succession of wrong streets. This was one of many similar incidents for Lucretia Mott, and her calm composure in a riot became legendary.

Sarah and Angelina Grimke, aristocratic women from the South, were among the earliest speakers and organizers of the abolitionist movement. I came across an interesting quotation from a speech by Angelina Grimke delivered before a Massachusetts legislative committee in 1832: 'As a moral being I feel I owe it to the slave and the master, to my countrymen and to the world, to do all that I can to overturn a system of complicated crimes built upon the broken hearts and prostrate bodies of my countrymen in chains and cemented by the blood, sweat and tears of my sisters in bond'.

Evidently Churchill knew a good phrase when he saw it.

Begin Organizing

Factional struggles inside the abolitionist movement led Lucretia Mott and Elizabeth Cady Stanton to call a convention for woman's rights in 1848.

Eight years earlier, a fight had taken place over the election of a woman to a business committee of the American Anti-Slavery Society. The vote was favorable to the candidate, Abby Kelly; and the anti-woman group seceded from the organization and formed their own anti-slavery society. A world-wide anti-slavery convention had been called in London. Purged of its reactionary elements, the American Anti-Slavery Society elected Lucretia and two other women to their executive committee and chose her and Charles Remond, a Negro, as delegates to the London convention. Lucretia also headed the delegation from the Women's Anti-Slavery Society.

Another delegation – one hundred per cent male, of course – was sent by the newly formed organization. In London every effort was made to keep peace by persuading the women delegates to withhold their credentials, but Lucretia insisted that the responsibility for rejection must rest with the convention.

Wendell Phillips opened the fight on the convention floor by proposing that all persons with credentials be seated. He pointed out that the convention's invitation had been addressed to all friends of the slave and Massachusetts had interpreted this to mean men *and* women. Clergymen at the convention were particularly eloquent in their opposition to seating women. 'Learned Doctors of Divinity raced about the convention hall Bible in hand, quoting words of scripture and waving their fists beneath the noses of disputing, brethren who did not know woman's place'.

The reactionaries won. Women were admitted as guests only and seated behind a curtain which screened them from public gaze. Garrison, the greatest figure in the abolitionist world, was scheduled to be the main speaker. On his arrival he climbed the stairs to the women's balcony, sat beside Lucretia behind the curtain, and remained there until the close of the convention.

It was on this trip to England that Lucretia met Elizabeth Cady Stanton, a young bride of one of the delegates. It was here that they decided to start a crusade for woman's rights on their return to America, although eight years passed before they were able to carry out their plans and call the Seneca Falls Convention of 1848.

This Equal Rights Convention, the first ever held in any country, was the official beginning of the suffrage struggle. The first day of the convention had been advertised as open to women only. When the women arrived at the Unitarian church they found they were locked out. A young professor climbed through a window and opened the door for them. On the spot, they decided to admit men, which turned out to be a fortunate decision for the suffrage cause.

James Mott was chairman of the meeting, as the women were still timid and did not know too much about parliamentary procedure. The Declaration of Sentiments adopted by the convention was signed by 68 women and 32 men. The resolution called for complete equality in marriage, equal rights in property, wages and custody of children, the right to make contracts, to sue and be sued, to testify in court – and to vote.

Elizabeth Cady Stanton introduced the suffrage amendment. It was opposed by Lucretia Mott because she considered it too radical and thought it would arouse public antagonism and ridicule. Frederick Douglass seconded Mrs. Stanton's motion and made one of the most eloquent speeches in history for woman's equality and her right to vote. His speech inspired the women to overcome their hesitation and pass the suffrage resolution. Within a year a National Woman's Rights Association was organized and state and national conventions were held regularly.

Persecution and Abuse

The woman's movement was met with a storm of abuse, particularly from the clergy, although a great many men just considered it funny. Within a few years, as it gained momentum, it met more serious opposition. Opponents of suffrage were divided as to whether the population would decrease because women were unsexed or illegitimately increase because of the practice of free love.

A typical example of the anti-suffrage point of view appears in a book by Dr. L.P. Brockett, quoted at some length in Hare's biography of Lucretia Mott. It gives a picture of just what would happen if women were allowed to vote and declares it will be a gala day for the prostitutes, as 'modest refined Christian women' would refuse to go to the polls in such company. Hare paraphrases the book:

> What a lesson of evil would be taught children on that day. Imagine the innocent offspring, clutching its mother as it stands in the presence of poor wretches, bedizened in gaudy finery, with bold, brazen faces, many of them half or wholly drunk and uttering with loud laughter, horrible oaths and ribald and obscene jests! What an impression the child would receive! And if the mother attempted to tell her daughter that these were bad women, the child might query: 'But mother, they are going to vote. If they were so very bad, would they have the same right to vote that you and other ladies have?' Unable to answer so precocious a question, the 'modest, refined Christian mother' would scurry home, leaving the polls to her male representatives and the women of the underworld.

'To drive home the lesson', says Hare,

> the book is illustrated with a picture showing the refined woman at the polls completely surrounded by a vicious group of derelicts of both sexes. The picture vividly warns any woman who is on the verge of becoming a follower of Lucretia Mott, the type of men and women with whom she must associate if she votes. It also discloses the unintentional fact that the voting male is the uncouth immigrant, the bowery heeler, and the pimp; the same male hailed by opponents of female rights as woman's natural representative in affairs of government. One glance at the men in the picture convinces the reader that woman's benign influence in the home had gone awry, despite this best chosen argument of the anti-suffragettes.

Dr. Brockett also predicts that some disastrous changes will occur in the appearance of women: 'The blush of innocence, the timid, half-frightened expression which is, to all right-thinking men a higher charm than the most perfect self-conscious beauty, will disappear and in place of it we shall have hard, self-reliant bold faces, and in which all the loveliness will have faded, and naught remain save the look of power and talent'.

The suffrage workers encountered additional ridicule at this time due to the introduction of the Bloomer costume. It was rather strange in appearance, consisting of trousers partly concealed by a full skirt that fell six inches below the knees. Elizabeth Cady Stanton, Lucy Stone and Susan B. Anthony probably suffered greater martyrdom, because of this costume than for any other phase of their crusade, and after a few years they discontinued wearing it, feeling that it did more harm than good. Nevertheless, the outfit did give much greater freedom of action and was adopted by many farm women of the period and recommended by doctors for use in sanitariums. It was the first step toward the freedom of the modern dress.

Mrs. Stanton became one of the most active suffrage leaders and it was in this period that her life-long collaboration with Susan B. Anthony began. She was the mother of five boys and two girls, and whenever her schedule of lectures, conventions and meetings became too heavy, she would threaten to interrupt it by having another baby. Lucy Stone, now best known as the woman who insisted on keeping her maiden name, also became prominent in the 1850s. Lucy's use of her own name grew out of her original opposition to marriage. When she did marry, the unusual ceremony attracted considerable comment, none of it favorable. She and Henry Blackwell opened the wedding with a statement:

> While we acknowledge our mutual affection by publicly assuming the relation of man and wife, yet in justice to ourselves and a great principle, we deem it a duty to declare that this act on our part implies no sanction of, nor promise of voluntary obedience to, such of the present laws of marriage as refuse to recognize the wife as an independent, rational being while they confer upon the husband an injurious and unnatural superiority, investing him with legal powers which no honorable man would exercise and no man should possess. We protest especially against the laws which give the husband:
> 1. The custody of the wife's person.
> 2. The exclusive control and guardianship of their children.
> 3. The sole ownership of her personal property and use of her real estate, unless previously settled upon her, or placed in the hands of trustees as in the case of minors, lunatics and idiots.
> 4. The absolute right to the product of her industry.

They continued with the regular marriage ceremony, omitting the word 'obey', but there was a popular feeling, especially since Lucy kept her own name, that they were not really married.

Many Negro women like Harriet Tubman, the extraordinary leader of the underground railway, and Sojourner Truth, also played an active role in the woman's rights movement. Tubman is reported to have been an amazingly eloquent speaker, but for reasons of personal safety the speeches were rarely recorded.

Not a Soft Occupation

Even a bare outline of the lives of these early women leaders arouses admiration. Lecturing for woman's rights was not exactly a soft occupation. Travelling was pretty rough then and the reception was likely to be rough, too. These women kept going at a remarkable pace in spite of large families and heavy domestic responsibilities.

Mrs. Stanton wrote most of her speeches after midnight while the children were sleeping – I don't know when she slept. Most of the women continued their work without let-up even when they were in their sixties and seventies. Lucretia Mott was 83 when she spoke at the 25th anniversary of the suffrage association. They were middle-class women but many of them faced economic hardships. Lucy Stone went to Oberlin College – the first to admit women – and worked her way through, sweeping and washing dishes at three cents an hour. Her life as an abolitionist and woman's rights speaker was not exactly a cinch either. She lived in a garret in Boston, sleeping three in a bed with the landlady's daughters for six and one-fourth cents a night. Constance Burnett in *Five for Freedom* describes a fairly typical meeting at which she spoke. (She was the outstanding orator of the woman's movement, a real spellbinder).

> Lucy posted her own meetings, hammering her signs on trees with tacks carried in her reticule and stones from the road. The first poster usually drew an army of young hoodlums who followed her up and down streets, taunting, flinging small missiles and pulling down her notices as soon as her back was turned ...
>
> For her ability to remain unperturbed through hoots, jeers and murderous assault, she had few equals. It was a common thing for her to face a rain of spitballs as soon as she stepped before an audience. Once a hymn book was flung at her head with such force it almost stunned her. On another night, in midwinter, icy water was trained on her from a hose

thrust through a window. Lucy calmly reached for her shawl, wrapped it around her shoulders and went on talking.

At an open air anti-slavery meeting on Cape Cod, the temper of the crowd seemed so dangerous that all the speakers, one after the other, vanished hastily from the platform. The only two left were Lucy and Abby Kelly's husband, Stephen Foster, a firebrand abolitionist of the same mettle from New Hampshire.

Before either of them could get to speak, Lucy saw the mob begin its advance. 'They're coming, Stephen. You'd better run for it', she warned him hurriedly.

Stephen no more than Lucy ever ran from danger. 'What about you?' he protested, and with that the surging, yelling mass was upon them. Overpowered, Foster disappeared in the melee, and Lucy, suddenly deserted, looked up into the face of a towering ruffian with a club.

'This gentleman will take care of me', she suggested sweetly, taking his arm, and too astonished for words, he complied. Reasoning calmly with him as he steered her out of the violence, she won his reluctant admiration and his consent to let her finish her speech. The platform was demolished by then, but he conducted her to a tree stump, rounded up the rest of the 'gentlemen' and preserved order with raised club until she was through talking. Lucy gave the whole gang a piece of her mind, not neglecting to collect twenty dollars from them to replace Stephen Foster's coat, which in their gentlemanly exuberance they had split in two.

The Alliance Ends

During the Civil War there was little activity in the woman's movement. All of the women were devoted to the abolitionist cause and enthusiastically entered into various types of war work. But the end of the war brought the end of the fifty-year alliance between the woman's cause and the Negro movement.

The split took place when Negro men got the vote. The Republican Party and the Negro leaders were both pressing for passage of the 14th and 15th amendments to the Constitution to enfranchise Negro men. The Republicans were not particularly interested in Negro rights but they wanted votes. The Democrats, who opposed the Negro vote, now gave lip service to woman suffrage in order to annoy the Republicans and hypocritically charge them with hypocrisy.

Negro leaders argued that this was the 'Negro's hour' and it was a matter of practical politics to push through the vote for Negro men while it had a chance of ratification. Adding woman suffrage to the amendment would inevitably result in its defeat. Negro and abolitionist leaders insisted that they were devoted to the woman's cause and would continue to fight for universal suffrage after Negro men got the vote.

Many of the women were embittered by what they considered a sell-out. Elizabeth Cady Stanton, in an argument with Wendell Phillips, said: 'May I ask just one question, based on the apparent opposition in which you place the Negro and woman? Do you believe the African race is composed entirely of males?'

For fifty years these women had fought for the abolitionist cause and they felt that they had won the right to be included in the suffrage amendment. They would not agree to being left out on grounds of political expediency. They got little support and the 15th amendment was passed, giving the vote to Negro men only.

At the American Equal Rights Association convention in 1869, a formal split occurred; with the majority, the more conservative grouping, supporting the Boston abolitionist wing. Among the majority were Julia Ward Howe and Lucy Stone, who formed the American Woman Suffrage Association. The radical minority, led by Susan B. Anthony and Elizabeth Cady Stanton, organized the National Woman Rights Association. For twenty years these two groups remained separate.

As I have indicated, the principal cause of the split was the division of opinion over supporting Negro suffrage while the question of woman suffrage was postponed. I've read some eloquent statements on both sides of this argument. Negro leaders like Frederick Douglass, the first man to speak up for woman suffrage in this country, felt that the Negro cause was jeopardized by the women who selfishly advanced their own demands instead of waiting until it was more 'practical' to advocate suffrage for women, too. Women felt this attitude was a great injustice on the part of the abolitionists, showing ingratitude to the women who had fought so long and so courageously for the Negro cause.

In Lucretia Mott's biography there is a description of the Centennial Anniversary of the Declaration of Independence: 'The newly enfranchised citizens appreciated what had been done for them – by their sex. Women on the sidewalks watched them carry banner after banner emblazoned with the names of Garrison or Phillips or Douglass. They searched in vain for a tribute to Lucretia Mott, or the author of *Uncle Tom's Cabin*, or any other woman of the anti-slavery conflict'.

Both the Negro and the woman's movement were greatly weakened by the split in their ranks and it was another fifty years before women got the vote.

In several accounts of this split written by men in sympathy with the Negro side of the argument, the women were held responsible for the delay because extremists in their ranks insisted prematurely on suffrage.

Historically there is not much point in speculating about what would have happened if the Negroes and women had stuck together – how long this would have delayed Negro suffrage (if at all) – and whether or not woman suffrage would have been won at an earlier date. Most Negro men were enfranchised in name only, and even to this day millions have not been able to exercise their constitutional right to vote. Personally I can't help sympathizing with the women who felt they had been deserted and betrayed. It's unfortunate that the reform movement was split as a result but I'm not sure this was entirely the fault of a few women 'radicals'. There were heterogeneous elements in the Equal Rights Association, many of whom felt that their cause, Negro emancipation and enfranchisement, had been won, and it is probable that this conservative element would have broken away in any case.

The history of the woman's movement from, this point on, divorced from the other reform struggles for which the women originally fought, becomes a bit dull. It is more bourgeois in character, exclusively concerned as it is with the vote.

The Struggle for the Vote

Immediately after the passage of the 15th amendment, Susan B. Anthony decided to test the new law, which was worded in such a way that it might possibly be construed to include women. In Rochester, N.Y., she and twelve other women armed with a copy of the Constitution demanded the right to vote. The election inspectors were so startled by this move that the women were allowed to cast ballots. They were promptly arrested for voting illegally. Susan was fined $100. She refused to pay the fine, hoping that she would be imprisoned and the case could be carried to the Supreme Court. But the judge was a shrewd politician and did not order her arrest. The fine has not yet been paid.

In the twenty-five years following the Equal Rights Convention of 1848, women achieved many of their original demands. More and more states passed laws giving married women the right to custody of their children, to disposal of their wages and their property.

Curiously enough, the first and most successful advocates of these laws were men whose interests were threatened. In upstate New York wealthy Dutch fathers-in-law became indignant when their daughters' property was squandered by spendthrift husbands. The Married Women's Property Bill was passed largely through their influence. In one of the Southern states a similar bill was introduced by a man who wanted to marry a wealthy widow. Heavily in debt himself, he knew her property could be attached to pay his debts if they got married. When the bill passed she could keep her property and they could both live comfortably on her income.

The Territory of Wyoming was the first to give women the vote in 1869; Utah followed the next year; Colorado and Idaho a little later. Pioneers in the West, accustomed to women who could load a gun, ride a horse and run a homestead as competently as a man, were more easily persuaded than Eastern men that women are not frail or feeble-minded. Twenty years later when Wyoming applied for statehood, the fact that women voted there became a political issue. Wyoming declared: 'We will remain out of the union 100 years rather than come in without woman suffrage'.

Susan B. Anthony continued to campaign for another thirty years. Her final speech to a Woman's Rights Convention was made in 1904 when she was 86 years old. An incident reported in *Five for Freedom* gives some idea of her remarkable energy:

> During this year Susan delivered 171 lectures, besides hundreds of impromptu talks. She traveled ceaselessly. The journey home through the Rockies in January became rugged when her train ran into mountainous drifts. Tracks had been recently laid, breakdowns were frequent and waits interminable. Passengers had nothing to eat but the cold food they had the foresight to bring. Many nights were spent sitting bolt upright.
>
> Susan did get back finally, in time for the annual convention of her National Woman Suffrage Association in the capital.
>
> 'You must be tired', they greeted her in Washington.
>
> 'Why, what should make me tired?' asked Susan. 'I haven't been doing anything for two weeks'.
>
> The restfulness of transcontinental rail trips in the 1870s was not apparent to others.

By 1900 the suffrage movement had become more powerful, but so had the opposition. The liquor interests, afraid that women would vote for prohibition, poured millions of dollars into campaigns to defeat woman suffrage. In state after state women lost out when the suffrage question came to a popular vote. The following circular published in Portland, Ore., is an example of how the liquor crowd worked:

> It will take 50,000 votes to defeat woman suffrage. There are 2,000 retailers in Oregon. That means that every retailer must himself bring in twenty-five votes on election day.

> Every retailer can get twenty-five votes. Besides his employees, he has his grocer, his butcher, his landlord, his laundryman and every person he does business, with. If every man in the business will do this, we will win.
>
> We enclose twenty-five ballot tickets showing how to vote.
>
> We also enclose a postal card addressed to this Association. If you will personally take twenty-five friendly voters to the polls on election day and give each one a ticket showing how to vote, please mail the postal card back to us at once. You need not sign the card. Every card has a number and we will know who sent it in.
>
> Let us all pull together and let us all work. Let us each get twenty-five votes.

This was signed by the Brewers and Wholesale Liquor Dealers Association. In this case the liquor interests were successful and woman suffrage was defeated. In spite of such defeats, the suffrage cause won more and more mass support. Jesse Lynch Williams gives a description of a suffrage parade which he watched from the window of a Fifth Avenue club:

> It was Saturday afternoon and the members had crowded behind the windows to witness the show. They were laughing and exchanging the kind of jokes you would expect. When the head of the procession came opposite them, they burst into laughing and as the procession swept past, laughed long and loud. But the women continued to pour by. The laughter began to weaken, became spasmodic. The parade went on and on. Finally there was only the occasional sound of the clink of ice in the glasses. Hours passed. Then someone broke the silence. 'Well boys', he said, 'I guess they mean it!'

In Albany, a representative from New York City said that not five women in his district endorsed woman suffrage. He was handed a petition signed by 189 women in his own block.

Turn to Militant Tactics

The split following the Civil War lasted twenty years. In 1890 the two suffrage organizations united as the National American Woman Suffrage Association. But in 1913 the movement split again, this time over the question of militant tactics imported from Great Britain.

The British suffragists started later than the American but once they got going, they really went to town. The militant suffragist movement in England, organized by Emmeline Pankhurst and her daughters in 1905, battled cops and hounded public officials. They chained themselves to posts or iron grillwork of public buildings and went on talking while the police sawed them loose. They climbed on rafters above Parliament and lay there for hours so that they could speak out at any opportune moment. Hundreds were arrested. In jail they continued to battle prison officials, went on hunger strikes, were subjected to forcible feeding.

A book written by one of Mrs. Pankhurst's daughters gives a colorful glimpse of the lively character of their protest. A poster, reproduced in the book, reads: '*Votes for Women* – Men and women, help the Suffragettes to rush the House of Commons, on Tuesday evening, the 13th of October'. (In the subsequent trial there was a good deal of debate as to just what the word 'rush' meant).

The title of Chapter 20, June and July 1909, is followed by a brief summary: 'Attempt to insist on the constitutional right of petition as secured by the Bill of Rights, arrest of Mrs. Pankhurst and the Hon. Mrs. Haverfield, Miss Wallace Dunlop and the hunger strike, 14 hunger strikers in punishment cells. Mr. Gladstone charges Miss Garnett with having bitten a wardress'.

Chapter 21, July to September 1909, gives this summary: 'Mr. Lloyd George at Lime House, 12 women sent to prison, another strike, hunger strikers at Exeter Gaol, Mrs. Leigh on the roof at Liverpool, Liverpool hunger strikers', etc. Some of the pictures have captions like 'Lady Constance Lytton before she threw the stone at New Castle'. 'Jessie Kenny as she tried to gain admittance to Mr. Asquith's meeting disguised as telegraph boy'.

Two American women, Alice Paul and Lucy Burns, took part in the English demonstrations, were imprisoned and went on hunger strikes. They returned to this country determined to introduce some new methods into the now rather conventional woman's movement.

In 1913 Miss Paul organized a suffrage parade in Washington, D.C. Some 8,000 women marched down Pennsylvania Avenue. As the procession approached the White House, it was blocked by hostile crowds. 'Women were spit upon, slapped in the face, tripped up, pelted with burning cigar stubs, insulted by jeers and obscene language'. Troops had to be brought from Fort Meyer. Afterwards the suffragists forced a Congressional inquiry and the chief of police lost his job.

Alice Paul concentrated on passing a federal amendment which the older suffragists had more or less shelved while they fought local battles from state to state. Miss Paul followed the political tactics of the English movement. This was to hold the party in power responsible for the delay in granting woman suffrage and to campaign against all candidates of that party regardless of whether or not they supported suffrage as individuals. By that time women had the vote in a number of states and Miss Paul systematically campaigned against *all* candidates of the Democratic Party, in power at the time.

Conservative elements in the suffrage movement did not accept this tactic and Miss Paul and others were expelled in 1913. They formed a new organization which took the name National Woman's Party in 1916. This organization also followed the British policy of putting a lot of pressure on top officials. (It got so that the British Prime Minister and cabinet officials were afraid to speak in public and only appeared at bazaars and social affairs). To get favorable action from Wilson, who saw numerous delegations but kept stalling, a picket line was thrown around the White House in January, 1917. It continued day after day. On Inauguration Day, in a heavy rain, 1,000 pickets circled the White House four times.

In April, war was declared but the picketing continued. In June patriotic mobs began to tear down their banners and maul the pickets. On June 22 police started arresting the women, who refused to pay their fines. Hundreds were sent to prison, including Lucy Burns and Alice Paul. A history of the National Woman's Party gives some details as to how they were treated:

> Instantly the room was in havoc. The guards from the male prison fell upon us. I saw Miss Lincoln, a slight young; girl, thrown to the floor. Mrs. Nolan, a delicate old lady of seventy-three, was mastered by two men ... Whittaker (the Superintendent) in the center of the room directed the whole attack, inciting the guards to every brutality. Two men brought in Dorothy Day, twisting her arms above her head. Suddenly they lifted her and brought her body down twice over the back of an iron bench ... The bed broke Mrs. Nolan's fall, but Mrs. Cosu hit the wall. They had been there a few minutes when Mrs. Lewis, all doubled over like a sack of flour, was thrown in. Her head struck the iron bed and she fell to the floor senseless.

As for Lucy Burns, 'They handcuffed her wrists and fastened the handcuffs over her head to the cell door'.

Alice Paul's hunger strike lasted twenty-two days. The authorities insisted on an examination of her mental condition. The doctor reported: 'This is a spirit like Joan of Arc and it's useless to try to change it. She will die but she will never give up'.

In the meantime, speakers of the National Woman's Party were arousing the whole country against the treatment of the prisoners. Suddenly, on March 3, they were released. They were promised action on the suffrage amendment;

but the following June, when Congress continued to stall, they started picketing again. Soon they were back in jail and on their hunger strikes.

The Senate finally voted on the amendment. It lost by two votes. The women transferred their pickets to the Senate.

Alice Paul started a 'watch fire' in an urn in front of the White House. Every time President Wilson made a speech abroad that referred to freedom even in a passing phrase, a copy of the speech was burned in the 'watch fire'. Invariably, police arrested the women who burned the speech. Evidently reports reaching Europe of the 'watch fire' embarrassed the President, for he cabled two Senators asking them to support the suffrage amendment.

In February, 1919, the Senate voted again and the amendment lost by one vote. In June it was finally passed. It still had to be ratified by the states and this meant a state-to-state struggle lasting another year. The women of the United States voted in the presidential elections of 1920.

I seem to have given most of the credit for final passage of this law to the National Woman's Party. The older suffrage organization continued its work during these seven years. It had a membership of almost two million as compared with a top membership of fifty thousand in the National Woman's Party. But it was this militant minority that gave the final push to the suffrage drive.

The Struggle Ahead

Since I have limited myself to the struggle of American women for legal equality, I have not attempted to describe their economic development in this hundred-year period, their entry into industries, office work, trades and professions, or their role in the trade-union movement. That story would require another article, but its close relationship to the growth of the woman's movement is obvious. As women achieved economic independence, their demand for the vote was taken more seriously. Laws change slowly and are generally a reflection of changes that have already occurred on the economic and social level.

Almost thirty-five years have passed since women got the vote. We are in position now to appraise what women achieved when they won the suffrage and what they did *not* achieve.

Many people are disappointed over the results of woman suffrage – for example, all those who believed that politics would be 'purified' by the participation of women. Reactionaries insist that suffrage and the entry of women into industry have actually achieved nothing, that modern women are miserably unhappy, frustrated and hysterical and go insane at a faster rate than ever before. (All this because women are allegedly emotionally passive and have been forced against their true nature into competition with men.) The solution, if we are to believe them, seems to be to hurry back to what's left of the home, which is something like going all out for the horse as a means of modern transportation. *Modern Woman – the Lost Sex* by a woman psychiatrist, Marya Farnham, is a good example of this reactionary trend.

Even people who approve of modern woman are disappointed at the results of the woman's rights struggle. Purdy in his biography of Mary Wollstonecraft says:

> All that has been done for women in the last century and a half has not saved them from the tragedies that afflicted Mary Wollstonecraft, Eliza Bishop and Fanny Blood. Inherited poverty, brutal or indifferent parents, disease following overwork and neglect, reluctant or faithless lovers, incompatible husbands, the struggle to wring a living from an apathetic world – has not been ended by female suffrage or any other abstract benefits women have recently achieved.

I can't help wondering just how many problems they thought woman suffrage could solve. The vote was, a simple question of democratic rights and not a magic formula that could dissolve all the bitterness and frustrations of women's daily lives. Men have been voting a hundred years longer than women and they've still got problems. That doesn't mean they should give up voting. If Negroes suddenly achieved complete equality with whites, they would still face unemployment, the threat of war, reaction and all the other difficulties that confront every worker, regardless of race or sex. That doesn't mean they should give up the fight for full equality.

I don't doubt that women are unhappy. The legal equality and other democratic rights for which they fought so heroically are meaningless as long as their position in economic and family life remains basically unaltered.

The economic status of women is undergoing change. This is bringing about the first fundamental difference in women's lives. Women now constitute one-third of the labor force and 25% of all married women are working. This is a revolutionary development that in the long run will mean a great deal more than the vote.

But the majority of women still face discrimination in wages and jobs. The average income of women workers is less than half that of men. They are also doubly exploited, as wage earners and as wives. A survey by General Electric revealed that the average work week of employed wives is 79 hours – 40 on the job and 39 at home.

This explains why women are not too enthusiastic about their so-called 'emancipation'. Women workers are obviously *not* emancipated, any more than male workers, Negro workers, or any other section of the working class.

The structure of the family is also undergoing change, partly as a result of women's changing economic position. Women are not as restricted in their sex and family relationships as they were when Mary Wollstonecraft first rebelled against marriage.

I believe it is significant that the first women who fought for equality and woman's rights directed a large part of their protest against bourgeois family relationships. Only at a later date did they center their attention on issues like the vote. It may be that in our re-examination of women's problems we will return to their starting point. In the light of modern psychological and anthropological knowledge, we should study the relations of husbands and wives, parents and children, in a society that is founded upon the institution of private property and where marriage laws and customs reflect this basic concept of private ownership.

Both the economic and sex status of women is changing, but these changes are only the first steps toward a revolution in human relationships which will take place in the future. The fight for freedom is indivisible and no basic change can be achieved in a society where men, as well as women, are not free.

When women are really emancipated from the economic exploitation and emotional restrictions of our society, men too will be freed from the frustrations and unhappiness which the same system inflicts upon them. Bull this can only be achieved in the cooperative atmosphere of a socialist commonwealth where our personal relationships will not be an expression of the property forms of a competitive society.

10 Feuerbach – Philosopher of Materialism[17]
(*1956*)

John G. Wright (Joseph Vanzler)

Ludwig Andreas Feuerbach, the fourth son of a famous German lawyer, was born at the beginning of the nineteenth century, July 28, 1804. His family was bourgeois. A native of Southern Germany, fiery and passionate by temperament, a born fighter, his natural element was the hurly-burly of public life; he needed the widest possible contact with people, the broadest possible arena. This was denied him by German reaction. The authorities drove him from his university post in 1832, refused to reinstate him in 1836, barred him from the main centers of German intellectual life and kept him penned up, in virtual exile, in a provincial corner of Bavaria, until his death September 13, 1872.

Many know Feuerbach by name; not a few have read about him, mainly in Marxist literature, but nowadays hardly anybody reads his books. His writings are not readily obtainable either in translation or the original German. Yet in the history of human thought he occupies an eminent place. For a whole decade, from 1840 to 1849, he dominated the field of advanced philosophy as only Hegel did before him and Marx and Engels after him.

Among the revolutionary-minded generation of his day, Feuerbach, the materialist philosopher and avowed opponent of theology, was naturally a hero. And just as naturally he was hated and hounded by reaction, not in Germany alone. In England, for example, one pillar of the church, William MacCall, publicly called for the physical annihilation of Feuerbach. 'Aye, annihilate; for this is not a matter in which we pretend to one morsel of tolerance', announced this British reactionary. It is the fate of thinkers like Feuerbach to be maligned and misrepresented long after their death. All the more incumbent is it upon us to restore his true stature and to place his teachings and accomplishments as well as his limitations and failures in their true historical context.

Feuerbach started out as a Hegelian. To be sure, he never was a wholly orthodox Hegelian, any more than were Marx and Engels who likewise started out as Hegelians. But Feuerbach was nonetheless an idealist at the outset.

---

17 Wright 1956. This article has been slightly edited and abridged.

His evolution is the conversion of a Hegelian into a materialist. The course of the development of Marx and Engels passes from Hegel through Feuerbach to dialectical materialism. Rosa Luxemburg somewhere says that dialectical materialism, the world outlook of Marxism, was the child of bourgeois philosophy, a child that cost the mother her life. At this birth Feuerbach may be said to have officiated as the midwife.

At the age of twenty and, ironically enough, a young theologian, Feuerbach came to Berlin to study under Hegel. After two years, he studied natural sciences at Erlangen. Philosophy became his lifework. His first book, published anonymously in 1830, *Thoughts on Death and Immortality*, shows that years before his definitive break with Hegel, he had already come under the influence of Spinoza, whose doctrine is materialist in its essence, despite its idealist modes of expression, as Feuerbach himself was later brilliantly to demonstrate.

In 1839 when Feuerbach published his *Zur Kritik der Hegelschen Philosophie* (A Contribution to the Critique of Hegelian Philosophy) he had broken with idealism. By 1841 when his monumental book *The Essence of Christianity* appeared, he was a materialist who waged war against idealism as the last refuge of theology and against Hegelianism as the last rational prop of theology.

Karl Marx hailed Feuerbach's ideas at the time as world-historic in their importance and inaugurating a new epoch. Why? Because they represented a decisive break with idealism and a rallying to materialism. As early as the eighteenth century, particularly in France, Marx pointed out in *The Holy Family*, materialism stood for the struggle not only against all metaphysical systems, against religion and theology, but also against the existing political institutions. To put it differently, materialist ideas were revolutionary.

If the credit for driving religion out of its last refuge in history belongs to Marxism, then the credit for launching the final struggle to drive theology out of philosophy belongs to Feuerbach. In this he was indisputably the first, although he did not thoroughly purge his own thought of idealist remnants.

There was nothing cut and dried about Feuerbach. With an eloquence rare in philosophic writings and with the zeal of a fighter for a correct line in philosophy – an intransigence and eloquence which captured the minds and hearts of revolutionists of his day – Feuerbach demonstrated that nothing exists save nature and mankind; that nature does not owe its existence to any power outside of itself, least of all to the power of an infinite subject, as idealists put it, or that nature is the 'self-estrangement' and 'other being' of the Spirit, as Hegel put it. Such claims, Feuerbach explained, are mere translations into philosophic language of the theological doctrine that God created the world.

'Our philosophers', he wrote, 'have up to now been nothing else but mediatizing theologians'. As for Hegel, 'the 'Absolute Spirit' is the 'departed Spirit' of theology which wanders like a ghost in and out of Hegelian philosophy'. This 'Absolute Spirit' remains as mysterious and unknowable as the God of the theologians, and Hegel actually tells as little about his 'Absolute' as theologians are able to tell about their divinity. Whoever fails to break with Hegelianism simply refuses to break with theology, concluded Feuerbach.

German idealism had forged powerful weapons; Feuerbach turned these weapons against idealism itself. 'Truth is concrete', was the banner raised by German idealism, in the first instance by Hegel. 'Philosophy is cognizance of whatever is', agreed Feuerbach. 'The supreme law and task of philosophy is to think about essence, about creatures and things as they really are'. He then proceeded to show how idealism violated its own fundamental premise.

Anticipating the conquests of natural science, the German philosopher Kant had introduced the doctrine of evolution into philosophy; Hegel was later to extend evolution into history. But evolution is unthinkable outside of time and space. And so Kant recognized time and space as forms of cognizance, that is, as indispensable premises for human reason.

With this Feuerbach agreed, only immediately to add that time and space must be much more than that. Are not time and space the necessary forms of existence, as well as the necessary forms of intuition and knowledge, the indispensable premises for the existence of all creatures and things, he asked. Of course they are. Space and time, said Feuerbach, can be forms of cognizance only because I myself happen to be part of whatever exists, only because I myself am a creature living in time and space.

'Space and time', he wrote, 'are the necessary forms of existence of all essence, of all creatures and things ... A timeless sensation, a timeless will, a timeless thought, a timeless essence – are absurd fictions. Whatever is located outside of time, has by this token no temporal existence and cannot strive either to will or think'.

According to Feuerbach, being could not possibly mean an existence in thought alone. Such a contention is meaningless. 'To prove that something exists means to prove that it exists not only in the mind', he insisted. It must exist in the outside world.

The starting point of idealism is that mind is prior to matter. Feuerbach concentrated his heaviest fire against this.

What divides the opposing schools of human thought is precisely their starting points. Arrayed here against each other in the field of theory, just as in politics and in economic life, stand hostile social forces, class forces representing progress on the one side, retrogression on the opposing side.

This historic controversy rages as fiercely today as it did in Feuerbach's day. Take the current crisis in science. Many modern scientists, physicists in particular, find themselves floundering, hopelessly divided over such issues as:

Is there a real outer world which exists independently of our acts of knowing?

Is the real outer world knowable or unknowable?

Is there objective lawfulness, objective causality, in nature?

These are the very same questions, it will be noted, which we are now discussing in connection with Feuerbach and to which he, as a materialist, gave affirmative answers.

Scientists today are divided into two warring camps. On the one side, a group who answers these questions in the affirmative; and on the opposing side, those who deny it.

Such denials follow consistently from the idealist standpoint that mind is prior to matter. And on this central issue Feuerbach in his day took the offensive.

Whoever maintains that mind is prior to matter is simply a theologian in disguise who seeks to deduce the objective world from some immaterial power, or the idea. To try, said Feuerbach, to deduce the objective world from one's idea is to show that one understands exactly nothing about nature or about the mind. The idealistic starting point is a false one.

'*Das Sein geht dem Denken voran*'. Being comes before thinking. Thinking does not determine being; just the contrary, it is being that determines thinking. Idealists reason like those who upon seeing crowds of people walking on a sunny day, conclude that the sun shines because people are out promenading. The correct conclusion is that people are out because the sun is shining. 'I do not generate the object from the thought', said Feuerbach, 'but the thought from the object'.

'I differ', he wrote with justifiable scorn, '*toto coelo* from those philosophers who pluck out their eyes in order that they may see better; for *my* thought I require the senses, especially sight'.

The idealist doctrine of the 'I', i.e., that the abstract 'subject' is the sole source of reality, is merely another way of saying that mind is prior to matter. It is a false doctrine, argued Feuerbach. He reasoned approximately as follows:

I am able to see, but I am not the only one gifted with sight. I am also seen by others. The real 'I' is invariably that 'I' which stands opposed to the 'You'. The real 'I' in turn becomes the 'You' that is to say, becomes the object for another 'I'. For itself the 'I' is naturally the *subject*; for others it is, just as naturally, the *object*. Therefore 'I' constitutes simultaneously both a subject and an object, or subject-object. This is not an identity, but a unity. Whoever analyzes consciousness independently of the rest of mankind does so only by ripping apart every single tie between consciousness and the outer world.

In *Capital* (page 61, Kerr edition) Marx develops and deepens the same ideas as follows: 'Since he [man] comes into the world neither with a looking glass in his hand, nor as a Fichtean philosopher to whom 'I am I' is sufficient, man first sees and recognizes himself in other men. Peter only establishes his own identity as a man by comparing himself with Paul as a being of like kind. And thereby Paul, just as he stands in his Pauline personality, becomes to Peter the type of genus homo'.

The outer world, said Feuerbach, is the necessary premise for consciousness. Our 'I' is not at all the abstract entity with which idealist philosophers try to operate. 'I' am a real being, a thing of the flesh. If you talk about my essence, please bear in mind that my body, too, belongs to this essence. What is more, it is my body, taken as a whole, that precisely constitutes my essence. It is my body that constitutes my 'I'. The process of thinking does not take place within some abstract being; it takes place exactly within my body, within your body. Before you or I can think we must exist. 'Before perceiving we breathe; we cannot exist without air, food and drink'. *Das Sein geht dem Denken voran.* Being is prior to thinking. Matter is prior to thought. Being determines consciousness, and not the other way around.

Feuerbach's motto was: 'Do not think as a thinker, but think as a real, living being in which capacity you are now swimming in the waters of the world ocean'. It is an excellent motto which Marxism has rendered more exact by specifying that individuals do not exist except within specific productive relations in society, i.e., as members of historically developed classes.

Opponents of materialism argue that consciousness cannot, after all, be explained by material phenomena. Thought is immaterial, spiritual, whereas material phenomena are just that – material and unspiritual. This argument (annihilating in the eyes of idealists) completely misses the mark; it does not even touch the materialist foundations of Feuerbach's doctrine. It is idealism that tries to do just the reverse; namely, to explain material phenomena by mental phenomena; in fact, to establish an identity between the two. It is wrong to do so, reasoned Feuerbach.

The domain of subjective events stands contraposed to the domain of objective events and these opposing sides can be understood only as a unity. Not an identity, but a unity. 'What is for me or subjectively, a purely spiritual, immaterial and unsensuous act, is by itself, objectively, a material, sensuous act', explained Feuerbach. The task is to differentiate between them in order then not to sever them asunder, nor falsely to identify them, but to relate them correctly as two sides of one and the same unified whole.

He carefully differentiated not only between consciousness and material phenomena but also between things as they really exist and things as they appear to us, things as we understand them. He differentiated in order to relate them correctly. Through our senses we obtain mental images of the objective world. These images are likewise products of nature but they are distinct from the actual objects of mental representation. In philosophic language, the thing-in-itself is distinct from the thing-for-us. The second, that is, the mental image, is only a reaction to the first, that is, it is an image of objective reality, just as man himself is only a fragment of the world of nature which is mirrored in his mind.

'My taste-nerve', explained Feuerbach, 'is just as much a product of nature as salt is; but from this it does not at all follow that the taste of salt as such would immediately be an objective property of salt; it by no means follows that the salt such as it appears only as an object of sensation would exactly be that in and-for-itself; that the sensation of salt on the tongue would also be the property of salt, as we think of it without sensation'.

Sensation or sense perception is the result of the objective action upon our sense organs of a thing in-itself which exists independently of us. Such is the materialist theory of Feuerbach; such is the theory of Marxism as well. Sensation is the subjective image of an objective world, a world which is simultaneously in-and-for-itself.

Idealists make quite a to-do about the theory of knowledge, gnosiology or epistemology as academicians call it. Is the thing-in-itself, that is, the outer world, really knowable? If so how do we know it? How can we prove it? Many modern scientists profess to be nonplussed by these questions.

In doing so they unwittingly follow in the footsteps of theologians who try to reduce logic to a mere instrument of proof. Actually, logic, even formal logic, is much more than that. It is one of the methods of proceeding *from* the known *to* the unknown, as was demonstrated by Bacon, the founder of modern materialism, with his method of induction as far back as the beginning of the seventeenth century.

The argument that it is not possible to prove by 'a priori arguments' that things are knowable has little weight in the progress of human knowledge, as all the advances of modern industry and technology have shown. It is a scholastic argument. The whole point is that the capacity of man to know reality can be, and has been, proved by other means. This problem of 'knowability', declared unsolvable by Kant, was, as a matter of record, resolved by Hegel who pointed out that as we learn more and more about the qualities of a thing, we get to know more and more about it. In other words, knowledge is derived from observation, from experience, from industry, technology, science, in brief, from the practical activity of man. As Marx pointed out, the problem of 'knowability' is not a theoretical question at all, but a practical one. And any scientist who, when he philosophizes, turns his back on such proof demonstrates thereby that his 'reason' is no better than the more or less diluted, more or less rarified 'reason' of the theologians.

We get to know things as we learn about their qualities, Feuerbach agreed with Hegel.

It is well worth pausing here to consider briefly how Feuerbach used Hegel's own arguments (against Kant) to demonstrate the inner inconsistency of the Hegelian system. Whatever lacks of qualities, said Feuerbach, 'has no effect upon me, has no existence for me ... To deny all the qualities of a being is tantamount to denying the being itself'. But this is precisely what Hegel does with regard to the category of 'pure being' with which his system starts.

'Pure being', as Hegel defines it in his *Science of Logic*, is 'without difference and without any characteristics'. It is 'pure indeterminateness', it is 'totally empty', otherwise, Hegel insists, 'its purity would be violated'.

'Pure being' is therefore without any real being, concluded Feuerbach. There is no being other than determinate being. What exists in space and time are particular species and individuals, solar bodies, stars, animals, plants, rocks and so forth. 'Space and time', said Feuerbach, 'are not simple forms of phenomena but essential conditions of existence'. Hegel's 'pure being' lies outside of time and space; it is without any characteristics; it is indeed, as Hegel himself put it, an 'empty abstraction'. It is a typical theological abstraction. Under the guise of 'pure being' Hegel simply smuggles in his 'Absolute Spirit'. Thus there is no evolutionary process in Hegel's logic at all; in reality, his reasoning is circular. He starts with the Absolute and ends with the self-same Absolute.

Feuerbach demonstrated without difficulty that other key categories of Hegel are likewise infinite and absolute in character, as for example the categories of *Wesen* (or Essence) and of *Begriff* (usually translated as Notion, this category figures in Hegel's system now as Spirit and now as Self-Consciousness). Because of this inner inconsistency Feuerbach discarded the dialectic altogether. He mistook the idealist form of the dialectic for the dialectic generally, a blunder which Marxism alone was able to rectify. In addition, by considering 'man' not as an abstraction transcending society but as a concrete expression of given societies, themselves in evolution, Marx and Engels transcended the idealist vestiges in Feuerbach's philosophy.

This brings us to the question of objective causality in nature. As Lenin pointed out, this question is of special importance in determining the philosophic line of any given system of ideas. ... Feuerbach ... recognized objective causality in nature which is mirrored only with approximate accuracy by the human representations of order, law and so forth. Human representations of nature are relative, but on the basis of these relative representations mankind gains knowledge of the objective lawfulness in nature. This recognition of objective causality is with Feuerbach inseparably connected with the recognition of the objective existence of the outer world of objects, bodies and things which human consciousness mirrors. His views on this question, as Lenin pointed out, are thus consistently materialist.

Frederick Engels wrote: 'One must himself have experienced the liberating effect of this book (Feuerbach's *Essence of Christianity*) to get an idea of it. Enthusiasm was general; we all became at once Feuerbachians'.

What liberated the young Marx and the young Engels? What made them so enthusiastic? They knew, as was said long ago, that without revolutionary theory there cannot be revolutionary practice. Marx and Engels were at the time trying to draw revolutionary conclusions from the Hegelian system and found themselves floundering in the self-contradiction of idealism. Feuerbach, as Engels put it, 'pulverized this contradiction at one blow' and enthroned materialism again in philosophy. This paved the way, as we shall see in our next article, for the elaboration of a correct line in sociology, in politics and economics. It enabled our great teachers to go beyond Feuerbach and to elaborate the scientific doctrine for socialism.

Today, when the fate of mankind sways in the balance, it is clearer than ever before that salvation for the workers lies only in revolutionary practice, in the struggle for socialism. For this, revolutionary theory is indispensable as the guide for action.

This struggle proceeds on three fronts – the economic, political and theoretical. Not three separate arenas, walled off from one another, but three interrelated fronts of one and the same struggle. The correct line is of supreme importance in all three. In the main, Feuerbach laid down the correct line in philosophy. Therein lies his historic achievement. Therein, too, lies our indebtedness to him.

11   Intellectuals and Revolution: The Case of C. Wright Mills (Letter to George Novack)[18]
(*1961*)

James P. Cannon

Dear George:

This is to acknowledge receipt of your letter and Evelyn's lively note of 9 February about your meeting with M[ills]. This is certainly interesting and important news. It is also gratifying to hear that a conversation between us about M[ills] a year or so ago led, in a chain of actions and reactions, to your visit at his home. ...

I think I agree entirely with everything you say in your letter in evaluation of M[ills]. He is different. As you know, I have always had a low, not to say contemptuous, opinion of the contemporary American intelligentsia. And that is not simply a carryover of the anti-intellectualism of my young Wobbly days. After I became a communist and recognized that the thinkers and leaders of the Russian Revolution, like their mentors before them, were all intellectuals, I made a serious effort at 'thought reform' on the subject. But I must say that the intellectuals of our time in this country, particularly those who have made pretentions to radicalism, have done their best to keep me from going overboard.

Experience and observation over a long time have taught me two things about the American intellectuals in general, and academicians in particular. They lack modesty, which is the precondition for learning things they don't already know, especially about the dark interiors of social problems which have been explored by others but remain an undiscovered country for them. Supplementary to that defect, and holding them back from serious exploration, is the plain and simple fact they have no guts. They want to keep out of trouble. ...

For quite a while I have regarded M[ills] as a maverick on the academic range; his manifest courage and honesty seemed to separate him from the herd. Then his book about Cuba showed another and most attractive side of his character. ... On one level it is an absorbing and moving exposition of the revolutionary process in Cuba, as the leaders of the revolution see it. And, to

---

18   Cannon 1992. This item has been edited and abridged.

my mind, reading between the lines of their letters transmitted through M[ills], they see more, and have studied and thought and reflected more about what they are doing, than they explicitly acknowledge in the letters. ...

They frankly say they are improvising as they go along. Bu the remarkable thing is that they have made the right improvisations almost every time, and keep in step with the revolution as it continues to develop. And this course has been continued since the book was written. Castro's speech at the United Nations on the mainsprings of imperialism was the speech of a man who has picked up Lenin's theory somewhere; maybe from the book itself. Then, in the press reports the other day Castro was quoted as saying – for the first time explicitly, as far as I know – that the socialist system is superior to the capitalistic system, and that in a resumption of normal diplomatic relations the United States would have to take this Cuban position into account.

From all of this I got the impression that the Cuban leaders knew more about revolutionary theory than they claimed to know when they were talking with M[ills], and that they know even more now, and are still learning.

On the other level, M[ills] revealed himself as a man more clearly in this book than ever before. I kept saying to myself as I turned the pages from his introduction to his summary: 'This intellectual really cares about the hungry people of the world. He worries, as he says himself, not about the sweeping revolution, but with it. He is even capable of anger – that holy emotion of rebels and revolutionists – about injustice, oppression, lies, and hypocrisy. What a dangerous wild man to be running loose on the American campus!' ...

I would like here to make a brief comment on the important point dealt with inconclusively at the end of your talk with M[ills]. For convenience, I will first quote a paragraph from your letter:

> 'If the Soviet economy is more productive, is it not then historically superior?' I asked. 'What do you mean by historically superior?' he asked. 'That it can produce more goods, more wealth, in less time with less labor per person'. 'Yes, I think it can be more efficient but that is not for me the only test of historical superiority. More important is the moral, cultural, and intellectual superiority'. The discussion ended when I added that without a superior capacity for material production there couldn't be a superior cultural superstructure.

I don't think the apparent disagreement should be left in that stalemate. The question is more subtle, more complicated. And, for my part, I can see merit in both your criterion and that of M[ills]. They should be reconciled, not contrasted.

It is elementary that 'a superior capacity for material production is the necessary basis for a superior cultural superstructure'. Even the Cuban leaders, who don't profess to be practicing Marxists, know that and are working night and day to improve productive capacities to provide the means for all the other things. But in my opinion, there is also merit in M[ills]'s concern for 'moral, cultural, and intellectual superiority', because it cannot be taken for granted that this will follow automatically from the reorganization of the productive system. This aim must be deliberately stated and consciously fought for all the time.

The fullest democracy in the transition period, institutionalized by forms of organization which assure the participation and control of the working people at every stage of development, is an indispensable part of our program. This has to be not merely stated, but emphasized. It distinguishes us from, and puts us in irreconcilable opposition to, the 'economic determinists' and the totalitarians. It is the condition for the most efficient and rapid development of the new productive process.

And no less important, perhaps even more important. This full and free democratic participation of the working people, in all stages and all phases of the social transformation during the transition period between the old society and the new, is the necessary condition for the preparation of the people for citizenship in a genuinely free society. It is not enough to learn to read and write and produce material things in abundance. That's only the starting point. People have to learn how to live abundantly. That means they have to learn how to be free in body, mind, and spirit. Where else can they learn that but in the school and practice of ever-expanding democracy during the transition period?

In view of the way things have turned out in the Soviet Union, Eastern Europe, and China, this part of our Marxist program – workers' democracy as the only road to preparation for the socialist society of the free and equal – must be given particular emphasis in all of our propaganda and all our arguments with people who are dissatisfied with capitalism, but don't want to exchange it for totalitarian slavery.

If we fail to emphasize this fundamental feature of our Marxist program; if we omit it or slur over it in our expositions of the superiority of nationalized and planned economy; if we neglect to speak of freedom as the socialist goal – we will never win the American worker and the new generation of intellectuals for the revolutionary fight. And we won't deserve to.

12 C. Wright Mills' *The Marxists*[19]
(1962)

William F. Warde (George Novack)

The Marxists was the last of C. Wright Mills' books to be published during his lifetime. His death at the age of 46 ended untimely a new beginning in his quest for sociological truth.

The Marxists is significant both for its opposition to the dominant trends in American social thought and for its place in the political and intellectual evolution of the author. This irreverent Columbia Professor of Sociology rejected the credo of his fellow faculty members that liberalism provides an adequate answer to Marxism.

Liberalism was once a fighting creed, he observed, but it has come to a dead end and now serves as a rationale and rhetoric for upholding the irresponsible rule of the Power Elite. It has been conscripted for this function because American conservatism has no philosophy of its own with which to defend the status quo.

Repudiation of the principal ideology for justifying the Big Money brought Mills face to face with Marxism, the foremost doctrine of the anti-capitalist forces. The Marxists records his debate with scientific socialism in order to define his own ideas and positions more precisely.

Mills accorded Marxism exceptionally high rank in the field of sociology. Marxism is more valuable for understanding today's social realities than all 'the abstractions, slogans and fetishisms of liberalism', he insisted. He wanted to break down the bias against Marxism in the halls of learning and encourage students to assimilate its indispensable contributions to social science.

Mills challenged another shibboleth of the professional liberals who, for their own cold-war purposes, accept the claim of Stalinism that it is a continuation of genuine Marxism and Bolshevism, rather than its distortion and negation. He sought to dissociate the ideas of Marx and Engels from the Stalin-

---

19   Warde 1962.

ist stigmas and, in line with this, to highlight the twin roles of Lenin and Trotsky who came together to form 'the Bolshevik pivot' in the October 1917 Revolution.

He contrasts these two with Marx, whom he one-sidedly portrays as a creative thinker but not a man of action, and with Stalin, Mao Tse-tung, Tito and Khrushchev whom he rates as purely practical politicians. Lenin and Trotsky were for him embodiments of the unity of theory and practice. 'Both are thinkers of high quality and both are among the most accomplished politicians of the last hundred years'.

In protest against 'the enormous ignorance and systematic distortion' of Trotsky's ideas, Mills calls upon the Soviet leaders 'to publish great editions of Trotsky's complete works and discuss widely and freely both his theoretical contributions and his political roles in their revolution. That will surely be most propitious', he writes, 'for new beginnings in Soviet Marxism'.

His recommendation that our countrymen find out what Marxism really teaches, his rejection of liberal complacency, his straightening-out of the roles of Lenin, Trotsky and Stalin in the Marxist tradition will act as antidotes to widespread prejudices in our national thought.

Mills' Appraisal of Marxism

Apart from selections of writings by socialist thinkers, from the founders of Marxism to the Yugoslav Kardelj, the Englishman G.D.H. Cole and the Cuban [sic] 'Che' Guevara, the axis of the work is an examination of the merits and demerits of Marxism. What is the substance of his critical appraisal?

Scientific socialism gave a theoretical picture of capitalist society which was better than any other in its day. However, classical Marxism is a conceptual reflection of the conditions of nineteenth-century Western capitalism. The matured, highly industrialized capitalist societies of the mid-twentieth-century and the Soviet types of society require a more complex type of explanation. Marxism is the Model T of sociology, Mills implies. It must be traded in for a higher-powered design which has kept up with the immense changes in the most advanced sectors of the world.

Most important among these new phenomena is the enormous scale of the aggregations of economic, political, military and cultural power with their extreme centralization, bureaucratization and tyranny over helpless masses of ordinary individuals. These trends are most fully incorporated in the two gigantic superstates, the US and the USSR, which so belligerently confront each other.

'The run of historical events', he writes, 'has overturned the specific theories and explanations' of classical Marxism. On the one hand, capitalism is stronger than ever in the industrialized West where Marx foresaw the workers coming to power. On the other hand, all the major revolutions of our century have occurred in predominantly peasant societies with autocratic governments where capitalism was weak. No proletarian revolution of a Bolshevik type has taken place in a democratic capitalist society and there are no substantial reasons to anticipate that one ever will.

Above all, Marxist theory has been invalidated, Mills argues, because its central proposition that the wage-workers would become more and more class conscious, anti-capitalist and revolutionary has not been borne out in the developed capitalist countries. 'To a very considerable extent, they have been incorporated into nationalist capitalism – economically, politically and psychologically'. The discrediting of 'the labor metaphysics', the keystone of the structure, entails the collapse of the rest of scientific socialism.

All that remains of the original Marxism as a lasting legacy to sociology is its method of work, he asserts. Everything else from its dialectical logic to its theory of the state has not stood the test of events and must be modified or discarded.

What does Mills propose to put in place of the classic liberalism and Marxism he has swept aside as obsolete? He does not give us much concrete information. In fact, he says he does not have to give any immediate alternative to the ideologies he has presumably demolished. He intended to work out his own theoretical positions and program of action subsequently together with those colleagues of 'The New Left' who shared the view that they had gone beyond the limitations of Marxism to some superior but still indeterminate type of social theory.

Science and Society

Despite his disclaimer, Mills did have a general method of thought which inspired and directed his entire evaluation of Marxism – and it was hardly new. That method was pragmatism, the predominant mode of thought in American culture. To be sure, he gave a leftward twist to his empirical thinking in the field of sociology. But he stubbornly adhered to its premises and prejudices.

This was evident in the footnote where he curtly waved aside the dialectical method, the mainspring of Marxist thought, as mysterious and useless.

'For us', he wrote, 'the 'dialectical method' is either a mess of platitudes, a way of doubletalk, a pretentious obscurantism, or all three'.

Yet the contrast between the shortcomings of his own method and the value of dialectical thinking can be shown in regard to his very first criticism of one of the cardinal principles of Marxist sociology. This is the distinction between the economic conditions constituting the material substratum of society and the cultural superstructure which arises out of it and rests upon it.

'Exactly what is included and what is not included in "economic base" is not altogether clear, nor are the "forces" and "relations" of production precisely defined and consistently used', he complains. 'In particular, "science" seems to float between base and superstructure ...'.

How does dialectical materialism approach the problem of the relations of science to the economic base and the cultural superstructure of society? This matter cannot be disposed of in a sweeping declaration, as Mills apparently demands. It is not so simple. The place and function of science in the social structure have not been the same in all historical epochs. They have changed in accord with the development of the forces of production and correlative changes in the mode of production.

Although the societies of savagery and barbarism nurtured embryonic elements of scientific knowledge, they contained as yet no science as a deliberate specialized pursuit of men, employing a rational method for investigating the phenomena of nature, society or the human mind. Science could emerge only when the powers of production had attained a certain height of development and the relations of production were of a special type (the commercial-craft relations of slave-holding antiquity).

These prerequisites were all brought together for the first time in Ionian Greece where science was born along with philosophy, materialism and mathematics. In this first stage of its existence, science, as part of philosophy, was situated exclusively in the cultural superstructure, even though it had been born of economic conditions and needs which set the elementary problems to be solved at that point in its growth.

So long as agriculture and craftsmanship remained the pillars of production under a system of slave labor, science could not and did not decisively react upon the social economy out of which it arose. This was further demonstrated by the fact that science continued to be cooped up in the cultural superstructure during feudalism, which likewise had an agricultural-artisan basis. Neither in Western Europe, India or China did science alter agriculture or craftsmanship to any real extent.

The great shift in the relations between science and production began with the bourgeois epoch. The economic needs and class interests of the merchants, mine owners, ship owners, manufacturers and their patron states not only promoted the growth of the sciences, especially in certain branches of physical knowledge such as astronomy, mechanics and optics, but changed the range and prospects of science in the social structure. This change was speeded up by the industrial revolution which became the technological basis of a matured capitalism. For example, the expansive power of steam, which was known in Greco-Roman antiquity but had been used solely for trivial purposes in temples and toys, became the prime motive force in the mechanism of production through applied science.

Since then science, through reciprocal action with industry, has grown like a giant. In the twentieth century the inventions and applications of science have transformed old branches of industry and even agriculture in the advanced countries. Scientific methods and discoveries have created wholly new, previously unknown industries such as electronics. In this way science is becoming the paramount factor in the progress of social production.

Thus we find that science has already passed through three distinct stages in relation to the rest of the social structure.

In precivilized communities science was too rudimentary and negligible to be counted as a separate social factor or productive force.

In the first period of its existence from Greece to the close of the Middle Ages, science was almost entirely confined to the upper reaches of society. It remained the possession of a few learned men aided by ingenious craftsmen, having little effect upon the production of wealth.

As capitalism grew, science grew with it in many directions. Breaking through the barriers between itself and the material foundations of social life, science has with the advent of nuclear energy become so revolutionizing a power that it has brought on the greatest crisis in human history.

Capitalism, which stimulated science in its progressive days, tends more and more to pervert and stifle its growth. The boundless potential of science can now be realized only through abolishing the outmoded capitalist mode of production and private property restrictions. Socialism means, in essence, the scientific illumination, planning and direction of all man's social activities from material production to the summits of intellectual creation.

∴

This may seem an overlong answer to a single objection. But Mills has not brought up an incidental point. The history of science is bound up with the science of history. When Mills doubts whether Marxism really knows where science belongs in the totality of social development, he is questioning the scientific solidity of its method. If Marxism cannot answer this correctly, its credentials as a scientific sociology become dubious since science in its workings is the most influential factor in our lives today.

It is worth noting that, while questioning the capacity of historical materialism to provide a clear solution to the problem of the place of science in social development, Mills offers no answers of his own. He, not the Marxist, is really the one who is 'floating' in empty space on this question.

Historical materialism approaches all aspects of social life from the standpoint of their connections with the development of the conditions of production. The evolution of science from primitive days to the present provides a prime example of this objectively conditioned process. Moreover, the reversal in the importance of science in the social order confirms the operation of two of the dialectical laws which Mills so scornfully dismisses: the law of the interpenetration of opposites and the law of the transformation of quantity into quality.

Science, once insignificant in production, has, through subsequent expansion of the forces of production, acquired the foremost place in production. Through the ages the relations between science and economy, the foundation of society, have changed into their opposite. Mankind is passing from a society dominated by routine, tradition, blindness and superstition to a society guided and controlled by conscious scientific method. And this qualitative change, to be perfected under socialism, has come about as the climax to the quantitative accumulation of scientific knowledge from savagery to the Atomic Era.

Do not the results of this dialectical and materialistic approach to the problem of social and scientific development offer some advantages over the skeptical empiricism of Mills?

The Laws of Social Development

The deficiencies of Mills' method can be seen in his one-sided approach to the laws of social development. Mills praises Marx for using the principle of historical specificity which means that 'each epoch must be examined as an independent historical formation in terms of categories suitable to it'. Mills however overlooked the fact that Marx not only studied the social formations of separate epochs but the entire evolution of society through all its stages. Every distinctive type of society from savagery to socialism was for him an interdependent link in a causal chain of social development which grew out of its predecessor and created the preconditions for its successor.

Marx was guided, not only by the principle of *historical specificity*, but equally by the principle of *historical generality*. As a dialectical thinker he understood the organic unity of the particular and the general and combined these two rules of method in all his investigations.

This is verified by Marx's Preface to *The Critique of Political Economy*, reprinted in *The Marxists*, which contains his broadest formulation of the materialist conception of history. There Marx set forth, as 'the *general* result' of his researches, fifteen propositions on the evolution of society. Twelve of these are not specific to any one social formation or historical epoch but apply to them all. Only in the last three does he refer to definite historical formations (the Asian, ancient, feudal and bourgeois modes of production and the transition of the latter to socialism).

It is understandable why Mills exalts the principle of historical specificity at the expense of the generalized conclusions Marx drew from his study of the successive stages of social development in their continuity and totality. It enabled him to lock Marx in a time-cage with other superannuated Victorian thinkers and to deny that his comprehensive laws of social evolution and revolution can be extended to cover the decline and downfall of capitalism while indicating the inescapable road to the next stage of human progress.

Mills is especially concerned to disqualify the foundation of the materialist conception of history which holds that production (and exchange) is the basis of every social organization; and that therefore, according to Engels, 'the ultimate causes of all social changes and political revolutions are to be sought not in the minds of men, in their increasing insight into eternal truth and justice, but in changes in the mode of production and exchange; they are to be sought not in the *philosophy* but in the *economics* of the epoch concerned'.

Mills denies there has been any one such central determinant of social movement operative throughout human history. Together with his tutors Weber and Mannheim and other liberal sociologists, he counter-poises the theory of multiple, independent and parallel causes to the unified Marxist conception of historical causation. According to historical materialism, all the aspects of social activity – from burial rites to witchcraft and from politics to philosophy – exert their own measure of influence upon events but throughout their reciprocal action economics is the most important and conclusive element.

This 'economic determinism' of Marx is too one-sided and dogmatic, he says, to do justice to the complexities of social evolution. Many factors other than economic conditions have been and can be fundamentally decisive in the course of development, not only within precapitalist societies but also under capitalism. Whereas, for example, economics may have been preponderant in early capitalism, political, military and other superstructural factors play an 'autonomous and originative' role in its later and contemporary stages.

The Welfare and the Warfare State

This thesis that economics is or can be subordinate to political and military forces will be familiar to readers of Mills' previous works: *The Power Elite* and *The Causes of World War III*. There he found the ultimate causes for the unprecedented expansion, imperialist policies and aggressive strategy of US militarism, not in the economic necessities of monopoly capitalism, whose servitors are the decision makers in Washington, but rather in the 'military metaphysics' which obsesses the statesmen and generals. Thus Mills reverted to the untenable viewpoint of idealism that the ultimate determinant of political events must be found, not in the economic framework within which the men at the top operate and within which they serve class interests, but in their mentality and outlook. From this sociological analysis flows the political conclusion that it is more realistic to try to change the thinking and policies of the people in power than to change the class possessors of power.

In *The Marxists* Mills goes on to affirm that the Welfare State, Siamese twin of the Warfare State, is likewise not 'determined by the mode of economic production, although of course it is made possible by economic developments'. The imperialist democracies of monopoly capitalism have supplanted the *laissez faire* regimes of competitive capitalism, just as the guided missile has replaced the cannon ball. The Welfare State, which combines Keynesian credit devices with social legislation, is the result of many interacting factors, from the exigencies of capitalist rulership to the pressures of the trade unions.

The serious question is: whose class interests do these policies primarily serve? Roosevelt, the improviser of the New Deal, granted reforms where Hoover did not, because, as he candidly admitted in 1936: 'liberalism becomes the protection of the far-sighted conservative'. By diverting a small fraction of the national revenue from its magnates to some of the more favored segments of the working people, the capitalist government is able to shore up its system. The masses more than pay for these restricted benefits by having to bear the penalties and burdens of continued exploitation and misrule along with misleadership by conservatized union bureaucrats.

The welfare provisions of the Warfare State can be sustained only by the wealthier capitalist countries, which can afford certain privileges for the labor aristocracy so long as these are offset by superexploitation of the underdeveloped continents. Whenever international competition tightens and corporation profits decline, the most liberal governments start whittling away at these social gains, as Belgium recently showed. Thus the extent and endurance of these concessions at bottom depend upon the economic resources and prospects of the national capitalism. Despite Mills' contention, the causal mechanism of the Welfare State is to be found in the specific necessities of capitalist rule and its mode of production.

The Longevity of Capitalist Rule

In accord with his thesis that 'political and military State of action and decision' can override economic laws, Mills maintains, against the Marxists, that contemporary Western capitalism can be readjusted without limit by the policies of the monopolists or by liberal and Laborite reforms. Despite his repugnance to their course, he agrees with its supporters that the capitalist system has enough resiliency to go on indefinitely.

This confidence that the political dexterity of the capitalists can control the harmful consequences of their rule does not fit the main facts of the twentieth century. The failure of the monopolist policy makers to solve the problems of markets, raw materials, colonies and world supremacy led to two global wars which prepared and provoked anticapitalist overturns from Russia to China. Since 1917 one-third of humanity has thrown off the economic and political control of world capitalism.

To be sure, the economies of the US and Western Europe have had no grave economic disturbances in the past two decades comparable to the crises of the 1930's. We have had the Cold War instead. But the US, mainstay of world capitalism, has passed through five recessions since 1945. Each one has lasted a little longer, leaving a larger residue of permanently unemployed and a growing anxiety about their material insecurity among sizeable sections of the workers.

Moreover, prolonged prosperity in the highly industrialized centers has been attended by chronic impoverishment in the less developed countries. The contrast between the economic levels and living standards of the rich and poor continents has become wider and deeper – and no Point 4 or Alliance for Progress programs can stem their inevitable consequences. The inability of the imperialist powers to overcome the disparity of rich and poor nations is at the root of the irrepressible surge and spread of the colonial revolution.

Meanwhile, the capitalist bloc confronts the workers' states, not only as military, diplomatic and political adversaries, but as economic rivals. These states have considerable distances to travel before catching up with the older capitalist nations, but, paced by the Soviet Union, they are experiencing a faster rate of economic growth.

If Western capitalism were considered by itself since the end of the Second World War, it would be easy to conclude with Mills and others that political maneuvers and measures can immunize it indefinitely from revolutionary convulsions. Yet even here, a caveat is in order. If, from 1944 to 1946 the Stalinist and Social-Democratic leaderships had not collaborated with Churchill, Roosevelt and de Gaulle to derail the workers' thrust toward power and to rehabilitate the shattered capitalist structure in Western Europe, history would have taken a different turn. Moreover, the respite did not save world capitalism from losing ground; it looks far less formidable on the world arena than it does from within the Atlantic Alliance.

It is true, as Mills emphasizes, that government intervention in the economic life of the capitalist countries has taken place on a massive scale. These measures have succeeded in delaying the advent of severe crises and will probably be stepped up in the years ahead. However, political regulation of the economy is a manifest symptom of the growing infirmity of capitalism which, in its monopolist-imperialist phase, can no longer rely upon the automatic operation of its forces for salvation. The plutocrats must utilize all the resources of state power to keep their system on an even keel, maintain their international positions, and forestall economic decline and political disturbances. Such intervention can alleviate the incurable ailments of the economy and attenuate their consequences but it cannot fend off the recurrence of more and more serious slumps.

Now, in this country government intervention is being extended to capital-labor negotiations where the Kennedy administration has held down wage increases in the steel industry under the pretext of 'protecting the national welfare', a pseudonym for corporation profits. This domestic policy is tied up with the worsening position of the US economy on the world market. The persistent deficit in the international balance of payments keeps draining the gold reserve, threatening more inflation and depreciation of the dollar.

The permanent overproduction crisis of US agriculture reflects the inability of the strongest capitalist government to counteract the workings of the 'free enterprise' system. Price-support measures and new farm programs concocted by successive administrations do not go to the root causes of the problem. They simply relieve the situation for the time being and postpone the final reckoning.

The most malignant offshoot of government policy has been the unending arms race. The $50-billion annual military budget keeps injecting artificial stimulants into our sick economy. But the changeover from planes to guided missiles tends to diminish the effectiveness of this economic stimulant. Equivalent appropriations generate fewer jobs, since it takes fewer workers and less plant space to build missiles than planes.

Technological developments in the military domain are only one aspect of the impact of automation and mechanization upon the capitalist economy.

These will reduce the industrial work-force as twenty-six million new young workers enter the job market in the next ten years. The cumulative consequences of these trends will serve to revive labor militancy, especially among the younger and less favored strata, and pose the issue of socialism versus capitalism more forcefully in bread-and-butter terms.

Mills' faith in the endurance of capitalist sovereignty and his underestimation of the capacity and will of the working class for independent action spring from his acceptance of the predominant economic and political conditions of the past fifteen years as fixed and final. He does not expect these to be altered and undermined by countertendencies in the capitalist economy or by fresh advances of the anticapitalist forces which in the coming years will abruptly upset the status quo. The brusque conversion of the Fourth Republic into de Gaulle's personal military regime indicates how rickety democracy can be when a national capitalism gets into difficulties. The most violent convulsions of capitalism lie ahead and are not safely buried in the past.

∴

In his assessment of the stability of capitalist rule, Mills for some reason fails to take into consideration the H-bomb crisis which he dealt with at length in other works. The political-military situation called forth by the development of nuclear devices provides striking proof of the Marxist proposition that the crisis of a social system is brought about and its downfall prepared by intensified conflict between new *forces* of production and outmoded *relations* of production. In the case of nuclear energy, this new force of production – or destruction, which is one and the same – is pounding against the national boundaries and property forms of monopoly capitalism. The development of this limitless source of power for beneficial social purposes is retarded and strait jacketed, while the major effort is concentrated on increasing its megatons of destruction.

This has involved the capitalist statesmen in the most excruciating of dilemmas. On one side, they must pile up nuclear arms as the indispensable instrument of their strategy to halt the progress of the workers' states and socialist forces and hold on to their possessions and power. On the other side, the incalculable consequences of dropping the bombs becomes a deterrent to their use.

How long can capitalism – and, even more, the people who live under daily threat of annihilation – go on this way? This intolerable 'balance of terror' keeps pressing for solution. It is a major factor in politicalizing and radicalizing the most sensitive segments of the population, from the youth to the mothers. Sooner or later their opposition to H-bomb diplomacy will extend into the ranks of labor, as it already has in Japan and England.

The Role of the Working Class

Mills clashes most profoundly with Marxism over the revolutionary role of the working class. He opposes the Marxist doctrine that the class struggle over the surplus product of the working force has been the prime mover and reshaper of history since the beginnings of civilization and private property. Asserting that class harmony and collaboration is 'as much a fact of class history as is a struggle', he extends this generalization to the monopoly capitalism of today. There collaboration between classes will remain predominant.

Mills acknowledges that the Marxist law of the capitalist concentration of wealth and power has worked out to the danger point in the US. But the corollary to this process, the deepening of the antagonism between the monied magnates and the hosts of labor, has not. Western capitalism may be stratified into classes but it has become stabilized, he argues. The workers in the affluent countries have neither desire nor need to do away with the existing system. They want nothing more than a larger share of the national income. Since their living standards have been improving wherever capitalist policies have been flexible and wherever democracy and unionism have been strong, they can have no reasons for revolutionary ideas or action.

Mills apparently arrived at his conclusion – that the workers are nonevolutionary and will forever be subordinate within Western capitalism – through an objective examination of present facts. But this conviction really rests upon a prior disbelief in the creative and directive capacities of the working people. Otherwise, why should he assume that a handful of monopolists could rule whereas the mass of workers never could?

This disqualification of the workers as potential leaders of society is the most flagrant expression of Mills' essential sociological conception that elites of one kind or another have been and will continue to be the principal history makers. He looks to the intellectuals for immediate salvation. He founds his hopes for peace, freedom and progress, not on the victory of the working masses over the plutocracy, but rather on the benign influence to be exerted by scholars, ministers, scientists and writers, the peripheral and not the central forces in our society.

In downgrading the workers Mills forgot that ascending social classes do not realize their full potential all at once. Classes undergo a prolonged development in which they are gradually transformed as the result of ceaselessly renewed efforts to satisfy their growing needs. Only after successive stages do they finally arrive at the point of a showdown with the ruling power that oppresses them. And history teaches that progressive forces do not make this challenge simultaneously and all together but in highly irregular sequence as necessity dictates.

In *The Marxists* Mills has demonstrated nothing beyond the obvious fact that up to now that part of the world working class which is directly dominated by imperialism and has shared its privileges has not mustered enough energy and clarity of consciousness to dislodge the monopolist masters from power. That is to say, the growth of the workers in the West as a revolutionary force has, for ascertainable reasons, been stunted and retarded. This is very different from the conclusion that their revolutionary qualities are non-prime or exhausted.

Two Incompatible Perspectives

Our argument with Mills does not center primarily on what the workers are today. We can agree that the political passivity, lack of militancy and dulled class consciousness of labor in the advanced countries stand in sharp contrast with the revolutionary ardor in the colonial areas. Our divergences revolve around what the workers can and must become in the further course of economic, political and cultural development.

Is the present state of affairs and alignment of class forces transitional or permanent? Mills foresees the prolongation of capitalist stabilization and harmony with labor. The revolutionary socialists envisage an erosion of the supports of monopoly capitalism which will lead to social conflicts and labor radicalization. Here two irreconcilable lines of capitalist and anticapitalist development are projected. Which is right?

The social scientist, even more than the political strategist, ought to measure vast social changes on appropriate scales. The contest between organized capital and its labor opposition concerns nothing less than the replacement of one global social regime by another. The direction and ultimate destination of the contending forces cannot be correctly and comprehensively apprehended at a single cross-section of time in a particular area of the world. They must be viewed in the context of their over-all evolution on the world arena.

Restricting our analysis to the past forty years, labor in Western Europe and North America does not present a picture of unrelieved stagnation or retrogression. The labor movement from Spain to Poland was crushingly defeated by fascism during the 1930's. At that time numerous former radicals asserted that European labor was forever pulverized, would never rise again as an independent force, and all its socialist perspectives were obliterated. Yet its economic and political organizations have been rebuilt to the point where Western European labor can again become the challenger of capitalist power.

US labor, on the other hand, passed from industrial atomization to union organization in one mighty leap during the 1930's – and has been marking time ever since. It now combines an immensely powerful organization and latent strength with an utterly reactionary officialdom and a crusty conservatism in its upper ranks.

Our trade unions are politically more backward than the newly emerging unions of Africa. Now that the Canadian unions have launched the New Democratic Party, ours is the only one among the major industrial countries that has not formed a political party of its own. Yet, in view of the recuperative capacities shown and the precedents set by labor in other lands, there is no reason to doubt that labor in this country will under changing conditions also shed its conservatism and resume its forward march.

Many skeptics regard socialist propaganda for a labor party as hopeless. They doubt whether the American workers can ever generate enough steam to cut loose from the Democrats and establish themselves as an autonomous political force. In the 1920's, an earlier generation of wiseacres had it figured out that the industrial proletariat was too divided, ignorant, downtrodden and leaderless to beat back Big Business and unionize the basic industries. It might be added that this was a tougher job to carry through than it would be to set up a national labor party with the resources of the existing unions.

Let us grant that US labor has a long way to go in catching up with its more advanced contingents in the rest of the world. Yet over the past hundred years our labor movement has grown into an economic, social and political power of a magnitude topped only by organized wealth itself.

Now the question is posed: should the partisans of the Old Left – or the New – take as their point of departure the achievements culminating in the militancy of the 1930's ... or should they base their estimates of the future upon the passivity of the Cold War period and look back upon the capacities displayed earlier as labor's last burst of creative energy? Which is the virile rising class and which is the senile and reactionary one – capital or labor?

Revolutionary socialists deduce from the international and national experiences of the past century, and the antagonistic tendencies of capitalist development, that the wiping out of the open shop in basic industry was not the final upheaval in the struggle between corporate wealth and organized labor. In reality, the industrial class battles in the first half of this century were only the opening chapters in a process of class struggle and social transformation which will find its sequel, and very likely its culmination, on the political plane during the second half. Just as the forward leap of the 1930's overcame the stagnation of the 1920's, so the advances of the coming period will erase the apathy of the 1950's and open up broader opportunities for radicalism and Marxism in the US.

Mills took his stand on the opposite alternative. He regarded any program depending on the independent action and heightened political consciousness of the workers as 'metaphysical moonshine'. This is the gravest decision a radical can make, for upon it hinges the main line of his political activity.

Significance of the Negro Struggle

In calculating the status and prospects of American labor, Mills unaccountably failed to reckon with the implications of the Negro struggle for equality which has the most direct bearing upon the movement for social change in this country.

Mills seemed to look upon the Negro movement as something essentially separate from the general labor struggle. To be sure, the fight against Jim Crow has its special roots in American history and has its own characteristics, aims, pace and channels of development. At the same time, it is an integral part of the conflict of American labor against the established order. Almost all Negroes belong to the working class and are the most abused section of it. Color discrimination is the most vicious instrument of class exploitation. That is why the Negroes have taken the lead in combating its consequences.

That is not all. Although the Negro movement arises from the disabilities suffered here, it is connected with the uprisings of the disinherited colored peoples in the colonial and semicolonial countries. The Negro demand for democratic rights is the most forcible and advanced expression to date within our own borders of this world-wide revolutionary process. This is understood, at least in part, by its most active participants who have been uplifted and strengthened by the Asian, African and Cuban revolutions.

The Negro struggle testifies that the rebellious mood which the imperialists fear so much and resist so fiercely is surging up in our very midst. It is far from its final expression. Even at this point it is the major source of instability in our social and political structure. As A. Philip Randolph has reminded the AFL-CIO heads, the white majority of the working class, and especially its leaders, is far from sharing the sentiments or even properly supporting the battles of their black brethren. Their indifference in this respect resembles the attitude of French labor toward the Algerian rebels.

It cannot be expected that all the potentially dissident elements will react to the same grievances and swing into action simultaneously. The most exploited and oppressed, those with the least to lose and the most to win immediately, move first and fastest both on the world arena and within our own country. Their initiatives serve to unbalance the forces of reaction and unloose effects which can, in time, reanimate the more sluggish sections of labor.

It is useful to recall in this connection that not so long ago the Negro minority was even more low-rated as a militant and effective agency for social change than the working class majority is today by Mills and others. If the first prejudice is harder to sustain nowadays, the second is more enduring. But it, too, will be shattered by events to come.

The Nature of Postcapitalist Societies

Mills held that Marx's prevision of the birth process of postcapitalist societies was as defective as his forecasts of capitalist development. Marx expected the workers in the most highly industrialized countries of Western Europe to abolish capitalism first and lead the way to socialism. Actually, capitalism has been overthrown only in backward peasant lands with autocratic regimes. According to Mills, this reversal of Marx's anticipated order of revolutionary victory invalidated all claims to the scientific character of his sociology.

This argument was first invoked (in the name of Marxism) by the Social-Democratic theoreticians against the legitimacy of the Bolsheviks taking power in October 1917. The opponents of Bolshevism shut their eyes to the real advancement of the revolution because it ran counter to their preconception of its predestined route. But the living Marxism of the twentieth century rejected such a scholastic approach, adjusted its outlook to the actual events and, what is more, comprehensively explained them.

The unexpected fact that the proletariat first attained supremacy, not in the advanced sectors of Europe, but in one of its most backward countries did indeed go counter to Marx's personal projection. But, far from nullifying the laws of historical materialism, the Russian Revolution extended the range of their application and enriched their content. This is certified by the fact that it was precisely the revolutionary Marxists who foresaw that probability years before it was realized and based their strategy upon it. Such was the political conclusion Trotsky drew from his theory of the permanent revolution applied to Russia as early as 1904–1906.

After 1917 Lenin explained that the socialist revolution had first triumphed in backward Russia for two main reasons. Under the stresses of imperialist war the chain of world capitalism had broken at its weakest link and let loose a peasant war of immense proportions and powers to back up the proletarian uprising. The interlocked struggles of these two classes enabled the Russian people to clean out, not only Czarism and landlordism, but bourgeois property and power and lay the foundations for a workers' republic.

The victorious socialist revolutions in Yugoslavia, China and Cuba after the Second World War have followed the same general pattern. They have taken place not in the richest but in the most backward lands where long-delayed agrarian revolution has meshed with the anticapitalist and anti-imperialist actions of a rebellious proletariat which has not been held back by its own conservatism.

Here we have examples of the operation of the Marxist law of uneven and combined development. This law states that, in order to break out of their misery and catch up with the more progressive sectors, historically backward peoples and classes are often obliged to take over the most up-to-date ideas and achievements, act upon them, and thereby for a time rush ahead of their predecessors.

Mills mistakenly maintains that the revolutions in the underdeveloped countries have been primarily anti-feudal. It is true that feudal survivals, because of their extreme oppressiveness, provoke the most violent explosions among the colonial peoples. From this fact it is easy to draw the conclusion, as Mills does, that the colonial revolution is primarily antifeudal in character. But this is an extremely superficial view.

The vestiges of feudalism in backward lands long ago ceased to have any independent character or significance. In extending its sway over the entire globe, capitalism incorporated the survivals of earlier modes of exploitation into its own system. Today they are inextricably intertwined. Hence, while the colonial peoples place great emphasis on the fight against 'feudalism', this is but a single aspect of their struggles. Fundamentally, and in essence, the colonial revolution is directed against exploitation by foreign and domestic capital which bars the colonial and semi-colonial peoples from the benefits of a modern economy and culture. The only way the Russians, Yugoslavs, Chinese and Cubans could gain access to these advantages was by knocking down capitalism and taking the road to socialism.

That is why the world socialist revolution in this first stage has conquered in the colonial and semi-colonial regions and is progressing from there toward the most advanced capitalist countries of Europe and North America. The fact that the proletariat, at the head of the peasantry, had to take power in the poorer countries, while imperialism retained its grip upon the more productive ones, has created tremendous practical difficulties for the socialist forces and introduced grave distortions into their regimes. But these problems, too, have been illuminated by Marxist theory.

What is the sociological character of the regimes that have issued from the great revolutions of our time in Russia, Yugoslavia, China and most recently in Cuba? Does Soviet society, despite its defects, hold a place in the historical progression of humanity superior to that of the capitalist regimes, whatever their formal democracy? Can its planned economy be more productive and efficient than capitalist economy?

From Mills' book we can learn what Lenin, Stalin, Trotsky, Hilferding, Kautsky, Mao Tse-tung and G.D.H. Cole think on these not unimportant matters. But, except for a few remarks on the bureaucratic character of the Soviet superstate, we cannot tell how Mills defines its social-historical nature.

Mills says that contemporary Marxists face the necessity of elaborating theories to explain the diverse types of Soviet-bloc societies. But beyond posing a series of questions about the prospects of de-Stalinization under Khrushchev, he refrains from telling us his views. He evidently had still to work out his solutions to these perplexing sociological problems.

Yet contemporary Marxism is not so impoverished or embarrassed in this field as he implies. The movement of the Fourth International has formulated and published views on all these questions, proceeding from Trotsky's analysis of the reasons for the degeneration of the Soviet state under Stalin and indicating the sources of its regeneration through the extension of the international revolution, the advances of Soviet economy and culture, and the political revitalization of its working masses.

But much as he esteemed Trotsky, Mills could not adopt his conclusions. He remained equally resistant to the Marxism of the nineteenth and of the twentieth centuries.

Through Mills we can observe the left flank of American liberalism undergoing a process of negation and dissolution. His thinking was a mass of contradictions. Repelled by the decay of liberalism and its apology for capitalist reaction and militarism, he nevertheless adhered to its fundamental pragmatic method of approach to the major social processes of our epoch. He was attracted by socialism but could not accept its scientific doctrine. He was a partisan of the Latin-American revolution who had no faith in a North American revolution. He opposed the autocracy of the Power Elite and aspired to a rebirth of democracy in our country. But he despaired of the capacities of the working people to clear the way for its realization.

Such an extremely awkward theoretical and political posture could not have been maintained for long. How these inconsistencies would have been resolved and his positions finally crystallized no one can say. But the example of his inquiring mind and courageous stands should inspire others among the New Left to go farther and cast off, not only the compromising policies of liberalism, but its false theories and methods in sociology and politics as well.

Mills won enduring honor for his impassioned defense of the Cuban Revolution. He saw in the young Cuban rebels a model for the New Left of the post-Stalin generation. He was not wrong. But while he was writing off Marxism as obsolete and Utopian, the *Fidelistas* were going forward from abstract humanism to Marxism and from bourgeois-democratic to explicit proletarian-socialist aims. As 'Che' Guevara told K.S. Karol: 'We are not the same men we were when we fought in the Sierra Maestra. I have always been a student of Marx. But now I realize that Marxism is not simply a doctrine – it is a science'. (*New Statesman*, May 19, 1961).

This postscript, written by the Cuban revolutionists to *Listen, Yankee*, is an ironic refutation of the skepticism about scientific socialism expressed in *The Marxists*. The Cuban experience will not be confined to Latin America. It prefigures the future on the whole Western hemisphere. The banner of Marxism and the socialist revolution today flying over Havana will yet be unfurled on the shores of North America.

Bibliography

Alexander, Robert J. 1991, *International Trotskyism, 1929–1985: A Documented Analysis of the Movement*, Durham, NC: Duke University Press.
Allen, Naomi and Sarah Lovell (eds) 1987, *A Tribute to George Breitman: Writer, Organizer, Revolutionary*, New York: Fourth Internationalist Tendency.
Allen, Robert L. 1983, *The Reluctant Reformers: The Impact of Racism on American Social Reform Movements*, Washington, DC: Howard University Press.
Allen, Robert L. 1990, *Black Awakening in Capitalist America*, Trenton, NJ: Africa World Press.
Anderson, Jervis A. 1986, *A. Philip Randolph: A Biographical Portrait*, Berkeley, CA: University of California Press.
Aronowitz, Stanley 2012, *Taking It Big: C. Wright Mills and the Making of Political Intellectuals*, New York: Columbia University Press.
Bair, Deidre 1990, *Simone de Beauvoir: A Biography*, New York: Simone and Schuster.
Baker, Melba 1962, 'Women Who Work', *International Socialist Review*, Summer.
Barnes, Jack 1999, *For a Workers' and Farmers Government in the United States*, New York: Pathfinder Press.
Barnes, Jack 2002, *Their Trotsky and Ours: Communist Continuity Today*, New York: Pathfinder Press.
Bell, Daniel 1976, *The Coming of Post-Industrial Society: A Venture in Social Forecasting*, New York: Harper and Row.
Belden, Jack 1970, *China Shakes the World*, New York: Monthly Review Press.
Benton, Gregor 2016, *Prophets Unarmed: Chinese Trotskyists in Revolution, War, Jail and Return from Limbo*, Chicago: Haymarket Books.
Berch, Bettina 1988, *Radical By Design: The Life and Style of Elizabeth Hawes*, New York: E.P. Dutton.
Blake, Jean 1954, 'The Continuing Struggle For Negro Equality: Will Supreme Court Ruling End Segregation?', *Fourth International*, Summer.
Bloom, Alexander and Wini Breines (eds) 2003, *Takin' It to the Streets: A Sixties Reader*, New York: Oxford University Press.
Bracey, John H. Jr., August Meier, and Elliott Rudwick (eds) 1970, *Black Nationalism in America*, Indianapolis, IN: Bobbs-Merrill Co.
Braden, Anne 1965, 'The Southern Freedom Movement in Perspective', *Monthly Review*, July–August.
Branch, Taylor 1988, *Parting the Waters: America in the King Years, 1954–63*, New York: Simon & Schuster.
Breitman, George 1953, 'How Stalinism Will Be Ended', *Militant*, June 29.
Breitman, George 1964, 'How a Minority Can Change Society', *International Socialist Review*, Spring.

Breitman, George 1965a, 'Malcolm X: The Man and His Ideas', *Militant*, March 22 and 29.
Breitman, George 1965b, *Marxism and the Negro Struggle*, New York: Pathfinder Press.
Breitman, George 1970, *The Last Year of Malcolm X: The Evolution of a Revolutionary*, New York: Pathfinder Press.
Breitman, George 1971, *The New Radicalization Compared with Those of the Past*, New York: Pathfinder Press (originally published in *International Socialist Review*, October 1970).
Breitman, George 1986, 'Introduction', *Don't Strangle the Party*, New York: Fourth Internationalist Tendency, online: https://www.marxists.org/history/etol/document/fit/dontstrangle.htm (accessed 22 June 2016).
Breitman, George (ed.) 1994, *Malcolm X Speaks*, New York: Grove Press.
Breitman, George and Joseph Hansen 1964, 'Exchange of Views on Deutscher Biography', *International Socialist Review*, Summer.
Breitman, George, Paul Le Blanc, and Alan Wald 2016, *Trotskyism in the United States: Historical Essays and Reconsiderations*, Chicago: Haymarket Books.
Brick, Howard and Christopher Phelps 2015, *Radicalism in America: The US Left*, Cambridge: Cambridge University Press.
Briffault, Robert 1927, *The Mothers: A Study of The Origins of Sentiments and Institutions*, 3 vols., New York: The Macmillan.
Bulletin in Defense of Marxism 1985, 'George Lavan Weissman (1916–1985), 49 Years in the Struggle for Socialism', at Marxist Internet Archive: https://www.marxists.org/history/etol/document/fit/viitoix.htm#section5 (accessed 22 June 2016).
Camejo, Peter 2010, *North Star: A Memoir*, Chicago: Haymarket Books.
Cannon, James P. 1953, 'Happy Birthday, Arne Swabeck!', *Militant*, September 21, online: https://www.marxists.org/archive/cannon/works/1953/hbaswab.htm (accessed 22 June 2016).
Cannon, James P. 1954, 'Trotsky or Deutscher? On the New Revisionism and Its Theoretical Source', *Fourth International*, Winter.
Cannon, James P. 1955, 'Engels on the American Question', Marxist Internet Archive, https://www.marxists.org/archive/cannon/works/1955/canonengonam.htm (accessed 17 May 2016).
Cannon, James P. 1958. *United Socialist Political Action in 1958*, New York: Pioneer Publishers.
Cannon, James P. 1960 'Trotsky on America', *International Socialist Review*, Fall, 21, no. 4.
Cannon, James P. 1973a, *Notebook of an Agitator*, New York: Pathfinder Press.
Cannon, James P. 1973b, *Speeches to the Party*, New York: Pathfinder Press.
Cannon, James P. 1983, *Don't Strangle the Party*, New York: Fourth Internationalist Tendency.
Cannon, James P. 1992, 'Intellectuals and Revolution', *Bulletin in Defense of Marxism*, October–November.

Cannon, James P. 1994, 'The Triple Revolution: Developing a Transitional Program for the Late 20th Century', *Bulletin in Defense of Marxism*, January.
Cantwell, Robert 1996, *When We Were Good: The Folk Revival*, Cambridge, MA: Harvard University Press.
Carlson, Grace 1944, 'The Myth of Racial Superiority', *Fourth International*, January.
Carson, Clayborne 1981, *In Struggle: SNCC and the Black Awakening of the 1960s*, Cambridge, MA: Harvard University Press.
Caute, David 2013, *Isaac and Isaiah: The Covert Punishment of a Cold War Heretic*, New Haven, CT: Yale University Press.
Charters, Ann (ed.) 1992, *The Portable Beat Reader*, New York: Penguin Books.
Clark, Steve and Paul Mailhot 1995, 'Bob DesVerney: Four Decades in the Fight for Communism, A Life to Emulate', *Militant*, November 13, available at: http://www.themilitant.com/1995/5942/5942_21.html
Coser, Lewis 1954, 'Sects and Sectarians', *Dissent*, Autumn, 1, no. 4.
Cowley, Joyce 1955, 'Women Who Won the Right to Vote', *Fourth International*, Spring.
Davidson, Basil 1978, *Let Freedom Come: Africa in Modern History*, Boston: Little Brown and Co.
D'Emilio, John 2003, *The Lost Prophet: The Life and Times of Bayard Rustin*, Chicago: University of Chicago Press.
Deutscher, Isaac 1967, *Stalin: A Political Biography*, second edition, New York: Oxford University Press.
Deutscher, Isaac 1968, *The Non-Jewish Jew and Other Essays*, New York: Oxford University Press.
Deutscher, Isaac 1970, *Russia, China, and the West, 1953–1966*, edited by Fred Halliday, London: Oxford University Press.
Deutscher, Isaac 2015, *The Prophet: The Life of Leon Trotsky*, London: Verso.
Dillard, Angela D. 2010, *Faith in the City: Preaching Radical Social Change in Detroit*, Ann Arbor: University of Michigan Press.
Dobbs, Farrell and Joseph Hansen 1963, 'Reunification of the Fourth International', *International Socialist Review*, Fall.
Duberman, Martin 2011, *The Saving Remnant: The Radical Lives of Barbara Deming and David McReynolds*, New York: The New Press.
Durham, Sukey and Melba Windoffer 1978, 'Sukey Durham Talks with Melba Windoffer', at the Freedom Socialist Party site, http://socialism.com/drupal-6.8/articles/sukey-durham-talks-melba-windoffer (accessed 22 June 2016).
Edwards, Theodore 1963, 'Kennedy's War in Vietnam', *International Socialist Review*, Summer.
Edwards, Theodore 1997, 'Myra Tanner Weiss (1917–1997)', *Against the Current*, November–December, https://www.solidarity-us.org/node/1984 (accessed 22 June 2016).
Elbaum, Max 2002, *Revolution in the Air: Sixties Radicals Turn to Lenin, Mao and Che*, London: Verso.

Evans, Leslie 2009, *Outsider's Reverie: A Memoir*, Los Angeles: Boyana Books.

Evans, Les and Russell Block (eds) 1976, *Leon Trotsky on China*, New York: Pathfinder Press.

Fairbank, John K. and Merle Goldman 2006, *China: A New History*, Cambridge, MA: Harvard University Press.

Farber, Samuel 2006, *The Origins of the Cuban Revolution*, Chapel Hill, NC: University of North Carolina Press.

Farrell, James J. 1997, *The Spirit of the Sixties: The Making of Postwar Radicalism*, New York: Routledge.

Ferry, W.H. et al. 1964, 'The Triple Revolution', in *Seeds of Liberation*, edited by Paul Goodman, New York: George Braziller.

Fitzgerald, Frank T. 1994, *The Cuban Revolution in Crisis: From Managing Socialism to Managing Survival*, New York: Monthly Review Press.

Flexner, Eleanor 1968, *Century of Struggle: The Women's Rights Movement in the United States*, New York: Atheneum.

Frank, Pierre 1979, *The Fourth International: The Long March of the Trotskyists*, London: Ink Links.

Frankel, Harry 1947, 'Three Conceptions of Jacksonianism', *Fourth International*, March.

Freedom Socialist Party 1993, 'Melba Windoffer, 1910–1993', *Freedom Socialist*, December, http://www.socialism.com/drupal-6.8/articles/melba-windoffer-1910-1993 (accessed 22 June 2016).

Fried, Albert 1996, *McCarthyism, The Great American Red Scare: A Documentary History*, New York: Oxford University Press.

Frieden, Jeffry A. 2006, *Global Capitalism: Its Fall and Rise in the Twentieth Century*, New York: W.W. Norton.

Garrow, David J. 1988, *Bearing the Cross: Martin Luther King, Jr. and the Southern Christian Leadership Conference*, New York: Vintage Books.

Georgakas, Dan 1992, 'Introduction', *Notebook of a Sixties Lawyer*, by Michael Steven Smith, Brooklyn, NY: Smyrna Press.

Gerassi, John 1963, *The Great Fear in Latin America*, New York: Macmillan Co.

Goldstein, Robert Justin 2001, *Political Repression in Modern American, from 1870 to 1976*, Urbana, IL: University of Illinois Press.

Goldstein, Robert Justin 2016, *Discrediting the Red Scare: The Cold War Trials of James Kutcher, 'The Legless Veteran'*, Lawrence, KS: University Press of Kansas.

Goodman, Paul (ed.) 1964, *Seeds of Liberation*, New York: George Braziller.

Gordon, David M., Richard Edwards, and Michael Reich 1982, *Segmented Work, Divided Workers: The Historical Transformation of Labor in the United States*, Cambridge: Cambridge University Press.

Gorman, William 1950, 'W.E.B. Du Bois and His Work', *Fourth International*, May–June.

Gorz, André 1982, *Farewell to the Working Class: An Essay on Post-Industrial Socialism*, Boston: South End Press.
Gosse, Van 2005, *Rethinking the New Left: An Interpretive History*, New York: Palgrave Macmillan.
Grant, Hedda 1962, 'Still a Man's World', *International Socialist Review*, Spring.
Grant, Joanne (ed.) 1996, *Black Protest*, New York: Fawcett Columbine.
Grey, V. 1957, 'China, Hungary, and the Marxist Method' (excerpt), *SWP Discussion Bulletin*, May.
Griswald, Deidre 1998, 'Some Aspects of Sam Marcy's Life', on the Workers World Party website, http://www.workers.org/marcy/cd/samtrib/marcybio.htm (accessed 22 June 2016).
Guerin, Daniel 1956, *Negroes on the March: A Frenchman's Report on the American Negro Struggle*, London: Grange Publications.
Habel, Janette 1991, *Cuba: The Revolution in Peril*, London: Verso.
Halstead, Fred 1962, 'The Jackson Freedom Ride', *International Socialist Review*, Spring.
Halstead, Fred 1978, *Out Now! A Participant's Account of the American Movement Against the Vietnam War*, New York: Monad Press/Pathfinder Press.
Hansen, Joseph 1945, 'Hayek Pleads for Capitalism', *Fourth International*, June.
Hansen, Joseph 1960, 'Deutscher's Life of Trotsky', *International Socialist Review*, Winter.
Hansen, Joseph 1961, 'Theory of the Cuban Revolution', *International Socialist Review*, Winter.
Hansen, Joseph 1964, 'Deutscher on Trotsky', *International Socialist Review*, Winter.
Hansen, Joseph 1974, *The Workers and Farmers Government*, edited by Fred Feldman, New York: Socialist Workers Party Education for Socialists Bulletin, April, https://www.marxists.org/history/etol/document/swp-us/education/1974-04-apr-Workers-and-Farmers-Government-EfS.pdf (accessed 6 July 2016).
Hansen, Joseph 1979, *Dynamics of the Cuban Revolution*, New York: Pathfinder Press.
Harrington, Michael 1973, *Fragments of a Century: A Social Autobiography*, New York: E.P. Dutton and Co.
Hawes, Elizabeth 1938, *Fashion is Spinach*, New York: Random House.
Hawes, Elizabeth 1943, *Why Women Cry, or Wenches with Wrenches*, New York: Reynal and Hitchcock.
Hawes, Elizabeth 1954, *It's Still Spinach*, Boston: Little Brown and Co.
Hirson, Baruch 2003, *Frank Glass: The Restless Revolutionary*, London: Porcupine Press.
Horowitz, David (ed.) 1971, *Isaac Deutscher: The Man and His Work*, London: Macdonald and Co.
Horowitz, Daniel 1998, *Betty Friedan and the Making of* The Feminine Mystique*: The American Left, the Cold War, and Modern Feminism*, Amherst: University of Massachusetts Press.
Howe, Irving 1981, 'The Boss' (Review of Milovan Djilas, *Tito: The Story from Inside*), *New York Review of Books*, January 22.

Huberman, Leo and Paul M. Sweezy 1969, *Socialism in Cuba*, New York: Monthly Review Press.
Hudis, Peter 2015, *Frantz Fanon: Philosopher of the Barricades*, London: Pluto Press.
Hugins, Walter E. 1960, *Jacksonian Democracy and the Working Class: A Study of the New York Workingmen's Movement, 1829–1837*, Stanford, CA: Stanford University Press.
Inman, Mary 1941, *In Woman's Defense*, Los Angeles, CA: Committee to Organize the Advancement of Women.
International Bolshevik Tendency 1997, 'Myra Tanner Weiss, 1917–1997: A Life in Struggle', http://www.bolshevik.org/1917/no2omtw1.pdf (accessed 22 June 2016).
International Communist League/Spartacists 1994, 'In Memoriam of Richard S. Fraser: An Appreciation of His Work', https://www.marxists.org/history/etol/document/icl-spartacists/prs3-fraser (accessed 30 July 2016).
Isaacs, Harold R. 2010, *The Tragedy of the Chinese Revolution*, Chicago: Haymarket Books.
Isserman, Maurice 1987, *If I Had a Hammer ...: The Death of the Old Left and the Birth of the New Left*, New York: Basic Books.
James, Frances 1960, 'Africa's Bid for Freedom', *International Socialist Review*, Spring.
Jamison, Andrew and Ron Eyerman 1995, *Seeds of the Sixties*, Berkeley, CA: University of California Press.
Jezer, Marty 1982, *The Dark Ages: Life in the United States 1945–1960*, Boston: South End Press.
Karnow, Stanley 1972, *Mao and China: Inside China's Revolution*, New York: Viking Press.
Karnow, Stanley 1997, *Vietnam: A History*, revised edition, New York: Penguin/Viking Books.
Karol, K.S. 1970, *Guerrillas in Power*, New York: Hill and Wang.
Kerry, Tom 1964, 'Maoism and the Neo-Stalin Cult', *International Socialist Review*, Spring.
Kirk, Richard 1963, 'Revolutionary Integrationism', *SWP Discussion Bulletin*, June.
Kirk, Richard and Clara Kaye 1965, 'Radical Laborism versus Bolshevik Leadership: The Organization Problem of the SWP', *SWP Discussion Bulletin*, 25/14.
Kovacs, Edmund 2000, 'The Weiss Group', the Weiss current in the SWP, made available through a site operated by Louis Proyect, http://lists.csbs.utah.edu/pipermail/marxism/2000-October/043492.html (accessed 22 June 2016),
Kutcher, James 1973, *The Case of the Legless Veteran*, New York: Pathfinder Press.
Lambert, Bruce 1993, 'Vincent Copeland, 77, is Dead; Led Anti-War Protests in the 1960s', *New York Times*, June 10, http://www.nytimes.com/1993/06/10/obituaries/vincent-copeland-77-is-dead-led-anti-war-protests-in-1960-s.html (accessed 22 June 2016).
Lavan, George (ed.) 1968, *Che Guevara Speaks*, New York: Grove Press.
Le Blanc, Paul (ed.) 1992, *In Defense of American Trotskyism: Revolutionary Principles and Working-Class Democracy*, New York: Fourth Internationalist Tendency, https://

www.marxists.org/history/etol/document/fit/revprinindex.htm (accessed 28 June 2016).

Le Blanc, Paul 2005, 'Writer, Organizer, Revolutionary: The Life and Legacy of George Breitman', in *Malcolm X and the Third American Revolution: The Writings of George Breitman*, edited by Anthony Marcus, Amherst, NY: Humanity Books.

Le Blanc, Paul 2007, 'On the Origins of the Cuban Revolution', *Against the Current*, January–February, https://www.solidarity-us.org/node/319 (accessed 22 June 2016).

Le Blanc, Paul 2015, *Leon Trotsky*, London: Reaktion Books.

Le Blanc, Paul 2016, *From Marx to Gramsci: A Reader in Revolutionary Marxist Politics*, Chicago: Haymarket Books.

Le Blanc, Paul (ed.) 2017, *Black Liberation and the American Dream*, Chicago: Haymarket Books.

Le Blanc, Paul and Michael Steven Smith 2000, 'Morris Lewit: Pioneer Leader of American Trotskyism (1901–1998)', in *Revolutionary Labor Socialist: The Life, Ideas, and Comrades of Frank Lovell*, edited by Paul Le Blanc and Thomas Barrett (Bias), Union City, NJ: Smyrna Press.

Le Blanc, Paul and Michael Yates 2013, *A Freedom Budget for All Americans*, New York: Monthly Review Press.

Lee, Paul 2002, 'Contributions of George Breitman', *Labor Standard*, http://www.laborstandard.org/Paul_Lee_on_MX/contributions_of_george_breitman.htm (accessed 16 June 2016).

Lenin, V.I. 2008, *'Left-Wing' Communism, An Infantile Disorder*, in *Revolution, Democracy, Socialism: Selected Writings*, edited by Paul Le Blanc, London: Pluto Press.

Lipsitz, George 1990, *Time Passages: Collective Memory and American Popular Culture*, Minneapolis: University of Minnesota Press.

Lovell, Frank 2000, 'Cecil Glass', in *Revolutionary Labor Socialist: The Life, Ideas, and Comrades of Frank Lovell*, edited by Paul Le Blanc and Thomas Barrett (Bias), Union City, NJ: Smyrna Press.

Lovell, Sarah (ed.) 1992, *In Defense of American Trotskyism: The Struggle Inside the Socialist Workers Party 1979–1983*, New York: Fourth Internationalist Tendency, https://www.marxists.org/history/etol/document/fit/struggleindex.htm (accessed 28 June 2016).

Lubitz, Wolfgang and Petra Lubitz 2004a, 'Joseph Hansen: Bio-Bibliographical Sketch', Lubitz' Trotskyana.Net, http://www.trotskyana.net/Trotskyists/Bio-Bibliographies/bio-bibl_hansen_j.pdf (accessed 22 June 2016).

Lubitz, Wolfgang and Petra Lubitz 2004b, 'Evelyn Reed: Bio-Bibliographical Sketch', Lubitz' Trotskyana.Net, http://www.trotskyana.net/Trotskyists/Bio-Bibliographies/bio-bibl_reed.pdf (accessed 22 June 2016).

Lubitz, Wolfgang and Petra Lubitz 2016, 'John G. Wright: Bio-Bibliographical Sketch', Lubitz' Trotskyana.Net, http://www.trotskyana.net/Trotskyists/Bio-Bibliographies/bio-bibl_reed.pdf (accessed 6 August 2016).

Malraux, André 1934, *Man's Fate*, New York: Modern Library.

Marable, Manning 2007, *Race, Reform, and Rebellion: The Second Reconstruction and Beyond in Black America, 1945–2006*, Jackson: University of Mississippi Press.

Marcus, Anthony (ed.) 2005, *Malcolm X and the Third American Revolution: The Writings of George Breitman*, Amherst, NY: Humanity Books.

Marcy, Sam 1953, 'The Global Class War and the Destiny of American Labor', *Internal Bulletin*, May.

Marcy, Sam 1996, 'Pages in My Life', in *A Tribute to Sam Marcy*, October 5, http://www.docfoc.com/sam-marcy-85th-birthday-journal (accessed 22 June 2016).

Marx, Karl 1972, *Capital: A Critical Analysis of Capitalist Production*, Volume 1, New York: International.

Mason, Paul 2016, *Postcapitalism: A Guide to Our Future*, New York: Farrar, Straus, and Giroux.

McGowan, Marjorie, Jeanne Morgan, and Joseph Hansen 1954, 'Debate on Cosmetics', *Discussion Bulletin*, October.

Meier, August and Elliott Rudwick 1972, *CORE: A Study in the Civil Rights Movement, 1942–1968*, New York: Oxford University Press.

Moody, Kim 2007, *US Labor in Trouble and Transition*, London: Verso.

Morgan, Ted 2004, *Reds: McCarthyism in the Twentieth Century*, New York: Random House.

Mullen, Bill V. 2016, *W.E.B. Du Bois: Revolutionary Across the Color Line*, London: Pluto Press.

New York Times 1981, 'Murry Weiss Dies, 66; a Marxist Theoretician', December 30 (accessed 22 June 2016).

Noble, David F. 1986, *The Forces of Production: A Social History of Industrial Automation*, New York: Oxford University Press.

Novack, George 1965a, *Origins of Materialism*, New York: Merit Publishers.

Novack, George (ed.) 1965b, *Existentialism versus Marxism: Two Conflicting Views on Humanism*, New York: Delta.

Novack, George 1971, *Introduction to the Logic of Marxism*, New York: Pathfinder Press.

Novack, George 1975, *Pragmatism versus Marxism*, New York: Pathfinder Press.

Novack, George 1978, *Polemics in Marxist Philosophy*, New York: Pathfinder Press.

Palmer, Bryan D. 1999, 'Before Braverman: Harry Frankel and the American Workers' Movement', *Monthly Review*, 50, January.

Pells, Richard H. 1985, *The Liberal Mind in a Conservative Age: American Intellectuals in the 1940s and 1950s*, New York: Harper and Row.

Peng Shu-tse 1980, *The Chinese Communist Party in Power*, New York: Pathfinder Press.

Pessen, Edward 1967, *Most Uncommon Jacksonians: Radical Leaders of the Early Labor Movement*, Albany: SUNY Press.

Phelps, Christopher 2002, 'Introducing Arne Swabeck', *Against the Current*, January–February, https://www.solidarity-us.org/node/1307 (accessed 22 June 2016).

Quinn, Patrick M. 1995, 'Hedda Garza, 1929–1995', *Against the Current*, November–December, https://www.solidarity-us.org/node/2565 (accessed 22 June 2016).
Reed, Evelyn 1954, 'The Myth of Women's Inferiority', *Fourth International*, Spring.
Reed, Evelyn 1964, 'The Feminine Mystique', *International Socialist Review*, Winter.
Robertson, James 1957, 'New Stage for the Youth', *International Socialist Review*, Fall.
Robertson, James 1964, 'The Centrism of the SWP', *Internal Information Bulletin*, January.
Robertson, James 1986, 'James P. Cannon Memorial Meeting', *Spartacist*, 38–39, Summer, http://www.regroupment.org/main/page_robertson_on_cannon.html (accessed 1 August 2016).
Robins, Harold 1955, 'Automation – Menace or Promise? The Unions Face a Crucial Problem', *Fourth International*, Spring.
Rousset, Pierre 2009, 'People's Republic of China at 60: 1925–1949 – Origins of the Chinese Revolution', *Links*, http://links.org.au/node/1268 (accessed 17 July 2015); 'People's Republic of China at 60: 1949–1969: Maoism and Popular Power', *Links*, http://links.org.au/node/1269 (accessed 17 July 2015).
Sale, Kirkpatrick 1973, *SDS*, New York: Random House.
Sanders, Lois 1959, 'The South's Dilemma', *International Socialist Review*, Winter.
Schneir, Miriam (ed.) 1972, *Feminism: The Essential Historical Writings*, New York: Vintage Books.
Schneir, Miriam (ed.) 1994, *Feminism in Our Time: The Essential Writings, World War II to the Present*, New York: Vintage Books.
Schrecker, Ellen W. 1998, *Many Are the Crimes: McCarthysim in America*, Boston: Little, Brown and Co.
Schwartz, Benjamin I. 1951, *Chinese Communism and the Rise of Mao*, Cambridge, MA: Harvard University Press.
Sell, Evelyn 1958, 'Really Beat?', *International Socialist Review*, Summer.
Sexton, Patricia Cayo 1991, *The War on Labor and the Left: Understanding America's Unique Conservatism*, Boulder, CO: Westview Press.
Shaikin, Harley 1985, *Work Transformed: Automation and Labor in the Computer Age*, New York: Holt and Rinehart.
Sheppard, Barry 2004, *The Party: A Political Memoir; The Socialist Workers Party 1960–1988, Volume 1: The Sixties*, Chippendale, Australia: Resistance Books.
Sheppard, Barry 2012, *The Party, The Socialist Workers Party 1960–1988, Volume II: Interregnum, Decline and Collapse, 1973–1988, A Political Memoir*, London: Resistance Books.
Simon, Jean 1952, 'Tom Paine – Revolutionist', *Fourth International*, March–April.
Snow, Edgar 1962, *The Other Side of the River: Red China Today*, New York: Random House.
Snow, Edgar 1994, *Red Star Over China*, New York: Grove Press.

Socialist Workers Party Political Committee 1963, 'Preparing for the Next Wave of Radicalism in the United States', *Internal Bulletin*, May.

Socialist Workers Party 1963, 'Freedom Now: The New Stage in the Struggle for Negro Emancipation and the Tasks of the SWP', *International Socialist Review*, Fall.

Socialist Workers Party National Committee 1965, 'The Organizational Character of the SWP', *SWP Discussion Bulletin*, January.

Srnicek, Nick and Alex Williams 2015, *Inventing the Future: Postcapitalism and a World Without Work*, London: Verso.

Starobin, Joseph R. 1972, *American Communism in Crisis: 1943–1957*, Cambridge, MA: Harvard University Press.

Stone, Ben 1978, *Memoirs of a Radical Rank and Filer*, New York, Prometheus Press.

Stone, I.F. 1969, *The Haunted Fifties*, New York: Vintage Books.

Stutje, Jan Willem 2009, *Ernest Mandel: A Rebel's Dream Deferred*, London: Verso.

Sugrue, Thomas J. 2008, *Sweet Land of Liberty: The Forgotten Struggle for Civil Rights in the North*, New York: Random House.

Swabeck, Arne and John Liang (Frank Glass) 1962, 'The Chinese Revolution – Its Character and Development', *SWP Discussion Bulletin*, March.

Tanner, Myra 1954, 'Sternberg vs. Karl Marx', *Fourth International*, Winter.

Thomas, Robert M. 1997, 'Myra T. Weiss, 80: Radical Who Ran Quixotic Campaigns', *New York Times*, September 20, http://www.nytimes.com/1997/09/20/us/myra-t-weiss-80-radical-who-ran-quixotic-campaigns.html (accessed 22 June 2016).

Thomas, Robert M. Jr. 1998, 'Sam Marcy, Marxist Writer, Dies at 86', *New York Times*, February 9, http://www.nytimes.com/1998/02/09/nyregion/sam-marcy-marxist-writer-dies-at-86.html (accessed 22 June 2016).

Trotsky, Leon 1994, *Leon Trotsky on Black Nationalism and Self-Determination*, edited by George Breitman, New York: Pathfinder Press.

Vernon, Robert 1963, 'Why White Radicals Are Incapable of Understanding Black Nationalism', *SWP Discussion Bulletin*, April.

Wang Fan-hsi 1991, *Memoirs of a Chinese Revolution, 1919–1949*, New York: Columba University Press.

Warde, William F. 1949a, 'A Suppressed Chapter in History of American Capitalism', *Fourth International*, January.

Warde, William F. 1949b, 'The Destruction of Indian Communal Democracy', *Fourth International*, April.

Warde, William F. 1957, *The Irregular Movement of History: The Marxist Law of the Combined and Uneven Development of History*, London: New Park.

Warde, William F. 1962, 'C. Wright Mills' *The Marxists*', *International Socialist Review*, Summer.

Weigand, Kate 2001, *Red Feminism: American Communism and the Making of Women's Liberation* Baltimore: Johns Hopkins University Press.

Weiss, Murry 1954, 'McCarthyism: Key Issue in the 1954 Elections After the Army-McCarthy Hearings', *Fourth International*, Summer.

Weiss, Murry 1956, 'The Vindication of Trotskyism: Khrushchev's Report on Stalin's Crimes', *Fourth International*, Summer.

Weiss, Myra Tanner 1962, 'Kennedy: The Candidate and the President', *International Socialist Review*, Winter.

Wilentz, Sean 1984, *Chants Democratic: New York City and the Rise of the American Working Class*, New York: Oxford University Press.

Williams, Guy 1973, *The YSA: How It Began*, New York: Bulletin Publications.

Wilson, William Julius 1997, *When Work Disappears: The World of the New Urban Poor*, New York: Vintage Books.

Wohlforth, Tim 1959, 'Youth Report to the SWP National Convention', *SWP Discussion Bulletin*, September.

Wohlforth, Tim 1962, 'Summing Up for Minority on World Movement', *SWP Discussion Bulletin*, December.

Wohlforth, Tim 1994, *The Prophet's Children: Travels on the American Left*, Atlantic Highlands, NJ: Humanities Press.

Wohlforth, Tim et al. 1963, 'Call for the Reorganization of the Minority Tendency', *SWP Discussion Bulletin*, April.

Wright, John G. 1956, 'Feuerbach – Philosopher of Materialism', *International Socialist Review*, Fall.

Wright, Richard 2008, *Black Power: Three Books from Exile*, New York: HarperCollins.

Index

Abenaki Indians   583
Abern, Martin   451, 518n22, 519, 521
Abernathy, Ralph D.   285, 293
abolitionists (opponents of slavery)   347, 540, 571, 572, 573, 600, 603, 640–1, 642–4, 647–9
Adams, James Truslow   617
Adams, John   616
Adams, Samuel   610, 617, 618
advertising   70, 76–7, 82, 121, 249, 251, 252, 267, 331
  See also Madison Avenue
Advertising Age   267
Africa   46, 51, 55, 59, 62, 239, 247, 303, 328, 383, 399, 481, 541, 542, 545, 602, 627, 682
  divisions: religious, tribal, cultural, linguistic   157
  imperialist oppression, exploitation, manipulation   156, 157–8, 159, 347, 539, 578
  influence on African American struggles   320, 322, 329, 331, 333–4, 339, 345, 400
  liberation struggles in   21, 139, 153–60, 176, 231, 239, 335, 352, 355, 367, 383, 407, 489, 683
  Malcolm X and Africa   270, 397, 398, 401
  shifts from "tribalism" to urbanization   154, 158, 159
Africa Digest (London)   154
The Age of Jackson (Schlesinger)   569, 573
The Age of Reason (Paine)   615, 616
Agger, Donald G.   144n11
agricultural revolution (neolithic revolution)   53
Akikuyus (East Africans)   59
Alexander, Robert J.   1
Alinsky, Saul   263
Allen, James   604
Almeida, Juan   334
Almond, J. Lindsay   279, 281, 282
Alvin, Milt   418
American Anti-Slavery Society   642, 643
American Century   139, 337
An American Dilemma (Myrdal)   595, 606

American Indians (Native-Americans, First Nations)   47, 55, 56, 58, 345, 541, 546, 548–9, 576–93, 612
America's Sixty Families (Lundberg)   181
American Federation of Labor (AFL)   257, 360, 361, 429, 602
American Federation of Labor-Congress of Industrial Organizations (AFL-CIO)   198, 212, 257, 301, 302, 683
American Federation of Teachers (AFT)   282, 284
American Revolution (1775–83)   367, 368, 537, 608, 610–13, 614, 618, 629, 639
American Socialist   115, 116, 536
American Theses   441–2, 451
American Woman Suffrage Association   649
American Workers Party   440
anarchists, anarchism, anarcho-syndicalists   117, 125
Angola   158
Anthony, Susan B.   641, 646, 649, 650, 651
anti-Communism   21–22, 163, 168, 225
anti-Semitism   35, 108, 331, 385, 563
Apache Indians   586, 590
Apithy, Sourou-Migan   156
Appeal to Reason   137
Arabs   541
Argentina   238
aristocracy   576, 591, 615
Aravaipa Apache Indians   583
Armstrong, Donald B.   144n11
Asia   26, 46, 55, 58, 228, 239, 270, 303, 381, 406–7, 481, 539, 541, 577, 580, 627, 675
  and Chinese Revolution   153, 489, 499
  and Vietnam (and Indochinese) wars   220, 221, 225, 227, 410
  liberation struggles in   21, 139, 231, 322, 335, 347, 355, 407
As Long as the Grass Shall Grow (Lafarge)   578
Australia   47–8, 58, 548
Australian aborigines   548
Austria   424, 560
automation and cybernation   89–99, 143–147, 210, 256, 258–60, 266, 358, 362, 433, 678

Automotive Industries 96
Aztec Indians 541, 580

Bakango people at the mouth of the Congo River 159
Baldwin, Hanson W. 227
Baldwin, James 16, 326, 327, 353, 376
Baltimore Afro-American 291–2
Bancroft, George 585–6
Banda, Hastings 159
Bao Dai 223
Barbaria, Frank 137
Barber, J. Max 601
Barlow, Joel 611
Barnes, Jack 141n5, 464
Bartell, Mike 520
Batista, Fulgencio 161, 165, 166, 167, 173, 235
Beals, Carlton 466–7n15
Beard, Charles A. 566, 569, 574, 576, 595, 597, 603, 605, 617
Beard, Mary 576, 603
Beat Generation ("beatniks") 23, 119–129
Belgium 241, 676
Bell, Daniel 145
Ben Bella, Ahmed 235, 239
Berger, Victor 137, 257
Bernstein, Eduard 507, 594, 634
Better Homes and Gardens 82
The Bible Defense of History (Priest) 540
The Big Sea (Hughes) 603
Bill of Rights 25, 530, 653
Billings, Warren K. 137
Binet, Alfred 546, 547
Bishop, Eliza 656
Black, Hugo 29
Black Bourgeoisie (Frazier) 331n13
Black Muslims. *See* Nation of Islam
Black Muslims in America (Lincoln) 332n14
Black liberation and civil rights struggles
  gains and victories 360–1
  See also racism
black nationalism and self-determination 264–5, 273, 274, 316–46, 385–7, 401, 404
  black nationalism defined 353–4, 399–400
  and black separatism 319, 329, 344, 353, 399
  challenged (revolutionary integrationism) 373–89

Blackwell, Henry 646
Blake, Jean 21, 25–32
Bleeker, Sylvia 22–3
Blood, Fanny 656
Boggs, James 23, 144n11
Bolshevik-Leninist. *See* Left Opposition
Bolshevism and Bolsheviks 5, 103, 106, 107, 109, 111, 137, 380, 381, 405, 422, 423, 441, 451, 468, 469, 495, 508, 512, 530, 602, 630, 669–71
  distortion of 117, 232, 428–35, 452, 504, 638
  hostility toward 452, 510, 635, 638, 684
  qualities of 6, 109, 171, 174–5, 258, 380, 530
  role in the Russian Revolution 167, 172–3, 176, 258, 310, 503, 634, 684
  Stalinist repression against 101
Bonaparte, Napoleon 616
Bonapartism 623, 624
Bonnevine, Marguerite 614
Bonnevine, Nicolas 616
Boston Guardian 596, 601
bourgeois (bourgeois-democratic) revolution 158, 170, 173, 404, 496, 497, 617, 687
bourgeois ideology 75, 572
Braverman, Harry 536, 537, 566–75
Brazil 238
Brecht, Bertolt 10
Breitman, Dorothea 6, 9
Breitman, George 1, 6–11, 13, 15, 16, 17, 140, 272, 273, 274, 298–315, 390–402, 461, 464, 465, 483–8, 517, 536, 537, 538, 620–4
Briffault, Robert 44
Brisbane, Albert 573
Britain 90, 156, 176, 221, 222, 232, 235, 241, 460, 540, 565, 585, 616, 627, 628, 633, 636, 652
Britton, Joel 531
Brockett, L.P. 645, 646
Broun, Heywood 265
Browder, Earl 386, 511
Brown, John 9, 599–600, 604, 606
Brown, Elmer 293
Brownell, Herbert 38
Bryan, William Jennings 568
Bukharin, Nikolai 108, 461, 508, 510, 511, 515

bureaucracy   1, 23, 238, 416, 417, 423, 446, 452, 453, 458, 472, 490, 509, 625, 670
  as parasitic caste   104, 230, 474, 622–3
  in China   498, 504
  in Communist movement   109–110, 240–1, 470, 515, 516
  in labor movement   37, 40–2, 97, 107, 113, 173, 187, 189, 205, 211, 212, 215, 218, 230, 265–6, 348, 351, 360, 361–2, 375, 379, 409, 442, 466, 507, 509, 513, 632, 676
  in Soviet Union (and Soviet Bloc)   103, 104, 106–7, 108, 109, 110, 111, 140, 171, 206–7, 220, 230, 240, 409, 413, 419, 442, 460, 473, 475, 483, 484, 499, 500, 505, 509, 511, 516, 538, 620–2, 623, 624, 686
bureaucratic collectivism   440, 478
bureaucratic conservatism   499
Burke, Edmund   614, 615, 616, 617
Burnett, Constance   647–8
Burnham, James   14n26, 436, 440, 451, 478, 518n22, 552, 557
Burns, Lucy   653, 654
Byrd, Harry F.   27, 283
Byrnes, James F.   27

cadres   12, 13, 142, 150, 204, 216, 217, 219, 237, 436, 438, 439, 440, 442, 458, 474n16, 480, 510, 518
Calhoun, John C.   572
Cambodia   226
Camejo, Peter   13, 14, 15, 17
Camus, Albert   480
Canada, Canadians   92, 94, 221, 242, 481, 581, 642, 682
Cannon, James P.   5–6, 9, 12, 13, 14, 19, 24, 67, 142–3, 144, 145–6, 147, 233, 235, 403, 421, 422, 423, 433, 437, 441, 461, 463–4, 465, 515, 536, 538
  criticized   410–2
  on regroupment   130–8
  on restrictions of party democracy   517–32
  on Triple Revolution   255–71
Capital (Marx)   78, 89n15, 609, 631, 633, 662
capitalism   1, 3, 8, 14, 16, 19, 23, 25, 147, 178, 191, 241–2, 298–9, 533–34, 550–65
  1 percent dominates 99 percent   300
  60 families dominate US capitalism (ruling oligarchy)   562

  achievements and benefits   19, 21n1, 66, 67, 68, 103, 171, 524, 559, 561
  commodity fetishism, consumerism   72, 77–9, 81, 82, 84, 87, 88, 174, 249–50
  cycles of economic booms (prosperity) and crises (depressions)   41, 142–3, 157, 200, 209, 435
  exploitation of labor   4, 8, 60, 135, 188, 192, 210, 214, 261, 278, 310, 408, 491, 536, 561, 572, 582, 588, 630, 632, 633, 656, 657, 676, 685
  gender inequality and oppression   43, 71, 82, 183–192
  imperialism, war and violence   30, 41, 155, 157, 158, 159, 160, 176, 204, 207, 253, 500, 539, 553, 629, 633, 676, 677, 685
  racism   8, 21n2, 25–32, 261, 299, 300, 304–5, 330–1, 351, 352, 355, 357, 358, 359, 361, 365, 366, 382, 534, 539–49, 683
  the state under capitalism   25, 38, 135, 136, 141, 177, 199, 200, 204, 211, 212, 213, 285, 299, 363, 364, 561
  strength in United States   21, 21n1, 82, 131, 132, 142–3, 241, 245, 412, 677
  unemployment under   30, 72, 98, 120, 145, 156, 157, 198–9, 453, 559, 562, 594, 633, 656
Capitalism and Socialism on Trial (Sternberg)   537, 635–38
capitalist libertarianism   550–565
Carlisle, Fred   506
Carlson, Grace   74, 533, 537, 539–49
Carnegie, Andrew   597–8
Castro, Fidel (and Castroism, *Fidelistas*)   16, 19, 126, 141, 164, 165, 167, 168, 169, 170, 174, 177, 194, 233, 234, 235, 238, 240, 334, 354, 377, 399, 415, 423n8, 416, 464, 498, 667, 687
Catt, Carrie Chapman   641
Center for the Study of Democratic Institutions   143, 256
Central America   93, 541
Central Intelligence Agency (CIA)   35, 194, 220, 221
centrism, centrists   233, 404, 418, 420–7, 433, 434, 444, 507
  defined   424, 434
"The Centrism of the SWP" (Robertson)   404, 420–5

INDEX 703

Ceylon (Sri Lanka)   239
Chalmers, George   616
Chamber of Commerce   550, 564
Chapple, Eliot D.   48
Che Guevara Speaks (Weissman)   140, 536
Cheetham, James   616
Chen Tu-hsiu (Chen Duxiu)   508
Cherokee Indians   587–8
Chevrolet   90, 259
Cheyenne Indians   583
Chiang Kai-Shek   100, 235, 354, 461, 489, 490, 508
Chicano   17, 18
Childe, V. Gordon   48, 50, 52, 53, 56, 62, 64
China   30, 51, 100, 102, 153, 157, 160, 166, 206, 221, 223, 236, 238, 240, 310, 354, 403, 406, 409, 417, 418, 431, 443, 461–2n4, 462n5, 481, 475, 489–501, 502–16, 531, 541, 628, 668, 672, 677, 685, 686
  Chinese Revolution (1925–27)   461, 489, 508
  Chinese Revolution (1949)   100, 153, 175, 176, 231, 239, 413, 461, 462, 475, 489, 495, 497
  Chinese-Soviet dispute (Moscow-Peking dispute)   207, 228, 230, 231, 238, 499, 500, 503, 504, 505
  Chinese Trotskyists   461, 508
  See also Chiang Kai-shek; Communist Party, in China; Kuomintang; Mao Zedong (Mao Tse-tung); Maoism
Chou Yang   502–3
Christ   541, 542
Churchill, Winston   643, 678
Civil War (U.S., 1861–65)   276, 280, 307, 336, 367, 368, 381, 536, 567, 574, 585, 586, 588, 594, 598, 599, 603, 604, 606, 648, 652
Civil War in France (Marx)   468
Clarke, George   421, 626, 637
The Class Struggle in France (Marx)   468
Clay, Henry   574
Cleage, Rev. Albert   9, 16, 305
coalitionism (political worker-capitalist alliance)   507–8
Cochran, Bert and Cochran group   1, 6, 403, 421, 428, 429, 432, 433, 436, 442, 451, 483, 487, 536, 638
Cohn, Roy M.   35

Cold War   14, 21, 131, 143, 157, 158, 160, 221, 228, 250, 348, 358, 390, 442, 460, 465, 535, 669, 677, 682
Cole, G.D.H.   670
collectivism   552, 553, 557, 558, 563
Collier, John   592
Columbus, Christopher   582, 592
"The Coming American Revolution" (Cannon)   421
The Coming of Post-Industrial Society (Bell)   145
Comintern. *See* Communist International
Committee to Aid the Monroe Defendants   431
Common Sense (Paine)   608, 610–11, 617
Communist International (Third International, Comintern)   110, 112, 140, 149, 174, 385–6, 470, 479, 451, 461, 507, 508, 510, 511, 512, 515, 523, 525, 623
Communist League of America   272, 386
Communist Manifesto (Marx and Engels)   84, 134, 523
Communist Party   312, 403, 440, 452, 504
  in China   461, 462, 489, 490, 508
  in Cuba   163, 164, 168, 170, 173
  in France   219, 221, 241
  in Germany   470
  in Soviet Union   100, 101, 206
  in the United States   109–10, 112, 113, 114, 170–1, 176, 199, 204, 215, 217, 255, 264, 299, 328, 336, 340, 355, 370, 377, 379, 422, 483, 485, 504, 506, 513–5, 518, 521, 523
  in Vietnam   220
Communist Party Opposition (Lovestone group)   1
Conant, James Bryant   576, 577, 579
Congo   53, 154–9, 333
Congress of Industrial Organizations, Committee for Industrial Organization (CIO)   29, 89, 93, 95, 96, 97, 263, 264, 265, 312, 336, 337, 360, 361, 368, 377, 384, 432, 441
Congress of Racial Equality (CORE)   273, 287, 288, 289, 290, 291, 292, 293, 295, 296, 297, 350, 351
Connor, Theophilus Eugene (Bull)   288, 289, 290
conscientious objectors   125

conservatives, conservatism (political ideology) 9, 23, 38, 132, 145, 170, 215, 253, 258, 280, 281, 302, 576, 615, 669
Constitution of the United States of America 21, 25, 276–7, 595, 639, 648, 650
Continental Congress 612
Coolidge, Calvin 602
Coon, Carlton S. 48
Cortés (Cortez), Hernán 592
Coser, Lewis 3–4, 5, 6, 16
cosmetics and cosmetics industry 23, 65–88
Mrs. Cosu (suffragist) 654
The Cotton Kingdom (Dodd) 574
Coughlin, Father Charles Edward 564
Cowley, Joyce 537, 639–57
Cox, B. Elton 297
Cox, Oliver C. 381
The Crisis (NAACP periodical) 601, 605
The Crisis (Paine) 611–2
The Critique of Political Economy (Marx) 675
Cross, Lonnie 343
Cruse, Harold 16
Cuba 126, 193, 194, 201, 207, 208, 213, 218, 230, 233, 235, 237, 334, 335, 338, 415, 416, 417, 419, 421, 428, 431, 433, 443, 498, 666, 667, 668, 670
  revolution in 16, 140, 141, 153, 161–79, 206, 211, 217, 231, 234, 236, 238–9, 240, 242, 306, 339, 355, 404, 405, 422, 423, 475, 499, 535, 666, 683, 685, 686, 687
  workers' state 230, 231, 234
Cuba – Anatomy of a Revolution (Huberman and Sweezy) 161, 165–71, 174, 176
Curtice, Harlow H. 97n18

Dahomey (Benin) 156, 158
Daily Worker 109
Dakota Indians 548
Dante Alighieri 468
Darwin, Charles. *See* Social Darwinism
Daumier, Honoré 10
Davis, Edward 333
Davis, Ossie 273
Day, Dorothy 654
Dean, James 120
De Beauvoir, Simone 7, 18, 141, 142n7, 180–2
Deck, Bert 417

Debs, Eugene V. 10, 134, 135, 137, 138, 391, 416, 537, 558, 601
Declaration of Independence (1776) 539, 611, 618, 649
De Gaulle, Charles 678, 679
democracy, democratic struggles 116, 126, 147, 157, 161, 163, 165, 170, 171, 178, 194, 210, 218, 225, 240, 302, 303, 306, 310, 349, 365, 366, 373, 374, 376, 397, 404, 491, 493, 496, 549, 576, 588, 589, 610, 614, 618, 623, 656, 683, 686
  bourgeois (capitalist) democracy 25, 26, 30, 136, 156, 157, 172, 173, 204, 205, 225, 306, 359, 365, 376, 452, 497, 500, 535, 539, 549, 551, 552, 566–75, 588, 597, 607, 638, 671, 676, 679, 680, 686, 687
  democracy in revolutionary party 107, 206, 230, 429, 438, 446, 448, 449, 450, 453, 454, 460, 505–6, 516, 525–6, 530–1
  democracy in unions 212, 218, 360
  proletarian (workers') and socialist democracy 1, 18, 101, 103, 140, 148, 163, 177–8, 182, 204, 230, 240, 310, 369, 422, 460, 466, 473, 474, 475, 498, 509, 511, 538, 622, 624, 636, 668
democratic centralism 206, 230–1, 234, 236, 436–7, 438, 439, 440–1, 442, 444, 449, 450, 451, 453, 459, 505, 515–6, 530–1
De Leon, Daniel 107
Democratic Party 29, 33, 34, 35, 36, 37, 38, 39, 40, 98, 109, 134, 141, 168, 195, 196, 197, 205, 211, 213, 214, 215, 217, 258, 273, 280, 285, 302, 309, 344, 347, 361, 363, 364, 422, 570, 571, 573, 600, 648, 654, 682
Dennis, Eugene 109
Derrick, Christopher 613–4
Des Verney (Vernon), Robert 274, 316–46
Detroit: I Do Mind Dying (Georgakas and Surkin) 10
Deutscher, Isaac 417, 460, 461, 466–88, 538, 620–4, 625, 638
  The Prophet Armed 461, 470
  The Prophet Outcast 461, 466–82, 483
  The Prophet Unarmed 461, 470
  Russia in Transition 417
  Russia: What Next? 484
Dewey, John 534, 597, 601, 605

INDEX

Dewey Commission   467n15, 534
dialectics, dialectical materialism   3, 14–5n26, 105, 231, 235, 237, 376, 432, 435, 438, 452, 468, 534–5, 553, 659, 664, 671–3, 674
   problematical version   502, 508–9
Diamond, A.S.   48
dictatorship of the proletariat as political rule by the working class   140, 174, 204, 312, 313, 364, 503, 533, 561, 604, 607
   See also democracy: proletarian (workers') and socialist democracy; workers' state
Dillard, Angela   9–10
Dobbs, Farrell   12, 13, 14, 137, 141, 142, 229–43, 403, 405, 428, 436–59, 463, 464, 465, 529, 532
   criticisms of   428, 431, 432–3, 463, 464
Dominican Republic   238
"Don't Strangle the Party" (Cannon)   465, 517–32
Douglas, William O.   29
Douglass, Frederick   596, 599, 600, 641, 644, 649
Dred Scott decision   25
dual unionism   388
Du Bois, William Edward Burghardt   139n3, 272, 533, 537, 594–607
   Black Folk, Then and Now (1939)   541
   Black Reconstruction in America (1935)   599, 600, 603–5, 607
   Dusk of Dawn (1940)   594, 601
   John Brown (1909)   599–600
   Philadelphia Negro (1899)   595, 597
   Souls of Black Folk (1903)   596, 598, 607
   Suppression of the African Slave Trade (1896)   595
Dulles, John Foster   114
Dunayevskaya, Raya   1
Dunlop, Miss Wallace (suffragist)   653
Dunne, Vincent Raymond   5, 13
Duquesne (Michel-Ange Du Quesne de Menneville)   585
Durocher, Leo   523
Duvalier, François   238

East German workers uprising of 1953   113, 206
Eastland, James O.   27

Eastman, Max   557
Ebony   328
Economist (London)   153
Ecuador   238
Edwards, Theodore   142, 220–8
Egypt   51, 176, 541, 542
The Eighteenth Brumaire of Louis Bonaparte (Marx)   468
Eisenhower, Dwight David   35
Emmett Till case   377
Engels, Frederick   5, 14, 18, 45, 61, 80, 103, 104, 108, 135, 140, 167, 181, 184, 403, 451, 466, 502, 504, 523, 524, 538, 558, 577, 637, 638, 658, 659, 664, 665, 669, 675
Eskimos   55
Esquire   121, 125
The Essence of Christianity (Feuerbach)   659, 665
Ethiopia   541, 542, 604
Eugene V. Debs Speaks (Tussey)   537
Europe   5, 26, 46, 51, 87, 88, 93, 124, 154, 156, 158, 159, 201, 235, 247, 260, 303, 325, 379, 549, 543, 546, 597, 614, 627, 634, 636, 640, 655, 677, 678
   ancient and feudal development   51, 55, 540, 541, 544–5, 591–2, 672, 673
   colonial and imperialist expansion   159, 539, 540, 542, 576–8, 579, 582–3, 584, 588, 604
   democratic revolutions   158
   labor, the left, working-class and struggle   16, 40, 106, 202–3, 241, 406–7, 481, 510, 512, 552, 559, 563, 601, 604, 635, 681–2, 684, 686
European Economic Community   202
Evans, Jessie Angelina   284
Evans, Leslie   12, 13, 14, 145–6, 463–4
Evolutionary Socialism (Bernstein)   507
existentialism   7, 182, 534n1

Fair Play for Cuba Committee   431
Fanon, Franz   139n3
Farmer, James   273, 287, 291, 292, 295
farmer labor party   569
farmers   36, 45, 62, 212, 213, 214, 224, 330, 561, 566, 567, 568, 574, 575, 585, 587, 595, 605, 611

well-to-do (planters) 566, 567, 568, 569, 570, 571, 572, 574, 575, 585
poor 212, 330, 374
working-class allies 364, 374, 569
See also peasants, tenant farmers and sharecroppers
Farnham, Marya 245, 256
fascism 40, 72, 101, 104, 260, 470, 471, 472, 479, 481, 485, 512, 525, 533, 549, 552, 553, 554, 555, 564–5, 634, 681
McCarthyism perceived as incipient fascism 22, 33–42, 215, 422
See also Hitler, Mussolini, Nazism
Faubus, Orval E. 275, 276, 279, 280, 281, 282
Fein, Lois 144n11
The Feminine Mystique (Friedan) 18, 141, 244–54
feminism 7, 18, 22, 23, 141, 180–2, 244–54, 405, 537, 639–57
Ferguson, Adam 609, 617
Ferguson, Duncan 21n2
Ferlinghetti, Lawrence 124, 125
Ferry, W.H. 144n11
Feuerbach, Ludwig 538, 658–65
First International. *See* International Workingmen's Association
First Nations. *See* Indians
The First Ten Years of American Communism (Cannon) 526
Five for Freedom (Burnett) 647–8
Flanders, Ralph 35
Flexner, Eleanor 22
Fontaine, W.T. 607
Ford, Ebenezer 570
Ford, Henry 256, 562
Fortune 97
Foster, Stephen 648
Foster, William Z. (and Fosterites) 386, 506, 507, 508, 510, 511, 514, 515, 516
Fourth International 11, 12n20, 229–43, 423, 461, 476–80, 486, 487, 515, 522, 529n26, 686
as World Party of Socialist Revolution 229
founding 149, 257, 460, 478, 481, 484, 488, 533, 537
fragmentation and factional struggle 142, 231–7, 404, 421, 533, 625
International Committee (fragment of Fourth International) 229, 231, 234, 235–6, 426
International Secretariat (fragment of Fourth International) 229, 231, 234, 235, 404
re-unification 11, 229–43, 423–5
United Secretariat 229
Fourth International 484, 625
Fourth Internationalist Tendency 465, 517
France 21n2, 77, 81, 176, 195, 221, 232, 241, 468, 479, 585, 611, 613, 614, 615, 616, 617, 628, 659
Franco, Francisco 104
Frank, Pierre 142n8, 233
Frankel, Harry. *See* Harry Braverman
Franklin, Benjamin 609, 613
Frankfurter, Felix 29
Fraser, Clara 1, 23, 142n7, 405, 428–35, 462
Fraser, Richard S. 1, 142n7, 274, 373–89, 404, 405, 428–35, 462, 519
Frazer, Sir James 47
Frazier, E. Franklin 331, 378, 381
Freedom Now Party 8, 9, 273, 274, 299, 300, 301, 302, 303, 305, 309, 364, 372, 394, 397, 431
Freedom Now: The New State in the Struggle for Negro Emancipation (1963) 16, 274, 347–72
Freedom Rides 242, 287–97, 317, 324, 325, 371
Freedom Socialist Party 142n7, 405
Freeman, William F. 96
Frieden, Jeffry 146
French Revolution (1789–94) 271, 614, 615–6
Freud, Sigmund, and Freudianism 181, 248, 253, 578
Friday Night Socialist Forum (Detroit) 9, 10
Friedan, Betty 18, 141, 142n7, 244–54
Fuller, Alex 302, 303
Fund for the Republic 143, 256

Gaither, Tom 293
Gandhi, Mohandas and Gandhism 323, 343, 350, 351
Also see pacifism
Miss Garnett (suffragist) 653
Garrison, William Lloyd 603, 641, 644, 649

INDEX 707

Garvey, Marcus (and Garvey movement) 301, 334, 384, 385–6, 391, 602–3
Garza, Hedda 141, 142n7, 180–2
Gates, John 422
Geismer, Maxwell 144n11
Gemmill, Henry 227–8
Georgakas, Dan 10, 11
Germain. *See* Ernest Mandel
The German Ideology (Marx and Engels) 598–9
Germany 37, 40, 90, 159, 241, 335, 337, 423, 435, 470, 512, 513, 540, 543, 544, 552, 553, 555, 556, 557, 561, 563, 594, 598, 606, 626, 631, 634, 635, 658, 660
    East 93, 104, 113, 206, 624
    West 93
Ghana 158, 159, 169, 176, 399, 400
Ginsberg, Allen 120, 121, 124
Gitlin, Todd 144n11
Gold, Herbert 127
"The Global Class War and the Destiny of American Labor" (Marcy) 403, 406–12
Goldenweiser, Alexander 44
Goldman, Albert 532
Goldwater, Barry 258, 261
Gompers, Samuel 257, 601
Gordon, Doug 517
Gordon, Rosemary 517
Gorman, William 533, 594–619
Gorz, André 23n8, 24
Gray, Jesse 16
Great Depression (1929–39) 104, 200, 262–3, 312, 358, 506, 510, 533, 634
Gregory, Dick 317
Greece 542, 672, 673
Green, Philip 144n11
Green, William 257
Greene, Nathaniel 612
Griffin, Marvin 279
Grimke, Angelina 643
Grimke, Sarah 643
Guinea 156, 159, 160, 399
Guerin, Daniel 21n2, 387
guerrilla struggles 173, 223, 224, 226–8, 230, 238, 490
Guevara, Ernesto (Che) 16, 140, 170, 174, 399, 536, 670, 687

Gunther, John 154
Guomindang. *See* Kuomintang
Gypsies. *See* Roma

Hacker, Louis M. 569
Hagan, Roger 144n11
Haiti 238, 592
Halberstam, David 289–90
Haldane, J.B.S. 540, 541
Halleck, Henry 586
Hallinan, Vincent 137
Halstead, Fred 13, 18, 273, 287–97
Hamilton, Mary 292
Hansen, Bill 293
Hansen, Joseph 12n20, 13, 23, 65–88, 140, 142, 161–179, 229–43, 461, 466–82, 483–88, 538, 550–65
Hansen, Reba 528
Hare, Lloyd C. M. 645
Harer, Asher 255
Harlem 264, 265, 269, 306, 325, 331, 333, 334, 338, 377, 384, 391, 393, 397
Harpers Magazine 81
Harriman, Job 137
Harrington, Michael 144n11, 145, 259
Hauser, Arnold 124, 125
Mrs. Haverfield (suffragist) 653
Hawes, Elizabeth 22
Hayden, Tom 144n11
Hayek, Friedrich A. 538, 550–65
Haywood, William (Big Bill) 257
Healy, Gerry 231, 233, 234–6, 237, 404, 443, 531, 532
Hegel, G.W.F. 73, 658–9, 660, 663, 664, 665
Heilbroner, Robert L. 144n11
Heine, Heinrich 468
Hendrix, Bill 28
Heredity and Politics (Haldane) 540
Herodotus 542
Herring, Frances 144n11
Herzen, Alexander 468
Hester, Hugh B. 144n11
Hilferding, Rudolf 686
Hill, Herbert 261
Hillquit, Morris 137
Hillman, Sidney 29
Hilton, Alice Mary 144n11
Hiroshima 128, 233, 527

Hiss, Alger   29
History of Civil Society (Ferguson, 1750)   609
History of the Communist Party of the United States (Foster)   514
The History of New England, 1691–1776 (Adams)   617
The History of the Russian Revolution (Trotsky)   468, 488
History of Tammany Hall (Myers)   570
Hitchcock, George   137
Hitler, Adolf   36, 101, 104, 163, 225, 245, 288, 470, 512, 513, 539, 543, 563, 635
   See also fascism, Nazism
Ho Chi Minh   221, 226, 228
Holmes, John Clellon   120, 121, 123, 127
Hollingsworth, Leta   547
Hollywood   85, 87, 132, 251
The Holy Family (Marx and Engels)   659
Hoover, Herbert   676
House Un-American Activities Committee   163
Howe, Irving   14n25, 144n11
Howe, Julia Ward   649
Howl (Ginsberg)   121
Huberman, Leo   161, 162, 165–76
Hughes, Charles Evans   276
Hughes, Everett C.   144n11
Hughes, H. Stuart   144n11
Hughes, Langston   603
Hungary (uprising of 1956)   113, 126–7, 150, 206, 403, 413–4, 474n6, 483

immigrants, immigration   22, 325, 337, 346, 588, 597, 645
Imperialism, the Highest State of Capitalism (Lenin)   628–30
In Defense of Marxism (Trotsky)   140n4, 150, 413, 518n22
Independent Socialist League (ISL)   11, 118
Independent Socialist Party   422
India   176, 221, 239, 247, 627, 672
Indians of the Americas (Collier)   592
The Indians of the United States (Wissler)   589
Indochina (Vietnam, Laos, Cambodia)   30
Indonesia   93, 239
Industrial Workers of the World (IWW, Wobblies)   125, 255, 256, 257, 292, 337, 464n5, 523, 596, 601, 666

Inghram, Louise   295
Inman, Mary   22
the Inquisition   555
Instruments and Automation   94
Intercontinental Press   12n20
International Brotherhood of Teamsters   13, 212, 261, 268, 432, 463
International Confederation of Free Trade Unions (ICFTU)   160
International Ladies Garment Workers Union (ILGWU)   189
International Workingmen's Association (IWA, First International)   604
intersectionality (interconnections of class, racial, gender, sexual and other forms of oppression)   8, 17, 16, 69, 70, 185, 244, 272, 311–4, 326, 365, 657, 683–4
Iron Age   90, 91, 92, 93, 95
Iroquois Indian confederation   585
The Irregular Movement of History: The Marxist Law of the Combined and Uneven Development of Society (Warde/Novack)   534–5
Italy   37, 40, 229, 241, 479, 486, 552, 553, 555, 604
IWW. *See* Industrial Workers of the World

Jackson, Andrew   536, 566–75
Jacobins   615
Jamaica   385, 592
James, C. L. R.   1, 272, 274, 314, 537
James, Frances   23, 139, 153–60
Japan   93, 127, 220, 239, 247, 260, 335, 461, 486, 489, 490, 495, 680
jazz   120, 122, 123, 127, 603
Jefferson, Thomas   568, 572, 613, 614, 616
Jet   295
Jews   102, 184, 280, 325, 331, 335, 337, 539, 540, 557, 563
Jim Crow (racist segregation and oppression)   26, 30, 72, 85, 215, 277, 278, 284, 285, 297, 336, 339, 343, 349, 350, 356, 357, 359, 683
   See also African Americans, racism, segregation
Jimenez, A. Nunez   334
Johnson, Gerald W.   144n11
Johnson, J.R. *See* C.L.R. James
Johnson, James Weldon   381

INDEX

Johnson, Lyndon B.   522
Johnson-Forest Tendency   537
Jones, Leroi   374
Jones, Robert L.   35
Jordan, Joan   137

Kahlo, Frida   467n15
Kant, Immanuel   660, 663, 664
Kardelj, Edvard   670
Karol, K.S.   687
Kautsky, Karl   507, 630, 686
Kelly, Abby   643
Kendall, Amos   573
Kennedy, John F.   141, 142, 143–203, 207,
    208, 209, 210, 212, 214, 215, 220–8, 238,
    239, 287, 295, 307, 330, 349, 350, 374,
    678
  Assassination   395, 434
Kennedy, Robert F.   194289, 291–2, 294, 295
Kenny, Jessie   653
Kenya   154, 155, 159, 367, 383
Kerouac, Jack   120, 124, 127
Kerry, Tom   13, 403, 405, 462, 463, 464, 465,
    502–16, 517
  criticisms of   428, 431, 432–3, 463, 464
Khrushchev, Nikita   240, 335, 502, 503, 504,
    505, 509, 670, 686
  report on Stalin   24, 100–111, 112, 113, 114,
    116, 150, 163, 206, 503, 506, 509
Kikuyu people (Kenya)   383
kill-ratios   225–6, 227
King, Martin Luther   173, 285, 289, 291, 295–
    6, 299–300, 301, 305, 333, 334–5, 350,
    351
King Philip's War (1675–1678)   583
Kipling, Rudyard   540–1
Kirov, Sergei   101
Klineberg, Otto   545, 546, 547, 548
Knights of Labor   523
Konikow, Antoinette   74, 75, 79, 80
Korea   30, 242, 489, 499
Korean War   131, 206, 252, 409, 410, 411, 433
Kovacs, Edmund. *See* Theodore Edwards
Krock, Arthur   227
Kugelmass, A. Newton   549
Ku Klux Klan (KKK)   27, 28, 261, 277, 301,
    356, 604
Kuomintang   489, 490, 491, 496, 497, 508
Kutcher, James   22

Labor and Monopoly Capital (Braverman)
    536
labor-Democratic coalition   205, 214, 215
  See also coalitionism; Democratic Party
labor party   72, 85, 78, 214, 216, 218, 285, 309,
    344, 362, 364, 376, 429, 430, 520, 682
Labor's Daily   34
Labor Youth League (LYL)   113, 115, 116, 117
Laclau, Ernesto   24
Lafarge, Oliver   578, 583
Lafayette, Gilbert du Motier   614, 615
Lambert, Jean-Pierre   404
Laos   226
Laski, Harold   602
The Last Year of Malcolm X (Breitman)   273
Laucks, Irving F.   144n11
Lee, Paul   8
Lee, Robert E.   34
Left Opposition   107, 108, 511, 523, 534
  in United States   204, 440, 515, 518, 519
Left-Wing Communism, An Infantile Disorder
    (Lenin)   4–5, 510
Leggett, William   573
Lenin, Vladimir Ilyich   4, 103, 104, 108–9,
    140, 171, 172, 257, 319, 329, 394, 403, 406,
    407, 411, 418, 423, 480, 493, 498, 499,
    502, 509, 510, 512, 513, 577, 558, 577, 627,
    637, 638, 684, 686
  leader of Russian Revolution   101, 173,
    258, 310, 311, 408, 635
  Lenin's "testament"
  democratic orientation   140, 240, 258,
    311, 460, 514, 530
  on imperialism   499, 628–9, 630, 637,
    667
  on philosophy   664–5
  on self-determination of oppressed
    nations   269, 380
  on the state   508
  revolutionary party   106, 107, 310, 436,
    437–9, 441, 450, 451–2, 507, 635
  relationship to Luxemburg   109
  relationship to Stalin   104, 107, 109, 167,
    446, 460, 504, 516
  relationship with Trotsky   14–5, 16, 107,
    109, 240, 311, 408, 441, 466, 523, 530,
    670
Leninism   14, 19, 107, 171, 237, 240, 386,
    411, 423, 432, 436, 437, 451, 503, 504

See also Bolshevism and Bolsheviks; democratic centralism; revolutionary party; Russian Revolution
Letters from Prison (Cannon)   532n27
Lewis, Jean   291
Lewis, John L.   263
Lewis, Mrs. (suffragist)   654
Lewit, Morris   463, 464
liberals, liberalism (political ideology)   33, 34, 40, 42, 109, 112, 114, 131, 132, 143, 156, 170, 197, 200, 214, 215, 218, 225, 247, 253, 265, 273, 286, 302, 303, 306, 309, 310, 323, 324, 328, 335, 337, 339, 340, 341, 343, 347, 348, 350, 352, 360, 361, 365, 366, 367, 378, 396, 517n21, 552, 558, 563, 564, 566, 568, 571, 573, 575, 576, 589, 590, 594, 598, 599, 600, 602, 603, 604, 607, 616, 617, 669, 670, 671, 675, 676, 677, 686, 687
Liberation magazine   292
Liberia   602
Lie, Trygve   471
Liebknecht, Karl   109, 149, 558
Mrs. Leigh (suffragist)   653
Life magazine   21, 120, 125, 267
Lincoln, Abraham   308
Lincoln, C. Eric   332
Lincoln, Miss (suffragist)   654
Listen Yankee (Mills)   161, 162–5, 535, 687
Lloyd George, David   653
Locke, Alain   381
Los Angeles Times   225
Lovell, Frank   6, 9, 11
Lovell, Sarah   6, 9
Lovestone, Jay   1, 510, 511, 514
Lovestoneites   1, 506, 514
Lowie, Robert H.   53
Lowry, John   293
Lundberg, Ferdinand   181, 245
Luxemburg, Rosa   109, 386, 558, 659
Lynes, Russell   81–4
Lyons, Eugene   557
Lytton, Constance   653

MacCall, William   658
MacDonald, Ramsey   602
Machiavelli, Nicolo   468
Madison Avenue (advertising, marketing, commercialism)   121, 122, 249, 329
Madison, James   611, 614
Mage, Shane   424, 443, 444
Mahoney, William   292
Mailer, Norman   127
Malaya   224, 239
Mali   156
Malcolm X   8, 9, 13, 16, 18, 140, 270, 273, 274, 290–402, 430, 536
Malcolm X Speaks (Breitman)   140, 273, 274
Mandel, Ernest   11, 142
   as Germain   233, 404
Mannheim, Karl   675
Mao Zedong (Mao Tse-tung)   173, 221, 240, 417, 461, 462, 493, 495, 496, 504, 505, 508, 535, 670, 686
Maoism   405, 462n5, 502–16
March on Washington Movement (1941)   301, 377, 601
Marcuse, Herbert   23
Marcy, Sam   1, 403, 406–12, 462
Marshall, John   276
Martinson, Robert   295
Marx, Karl   14, 16, 45, 77, 80, 89, 91, 103, 104, 108, 135, 140, 142, 167, 280, 310, 311, 319, 329, 399, 403, 451, 466, 468, 488, 502, 504, 523, 524, 527, 535, 537, 538, 558, 577, 598, 609, 629, 630, 631, 632–3, 634, 637, 638, 658–9, 662, 664, 665, 669–70, 671, 674–5, 684, 687
Marxism   15–6, 369, 669–87
Marxist-Leninist Quarterly   506
Mason, Otis Tufton   46–9, 50, 51, 55, 56, 59, 60, 61
Mason, Paul   147
Matriarchy   44, 64, 181
Matzkin, Norma   293
May, Samuel   642
Mayan Indians   541, 580
Mayfield, Julian   16
Mboya, Tom   155, 159, 160
McAvoy, Clifford   137
McCarthy, Joseph and McCarthyism   22, 29, 33–42, 120, 164, 215, 231, 241, 253, 422
McCrummel, James   642
McGowan, Marjorie   23, 65–9, 84–5
Meacham, Stewart   144n11

INDEX   711

Mead, Margaret   248
"Meet the Press" (NBC-TV program)   27
Menshevism and Mensheviks   109, 137, 310,
    508, 638
Mexico   124, 467n17, 528n26, 541, 592
middle class
    class   17, 36, 41, 67, 69, 123, 126, 127, 214,
        218, 244, 245, 246, 247, 252, 323, 330,
        348, 350, 358, 359, 378, 379, 413, 535,
        594, 596, 598, 603, 605
    politics/ideology   42, 112, 169, 173, 214,
        245, 350, 378, 379, 443, 605
    See also petty bourgeois
Mifflin, Thomas   613
Militant   12, 65, 73, 74, 84, 85, 103, 136,
    146, 267, 412, 421, 422, 426, 430, 484,
    515
Militant Labor Forum   398, 399
Mill and Factory   90, 91, 93, 95
Miller, John C.   617
Miller, Kelly   290
Millerand, Alexandre   507
Mills, C. Wright   23, 140, 161, 162–5, 169, 170,
    178, 535, 536, 666–8, 669–87
Minneapolis General Strike (1934)   13, 263,
    432
Minton, Sherman   29
Mississippi Freedom Democratic Party
    430
Mohegan Indians   590
Monroe, James   616
Monthly Review   114, 140, 165, 166, 171, 536
Moody, Kim   146–7
Morgan, Jeanne   23, 70–2, 75–6, 85
Morocco   160
Morris, Gouverneur   615
Morrow, Felix   532
Moscow Trials. *See* Stalinism
The Mothers (Briffault)   44
Mott, James   643, 644
Mott, Lucretia   641, 642, 643, 644, 645, 647,
    649
Mouffe, Chantal   24
Mozambique   159
Muhammad, Elijah   301, 351, 363, 392, 393,
    394–5, 396, 397
Munis, Grandizo   520
Murrow, Edward R.   258, 266
Mussolini, Benito   104

Muste, A.J.   114, 144n11
Musteites (American Workers Party)   163,
    164, 263, 264
Myers, Gustavus   570
Myrdal, Gunnar   144n11

Nagasaki   128, 233, 527
Nash (Bevel), Diane   289, 290, 305
Nation   119, 124, 295, 599, 600, 604
Nation's Business   189
Nation of Islam ("Black Muslims")   235, 323,
    325, 332n14, 343, 344, 345, 375, 384–5,
    392–96, 397, 399
National American Woman Suffrage Associ-
    ation   652
National Association for the Advancement of
    Colored People (NAACP)   26, 28, 30, 31,
    261, 291, 340, 350, 373, 377, 384, 388,
    599, 600–2, 605
National Civic Federation   601
National Coordinating Committee to End the
    War in Vietnam   517n21
National Farmers Organization (NFO)   213
National Guardian   115, 136, 137, 422, 430
National Liberation Front   228
    See also Viet Cong
National Woman's Party   654, 655
National Woman's Rights Association   644,
    649
Native Americans. *See* Indians
Nazism   36, 85, 245, 268, 471, 543, 551, 552,
    555–6, 557, 558, 563
    See also fascism, Hitler
Neff, Walter   547
Negro American Labor Council   301, 351,
    362
Negro Digest   606
Negroes. *See* Africans, African Americans
Negroes on the March (Guerin)   387
Nettels, Curtis   617
Neuschel, R.T.   93–4
The New Course (Trotsky)   531
New Deal   169, 205, 214, 264, 603, 605, 606–
    7, 638, 676
new left   139, 526–7, 535, 671, 687
New Left Review   535
New Masses   604
New Democratic Party   682
The New Reasoner   535

New Republic 604
New York Times 35, 193, 195, 196, 197, 220, 224, 227, 228, 294, 333, 410, 550, 552, 560, 564, 565
New York Herald Tribune 35, 93, 95, 96, 97, 223, 576
Newspaper Guild 265
Newsweek 222, 225
Ngo Dinh Diem 221–3, 224, 225, 226, 227, 228
Ngo Dinh Nhu 222, 223, 224
Nguyen Thau Bihh 225
Nicaragua 222
Nigeria 158, 160
Nixon, Richard M. 22, 214
Nkrumah, Kwame 159, 160
Nobody Knows My Name (Baldwin) 326, 328
Mrs. Nolan (suffragist) 654
North Vietnam 226, 228
Norway 471
Noske, Gustav 635
Novack, George 13, 23, 396, 405, 436–59, 464, 534, 535, 536, 538, 576–93, 666–8, 669–87
nuclear energy 50, 89, 96, 673, 674, 679
nuclear weapons 16, 21, 119, 120, 126, 128, 139, 143, 175, 193, 195, 207–8, 232, 233, 253, 306, 450, 479, 527–8, 607, 679
Nyasaland 156, 159

October Revolution. *See* Russian Revolution
Oehler, Hugo 1, 386
Oganesoff, Igor 223
Oldys, Francis. *See* George Chalmers
Olshausen, George 137
Omaha Indians 581
Ona Indians 54
On the Road (Kerouac) 120, 127
opportunism 233, 234, 235, 257, 312, 384, 404, 423, 424, 439–40, 489, 501, 504, 509
Organization of Afro-American Unity (OAAU) 397
"The Organizational Character of the Socialist Workers Party" (Dobbs and Novack) 405, 436–59
Orwell, George 114
The Other America (Harrington) 259

Out Now! A Participant's Account of the Movement Against the Vietnam War (Halstead) 18
Ovington, Mary White 601
Owen, Robert 570
Owen, Robert Dale 570

Pablo (Raptis), Michel and "Pabloites" 233, 404, 417–18, 421–2, 423, 426, 427, 461, 625, 626, 630, 635, 636, 637, 638
pacifism 211, 2114, 273, 306, 350, 599
Palmer, Bryan 533–8
Pan-African independence movement 155, 159
Pankhurst, Emmeline 653
Paris Commune (1871) 523
Parker, Charlie 120
Parrington, V. L. 569, 597, 605
Paul, Alice 653, 654, 655
Pauling, Linus 144n11
Paxson, F. L. 568
peace movement 211, 214, 215, 216, 217, 218, 233, 341, 430
peasants 159, 167, 230, 408, 493, 495, 596, 598–9, 671, 684
  China 461, 462, 475, 489, 490, 491, 492, 493, 494, 495, 496, 497, 498, 508
  Cuba 165, 167, 172, 173
  Latin America 238
  Russia/Soviet Union 102, 106, 108, 167, 172, 176, 258, 268–9, 311, 315, 504, 511, 622, 685–6
  kulaks (rich peasants) 108, 167, 493, 511
  middle 492, 493, 511
  poor peasants and agricultural laborers 492, 493, 511
  Vietnam 221, 222, 223–5, 226, 227, 228
  working-class allies 141, 165, 173, 174, 176, 178, 258, 268, 311, 387, 408, 492, 497, 685
  democratic dictatorship of the proletariat and the peasantry 165, 422
  See also farmers
Peck, James 287, 288
Peking Review 502
Pennsylvania Magazine (1775) 610
People's Front 173, 508, 513, 604

INDEX 713

permanent revolution   2, 109, 172, 310, 313, 404, 472, 475, 684
Peress, Irving   34
Peru   238, 592
Petrick, Howard   22n3
petty bourgeois
  characterization of 1939–40 opposition in SWP   431, 440–1, 518, 519, 532
  class   174, 269, 374, 378, 452, 481, 490, 550–1, 566, 568, 575
  ideology, politics   173, 174, 340, 354, 432, 452, 456, 563–5, 571, 575, 594, 599, 601, 625
  See also middle class
Piel, Gerald   144n11
Philippines   53
Phillips, Albert   443
Phillips, Wendell   641, 644, 649
Pittsburgh Courier   28
Pizzaro, Francisco   592
The Plague (*La Peste* – Camus)   480
Playboy   124, 125
Plekhanov, George   80, 81
Pliny   542
Poland   113, 150, 206, 221, 460, 681
Popular Front. *See* People's Front
Populists, Populist Party   568, 594
Posadas, Juan   231, 232, 233, 234, 236, 237
POUM (Partido Obrero de Unificación Marxista – Workers' Party of Marxist Unification)   5
Pound, Ezra   121
Powell, Adam Clayton   363
pragmatism (philosophical)   534, 671
prejudice (ethnic and racial). *See* racism
Priest, Josiah   540
Progressive Party   377, 520
Progressive Labor Movement   504–5
Progressive Labor Party   462n5, 517
Ptolemy   542
Puerto Rico   86, 188

Race Differences (Klineberg)   545
racism, race prejudice, racial chauvinism   4, 8, 17, 21, 35, 108, 124, 145, 242, 272, 276, 279, 284, 285, 287, 290, 291, 300, 301, 312, 321, 337, 339, 342, 344, 350, 351, 357, 359, 361, 362, 364, 365, 368, 369, 370, 374, 378, 382, 383, 385, 387, 388, 391, 396, 399, 401, 533, 534, 537, 540, 571, 589, 595, 604, 563
  essential to specifics of US capitalism   359
  socio-economic racism embedded in US capitalism   358
Raleigh, Walter   592
Randolph, A. Philip   273, 301, 351, 683
Randolph, John   530, 614
Reader's Digest   95
Reagan, Michael D.   144n11
Reconstruction: The Battle for Democracy (Allen)   604
Red Army (China)   495
Red Army (USSR)   101, 413
Reed, Evelyn   23, 43–64, 141, 244–54
Reed, Stanley Forman   29
Reflections on the Revolution in France (Burke)   614
regroupment on US left (late 1950s, early 1960s)   24, 113, 114, 115, 117, 118, 133, 139, 150, 151, 206, 217, 239, 417, 421, 422, 428, 430
Remond, Charles   643
Report on Automation (UAW-CIO)   89n17, 93, 95, 96, 97, 98
Report on an Investigation into the Peasant Movement in Hunan (Mao, 1927)   495
Reporter   123, 223, 226, 289, 295
Republican Party   22, 29, 33, 34, 35, 36, 37, 38, 39, 40, 135, 168, 197, 213, 258, 280, 285, 302, 309, 336, 363, 606, 648
Reuther, Walter   95, 97, 98, 212, 266, 351, 361
The Revolution Betrayed (Trotsky)   106, 472–3
Revolutionary Union Movement   10
Rexroth, Kenneth   124
Reynolds, Ike   293
Rhodesia   154, 155, 156, 159, 160
The Rights of Man (Paine)   614, 615
Rike, David   125, 126
Ring, Harry   13
The Rise of American Civilization (Beards)   569, 576, 617
Rivera, Diego   466–7n15
Roa, Raul   193, 194
"The Road to Peace According to Lenin and According to Stalin" (Cannon)   410–1
The Road to Serfdom (Hayek)   538, 550–65

Roanoke Times 283
Roberdeau, Daniel 612
Robertson, James 1, 23, 112–8, 144, 145n12, 404, 420–5
Robertson faction 436, 437, 443–46, 448, 449
Robeson, Paul 606
Robins, Harold 23, 89–99
Rockefeller, Nelson 330
Roosevelt, Franklin D. 167, 201, 222, 301, 565, 571, 575, 638, 676, 678
Roosevelt, Theodore 599, 617
The Roots of American Civilization (Nettels) 617
Rose, Jerry A. 226
Routledge, Katherine 59
Routledge, Scorsby, W. 59
Russell, Bertrand 527–8
Russell, Charles Edward 601
Russian Civil War 106, 491, 531
Russian Opposition. *See* Left Opposition in Russia
Russian Revolution of 1905 109, 472
Russian Revolution (October 1917) 14, 18, 22, 100, 101, 103, 104, 106, 108, 109, 110, 112, 140, 167, 172, 242, 258, 268, 310, 311, 339, 379, 408, 452, 460, 468, 472, 475, 480, 489, 503, 510, 512, 523, 525, 605, 666, 670, 677, 684
Rustin, Bayard 144n11, 273, 305
Rykov, Alexei 511

Sailors Union of the Pacific (SUP) 432
San Francisco General Strike (1934) 126, 263
Saunders, Lois 273, 275–86
Sartre, Jean-Paul 172
Satterthwaite, Joseph C. 156
Saville, John 535
Scheidemann, Philipp 635
Schine, David 34
Schlesinger, Arthur Jr. 569, 571, 573, 603
Schlesinger, Arthur Sr. 569, 603
Science of Logic (Hegel) 664
Scully, François 222, 223
Second American Revolution. *See* Civil War (U.S., 1861–65)
Second International (Socialist International) 109, 507
The Second Sex 7, 18, 141, 180–2

sectarianism (cutting one's self off from living struggles) 3–6, 115, 117, 172, 235, 266, 270, 431, 434, 440, 460, 502, 509, 524
  sectarian abstention 3–4, 6, 385, 439, 443
  sectarian appearance to some may not be sectarian 4, 9, 419, 479, 481, 536, 638
  sectarian exploitation of mass struggles 217
  sectarian vegetation 205
  sectarian vs revolution Marxism 257–8
segregation 31–32
  See also Jim Crow
Seligman, Ben B. 144n11
Sell, Evelyn 6–12, 23, 119–129
Seneca Falls conference on women's rights (Equal Rights Convention, 1848) 141, 644, 650
Sexton, Patricia Cayo 146
Shachtman, Max and "Shachtmanites" 1, 11, 12, 14n26, 115, 118, 149, 273, 422, 436, 440, 451, 518n22, 519, 521, 529
  See also Independent Socialist League (ISL)
share-cropping. *See* tenant farmers
Sharon, Art 531
Shaw, Ed 13, 528
Shaw, George Bernard 267
Shawnee Indians 581
Shelley, Percy Bysshe 271
Sheppard, Barry 13, 464
Sheridan, Philip 586
Shoshone Indians 47
Shuttlesworth, Frederick L. 287, 288, 290
"Silent Generation" 119, 120
Simon, Jean. *See* Jean Tussey
Singler, Melissa 7
sit-down strikes 263, 305, 442
Sklarewitz, Norman 223–3
slavery and anti-slavery 25, 43, 60, 239, 307–8, 347, 357, 368, 381, 382, 533, 539, 540, 542, 543, 566–70, 572–5, 582, 586, 587, 588, 592, 595–6, 599, 600, 603–4, 606, 607, 618, 640–1, 642, 643, 644, 648, 649
  See also abolitionists
Smith Act (1940) 421, 534, 537
  Minneapolis Smith Act Trial 520, 537
Smith, Adam 609, 617

INDEX   715

Smith, Howard K.   288, 289
Smith, Kelley Miller   290
Smith, Margaret Chase   35
Social Darwinism   594, 595, 599
social democracy, social democrats   11, 114,
    117, 149, 152, 204, 205, 206, 230, 238,
    259, 310, 337, 352, 370, 386, 387, 423,
    424, 435, 471, 507, 510, 512, 513, 523, 525,
    626, 630, 634, 635, 678, 684
Social-Democratic Federation (U.S.)   114, 118
social-fascism   512, 513
Social History of Art (Hauser)   124
Social Justice   564
socialism   13, 14, 16, 22, 42, 72, 85, 99, 116, 150,
    178, 230, 239, 674, 679, 686, 687
    democracy essential   18, 178, 182, 240,
        460, 668
    development of   66–7, 69, 134
    global system   100, 103, 104, 243
    illusions regarding Soviet "socialism"
        113–4, 171
    relationships and   79–80, 84
    social-economic stages toward   675, 684,
        685
    socialism or barbarism   478, 479
    thoughts on its "essence"   493, 673
    utopian   570, 605, 641
    withering away of the state   105
Socialist Call   114
Socialism on Trial (Cannon)   520
Socialist Educational League   242
Socialist Equality Party   404
Socialist Labor Party   113, 118, 137, 299, 370
Socialist Labour League (SLL)   234, 235, 404
    See also Workers Revolutionary Party
Socialist Party of America   112, 114, 118, 137,
    257, 264, 299, 370, 436, 462n5, 510, 523,
    601
    entry of Trotskyists into   440
    Norman Thomas socialists   215
    regroupment in 1950s   11, 114, 115
Socialist Revolutionary Party (SRs)   258
Socialist Workers Party
    achievements   521–8
    cadre development   150, 152, 439–40
    electoral campaigns   12, 136–8, 146, 216–
        7, 429–30, 431, 520
    internal democracy   454–5, 525–6, 530–
        1

    organizational and programmatic per-
        spectives   204–19, 436–59
    organizational routinism   11–13, 145–6
    party-youth relations   150–2
    perceptions of decline, degeneration
        420–7, 464
    tensions within   141n5, 403–435, 463–
        465
Somoza, Anastasio   222
Souls of Black Folk (DuBois)   596, 598, 607
South Africa   55, 154, 155, 156, 157, 367, 462n5
South America, Latin America   51, 139,
    140n3, 153, 162, 164, 173, 176, 178, 179,
    212, 231, 232, 233, 238, 239, 242, 322, 345,
    347, 355, 406, 481, 588, 686, 687
South Vietnam   207, 220–8
Southern Christian Leadership Conference
    (SCLC)   273, 289, 291, 296, 350
Southern Conference for Human Welfare
    29
soviets as democratic councils   258, 511, 624
Soviet Union (Union of Soviet Socialist
    Republics – USSR)   100–1, 117, 157, 163,
    175, 207, 231, 232, 240, 269, 343, 403,
    408, 413, 460, 468, 472, 481, 489, 500,
    501, 503, 511, 512, 513, 525, 559, 638, 668,
    670, 677
    achievements of and gains within   100,
        110, 206, 412, 480, 543, 552, 554
    afflicted with repressive bureaucratic dic-
        tatorship   100–4, 105, 106–7, 113–4,
        140, 167, 171, 408, 412, 473, 474, 493, 498,
        505–6, 525, 622
    as bureaucratic-collectivist   440, 478
    as degenerated workers' state   110, 140,
        230, 440, 472–3
    as state capitalist   176, 234
    defense of gains   112, 230, 412, 413, 440
    political revolution needed within   140,
        413, 417, 473, 474, 475, 476, 538, 622, 623,
        624
    self-reform of bureaucracy   442, 460,
        474, 483, 538, 622, 623
    See also Stalinism
Spain   37, 40, 102, 126, 241, 541, 681
Spartacist League   144, 404
Spartacus Youth League   112
Spencer, Herbert   594
Spingarn, Joel   601

Spinoza, Baruch   659
Spock, Benjamin   250
Srnicek, Nick   147–8
Stalin, Joseph   1, 100–11, 116, 163, 167, 171, 173, 175, 221, 241, 385, 411, 416, 421, 440, 460, 461, 466, 469, 470, 479, 484, 490, 503, 622, 670
Stalinism   15, 21, 24, 100–11, 112–4, 117, 118, 125, 140, 143, 150, 152, 163, 164, 165, 171, 174, 204, 206, 230, 231, 239, 241, 386, 406–9, 411, 412, 416–19, 422, 440, 444, 446, 452, 462, 472–3, 474, 480, 481, 483, 485, 620–4, 625, 669
  authoritarian grip in Communist parties   207, 385, 504, 514, 515
  authoritarian organizational practices   101, 163, 460, 511, 516
  bureaucratic dictatorship in Soviet Union   101, 230, 460, 498, 504, 509, 622–3
  conception of "socialism in one country"   109, 171
  conception of "Third Period"   386, 471, 510, 511–2, 513, 515
  opportunist and reformist tendencies   40, 41, 205, 489, 490, 508, 678
  repression, show trials, executions in Soviet Union   24, 100–1, 163, 171, 471, 481, 493, 504, 505, 506, 511, 624
  ultra-leftist tendencies   470, 513
  See also People's Front
Stanton, Elizabeth Cady   641, 643, 644, 646, 647, 649
State and Revolution (Lenin)   508
state capitalism   176, 234
Stein, Morris. *See* Morris Lewit
Stevens, Robert T.   34
Stevenson, Adlai   118, 194
Stone, Lucy   641, 643, 646, 647, 649
Stowe, Harriet Beecher   649
strategic hamlets   224
Strategy of Peace (Kennedy)   194, 195
The Struggle for Socialism in the 'American Century' (Cannon)   532n27
Student Nonviolent Coordinating Committee (SNCC)   273, 289, 351, 373, 423
Students for a Democratic Society (SDS)   430
The Struggle for a Proletarian Party (Cannon)   441, 518n22

The Subterraneans (Kerouac)   120–1
Supreme Court of the United States   21, 25, 26, 28, 29, 30, 31, 32, 275, 277, 278, 280, 281, 284, 285, 287, 358, 650
  Brown *v.* Board of Education   272
  Plessy *v.* Ferguson   26
"Survival of the Fittest" (Spencer)   594
Swabeck, Arne   427, 462, 463, 489–501, 517, 519, 520, 531, 532
Swanson, Gloria   85–8
Sweezy, Paul M.   23, 114, 140, 161, 162, 165–76

"Talented Tenth" (Du Bois)   597–8, 599, 600, 602, 603, 605, 606
Talmadge, Herman Eugene   27
The Tastemakers (Lynes)   81
Teamsters Union. *See* International Brotherhood of Teamsters
tenant farmers and sharecroppers   212, 278, 381, 596
Tecumseh   581
Tenney, Jack   35
Terman, L. M.   547
Thaelmann, Ernst   470
"third camp"   433
Theobald, Robert   144n11
Thomas, Dylan   120
Thomas, Henry   287, 291
Thomas, Norman   215
Thompson, E.P.   535
Thompson, Robert G.K.   224
Thoughts on Death and Immortality (Feuerbach)   659
Thucydides   468
Time magazine   119, 120
Tito, Josep Broz   173, 421, 670
Togoland   158
Toledo General Strike (1934)   263
Tom Paine: America's Godfather (Woodward)   617
Tomsky, Mikhail   511
totalitarianism   113, 240, 325, 374, 376, 409, 556, 558, 563, 565, 623, 668
Touré, Sékou   159
Trade Union Unity League (TUUL)   513
Trainor, Larry   13–4
Tran Van Tung   224–5
Transitional Program   230, 266, 267, 268, 270, 439, 442, 451, 624

INDEX 717

Tribovitch, Manny 520
Triple Revolution 143–8, 255–71
Triumph of Freedom (Miller) 617
Trotsky, Leon 2, 13, 14, 102, 103, 109, 112, 140, 161, 172, 173, 229, 230, 240, 257, 258, 266, 272, 274, 310, 311, 312–3, 314, 386, 390, 403, 404, 413, 416, 418, 420, 424, 434, 440, 451, 461, 466–88, 511, 515, 518, 521, 531, 533, 535, 549, 554, 558, 623, 638, 670, 684, 686
  on ideas in head *vs* ideas in flesh and blood 524
  on priority of political over organizational questions 518–9
  relations with comrades near end of life 477, 481
  relationship with Lenin 14–5, 16, 107, 109, 240, 311, 408, 441, 466, 523, 530, 670
  role in Russian Revolution and Civil War 172–3
  resistance to Stalinism 106, 107, 511, 565, 623–4
  slanders against 108, 511, 515, 534, 670
  unity of political outlook and action 481
  See also permanent revolution
"Trotsky on America" (Cannon) 14
Trotskyism 240
  defined
  denigrated
Trotskyism in the United States (Breitman, LeBlanc, Wald) 1
Trotter, Monroe 596, 601
Trujillo, Rafael 238
Truman, Harry 38
Truth, Sojourner 647
Tubman, Harriet 647
Turkey 242, 312
Tussey, Jean. 528, 537, 608–19
Turner, Frederick Jackson 566, 567, 568, 569, 574
Turner (frontier) thesis 566–7, 568
Turner, Nat 600

Uganda 159
ultra-leftism, ultra-leftists 4, 69, 257, 396, 439, 509, 510–4, 604
Uncle Tom's Cabin (Stowe) 649
Underground Railroad 600, 604

Unemployed Leagues 263, 264
unemployed movement 261, 264, 266, 269–70, 456, 562
uneven and combined development 2, 3, 685
Union of Soviet Socialist Republics (USSR). *See* Soviet Union
United Arab Republic 160
United Auto Workers (UAW) 90, 93, 95, 96, 97, 259, 526, 433
United Packinghouse Workers of America 284
united front 18, 428, 490, 512, 513, 515, 610
  united front from below 512, 513
Universities and Left Review 535
US News and World Report 103

Van Vechten, Carl 603
Vanzler, Joseph. *See* John G. Wright
Veblen, Thorstein 597
Viet Cong 222, 223, 224, 227
Viet Minh 221
Vietnam war 16, 17, 18, 142, 207, 220–8, 239, 435, 517n21, 531
  See also North Vietnam, South Vietnam
Villard, Oswald Garrison 599, 600
Vindication of the Rights of Woman (Wollstonecraft) 639
Voice of America 26, 29
Voice of the Negro 601
Voltaic Republic 158
Voz Proletaria 233

Wadsworth, James J. 193
Wald, Alan 1
Wall Street Journal 223, 225, 227
Wallace, Henry 520
Wallace, Miss (suffragist) 653
Walling, William English 601
Ward's Automotive Report 96
Ward, John William 144n11
Warde, William F. *See* George Novack
Warner, Denis 223
Warren, Earl 26, 276
Washington, Booker T. 596, 597, 599, 601
Washington, George 334, 614
Watson, T.J. 95
Watts, Daniel 16
Webb, Beatrice 602

Weber, Max   675
Weekly People   430
Weiss, Murry   22, 24, 33–42, 100–11, 142, 403, 405, 417, 422, 424, 427, 428, 463
Weiss, Myra Tanner   23, 24n9, 137, 141, 142, 193–203, 403, 405, 424, 428, 533, 537, 625–38
Weissman, George L.   21n2, 140, 536
Wensel, Louis O.   283
West Indies   345, 391
   See also Jamaica, Trinidad
When the West Is Gone (Paxson)   568
Whig Party (England)   614
Whig Party (US)   573, 574, 575
White, Mrs. Charles E.   283
White, Geoffrey   443, 444
White, Walter   605
White Citizens Councils   277, 366
white chauvinism. *See* racism
"The White Man's Burden" (Kipling)   540–1
Wilkins, Roy   295, 385
Williams, Alex   147–8
Williams, Jesse Lynch   652
Williams, John Bell   27
Williams, Robert F.   16, 297, 338, 351, 373, 374
Williams, Roger   583
Wilson, Woodrow   599, 600, 601, 654, 655
Windoffer, Melba   143, 183–192
Witty, Paul   547
Wobblies. *See* Industrial Workers of the World
Wohlforth, Tim   1, 11, 12, 14, 15, 22, 23, 139, 149–52, 404, 415–9, 426–7, 443
Wollstonecraft, Mary   639, 642, 656, 657
Women's Anti-Slavery Society   642, 643
women's liberation. *See* feminism
Woodward, W.E.   612, 617
Wordsworth, William   271
workers' and farmers' government   42, 140–1
Workers League   404
Workers Party   11, 424
Workers Revolutionary Party   404
Workers World Party   403
workers' state   102, 104, 140, 141, 171, 230, 231, 232, 234, 235, 412, 466, 472, 475, 491, 494, 677, 679
   deformed   423, 497
   degenerated   110, 140, 230, 440, 472–3
   See also dictatorship of the proletariat

working class (proletariat)   4, 14, 16, 23, 36, 37, 40, 41, 42, 71, 72, 88, 98, 99, 103, 109–11, 118, 140, 147, 154, 160, 163, 177, 185, 199, 208, 214, 215, 233, 258, 263, 268, 304, 311, 318, 322, 323, 324, 341, 354, 366, 369, 373, 376, 387, 388, 406, 408, 409, 412, 415, 416, 419, 437, 439, 441, 442, 454–8, 462, 470, 477, 490, 491, 496, 497, 503, 505, 507, 512, 513, 514, 523–7, 536, 553, 554, 555, 571, 573, 598, 601, 603, 605, 631–5, 679, 680–1, 684
   class consciousness   4, 8, 42, 85, 118, 152, 189, 202, 216, 218–9, 312–3, 353, 362, 366, 368, 376, 377, 379, 398, 441, 524
   de-radicalization and "false consciousness"   12, 14, 106–7, 109, 118, 128, 142–3, 175, 230, 252, 262, 285, 322, 357, 379, 407, 431, 452, 526
   labor aristocracy   312, 624, 676
   occupational shifts though technology and globalization   89–99, 146–8
   struggles of   5–6, 42, 104, 110, 114, 152, 171, 202, 205, 216, 264, 268, 312–3, 373, 380, 384, 416, 421, 450, 451, 453, 478, 495, 524, 622, 624, 685
   vanguard layer of   4, 5–6, 106, 152, 192, 204, 205, 310, 312–3, 368, 389, 423, 453, 551
   sectors
      agricultural workers   63, 124, 173, 188, 213, 310, 494, 596, 639, 672
      craft (skilled) workers   57, 59, 61, 63, 186, 189, 212, 262, 281, 388, 425, 547, 593, 602, 603, 627, 672, 673
      industrial workers   12, 63, 70, 74, 89, 91, 93, 95–6, 104, 106, 107, 110, 126, 142, 146–7, 158, 183, 184, 186, 187, 190, 211–2, 214, 244, 262, 263, 264, 268, 281, 284, 351, 360–1, 456, 498, 526, 564, 566, 570, 596, 597, 601, 604, 639, 640, 655, 678, 679, 682
      unemployed workers   125, 210, 214, 258–61, 264, 266, 269–70, 456, 562, 564, 633
      white collar, service and "professional" workers   82, 125, 186, 187, 188, 191, 244, 358, 378, 535, 536, 655
   See also intersectionality

Workingmen's Party (1829)   570
World Federation of Trade Unions (WFTU)   160
World War I   104, 112, 119, 137, 149, 257, 262, 423, 478, 507, 546, 548, 601–2, 604, 627, 634, 637
World War II   12, 22, 82, 89, 104, 110, 112, 119, 127, 128, 131, 145, 153, 157, 182, 200, 202, 206, 220, 230, 245, 263, 336, 358, 385, 432, 440, 461, 472, 478, 479, 480, 499, 533, 563, 627, 634, 635, 636, 638, 677, 685
Worthy, William T.   16, 144n11, 255, 363, 376
Wounded Knee (1890)   583
Wright, Frances (Fanny)   573, 641, 642
Wright (Joseph Vanzler), John G.   530, 658–65
Wright, Richard   139n3

Young Peoples Socialist League (YPSL)   112, 115
Young Socialist   149, 151, 398, 400
Young Socialist Alliance (YSA)   11, 12, 13, 16, 18, 139, 520, 528, 404, 434
Young Socialist League (YSL)   11, 115, 116, 117, 149, 150, 422
youth radicalization   7, 14, 16, 17, 23, 112–8, 119–29, 139, 149–52, 206, 210–211, 218, 238, 242–3, 279, 283, 297, 306, 348, 371, 373, 393, 401
Yugoslavia   102, 176, 206, 236, 416, 417, 418, 685, 686

Zanzibar   399
Zen Buddhism   120
Zulu   60
Zwerg, James   291
Zwicker, General Ralph Wise   34

Dissident Marxism in the United States

This book is Part III of a documentary trilogy on US Trotskyism. It is also the fourth volume of a six-volume series on Dissident Marxism in the United States, published within the Historical Materialism (HM) book series:

1. *The 'American Exceptionalism' of Jay Lovestone and His Comrades, 1929–1940. Dissident Marxism in the United States: Volume 1.* HM 83, ISBN 9789004224438 (Brill 2015).
2. *US Trotskyism 1928–1965. Part I: Emergence. Left Opposition in the United States. Dissident Marxism in the United States: Volume 2.* HM 156, ISBN 9789004224445 (Brill 2017).
3. *US Trotskyism 1928–1965. Part II: Endurance. The Coming American Revolution. Dissident Marxism in the United States: Volume 3.* HM 183, ISBN 9789004224452 (Brill 2019).
4. *US Trotskyism 1928–1965. Part III: Resurgence. Uneven and Combined Development. Dissident Marxism in the United States: Volume 4.* HM 184, ISBN 9789004224469 (Brill 2019).
5. *'Leftward Ho!' Revolutionary Intellectuals, 1928–1948. Dissident Marxism in the United States: Volume 5* (Brill, forthcoming).
6. *Independent Marxism in the American Century, 1949–1965. Dissident Marxism in the United States: Volume 6* (Brill, forthcoming).

CPSIA information can be obtained
at www.ICGtesting.com
Printed in the USA
JSHW020208090221
11731JS00002B/5